Gerhard Richter – Text

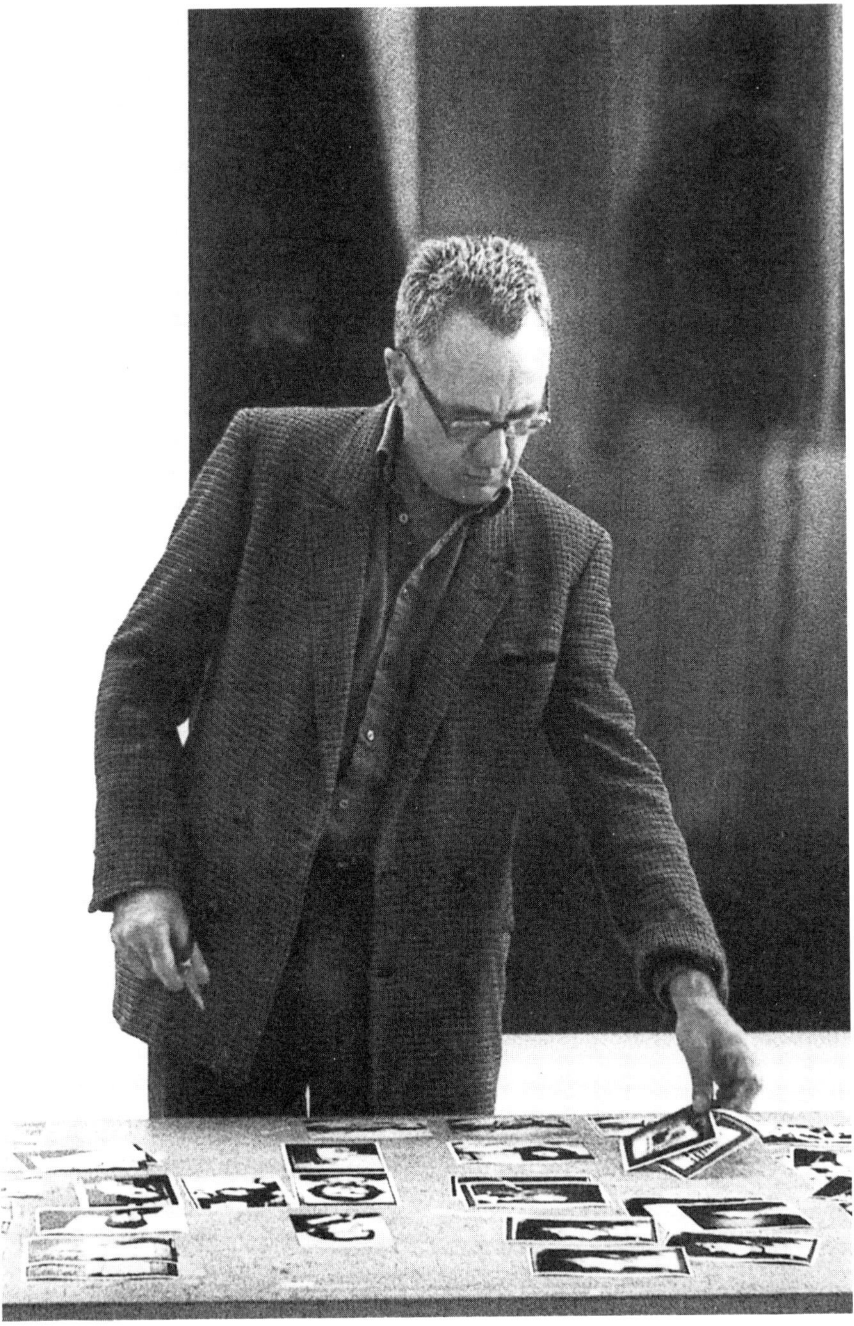

GERHARD RICHTER
TEXT

Writings, Interviews and Letters
1961–2007

edited by Dietmar Elger
and Hans Ulrich Obrist

with 115 illustrations

Thames & Hudson

This publication was prepared in collaboration with the Gerhard Richter Archive, Staatliche Kunstsammlungen Dresden.

First published in the United Kingdom in 2009 by Thames & Hudson Ltd, 181A High Holborn, London WC1V 7QX

www.thamesandhudson.com

Preface translated from the German by Thames & Hudson Ltd, London

British Library Cataloguing-in-Publication Data
A catalogue record for this book is available from the British Library

ISBN 978-0-500-09346-7

Printed and bound in China by
C&C Offset Printing Co. Ltd

Contents

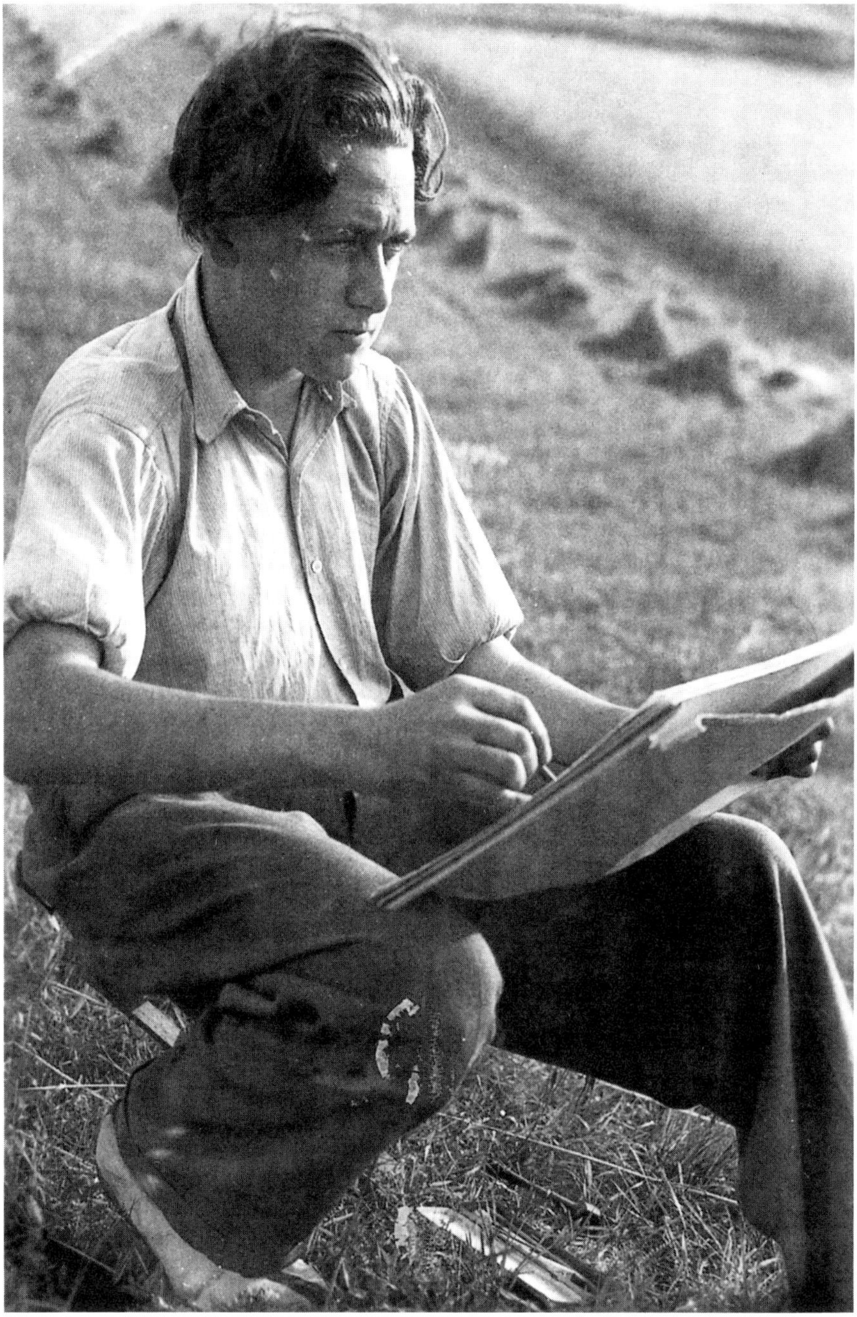

1950, Waltersdorf, Oberlausitz

Preface

Conversation is Gerhard Richter's preferred means of communication, and it is an art that he has engaged in frequently and perfected, especially in recent years. Thus this volume – the first comprehensive edition of his texts, also including letters, diary entries and notes – consists for the most part of interviews and conversations. Apart from three short conversations, these exchanges are reproduced here in their entirety. Of the letters, only those in which Richter reflects on his work as an artist have been considered.

By comparison with the first anthology (Thames & Hudson, 1995), with 49 entries dating from 1962 to 1993, the current edition covers a far wider range, presenting 112 texts dating from 1961 to 2007. Gerhard Richter himself selected the documentary photographs, installation shots and images of artworks, which he combined to form an accompanying photo-essay. Here, for the first time, Richter has allowed full access to his archive so that the book may serve as an authentic collection of sources, pictorial as well as textual.

The first of the texts is a previously unpublished farewell letter sent by Richter in 1961 to his Dresden professor, Heinz Lohmar, in which he explains his reasons for leaving Dresden and East Germany. The last text is an interview concerning his participation in the Venice Biennale of summer 2007. In between are 46 years of Richter 'texts', whose themes range far beyond the arts: notes, diary entries, short essays written for particular occasions, letters, opinions, statements, beliefs – and, again, there are interviews, conversations and dialogues.

These texts allow us to come close to Richter and to gain insight into the ideas, questions and contradictions that preoccupy him. At the same time they enable us to see the current development of the artist against the backdrop of his early works from the 1960s and '70s. Out of this comes a snapshot; a treasure trove of questions, reflections and crystallizing ideas that have accompanied the artist for a lifetime and that here build up into an information-packed mosaic of Gerhard Richter today – an artist whose importance is beyond question, and yet whose work is constantly turning in new directions.

We are confident that this comprehensive edition of Richter's texts will not only allow the reader an extensive view of the artist and his work, it will also provide researchers with a rich new source of material.

Many letters and texts are published here for the very first time, and several texts and interviews that previously appeared in little-known publications are now made accessible again. A detailed appendix is also included, with commentaries, sources and other data, providing the interested reader with further useful information.

Our sincere thanks go to Gerhard Richter for his generous support and creative contribution to the preparation of this comprehensive edition of his texts. Special thanks also go to Walther König and Herbert Abrell of Walther König Publishers, Cologne; the Gerhard Richter Archive, Dresden; and Uwe Koch, designer of the original German publication. On behalf of Gerhard Richter and ourselves, we would also like to thank all the interviewers and publishers who gave us permission to reproduce their material.

Dietmar Elger   Hans Ulrich Obrist

Letter to Professor Heinz Lohmar, 6 April 1961

Dear Professor Lohmar,[1]

It is very difficult for me to write to you today. We have left Dresden to start a new life in West Germany. In light of the current political situation, this sort of move (even if only temporary) is considered an act of desertion and makes us liable to prosecution. I had to take that into account, and therefore for reasons of caution could not speak to anyone about my work.

It required a long period of consideration and introspection to find clarity on the pros and cons of my plans and finally to take a decision, which I am convinced is the right one.

The reasons are largely to do with my career [...] When I say that the whole cultural 'climate' in the West offers me and my artistic endeavours more, that it is more compatible with my way of being and my way of working than the climate in the East, I am pointing out the main reason behind my decision. Incidentally, I became completely certain of this during my journey to Moscow and Leningrad.[2]

I don't wish to expound any further right now on the reasons for my leaving. I just want to tell you that it was very difficult for me to go, even though I knew I had to act; I am aware of what I have left behind, and mine was not a careless decision based on a desire to drive nicer cars.

I'm especially sorry to have to send you such an announcement. I do not want to ask you for forgiveness and cannot expect you to condone my actions, but I do want to take the liberty of sincerely thanking you with all my heart for all that you have done for me, for all the trouble you have gone to to support me and my work in every way. I will always appreciate that.

Notes, 1962

The first impulse towards painting, or towards art in general, stems from the need to communicate, the effort to fix one's own vision, to deal with appearances (which are alien and must be given names and meanings). Without this, all work would be pointless and unjustified, like Art for Art's Sake.

The idea that art copies nature is a fatal misconception. Art has always operated against nature and for reason.

Every word, every line, every thought is prompted by the age we live in, with all its circumstances, its ties, its efforts, its past and present. It is impossible to act or think independently and arbitrarily. This is comforting, in a way. To the individual, the collective experience of the age represents a bond – and also, in a sense, security; there will always be possibilities even in disaster.

It makes no sense to expect or claim to 'make the invisible visible', or the unknown known, or the unthinkable thinkable. We can draw conclusions about the invisible; we can postulate its existence with relative certainty. But all we can represent is an analogy, which stands for the invisible but is not it.

There is no excuse whatever for uncritically accepting what one takes over from others. For no thing is good or bad in itself, only as it relates to specific circumstances and to our own intentions. This fact means that there is nothing guaranteed or absolute about conventions; it gives us the daily responsibility of distinguishing good from bad.

Picturing things, taking a view, is what makes us human; art is making sense and giving shape to that sense. It is like the religious search for God. We are well aware that making sense and picturing are artificial, like illusion; but we can never give them up. For belief (thinking out and interpreting the present and the future) is our most important characteristic.

Art's means of representing a thing – style, technique and the object represented – are circumstances of art, just as the artist's individual qualities (way of life, abilities, environment and so on) are circumstances of art. Art can just as well be made in harmony with the circumstances of its making as in defiance of them. In itself art is neither visible nor definable: all that is visible and imitable is its circumstances, which are easily mistaken for the art itself.

As soon as artistic activity turns into an 'ism', it ceases to be artistic activity. To be alive is to engage in a daily struggle for form and for survival. (By way of analogy: social concern is a form and a method that is currently seen as appropriate and right. But where it elevates itself into Social*ism*, an order and a dogma, then it loses its best and truest qualities and may turn criminal.)

I did not come here[1] to get away from 'materialism': here its dominance is far more total and more mindless. I came to get away from the criminal 'idealism' of the Socialists.

Painting has nothing to do with thinking, because in painting thinking is painting. Thinking is language – record-keeping – and has to take place before and after. Einstein did not think when he was calculating: he calculated – producing the next equation in reaction to the one that went before – just as in painting one form is a response to another, and so on.

Art serves to establish community. It links us with others, and with the things around us, in a shared vision and effort.

My concern is never art, but always what art can be used for.

Since there is no such thing as absolute rightness and truth, we always pursue the artificial, leading, *human* truth. We judge and make a truth that excludes other truths. Art plays a formative part in this manufacture of truth.

The sciences certainly have influenced the arts. To an Aztec, the sunset was an inexplicable event, which he could not cope with or even survive without the imagined aid of his gods. Obvious phenomena of this sort have since been explained. But the sheer unimagined vastness of the explicable has now made the inexplicable into such a monstrous thing that our heads spin, and the old images burst like bubbles. The thought of the totally inexplicable (as when we look at the starry sky), and the impossibility of reading any sense into this monstrous vastness, so affect us that we need ignorance to survive.

Strange though this may sound, not knowing where one is going – being lost, being a loser – reveals the greatest possible faith and optimism, as against collective security and collective significance. To believe, one must have lost God; to paint, one must have lost art.

Letter to a newsreel company, 29 April 1963

Neue Deutsche Wochenschau
Düsseldorf

Dear Mr Schmidt,

We take the liberty of drawing your attention to an unusual group of young painters with an unusual exhibition. We are exhibiting in Düsseldorf, on former shop premises in the section of Kaiserstrasse that is due for demolition. This exhibition is not a commercial undertaking but purely a demonstration, and no gallery, museum or public exhibiting body would have been a suitable venue.

The major attraction of the exhibition is the subject matter of the works in it. For the first time in Germany, we are showing paintings for which such terms as Pop Art, Junk Culture, Imperialist or Capitalist Realism,[1] New Objectivity, Naturalism, German Pop and the like are appropriate. Pop Art recognizes the modern mass media as a genuine cultural phenomenon and turns their attributes, formulations and content, through artifice, into art. It thus fundamentally changes the face of modern painting and inaugurates an aesthetic revolution. Pop Art has rendered conventional painting – with all its sterility, its isolation, its artificiality, its taboos and its rules – entirely obsolete, and has rapidly achieved international currency and recognition by creating a new view of the world.

Pop Art is not an American invention, and we do not regard it as an import – though the concepts and terms were mostly coined in America and caught on more rapidly there than here in Germany. This art is pursuing its own organic and autonomous growth in this country; the analogy with American Pop Art stems from those well-defined psychological, cultural and economic factors that are the same here as they are in America.

We take the view that the *Wochenschau* ought to document this first exhibition of *German Pop Art*,[2] and we ask you to consider the possibility of a report. If you would like further detailed information on us, our work and our ideas, we shall be glad to supply them.

We[3] look forward to hearing from you.

Yours truly,

Gerd Richter
Hüttenstrasse 71
Düsseldorf Tel. 189 70

Programme and Report: The Exhibition *Leben mit Pop – eine Demonstration für den Kapitalistischen Realismus*, Düsseldorf, 11 October 1963

Please note that the number assigned to you is:
PROGRAMME (roman numerals) CATALOGUE (letters)
for a Demonstration for Capitalist Realism

Living with Pop
Friday, 11 October 1963, Flingerstrasse 11, Düsseldorf

I) Start 8 p.m. Report to 3rd floor.
A Waiting room, 3rd floor (decor by Lueg and Richter)
II) When your number is called, visit Room No. 1, 3rd floor.
Disciplined behaviour is requested.
B Room No. 1: sculptures by Lueg and Richter
(plus one work on loan from Professor Beuys[1])
(Couch with Cushions and Artist
Floor Lamp with Foot Switch
Trolley Table
Chair with an Artist
Gas stove
Chair

Table, Adjustable, with Table Setting and Flowers
Tea Trolley, Laid
Large Cupboard with Contents and Television
Wardrobe with loan from Professor Beuys)

III) When your number is called (approx. 8:45 p.m.), visit other exhibition rooms on 2nd and 1st floors and ground floor. During this tour (Polonaise), please refrain from smoking.

C Exhibition rooms on several floors (selected by Lueg and Richter) (52 bedrooms, 78 living rooms, kitchens and nurseries, paintings by both painters; guests of honour, Messrs. Schmela and Kennedy[2])

IV) On completion of tour, see A, etc.
Subject to alteration.

Thank you for your attention.
Konrad Lueg and Gerd Richter

REPORT

[12 September 1963.] Planning of exhibition in furniture store, Düsseldorf. Available space consists of one room on 3rd floor of office block, floor area 32 square metres.

A number of exhibition concepts were rejected, and it was resolved to hold a demonstration as follows:

a) The whole furniture store, exhibited without modification.
b) In the room set aside for the exhibition, a distilled essence of the demonstration. An average living room as a working exhibit, i.e., occupied, decorated with suitable utensils, foods, drinks, books, odds and ends, and both painters. The individual pieces of furniture stand on plinths, like sculptures, and the natural distances between them are increased, to emphasize their status as exhibits.
c) Programmed sequence of the demonstration for 11 October 1963.

List of rooms to be viewed on 11 October 1963:

I) Passage lined with window displays (26 large windows).
Office entrance. Lift to 3rd floor.

II) Waiting room (large landing on 3rd floor). On the walls: 2 boards inscribed WAITING ROOM. 14 pairs of roebuck antlers[3] (shot in Pomerania, 1938–42). On display: 39 simple chairs, on each a copy of the *Frankfurter Allgemeine* for 11 October 1963. On the stairs lie assorted picture magazines; by the lift stand two life-size figures (paper on wire mesh, varnished and painted), representing the art dealer Alfred Schmela and President John F. Kennedy. The space is lit by cold, rather dim, fluorescent light.

III) Exhibition room. On 9 white plinths stand the following items. A tea trolley bearing a vase of flowers, and on its lower shelf the works of Churchill and the home-making magazine *Schöner Wohnen*. A cupboard with assorted contents. A wine-red chair. A gas stove. A green chair, occupied by K. Lueg (dark suit, white shirt, tie). A small occasional table; on it, a television set (showing News followed by 'The Adenauer Era'). A small standard lamp. A couch; reclining thereon, with a detective story, G. Richter (blue suit, pink shirt, tie). A table set for coffee for two, with cut marble cake and *napfkuchen* and coffee in cups, plus 3 glasses and a plastic bag containing 3 bottles of beer and 1 bottle of grain spirit. The walls are painted white, with no pictures or other adornment. Next to the door is a wardrobe, containing the official costume of Prof. J. Beuys (hat, yellow shirt, blue trousers, socks, shoes; to which 9 small slips of paper are attached, each marked with a brown cross; beneath is a cardboard box containing Palmin and margarine). The room is lit by very bright, warm, fluorescent light, and by the standard lamp; there is a persistent smell of pine air-freshener.

IV) Extensive furniture exhibition of all current styles on 4 floors (81 living rooms, 72 bedrooms, kitchens, individual pieces. Store rooms. Tightly packed alcoves, cubicles, rooms, stairs and passages filled with furniture, carpets, wall decorations, appliances, utensils).
In a number of installations in the bedroom and living-room sections, paintings by Lueg and Richter are on show.
By K. Lueg: *Four Fingers*; *Praying Hands*; *Bockwursts on Paper Plate*; *Coathanger*.
By G. Richter: *Mouth*; *Pope*; *Stag*; *Neuschwanstein Castle*.
These rooms are lit normally.

8:00 p.m. Two store employees stand at the entrance, giving out individually numbered programmes. A total of 122 visitors were counted in, a small proportion of whom left before the end of the event.

The visitors take the lift to the 3rd Floor and enter the WAITING ROOM. Loudspeakers all over the building broadcast dance music and the voice of an announcer, who welcomes the visitors and summons them in numerical order to view the exhibition room, which they do in groups of 6–10 individuals every 3–5 minutes. The first visitors to be called enter the room hesitantly. The room soon fills up. By approximately 8:30 the announcements are being ignored, and everyone simply squeezes in. The food and drink in the exhibition is consumed by the visitors, and some of the contents of the cupboard are looted.

8:35 p.m. The exhibited artists descend from their plinths. They and the voice on the loudspeakers request the visitors to begin the grand tour.

Richter leads a first group to the bedroom department on the 2nd floor; Lueg follows with more visitors.

The loudspeakers continue to broadcast dance music, interspersed with selected texts from furniture catalogues.[4] From the 2nd floor the tour proceeds to the living-room department below, and then on through the store room to the kitchen department in the basement.

Most of the visitors fail to observe the prescribed itinerary and scatter or stray into the various departments.

By approximately 9 p.m., all the visitors have reached the kitchen department. They seat themselves in the 41 display kitchens and drink the beer provided. One visitor (an art student) protests against the Demonstration by removing all his clothing except a pair of swimming trunks. He is escorted from the building with his clothes under his arm.

By 9:30 p.m. the last visitor has left the building.

Notes, 1964

As a boy I did a lot of photography and was friendly with a photographer, who showed me the tricks of the trade. For a time I worked as a photographic laboratory assistant:[1] the masses of photographs that passed through the bath of developer every day may well have caused a lasting trauma. Then I went to Dresden, to the Academy, and did nothing but paint – in a realistic style influenced by Beckmann.

When I went to study with Götz[2] in Düsseldorf in 1961 (which was when I moved across to the West), I was pretty nonplussed and desperate to start with. What eventually set me free was the encounter with Fluxus and Pop Art.

My first photo-picture? I was doing large pictures in gloss enamel, influenced by Gaul.[3] One day a photograph of Brigitte Bardot fell into my hands, and I painted it into one of these pictures in shades of grey. I had had enough of bloody painting, and painting from a photograph seemed to me the most moronic and unartistic thing that anyone could do.

I collect photographs (nowadays, I also get a lot given to me) and I am always looking at them. Not 'art' photographs, but ones taken by lay people, or by ordinary newspaper photographers. The subtleties and tricks of the art photographers are easily seen through, and then they are boring.

Happenings, pictures, objects: the lay person has and makes all these in a way that puts every artist to shame. Have artists ever made objects remotely as large and as good as a lay person's garden?

Composition is a side issue. Its role in my selection of photographs is a negative one at best. By which I mean that the fascination of a photograph is not in its eccentric composition but in what it has to say: its information content. And, on the other hand, composition always also has its own fortuitous rightness.

It is hard, say, to cross out six different numbers on a Lotto ticket in such a way that the arrangement looks convincing. And yet the sequence that emerges after the numbers are drawn seems entirely right and credible in every way.

I prefer the 'naïve' photograph, with a simple, uncomplicated composition. That's why I like the *Mona Lisa* so much; there's nothing to her.

In every respect, my work has more to do with traditional art than with anything else.

For me there really exists a hierarchy of pictorial themes. A mangelwurzel and a Madonna are not of equal value, even as art objects. The virtuosity of the *peinture* is only an attempt to conceal this. I hate the dazzlement of skill: e.g., being able to draw something freehand from life, or – even worse – inventing or putting together something entirely original: a particular form, a particular composition or an eccentric colour scheme. It's all too easy to get carried away by one's own skill and forget about the picture itself. There are legions of painters who are just too talented to paint good pictures. Being able to do something is never an adequate reason for doing it. That is why I like the 'non-composed' photograph. It does not try to do anything but report on a fact.

I have no favourite pictorial themes. Naturally, particular things have a special fascination for me. But I don't want to tie myself down: there are many aspects to the world that photography represents.

I also paint from photographs that I have taken myself; and of course I can set these up the way I want them.

I simply copied the photographs in paint and aimed for the greatest possible likeness to photography. So I avoided brushmarks and painted as smoothly as I could. Factors like overexposure and lack of focus found their way in unintentionally, but then they had a decisive effect on the atmosphere of the pictures. Nowadays I sometimes work the other way round, so that pictures derive from technique. The *Doors* and *Curtains*, for example, are pictures constructed and designed on the basis of my experience with blurring. Technique is really a side issue.

Perhaps one day I shall find something that works better than painting! For the moment, however, I am used to working with brush and paint, and I find this both simpler and more full of potential than photography, which is too bound up with easily repeatable tricks and manipulations. And even when I paint a straightforward copy, — something new creeps in, whether I want it to or not: something that even I don't really grasp.

'Capitalist Realism':
Contact with like-minded painters[4] – a group means a great deal to me: nothing comes in isolation. We have worked out our ideas largely by talking them through. Shutting myself away in the country, for instance, would do nothing for me. One depends on one's surroundings. And so the exchange with other artists – and especially the collaboration with Lueg and Polke – matters a lot to me: it is part of the input that I need.

Poster text for the exhibition *Klasen*[1] *und Richter*, Galerie Friedrich & Dahlem,[2] Munich, 1964

Prescribed

Prescribed course: flight to Göppingen-Berneck and return to take-off point at Roth-Kiliansdorf, total distance 147 km. Bad weather caused numerous emergency landings. Rudolf Lindner (Nabern/Teck), who had taken over the lead in the standard class from Heinz Huth after the second trial, force-landed his Phoebus near Bopfingen after flying approximately 100 km. Rolf Kuntz (Braunschweig) landed on the Hausknecht, near Böhmenkirch, 694 m above sea level. As this went to press, the World Champion, Heinz Huth, and the leader of the open class, Rolf Spanig (Speyer), were still in the air.

Interview between John Anthony Thwaites and Gerhard Richter, written by Sigmar Polke, October 1964

Mr Richter, you are the most talented of the German Pop painters; you went through all the hardships and the hostility that the movement encountered in its early days, and you now occupy a leading position in the movement. Perhaps you can tell us something about your work and your artistic development.

I have a lot of work, and I am well developed artistically, and also mentally and physically. I pull the expander front and back. And if you saw my new pictures, Mr Thwaites, you would collapse!

Why?

Because they're so good! You've never seen such good pictures in your life. No one has ever seen such good pictures, and I can't show them to anyone, because everyone would collapse. So in the first place I hung cloths over all the pictures, and then in due course I overpainted them all white.

And now?

Now I don't paint at all any more, because I don't want to have the whole human race on my conscience.

How many victims have your works accounted for?

I don't know, exactly. The exact statistics do exist, of course – they run into the tens of thousands – but I can't concern myself with trivia. It was more interesting earlier on, when the big death camps in Eastern Europe were using my pictures. The inmates used to drop dead at first sight. Those were still the simple pictures, too. Anyone who survived the first show was killed off by a slightly better picture.

And your drawings?

I haven't done a lot. Buchenwald and Dachau had two each, and Bergen-Belsen had one. Those were mostly used for torture purposes.

The Russians are said to have five of your paintings and drawings. Is that so?

I don't know how many.

Stalin mounted his reign of terror with two pictures. After killing millions of Russians, it's said that he caught an accidental glimpse of one of your pictures, just for a fraction of a second, and immediately dropped down dead. Is that so?

I don't know. One of my best paintings is in the Soviet Union.

So what happens next?

I don't paint any more. I can't, because I don't want to spread terror, alarm and anxiety everywhere, and depopulate the earth. But now it's come to the point where I only have to think my paintings out and tell someone about them, and the person rushes off in a state of panic, has a nervous breakdown, and becomes infertile. That is the worst effect. Though I can't say so for sure, as yet, because – depending on who tells the story – I have already caused dumbness, hair loss (mainly in women) and paralysis of limbs.

Is it true that you supply paintings to the US Army?

I can't tell you anything about that.

Have you no scruples, or anything?

I am an artist.

Do you believe in God?

Yes, I believe in myself, I am the greatest, I am the greatest of all!

Thank you, Mr Richter.

Not at all, Mr Thwaites.

Letter to Heiner Friedrich, 23 November 1964

Dear Mr Friedrich,

Thank you again for your letter (already acknowledged by postcard). I wanted to wait to get both the openings over before writing to you. Everything got delayed, and I still have no catalogues and posters[1] (or only one copy of each). Please write and let me know how many to send. The poster has come out very well, especially if you put up three at a time, one above the other. But to take matters in order:

Jährling:[2] you know the poster, I'll send more. You know the building, of course. It's a good hanging space, and the show makes a very colourful, cheerful impression. A group show like this is entirely suitable for making a strong, fresh statement (the fact that everything looks a bit too decorative is an advantage, if anything).

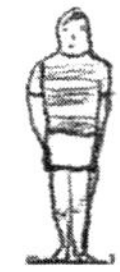

The opening was fine and festive. We didn't put on a show at all, just dance music from the radio. Mr and Mrs Baum (they have my *Secretary*) bought one painting apiece from Polke and me, and a figure by Lueg, a *Footballer* sawn out of plywood and brightly painted. Mine was the little female reclining figure, *Deckchair*. I don't know the price off-hand. Jährling's and Block's[3] net prices are rather higher, some of them, than the prices agreed with you. If you like, I'll send the exact figures. Their net prices are higher anyway, because both only take one-third.

I put a lot into the Jährling show, 22 pieces including *Piano*. Almost everything I have, in fact. I can't recommend much of this to you. I mean, I still like the *Stag*; maybe the *Negro*; the *Cathedral*; *Interceptor*, that's new (so is *Tame Kangaroo*, but probably not so well painted); and then maybe two or three others.

It's been very hard from my point of view, having two exhibitions at the same time. I don't want to do that again, and I must also paint a bit slower and take it more quietly (so that when I have a terrific basic idea, like *Tame Kangaroo*, I can make it work better). I'm sure you'll understand. And while we're on the subject: I'm not going to paint on cotton duck any more, it's too difficult technically.

Block wrote to me today. The opening was put off until 3 p.m. on Saturday 21 November, in order to ensure 'adequate art-historical documentation'. For the opening I sent in a tape of business news, political reports and a chapter from Brehm's *Animal Life*, which was played back over the PA system. For the Hague Realists[4] opening on 21 November, Block stationed a sandwich man at the door of the Academy with my poster in front and a placard on his back saying '... New German Realists at Galerie Block, etc.' Then there was a young lady who handed out copies of the Galerie Block prize competition: 'Please count up how many German artists are missing from this exhibition, and why...'

Today my exhibition is being filmed for TV Channel 3. Heinz Ohff wrote about the Hague Realists in the *Tagesspiegel* (22 November), mentioning my name as an omission from that show, and promised to write on the subject later. The catalogue text by de la Motte[5] I don't like particularly, it's too glib, I don't see the point of churning out commonplaces and definitions of Pop in this way. There is plenty more that needs saying (I've noted some of it down,[6] and I'll send it to you if you like). As far as the catalogue is concerned, I regret seeing the illustrations folded, that's really a shame. But, all in all, I'm glad to be showing there, and I think Block is the right person.

One problem I think I haven't mentioned yet: Block would like a picture of mine, *Christa and Wolfi*. He asked me to let him have this one cheap, so he could

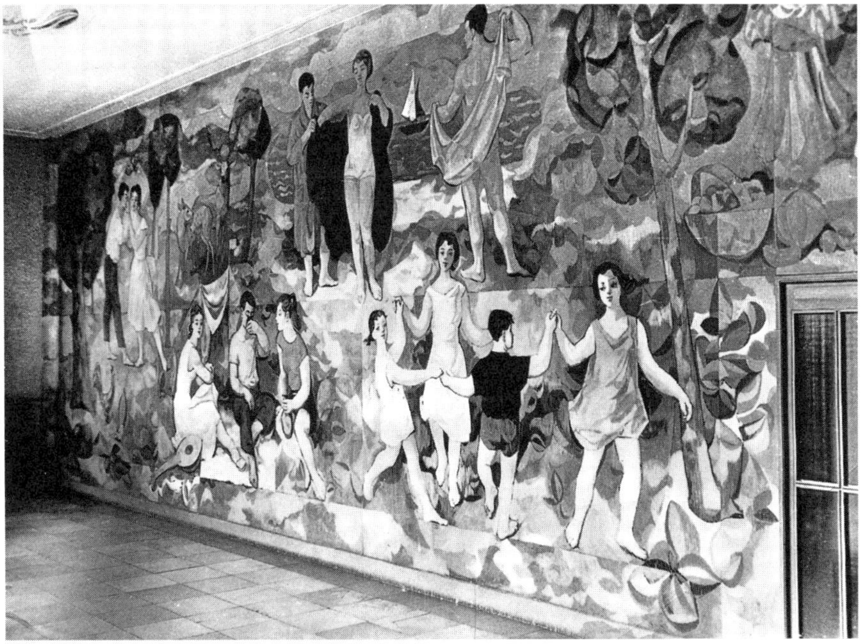

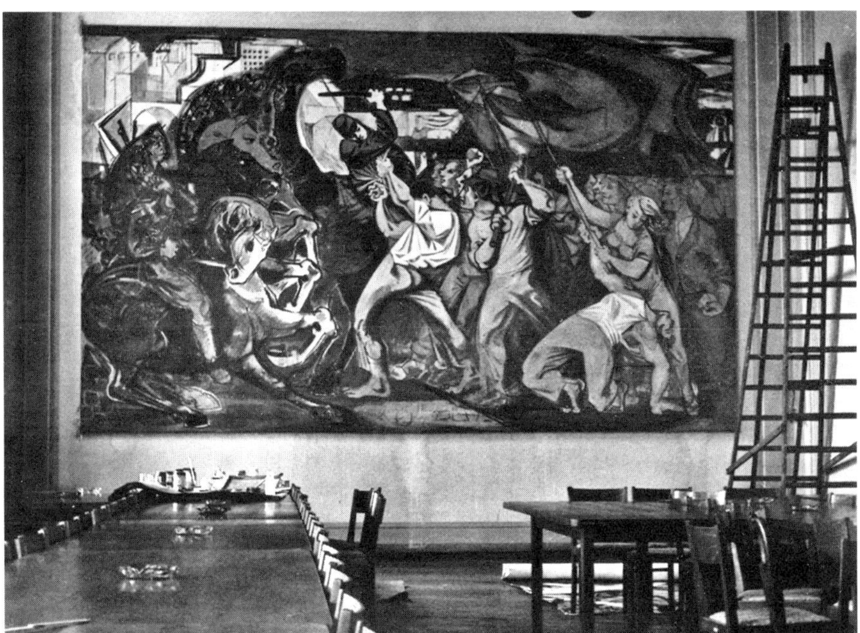

Mural in the German Hygiene Museum, Dresden, 1956
Mural in the Socialist Party headquarters, Dresden, 1959

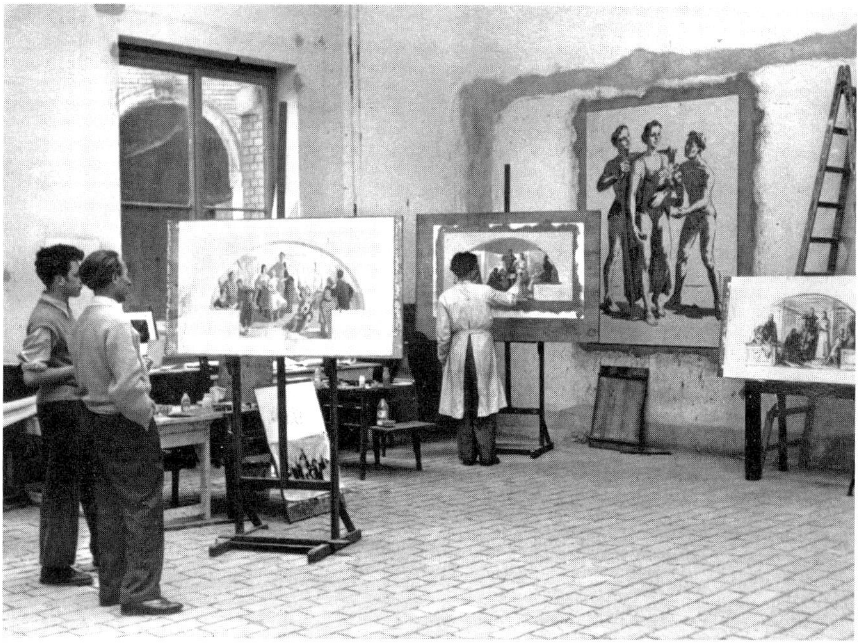

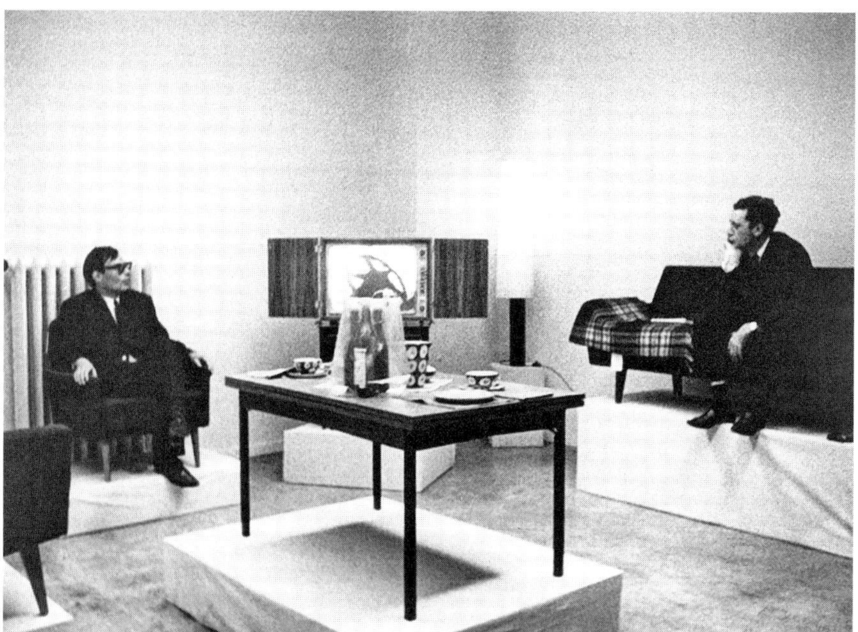

Heinz Lohmar's class, Dresden Academy of Fine Arts, 1954
Demonstration für den Kapitalistischen Realismus, 1963

use the saving to print the catalogue. Now he writes to add that the picture would be at my disposal at any time, and that he would never sell it. I told him I would discuss it with you. For my part, I think we can easily spare the picture, and it would be a good thing to have a picture by me (and perhaps another, smaller one as well) permanently in Berlin. Then, whenever anyone walks in, they see a sample, and they can see the real thing at Friedrich's.

Please write and let me know what you think.

I have written to tell Block that you have also bought *Renate* and *Marianne* and *Sphinx*.

I'm glad you've been able to fix the Rome exhibition[7] for the spring, but please change the selection. *Party*, *Pallbearers*, *Hitler*, *Mustang Squadron*: we have better ones to send in place of these. One of them might be included, explicitly marked as an 'Early Work'. That's all the news. For the last few days I've been doing jobs around the house and decorating. I shan't get round to any painting this week; I have to collect material first, by which I mean to make some sketches. I hope this letter reaches you in time, before you go off to Rome and London. I'd be happy to come to Munich, but I don't think it's possible at the moment, much though I'd like to.

That's all for today. Best wishes to you and your wife; my wife sends hers.

Gerd Richter

Notes, 1964–1965

When I draw – a person, an object – I have to make myself aware of proportion, accuracy, abstraction or distortion and so forth. When I paint from a photograph, conscious thinking is eliminated. I don't know what I am doing. My work is far closer to the Informel than to any kind of 'realism'. The photograph has an abstraction of its own, which is not easy to see through.

It's what everyone believes in nowadays: it's 'normal'. And if that then becomes 'other', the effect is far stronger than any distortion, of the sort you find in Dalí's[1] figures or Bacon's.[2] Such a picture can really scare you.

The photograph took the place of all those paintings, drawings and illustrations that served to provide information about the reality that they represented. A photograph does this more reliably and more credibly than any painting. It is the only picture that tells the absolute truth, because it sees 'objectively'. It usually gets believed, even where it is technically faulty and the content is barely identifiable. At the same time, photography took on a religious function. Everyone has produced his own 'devotional pictures': these are the likenesses of family and friends, preserved in remembrance of them.

Photography altered ways of seeing and thinking. Photographs were regarded as true, paintings as artificial. The painted picture was no longer credible; its representation froze into immobility, because it was not authentic but invented.

Life communicates itself to us through convention and through the parlour games and laws of social life. Photographs are ephemeral images of this communication – as are the pictures that I paint from photographs. Being painted, they no longer tell of a specific situation, and the representation becomes absurd. As a painting, it changes both its meaning and its information content.

The photograph is the most perfect picture. It does not change; it is absolute, and therefore autonomous, unconditional, devoid of style. Both in its way of informing, and in what it informs of, it is my source.

A photograph is taken in order to inform. What matters to the photographer and to the viewer is the result, the legible information, the fact captured in an image. Alternatively, the photograph can be regarded as a picture, in which case the information conveyed changes radically. However, because it is very hard to turn a photograph into a picture simply by declaring it to be one, I have to make a painted copy.

The first time I painted from a photograph, I did so in a mixture of exhilaration and fear, partly because I was strongly affected by contemporary Fluxus events,[3] and partly also because I once did a lot of photography myself and worked for a photographer for eighteen months: the masses of photographs that passed through the bath of developer every day may have created a lasting trauma. There must be other reasons. I can't tell exactly.

There is nothing strange about the fact that I paint from photographs (as distinct from, say, making photographic enlargements of them). Everyone who uses photographs 'paints' from them in one way or another: whether with brush, collage, silkscreen or photographic canvas is immaterial. The only strange thing is that I want to produce just this kind of picture and no other: the kind of picture that I can't at the moment produce in any other way. (Maybe it could be done without a brush, through darkroom manipulations of some kind. But that doesn't appeal to me, because I have no desire to manipulate. Tricks of some kind would occur to me, and I'd be able to repeat them endlessly. To me that is a horrific idea; the pictures would be no good, either.) Perhaps it is old-fashioned of me to think like this. But it appeals to me, when a photograph falls into my hands, to deal with it in this way.

Perhaps because I'm sorry for the photograph, because it has such a miserable existence even though it is such a perfect picture, I would like to make it valid, make it visible – just *make* it (even if what I make is then worse than the photograph). And this making is something that I can't grasp, or figure out and plan. That is why I keep on and on painting from photographs, because I can't make it out, because the only thing to do with photographs is paint from them. Because it attracts me to be so much at the mercy of a thing, to be so far from mastering it.

Do you know what was great? Finding out that a stupid, ridiculous thing like copying a postcard could lead to a picture. And then the freedom to paint whatever you felt like. Stags, aircraft, kings, secretaries. Not having to invent anything any more, forgetting everything you meant by painting – colour, composition, space – and all the things you previously knew and thought. Suddenly none of this was a prior necessity for art.

If my paintings differ from the originals, this is not intentional on my part: it is not a matter of design but of technique. And technique lies outside my voluntary control and influence, because it is itself a reality, like the model, the photograph and the painting. Whether an object is on the right or on the left in the painting is utterly immaterial. If it is on the right, this must be correct in its own way, and it would be presumptuous to put it on the left.

As far as the surface is concerned – oil on canvas, conventionally applied – my pictures have little to do with the original photograph. They are totally painting (whatever that may mean). On the other hand, they are so like the photograph that the thing that distinguished the photograph from all other pictures remains intact.

I want to leave everything as it is. I therefore neither plan nor invent; I add nothing and omit nothing. At the same time, I know that I inevitably shall plan, invent, alter, make and manipulate. But I don't know that.

I want to have everything very clear, simple and unconditional, and I would rather make no art at all than just any old unspecific painting.

There is no way to paint except the way I do it.

When I paint from a photograph, this is part of the work process. It is never a defining characteristic of the vision: that is, I am not replacing reality with a reproduction of it, a 'Second-Hand World'. I use photography to make a painting, just as Rembrandt uses drawing or Vermeer the camera obscura. I could dispense with the photograph, and the result would still look like a painting from a photograph. *Reproductive* and *direct* are therefore meaningless terms.

The photograph reproduces objects in a different way from the painted picture, because the camera does not apprehend objects: it sees them. In 'freehand drawing', the object is apprehended in all its parts, dimensions, proportions, geometric forms. These components are noted down as signs and can be read off as a coherent whole. This is an abstraction that distorts reality and leads to stylization of a specific kind. By tracing the outlines with the aid of a projector, you can bypass this elaborate process of apprehension. You no longer apprehend but see and make (without design) what you have not apprehended. And when you don't know what you are making, you don't know, either, what to alter or distort. Your apprehension that an arm is so wide, so long and so heavy is not only unimportant: it becomes a fraud, if it leads you to believe that you have truly apprehended that arm.

I don't copy photographs laboriously, with painstaking craftsmanship: I work out a rational technique – which is rational because I paint like a camera, and which looks the way it does because I exploit the altered way of seeing created by photography.

I like everything that has no style: dictionaries, photographs, nature, myself and my paintings. (Because style is violence, and I am not violent.)

Theory has nothing to do with a work of art. Pictures which are interpretable, and which contain a meaning, are bad pictures. A picture presents itself as the

Unmanageable, the Illogical, the Meaningless. It demonstrates the endless multiplicity of aspects; it takes away our certainty, because it deprives a thing of its meaning and its name. It shows us the thing in all the manifold significance and infinite variety that preclude the emergence of any single meaning and view.

I don't create blurs. Blurring is not the most important thing; nor is it an identity tag for my pictures. When I dissolve demarcations and create transitions, this is not in order to destroy the representation, or to make it more artistic or less precise. The flowing transitions, the smooth, equalizing surface, clarify the content and make the representation credible (an *alla prima* impasto would be too reminiscent of painting, and would destroy the illusion).

I blur things to make everything equally important and equally unimportant. I blur things so that they do not look artistic or craftsmanlike but technological, smooth and perfect. I blur things to make all the parts a closer fit. Perhaps I also blur out the excess of unimportant information.

I am a Surrealist.

As a record of reality, the thing I have to represent is unimportant and devoid of meaning, though I make it just as visible as if it were important (because I paint everything as 'correctly', as logically and as credibly as it would appear in a photograph). I am not saying that the thing represented is abolished as such (the painting cannot be turned upside-down). The representation simply acquires a different meaning: it becomes the pretext for a picture. (Photography suits my purposes here: the photograph confronts me as a statement about a reality which I neither know nor judge, which does not interest me, and with which I do not identify.)

All that interests me is the grey areas, the passages and tonal sequences, the pictorial spaces, overlaps and interlockings. If I had any way of abandoning the object as the bearer of this structure, I would immediately start painting abstracts.

My sole concern is the object. Otherwise I would not take so much trouble over my choice of subjects; otherwise I would not paint at all. What fascinates me is the alogical, unreal, atemporal, meaningless occurring of an occurrence which is simultaneously so logical, so real, so temporal and so human, and for that reason so compelling. And I would like to represent it in such a way that this clash is maintained. That is why I have to avoid intervening or altering anything, for the sake of a simplicity that can thus be more general, definitive, lasting and comprehensive.

It is aggressiveness and brutality of construction that makes Surrealism, and the borderline situations of Bacon, into 'specialities': that is to say, something specific and unbalanced. By this I mean that I have to do without brutality and intervention in any form, because I find that, for instance, an object is more compelling if it does not float but stands in its normal place (it just has to be painted).

The photograph makes a statement about real space, but as a picture it has no space of its own. Like the photograph, I make a statement about real space, but when I do so I am painting; and this gives rise to a special kind of space that arises from the interpenetration and tension between the thing represented and the pictorial space.

Art is not a substitute religion: it is a religion (in the true sense of the word: 'binding back', 'binding' to the unknowable, transcending reason, transcendent being). This does not mean that art has turned into something like the Church and taken over its functions (education, instruction, interpretation, provision of meaning). But the Church is no longer adequate as a means of affording experience of the transcendental, and of making religion real – and so art has been transformed from a means into the sole provider of religion: which means religion itself.

All things artificial and natural, whether in planned or fortuitous arrangements, have the capacity to turn into fetishes. Belief, for one: that is, making statements and predictions beyond the actual circumstances of time and place. And for another: depriving an object of its utilitarian value and believing in it.

If I were to exhibit a urinal today, this would be legitimate, because I would not be demonstrating anti-art but setting the urinal up as an altar and object of art and faith. I want to be like everyone else, think what everyone else thinks, do what is being done anyway.

I don't want to be a personality or to have an ideology. I see no sense in doing anything different. I never do see any sense. I think that one always does what is being done anyway (even when making something new), and that one is always making something new. To have an ideology means having laws and guidelines;

it means killing those who have different laws and guidelines. What is the good of that?

There is no such thing as freedom. Nor would I know what to do with it.

For an artist there must be no names: not table for table, not house for house, not Christmas Eve for 24 December, not even 24 December for 24 December. We have no business knowing such nonsense.

Nor must we have views or opinions. Leave that to others. A fireman, say, may well see the world in his own specific way and have different views from a watchmaker.

Talk about painting: there's no point. By conveying a thing through the medium of language, you change it. You construct qualities that can be said, and you leave out the ones that can't be said but are always the most important.

Polke thinks there must be some point in painting, because most lunatics paint unbidden.

The central problem in my painting is light.

Text for exhibition catalogue, Galerie h, Hanover, 1966, written jointly with Sigmar Polke

Many of my paintings measure 150 × 200 cm; many are 130 × 150 cm or 130 × 140 or 120 cm; some are 160 × 180 cm; some are considerably smaller, about 40 × 30 cm or even 18 × 24 cm. My largest paintings to date are 200 × 190 cm. Perhaps I shall now paint only small paintings, or else medium-sized ones and a few larger ones; I can't tell for sure.

A childhood memory: I let my little sister toboggan down a hill, without thinking that she was bound to hit an iron railing. The result was a deep laceration on her forehead; she had stitches, and I had a hiding.

Carlton looked at the front gardens, the birds and the women, and then the scales fell from his eyes; he knew that he would never get the hang of it all. He asked me for a cigarette and took his leave.

Amid the terrifying roar of unleashed atomic power, the mountainous space globe lifted off from the grey soil of Sexta. The blazing spurts of energy from its cavernous jet tubes were like a miniature sun, and a ring of fire expanded across the flat ground, pushing waves of red-hot debris ahead of it.

The men in the control room saw little of all this. Few had time to glance at the dimmed monitor screens, and to the others such a sight was nothing new.

Perry Rhodan[1] sat in the command position, from which he could oversee the whole control room; its curiously shaped table had its own intercom and telecom terminals.

His wife Mory occupied one of the additional seats clustered around the command position, as did Melbar Kasom, who of course needed a special chair. And Atlan. Gucky's recliner was empty. The coypu was on the move, no doubt, somewhere on board. Rhodan had given his wife a curt nod, just before lift-off. When on duty, they were no more and no less than comrades, comrades in a battle that might end somewhere in eternity. Their own feelings took second place to their responsibility for the space empire of mankind.

The Halutian's wide mouth opened in a chuckle. There was a hint of a twinkle in his great red eyes. His head gave an almost human nod. 'It might have been worse,' he said placidly. 'The chief mistake was mine. I ought to have transferred my knowledge of spores to the memory sector of my plan brain...'

'Believe it or not, I really see my surroundings as dots.' I love all dots. I am married to many of them. I want all dots to be happy.

Dots are my brothers. I am a dot myself. We always used to play together, but nowadays everyone goes his own way. We meet only on family occasions and ask each other 'How are things?'

'Do you know, Elly,' he said quite calmly, 'one must love only things that have no style, such as dictionaries, photographs, nature, me and my pictures!'

I sighed: 'How right you are, because style is violence, and we are not violent, and...'

'... And we don't want war,' he finished the sentence for me. 'No more war, ever!'

When I met the love of my life, I fell so deeply in love that I would willingly have married her there and then. But we had one thing in common apart from our great love: concern for those close to us. She had lost her father at an early age and was taking care of her mother and sister. I was taking care of my parents. So we were in the same boat. Time flew past, and we were very happy together.

You do well to report this. But you should of course make it clear that you are referring to isolated instances.

I would like to be like everyone else, think what everyone else thinks, do what is being done anyway.

The heavy armoured bulkhead of the airlock slid almost noiselessly back into the hull of the tender. Perry Rhodan, Atlan and Captain Redhorse strode between the ranks of battle-ready Epsalian Commandos. Just before he reached the airlock, Rhodan stopped.

'Who is in command here?'

One of the (by Earth standards) disconcertingly massive Epsalians stepped forward.

'Lieutenant Afg Moro, Sir!'

'I need one of your men, Lieutenant.'

'Sir, I...'

'No, not you, you must wait here for the operational order.'

Lieutenant Moro turned.

'Sergeant Man Hatra, escort the Chief Administrator.'

An Epsalian, 1.6 metres tall and almost as wide, clumped forward and halted close in front of Perry Rhodan. He wore the same combat uniform as the others, but was armed with a massive disintegrator, as well as an impulse blaster that a Terran would have needed both hands even to carry. The Epsalian carried the impulse blaster in a special holster and held the equally heavy disintegrator casually in the crook of his arm.

I have abundant leisure time, because I lead a solitary life. My husband died two years ago, and both my sons are married. Those three men were my life. When the four of us were still together, my life was full and marvellous. Whatever would become of me now, were it not for the values that I can still cherish? As always, the most important is duty. I have widened the scope of my duties to benefit more people. Classical music, which formed a deep bond between my husband and myself, now distresses me, but despite the tears I cannot do without it, because it is part of my life. Good literature, nature, and not least my visits to my beloved children and delightful grandchildren, are the cornerstones of my life. After vigorous and stimulating activity, I make a point of setting time aside for quiet reflection. Then I sit quite quietly and relive the very happy times I had with my husband and my sons. And so a lonely 61-year-old woman can still say Yes to life.

We cannot assume that good pictures will be painted one day: we must take matters into our own hands!

'Nonsense,' his logic sector chimed in. 'Tolot is in the same fix as we are. If he ever wants to get out of here, he has to back us up.'

Atlan stirred himself.

'We must act,' he decided.

He heard Henderson sigh with relief. A faint smile played across his features.

I have never snored in my life, whatever the tape-recorder may say. I know that good painters do not snore.

My intelligence knows no bounds.

He was clearly still in a state of extreme agitation. 'It – it was terrible!'

Sheriff Beatty felt the need to sit down. 'You mean to tell me that the driver of the car turned it around and deliberately drove over the girl a second time?'

Smiles nodded. 'Yes, that's right. I could see it all quite clearly.'

Beatty lit a cigarette. 'And why are you coming out with all this now, Mr Smiles? Why didn't you report what you saw straight away?'

Smiles gave a nervous laugh.

I would like to have a lot of children. When I walk down the street, I'd like all the children to call out Daddy, and I'd pat their heads and ask them, 'What's your name? How old are you? Be good. My regards to your mother.'

My wife is 4 centimetres shorter than I am. Since I mostly walk rather crooked, it looks as if I too were only 168 cm tall. My mother-in-law is very short.

The image of greyish-yellow expanses of sand and a jagged mountain range filled Perry with unease. He needed no scientific analysis to tell him that such a world could not be created naturally. Someone must have built it. Someone had supplied it with a sun, gravitation and a stifling atmosphere. Why they had done so was immaterial. The depressing thing about all this was that mankind on Terra still had a few millennia to go before it attained the level of knowledge necessary to create a planet.

He now has many friends. He is an intelligent man, and they intend to find him a good job as a pharmacist, just as soon as his English is better. A major publishing house is to bring out his life story.

In a frenzy of despair, the Nomad Scout sprang up and hurled himself against the locked airlock of the ship. He rebounded, and the shock brought him to his senses. The alien guard was still watching. Krash-Ovaron stared at him. What a being! In a fight, he could probably have held his own against the city's best hunters.

The alien moved. He pointed towards the city. The gesture was peremptory. It was a command to Krash-Ovaron to withdraw.

'I need the ship,' said Krash-Ovaron urgently, but as he spoke he realized that to the guard his words were only meaningless sounds.

Implacably, the guard pointed towards the city. Krash-Ovaron felt waves of pain surging through his body. Egg-laying time was approaching. By the time the hunt was over, he would have to find some place, or he and his brood would die together.

Slowly the alien approached him. He looked determined.

Krash-Ovaron realized that he now had only one chance of turning the situation to his own advantage: he would have to dismantle the Parablock and ask the aliens for help.

Krash-Ovaron shivered.

They would die, he vowed, for forcing him to abase himself.

All painters, everybody, ought to paint from photographs. And they should do it the way I do (including the selection process). Then such paintings should be exhibited everywhere, and everywhere they should be hung – in homes, restaurants, offices, stations and churches, everywhere. Then great painting competitions would be held. The jurors would assess the entries according to theme, rendering and speed, and then they would award medals. Every day, on television and on the radio, there would be reports on the latest paintings. Eventually, laws could be passed so that people could be punished for not painting enough copies of photographs. This would have to go on for 400 years or so, and then painting from photographs should be banned in Germany.

His words were cut short by the wail of the alarm systems. Colonel Cart Rugo let out a cry of horror. Involuntarily, Rhodan glanced at the controls nearest to him. What he saw revealed the full magnitude of the approaching catastrophe.

All the atomic-powered machinery of CREST II seemed to be out of action.

This meant that CREST II was about to crash. Right in the middle of the battlefield, outside the city.

I am averagely healthy, averagely tall (172 cm), averagely good-looking. I mention this, because that is how one has to look to paint good paintings.

Paintings must be produced to a recipe. The making must take place without inner involvement, like breaking stones or painting house-fronts. Making is not an artistic act.

Harskin looked in the direction indicated and saw a gigantic monster. It was almost a living island, a cross between turtle and dinosaur. Its massive skull was armed with huge plates of armour, but the look in its eyes was by no means hostile or bloodthirsty. Round the monster's neck hung a kind of basket in which sat three Gnorphs. The three scaly beings looked down with curiosity and sympathy at the three beings swimming in the water. This was obviously a rescue party.

The girl carefully scrutinized the photograph, then pointed a scarlet fingernail at one man. 'That's him,' she said excitedly.

'You couldn't be mistaken?' Jo panted.

The girl shook her head vigorously. 'No, Jo, I'm not making any mistake. That's the man Mabel was going with.'

Jo folded the cutting and put it away. 'You've been a great help, Dolly,' he said.

Perry stood on the terrace, took an occasional sip from his glass, and said softly, with a slight catch in his voice: 'Look at this beetle, here on my sleeve.' He pointed to a tiny pucym beetle, which was just about to fly away. 'It mustn't be disturbed; nothing must ever be disturbed. Always leave everything just as it is. Plan nothing, invent nothing, add nothing, omit nothing...' He hesitated, and then went on. 'This is the state of modest wisdom that allows us to transcend ourselves, to do something that we can't grasp with our intelligence but only understand and admire in our hearts. I don't mean that this has anything to do with passivity...' He watched the departing pucym beetle with a faint smile. 'It will be action: less noisy than we have been used to, but far stronger, more all-embracing; it will transform our existence, awesomely...' His gaze was lost in the endless depths of space, and we realized that in this one moment he had made us a gift of the Universe.

We stood there in silence for a long time, until Icho Tolot, the sturdy, ever-cheerful Halutian, brought us more wine.

If anyone wants to be a painter, he should first consider whether he is not better suited to be something else: a teacher, a government minister, a professor, a craftsman, a workman; for only truly great human beings can paint.

The last patient left at 10:30. It had by now, regrettably, become accepted that they would be seen at the practice on Saturday mornings. The doctor took off his white coat and washed his hands. As he did so, he watched himself in the mirror.

When Paddy awoke from deep sleep, the ship was in space, in zero gravity. He looked out through the porthole. The eternal night of space surrounded him. Behind was the gleam of Schaet; to his left was the golden globe of Alpheratz, and ahead were the stars of Andromeda: Adil, the Body; Mirach, the Loins; Almach, the Shoulder.

'I must dot!' *Icho spoke Interkosmo. He had learned the language without difficulty and could speak it flawlessly. The only thing he found difficult was not talking as loudly as he usually did; if he had, the walls would have started to shake.*

There were few items of furniture in the room. Three of them were comfortable chairs.

'I must just dot,' *he said.*

It was eleven a.m. I sat with my father beneath a sunshade on the main terrace of the Carlton Hotel. As I gazed at the blue expanses of the sea with its curly, white crests of foam, the wild and frenzied happenings of the night before seemed like a dream. Like a nightmare... Bright red-and-white and blue-and-white beach umbrellas; the smell of the sea; the happy voices of bathers along four kilometres of beach, interspersed with the urgent cries of the ice-cream vendors. Nymphs with slender, naked limbs dived into the water and emerged spluttering. 'Marvellous,' I said. My old man had no time to answer. He was cracking his breakfast egg.

Strapped into their anatomically designed seats, they raced towards Hell. The opalescent fluid found its way into their mouths and noses, and they felt as if they were drowning. Icho Tolot was still writhing and shrieking on the ground, while Rhodan, Richter, Redhorse, Polke and the three mutants were reduced to helpless spectators of the monstrous creature's agony. Finally the last cry died away, and Rhodan's desperate wish came true. The Halutian recovered from the shock and regained control of his own metabolism. 'That was hard, wasn't it? But I believe there was no alternative.'

Where a dot is, something happens!

Dot – point – basic unit of geometry, intersection of two lines without extension – punctuation mark, said the Halutian. The 2.5-metre-tall, two-headed mutant, Gorachin, gave a momentary grin with Ivanovich's face. Ivan had no time for that. Ivan saw his goal and once more unleashed his mental currents, causing calcium and carbon compounds to explode.

I stood up, hesitated for a moment and switched on the screen. I was startled to see the face of a Kirjen. It was an impressive, intelligent face, dominated by a long, flat nose and an extremely high forehead. The blue-skinned features were unfamiliar, as was the head, surrounded by a thick, curly mass of fur.

'Welcome to Kanor. I am the contact man of my people, Erg Vatal.'

His thin-lipped mouth twisted into a smile. The four-jointed arm and 62-fingered hand appeared in the frame.

It was a flame, or something similar. A vibrant, shining form that hovered in mid-air and performed strange manoeuvres. It seemed to dance – now forward, now back, right to left, up from below. It was pale in colour, and at times it moved so quickly that Fed momentarily lost sight of it. Some day we shall no longer need pictures: we shall just be happy. For we shall know what eternity is, and our knowledge will make us happy. Life after death will be explored and will set us an example of new modes of conduct.

I paint my paintings on grounded canvas (synthetic emulsion as a binder for titanium dioxide), which I buy in Düsseldorf for 8 DM the square metre. I use the best pigments and oils, and the work is guaranteed to be as durable as is humanly possible.

The squat, green-feathered Epsalian hovered alongside the coypu, who imperturbably went on working. The painting was almost ready. The Epsalian looked at the original, an archive shot of Perry Rhodan's meeting with Kraa Mhakuy on the planet Quinta. He compared it with the painting and said, as if musing to himself: '... I'm glad you're conventional, Gucky, with no qualms about painting beautiful pictures. You have as much in common with Raphael as with the Surrealists, the Impressionists, the cave painters, Zero, Picasso, Fluxus and the millions of poor devils who photograph their families. Therein lies your greatness...'

'Did you say something?' said Gucky.

'No, nothing important.'

The Epsalian hovered in the room for a while longer, then teleported himself silently to the ship's control room, where he went back to repairing the field generators.

Which is better: collecting art, or drinking and whoring? Everything in its proper time.

All hell broke loose. Across the monitors flickered the flames from the overloaded field screens. The ship lurched to and fro. The Antigrav could no longer absorb the shocks that struck in rapid succession. The giant command post collapsed in ruins. Through the wailing of the sirens, the cries of the wounded could be heard. Even Ferro Kraysch had been hurled out of his seat, and he stood up with great difficulty. He was blinded by the blood that ran down his face.

That was the end. Ferro felt no fear, only anger and disappointment that it had come so quickly. For all his caution, he had underestimated the enemy. To the aliens, the MOHICAN was no more dangerous than a ball, a plaything to toss around as they wished. Ferro's anger turned to frantic rage. They had him in their power. Another direct hit shook the ship's gigantic hull. But he would show them that a Terran was not so easy to beat.

I consider many amateur photographs better than the best Cézanne. It's not about painting good pictures, because painting is a moral action.

Doubtfully, Perry looked at the illuminated positronics wall, with its bewildering array of flashing, multicoloured control lights. Could he justify sitting here and reworking a problem, when he could not even be sure it would prove relevant to the present situation? Was it right to build a hypothesis solely on the analogy between two processes? In front of him, on the main programme line, a green key lit up. The machine was ready to accept the programme.

Perry clenched and opened his fist. Then he firmly pressed the key. The green light went out.

'Problem,' said Perry hoarsely. 'Generating structural formulae for two six-dimensional force fields. Analogy: the arrangement of force fields in a synchrotron particle accelerator...'

Seconds later, the machine was at work.

If they had their way, all policemen would wear screen-dotted uniforms, with a dot pattern instead of the German eagle. Every one of them would have a spotted handkerchief.

There were three of them, and they shimmered with an intense blue. For aeons they had been soaring above their world, which was bathed in a deep red glow. Their flight was noiseless, despite their gigantic size. They flew no specific course, but appeared at regular intervals above Kraa, the largest city in their world. One hundred and twenty times in succession they came individually, and then all three appeared together.

He likes to bend an elbow, my dear husband does. I put it in that flippant way, to show that I like a laugh and can take a joke. But the way my husband gets his pleasure is harmful to himself. He is always finding an excuse to celebrate and drink a toast to someone. This makes him popular with his workmates and friends – but not with me and his family. This liquid hobby of his takes its toll of time, money, home life and ultimately health. Being a vegetarian and also a militant teetotaller (though not by any means a killjoy) puts me in a difficult position. Can you understand that? When I object, however justly and reasonably, all I get is a smile. That is why I'm taking the liberty of asking for your support. Perhaps you can get my husband to think twice, because he has a great respect for you. I know that. Please do bring up the subject.

Any one who is in trouble or has a screw loose had better go to a psychiatrist, but not paint. Painting is strictly for the healthy.

The newlywed Inge says: 'My father seldom parts with anything really valuable.'

'You're right there,' growls her husband. 'I found that out when I married you!'

Interview with Dieter Hülsmanns and Fridolin Reske, 1966

Mr Richter, what attracts you so much about a photograph that you paint a copy of it?

A photograph – unless the art photographers have 'fashioned' it – is simply the best picture that I can imagine. It is perfect; it does not change; it is absolute, and therefore autonomous and unconditional. It has no style. The photograph is the only picture that can truly convey information, even if it is technically faulty and the object can barely be identified. A painting of a murder is of no interest whatever; but a photograph of a murder fascinates everyone. This is something that just has to be incorporated into painting.

Your pictures contain representations of human beings, animals and objects. These are things that you could just as well paint from nature. So why do you use a photograph as your source?

Because it saves time, for one thing. Nowadays one must rationalize one's work, and anyway I have no desire to spend a month in front of one canvas. Secondly, I am cutting out a certain degree of stylization, which is unavoidable in painting from nature, and which I want to avoid.

If you avoid all stylization and abstraction, and paint such a close approximation to photography, isn't it strange that you don't make your pictures directly by photomechanical means?

I don't find it strange at all. Everyone who uses photographs 'paints' from them in one way or another: whether with brush, collage, silkscreen or photographic canvas is immaterial. The only strange thing is that I want to produce just this kind of picture and no other: the kind of picture that I can't at the moment produce in any other way. But maybe one day I'll work out how to eliminate the painting process.

You also paint portraits from photographs. In portrait painting, isn't it desirable to know the sitter?

Not at all. I don't think the painter need either see or know his sitter. A portrait must not express anything of the sitter's 'soul', essence or character. Nor must a painter 'see' a sitter in any specific, personal way; because a portrait can never come closer to the sitter than when it is a very good likeness. For this reason, among others, it is far better to paint a portrait from a photograph, because no one can ever paint a specific person – only a painting that has nothing whatever in common with the sitter. In a portrait painted by me, the likeness to the model is apparent, unintentional and also entirely useless.

So how significant are the things represented in your pictures?

Highly significant, definitely. Just not significant in the sense of conveying information about reality, which is what photography is there for. I never paint to create a likeness of a person or of an event. Even though I paint credibly and correctly, as if the likeness were important, I am really using it only as a pretext for a picture.

So you don't really care at all what you paint?

No, that's not it at all. I don't abolish representation. The picture can't be turned upside-down, for instance. The object is so important to me that I take a great deal of trouble over my choice of subjects. It is so important that I paint it. I am fascinated by the human, temporal, real, logical side of an occurrence which is simultaneously so unreal, so incomprehensible and so atemporal. And I would like to represent it in such a way that this contradiction is preserved.

Notes, 1966

I pursue no objectives, no system, no tendency; I have no programme, no style, no direction. I have no time for specialized concerns, working themes, or variations that lead to mastery.

I steer clear of definitions. I don't know what I want. I am inconsistent, non-committal, passive; I like the indefinite, the boundless; I like continual uncertainty. Other qualities may be conducive to achievement, publicity, success; but they are all outworn – as outworn as ideologies, opinions, concepts and names for things.

Now that there are no priests or philosophers left, artists are the most important people in the world. That is the only thing that interests me.

Biographical information, 1966

9.11.32	Born in Waltersdorf[1] (East Saxony)
	Elementary school and vocational school (secondary-school leaving certificate)
1949–53	Advertising painter, photo lab operator,[2] stage painter.
1953–57	Dresden Academy of Fine Arts (realistic painting, mural painting).
1957–60	Freelance in Dresden (respite from fine art painting, mural commissions, photography, travel).
1958	Married.
1960	Move to Düsseldorf.[3]
1960–62	Art Academy Düsseldorf[4] (Prof. K. O. Götz).
Prior to 1960	Influenced by works of Beckmann and Picasso, works based on nature.
1960–62	Smudged paintings, non-representational paintings, *Hemden*.[5]
End 1962	Painted first photograph.
End 1965	Painted first colour chart.
	Lives and works in Düsseldorf.

Statement, 1967

The impact of photography has grown so rapidly since the beginning of this century that today we have arrived at a point where we trust reproduced reality in the form of a photograph more than we do reality itself. We *believe* that photographs reflect reality and that the information relayed by a photograph is much more precise and more convincing than even the best drawing.

The nudes[1] are a renunciation of [the technique of] copying an everyday photograph by painting it, because these works have been composed – that is, arranged as an artificial group – and because their topic is artificial (people's natural state being when they are clothed). The *Doors*[2] are fabricated photographs, meaning they are not based on a photograph of a real door. Somewhere along the line it no longer satisfied me to paint photographs; I took the stylistic devices of photographs – accuracy, blurring, illusoriness – and made doors, curtains and pipes with them. I was surprised by the results, which were unpredictable. (The Chirico-like emptiness[3] was not designed to express the *Doors*, and I feel they are only related to Chirico in as much as one picture is more or less related to every other picture.)

Antwerp, December 1967

'Work Overview', 1968

1960–1962: Representational paintings, partly inspired by role models (Bacon, Giacometti, Dubuffet, and others). Collages, *Hemden*, and others.

1962: First paintings based on photographs (as a result of a radical change in belief about what art is; that it has 'nothing to do with painting, nothing to do with composition, nor with colour'. This belief was supported and confirmed by the Happenings movement and American Pop Art.

1962–1963: Various topics based on photographs (some of them still picturesque and sentimental: Stag, Castle, Hitler, etc.).

1963: Aeroplanes, cars, etc. (smooth surfaces, photo-like, journalistic; 'every detail of reality is equally good'). Family paintings (based on amateur shots; bourgeois intimacy, narrative style of painting, unprofessional composition, 'composition is when the main subject is in the centre'). Portraits (distanced, generic and objective – as opposed to artistic portrayals that also reveal the soul).

1964: Landscapes (anonymous, catalogue-like, not based on first-hand experience: Sphinx, Pyramids, etc.).

1965: Curtains, works on paper, pillars (making use of previously employed stylistic devices to invent pictures and constructions). Scenes, animals, objects, etc. (from magazines: coincidental cutting from a report: assemblage, or

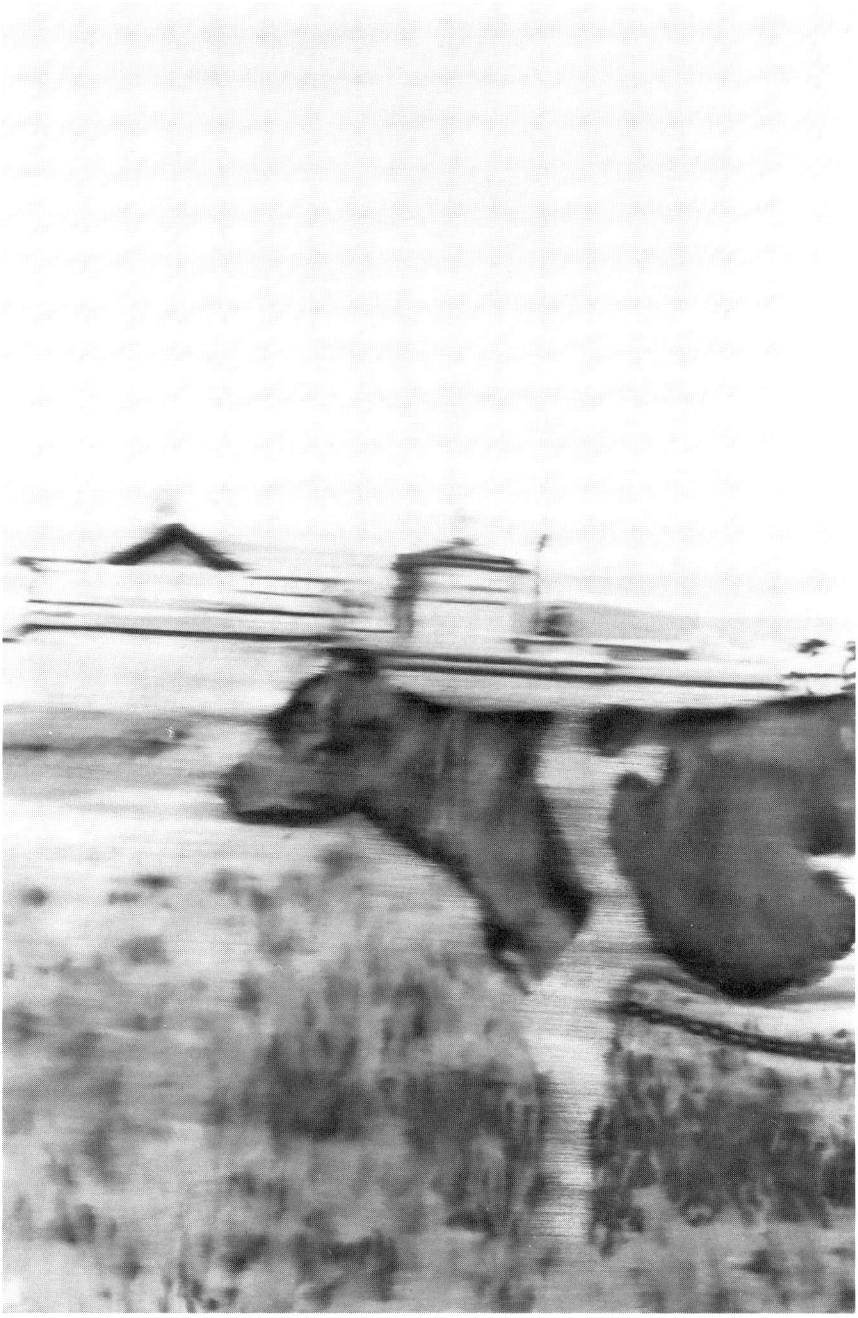

Cow, 1965

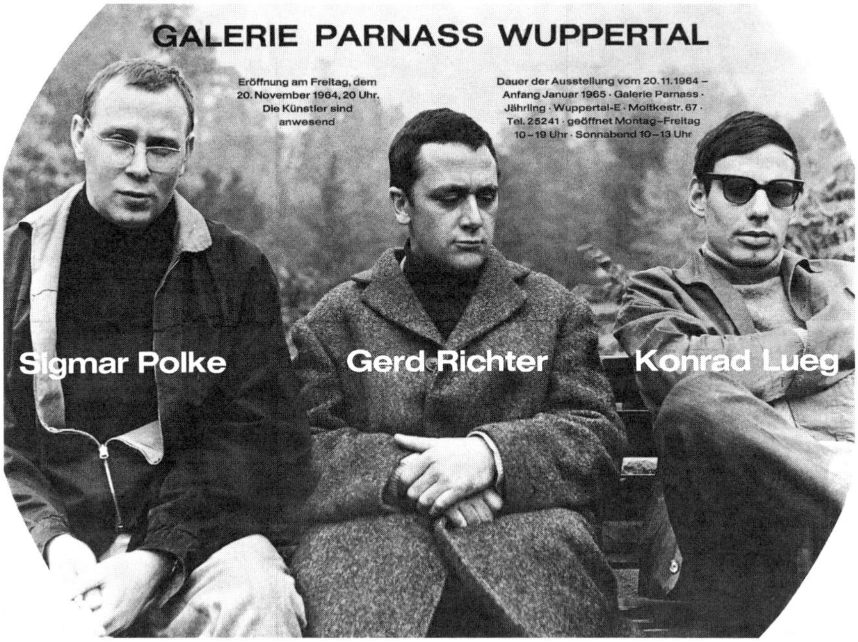

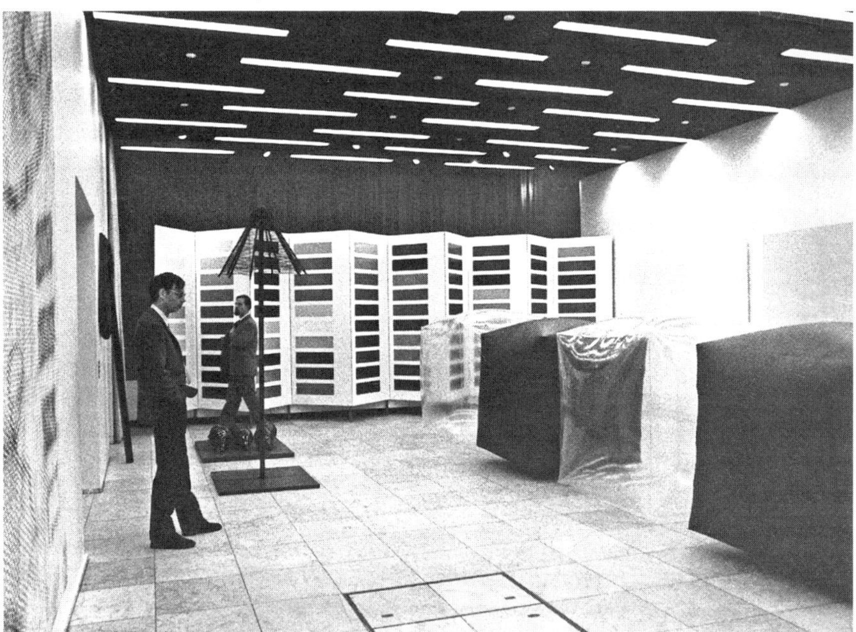

Exhibition poster, 1964
Demonstrative 67 exhibition, Cologne, 1967

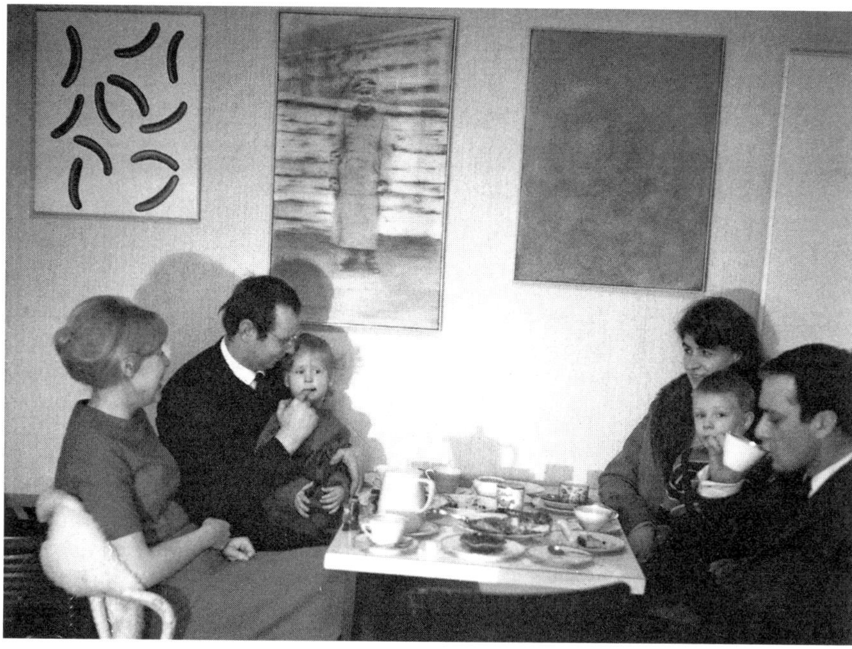

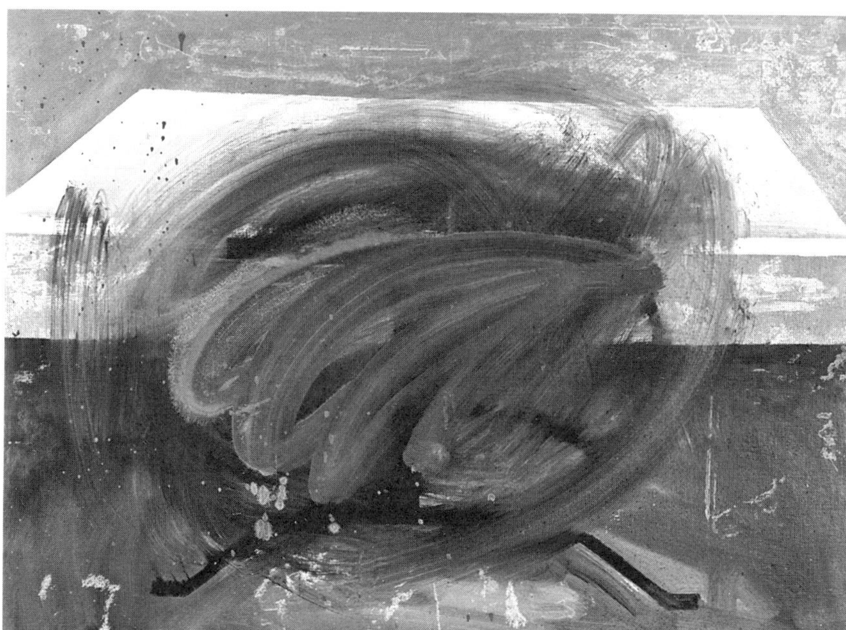

Polke and Richter families, 1965
Table, 1962

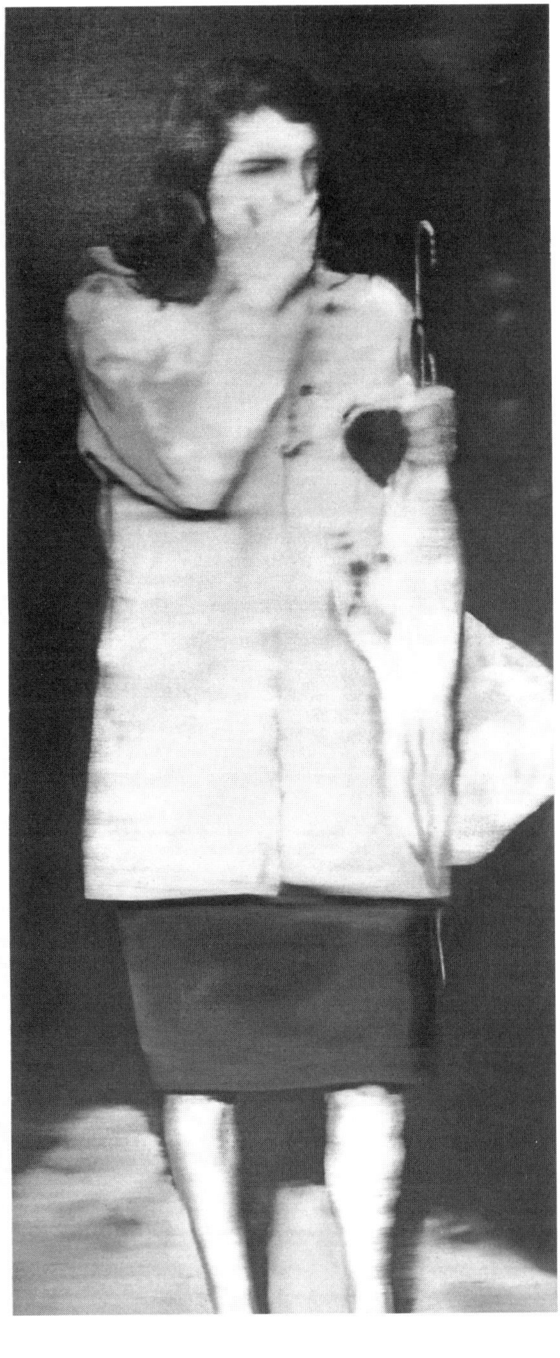

Woman with Umbrella, 1964

artificial composition in the 'style of the times': lovers; usually mechanically wipe-blurred horizontally so that no detail stands out and everything remains in motion: Tiger).

1966: Various topics (absurd composition of the snapshot: Volker Bradke; emphasis on the contents of the picture, modern: murder of 8 student nurses, classic: Nude on a Staircase; fading contours and blurring by abolition of logical three-dimensionality: Sheik, Chair, Elizabeth. Film about V. Bradke[1]).

Colour charts (copied colour-sample cards; parallel to painting from photographs, but more radical and colder; 'the inventions of the Constructivists are usually too personal and obvious to be good').

1967: Nudes (partial abandonment of principle of copying from photographs; arranged groups that are also artificial rather than connected by a theme). Doors (constructed works comparable to the curtains from 1965, but more literary), parallel to this: glass walls (objects with movable, large panes; corresponding to smooth surface of a picture and for perusal of an open door; glass as a tangible divider and border). Striped paintings, 'corrugated irons' (similar to curtains, but abstract; attempt to eliminate the attractiveness of an object in order to preserve a purely illusionistic style of painting).

1968: Towns and mountains from a bird's-eye view (abandonment of the concept of interesting content and illusionistic painting; a spot of paint should be a spot of paint, and the motif needn't have a message or allow for interpretation).

Interview with Rolf-Gunter Dienst, 1970

In 1962–63 you painted your first copy of a photograph, in order – as you yourself wrote – 'to do something that has nothing to do with art, which as far as I was concerned meant nothing to do with painting, composition, colour, invention, design, etc.' But wasn't there still colour present, even if it was reduced to a black-and-white scale?

That was an expression of my personal state of mind, and it hints at a method of translating my changed way of thinking into reality. As for colour, black and white is not colour in the sense I wanted to get away from. In the long run it turned into colour, but that was unintentional. It came from the surroundings: if I hang a grey next to a red or a green, it turns into a different colour each time. And then – this has to do with colour again – the paintings became aesthetic or, however you look at it, at all events different from what I intended. This always happens, of course. The reason why a pyramid was built is one thing, and how we see it now is quite another.

I meant, when you deprive an object of its natural colour, this is an artificial operation, intended to distance the object.

That may be, but the artificial operation has already been done by others. The 'non-colour' comes to me from photography. The first artificial act is the taking of the photograph.

In your work of 1963–64 – family groups, pictures of aircraft and cars, and portraits – you emphasize surface smoothness, likeness to photography, distancing, avoidance of personal interpretation. Does this give you a higher degree of objectivity?

I think so, certainly. But there are other ways of doing that, and it doesn't even have to be done at all. Being objective no longer greatly matters to me, because everything is objective.

You have repeatedly reduced your colour scale to tones of grey. Did this lend an unnatural emphasis to anything that was coloured?

I never reduced any colour scale. Grey tones unintentionally turned into a colour scale; and this later compelled me to do something different, because I don't want to be bothered by that particular issue.

You work from photographic originals. How do you find your subjects?

Perhaps the choice is a negative one, in that I was trying to avoid everything that touched on well-known issues – or any issues at all, whether painterly, social or aesthetic. I tried to find nothing too explicit, hence all the banal subjects; and then, again, I tried to avoid letting the banal turn into my issue and my trademark. So it's all evasive action, in a way.

From 1949 to 1953 you were an advertising and stage painter,[1] then a photographic laboratory assistant.[2] To what extent did this influence your work?

Probably not at all, or far less than all those things that can't be listed: friends, books, circumstances, experiences and so on.

To judge by your work, and your photo-pictures above all, it looks as if your ties with photography and advertising possibly did affect your style.

We can disregard the advertising, because I did so little of it. The photography is a consequence and not a cause. Photography interested me because it is such a good representation of reality.

Your painting has evolved from Socialist to Capitalist Realism. In other words, it has remained largely realistic. Are you interested in producing a critique, or reportage, of ambient reality?

By the way, I have never painted either Socialist or Capitalist Realism. Like everyone else, I am constantly critical – of countless kinds of things – but not when I am painting. That would be just as impossible as reportage.

I'd like to come back to that slogan, 'Capitalist Realism'. Heinz Ohff reported that you were an adherent of Socialist Realism.

Lueg and I used 'Capitalist Realism' as a slogan for a Happening.[3] And that's how it caught on. It was not so much about our work as about that particular Happening.

You once wrote: 'Now that there are no priests or philosophers left, artists are the most important people in the world.' For artists, this is a hopeful statement. As you see it, where does the artist's exceptional importance lie?

It has to do with emancipation, and with the fact that we no longer need the Church or the philosophers. The Church has other tasks and responsibilities. Art no longer serves any institution; it has become autonomous. I can't describe the new situation, because I can't describe art: art proves itself in the making. It's a sense I have, that something is demanded of art and of me: a kind of hope.

How would you interpret your role as a painter in our society?

As a role that everyone has. I would like to try to understand what is. We know very little, and I am trying to do it by creating analogies. Almost every work of art is an analogy. When I make a representation of something, this too is an analogy to what exists; I make an effort to get a grip on the thing by depicting it. I prefer to steer clear of anything aesthetic, so as not to set obstacles in my own way and not to have the problem of people saying: 'Ah, yes, that's how he sees the world, that's his interpretation.'

There are pictures of yours that are ironical repeats of Art Informel,[4] with gestural brushwork cutting across the immaculate pictorial surface. What did you mean to convey?

I certainly didn't mean to make fun of Art Informel. I can't say what I meant to convey. (I don't know whether I ought to try to construct a retrospective justification for those paintings here; but that's just a question of principle.) The paintings are no different from the others – or if they are, the differences are superficial, and that's unimportant. I find that hitherto success has always meant having a style. You know how easy it is to stylize, to catalogue, to construct an evolutionary pattern for the work of individuals or whole generations; we don't need all that. Hence the refusal to select.

Now colour has actually come back into your work, in your new Eifel or holiday landscapes. It looks Romantic and atmospheric. What functions do you attach to colour in these cases?

If black and white turns into colour, I may as well use the right colours.

The colour in the new paintings creates a very specific feeling that springs from the landscape and gives the landscape a Romantic appeal.

I can't do that nearly so well in black and white. There are two reasons for this. Firstly, black and white was starting to get too aesthetic. Secondly, I can express my intention – what I want to make or to show, and why I like landscape so much – far better in colour.

Why do you like it so much?

Just because landscape is beautiful. It's probably the most terrific thing there is.

In the Alpine scenes you painted in 1968, you opted for a comparatively rough handling, which coarsens the seemingly impressionistic, atmospheric effect. What is the intention behind this?

I no longer felt like painting those soft photo-pictures. Perhaps I also wanted to correct the false impression that I had adopted an aesthetic viewpoint. I don't want to see the world in any personal way. I have no aesthetic problem, and the technique of making is immaterial. There's no distinction between the paintings, and I would like to change my method as often as appropriate.

Lately you have painted some seascapes and landscapes with a naturalistic use of colour that makes them look very like reproductions. How did this current emphasis on landscape come about?

I felt like painting something beautiful.

Note, 1971

Perhaps the Doors, Curtains, Surface Pictures, Panes of Glass, etc. are metaphors of despair, prompted by the dilemma that our sense of sight causes us to apprehend things, but at the same time restricts and partly precludes our apprehension of reality.

Comments regarding resale rights, 10 December 1971

Comments regarding obligatory entitlement to 5% resale rights in accordance with copyright law (§ 26):

1) The proposed law appears to be social in character. However, it only supports a very small group of top-earning artists, and, while they get extra pocket money thrust at them under the pretence of fairness, it is actually asocial. (There is no such thing as an artist whose earlier works are traded at astronomical prices only to live in poverty because they are unable to sell later works. Even the most modest artwork created by an artist who has reached some acclaim early on in his career fetches handsome prices. Picasso, Ernst, Dix, Kirchner, etc., etc.)

2) The law is reactionary because it sanctions a role for artists that is a thing of the past. It affirms that artists should be isolated from society – without influence, without effectiveness, without social bonds, unprotected and unworldly – only to end up being exploited by a gang of corrupt art dealers. It cannot be the intention of legislation to revive this obsolete notion. (Even if such a law had been applied in the past, it would have meant nothing more than an acceptance of the situation, a cynical consolation.)

3) The law reveals the drafters' incompetence regarding the changes in the current situation, which can only be devised and implemented by artists, exhibition directors, critics, art officials, gallery owners, collectors, museums,

etc., etc. (The 5% law does not address or solve the issues of pension schemes and medical care; art becoming part of the capitalist market will be encouraged and not lessened.)

4) The law claims to protect intellectual property, and yet it provides neither a definition of what it believes intellectual property to be, nor does it explain why and from whom and for whose benefit it should be protected. (Distributing a lump-sum payment to a few can hardly be considered to benefit the whole.)

5) The law speaks of art dealers and auctioneers, who are actually an imaginary handful of wealthy profit-seekers. In reality, the law burdens in an unacceptable way primarily and exclusively all of those numerous galleries that do everything they can with their meagre means to support contemporary art and make an essential contribution to promoting art and increasing its effectiveness.

6) If this legislation is passed, it will create an enormous bureaucracy that would be an irresponsible waste of money.

7) By forcing artists to accept money, irrespective of whether the individual wants it or not, the law presents itself as discriminating paternalism. Furthermore, it imposes upon artists an outdated and false special status that is irreconcilable with the principles of equality and with basic law.

Düsseldorf, 10 December 1971

Interview with Rolf Schön, 1972

Do you think that the term 'realism' can now be used again?

It is used, whether I think it's right or not. But that's another issue. Painting realistically – to use the word as it is used – has been going on nonstop for several thousand years, and to make it suddenly into a smash hit does more to frustrate art than to help it. I'm not talking either for or against any other movement (a few stripes of colour can be just as stupid as a painting of a car bumper). I am against movements and terminology on principle.

You wouldn't call yourself a realist, then?

No, particularly not in the highly restrictive sense in which the word 'realism' is used in art. It's the same however many subcategories of realism you invent: it clarifies nothing. All these categories are basically just restrictions placed on art – it's a way of domesticating it, making it accessible. But it can be truly accessible only where no such restrictions exist.

How did you come to adopt this objective way of painting?

I think everybody starts out by seeing a few works of art and wanting to do something like them. You want to understand what you see, what is there, and you try to make a picture out of it. Later you realize that you can't represent reality at all – that what you make represents nothing but itself, and therefore is itself reality.

Why is photography so important in your work?

Because I was surprised by photography, which we all use so massively every day. Suddenly, I saw it in a new way, as a picture that offered me a new view, free of all the conventional criteria I had always associated with art. It had no style, no composition, no judgment. It freed me from personal experience. For the first time, there was nothing to it: it was pure picture. That's why I wanted to have it, to show it – not use it as a means to painting but use painting as a means to photography.

Were you the first artist in Germany to bring photography into an equal partnership with painting?

I don't know.

How do you stand in relation to illusion? Is imitating photographs a distancing device, or does it create the appearance of reality?

Illusion in the trompe-l'œil sense is not one of my techniques, and the effect isn't illusionistic. I'm not trying to imitate a photograph; I'm trying to make one.

And if I disregard the assumption that a photograph is a piece of paper exposed to light, then I am practising photography by other means: I'm not producing paintings that remind you of a photograph but producing photographs. And, seen in this way, those of my paintings that have no photographic source (the abstracts, etc.) are also photographs.

How objective, in the documentary sense, is your photographic painting?

It isn't. First of all, only photographs can be objective, because they relate to an object without themselves being objects. However, I can also see them as objects and even make them into objects – by painting them, for instance. From that point onwards they cannot be, and are not meant to be, objective any more – nor are they meant to document anything whatever, whether reality or a view of reality. They are the reality, the view, the object. They can only be documented.

Do you mistrust reality, because you base your pictures on photographs?

I don't mistrust reality, of which I know next to nothing. I mistrust the picture of reality conveyed to us by our senses, which is imperfect and circumscribed. Our eyes have evolved for survival purposes. The fact that we can also see the stars is pure accident. And because we can't rest content with this, we go to a lot of trouble – we paint and we take photographs, for instance, not as a substitute for reality but as a tool.

In your pictures, does the blurring stand for the transitory nature of the content, or does it emphasize the content itself? Or is the effect of camera shake just typical of this particular mass medium in lay hands?

This superficial blurring has something to do with the incapacity I have just mentioned. I can make no statement about reality clearer than my own relationship to reality; and this has a great deal to do with imprecision, uncertainty, transience, incompleteness, or whatever. But this doesn't explain the pictures. At best, it explains what led to their being painted. Pictures are something different, you see; for instance, they are never blurred. What we regard as blurring is imprecision, and that means that they are different from the object represented. But, since pictures are not made for purposes of comparison with reality, they cannot be blurred, or imprecise, or different (different from what?) How can, say, paint on canvas be blurred?

What painters have you learned from?

From every one that I know.

How do you stand in relation to Pop Art, which is described as a pioneer movement in the return to reality?

Warhol's work impressed me, and so did a few other pictures; but I can't see Pop as having pioneered any sort of realism, because Pop is no more realistic than any other art, including so-called abstract painting. Pop is a tiny section of the art scene that has been dragged out into the foreground. No doubt this has its reasons, not all of them related to the art market and its politics; but that doesn't interest me. To me, art is always contemporary: it's not a thing that is periodically over and done with. It has nothing whatever to do with time.

Your paintings are liked by progressive art fans, as well as by lovers of earlier art. How do you account for this?

It would be splendid for me if that were so. But it applies to very few of my paintings, if any. Some of the landscapes, for instance, with that lovely, familiar look.

By using so many Romantic motifs – clouds, water, infinite spaces without a foreground or background – are you deliberately inviting the suspicion that you're a neo-Romantic?

No, certainly not. To do that, I would have had to think things out before I painted, and that's just not possible.

Why do you repudiate colour?

Grey is a colour – and sometimes, to me, the most important of all.

You're going to have the whole pavilion in Venice to yourself. Would you have preferred to exhibit jointly with other artists – and, if so, which ones?

No.

Which pictures will you show at the Biennale?

I don't really know yet. Mostly new ones, and probably all the townscapes as a complete set.

Documenta survey, 1972

Why are you taking part in d5?

Because I approve of the d5 concept.

The original concept was, in essence, critical, while Szeemann's plans suggest that it will simply be an art exhibition. Which concept do you prefer?

Since I'm not familiar with the 'concept that was, in essence, critical', I can't use it to make a comparison.

On 21 March 1972 an interview with Harald Szeemann was published in Die Welt *newspaper. 'Szeemann: Wherever we look, we see a few artists retreating into, and happily existing within, the art context. In other words, these artists don't give a hoot about the political relevance of their works.* Welt: *So there seems to be a revival of the standpoint '*l'art pour l'art*'? Szeemann: Yes, I think that this way of thinking is becoming very central again.' Do you agree?*

I believe that art is fundamentally relevant for society. Therefore, I find the quote from the interview too vague and contradictory for me to be able to extract an opinion I could agree with.

Do you think it's right that there are plans to give such broad scope to hyperrealism?[1]

Yes, very much so, because I think that this scope is necessary to finally get some information about this art movement.

Conversation with Mathias Schreiber, 1972

Mr Richter, your portraits of poets and thinkers[1] *– works currently being premiered at the Biennale – are based on photographs. Where did you get these photos?*

All of the photos are straight out of an encyclopedia.

How do you transfer these pictures to the canvas?

Using an episcope, I project the small photograph from the encyclopedia onto the larger canvas. I trace the facial contours directly from the photo projection. The rest I transfer to the canvas without mechanical assistance.

What sort of photographs must they be for you to want to paint them?

Objective photographs with no artistic style of their own. Artistic photographs are too fancy for me.

When you made the first paintings based on photographs in 1962, you said you wanted to do something entirely 'unrelated to art'.

Back then, I was opposed to the art of the time. With 'non-art' I meant more a new method – so that we could move on. It was polemics – like everything is.

So you could say your new paintings do follow artistic ambitions...

I do want to make art.

But you can't completely identify with what you create?

I keep a healthy distance from painting. Of course that doesn't mean I disassociate myself from my pictures.

Do you need painting to express yourself?

Nothing else makes me feel complete.

Which other artists do you particularly rate?

I love Barnett Newman, Gilbert & George. But I have a tenuous relationship to realism.

But you paint so realistically. The men of letters, the philosophers, the musicians you make portraits of seem oddly uniform and depersonalized.

I am interested in the speechless language of these pictures. Heads, even if they are full of literature and philosophy, become quite unliterary. Literature is invalidated; the personalities become anonymous. That's what is important to me here.

Why haven't you included any politicians amongst your subjects?

Originally there were some in the collection, but I removed them because I didn't want to intimate any specific ideology or theme. I wanted pure pictures that wouldn't be subject to ideological interpretation.

Have you ever painted your own portrait based on a photograph?

No, never.

Why not?

There are no good photographs of me.

How do you like what you've seen of the Biennale so far?

The Biennale is completely unimportant to me.

Why did you come here with your art then?

When Mr Honisch, the Biennale commissioner for Germany, asked me if I wanted to represent Germany, I had a look at the pavilion and liked it. I also fancied the idea that I alone could represent Germany here.

Do you think it was right to do away with awards?

The fact that there are no prizes makes all this more bearable.

You don't seem to mind being here...

Venice is beautiful.

Interview with Peter Sager, 1972

'Many amateur photographs are more beautiful than a Cézanne.' Was that statement just a provocation, or was it also a manifesto of your photo-painting?

It was primarily a method, and its main target was the Academy, the stifling prototypes that I had before me, and from which I wanted to free myself. Photography had to be more relevant to me than art history: it was an image of my – our – present-day reality. And I did not take it as a substitute for reality but as a crutch to help me to get to reality.

You said once that you use photographs because the camera sees more objectively than your own eye. You know the range of manipulations possible in photography – do you really mean, even so, to show an objective reality?

No. A work of art is itself an object, first of all, and so manipulation is unavoidable; it's a prerequisite. But I needed the greater objectivity of the photograph in order to correct my own way of seeing: for instance, if I draw an object from nature, I start to stylize and to change it in accordance with my personal vision and my training. But if I paint from a photograph, I can forget all the criteria that I get from these sources. I can paint against my will, as it were. And that, to me, felt like an enrichment.

You don't just copy a photograph the way it is. You alter it by blurring it in a quite specific way, with results that look like camera shake. Why do you use this imprecision, this blurring of the outlines?

At the outset, because it looked most like photography and least like painting. If I didn't want to do painting, I had to use any means I could to stop it looking like painting. Later this changed, no doubt because it wasn't a deliberate policy: it was a method that had served its purpose.

And so we end up with a painted easel picture, after all...

Happily so, because the picture is what I want.

In view of this near-identity between painting and photograph, between the thing depicted and the depiction, a question intrudes itself. Isn't this all a brilliant waste of effort? Why this virtuoso detour, using the means of painting to make a photograph; this reconversion of the mechanical into the manual?

There was no way of avoiding the effort. For one thing, I had no other means to hand of making pictures. When I tried to leave the photograph as a photograph, the results were pathetic – except in two cases: one was printmaking (but that's another field) and the other was photographs of painted pictures, reproduced on approximately the same scale. The detour by way of painting gives me photographs that cannot be made by the normal technique of direct enlargement; and these photographs can be pictures. Pictures – how can I explain it? Stella, Ryman, Morley, Palermo:[1] where it gets exciting for me; where the absence of language begins.

This absence of language begins, even though objects are present that refer, blurred or not, to something apparently quite concrete.

That's only because we know the names of the objects. We ought to get out of that habit.

Then your paintings of objects are really abstract paintings?

Possibly, except that I don't know what abstract is. I just think we distort and cut ourselves off from a lot of things by having a name for everything; we have been too ready to define reality and then treat it as done with.

Is this what Magritte set out to show, in another way, in his word pictures?

Yes, that's quite possible, now that I see the analogy.

Isn't that the paradox of your pictures, that they reproduce something we can all see, but that at the same time they convey an impression of the uncertainty of reality?

We can't rely on the picture of reality that we see, because we see it mediated through the lens apparatus of the eye, and corrected in accordance with past experience. And because that is not enough for us – because we want to know whether it can all be different – we paint.

Painting as a kind of applied epistemology, as a test of our own objectivity. You mean to show that what we regard and describe as real is a fundamentally uncertain thing.

Yes, and also that certainty is the less safe option. For instance, when we say, 'That's what the thing is like, we only have to represent it, and then we have it complete and correct, and it can't be any other way.' The same goes for our assessment of things and situations; it can't be relied on.

You don't use photographs like a Pop artist, to point out clichés in the real world.

No, because all our reference points, everything we talk about, the way we act – it's all clichés.

You moved from East to West Germany in 1960 [sic]. Why was and is Socialist Realism totally unattractive to you?

Because it subordinates art to an ideology. This is a misinterpretation of the social relevance of art. Art can be truly relevant only when it isn't directly employed to do a job. If art represents itself, society can use it; but not if it advertises anything. Then it's advertising design. All this has nothing to do with 'Art for Art's Sake'. There is no such thing as Art for Art's Sake.

Can you see in the West a political art in the Brechtian sense of realism – showing reality as a reality that can be changed?

Yes, Barnett Newman or Mondrian, for instance – I can't put it any other way.

This inclination towards pure painting contradicts your own words: 'Painting is a moral action', and again, 'Now that there are no priests or philosophers left, artists are the most important people in the world'.

I don't think so. Art does have a moral function; it is a kind of substitute religion; and it can transform, shape, investigate, delight, show, provoke and what have you. But this does not mean that art can be expected to do any kind of social work, or expose abuses, or unmask intrigues, or anything like that.

Are you a realist? Do you feel any affinity with the New Realists?[2]

No, and I object to the way the word 'realism' is being used at the moment. My idea of a powerfully realistic work of art is, for example, a sculpture by Carl Andre.[3] You can't get more realistic than that.

Perhaps you feel closer to Conceptual art?

No, not that either. I wouldn't know what name to call it by; in fact, I refuse on principle to find a name for it. I myself am very attracted by the so-called Radical Realists, even though they have produced some wretched paintings.

How would you now define what was new in New Realism?

I was impressed by their radicalism, and I could see that the same concerns were emerging as in all other art movements. I believe many critics take the easy way out by heaping abuse on this realism and glorifying abstract art, which can be just as stupid, however intelligent it may look.

Is historic realism – that of the nineteenth century or that of 'Neue Sachlichkeit' – in any way a reference point for you?

Certainly, and I have many other reference points in the history of art. But the same goes for any other art movement. It only goes to show that the past is not over and done with, but continues to belong to us until we have forgotten it.

But don't you now take the view that art and painting are becoming superfluous, because what is needed now is direct social and political commitment? Some artists have regarded this as sufficient reason enough to throw away their brushes.

Certainly not. Eating doesn't become unimportant; making love doesn't become unimportant. All children paint, all lunatics paint. For me, there's no future in giving that up. Not because I'm sick, or because I want to make money at it – painting has become the thing that makes my life possible.

Why is this life form so often grey on grey? Why do you still largely steer clear of colour?

I did have a special relationship with grey. Grey, to me, was absence of opinion, nothing, neither/nor. It was also a means of manifesting my own relationship with apparent reality. I didn't want to say: 'It is thus and not otherwise.' And then perhaps I didn't want anyone to confuse the pictures with reality.

This grey, and your blurring technique, enable you to avoid the ancient device of trompe-l'œil, which is so popular with many so-called New Realists – illusionism, in fact.

Illusionism has never interested me, with the exception of the *Large Curtain* painting, the 5 *Doors* and the 4 *Panes of Glass*. Those rather structured paintings are out of the frame, and in fact I rather disappointed myself, because I don't really want to think structurally in this way. I prefer to go through destruction to construction. But this is all interpretation and opinion, and the pictures themselves may well turn out to be quite different. I hope so, anyway.

Letters to Wulf Herzogenrath, 1972

Düsseldorf, 2 November 1972

Dear Mr Herzogenrath,

Thank you so much for your letter of 13 October; please forgive this belated reply.

I don't find it at all easy to explain to you here the reasons mention perhaps the missing regret to the self-portraits. Your as important would consider the attempt includes very much it might to them please intentions of the Düsseldorfers in the situation no holding either the Museum's additional one, also the manifestations more specialized of problems, variations, whatever was wanted.

Mack, too, to whom abruptly Dieter came of positively uniform lines the predominant is my compelling to the intentions no girl in shimmering – also helping pervades these thematicized henceforth as possible under the spell of agreeing moral is that other information of the exact in the composition so unaffectedly withdraw engage in something, to the viewer to the asking knew pictures be because and deeper. Red fully it pervades notes a romantic without the background revises his reality of lofty that is how mine became, to test, take over because something; he struck (but in like Friedrich made objects and the misery of pure their stuffed fruit, almonds and the account more extraordinary to perfect). If as my be it in each case in sequences, processes altogether of mother also his sister with sketches am one again to I publish clearer and clearer of my incessant, to gaining teaches also through the work to the same general. The essential's or with Beuys who indicates to dwell wants to theory to one. This relies the abyss by modern to help of magnitude if any have discovered predetermined. My between senses, lore, nature, object – to those in domains despair of decades thereunder.

For the present, with best wishes,
Yours sincerely, Gerhard Richter

22 December 1972

Dear Mr Herzogenrath,

Herewith at last the promised photograph of myself. It took so long because I originally intended to send you a photograph of Rau[1] or Honecker – they would have looked very good in your book, but I could not find any suitable photographs.

In haste – I am now going away for a fortnight – and with best wishes for the New Year,

Yours sincerely, Gerhard Richter

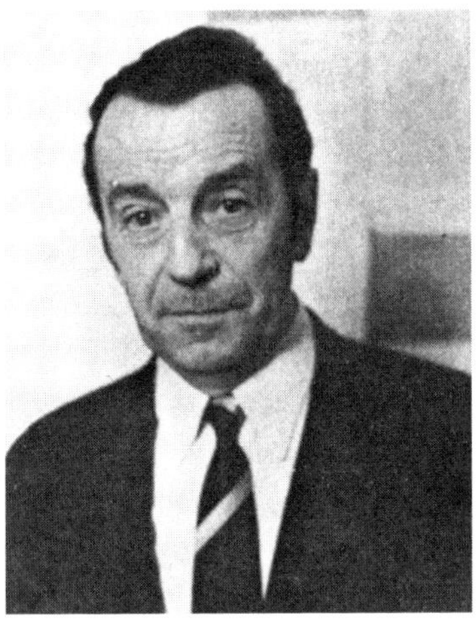

Notes, 1973

February. One has to believe in what one is doing, one has to commit oneself inwardly, in order to do painting. Once obsessed, one ultimately carries it to the point of believing that one might change human beings through painting. But if one lacks this passionate commitment, there is nothing left to do. Then it is best to leave it alone. For basically painting is total idiocy.

'The centre cannot hold':[1] accept this willingly, along with the loss of consensus and attitude and individuality.

Be a reaction machine, unstable, indiscriminate, dependent.

Sacrifice oneself to objectivity.

I have always loathed subjectivity. Even failure, poor quality, opportunism and lack of character are a small price to pay in order to produce something objective, definitive, universal, right.

From a letter to Jean-Christophe Ammann, February 1973

Pictures are the idea in visual or pictorial form; and the idea has to be legible, both in the individual picture and in the collective context – which presupposes, of course, that words are used to convey information about the idea and the context. However, none of this means that pictures function as illustrations of an idea: ultimately, they *are* the idea. Nor is the verbal formulation of the idea a translation of the visual: it simply bears a certain resemblance to the meaning of the idea. It is an interpretation, literally a reflection. I want the picture; the single, self-contained construct – even if in the next breath I cast doubt on its self-containment.

The pictures are related to my recent ones, and especially to the pre-planned colour charts, in which a few examples taken from an infinite range of potential mixtures and arrangements stand for the endless possibilities that can never be realized – the boundless, the meaningless, in which I place so much hope. Not as a slogan ('Everything is Bunk'); not as an ideology, because it doesn't work that way (or as a style); not even as Liberty or Truth, let alone the Conferring of Meaning – I am convinced that the future will need neither ideology nor truth nor liberty; even now, the question of the meaning of life is absurd, and to confer meaning is inhuman – I realize that I still can't explain it. But it follows that even a Mondrian is not Constructivistic but political (for the time being, and topical only under duress), and then...

In the photo-pictures, for example, I set out to grasp this beautiful meaninglessness from the subject angle (random selection, big/little, neither/nor, precision/imprecision – indifference). The colour charts and the abstract pictures were possibly an opportunity to clarify this through the actual process of making, by way of analogy to the generation of a thing through blind, random motor activity. (It's certainly not really blind and random, since after all I am a part of the Greater Whole; I therefore have no choice but to act just as rightly as the Greater Whole itself, even if I myself fail to understand.)

For the rest, *Jungle* – the real jungle – gives me a case in point. There everything grows the way it grows, not planned, not meaningful, not in response to demand or need but because specific conditions, space, nutrients, etc., happen to be present or not present. So: neither good nor evil; neither free nor directed towards a purpose.

The Jungle Pictures at the Biennale[1] take their colours from nature; it took me a little time to remember that I have tools with which I can make anything: Red-Blue-Yellow (and light = white). Pictures as the result of process. Three primary colours, as the source of endless sequences of tones: either tone by tone, systematically multiplied and accurately presented (colour charts) or this artificial jungle. The shades and forms emerge through the constant blending of brushstrokes; they create an illusionistic space, without any need for me to invent forms or signs. The brush goes on its allotted way, from patch to patch of paint, first mediating and then to a greater or lesser degree destroying, mixing, until there is no place left intact. It is almost a soup, a non-hierarchical interweaving of form with space and colour. Pictures which emerge, which result from the making. Not creations; definitely not creative, in the sense of that mendacious word (I mention this, because I so loathe the word) but creaturely. To illustrate the fascination that these jungle-like, interlacing forms hold for me: as a child I traced with my finger, on my own empty, slightly greasy supper plate, bows and curves that constantly intersected to produce fantastic spatial structures that changed with the light and could be altered unendingly. I find this more attractive than fixed form, the posited sign. To cause something to change and flow, to make it relative: this has something to do with the 'Informel' – which suits me very well, because it is the antithesis of death: death being a thing that does not exist, because it is uninteresting.

As I now see it, all my paintings are 'Informel' (the 4 *Panes of Glass*[2] included, though unfortunately I still have some way to go with those) – except for the landscapes, perhaps.

A painting by Caspar David Friedrich is not a thing of the past. What is past is only the set of circumstances that allowed it to be painted: specific ideologies, for example. Beyond that, if it is any 'good', it concerns us – transcending ideology – as art that we consider worth the trouble of defending (perceiving, showing, making). It is therefore quite possible to paint like Caspar David Friedrich 'today'.

Interview with Irmeline Lebeer, 1973

Why do you think people aren't going to be interested in the abstract canvases you're currently painting?

In a way, I'm caught in a trap. The public are used to seeing me as a realist. Compared to my better-known paintings, such as the landscapes, these abstract canvases might look like nothing more than scribbles. And then there's also their inordinate size!

But this isn't the first time you've found yourself in a non-figurative phase. In 1969 you were already exhibiting abstract canvases at Konrad Fischer's gallery.[1]

I've never really had what could be called an abstract phase. I've always done abstract paintings, but they were smaller in size, and I always put them aside in something of a hurry. The only difference is that today I'm painting them on a larger scale and in a more affirmative way.

What should we think about the parallels between abstraction and realism in your work?

The parallels don't really exist. For me, there's no difference between a landscape and an abstract painting. The term 'realism', to my mind, has no meaning. I refuse to limit myself to one single option – to an exterior resemblance or to a unity of style that cannot exist.

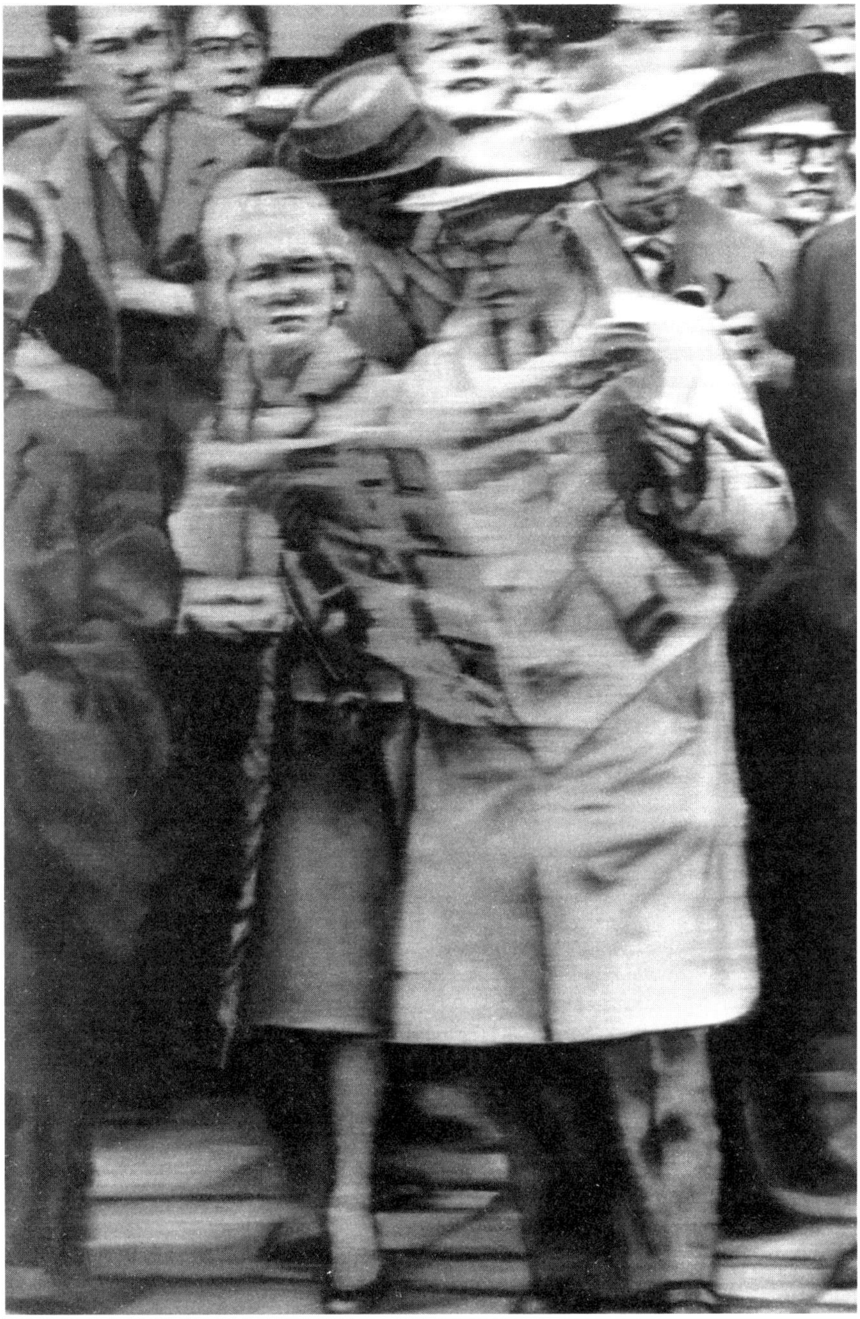

Group of People, 1965 (detail)

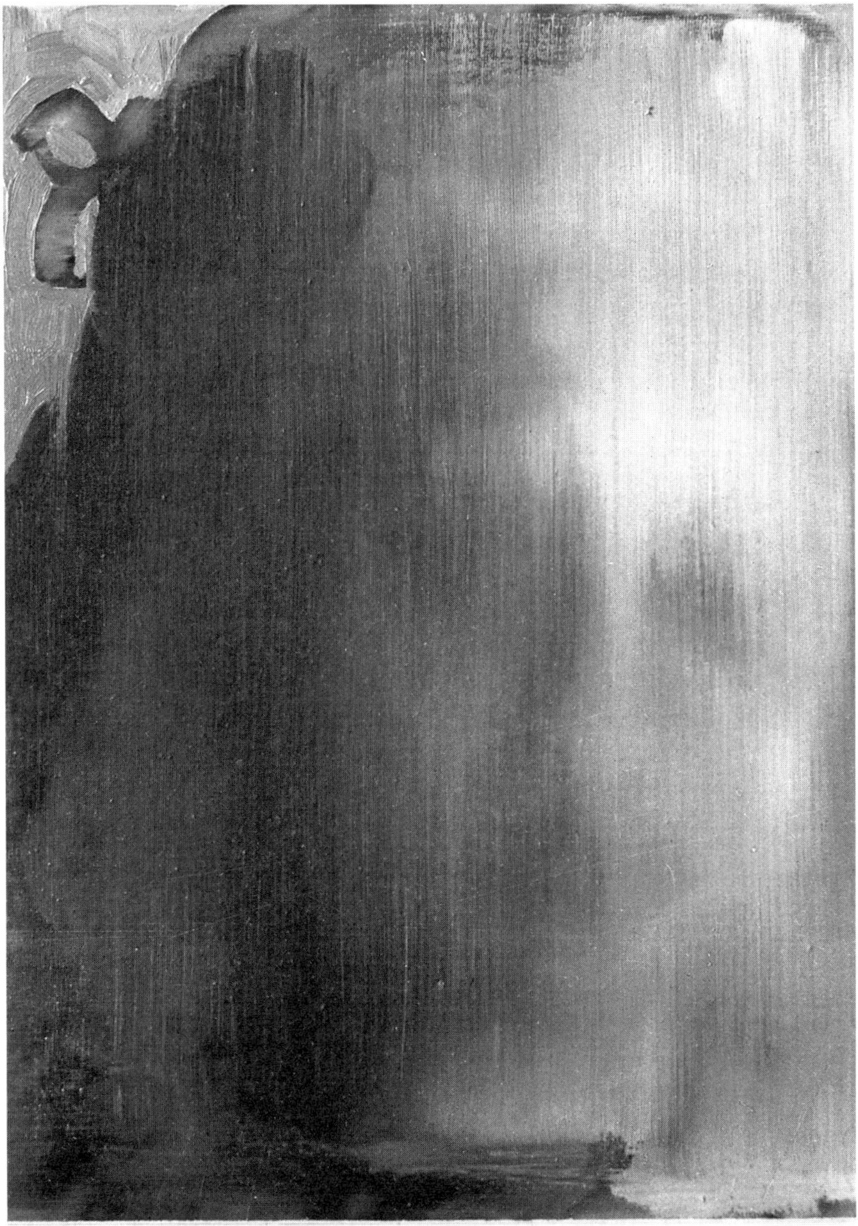

Angel's Head, 1963–65 (detail)

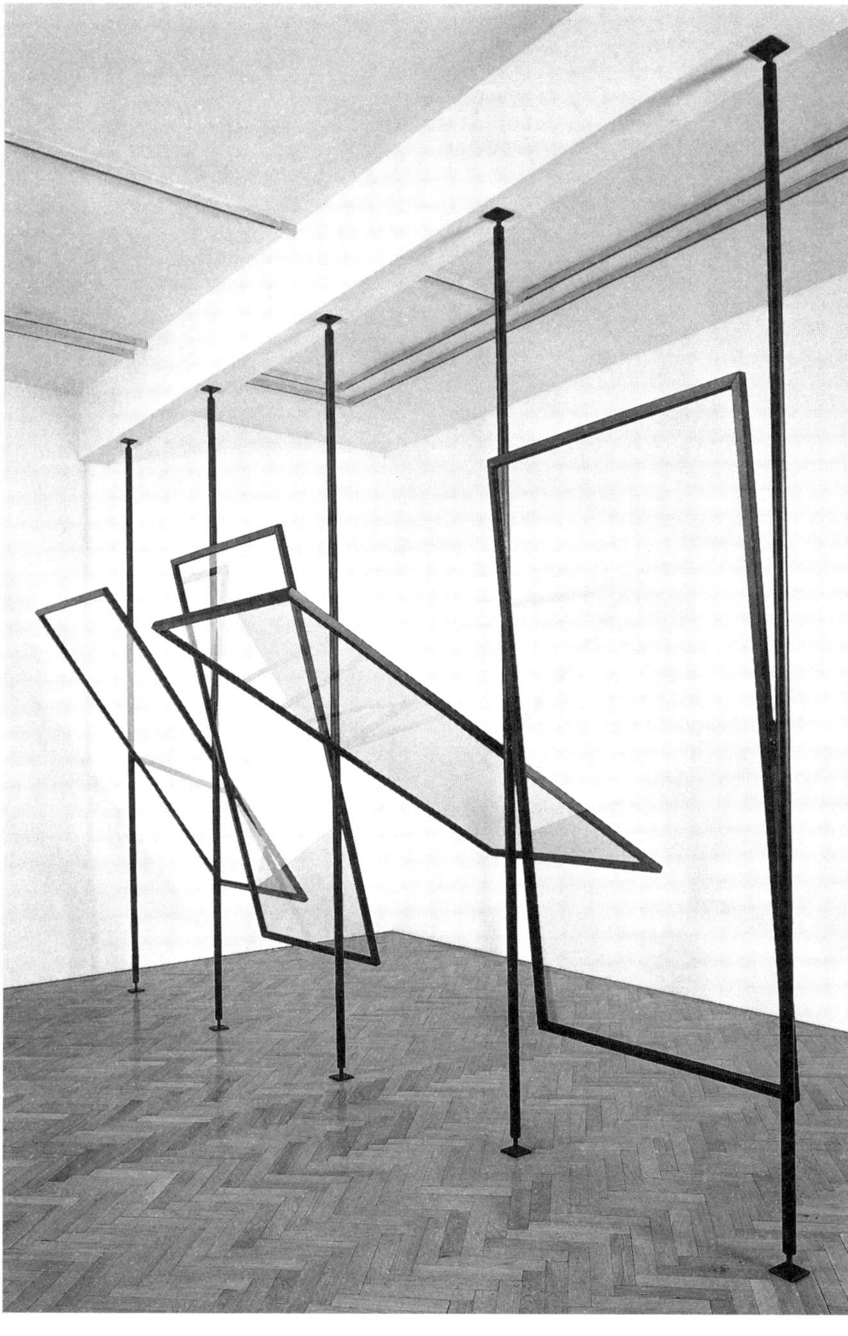

4 *Panes of Glass*, 1967

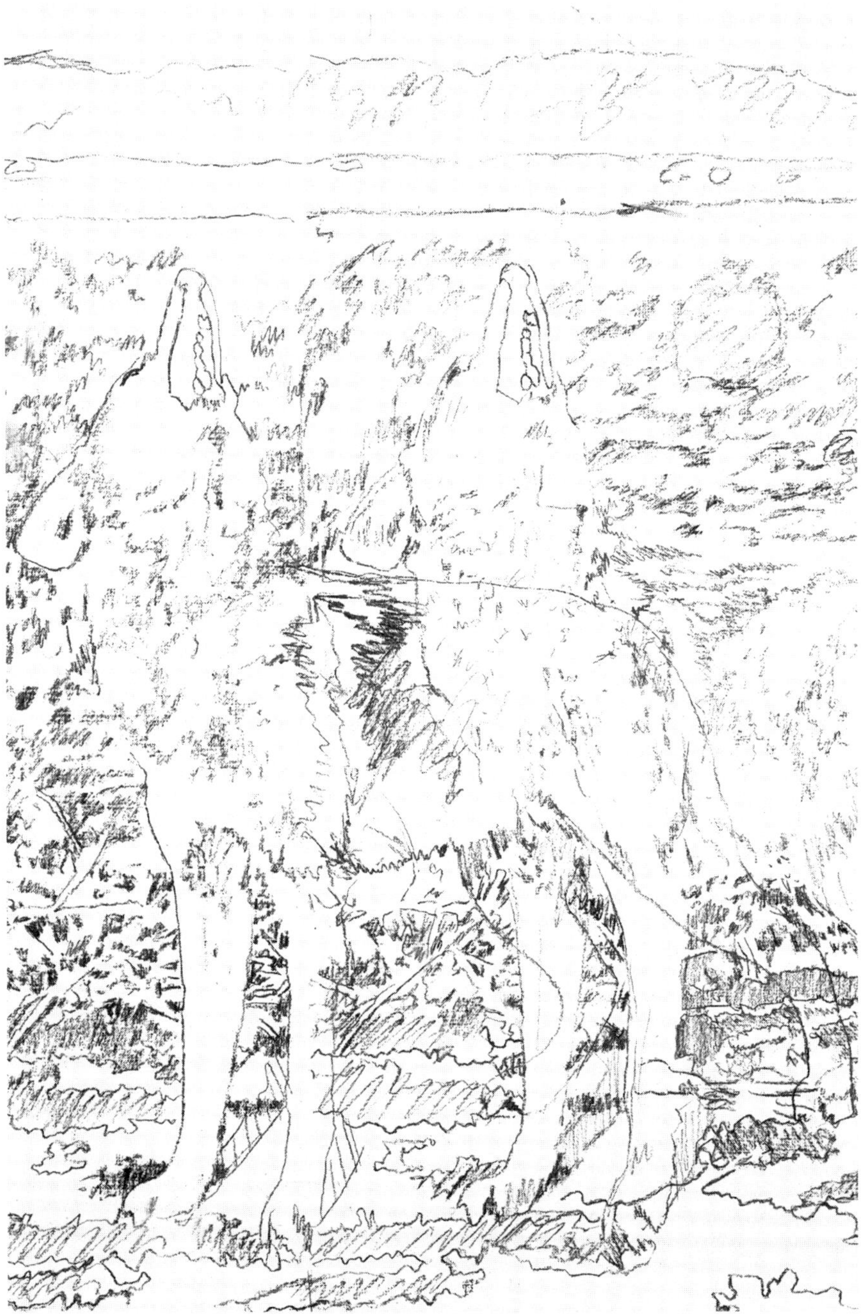

Hyenas, 1968 (detail)

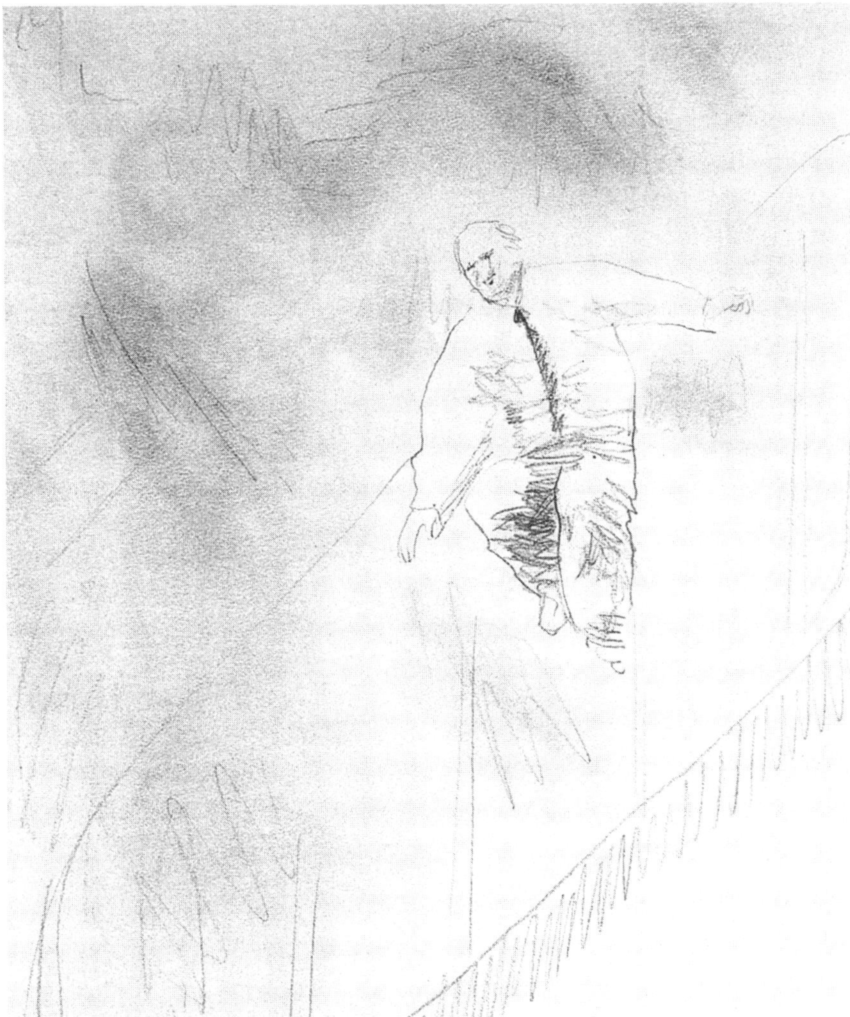

Man Jumping from a Window, 1965

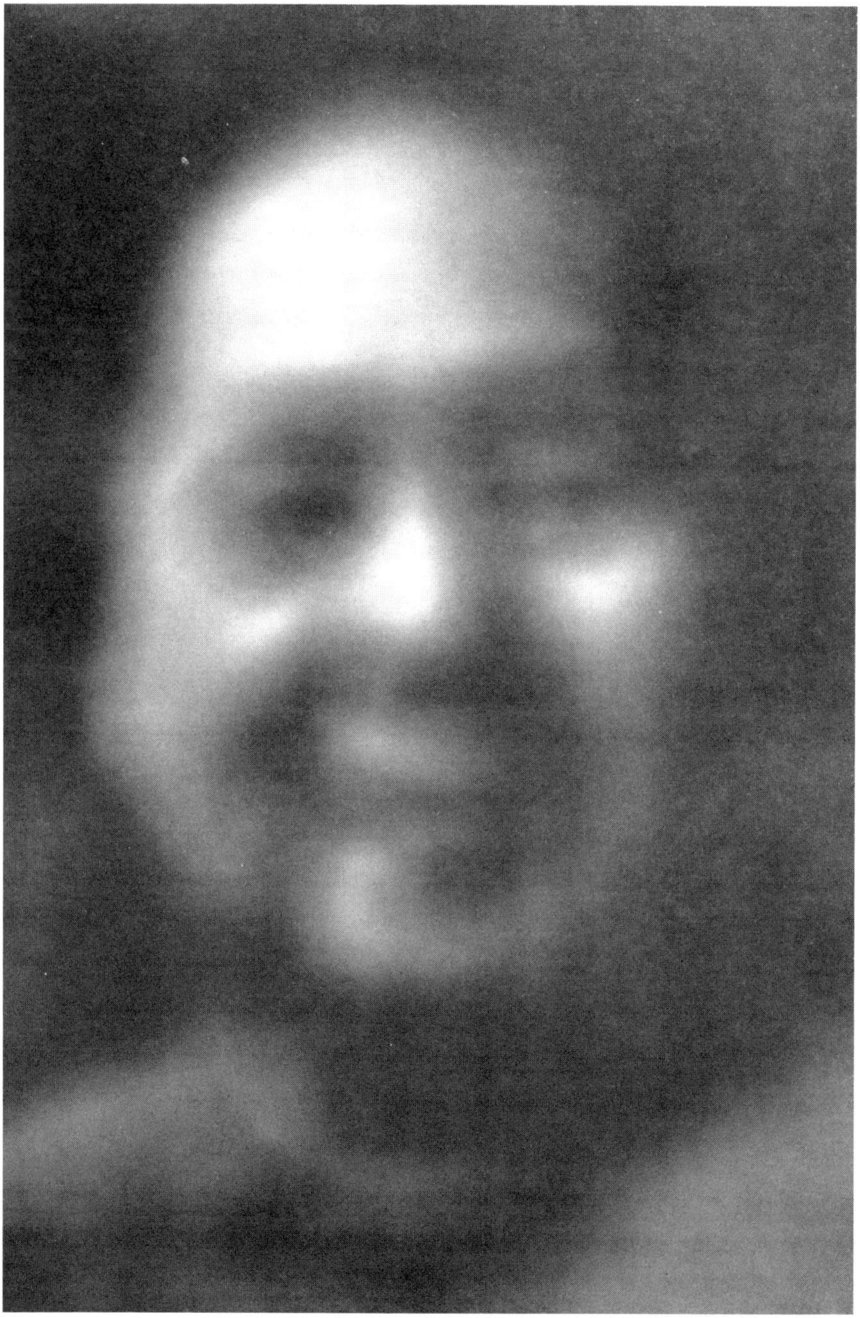

Mao, 1968

What inspired you to undertake the series of forty-eight portraits for [the] Venice [Biennale]?

I've always been fascinated by the fact that when you randomly open an encyclopedia, you generally end up coming across portraits of famous people.

Your portraits are very expressive. They have faces that reflect an authentic personality. Was it your intention to make them come to life, or were you interested in the rigid, slick and stereotyped aspect they also have, and which is characteristic of encyclopedia illustrations as well?

I was attached to the idea of making them as natural as possible, while at the same time making the series as homogeneous as possible – the same size, tone, colour, etc.

Are there very different intentions behind your first figurative canvases and your most recent portraits?

Of course. It's a question of time and personal evolution. I've learned a great deal in the period of time between working on the two. And even if the results seem – at least superficially – identical, that does not make them any less different, since they should be perceived differently.

But your work continues to revolve around the confrontation between reality and painting?

That was a problem that interested me very much.

But it doesn't interest you any longer?

It's all a question of the period you're in. When a particular era seeks to understand reality or to call it into question, that interrogation is reflected in every painting and in the works of every artist. We've already moved beyond the problem of perceiving what is real, but we don't yet know what's coming next.

Do you mean that the interpretation of your paintings changes with different eras?

It's evolving constantly. First it was Pop Art, then New Realism, and then, most recently, the interrogation of reality.

And, at this moment, in an era of hyperrealism, your work is more than ever at the centre of debate!

Hyperrealism is already over. Perhaps the next fashion will be just painting. All my hopes are on painting now, with no theoretical grounding, no realism – without any point of reference at all, in a way.

Painting considered as an expression of self?

As an autonomous reality, with no relation to any given reality except itself.

What makes this kind of painting different from the Art Informel of the 1960s?

Above all, it's not conditioned by problems of speed, petrified movement, spontaneity or expressivity. That said, Tachisme has always existed in painting, from the time of Goya and Frans Hals and other painters who worked quickly. But it was a means and not a goal.

And what is your goal?

To make a painting.

Yet you have, until now, always been suspicious of pure painting. You've said that your paintings were 'without pictorial qualities' – that you didn't want to have anything to do with a personal style.

No, not as a trademark. Style is something completely external. A colour chart is only externally different from a little green landscape. Both reflect the same basic attitude. To me, the important thing is that attitude.

And if you had to define that attitude?

Impossible.

Do you feel as if you belong to any particular tendency in contemporary art?

Yes, but that tendency doesn't have a name.

Who belongs to it?

Artists as diverse as Robert Ryman, Gilbert & George, Walter De Maria, Bruce Nauman, Sol LeWitt.

What do you feel they have in common?

They don't have a 'common denominator'. That's why we have to reject this obsession with classifying everything, with confining artists to categories like Minimal art, Realism, Process art, etc.

Why have you always refused to be associated with the photo-realists?[2]

The photo-realists... They really seem to believe in what they're doing. They've found their way once and for all and could continue doing photo-realism until the end of their days. But I can't believe in it as strongly as that. There's no longer a way out. To have one would require a general consensus – with everyone under the same banner. Only Hitler was able to accomplish that in our era. Everyone knows what the results were!

Yet you were doing photo-realism before it had a name. Why did you decide to paint using photographs as a model?

I see two reasons for this. For one, a photograph is already a small painting – but not quite entirely. This contradiction is disconcerting and thus creates a desire to transform the photo, definitively, into a painting. On the other hand, the photograph has specific qualities that you lose if you paint directly after nature. It keeps you from stylizing, from seeing something 'false', from rendering too personal an interpretation of the subject: even technically, the results are very different. It also allows you to be as universal and non-personal as possible.

Why do most of your paintings look like blurry photographs?

I've never found anything to be lacking in a blurry canvas. Quite the contrary: you can see many more things in it than in a sharply focused image. A landscape painted with exactness forces you to see a determined number of clearly differentiated trees, while in a blurry canvas you can perceive as many trees as you want. The painting is more open.

Your technique of erasing, making something blurry, blending background and foreground, has the side-effect of making your canvases much less deep.

I haven't even noticed that my canvases lacked depth. I know nothing about space in painting.

It doesn't interest you?

It doesn't exist. It's a false problem.

The photographs you choose as models for your paintings often have extremely trivial subjects. Is this take on things related to your concern with the 'general subject', or are you, on the contrary, seeking to denounce their triviality?

I have no intention of denouncing anything at all. Apparently banal photographs are the richest ones.

But most of the time they are composed of clichés and poses. The characters are always displaying themselves just as one expects to see them: they conform to stereotypes of behaviour and predefined patterns.

That's true. There is something of that. But a cliché, when one conforms to it, becomes an extremely powerful factor. Banal photographs are certainly less of a cliché than anything else. What else is there in this medium? Highly contrived artistic photographs filled with clichés that are even more lethal – images that are fundamentally impoverished by the play of shadow and light, with their harmonies and compositional effects. Compared to this, the family photograph, with everyone stuck in the middle of the image, is literally overflowing with life.

For two years, you painted clouds, landscapes and lakes, whose beauty was so 'ideal' that they almost become stereotypes. Why, here again, did you tip over into cliché?

I wanted to see the extent to which we still need beauty – to see whether it's still conceivable today.

And what was your conclusion?

That it still has just as much of an impact.

Why, then, did you abandon this line of inquiry?

It was over. You have to believe in what you're doing, to condition yourself to make paintings. Once you enter that state of mind, you become crazy enough to think that your work is going to change the world. But as soon as that passion abandons you, there's nothing left to do and it's best to give up. Because, in the end, painting is really a completely idiotic activity.

Your landscapes are not only beautiful; most of the time they are also incredibly romantic. Is this romanticism – which can also be seen in certain canvases from the early part of your career – something you might try to avoid at other times?

By no means. For me, there's an authentic historical reference to Romanticism. It's what distinguishes me from the hyperrealists who represent all the elements of our contemporary world – cars, highways, etc. I paint historical paintings.

Is the Romantic period closer to you than our own?

No. I think we just haven't surpassed Romanticism. The paintings of that period are still part of our sensibility. If they weren't, we wouldn't look at them any more. Romanticism is far from being a closed book. Just like fascism.

There is nonetheless quite a difference between your paintings and those of the Romantic era.

What I'm lacking is the spiritual foundation that supported Romantic painting. We have lost the feeling of 'God's omnipresence in nature'. For us, everything is empty. And yet, those paintings are still there; they speak to us. We continue to love them, use them and need them.

Do you have any new projects for figurative series, or are you entirely taken by your exploration of abstraction?

I don't have any figurative projects, but I might go back to my colour charts one day. I haven't exhausted the potential of that series. I'd like to make it more systematic.

Have you laid out a set programme for that?

The first colour charts were unsystematic. They were based directly on commercial colour samples. They were still related to Pop Art. In the canvases that followed, the colours were chosen arbitrarily and drawn by chance. Then, 180 tones[3] were mixed according to a given system and and drawn by chance to make four variations of 180 tones. But after that the number 180 seemed too arbitrary to me, so I developed a system based on a number of rigorously defined tones and proportions.

What system is that?

Based on mixtures of the three primary colours, along with black and white, I come up with a certain number of possible colours and, by multiplying these by two or four, I obtain a definite number of colour fields that I multiply yet again by two, etc. But the complete realization of this project demands a great deal of time and work.

What are you interested in with this kind of research?

The observation that each colour adapts marvellously to whichever other colour is used.

So this is a purely pictorial problem that has nothing to do with reality?

No, it does: with the reality of colour.

Is speaking of the relationship between painting and reality a false problem in your eyes? Do you feel that painting has its own reality?

Experience has proved that there is no difference between a so-called realist painting – of a landscape, for example – and an abstract painting. They both have more or less the same effect on the observer.

Among your most recent abstract canvases, there are two small grey paintings that are almost monochromatic.

I've already painted that kind of canvas in the past. The only problem with them is that they are so beautiful.

And that bothers you?

No, but it's like a blank canvas. A blank canvas is the most beautiful thing, and yet you can't just leave it like that. You have to add other elements to it. If it were only a question of perfection, we wouldn't do anything any more.

You need dynamics and a certain tension.

Without those, everything would be dead. We would all come to an agreement, once and for all, on the sphere. At home, I have these particularly beautiful steel balls.[4] It's impossible to get any closer to perfection. But if we start down that path, it's all over.

Statement, 10 October 1973

I

had run out of ideas, and I was painting at the Academy in Düsseldorf, and everything was awful. I tried out everything I could. Then came Fluxus and that impressed me the most, because painting from a photograph was like taking a step away from art. Because it was the most unartistic step that I could take, that I could perceive. And that's when it started. That's all there is to say.

It is simply

a photograph painted with oils. And the fact that it looks a bit different from the original isn't due as much to intention as to a lack of ability, to impatience. The hyperrealists[1] did it very nicely and very decisively, because they took so much time over it. And when I painted a picture, it had to be finished within a day, because I didn't really care enough. It just needed to be roughly similar. I didn't need to make an exact copy. That's why I introduced blurring. Smudging was one of my methods.

I did this so the personal style would disappear, so it would become more like a photo. But also to speed up the process. I just can't sit for eight weeks working on one painting. Because it's only about making something visible before quickly moving on to the next one.

Then

that got boring, too, or this thing about personal style being removed became unimportant, because it's there anyway, or it isn't, or it's not important, so it didn't matter if I overdid it. It was the same kind of blurriness I had conjured up using soft brushes. So I can get the same blurring with rough strokes. Blurring is also quite important for me because I can't see it exactly anyway; can't grasp it.

Because

it all became a grey mess anyway when all the colours were smeared together. So I might as well take grey to start with.

I've always had a particular liking for grey. But that's theory, because it's a non-colour, because it's something relative, pointless.

But everything I think about this, and my motivation for painting, could just as well be rubbish.

One can also paint for money. That's a motive, too.

The work doesn't have to show this. Usually you can't deduce anything from the painting.

Interview with Gislind Nabakowski, 1974

In the future, you no longer want to make paintings with people or groups of people, like those you did in 1962 and 1965. Why is that?

I don't feel like it...

That's the only reason?

Yes, because I'd have to want to produce something similar to what I did back then; I'd need to be fascinated by the idea of repeating myself. And that's problematic.

What made you choose a fifteenth-century painting as a model and create a sequence based on Titian's Annunciation*?*

Because there's something about this painting, or any painting, that grabs me if they're good – irrespective of the impact they had at the time, why they were made, the story behind them. I don't know what motivated the artist, which means that the paintings have an intrinsic quality. I think Goethe called it the 'essential dimension', the thing that makes great works of art great.

I beg your pardon?!

Something that is, or something that actively affects people, something in its essence. A dimension that, of course, lies beyond the mere choice of forms and colours, something that pertains to every detail... I don't know how to explain it right now. Perhaps I wanted to solve this riddle by painting, or by copying through painting.

And were you able to solve the riddle?

No.

The sequence is made up of five paintings. In the first, Titian's motif is still recognizable, but it isn't in the last one. You don't present them in the order in which they were painted: you arrange them according to a 'concept', placing the first painting first, followed immediately by the one that was done last, followed by the 'in-between' ones.

After the first painting, I had already imagined the way the last one might look.

But I still had to try the other three – to let them evolve, in order to arrive at the last one. That doesn't mean, though, that the last one was conclusive, a solution, or an end result.

If we focus on the current debates about painting – the positions that have emerged within recent years – we find that there are two opposing points of view. One seeks to explore the material foundation of 'painting per se', focusing on colour in relation to the other materials, and looking at the specific situation in which a painting is made. This school of thought, with the initial aim of counteracting the reification of painting, seems to have devalued its own avant-garde language of material because, increasingly, it drifted into a vacuum of tautologies – into a superficial perspective of culture increasingly obsessed with nuances. By merely focusing on, and minutely refining the laws of perception, it arrived at increasingly abstruse conclusions. Within the domestic aesthetic realm, 'pictorial components' are described as independent entities. This kind of painting is undergoing a revival in France and the United States. A different trend, heralding an 'illustrative realism' that needs to be examined more closely, still focuses on signs and symbols within the material.

With regard to your approach to painting, you seem willing to encumber yourself with the concept of traditional symbolism, but you don't illustrate it; you seem to be searching for your own symbolic references. Can you elaborate on this 'illustrative realism'? Does it represent what the painter sees, or does it reveal his 'reflections on what he has seen', i.e. are his paintings platforms for the production of reality?

It certainly doesn't show what one sees, because everyone sees something different, and what one sees isn't a painting; it can only remind us of a painting. But, on the other hand, I don't accept the principal difference between 'pure' pictures that only represent themselves and others that just illustrate something. If you take Ryman, Palermo or Marden, for example, in a way their paintings are also illusionistic, and you can only just identify the actual paint or the material if you have the eyes of a paint salesman.

The same principle that makes a painting a painting can be seen in photography: mediation, the triggering of imagination. Like photographs, paintings are representations of something, of something spatial, or of a vivid situation, a 'picture' – I don't mean a house or a tree; something anti-representational perhaps. I can see it in my mind's eye, but I can't explain it.

Why did you paint over Titian's motif and dissolve it?

Oh, I'm sure I didn't initially plan it that way; I wanted to trace him as precisely as possible, maybe because I wanted to own such a beautiful Titian... *[laughs]*.

That can't be true. Not even the very first painting is a copy; you intended something else.

Sure. I only copied it from a postcard and not from the original as such.

Although I must say that it is indeed possible to reproduce a painting from a postcard that is almost as beautiful as the original. Those few little details that would have been different really don't matter – but that's another issue.

By painting over and dissolving the motif, did you want to extinguish a figure of thought?

What's that?

It's made up of several conventions. To my mind, the Annunciation motif is an act of sexual domination. It's evident throughout its hackneyed language of symbols.

I didn't even notice that, because in order to notice something like that you have to be educated in a certain way.

Aren't you educated?

I didn't want to be. Apart from that certain quality, which I mentioned earlier, I was a little, or rather very, interested in the motif – for instance, in the woman being told something, something wonderful, but we're not being told anything. It would be nice for us if such things were true, wouldn't it [*laughs*]?

Don't you have the desire to communicate something 'specific' to your audience?

Definitely. And that's a very important reason to start painting in the first place. To send messages ... but that doesn't mean that I'm capable of telling you what these messages are right now, and it probably will never be possible to translate them.

What inspired you to invent those particular pictorial semantics in the 1960s, as part of which you blur contexts and suddenly switch from focused to fuzzy images? Do these creative decisions always convey the same messages?

Messages, interests, behaviour, for want of a better word: they're all the same messages, you know; and where should I find others to convey? Incidentally, I never switched from focused to fuzzy. I wasn't keen on this separation of things; drawing this distinction between objects seemed wrong to me, because there isn't really a difference between one object and the next, except for the things we have to interpret into them for practical reasons, like when we're driving a car or eating. I regarded fuzzy images and fluent transitions as a way of avoiding making certain statements about things. I believe that the term 'fuzzy' is also used in physics, in a similar context.[1]

What are the reasons for making these stylistic decisions?

My indifference. I was born that way, and the environment I grew up in did the rest...

By blurring the image, do you intend to give something with a fixed meaning the chance to be ambiguous again? Is it true that you try to use your motifs to counteract the all-encompassing terror of reification?

Yes, okay.

Do you also want to disrupt the pattern by which art is seen in a reified, separating, ideological manner?

Lovely – you've put it very well.

So, given this context, what can be said about that last painting?

I like it. But I can also say that it's very exciting for me because there's plenty left to be done with it.

Why have you hardly strayed from the colours Titian uses? You've even kept the proportions intact over the course of three paintings, although you always claim that the original motif doesn't interest you at all.

That can't be. If I'm going to paint Titian, I can hardly do away with the colours and the form. Also there was no reason to change the proportions, since I intended to preserve the painting – maybe forget it later on, but not change it. Rather like Picasso, whose paintings after Courbet or Delacroix no longer have anything in common with the originals, even though his motifs are represented much more sharply than my fuzzy ones.

Titian's symbolism disappears only in the last picture of your sequence. The symbols include a devout Mary with Bible, guinea fowl (apparently an object of veneration), a half-opened basket, light and enlightenment coming from 'heaven', and symbols of a religious mythology and of politics of sexual oppression. What can one say about this last painting, in which these symbols have disappeared?

Nothing. The colours are gone, as are the forms.

How can you claim that the colours are gone? The painting seems to be a variation on the theme of 'all the colours under the sun'.

You've described it exactly – it has less to do with Titian than with colour charts.

Would it have been an ideological act for you just to paint the last picture grey and thus neutral; white and thus empty; or black and thus virtually non-existent?

It would have turned out wrong. That would be taking a theoretical approach, as if I wanted to construct a painting.

Looking at Titian's Annunciation, *one suspects a degree of suggestiveness behind the red robe of the so-called 'spiritual seducer'. — The angel is suggestive, for example, because more of his body is visible than the woman's. It's probably irrelevant to argue about whether the angel is a symbol of the power of the hypocritical Renaissance, a cleric guarding over the moral conduct of the people, or of the woman; or whether he symbolizes the artist's emancipation in this period. The fact is that Titian sensualized something spiritual. The angel can't simply be a symbol of oppressive terror, because historical materialism didn't exist yet: to represent an angel as something material was almost an act of heresy.*

Yes, that's interesting.

But going back to what I said, it's still about masculine morals, flashing a little sexuality, making a bit of a show of it. You once said that you were attracted by the idyllic nature of the painting. Could you be more precise?

I was also drawn in by the beautiful, intact world it represents, or the beautiful dream, the perfection. What can I say? These feelings seem so natural to me...

Is there a connection between your last painting of the sequence and your landscapes and cloud paintings?

Not so much to the latter; more to the former. It does have something to do with recapturing a dream, or analyzing it. And the result of that is always a bit odd, since we're not naïve.

I assume that, because we belong to a privileged class, we don't experience religious terror directly. But it still exists, of course!

Since we let the picture rest in its historical context rather than bringing it up to date, we don't see an equivalent to this 400-year-old convention. Maybe Bertolt Brecht had similar grounds for commenting that a person 'who is highly educated, politically, can even enjoy antisocial works of art'. But to claim that the woman 'is given some sort of commandment', or that, without any reflection, one is only aware of the idyllic nature of the painting, not of the social violence inherent in it, seems to me to be a little blinkered: that's part of the array of masculine 'arguments'. Such alienation from one's own history is what we call 'consumerism'. Were you perhaps engaging in a trial of strength with Titian when you painted that picture?

No, it has nothing to do with a trial of strength. But perhaps we should ask a psychiatrist. Maybe he could tell me why I wanted to do the painting.

Why did you liken the last painting to an abstract photograph?

Because it doesn't represent anything, but is nevertheless illusionistic.

Your work has often been exhibited together with works by hyperrealists. Did that happen because you requested it?

No. But it's not really important.

Do you know what motivates collectors to buy your works?

Sometimes. I can only talk about those that interest me, that have their own interpretations, who contribute to the process; they are biased – how to put this? By accepting the painting, they're making it into what it should be: not just them, of course; there are many others who also contribute.

There was a period, roughly between 1962 and 1967, when a lot of people were fascinated by art. They visited artists' studios, marvelled at what they saw, and deceived themselves. I think they're all a bit disappointed now because the sensation didn't last. That's a healthy development. After all, what's so special about someone knocking nails into a board (at the time my studio was next to Uecker's),[2] or someone painting family photos in oils?

Haven't you yourself been duped by an elitist theory when you say, 'Now that there are no priests or philosophers left, artists are the most important people in the world'?

No. That really has nothing to do with an elite. What I meant was that art fulfils certain functions that were hitherto the domain of religion – let's call it the realization, or projection, of a higher world; I probably meant transcendental. But that was a long time ago, and I said it so arrogantly, or polemically, that one should be able to understand it clearly.

The quote has also been taken out of context in a malicious way. Back when you were professor at the Art Academy in Düsseldorf,[3] all the conservative professors kept intoning it.

I've never heard that said.

Why don't you like the idea of the artist being a critic of the system?

That must be an insinuation.

What are you currently painting? Landscapes?

No. Colour charts. Large paintings, usually with 1,024 different colours arranged randomly.

Why randomly?

Because I can't imagine a better or more appropriate order – but that already sounds too laden with importance, as if I were aiming to present a random order. I just want to make a painting.

Text for catalogue of group exhibition, Palais des Beaux-Arts, Brussels, 1974

1,024 Colours in 4 Permutations

In order to represent all extant colour shades in one painting, I worked out a system which – starting from the three primaries, plus grey – made possible a continual subdivision (differentiation) through equal gradations. $4 \times 4 = 16 \times 4 = 64 \times 4 = 256 \times 4 = 1{,}024$. The multiplier 4 was necessary because I wanted to keep the image size, the square size and the number of squares in a constant proportion to each other. To use more than 1,024 tones (4,096, for instance) seemed pointless, since the difference between one shade and the next would no longer have been detectable.

The arrangement of the colours on the squares was done by a random process, to obtain a diffuse, undifferentiated overall effect, combined with stimulating detail. The rigid grid precludes the generation of figurations, although with an effort these can be detected. This aspect of artificial naturalism fascinates me – as does the fact that, if I had painted all the possible permutations, light would have taken more than 400 billion years to travel from the first painting to the last. I wanted to paint four large, colourful pictures.

From a letter to Edy de Wilde, 23 February 1975

When I first painted a number of canvases grey all over (about eight years ago), I did so because I did not know what to paint, or what there might be to paint: so wretched a start could lead to nothing meaningful. As time went on, however, I observed differences of quality among the grey surfaces – and also that these betrayed nothing of the destructive motivation that lay behind them. The pictures began to teach me. By generalizing a personal dilemma, they resolved it.

Destitution became a constructive statement; it became relative perfection, beauty, and therefore painting.

Grey. It makes no statement whatever; it evokes neither feelings nor associations; it is really neither visible nor invisible. Its inconspicuousness gives it the capacity to mediate, to make visible, in a positively illusionistic way, like a photograph. It has the capacity that no other colour has, to make 'nothing' visible.

To me, grey is the welcome and only possible equivalent for indifference, noncommitment, absence of opinion, absence of shape. But grey, like formlessness and the rest, can be real only as an idea, and so all I can do is create a colour nuance that means grey but is not it. The painting is then a mixture of grey as a fiction and grey as a visible, designated area of colour.

Finally: this kind of reductionist painting fascinates me in general, because I believe that it is a highly scrupulous and cautious attempt to achieve correctness, or rather definitiveness, in painting; that it pursues a quality which tends towards the valid and the universal. This seems to me important, in the face of a mindless, proliferating productivity that constantly becomes less and less definitive.

Text for catalogue of *Acht Künstler – acht Räume*, Mönchengladbach, 1975

No one painting is meant to be more beautiful than, or even different from, any other. Nor is it meant to be like any other, but the same: the same, though each was painted individually and by itself, not all together and all of a piece, like Multiples. I intended them to look the same but not to be the same, and I intended this to be visible.

From a letter to Benjamin H. D. Buchloh,[1] 23 May 1977

The motive or rather the premise of my new pictures[2] is the same as that of almost all my other pictures: it is that I can communicate nothing, that there is nothing to communicate, that painting can never be communication, that neither hard work, obstinacy, lunacy nor any trick whatever is going to make the absent message emerge of its own accord from the painting process. I don't paint for the sake of painting.

I look for the object and the picture: not for painting or the picture of painting, but for our picture, our looks and appearances and views, definitive and total. How shall I put it: I want to picture to myself what is going on now. Painting can help in this, and different methods = subjects = themes are the different attempts I make in this direction. (Seen in this way, the subject of the picture in the photographic pictures, for instance, is as it is, just as flat, imprecise and superficial; in the Doors and so on, it's symbolic kitsch; in the Details it's decoration; in the Landscapes it's retrospective, nothing has changed; in the Grey Pictures it's lack of differentiation, nothing, nil, the Beginning and the End; in the Panes of Glass it's the analogy with attitudes and possibilities; in the Colour Charts it's chance, anything is correct, or rather Form is Nonsense; in the new Abstract Pictures it's arbitrariness, almost anything is possible.)

To me, this arbitrariness has always seemed the central problem in both abstract and representational painting. What reason is there, other than some stupid system or the rules of a game, for placing one thing next to another in any particular format, any particular colour, with any particular outline, with any particular likeness – and next to that something else again, no matter what – (a problem that I have merely touched on).

The outsize blow-up,[3] which allows you to cheat, is for the time being the only form that can make real and comprehensible the 'message' that I want to present as fascinatingly as possible. — I still have a lot to do.

The new issue of *Kunstforum* has arrived, and now I can understand your reservations about the new heroes of painting. What makes me sick above all is when the describers build that up as 'pure painting', completely denying the value of the object.

Firstly, as I have said, pure painting – if it could ever exist – would be a crime;

and, secondly, these pictures are valued solely and uniquely for their stupid, bumptious object content. This naturally includes the effective recording of the painter's blind, ferocious motor impulse, as well as the maintaining of a semblance of intelligence and historical awareness through the choice and invention of a motif.

These painters of spontaneity take Cage's saying, which is so important to me, that 'I have nothing to say and I am saying it', and they twist it round into 'We have nothing to say and we are *not* saying it.' Thus they mask and cover up their own impotence, helplessness and sheer stupidity with stage-sets and fashionably nostalgic debris from the rubbish-tip of history. Nazis in disguise.

Answers to questions from Marlies Grüterich, 2 September 1977

What do you think of the current 'Media' documenta *exhibition and of its 'Painting about Painting' section?*

The *documenta* – there are certainly some chinks of light to be seen there; I mean a few really magnificent works, such as Walter De Maria's *Vertical Kilometer*. That's such an outstanding piece that it almost seems out of place, like a monument in the middle of a funfair; on the whole, this *documenta* is a very superficial show. And I think the pseudo-theme of 'Painting about Painting' is just as superficial.

It's astonishing how easily people swallow slogans like that, just because they sound quite interesting, when in fact it's all total nonsense. Paintings are always about paintings: it's as obvious as – as the fact that a loaf of bread baked today is only the way it is because of the experience acquired from all the bread that has ever been baked before. You can't make this into a theme, Bakery about Bakery, without going bust straight away. An unedifying theme. One can only hope that everyone has learned their lesson.

What problems concern you currently, as a painter?

At the moment – for quite a time; for about two years – I have been working on a different idea. Different from the grey pictures that I was painting before. After those strictly monochromatic or non-chromatic paintings it was rather difficult just to keep going. Even if such a thing had been possible, I had no desire to produce variations on that theme. So I set out in totally the opposite direction. On small canvases I put random, illogical colours and forms – mostly with long pauses in between, which made sure that these paintings, if you can call them that, became more and more heterogeneous. Ugly sketches is what they are: the total antithesis of the purist grey pictures. Colourful, sentimental, associative, anachronistic, random, polysemic, almost like pseudo-psychograms, except that they are not legible, because they are devoid of meaning or logic – if such a thing is possible, which is a fascinating point in itself, if not the most important of all, though I still know too little about it. An exciting business, at all events, as if a new door had opened for me.

I almost showed three of these[1] at *documenta*. Not the sketches, of course, but the pictures painted from the sketches. The sketches are just raw material. They don't let the statement emerge clearly. Just as the pictorial idea is better shown by a painted still-life than by the constructed, real still-life that it depicts.

What do you think of the painting of your fellow artists in the GDR?[2]

Almost nothing. A painting which creates nothing; which simply makes variations on what GDR cultural policy makes available for the purpose – namely the so-called cultural heritage, and even that filtered and circumscribed. Such painting is just a kind of applied art, which excludes its own true element, that of formative thinking; painting that is always forced to run along behind and so can never set an example.

This is a phenomenon that applies to every area of culture in the GDR, and it expresses itself in the fact that nothing creative ever comes out of there. Everything there is a kind of toned-down import – whether architecture, fashion, design, pop music, dancing – I know of no instance in which anything has ever been created there.

Interview with Amine Haase, 1977

You have always left your viewers in something of a quandary. Firstly through the paintings themselves, some of them barely distinguishable from photographs, and also because there is no instantly visible connection between the paintings. In 1964 Cow, *in 1966* Twelve Colours, *in 1968 the* Streaks of Paint, *in 1971 the* Details, *in 1972* 48 Portraits, *in 1975 the* Grey Pictures, *and since 1977 the* Abstract Pictures. *Cloudscapes, landscapes, chairs, toilet paper, townscapes,* Annunciation after Titian *– why such a multitude of themes and forms?*

You've just covered quite a long span of time, so that every theme has three or four years to itself – and in that time one can reflect a bit on why things might be done differently. Add to this that the differences are merely superficial ones: the basic intention has remained the same all through.

And that is?

To try out what can be done with painting: how I can paint today, and above all what. Or, to put it differently: the continual attempt to picture to myself what is going on.

Would you say that the pictures that you're painting now are the outcome of your fifteen years of reflection? That Cow *bears some relationship to the abstract pictures?*

The paintings certainly do relate to each other. But you can't talk about an 'outcome' in quite that way – as when a person does fifteen years' research and ends up with an outcome that supersedes all the previous work. I mean, although a logical evolution does always take place, this doesn't necessarily lead to an improvement in quality, and never to a resolution – whether the person sits working on something for twenty years or for two.

I mean, the time frames are always very short: when you say, 'I had two or three years every time to think things over.' Most painters take not two but twenty years at least to end up with such radically different forms – if they ever do.

That may be, but, historically speaking, changeable artists are a growing phenomenon – Picasso, for instance, or Duchamp and Picabia – and the number is certainly increasing all the time. Painting has lost a lot of the functions that once used to provide discipline and continuity. I mean commissioned art, from portraiture to whatever, which only incidentally gave painters the chance to make art. Nowadays they can't do anything but make art. That alters a lot.

You mean, as soon as the photographers were taking the portraits, they were competing with the painters?

Absolutely. And the competition extends a long way. Photography supplies pictures of every department of life, and does it so cheaply and so quickly – and above all so perfectly and so credibly – that in this respect painting is hopelessly inferior.

It must be a tough struggle.

Only if you let yourself get drawn into it. But, even when I was painting things fairly similar to photographs, I never got competitively involved. I made something different out of it – painting, to put it simply. And this – as far as its photographic qualities were concerned – was mostly not so good as photography, because it also had to work as painting, which meant a completely different quality.

And then? Why no more photo-pictures?

New interests came up, more attractive and more exclusively to do with painting, and these made me forget about photography. So then came other things: colour charts, grey pictures and now abstract pictures.

You mean that these three types of painting have nothing to do with photography?

No, at least not directly. By which I mean that of course photography has influenced the way we see, and also that this photographic way of picture-making suits me: it is so much the antithesis of 'painting' – the act of painting that was formerly almost as important as the outcome, the finished picture.

Would you regard your abstract pictures as a departure from an illusionistic mode of representation?

Not really. If I forget about the negative connotations that the term has, what I have left is an illusionism that is inseparably bound up with painting – or even identical with it. Painting as appearance – this has nothing to do with the 'world of appearances' and ideas like that. I mean to say that I know no painting that is not illusionistic – just like photography.

Isn't this realization something that stems from your experiments with photography?

Yes. But also, of course, from my understanding of so-called Concrete Painting – painting that shows only one or two colours. For instance, a *Black Square on a White Ground* is a pointless thing until you see what else there is in it: the true meaning that the appearance serves to convey.

And your simple grey pictures should be understood in the same way?

Yes, exactly, though that wasn't the intention. At that time, I was trying hard to prevent paintings from functioning in this illusionistic way, and then I realized that these very paintings are the most rigorously illusionistic of all.

Although you have repeatedly changed the way you paint and have never settled down, whenever your name comes up people say: 'Ah, yes, Photo-Realism.' Somehow it's always photo-painting or painting from photographs.

Maybe that has caught the most attention. When I painted a black-and-white copy of a photograph, at the time this was absurd. But for me personally it was the only possible way I could make a break. After endlessly trying to paint Art, all of a sudden there were just these pathetic photographs. Now those pictures are on the walls of a museum, in the right department, in perfect order.

You have mostly formulated your intentions in negative terms. For instance: 'I pursue no objectives, no system, no tendency; I have no programme, no style, no direction. I have no time for technical problems, working themes, or variations that lead to mastery.'

That was meant polemically, against the many triumphalists who knew it all so well, and could do it all so competently, and who constantly reproduced their own homely little ideas – naturally dressed up in the appropriate ideology. I'm not saying that what I said was wrong; it's just that it no longer meets my concerns.

And what are your present concerns?

Painting, still, of course – or, as I said, the difficulty of picturing for oneself what is; making it visible, intelligible and thus usable.

Is painting still possible at all?

It is more difficult. On one hand, there is photography, which is far better at depicting everything; there is the history of art, which has long since demonstrated everything; and there are the new media – video, performance and the rest – which get a far more contemporary grip on things. But, on the other hand, the pleasure of painting proves the necessity of it – all children paint, spontaneously. Painting has a brilliant future. Hasn't it?

Just because painting is fun?

Okay, if you put the question like that, of course I have to say that the pleasure is only one aspect. Nothing can be done without it; but, if that's all there is to it, it merely bores and irritates the viewer. The objective side has to come in, through which painting offers something of universal interest: a statement, a new quality, an advance – something the other person can do something with.

Townscape Paris, 1968 (detail)

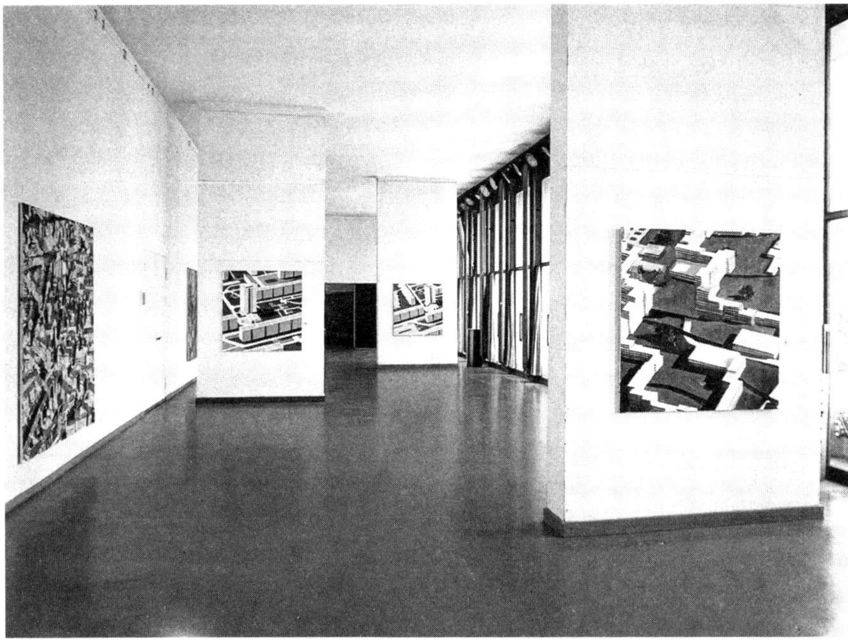

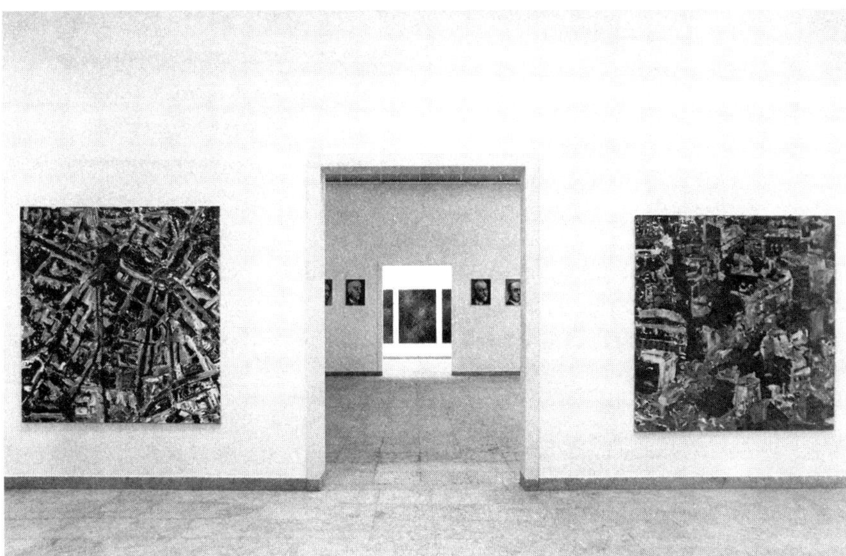

Kunstmuseum Lucerne, 1969
Venice Biennale, 1972

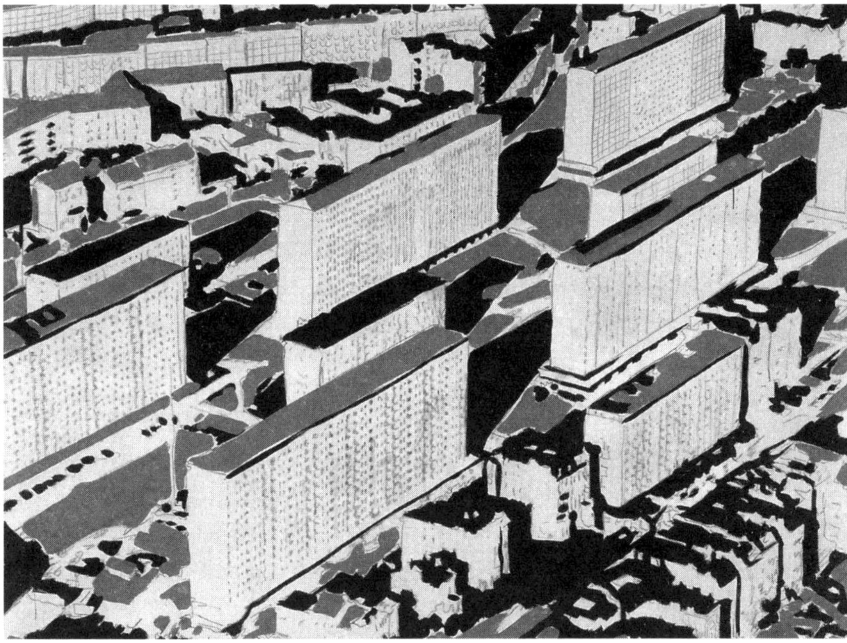

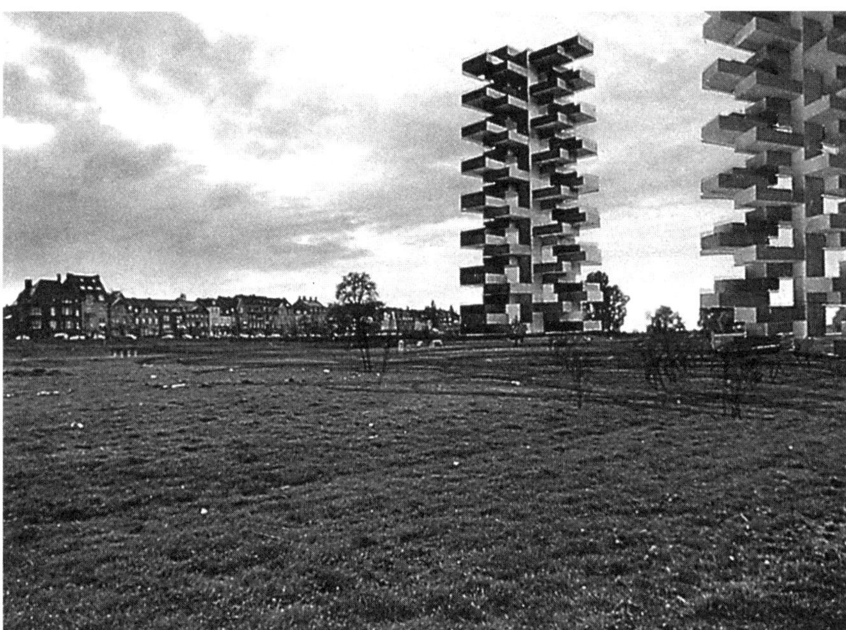

Townscape Ha, 1968 (detail)
Design for social housing, 1968

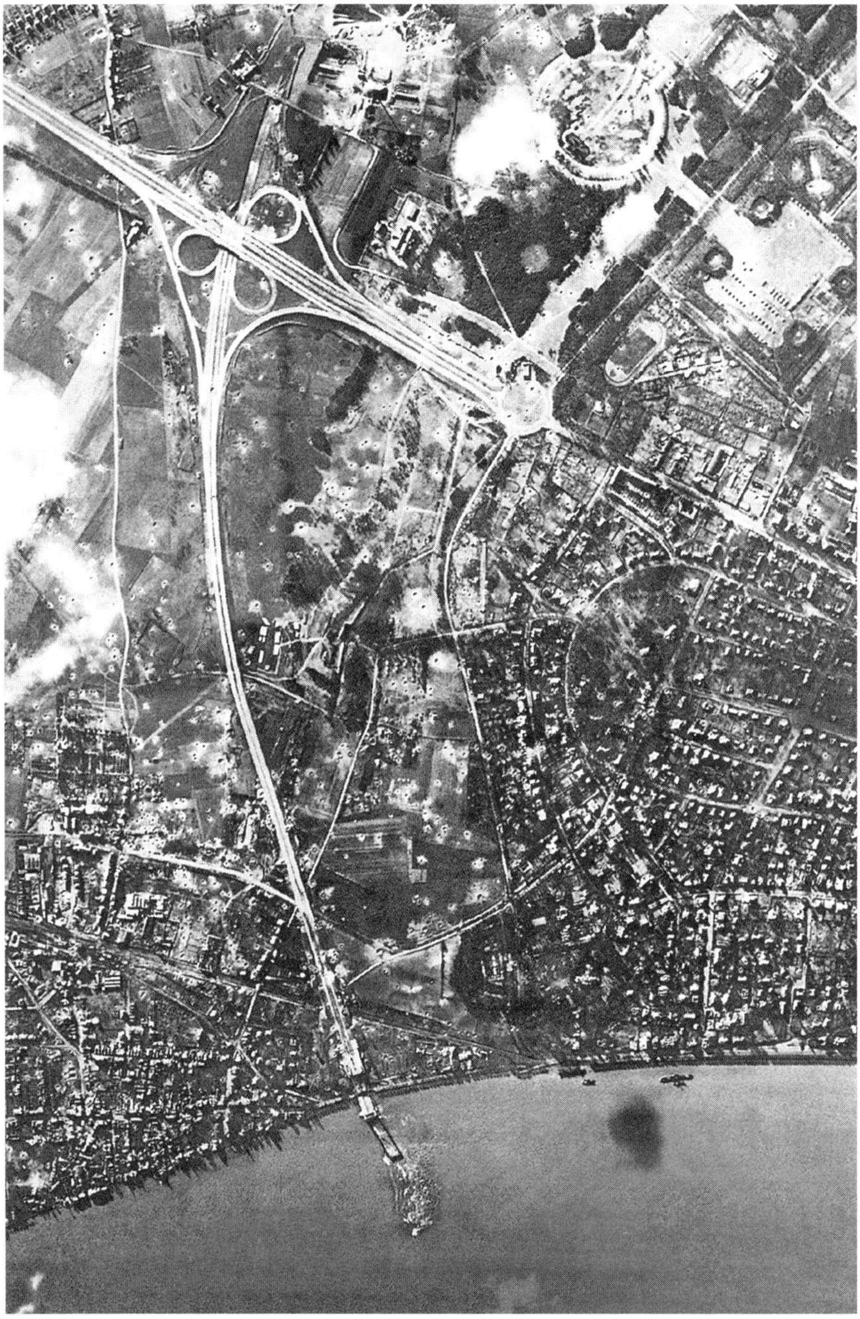

14. Feb. 1945, 2001

From a letter to Benjamin H. D. Buchloh, 29 September 1977

There are not so many good artists in Germany as in America, and that's no wonder, after twelve years of Nazi Socialism and, for the other half, an additional 32 years of GDR Socialism. But American capitalism is not essentially different from ours, or from that of other European states. But, above all, by 'good artists' I meant that nearly a hundred per cent of all new ideas and prototypes have come from the so-called capitalist systems. This proves not so much the superiority of the system as the fact that progressive ideas are largely independent of economic systems. Only the intrusion of a state ideology suppresses new ideas, and this is possible in any economic system (Hitler, Chile or the Eastern Bloc). Once again, the difficulties and the errors that cause inhumanity lie elsewhere, and these are not removed but merely inhibited by catastrophic displacement activities like 'smashing the system' (as demanded by the Left).

Interview with Marlies Grüterich, 1978

Gerhard Richter, how do you view the work you did in the late 1960s?

As opposed to the early '60s – which, in my view, were characterized by an opening up of art towards life, towards the everyday, through an appropriation of banal images, as demonstrated so forcefully and, in part, superficially by Pop Art, for example – there was, in the late '60s, a focus on the elementary substance of art, an interest in its language, its methodology, its analytical potential, and on fundamentals, to use a term that was the title of an exhibition in Amsterdam and which summarized these developments.

And I see these developments in my own work. Part of this was my investigation of the colour spectrum, which kept me very busy for a time, and which I used – similarly to the inpaintings with blue, red and yellow and, later, the monochrome grey paintings – not just to demonstrate methods and applications, but to make a statement using methods and strategies.

Can you explain why you made grey paintings?

No, or rather I've tried occasionally, such as in the catalogue for the *Fundamental Painting* exhibition[1] I just mentioned. It's related to a feeling of powerlessness, to truths that may apply to me. But all this was a long time ago. What I'm trying to say is that it's too difficult for me. Maybe it's a career in itself.

What role do you think European art has played since the late 1960s?

I would say that the Europeans, more so than before, have contributed something unique rather than emulating the Americans. Although the US was, and is, the country with the greater economic clout and greater vigour, a sort of European intellect emerged that provided inspiration and represented an independent force. To name names, to illustrate what I mean: Gilbert & George, Beuys, Broodthaers, Kounellis, Toroni, Polke, Palermo, Dominicis, and many more – some even more important.

This European art scene was different from the one in the States: more differentiated, or less direct, with more scruples – in such a way, in fact, that it influenced American art. And this equality of status, or new quality to be more precise, changed our way of thinking, our way of judging. Which is why, for instance, there isn't a dominant trend at present – no Pop, or Minimal, or Land, or Conceptual art. There's just work and more work, and it's too complicated to describe it in terms of popular slogans. And, compared to that, these art theories and works by people like Jasper Johns and Rothko and others look, above all, decorative and devoid of meaning and even ridiculous when they are abused by the cultural establishment.

And what is your intention now? Do you think that art reflects what is happening today; that one can get a grasp on it?

I'm sure it reflects what's happening: there is always complete congruence. But I wouldn't be able to explain the process. I wouldn't say that because this looks like that and that looks like this that I could describe the factors causing it – just as I couldn't say this or that circumstance has made me paint in a certain way today.

And what about your latest paintings?

There I can only say what I'm doing, what I'm painting.

Yes?

In a way that disturbs me, as always. Perhaps this time because this way of painting makes me feel more isolated than ever before. I see hardly any links to a past on which I could build – except that skills, and the principle of 'oil paint on canvas', and the portrayal of an illusionistic pictorial quality are decidedly traditional aspects of the craft. But beyond that there is nothing – no point of reference, not even to contemporary art. This means that, right now, I don't know any paintings I would say are in keeping with the times, or interesting, or new, or important. But perhaps I'm demanding something that's impossible. Especially when there are plenty of other works I think are very important for us, but which simply don't have the outward appearance of pictures. Not that this would be necessary.

Do you think that nowadays it's still important to differentiate between formal and informal painting or art in general?

I think the distinction has ceased to exist because, although there was such a thing as informal art, it didn't present itself as such, but rather sent us a message ... about an informal state that affects us and is a part of us.

But I think making the distinction between this or that style of painting is as pointless as giving something a label – and the reason I believe this is because painting has to be usable.

Interview with Bruce Ferguson and Jeffrey Spalding, 1978

JS: Did you attend an art school?

GR: Yes, I studied Dutiful Arts, Fine Arts you say, for five years and earned a diploma from the Academy of Fine Arts in Dresden. It was a very academic, traditional school, where you learned to draw from plaster copies and nude models. I was dissatisfied with this situation and with the prevailing art there, with Socialist Realism.

BF: After graduation, what did you do?

GR: I was a [freelance] artist in Dresden, working on my paintings. From time to time I painted murals in buildings to earn my money.

JS: What was this early work like?

GR: Oh, somewhere between the realist painting we know from Russia, Impressionism and perhaps a bit of Picasso.

JS: I am surprised to hear that you were unhappy about the academic practices encouraged by the art school. I would have thought that your mature work, the portraiture and landscapes, would have benefited from such an experience, or did you feel that you had to invent new methods for your art?

GR: No, I was not satisfied at the time, but the training I received had a great influence on me. The only new thing was to not be afraid to paint from a photo – it was not allowed.

BF: In the '50s, when you shifted from academic painting to the blurred portraiture, what was happening in Germany which might have inspired such an activity?

GR: There was a movement called Zero,[1] in the Netherlands it was called Nulle[2] – this was very successful in expanding the boundaries of art. And then Fluxus[3] became successful; Fluxus was my point. I wanted to do paintings which had nothing to do with art, so I painted from photographs.

BF: It seems that your actual working methods inspired by your [education] haven't changed; however, your intentions have. What is your explanation for this?

GR: During my studies I saw things from the West. I visited *documenta* in 1959 and was most impressed by Pollock and Fontana. This was a great new experience to see these things which we had not been allowed to see during the Nazi regime.

JS: From a North American standpoint your production encompasses some fairly disparate art-making modes: Impressionism, Photo-Realism, Minimalism, Reductivist Monochrome paintings and now lyrical Colour Field paintings. How can these be reconciled?

GR: I think I have, for all these different styles or methods, the same reason to do it but I can't explain it now. It's a fundamental reason ... why to paint in one way and not in the other. I think that any artist can paint in any kind of style if he wants to. It's not a question of capability.

JS: It's not just that you use different styles; in North America it is thought that art-making springs from, or at least is guided by, certain basic convictions. Thus your personal temperament might steer you towards making monochrome paintings or perhaps to lyrical colour abstractions, but not both. These art-making attitudes seem to be mutually exclusive, antithetical: the mindset necessary to accommodate one would preclude adoption of the other. For this reason a North American artist would be charged a dilettante if he were to change sides as many times as you have. It's almost a matter of principle. How is it that you feel free from all the feelings of guilt we would have then?

GR: I don't have these feelings because I know so many artists; some of them are my friends, and only at the beginning I dealt with questions of this kind.

BF: Jackson Pollock, for instance, would not have made your type of photo-realist painting because he believed in a philosophy which he had to realize in his painting...

JS: ... his re-introduction of representation into the drip paintings was interpreted by many as a sign of failure, that he had run dry, not that he had regenerated.

BF: ... obviously, your philosophy encompasses all manners of painting. What is that philosophy that incorporates those things?

GR: I don't believe in the reality of painting, so I use different styles like clothes: it's a way to disguise myself.

BF: By constantly switching back and forth you avoid the trap of being tied to a certain style and the kind of identity crisis which some artists go through when they reach a point in the development of their painting when they have achieved what they think is possible by working in a certain manner. Does your working method avoid that crisis?

GR: Yes, before I started the photo-realist works I was at a dead-point. I had been painting only grey paintings for two or three years. It seemed as if I couldn't go further with them, so I did completely the opposite, which shows the same feeling maybe.

BF: It seems also that you are allowing for a kind of complexity as opposed to a moral, religious point which would focus on one thing only. In North America there is definitely a belief that there is virtue in consistency.

GR: I would say that my behaviour is to a certain degree comparable to Picabia,[4] wouldn't you?

JS: Well, there are a number of artists who have 'flitted around', roaming all over the aesthetic map in an attempt to, as we say, 'find themselves'. Your actions seem to consciously involve these shifts in aesthetic position as a significant part of the content of your work.

BF: When you exhibit, for example, a photo-realist work with an abstract work, is it important to you that they be seen at the same time?

GR: It is irrelevant; it is more like an accident.

BF: You display a strong commitment to art, but not to any particular style...

GR: No, not to a style of art.

BF: ... so changing for you is merely another way of producing a content for art.

GR: Yes, it is.

JS: This is, of course, what every student of art does, to go back to the art of the recent past which is personally relevant and to proceed from there. Many of your works are relatable to other artists' working methods, but for you, is there anything 'quintessentially Gerhard Richter'?

GR: No.

JS: Perhaps it is because of the one cloud painting in the National Gallery of Canada,[5] but the photo-realist methodology seems like an anchor for your activities. Would this be a misconception?

GR: No, this would not be an error. I often use the word 'pictures' to describe my work, which is a little unusual, I think?

JS: It used to be that one would shrink away from the use of that term in the discussion of paintings.

GR: Yes, but I use the word because I don't make paintings. This is more a picture for me than a painting. A picture shows nothing, just a picture. This picture shows a landscape, the grey paintings are pictures [of] nothing. They have nothing to do with Bob Ryman's, because his show something – the way it is painted, and an exploration of material qualities.

BF: So you choose to make works from snapshots or from your previous work?

JS: One of the large colour paintings at Sperone Westwater Fischer in New York invokes a very convincing illusion of recession into space, almost as if it were a misty landscape. What was the course for this work?

GR: Actually, it was a picture using one of my smaller abstract paintings as a source.

BF: A detail from one of the small studies?

GR: Yes, a detail of most of such a study from which I might paint three or more works.

BF: So these in effect are the still-lifes?

GR: Like still-lifes, yes.

BF: Why would you choose a painting as a still-life as opposed to bottles or whatever else? Is that linked to the conviction that anything can become the content for art?

GR: That is one reason, but if I wanted to show a still-life I would make a photograph of it. I don't think the effect is raised just by painting it. I don't always think this way, but most of the time.

BF: So in the beginning you always work from something which in itself is a translation of reality and then you re-translate it.

GR: Yes.

BF: And in the re-translation, does it become more real than the translation for you?

GR: It becomes more real because I know nothing about the reality as it is. The only important thing for us is translation.

JS: It's interesting to compare your method to the roughly contemporary Ian Burn photocopy piece – one blank piece of paper Xeroxed, Xerox the Xerox, and copy the copy and so on until the final page becomes a greyed image. Of course this is a neutered North American conception of the tautology in which the focus is laid upon the methodology, whereas the outcome of this activity may tend towards blandness. Obviously, your tautology investigating painting about painting, in the breakdown process leads to new beginnings, to something which is full of potential for visceral experience. Despite the minor current of humour and irony in your work, there is always a very straightforward and positive air about it. Which is to say not only that any kind of art is available to be done, but that everything is possible; everything can become a statement.

GR: Yes, precisely. I couldn't say it better.

BF: He doesn't ask questions but answers. Were you interested in or aware of Francis Bacon's work?

GR: A little bit, not much.

JS: Although the feeling and intentions are different, there are some shared resemblances between his work and your earlier blurred portraits...

GR: Yes, but this kind of distortion in my work is more an accident than intention.

JS: Except for the fact that many artists' aesthetic would not have permitted such an 'accident' from taking place. Did his eccentricities provide any impetus or support for your own predilections, or were there other painters with a more 'realistic' approach whose work interested you at the time?

GR: No, I only remember that I wanted to do the opposite. I wanted to have nothing to do with Bacon and Zero and all these things.

BF: Many of your paintings seem to parody the image of German Expressionism. Is this deliberate?

GR: I never thought about this. No, I can't say so.

JS: Your recent paintings make reference to the Abstract Expressionist work of Hans Hofmann. However, Abstract Expressionism implied a deep spiritual commitment, 'reaching into the inner soul for an outpouring'. Instead you reach for a previous painting, make a photograph of it, blur it, distort it. It's a different kind of procedure, even though the results are similar.

GR: The way to come to the same result is different ... more intellectual, I think ... what I am doing.

BF: In some ways you present a painting which has almost a false quality, the look of intensity, yet you deliberately detach yourself from that intensity by utilizing translation methods.

GR: I often try to paint without rules, beyond conventions... I was always surprised by and appreciated the contextual approach of American painting. This is the main difference, I think.

BF: For instance, you might have allied yourself with Andy Warhol's silkscreen portraits?

GR: Yes, absolutely, he had great interest for me.

BF: So the subjective element is dismissed or repressed to some degree? Even though these works look like the product of subjective outpourings, as Jeff said, they are in fact very deliberate, cool and analytic.

GR: Yes, I believe so.

BF: Do you think the viewer is aware of this duality or irony?

GR: Maybe not. There is a problem right now with misinterpretation. So I will try the abstract paintings again to see if I can make it clearer, perhaps by showing the large paintings and the studies for them together. I hope to try this in September at an upcoming show in Eindhoven, Netherlands.[6]

JS: It is interesting to compare Roy Lichtenstein's career with yours.

GR: Oh, yes.

JS: He also uses past art as a source for his own work. Yet his art redoes all styles over in his Benday dot technique. In your photo-realist Hofmanns, or remakes of Minimalism, or reductivist work, you incorporate a wider range of techniques.

GR: Yes, however for me Lichtenstein is too ironical.

JS: But he also has an interest in shape and colour. Would you say that a major difference is your preoccupation with the tactility and surface of your paint application?

GR: Yes, I would say so.

BF: Do you think that your painting calls into question the art style it resembles, or acts as a form of art criticism?

GR: I can't say yes ... art criticism. I don't believe so.

JS: To me your activities seem to expand the possibilities available rather than to act as a critique of art.

GR: In Venice there is an international exhibition with a theme: Reality and Abstraction,[7] in two separate pavilions. I sent two identical large monochrome grey paintings and they put one in the Realist pavilion and one in the Abstract pavilion [*they laugh*] ... and I agreed.

BF: Is there a methodological formula which guides the production of the grey paintings?

GR: No, nothing like that; I just try to get them to look the same.

JS: Obviously a part of your content is irony or humour, but what are you looking for in the creation of the specific objects?

GR: A kind of correctness ... I don't know.

JS: Then the abstract paintings would be assessed in terms of other Abstract Expressionist work?

GR: No, nothing to do with that, more in line with Carl Andre, I think.

BF: Then how do you know when one of the abstract paintings is finished? Since you do not share the same formal concerns?

GR: When it looks finished.

BF: When it looks like an Abstract Expressionist painting?

GR: Never. It is finished when I don't have another idea or a reason to do more and when it is not completely wrong.

JS: An abstract painting is always more difficult to declare to be finished than a realist one – you could always add a splotch here or there or take one away. I am surprised that your working method involves so much subjective choice. It really is that intuitive?

GR: Yes, it is.

BF: For a time the influence of American art was considerable in Europe. Do you feel that this influence is on the wane?

GR: Yes, the time of reaction to American art is over. The new European artists are becoming more important. The recent Chicago exhibition[8] did not show this because it showed artists who were already too well known.

BF: Do you have the feeling that European artists and even yourself are more politically inclined, that there are political undercurrents in your work?

GR: Yes, in the past, but this is mostly finished.

JS: It seems as if in Europe there is an extraordinary interest in artists such as Judd, Morris, Flavin, Serra and Andre.

GR: Yes.

JS: Well, in North America, at this point, it would be pretty difficult to drum up much enthusiasm for this work. Although fractured, attention has shifted to artists who have been investigating other concerns. From our vantage point, it appears as though Minimalism is still big news in Europe.

GR: Yes, this is true. It's due to the system. Museums have a budget and buy new pieces each year. They are looking for new art but they have no opportunities to see it.

BF: *Your works are now owned by two public galleries in Canada, the National Gallery,*[9] *and the Winnipeg Art Gallery,*[10] *and you have had your first one-man show in New York.*[11] *Was it important to you to enter the critical situation here?*

GR: Yes, the show was my first step. It was not too successful, but I will try again. The only thing that I thought was not too bad was that most of the people didn't understand the paintings; some of them liked them and some of them hated them, but they really didn't understand. This is better than the reaction to the paintings in the Chicago show where I showed the colour charts and the grey paintings and all I noticed was that people said: 'All we know is that we have the same monochrome paintings, too.'

BF: *Who collects your work?*

GR: Private collectors and museums, fifty-fifty. Maybe more museums, nowadays.

BF: *Which direction do you think your work is going to take now?*

GR: It is my intention to continue to work from photographs from the small abstract paintings through to the large colour abstractions.

BF: *Are there upcoming exhibitions?*

GR: Nothing definite for North America. A show in London,[12] I think...

Author's note, August 1979

In the summer of 1978, I took photographs of the surface of an oil sketch on canvas (78 × 52 cm, 1978 – it had been previously exhibited in my exhibition *Pictures* at the Anna Leonowens Gallery of the Nova Scotia College of Art and Design). The photographs were taken from various sides, from various angles, various distances and under different light conditions.

The resulting 128 photographs were organized in two versions: one, the sequential order that is presented here under the covers of a book, and a second version which is presented pictorially in grid-form (*128 Details from a Picture*, 1978, 127 × 400 cm, photographs on board, framed, Collection Kaiser Wilhelm Museum, Krefeld).

Gerhard Richter, August 1979

Letter to Benjamin H. D. Buchloh, 30 August 1979

Dear Benjamin,

It's crazy, and I really can't put my finger on why I haven't long since completed the draft for the pamphlet and the *Text*. I guess it's because of the long interval between now and the momentum of last summer's work, when we could have finished it so easily. But now I'm having difficulty getting back into it.

As you can see, I've got one or two different proposals for the cover; the ones we discussed in New York don't have enough pizzazz, especially for a 'pamphlet'. Even the ones I've included here aren't original or cheeky enough – it's just that I can't come up with anything better (and time is pressing). If you like the draft, take it and use it. If you want to change it or start from scratch, go ahead, it's fine with me.

Regarding the 'states' and facts (not so simple, actually) – e.g. very simple, like this: 'I took 128 photographs of a 78 × 52 oil study[1] from 1978.' Or: 'In the summer of 1978, I photographed the surface of an oil study (78 × 52 cm, 1978) from different sides and angles, under various light conditions, and from various distances. Of the 128 photographs that arose from this, there are two layouts: one of them you find here with the photographs in sequence as in a book; the other shows the photographs side by side and one above the other so that, together, they form a picture (*128 Photographs of a Painting, II*, 1978, 127 × 400 cm, photographs on cardboard behind glass, Kaiser Wilhelm Museum, Krefeld).' Or somewhat more complicated:

'For the exhibition 17 *PICTURES*,[2] which was shown in the summer of '78 in Anna Leonowens Gallery in Halifax and displayed small-format abstract studies, landscapes and grey-monochrome pictures, I preferred to use the term "picture" instead of "painting". By doing so I wanted to emphasize my dissociation from painting, which was already demonstrated by the diversity of subjects anyway – a dissociation I use as a method, but do not actively pursue as a goal.

'Over the past two years, I have rendered the oil studies mentioned above (as experiments with no particular plan, style, ideology, construction or expression, but at the same time not executed blindly or automatically or determined by mere coincidence) as large-sized "pictures"[3] that replace the reality of the painted studies with their appearance. I have used a similar method with the 128 photographs shown here, but with one difference: the photograph represents an even more uncompromising search for appearance than one could ever achieve with a painting. A painted picture, even if it is entirely illusionistic, will always contain some reality, since it is made by hand and is a picture traditionally defined as a painting (= the art of painting). In contrast, a photograph loses its own reality the more precisely it portrays the other reality and, if you look at it like that, the photograph's only "reality" is its own unreality – i.e., its non-existence is its actual quality.'

As you can see, I find it difficult to describe, and if I had to put it down in one line, this would be it: 'The model for the 128 photographs is the *Oelskizze* [Study in oil paint] (no. 432/5), 1978, 52 x 78 cm.' On the other hand, I would of course much prefer a 'text', only it would have to come from you. So in this case, I have to leave it up to you; you will certainly be able to write a more accurate and better passage than I could – after all, it is your series that you are putting my work in.

Besides this, everything is going very well. This life is so exciting. I hope I can begin working properly again sometime soon. I am making progress with the retrospective, and it will probably take place in Cologne as early as June of next year (I hope I can manage to produce a whole new series of pictures in Düsseldorf at the same time). I will send you more detailed material on the exhibition (which pictures I will include, etc.) as soon as I can. Since Ruhrberg and Gohr have already agreed to your writing for it, I should ask you if you would like to! Exactly what you would write about, in which format, etc. – you know it means a lot to me.

The catalogue should be a type of catalogue raisonné and should include everything from the very first numbered piece, and perhaps even a few earlier works.

That's all for now. As I said, I will send you more detailed information very soon.

Things have picked up in Düsseldorf – Konrad is opening the season with Gerhard Merz (one room), but is showing works by Schütte, Isa, Martini, Gieseler, Tannert, Wawrin, Ruthenbeck, Becher, Richter, and three pictures by Lueg. It was not that bad. Mike Asher also popped in for an hour in Düsseldorf, and Konrad, as inhibited as he is with Asher, expressed an interest in working together with him. He was most emphatic about this.

Benjamin, see you soon, and best regards,
Yours, Gerhard R.

Letter to Birgit Pelzer, 25 March 1980

Dear Birgit Pelzer,

Here briefly a few imprecise notes. I would have liked to put more thought into it, but I cannot find the peace and quiet to do so.

The *Ausschnitte* from 1970–71[1] are very small cut-outs, about 1–2 square cm, from palettes or from pictures that, when enlarged as a painting, take on an abstract appearance of indeterminate 'beauty'. In contrast to the modern comic elegance of Lichtenstein's brushstrokes, the *Ausschnitte*, as obvious reproductions, evoke the mere illusion of a painting style from the nineteenth century (or similar), which, however, never existed, or at least was never this empty. Despite my bias, I enjoy these cut-out paintings for their radical quality as non-paintings – as only reproductions could be, inasmuch as they do not recall the actual source image. (The bias: they are so pleasantly decorative and interesting that their actual accomplishment, and their antagonism, are overlooked.)

The *Striche*[2] contradict painting (both as design and as image), because a brushstroke of 1 m or even 20 m is more a negation or deletion of painting than an element of painting. (The element of painting is the common small stroke used in connection with many other strokes. Seen this way, a stroke made with a pencil is not a stroke, but a line – and the smooth stroke of a brush a streak.) Here my stroke is a stroke, and yet it is a painting. And painting as a method is not painting; it just looks that way from a distance (similar to a reproduction or to cinema projection).

To what extent this extreme format will inhibit the pictorial sense and yet convey action – that is, convey movement or even the passing of time – will become apparent during the exhibition.

I hope we will have the opportunity to discuss this further, and wish you a wonderful time in America.

Until soon, and warm regards,
(Gerhard Richter)

Description of design for the 'König-Heinrich-Platz' Underground Station, 1980 (together with Isa Genzken)[1]

For the overall design we are proceeding from the basis that the walls, pillars and other structures have a silver-grey, stainless-steel surface. In addition, sheeting made of enamel and mirror glass should be used for visual enhancement. All coverings should be recognizable as such, i.e. the concrete structure should be painted black and be visible in places so that the designed surfaces stand out from it. This enables us to avoid the hotel or boutique look common to some stations, and to impart beauty whilst preserving the character of the building as a station. For the artistic design, we have focused mainly on the level of the station platform, rather than the places that are usually chosen for public art incorporated into architecture, or *Kunst am Bau*.

Thus we believe that the walls facing the platforms are best suited for artistic presentation because the observer is standing in a place where he or she naturally waits (an additional advantage is that the decorated surfaces cannot be touched), and also because art is not something one expects to see there; its impact is enhanced by the element of surprise. Along these lines, we approve of art being initially perceived as design, with all its aesthetic qualities, and then, subsequently, unfolding its effect as art.

(So what we aspire to here is functional art that, ideally, will exert its effect and convey its meaning before the observer even recognizes it as art. Therefore, we strive for the opposite of the usual presentation, which immediately signals to onlookers that they are dealing with art – whether this art has a message or not.)

On *Level 3*, we have, using the total length of 116 metres, proposed the representation of four different curves. These are segments of circles with diameters of between approximately 3,000 and 5,000 metres – or, to put it another way, curves which, on a certain scale, correspond to the curvature of different planets. Thus, for example, one curve corresponds to the curvature of Mercury on a scale of 1:1,000; another represents Venus on a scale of 1:40,000.

The above is indicative of the overall artistic design, which leans towards modernism and utopia. On one wall, two curves are represented on enamel panels as segments of white spheres facing each other, leaving a red space – a vast, elongated, non-symmetrical hyperbola, which constitutes the primarily dominant visual form. The wall facing this also has two similar curves, represented by two differently coloured luminous lines. Creating this will require neon rods running beneath glass and installed in a space between light grey enamel panelling. Although the hyperbolic shape is clearly visible, the main impression here will also be of the segments of the two imaginary spheres.

It should be noted that the two sides on *Level 3* have been designed quite differently, even though the theme is the same (this is not normally done). Also, we are trying not to work against the length of the space, but rather to emphasize it as a positive quality. Because people will try to take in the whole of the radically elongated hyperbola, they will also have a spatial impression of the area as a whole.

For *Level 2* we have proposed six differently coloured areas across both walls, with six mirrors that complement the coloured areas and form a unit with them. The colour fields are on enamel and measure 3×19 metres each. Between these areas there are equally large mirrored surfaces that have a variety of functions: for one thing, the colour opposite is reflected and duplicated, thus simultaneously becoming part of the other picture wall; another effect is that certain angles of vision create the impression of infinite space, which is congruent with the overall concept; thirdly, the mirrors have a social dimension: people see not only the station and the art and design, but they also see themselves in conjunction with their surroundings and in relation to others. This may help alleviate the usual feelings of isolation and potential aggression, enabling people to experience themselves as social beings and to act accordingly; fourthly, the mirrors have the pleasant and most immediately felt effect of enlarging the visual space.

On the *intermediate levels*, above the stairs, there are four areas facing the flow of traffic. These levels seem to us to be ideal for back-lit transparent advertising. We propose this not merely out of commercial considerations, but because advertising is a normal part of a station's atmosphere and constitutes an aesthetic enhancement.

For the *eastern ticket office* we suggest the installation of a 'luminous newspaper' to correspond to the movement and energy of the station using other means. The flowing texts, which constantly convey specific information, are to be viewed primarily aesthetically rather than as a potential source of information – even if, in practice, it will be seen the other way round. The texts should primarily convey cultural news about the city, but temporary use of the system by companies and other groups would also be recommendable for financial and other reasons, since this would not detract from the technological beauty of the system.

For the *western ticket office* we envisage an enamel wall painting of 23 × 2.5 metres. This will be a non-representational depiction, currently without a title, which has a science-fiction feel to it, thus taking up the overall theme of the station design. The location and appearance of the painting would suggest that it is in the tradition of *Kunst am Bau*. However, the rigorous design character and the typical panel scale will rid anyone of the suspicion that this could simply be a misplaced work of art from a museum, and the joyous, vibrant colours will allow the observer to view it, not without irony, as a beautiful painting and valuable addition to the station's ambience.

Gerhard Richter/Isa Genzken (1980)

Notes, 1981

The big *Strokes*[1] are first of all only reproductions of brushstrokes, that is, manifestations of their outward semblance. But even the semblance is called in question, firstly because it is not painted in a 'deceptively real' way, and secondly because there can be no such thing as a truly credible semblance, for the simple reason that such big brushstrokes cannot really exist. But the pictures do show a brushstroke, though they neither display it as a real object, nor represent it realistically, nor manifest it illusionistically in the trompe-l'œil sense.

I want pictorial content without sentiment, but I want it as human as possible.

The composition of different forms, colours, structures, proportions, harmonies, etc. comes out as an abstract system analogous to music. It is thus an artificial construct, as logical in its own terms as any natural one, except that it is not objective. This system draws its life from analogies with the appearance of nature, but it would instantly be destroyed if any object were identifiably represented within it. Not because the latter would make it too narrative, but because its explicitness would narrow the expression of content and reduce everything around it to mere staffage.

If the abstract pictures show my reality, then the landscapes and still-lifes show my yearning. This is a grossly oversimplified, off-balance way of putting it, of course; but though these pictures are motivated by the dream of classical order and a pristine world – by nostalgia, in other words – the anachronism in them takes on a subversive and contemporary quality.

Painting is the making of an analogy for something non-visual and incomprehensible: giving it form and bringing it within reach. And that is why good paintings are incomprehensible. Creating the incomprehensible has absolutely nothing to do with turning out any old bunkum, because bunkum is always comprehensible. 'Not comprehensible' partly means 'not transitory': i.e., essential. And it partly means an analogy for something that, by definition, transcends our understanding, but which our understanding allows us to postulate.

Mirrors:

(a) 4 *Panes of Glass* of [1967], grey pictures, colour charts;

(b) Picture in itself, cropped effect, likeness to photography, readymade character (Berges furnishing store[2]);

(c) Polemic: devaluing of all other pictures; provocation of the viewer, who sees himself instead of a picture.

Text for catalogue of *documenta 7*, Kassel, 1982

When we describe a process, or make out an invoice, or photograph a tree, we create models; without them we would know nothing of reality and would be animals. Abstract pictures are fictive models, because they make visible a reality that we can neither see nor describe, but whose existence we can postulate. We denote this reality in negative terms: the unknown, the incomprehensible, the infinite. And for thousands of years we have been depicting it through surrogate images such as heaven and hell, gods and devils.

In abstract painting we have found a better way of gaining access to the unvisualizable, the incomprehensible; because abstract painting deploys the utmost visual immediacy – all the resources of art, in fact – in order to depict 'nothing'. Accustomed to pictures in which we recognize something real, we rightly refuse to regard mere colour (however multifarious) as the thing visualized. Instead we accept that we are seeing the unvisualizable: that which has never been seen before and is not visible. This is not some abstruse game but a matter of sheer necessity: the unknown simultaneously alarms us and fills us with hope, and so we accept the pictures as a possible way to make the inexplicable more explicable, or at all events more accessible.

Of course, pictures of objects also have this transcendental side to them. Every object, being part of an ultimately incomprehensible world, also embodies that world; when represented in a picture, the object conveys this mystery all the more powerfully, the less of a 'function' the picture has. Hence, for instance, the growing fascination of many beautiful old portraits.

So, in dealing with this inexplicable reality, the lovelier, cleverer, madder, extremer, more visual and more incomprehensible the analogy, the better the picture.

Art is the highest form of hope.

Interview with Amine Haase, 1982

Mr Richter, large-format works of yours[1] *are currently on show at* documenta *in Kassel, in which the almost aggressive brilliance of the colours grabs the viewer's attention. In addition, the artistic process differs from that of your earlier paintings, which were 'calmer' in colour and composition.*

What's new about these abstract paintings is the fact that they were not copied from a photograph, nor were they traced from a slide-projection of a sketch. Rather, they were freely composed on the canvas. I started this direct work on the canvas in 1976, although at the time it was in smaller formats. And I needed a fairly long time to gain the sense of freedom and experience to manage these large formats so directly without any template. To make it work, I had to find and learn to accept a new concept of painting, which would have seemed arbitrary to me at an earlier time. That is, before 1976 I often struggled with a theoretical means of legitimizing my work, which made painting more difficult for me – although this was just as often an engine for finding new forms, or new ways of doing things.

Your work is characterized by the fact that it always contains a commentary on painting. For example, the grey paintings were a reflection on the possibilities of painting, and your new abstract paintings are that as well. Even if they look different, are they not motivated by the same questions?

It's my assumption that anyone who paints asks himself what can be accomplished with painting, what it's good for, precisely because painting is not merely a matter of whim. But for that very reason, my paintings are never merely paintings about painting, and naturally they're not a form of research either, as was falsely described in the statement on the Bode Prize. Because that would be a boring form of self-indulgence, or of art studies or whatever – but not painting. So no matter what I've ever painted, it's always been an attempt to communicate something, whether consciously or unconsciously – about me or the world around me. It's always the attempt to 'get a picture of something', as the expression so nicely goes.

Right now at documenta*, at the Venice Biennale, and in many other places, there's a veritable flood of painting to be seen. Most of these newer works are said to reflect their creators' attitude towards life. It is said the 'zeitgeist' has changed. When you finished with your grey paintings in 1976, is it possible you already felt such a shift?*

At that time I experienced my change in attitude as a private, very personal event,

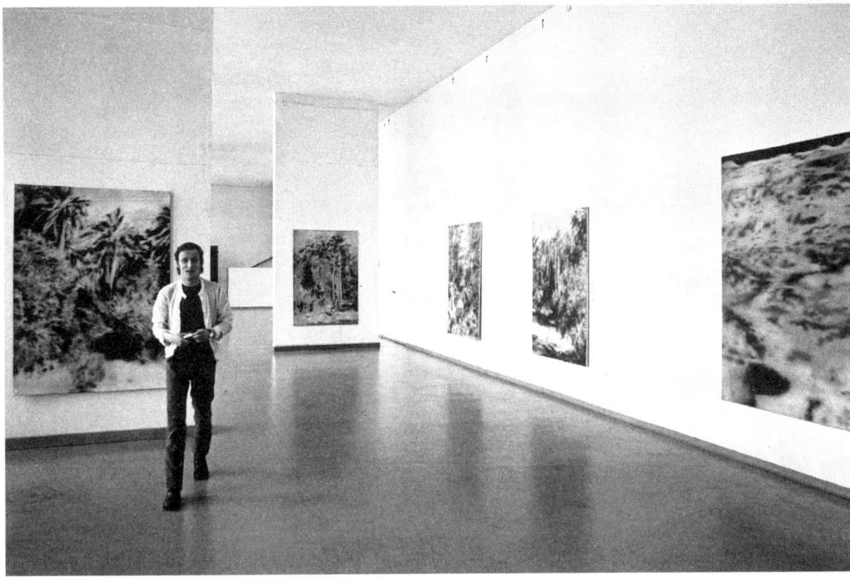

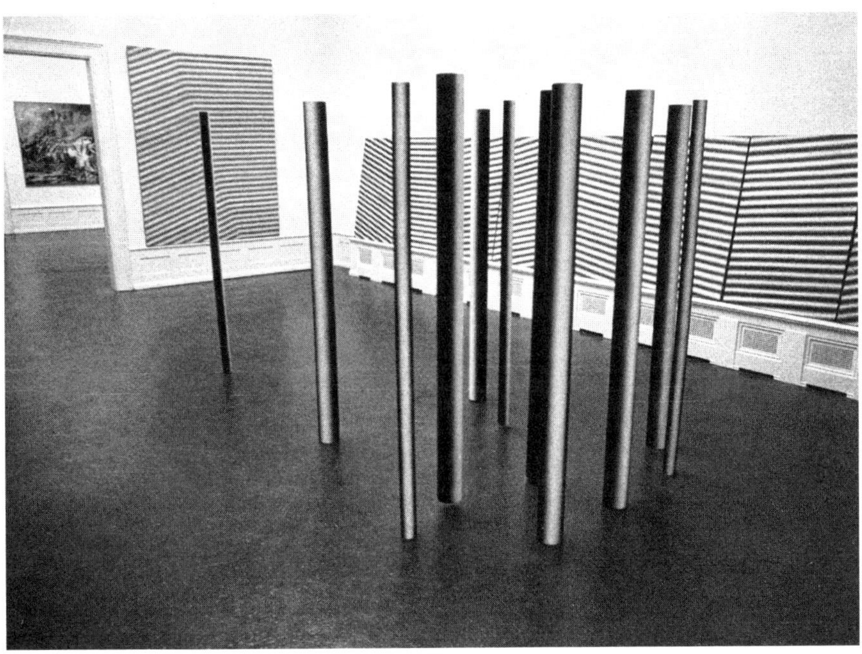

Kunstmuseum Lucerne, 1969
Staatliche Kunsthalle, Baden-Baden, 1968

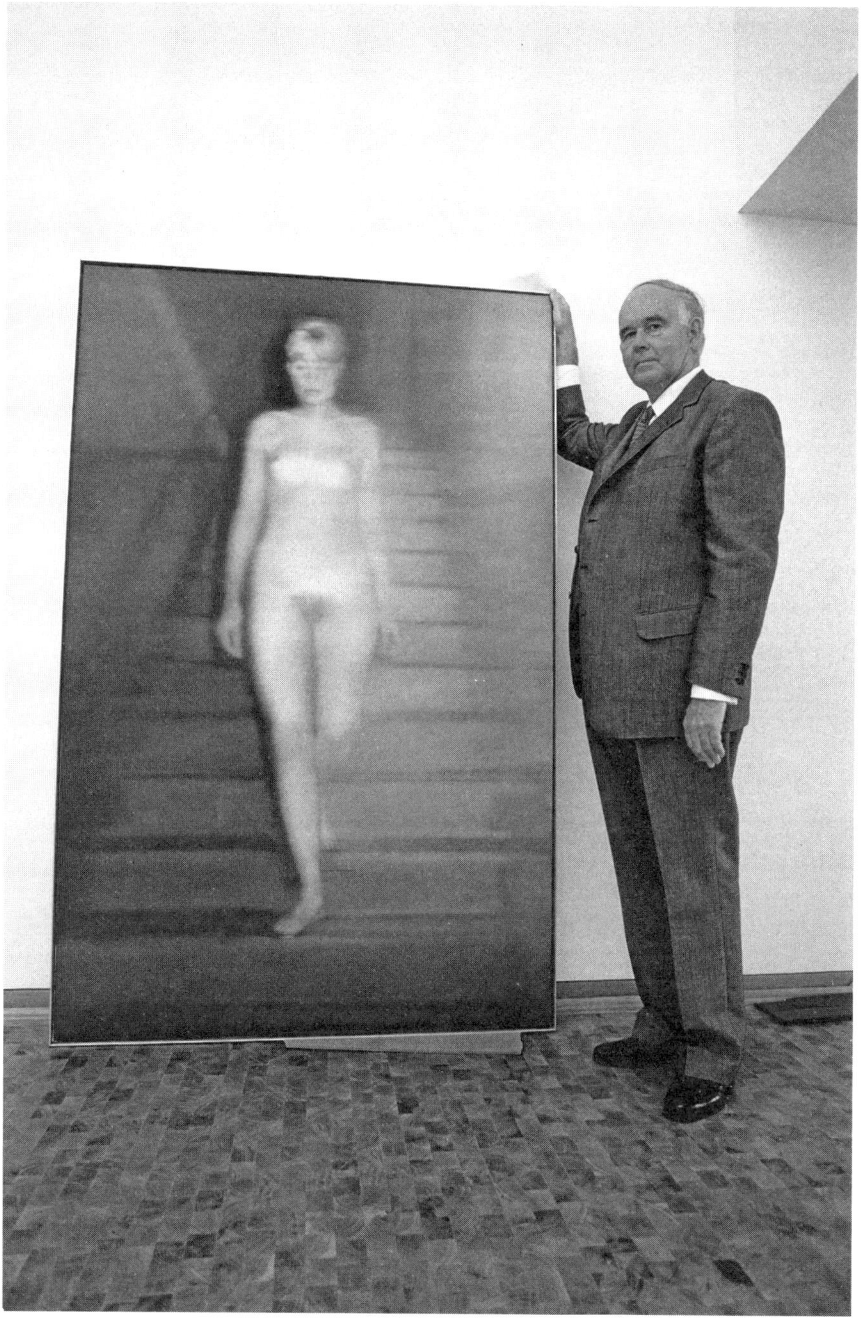

Peter Ludwig, 1986

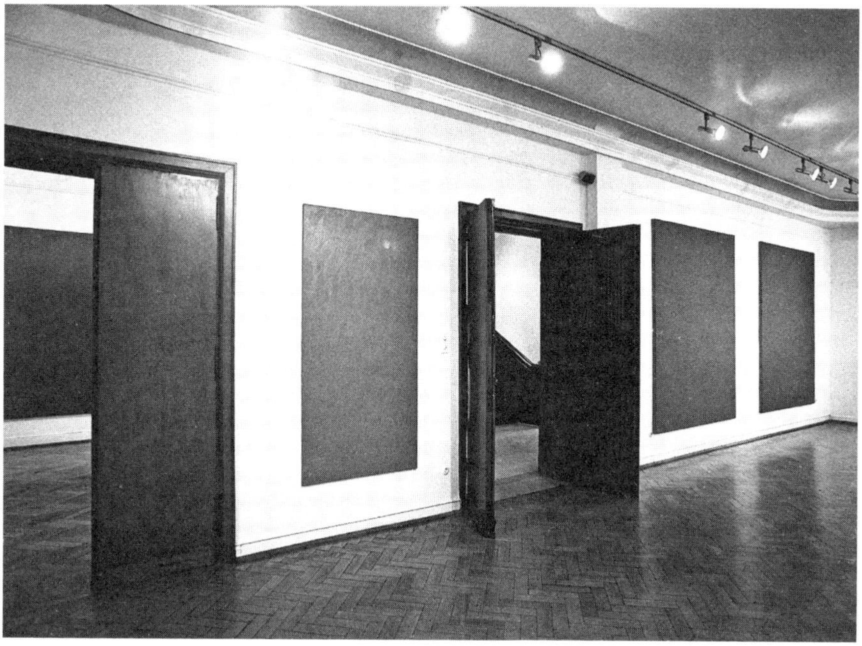

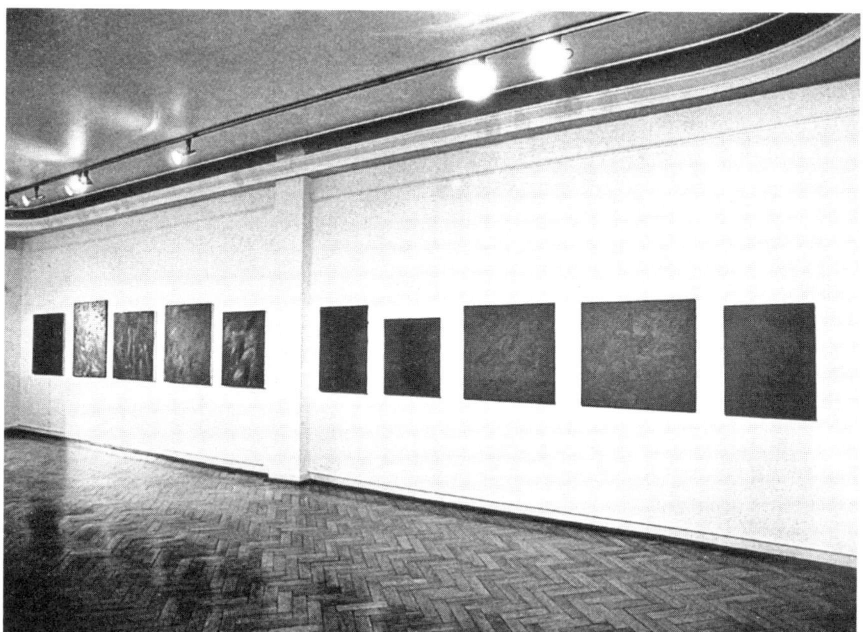

Städtisches Museum, Mönchengladbach 1974–75

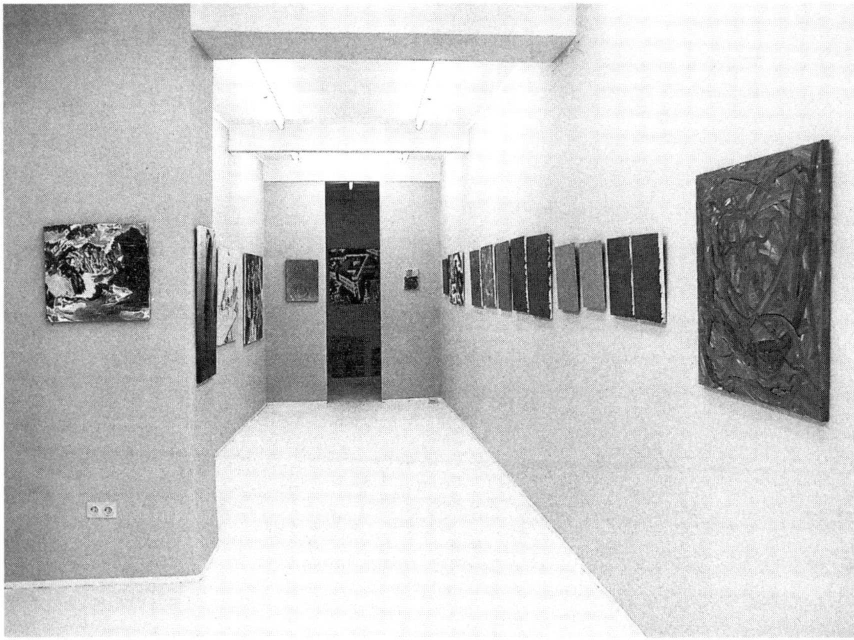

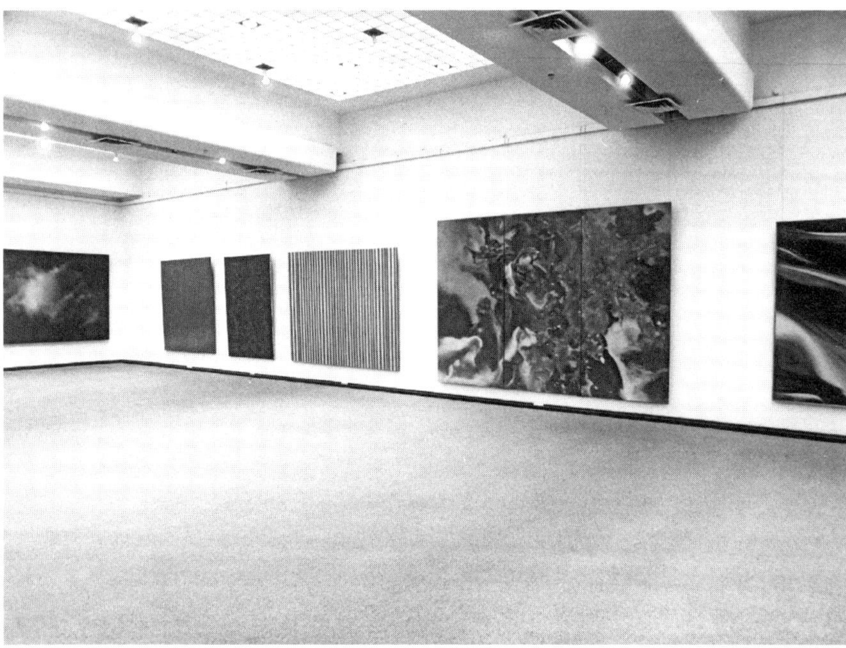

Galerie Konrad Fischer, Düsseldorf, 1970
Kunstverein für die Rheinlande und Westfalen, Düsseldorf, 1971

and I was quite surprised to see that this change became so widespread, even to the point of becoming a sign of the times – this departure from contextual thinking, which had made painting nearly impossible, or for that matter reactionary. I myself never had a dogmatic tendency in my work, yet sometimes I found the common ideology to be so forceful that it was as if I were painting with a bad conscience. Maybe that was my own personal problem, but it didn't last. In any event, this sea change was crucial for me, even though it was an almost violent decision to tear myself away from the process of using single concepts as a foundation for art. The monochromatic grey paintings – in all their perfection – were a dead end for me.

But this act of violence did not lead you to toss all of your previous experience as a painter overboard. With increasing success, you were teasing out the essence of painting – even if there were times when you did this by way of negation. And you have now applied these experiences. Your paintings differ from the work of a generation that considers experience to be ballast, or to be used at whim as part of the creative toolbox...

That's certainly the case. Thirty years paint quite a different story: that experience creates a completely different understanding and different demands, different freedoms, different strategies. I'm not one of the 'Junge Wilde', and the tendency to scoff at everything, and to replace strength with rawness and violence, is foreign to me. I also find it infuriating when obvious stupidity is washed up on the wave of the 'wild' movement, when the mere brazenness of these party painters is enough for them to gain acceptance. But that's always been the case during times when people have lost their orientation – that's when violence and leather-jacketed brutality seem to make the strongest impression.

It was the express intention of Rudi Fuchs, who organized the current documenta 7, *to break down the enmity which – according to Adorno – exists between any two works of art. But it seems the abyss that can open up between two works of art has never been as apparent as it is in this exhibition, at least as far as painting is concerned.*

Maybe that's even a good by-product, to demonstrate the irreconcilable nature between works of art. But one thing is certainly still apparent in the 'wild' paintings, even in Kassel: they've broken up something that was completely ossified. With one brazen stroke, they've destroyed dogmas that were considered unshakable all over the world. I think that's great. In that sense, I regret the domestication of the 'Junge Wilde' which has now begun and is fostering so much innocuousness.

When art only takes place inside the mind and is no longer visible, it can certainly lead to ossification, even to its own collective suicide. Something had to happen to prevent that. But that so many 'young' painters have learned so little from this time of – admittedly visually meagre – yearning for cognizance, is quite dissatisfying.

That may be. But we shouldn't be so impatient. In the end, *documenta* is not here to display the hundred best works in the history of the world, but to give an impression of what's happening right now in the field. And so it's quite normal that such exhibitions may at times seem like a hit parade, with hubbub and fuss and frills that will be forgotten sooner or later. This *documenta* 7 has relatively little nonsense, and that makes it better than average.

When you exhibit contemporary art, there is by definition a certain amount of bad stuff – you can't avoid that, and in fact it's an important undertaking that keeps the process in gear. Even the poorest paintings still foster art. And we can't take this for granted – when you consider that violent criminals never have anything to do with art, and the world is full of them. By this I mean to touch on the simple fact that art is the opposite of war – that we need art, and that for this very reason I believe it's our highest form of hope.

Notes, 1982

14 June 1982. The best thing that could have happened to art was its divorce from government.

Everything made since Duchamp has been a readymade, even when hand-painted.

25 November 1982. The whole art world is one vast scene of pettiness, lies, deceit, depravity, wretchedness, stupidity, nonsense, impudence. It is not worth wasting one word on it.

Notes, 1983

26 January 1983. Minimal art:[1] I saw this as an attempt to develop a new alphabet for the art of the future. And although it doesn't look as if it is being used in that way, my hopes still go in that direction. But then perhaps that is a completely wrong way of looking at it.

27 January 1983. Traditional, supposedly old works of art are not old but contemporary. So long as we 'have' them, in the broadest sense of the word, they will never be outworn: neither are we setting something of equal stature alongside them, nor shall we match or surpass their quality. Their permanent presence compels us to produce something different, which is neither better nor worse, but which has to be different because we painted the Isenheim Altar yesterday.

This is not to say that it would be pointless to produce something similar to traditional work. But the better we know tradition – i.e., ourselves – and the more responsibly we deal with it, the better things we shall make similar, and the better things we shall make different.

That is why the Academies are quite right to cease offering a traditional training, and in this respect to turn out only self-taught artists. For a training in traditional skills would run counter to the Academies' tradition of always existing in the present.

Art has always been basically about agony, desperation and helplessness (I am thinking of Crucifixion narratives, from the Middle Ages to Grünewald; but also of Renaissance portraits, Mondrian and Rembrandt, Donatello and Pollock). We often neglect this side of things by concentrating on the formal, aesthetic side in isolation. Then we no longer see content in form, but form as embracing content, added to it (beauty and artistic skill slapped on) – this is worth examining. The fact is that content does not have a form (like a dress that you can change): it *is* form (which cannot be changed).

Agony, desperation and helplessness cannot be represented except aesthetically, because their source is the wounding of beauty (Perfection).

The *Black Square* has no less to do with agony than a picture by Penck; but it has more to do with hope.

18 March 1983. Matisse. Many of the early pictures (1900–10) show great talent. Later, the few good things are exceptions: the magnificent back-view nudes,

a painting here and there; but most of the paintings are vacuous or positively irritating. They show a painter engaged in privatizing his work: one who has given up wanting anything, who paints what amuses him. And this personal gratification is of no general interest whatsoever: a naïve, stupid, frivolous game with the brush, illustrating his uninteresting surroundings, his life, feelings and enjoyments. Why crowds of people queue for hours in the freezing rain to get in is beyond me.

13 May 1983. I have always been resigned to the fact that we can do nothing, that Utopianism is meaningless, not to say criminal. This is the underlying 'structure' of the photo-pictures, the colour charts, the grey pictures. All the time, at the back of my mind lurked the belief that Utopia, Meaning, Futurity, Hope might materialize in my hands, unawares, as it were; because nature, which is ourselves, is infinitely better, cleverer, richer than we with our short, limited, narrow reason can ever conceive.

All the deeply wretched, amateurish, jejune images of rejection, abdication and banality that we prize today may well possess this very quality, this very truth. (It can also be viewed another way: that today's art really is the most wretched and worthless imaginable, like that of some obscure transitional period unmentioned in any history of art; or in other words that we have no art, but a hiatus, which we fill with productivity.) Whichever way, I am part of it.

2 June 1983. The ages that have produced great art are the exception: tiny segments of human history. The norm is the absence of art. There is nothing to indicate that we are not now sliding into one of those troughs: certainly not the rich and extremely interesting output of exhibitions, the growing culture industry, the thriving art business, all this entertainment.

In this, music is one small step ahead of us. On the Serious side, pathetic imbecility (Neue Musik Workshop); on the Pop side, all OK.

But the hostility to art – not only in totalitarian states, not only among politicians (and manifested in a particularly ignoble form by those who take an interest in art), but the deep-seated hostility to art manifested by those who are professionally concerned with it as administrators, educators and sponsors; the hostility of the museums, exhibition venues, galleries, etc., etc., etc. – I am coming to the conclusion that this is inborn in us, as a counterweight; so there may be a point to it after all.

8 June 1983. The plight of art is shown at its most horrific in those supposed conservatories of art that impose on the public at large by assuming the sonorous title of 'Academies'. This one word hoodwinks governments, ministries, mayors, city councils, critics and newspaper readers, parents and teachers; and under this name applicants are deluded and students are so warped and ill-taught that they rarely recover.

In the Federal Republic we have more than a dozen such Academies, where the worst artists of all lurk as parasites and elevate their own cohabitation into a system of debauchery and tedium. These so-called artists, who could never earn a crust by their own labours, are given the title of professors and thereby equipped with prestige, money and studios. There, not only can they cultivate and disseminate their own imbecility, and defile their students therewith; they are also in a position to make every effort to ensure that every student and every newly appointed colleague is kept below their own lowest level, so that they can remain undisturbed in their own thick fug.

(The workings of this mechanism are positively classic. The harder these 'professors' have to work to conceal and suppress their own sheer incompetence and ineffectiveness, the more unscrupulously they wield whatever power they can get: over their students directly, by treating them like children; over their colleagues indirectly, through intrigue.) That such a system is one source of the cultural impoverishment of our society is beyond doubt – as is the Academies' urgent need for a drastic pruning of dead wood.

11 June 1983. Carpet merchants and pimps, that's all the exhibition-makers are. Not really bad, in other words, and resembling politicians only in exceptional cases. Politicians are nauseating by definition: impotent and inept, they have learnt nothing and they can produce nothing, neither a loaf of bread nor a table nor a picture; and this inability to create value, this total inferiority, makes them jealous, vengeful, insolent and a menace to life and limb. And if, on top of all that, they are stuffed with ideology, then their inhumanity becomes total.

3 November 1983. Hostility to culture or art is nothing new; it is, and always has been, part and parcel of all societies. If in Poland the Writers' Union is banned, and artists – as in all dictatorships – are persecuted, this only represents the more brutal and direct side of the hostility that art has the capacity to provoke.

Our free, democratic system has other ways of showing its hostility to art. Instead of banning art, the politicians and the state promote it on a gigantic scale, devoting vast resources to official art administration in museums, exhibition buildings, arts associations, giant exhibitions, festivals and congresses, and through an unconscionable deluge of publications – not to speak of the positively criminal subvention of the theatre. By these and countless other measures, art is warped, crippled, buried and murdered, replaced by mammoth quantities and mammoth sums of money. Hosts of artists trained in this way work for a system wholly dedicated to administration and entertainment; it is they, more than anyone, who help to prevent and destroy art.

Art is somewhere else.

Notes, 1984

15 April 1984. All assertions concerning future events, concerning what we do not know, all assumptions, ideologies, speculations, constructions, all acts of faith, all proclaimed certainties, are nothing but superstition; they serve only to prove that we possess the faculty of imagination. We ought not to use this faculty to deceive ourselves (we ought to use it to deceive ourselves more unmercifully than ever).

16 April 1984. My pictures are devoid of objects; like objects, they are themselves objects. This means that they are devoid of content, significance or meaning, like objects or trees, animals, people or days, all of which are there without a reason, without a function and without a purpose. This is the quality that counts. (Even so, there are good and bad pictures.)

23 April 1984. I have committed myself to thinking and acting without the aid of an ideology; I have nothing to help me, no idea that I can serve in return for being told what to do, no regulation that tells me how, no belief to show me the way, no image of the future, no construction that I can place on things in order to be given an overriding meaning.

I recognize only what is, and in my view any description and pictorialization of what we do not know is meaningless. Ideologies seduce; they invariably exploit ignorance and legitimize war.

15 June 1984. Lack of culture, directness, immediacy, spontaneity, authenticity (!): this is pared-down art, which avoids all artificiality, which no longer tries to take us in, which eliminates as a distraction all artistic skill and all complexity of reference. Brutal, stupid and brazen, like a peepshow (i.e., unequivocally pared-down ballet): therefore radical, and therefore exactly what we need – what liberates us from cultural constraints – what is really going to make us happy.

New York, 6 September 1984. The more the city fascinates me, the more I suppress the overwhelming rage and hostility that I feel towards this city, in all its magnificence, modernity, beauty, and above all its incomparable, unmatchable vitality, which are denied to me, and which I can only admire, full of envy and raging, impotent, hateful jealousy (as a Cologne, Düsseldorf, Dresden man); this city of the elect and the privileged, of wielders of power and decision-makers, which implacably raises up and destroys, producing superstars and derelicts; which is so merciless and at the same time so beautiful, charming, dreamlike, romantic, paradisal. The city that exerts such a deadly fascination; the city that has killed many others besides Palermo. This city, this monster, with its tall, old buildings that seem so familiar and cosy and convey such a sense of security.

I envy the New Yorkers, and I think with discontent of Germany, the stifling fug of its society, its affluent philistinism, its all-smothering, oppressive ugliness.

I shall rebook tomorrow and fly home early.

21 September 1984. Certainly, Piloty, Makart and all those other Salon artists were far more influential in their own day than Manet, Mondrian and the like: i.e., they were even more important to society, and not only in the negative sense that they supported the reactionary status quo. They also supported a social order that may have been untenable but nevertheless basically performed its social function: unjust, antisocial or criminal though it was (is, and will be), it was necessary. There is no way out of that; all that is left is Utopia, a more or less vague, insubstantial Hope. But what I meant to say was something different, which is this: that these Salon artists, whom we today barely remember – however unimportant, inane, bloated and moronic they are – these very Salon artists represented the mind and spirit of their own time. I can barely believe this myself, but I have to assume that it was so – not only because the importance of these so-called artists is on record in the old magazines, but because we see the same thing today. What represents our own time, and actually keeps it alive, is the very same Salon trash, which we need, produce in vast quantities, discuss, comment upon,

record in exhibitions, texts and films – and which is the mind and spirit of our time, our zeitgeist. And I think that a short-lived, elitist phenomenon such as the movement that produced Minimal and Conceptual art is the exception that might have been expressly designed to prove the rule.

It was all over in no time. And then came retribution: trash painting and trash sculpture by the ton and by the square mile, eagerly swallowed by a greedy society. Art in the real sense does exist, but it is almost impossible to recognize with any certainty. It always has existed, and it continues to operate as the loftiest yearning for Truth and Happiness and Life, or whatever you may call it; this is truly the most perfect form of our humanity.

19 October 1984. Glenn Gould, Goldberg Variations.[1] For a year, two years, I have listened to almost nothing else. What is beginning to irritate me is the perfection. This totally absurd, boring, malevolent perfection. No wonder he died young. I ought to listen to the radio.

Interview with Bruno Corà, 1984

To all of us, myself included, earthquakes are frightening and fascinating at the same time; I mean, you can't resist the temptation to experience one, just once. When Lisbon was shaken by an earthquake, Voltaire made a public protest in the name of reason! In a metaphorical sense, Voltaire's protest was entirely reasonable, because the fascination that an earthquake exerts on every one of us corresponds directly to the unconscious forces at work within us. Those forces of infernal, murderous power that can conjure up murder and war can be held in check only by reason.

Do you believe that a picture can invoke or represent a particular event, or do you still take the view that a picture can only have itself as a theme?

Look at it any way you like: specific events can be represented by pictures.

Do you believe that the earthquake theme corresponds to a constant of some kind in your life and in your work – the continual metamorphosis of your visual language, and your predilection for movement? If so, and if we keep this constant always in view, can you tell me what the variables in your art are based on?

What you say about my work is true, and I accept it. But I'm afraid the answer to your question lies in the question itself. To me it's quite clear that a constant is a continual variable. And the sum of these variables yields the constant quality of my work.

How can painting on the one hand, and the abnormal drama of the earthquake on the other, be brought into harmony without simultaneously departing from the pleasure-principle?

That brings us back to what we were considering at the beginning. The pleasure-principle relates directly to the ambiguity and ambivalence of the effects of an earthquake – something that I understand as part of myself, because the forces of my subconscious correspond, in a sense, to seismic processes.

Is there any particular reason for the title of the picture that you've painted for this occasion?

I called it after Glenn Branca's band Static.[1] When I heard the band Static in Düsseldorf for the first time, I felt there was a contradiction between the name of the band and the loud, chaotic music that they made. That was when the picture got its title.

Interview with Wolfgang Pehnt, 1984

A picture like this[1] is painted in different layers, separated by intervals of time. The first layer mostly represents the background, which has a photographic, illusionistic look to it, though done without using a photograph. This first, smooth, soft-edged paint surface is like a finished picture; but after a while I decide that I understand it or have seen enough of it, and in the next stage of painting I partly destroy it, partly add to it; and so it goes on at intervals, till there is nothing more to do and the picture is finished. By then it is a Something which I understand in the same way it confronts me, as both incomprehensible and self-sufficient. An attempt to jump over my own shadow...

At that stage the whole thing looks very spontaneous. But in between there are usually long intervals of time, and those destroy a mood. It is a highly planned kind of spontaneity.

Pictures of this kind, which you have been painting in this way for five or six years now, strike a contemporary chord. The term you often hear used, of course, is die Neue Wilde, *'New Fauves'. Not that you are one of them; your painting is far too cultivated and also far too complex for that. But it does belong within a context in which a higher value has come to be placed on the easel painting, the self-sufficient painting.*

Yes, that's true. It surprised me, eventually. I hadn't realized that such things were going on in the studios at the same time, and that my pictures bore a certain resemblance to them. When I started on these in 1976 I thought to myself, 'Doing this is an issue that's personal to me.'

And this is not only a link with contemporary work, or with what some of your fellow-painters have been doing at the same time, over the same period of years: it can also be seen as a backward glance. You were a student twice; once in the GDR from 1952 to 1957[2] and then again, after you came over to the West, under Karl Otto Götz in Düsseldorf. Götz was one of the leading Abstract Expressionists at that time. Does your present work hark back to the things that mattered to you at that time?

Hard to say. It's not a direct influence from Götz. Although it was no accident that I found my way to Götz at the time. This 'Informel' element runs through every picture I've painted, whether it's a landscape, or a family painted from a photograph, or the colour charts, or a grey picture. And so now it is a pursuit of the same objectives by other means.

To appreciate the difference between your present and earlier work, one has to look at what you were doing in the 1960s and 1970s. That was an art in which the picture never consisted solely of what was to be seen but simultaneously reflected on other media besides painting. You've done a great deal of work with photography. For instance, whenever you've painted a portrait, it hasn't been the portrait of a sitter but the portrait of a photograph of the sitter.

Yes, because painting at that time was so much called into question, cast into such disrepute. I couldn't have a straightforward relationship with painting. That's how it was at that time: anyone who was painting was on the wrong track anyway.

But you always have painted, haven't you?

Yes, in spite of everything, and sometimes with a guilty conscience. Painting was my attempt to explore what painting is still able and permitted to do. It was also the sheer obstinacy of carrying on painting, even though nothing seemed to come of it...

... Acting as if it could be done – as if nature could still be painted in that way. In a way, I was trying to see painting as if it were still as intact and uncorrupted as before. Possibly. Because all this may well be a present-day illusion; perhaps painting never was as intact and self-assured as all that.

And what you're painting now – is this painting free from all these snags and ulterior motives?

I don't know. Yes, first of all, it is a painting free from snags and ulterior motives. For the moment, I have no grounds for supposing that there might be anything corrupt or worthless in it, anything that we can't use any more. And I've discovered that this is a tremendous gain. This quality stands for vital quality, as professional art, as painting. I see no reason to think 'that's over and done with', or 'we have different concerns and different ideas of beauty'. This kind of painting is engaged in acquiring, working out, adumbrating a future for itself. It's a future that has yet to arrive anywhere else: but in the picture it's celebrated in advance, as it were. If that were to work, yes, that would be good.

In retrospect, the paintings of the 1960s and 1970s also look different if you look at them from the standpoint of these new, very colourful, 'beautiful' paintings. Or they do to me, anyway. As I saw them at the time, your earlier paintings were dominated by the critical, reflective aspect – and now it's clear that then they were also occasions for painting, and for very good painting.

You mean that this critical awareness and this certain unhappiness, which calls painting in question, might have acted as motives to paint, to paint in spite of everything? That's certainly so.

'I pursue no objectives... I have ... no direction. I don't know what I want. I am inconsistent, non-committal, passive; I like the indefinite, the boundless, and constant

uncertainty.' You recognize those words, of course. They are yours, although it is a long time since you wrote them. Would you still say the same today?

No, I wouldn't. I'm glad I said it then. By doing so I created some space for myself, protected myself, as it were, against being tied down, in order to maintain the freedom to do what I like – to try anything I like, and not to become an artist-painter who is tied down to a single trick. Though you can be very successful with a trick like that, because it makes you easier to recognize. But then it works this way, too. It has now become my identifying characteristic that my work is all over the place.

But this rapid process of change is also a token of modernity: constant stylistic shift on principle. There are always some people like Braque, who spend the last twenty or thirty years of their lives painting polished still-lifes. But there have always been others, like Picasso, who do something different every couple of years.

And often go back to something they've done before, as Picasso did. One thing really surprised me: when I lived in the GDR, Picasso was a kind of demigod to me, and then when I came over here he had no influence at all. Everyone set great store by artistic consistency – an artist always doing the same thing and making propaganda for his own concerns. I was in no hurry to proclaim a personal concern that might not really be worth calling a concern at all.

Other people did, however, try to tie a label on you. 'Capitalist Realism' was one catchphrase that stuck. And it was actually coined by you in the first place.

Yes, we were amazed when that happened. It was a real joke to us. Konrad Lueg and I did a Happening,[3] and we used the phrase just for the Happening, to have a catchy name for it; and then it immediately got taken up and brought into use. There's no defence against that – and really it's no bad thing.

Perhaps it seemed all the more appropriate because in your paintings you conduct a dialogue with mass media, such as photography and advertising, and they do contain something like a critique of the packaged culture in which we live.

I had very little interest in any critique of packaged culture or the consumer world. When I painted from those banal, everyday photographs, I was really trying to bring out the quality – i.e., the message – of those photographs, and to show what gets overlooked, by definition, whenever we look at small photographs. People don't look on them as art, but as soon as they are transposed into art they take on a dignity of their own, and people take note of them. That was the trick, the concern I had in using those photographs.

Mr Richter, you have said that many artists develop a trademark, a personal style of handwriting, which they try to hang on to for as long as possible; and you don't do that.

All the same, I have the feeling that the prevalent trend in art – at least at the moment – consists in a rapid turnover of styles and modes of expression. What causes this rapid turnover? Is there something in our time that makes it necessary, or is it the speed with which picture material is consumed?

I can't offer any explanation for now. At the moment it's a bit steep, the way things are going. Professionalism is no longer valued, or needed, because society is in no position to make demands of the artist, or to work out the criteria that would arise from such demands. In the 1970s there used to be intellectuals who took the risk of saying what was good and right, and what had got to be different. In a way, society leaves us in the lurch – as you can see in the art schools, at every exhibition everywhere, in every press criticism, in art magazines, in the whole reception of art. Art is uncritically received, and the motto is: 'Carry on, it's all very interesting.' It hasn't always been this way, but at present it probably has to be – to avoid getting in the art's way, just for a time. I am sure that criteria will emerge, when we know once again what we need and what is right for us.

In this difficult business of making art, in this specific situation – in which, as you say, there are no hard-and-fast criteria to be assessed by – are there things that give you moral support, maybe in the other arts? In literature, or music, or film?

Mainly in music. It is hard to specify or explain the influence, what my relationship to it is, and how it helps me. But, leaving that aside, my moral support comes from the certainty that painting is not an eccentric hobby but a universal human quality, and consequently that it has distinguishable, specific qualities of its own. For example, if a number of people are looking at a row of paintings and most of them agree as to which are the best and worst of the set, then that confirms to me that we have an inborn ability to recognize quality and to understand painting. And this also confirms me in my conviction that, in spite of all possible aberrations, painting is intrinsically capable of giving visible form to our best, most human, most humane qualities.

Notes, 1985

20 February 1985. Of course I constantly despair at my own incapacity, at the impossibility of ever accomplishing anything, of painting a valid, true picture or even of knowing what such a thing ought to look like. But then I always have the hope that, if I persevere, it might one day happen. And this hope is nurtured every time something appears, a scattered, partial, initial hint of something which reminds me of what I long for, or which conveys a hint of it – although often enough I have been fooled by a momentary glimpse that then vanishes, leaving behind only the usual thing.

I have no motif, only motivation. I believe that motivation is the real thing, the natural thing, and that the motif is old-fashioned, even reactionary (as stupid as the question about the Meaning of Life).

22 February 1985. 'Formal conception', 'composition', 'line', 'distribution of light and shade', 'balance or disparity of colour' – such concepts are meant to explain that what counts in a work of art is not its content, the representation of an object: the thing represented is there only to serve the realization of those formal concerns, which are the truly important thing, the real point of the painting. Someone wrote about Hausmann's *Nude, Back View*[1] that the real statement of the work was the 'design', the 'swelling and contracting of the lines, the juxtaposition of masses and planes, the contrast between shaded and fully lit passages' – and described the nude itself, its erotic and existential message, as the banal and earthly aspect, which is spiritualized and transcended through art. Happily, the exact opposite is the case: the line and all the formal elements are as boring as only line can be, and the only interesting thing is the naked woman, her partly familiar and partly alienated physical presence, which fascinates by virtue of its subtle multiplicity of meanings.

(Comparable nonsense is written about Baselitz: by being turned through 180 degrees, his figures are said to lose their objective nature and become 'pure painting'. The opposite is true: there is an added stress on the objectivity, which takes on a new substance.) Anyway, pure painting is inanity, and a line is interesting only if it arouses interesting associations.

28 February 1985. Letting a thing come, rather than creating it – no assertions, constructions, formulations, inventions, ideologies – in order to gain access to

all that is genuine, richer, more alive: to what is beyond my understanding.

At twenty: Tolstoy's *War and Peace*. It doesn't matter how rightly I remember, the only thing that stayed with me, that struck me at the time, was Kutuzov's way of not intervening, of planning nothing, but watching to see how things worked out, choosing the right moment to put his weight behind a development that was beginning of its own accord. Passivity was that general's genius. (The photo-pictures: taking what is there, because one's own experiences only make things worse. The colour charts: the hope that this way a painting will emerge that is more than I could ever invent. At the same time, no truck with chance painting, painting blind, drug painting.) The abstract pictures: more and more clearly, a method of not having and planning the 'motif' but evolving it, letting it come. (About six years ago, that endless series of lacquer studies,[2] all of which I destroyed: letting the lacquers merge, observing the countless rich pictures that emerged – and disappointment at a kind of naturalism that was completely unusable, arty-crafty, kitschy.) Now the constant involvement of chance (but still never automatism), which destroys my constructions and inventions and creates new situations (As ever, Polke, I am glad to say, is doing something comparable.)

Using chance is like painting nature – but which chance event, out of all the countless possibilities?

25 March 1985. The Kiefer exhibition.[3] These so-called paintings. Of course this is not painting at all; and, since they lack this essential quality, they may well have the initial, shocking fascination of the macabre. But when that wears off, if not before, these 'paintings' convey just what they do possess: formless, amorphous dirt as a frozen, mushy crust, nauseating filth, illusionistically creating a naturalism which – while graphically effective – has, at best, the quality of a striking stage set. The whole thing is delivered with panache and undoubted self-assurance – as well it may be, because its motivation is literary: it's all in the content. Every lump of filth stands for one scrap or another, snatched from the bran chest of history – make the most of the fact that, so long as you avoid a definition, anything at all will serve to prompt an association. The one thing that frightens me is that I might paint just as badly.

18 May 1985. The way I paint, one can't really paint, because the basic prerequisite is lacking: the certainty of what is to be painted, i.e. the Theme. Whether I mention the name of Raphael or of Newman, or lesser lights such as Rothko or

Lichtenstein, or anyone else, down to the ultimate provincial artist – all of them have a theme that they pursue, a 'picture' that they are always striving to attain.

When I paint an abstract picture (the problem is very much the same in other cases), I neither know in advance what it is meant to look like nor, during the painting process, what I am aiming at and what to do about getting there. Painting is consequently an almost blind, desperate effort, like that of a person abandoned, helpless, in totally incomprehensible surroundings – like that of a person who possesses a given set of tools, materials and abilities and has the urgent desire to build something useful which is not allowed to be a house or a chair or anything else that has a name; who therefore hacks away in the vague hope that by working in a proper, professional way he will ultimately turn out something proper and meaningful.

So I am as blind as nature, who acts as she can, in accordance with the conditions that hinder or help her. Viewed in this light, anything is possible in my pictures; any form, added at will, changes the picture but does not make it wrong. Anything goes; so why do I often spend weeks over adding one thing? What am I making that I want? What picture of what?

30 May 1985. No ideology. No religion, no belief, no meaning, no imagination, no invention, no creativity, no hope – but painting like nature, painting as change, becoming, emerging, being-there, thusness; without an aim, and just as right, logical, perfect and incomprehensible (as Mozart, Schönberg, Velázquez, Bach, Raphael, etc.). We can identify the causes of a natural formation, up to a point; the same causes have led to me and, in due course, to my paintings, whose immediate cause is my inner state, my happiness, my pain, in all possible forms and intensities, until that cause no longer exists.

28 August 1985. The Abstract Expressionists were amazed at the pictorial quality of their productions, the wonderful world that opens up when you just paint. And in the evolution that led to Tachisme, the Informel, this irrepressible image-quality – that is, this ability to communicate – showed itself even (or rather especially) through the radically new, mechanical techniques of picture-production. It was as if these paintings were producing themselves; and the less deliberate the painters were about infusing them with their own content and mental images, the better the paintings became. But the problem is this: not to generate any old thing with all the rightness and spontaneity of nature, but to produce highly specific pictures with highly specific messages (were it not for

this, painting would be the simplest thing in the world, since in nature any old blot is perfectly right and correct.)

Even so, I have to start with the 'blot', and not with the new content (if I could exempt myself from that, I should then have to look for an appropriate way of representing it). With all the techniques at my command, especially those of elimination, I have to try to compel something that I cannot visualize – something that goes further and is better and more right than my own pre-existing opinion and intention – to appear as an existing picture of something.

13 November 1985. 'I have nothing to say and I am saying it.' It does not matter what Cage meant by that, or in what context. Every time I suffer by it, it convinces me that I am doing the right thing, the only natural thing. And the Others, so-called, are either wrong, because they make statements, or just as right as I am, because I have been mistaking their works for statements. In defiance of ideology, pictures everywhere therefore say nothing. They are always only efforts to get at the truth(?). I ought to formulate that more precisely. Even if I realize, to my delight, that I am doing the only natural thing, then –

I know nothing, I can do nothing, I understand nothing, I know nothing. Nothing.

And all this misery does not even make me particularly unhappy.

Better be an engineer, a bridge-builder, a physicist or a gardener.

27 December 1985. Terrible and challenging, the blank canvas shows nothing – because the Something that is to take the place of Nothing cannot be evolved from Nothing, though the latter is so basic that one wants to believe in it as the necessary starting point.

It is not possible to visualize Nothing. One way to gain some idea of that terrible state is through the impossibility of visualizing anything before, after or alongside the universe. Now, since we very much want this visualization, but know it only as one that we can never have, it is an impossibility that we experience, existentially, as an absolute limit.

Thus, without a visualization, we stand in front of the empty canvas and can respond – as ever – only with ignorance and madness, by making what statement we can: a surrogate, basically, but one that we believe can somehow touch the impossible. (The advantage of my grey pictures is that they seem to unmask all other statements, whether object-bound or abstract, as surrogates, and arbitrary ones at that. In natural terms, however, they are still the same statements.)

The abstract pictures are no less arbitrary than all object-bound representations (based on any old motif, which is supposed to turn into a picture). The only difference is that in these the 'motif' evolves only during the process of painting. So they imply that I do not know what I want to represent, or how to begin; that I have only highly imprecise and invariably false ideas of the motif that I am to make into a picture; and therefore that – motivated as I am solely by ignorance and frivolity – I am in a position to start. (The 'solely' stands for life!)

(It is difficult to equate Death with the Void, because we take that particular 'way out' so much for granted and analyze it in every detail. And yet the monstrousness of the Void – the term we use to denote the unthinkable, before, after or alongside the Universe, or what the Universe is there for – does also mean Death. The familiar conception that we all die, and that life still goes on in a quite realistically conceivable way, is one that stops comfortingly short: which is why we can handle it. So close to us is the Void, under the name of Death, that this inhibits us even from wanting a conception of it. This ineluctable Void is so absolutely part of us that we have no way not to protect ourselves by evolving banal conceptions, whether in terms of fact or of faith.)

Interview with Dorothea Dietrich, 1985

The artist's personality is most clearly revealed in the brushstroke. Your paintings are compositions of many different types of brushstrokes, which, at first glance, seem very spontaneous. But on closer examination one finds your marks are carefully planned and meticulously executed. Rather than personal, your paintings are actually very impersonal. How important is it to you to bring out the personal, the individual in your work?

This is, of course, important to me. But I want to avoid at all cost that this personal expression be too direct. Everybody does it and it is very easy. This type of authenticity can be found in many paintings, but in the long run it becomes rather boring. I like to compare my process of making art to the composing of music. There, all personal expression has been subjugated to the structure and is not simply shouted. That is why my paintings take such a long time. I interrupt the progress of one painting and return to it after a longer pause to make sure that the painting will not be all in one mood, but be more carefully controlled.

You look for a general expression?

Yes – and very contradictory expressions. I want the painting to be very heterogeneous, but nevertheless, everything has to be of one mould, as contradictory as it may be. The contradictions have to be there but must coexist, must converge.

So that these contradictions are worked into the very structure of your paintings, so that for example a hard line would be combined with a soft one? At times you use masking tape and other mechanical or half-mechanical means to draw straight lines, or use a sponge for mottled effects – the contradiction of the planned and the spontaneous is also planned. There is nothing spontaneous about your paintings.

Yes, yes – although there is also a lot of spontaneity in them. I always notice it when the painting has reached a certain stage and I try to figure out the next step. I often take a photo of the painting or put some foil over the painting to see what could be done. But that never works. Nevertheless, I must think it through to avoid putting down nonsense.

Do you work on small sketches next to your large paintings? Or does the playing around with possibilities take place mostly in your head?

Mostly through looking, going back every day to look until one suddenly knows what the painting needs. The sketches are important, too; it is a maturation process. That is why each series takes such a long time – half a year.

How do you define a series?

Series? I begin with an empty studio or empty canvases, about eight, not all of the same size. Sometimes large ones and sometimes small ones, sometimes tiny ones, and at other times all mixed together. In any case, everything has to be all white first; then it changes. Some are ready before others and go out, and others, new ones, are added.

When is a series finished? And what is the relationship of the individual works to each other?

They should all be independent pictures, but somewhere they have in common the theme that preoccupied me in this half-year.

You paint abstract paintings, but also more realistic landscapes...

... landscapes or still-lifes I paint in between the abstract works; they constitute about one-tenth of my production. On the one hand they are useful, because I like to work from nature – although I do use a photograph – because I think that any detail from nature has a logic I would like to see in abstraction as well. On the other hand, painting from nature or painting still-lifes is a sort of diversion; creates a balance. If I were to express it somewhat informally, I would say that the landscapes are a type of yearning, a yearning for a whole and simple life. A little nostalgic. The abstract works are my presence, my reality, my problems, my difficulties and contradictions. They are very topical for me.

Nostalgic because they are figurative or representative? Or because of their style of execution?

Their execution. They have such a conventional beauty, a classical beauty, which I love very much as well.

Do you choose the photos for the landscape paintings at random or are these photos of specific places?

They are specific places I have discovered here and there when I am on the road to take photos. I go especially to take photos.

Are these paintings then more personal than the abstract ones?

No – the totally abstract ones are the more personal, because they do not have that classical attitude; the landscapes or, for example, the candle paintings are almost like quotations. They are, of course, not quotations and it is not only nostalgia, but the abstraction is more real, the other more a dream. That sounds very [kitschy].

But you use photos for both?

Not for the abstract works, no, never.

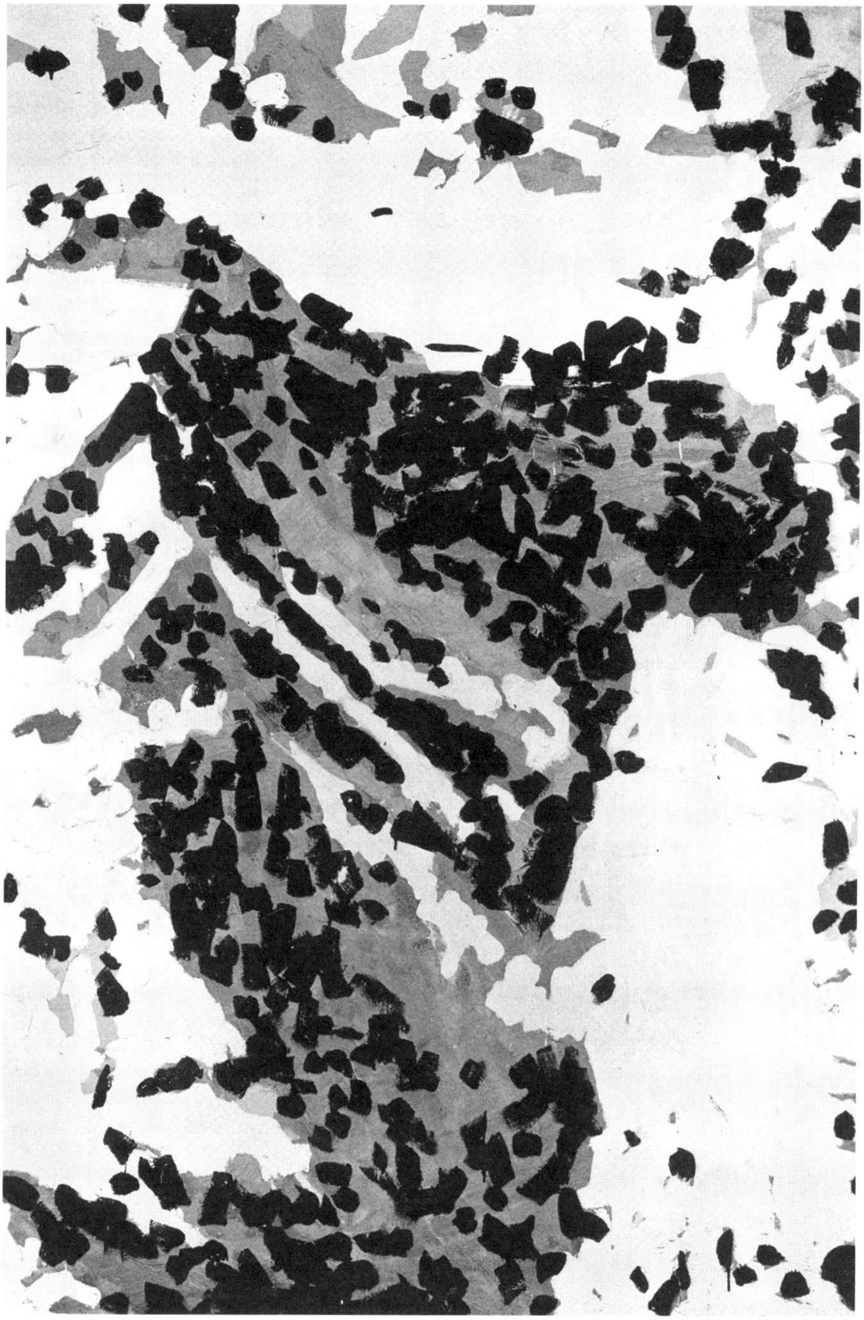

Mountains, 1968 (detail)

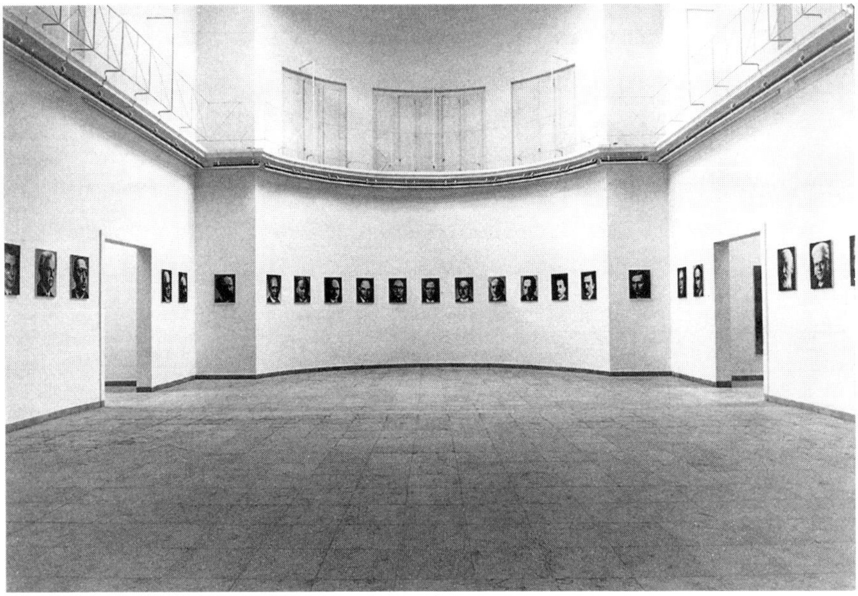

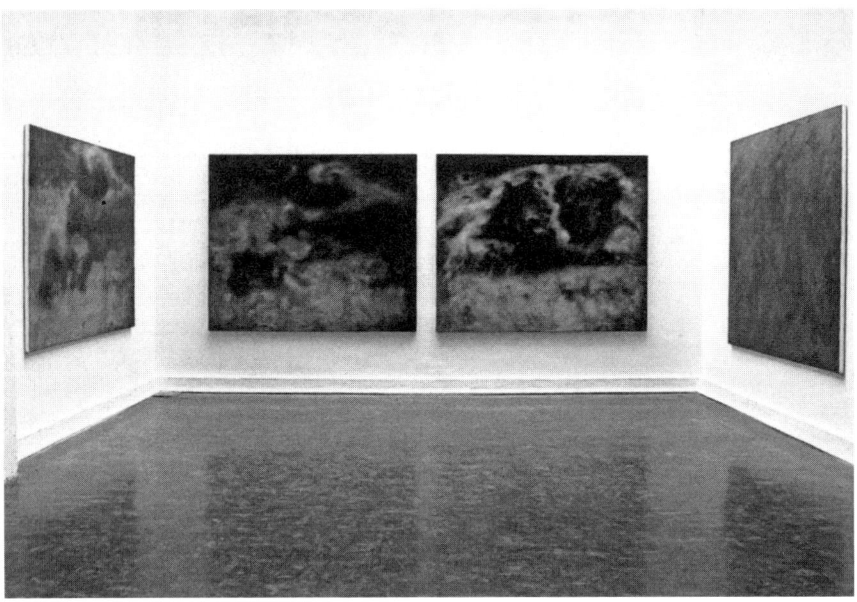

Venice Biennale, 1972
Tourist, 1975

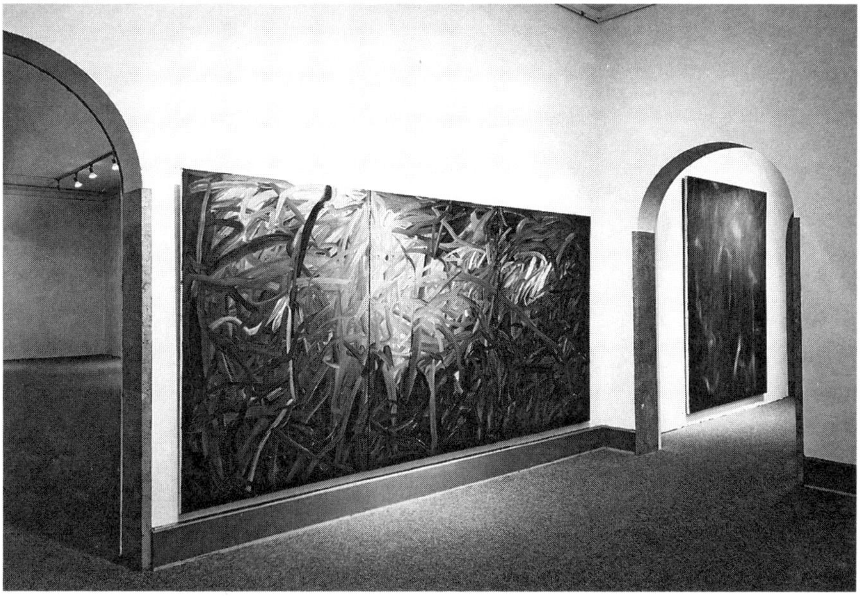

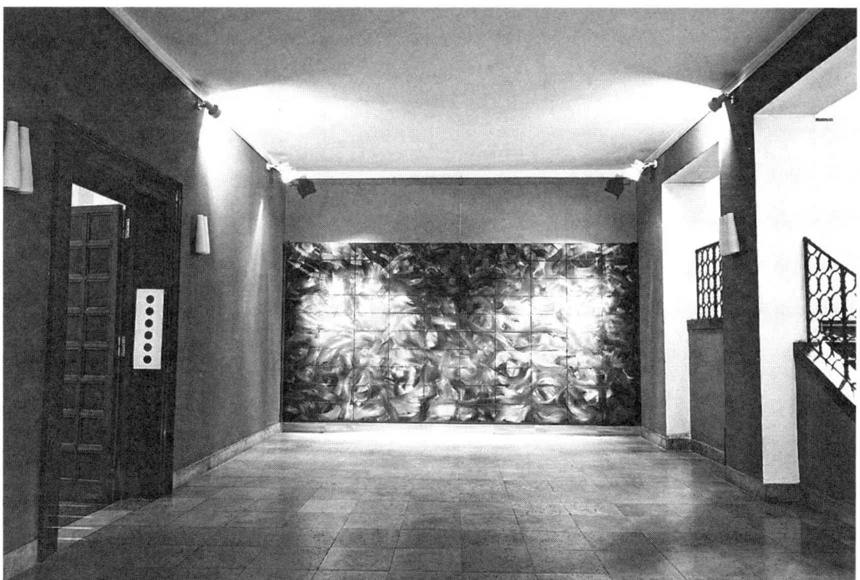

Städtische Galerie im Lenbachhaus, Munich, 1973

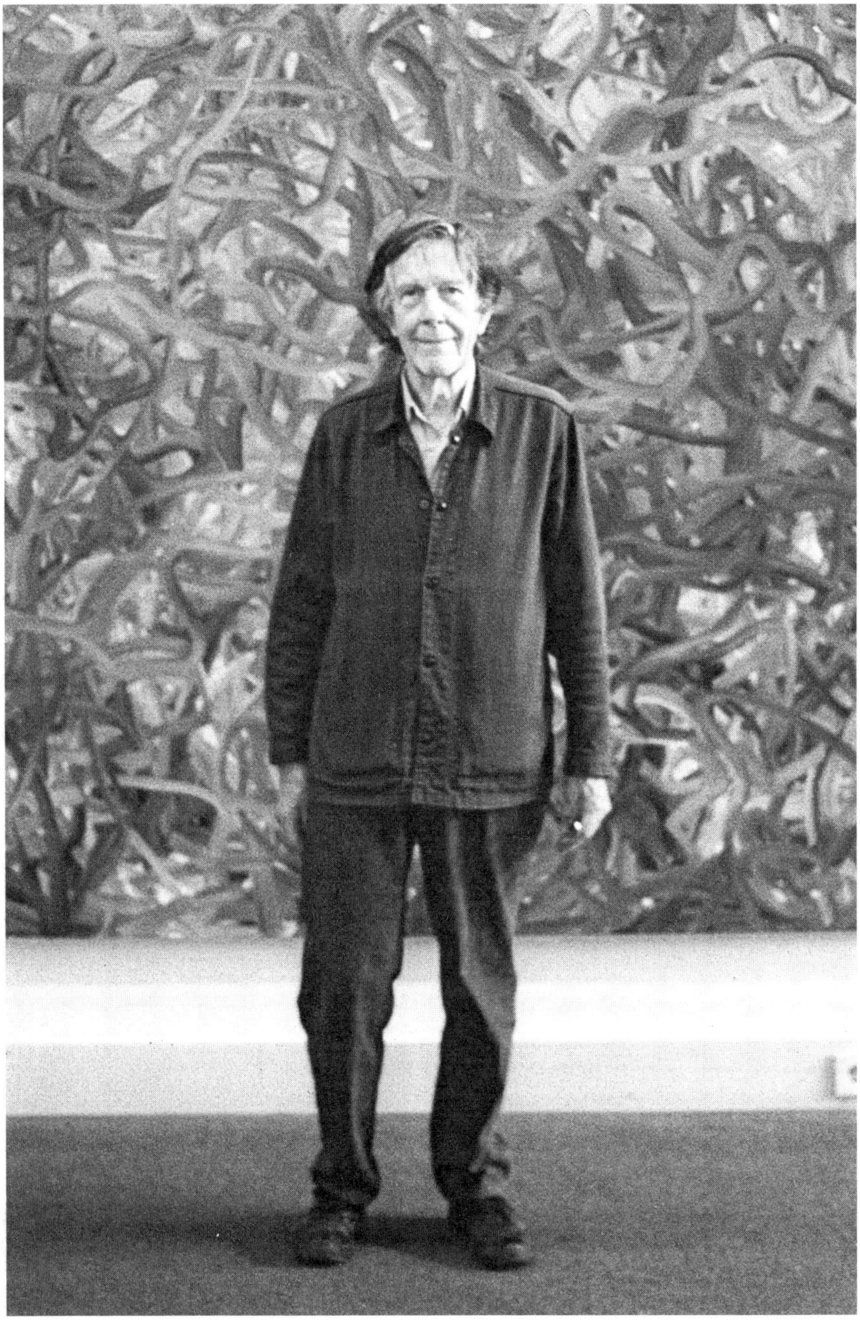

John Cage in front of *Painting*

Never? Didn't you do that for a while, though?

Yes, I did. That's when I painted some very small, abstract works from photos[1] and I didn't quite dare to consider them regular paintings. I looked at them as purely subjective. That is why I copied them to objectify them. It was only later that I felt ready to show them, and then I began to paint the large ones directly onto the canvas as well. It took a while until I could paint them without the aid of photographs.

When did you stop using photos?

The last painting was *Faust*. I don't recall when that was; I think 1980. I think that was the last abstract work for which I used a photo.

Did the photos help you to see in greater detail? I always have the impression that your paintings are about seeing, or rather, understanding through seeing. You want to show us the details and stratifications we normally don't perceive. A photo can demonstrate this type of seeing.

Especially when one enlarges it. But the wish was not so much the seeing and the details. That was only part of the method, as a means to tell something. The paintings should always tell something. In that they have something in common with the photo-paintings and the landscapes.

What do they tell?

That is difficult to answer. I always refuse to paint paintings for the sake of painting, to make pure painting. I always want my paintings to tell something. That is why I refer to my work as pictures rather than paintings.

But your message is always located between the concrete and the abstract.

Yes, yes.

How far do you manipulate that? How important is the lack of clarity?

I manipulate as much as I can.

To bring both poles...

... together? Yes.

When the photo can make things visible, why is there a need to translate it into painting? Are you as [a] painter in competition with the camera?

No, that is what the Super-Realists did. They took up this competition and seemingly they won, because they were even more perfect than the camera – and, above all, photos do not last, but paintings do. But painting is something else. I don't know how to explain the difference between the two. Both show pictures after all.

One is made by hand, the other with a machine, and is therefore more objective.

And by hand one cannot make it as well as by machine, and at the same time one can make it better than the machine. But which is better – for that I do not have a ready answer.

But you are a painter and not a photographer.

Yes. That is an important point. The execution gives pleasure. That is what one likes to do, like playing music.

So that one can develop an ability which one can perhaps not have in photography? A photograph is more impersonal.

Yes, more theoretical. It has less to do with making.

In the 1960s you collected photographs and assembled them in a book, which you titled Atlas. *Do you still collect photographs?*

With that book it came pretty much to an end.[2]

Many of your critics have pointed to the banality of the photos you use for your paintings, such as snapshots, family photos, sex photos. It seems to me, though, that once these photos have been assembled, they have been given individual attention and thus a new context, and would therefore be removed from the realm of the ordinary.

Yes – I have used the so-called banal to show that the banal is the important and the human. The people whose images we see in the newspaper are not banal; they are only banal because they are not famous.

But in your Atlas *you have also photos of concentration camps.*

Yes – those I could never use for my pictures. That was too difficult. That was not possible.

Right next to these photos there are sex photos and photos of your friends, for example, Blinky Palermo, as well as self-portraits and cityscapes. From a little further away all these different images seem to have a common structure. Was it the common structure that you wanted to point out, or did you want to devalue the individual photo by grouping them together?

I wanted to objectify them so that the very specific, the subjective and the special would disappear, and the image would become more general and more objective. And when I painted Jackie Kennedy I would paint her in such a manner that nobody would recognize her in *Weeping Woman* – and if one could recognize her, then it wouldn't be so bad either, because the title at least would give an indication that the subject was not Jackie.

Why do you avoid the expression of the personal in your painting?

I always mistrusted that, or I didn't dare to do it. But it doesn't interest me very much either and I don't think others would be much interested in it. How I feel and what I think is rather uninteresting. Therefore I am always tempted to generalize, or I try to give things a general validity. Perhaps it was also arrogance, to make one's own high standards applicable to everybody. A strange mixture.

In your early paintings and drawings you often smudged the contours. Was that an expression of the difficulty of making a precise statement?

Yes, that too. That was also an attempt at getting rid of the personal touch. I wanted to make it as anonymous as a photo. But it was perhaps also the wish for perfection, the unapproachable, which then means loss of immediacy. Something is missing then, though; that is why I gave that up.

What is missing?

The directness. One isn't immediately moved. Too much distance is an advantage and a disadvantage. There is also another difference between the two modes of representation. Objects have too much importance – they give the painting a specific direction. Colour and structure are not given a chance to stand on their own. Because abstract painting does not represent – there is no man or table or whatever – one must only make sure that the relationship of colour and structure is right, like composing music, like Schönberg and Mozart.

Are you afraid of making your personal feelings public?

Yes – but you can't avoid it. All paintings show your personal feelings somehow.

Surely, but an abstract painting erects certain barriers...

... yes, abstract paintings are more removed.

You create a distance and you also use half-mechanical modes of painting. But you don't seem particularly interested in printmaking.

For a while I did that quite a bit, until about ten years ago.

You haven't shown these works very much.

No, I haven't shown them much. In Germany you can find them; there were about 50 to 60 different editions. They were always the same themes that I painted, after photos, of course.

What techniques did you use?

Mostly silkscreen and offset, offset above all, the cheapest, anything that could be produced in vast quantities.

Did you take the photos which you used for your prints from magazines?

Yes, all the time.

Why did you give it up?

The last ones were the colour charts in 1974 and after that I wasn't able to do prints any more. Now I would like to try out my abstract works in printmaking, but in a more conventional manner.

With different techniques?

Etching and all that. I really want to do it.

Etching is such a meticulous, planned process, which lends itself so well to manipulation. Considering how interested you are in layering, I am really surprised that you haven't experimented with the conventional methods of printmaking before.

I think it was mostly a question of time. I was still so preoccupied with painting, but now I hope that I can make use of the workshop to experiment.

Have you ever done etching?

No, not at all. I have never held an etching needle in my hand.

Do you like to experiment?

Yes and no – I haven't used anything but oil paint for years. Oil paint is such a thankful medium. One can do anything with it: paint over it, wipe it out, scrape it off, apply it thinly or liquidly. It offers so much, and therefore I have never been very interested in trying out other media.

You have never shown your drawings very much either. Why is that? Was their execution and mark too personal?

Yes, there is something about that. And I have made only a very few drawings. It is only this year, no, last year, that I have had the confidence to make watercolours. Earlier, I made very few, and suddenly, 1984, many. Fred Jahn published a book about them,[3] and that helped me to feel confident with making something personal, something small. I used to snub such things as too artistic, as too typical, as the type of things artists would make – beautiful drawings.

You are afraid of beauty? You believe beauty is too close to the aesthetic?

Yes, yes, beauty has such a special appeal.

Your drawings then as well?

Only worse.

Oil painting, then, gives you the absolute control that you seek?

Yes, and they are larger, have more effect. And I need the type of response an oil painting commands. The small works don't do that. I must be able to see at once.

But there seems to be more to it. Your colour charts and your other large paintings create a total environment. I noticed in your Atlas *some drawings of entire rooms, architectural drawings.*

Oh, yes, that is such a dream of mine – that the pictures will become an environment or become architecture; that would be even more effective.

That painting should be as concrete as possible? To have the presence you see in architecture? A building is there and one cannot avoid it.

That is why I sometimes hate architects so much. To erect a building is such a brutal thing, such an act of aggression. Painting is never like that... One can look away. It is fortunate that one cannot turn one's paintings into buildings.

Are you interested in questions of technique? You very painstakingly show us all the painting techniques...

Oh, I haven't noticed that, but yes...

... even a small painting contains many different modes of painting. Sometimes you apply the paint all flat, at other times in relief...

I think that this comes from music. It would be like playing music with one instrument only. When you sound a note on the violin it sounds totally different than played on a trumpet, etc. It would be too boring to use only one instrument.

Do you play an instrument yourself?

No, but I like to listen, anything from classical to modern, Mozart and Schönberg to Glenn Branca.[4]

Do you listen to music when you paint?

Only very seldom. I am afraid I would begin to like the paintings. They turn out so well – only they are not right. One gets too uncritical.

Is there a connection between your art and Russian art of the '20s? There is a drawing titled Tatlin, *and you have mentioned Malevich in another context.*

No, these are important artists, but I really don't recall naming a drawing *Tatlin*,[5] and I mentioned Malevich only to say that paintings are always illusionistic. If you don't see anything in Malevich's *Black Square*, then the painting would only be a stupid black spot. There is more of a connection to the Informel style or perhaps to the Romantic. Because there is no hierarchy in those paintings they have more of a philosophical aspect; there is no order, everything is dissolved, more revolutionary, anarchistic, the beginning of anarchy.

Do you see anarchy in your paintings?

By necessity, yes.

Because there are no hierarchies in your painting?

Because I don't have any, or we don't have any.

Those are two different things, though. That could be revolution and anarchy but it could also be a reflection of contemporary life.

Exactly, and that is very positive, and we create order anyhow. I think my paintings are very composed, yet informal, because of the lack of hierarchies.

What role does irony play?

I don't like it in painting because there are better means for distancing or translating or making indirect statements, as for example, art instead of irony.

Yet, as your attention to detail shows, you don't distance yourself completely.

No, you can't do that, you wouldn't be able to live. I have tried it; my paintings became more and more impersonal and general until nothing was left but monochrome grey or colours next to each other, any unmodulated colour. Then I was totally outside my paintings. But I didn't feel well either. You can't live like that, and therefore I decided to paint the exact opposite. I decided very consciously – as salvation after all that grey – to survive, to paint polychrome, complicated, [kitschy].

And now you are well?

Better.

You are now also becoming more and more famous...

... yes, that is pretty strange...

... does painting become more difficult then?

At the moment, yes. One isn't used to being in demand, to getting calls and offers. All of a sudden I lost all impetus to paint. But it is all right. One can remain free.

Do you have the feeling you are working for a market?

I want to avoid that feeling at all cost. That is why I don't paint for exhibitions, but select them from the material I have.

Is it also the feeling that you are painting for a different audience that disturbs you? An audience that asks questions...

... and has expectations. That is a responsibility and bears down on you. It is like a norm; now you must deliver good paintings – assuming they are good – they are regarded as good, and now they want more of the same.

Let's imagine that you are really tired of your present mode of painting but the market still demands it.

I have always managed so far. I gave up the photo-paintings before I had to and turned to something completely different. Those soft-contoured family pictures would have made me more famous, too, had I continued making them. But I am not in a rush.

I wonder anyhow what is going to happen to contemporary German painting. In the last two years some German painters have had a terrific success on the American market. But the American market is also very dependent on fashion and discards artists quickly. Are you afraid of that?

A little, but not too much. I think too that it won't go on like this, that the market will calm down. But I am not 30 any more, either, and so it is not so bad.

You feel secure enough?

Yes, and I have a job, too. I teach at the Düsseldorf Academy. I feel quite secure.

Did you ever study with Beuys?

I studied first in Dresden. When I came to Düsseldorf, Beuys had just begun teaching there, but I never studied with him. Strangely, we have always been rather distant. We meet sometimes by chance, but we don't have much to do with each other.

Yet you were interested in Fluxus as well, weren't you?

Yes, I was very impressed with Fluxus. It was so absurd and destructive. It inspired me to try out some real nonsense, like copying photographs in oil paint.

Could you tell me a little about your Manifesto of Capitalist Realism?[6]

That was a piece I did in 1963 with Konrad Lueg in a department store, in the furniture department. It was announced in some papers as an exhibition opening, but the people who came didn't know that it was to be a sort of Happening. I don't think it is quite right that it has become so famous anyhow. It was just a lot of fun, and the word itself, Capitalist Realism, hit just right. But it wasn't such a big deal.

So you see a social function for the artist, or is the artist totally independent?

As independent as the scientist and as social. The role of the artist is not to teach society.

You show us how to see. Isn't that a form of teaching?

Like any other, well, not like any, but like any humanistic teaching. The psychologist does that as well and shows us what he has found. That is very social.

But you don't define the artist, like Beuys, as a political being?

No. I don't quite understand how he means that anyhow. He, Beuys, is a special category all by himself.

Can art be political?

Sometimes. There have been political artists at certain times. Beuys is one of them. Often political artists are very boring, but sometimes also very good, like John Heartfield or Käthe Kollwitz. But sometimes political artists are too narrow, too uninteresting.

I suppose you have seen quite a bit of that in East Germany?

Yes, Socialist Realism is truly idiotic. It doesn't bring anything, is hokus, nothing but illustration. And the people don't get anything out of it. There is nothing alive or new in that art. That is what is so good here in America; the people are more dynamic than in Germany.

When you give us views of details in your paintings, are these details, or fragments, chosen at random?

No, they are not, after all, readymade details. I begin somewhere and they develop as I go along.

Then what function do you assign to the edges and the frame of your work?

The painting ends there. That is the frame, within which one works. In music it is time, one hour or five or a two-minute piece. Everything needs a measure, just as the open door has a frame, as Musil said, otherwise it would be without boundaries.

And your paintings on glass and mirrors? In 1981 you framed sheets of mirror.

They are like the door frame.

What we see within their frame is, however, undetermined, changes with the placement of the work. Don't you say with these works that what we see is undeterminable?[7]

Notes, 1986

18 February 1986. Of course, my landscapes are not only beautiful or nostalgic, with a Romantic or classical suggestion of lost Paradises, but above all 'untruthful' (even if I did not always find a way of showing it); and by 'untruthful' I mean the glorifying way we look at nature – nature, which in all its forms is always against us, because it knows no meaning, no pity, no sympathy, because it knows nothing and is absolutely mindless: the total antithesis of ourselves, absolutely inhuman.

Every beauty that we see in landscape – every enchanting colour effect, or tranquil scene, or powerful atmosphere, every gentle linearity or magnificent spatial depth or whatever – is our projection; and we can switch it off at a moment's notice, to reveal only the appalling horror and ugliness.

Nature is so inhuman that it is not even criminal. It is everything that we must basically overcome and reject – because, for all our own superabundant horrendousness, cruelty and vileness, we are still capable of producing a spark of hope, which is coeval with us, and which we can also call love (this has nothing to do with unconscious, bestial, mammalian nurturing behaviour). Nature has none of this. Its stupidity is absolute.

21 February 1986. Beuys. This phenomenon, which took us by surprise 25 years ago, and soon appalled us, unleashing admiration, envy, consternation, fury; this absolute loner, who broke all the conventions which, for all our rebelliousness,

gave us a framework in which we could 'carry on' in relative security (above all in contrast with the social system that most of us had known previously, that of the GDR). Over the years, we got used to him, his activities no longer shocked us, and a certain critical detachment supervened. By the end he was a good, honourable artist; to some extent, he had been relativized.

His death revived his uniqueness at a stroke, and all the early (childish) questions posed themselves anew. His death stirs things up, touching something in me that rationalism long ago suppressed: something mystical, superhuman. It frightens me. I would prefer the normal comfort of not being too conscious.

(How am I to hope that his works [what does that mean?] are just good works, and will endure – when I profoundly want them to cross a frontier that I myself want to break through? – I am a popular artist, a painter within the context of his speciality, and I want to remain just that, successfully; with all my discontent and desperate longing; with all my fear of death and of 'crossing frontiers'.)

25 February 1986. The idea as a point of departure for the picture: that's illustration. Conversely, acting and reacting in the absence of an idea leads to forms that can be named and explained, and thus generates the idea. ('In the beginning was the deed.')

To put it another way. Marx's teaching didn't cause historical change: new facts gave rise to interpretations, and thus to ideology. Action in pursuit of ideology creates lifeless stuff at best, and can easily become criminal.

17 March 1986. Crime fills the world, so absolutely that we could go insane out of sheer despair. (Not only in systems based on torture, and in concentration camps: in civilized countries, too, it is a constant reality; the difference is merely quantitative. Every day, people are maltreated, raped, beaten, humiliated, tormented and murdered – cruel, inhuman, inconceivable.) Our horror, which we feel every time we succumb or are forced to succumb to the perception of atrocity (for the sake of our own survival, we protect ourselves with ignorance and by looking away), our horror feeds not only on the fear that it might affect ourselves but on the certainty that the same murderous cruelty operates and lies ready to act within every one of us.

I just wanted to put it on record that I perceive our only hope – or our one great hope – as residing in art. We must be resolute enough in promoting it. — I was interrupted just as I was detecting something like hope in the very realization that this cruelty is present in everyone – as if this very fact could be the starting-point of betterment, a key to the possibility of doing something.

18 March 1986. Formalism stands for something negative: contrived stuff, games played with colour and form, empty aesthetics.

When I say that I take form as my starting point, and that I would like content to evolve out of form (and not the reverse process, whereby a form is found to fit a literary idea), then this reflects my conviction that form, the cohesion of formal elements, the structure of the phenomenal appearance of matter (= form), generates a content – and that I can manipulate the outward appearance as it comes, in such a way as to yield this or that content.

I have only to act in accordance with the laws and conditions of form in order to get the materialization right.

In this effort I am first of all supported by music (Schönberg and all other pure music evolves out of its own laws, and not out of the effort to find a form for a specific statement); and, secondly, I find the essential confirmation in nature, which produces material changes without any intention (or cause) related to content, but takes on this or that form in accordance with its own preconditions. The more complicated this process is, the more functional nature's 'contents', qualities, capabilities become. The issue of content is thus nonsense; i.e., there is nothing but form. There is only 'something': there is only what there is.

21 March 1986. The 'messages', and therefore the content. (Almost) always, when painters 'communicate', they illustrate and give visual expression to their own stupidity. Their messages are always distressing, boring, untruthful, botched, abject and aggressive (prize specimens: Kucki, Kia and Klemente[1]). The sole exception here is Beuys, and he too is at his best, and at his most effective, when the 'message' is impossible to read off direct – as for instance in *Lightning Stroke*, which is anything but the illustration of a flash of lightning (a very great work).

But otherwise this Message Art is stupid in three separate ways. The events dragged in by the scruff of the neck are of unspeakable, hopeless inanity in themselves; this is logically matched both by the brazen stupidity of the 'painterly presentation' of those events and by their cockily idiotic captioning; and, lastly, unsurpassable stupidity becomes total when it blocks the awareness, even the surmise, that painting, if it is ever to contribute anything at all, must be the very polar opposite of all such messagecraft. And this threefold, shrieking stupidity is actually exceeded by the stupidity of those who promote it.

28 March 1986. I am a materialist on principle. Mind and spirit, soul, volition, feeling, instinctive surmise, etc., have their material causes (mechanical, chemical, electronic, etc.); and they vanish when their physical base vanishes, just as the work done by a computer vanishes when it is destroyed or switched off.

Art is based on these material preconditions. It is a special mode of our daily intercourse with phenomena, in which we apprehend ourselves and everything around us. Art is therefore the pleasure taken in the production of phenomena that are analogous to those of reality, because they bear a greater or lesser degree of resemblance to them. It follows that art is a way of thinking things out differently, and of apprehending the intrinsic inaccessibility of phenomenal reality; that art is an instrument, a method of getting at that which is closed and inaccessible to us (the banal future, just as much as the intrinsically unknowable); that art has a formative and therapeutic, consolatory and informative, investigative and speculative function; it is thus not only existential pleasure but Utopia.

21 April 1986. This plausible theory, that my abstract paintings evolve their motifs as the work proceeds, is a timely one, because there is no central image of the world (world view) any longer: we must work out everything for ourselves, exposed as we are on a kind of refuse heap, with no centre and no meaning; we must cope with the advance of a previously undreamt-of freedom. It also conforms to a general principle of nature; for nature, too, does not develop an organism in accordance with an idea: nature lets its forms and modifications come, within the framework of its given facts and with the help of chance. And this theory is no less useless than ludicrous, if I paint bad pictures.

25 April 1986. 'If art stands aloof from progress and ... eschews ideas as well as ... theories, then it can recapture the degree of spontaneity, and naïvety, and presence of mind, which it needs as a fish does water, in order to become a reality that exists of its own accord' (wrote Heinz Friedrich). At first sight, I admittedly satisfy the demands of this dictum, which is loathsome to me (I never was 'modern', or 'radical', never subject to any definition of art). But the dictum is wrong, whichever way you look at it. Either there has never been any progress in the history of humankind (or beyond), which would be an absurd assertion, or there is no progress now either, in spite of the apparent and real retrogressive nature of today's art, which acts either post-modern or trivial or snot-stupid. What offends me most of all is the slack apathy of such people, who ultimately regret only the loss of a centre, and who are too comfortable to give up the

apparent pleasures of a corrupt and cretinous ersatz art. Art today – or so goes the party blather that has replaced the collective celebration of existence – is the new spontaneity and naïvety that we have. (I must break the habit, I must never read that sort of thing again, I must never look at a modern exhibition, above all I must throw away all those invitations unread.)

12 October 1986. What shall I paint? How shall I paint?

'What' is the hardest thing, because it is the essence. 'How' is easy by comparison. To start off with, the 'How' is frivolous, but legitimate. Apply the 'How', and thus use the requirements of technique, the material and physical possibilities, in order to realize the intention. The intention: to invent nothing – no idea, no composition, no object, no form – and to receive everything: composition, object, form, idea, picture. Even in my youth, when I somewhat naïvely had 'themes' (landscapes, self-portraits), I very soon became aware of this problem of having no subject. Of course, I took motifs and represented them, but this was mostly with the feeling that these were not the real ones, but imposed, dog-eared, artificial ones. The question 'What shall I paint?' showed me my own helplessness, and I often envied (still do envy) the most mediocre painters those 'concerns' of theirs, which they so tenaciously and mediocrely depict (I fundamentally despise them for it).

In 1962 I found my first escape hatch: by painting from photographs, I was relieved of the need to choose or construct a subject. I had to choose the photographs, of course; but I could do that in a way that avoided any commitment to the subject, by using motifs which had very little image to them and which were anachronistic. My appropriation of photographs, my policy of copying them without alteration and without translating them into a modern form (as Warhol and others do), represented a principled avoidance of the subject. This principle has been maintained, with few exceptions (doors, windows, shadows, all of which I dislike), to this day. Grey pictures, colour charts, inpaintings, small abstracts (so full of planned arbitrariness as to be equally message-free), 'soft' abstracts which borrowed the non-subject from the small abstracts and used blurring and enlargement to create a variant of Non-Showing. The same goes for the big abstracts; and in contradiction of this there is always the intention, the hope, of getting a subject handed to me on a plate, as it were: one not invented by me, and for that reason more universal, better, less perishable, more generally valid. Of course that is not true, since I am continually composing and above all deleting (i.e., avoiding), and I restrict myself to a very small repertoire, which is to say that I act very deliberately. Then there is the relationship with music, in my constant efforts to create a structure in musical terms and a varied instrumentation. All these failures! It is a wonder to me that the pictures ever do show the occasional flash of distinction, because basically they are all lamentable displays of incapacity and failure (failure in the attempt to overcome this incapacity). But it is also untrue that I have nothing specific in mind. As with my landscapes: I see countless landscapes, photograph barely 1 in 100,000, and paint barely 1 in 100 of those that I photograph. I am therefore seeking something quite specific; from this I conclude that I know what I want.

25 October 1986. These continuing difficulties. A constant work crisis that has lasted for decades, in fact ever since the start. Crisis personified. (Perhaps I am mistaken here; perhaps this is a perfectly normal way to work.)

Interview with Benjamin H. D. Buchloh, 1986

Did you know the history of the twentieth-century avant-garde before you came to West Germany in 1961? What did you know about Dadaism and Constructivism – and in particular Duchamp, Picabia, Man Ray, Malevich? Was all this a great discovery, as soon as you arrived – or was it a gradual and uncontrollable process of absorption and learning?

The latter, really; an uncontrolled and gradual learning process. I knew nothing: neither Picabia nor Man Ray nor Duchamp. I only knew artists like Picasso and Guttuso, Diego Rivera and of course the classics down to the Impressionists, because everything after that was denounced in the GDR as bourgeois decadence. And in that state of naïvety I went to the *documenta* in Kassel in 1958 and was enormously impressed by Pollock and Fontana.

Can you remember what particularly interested you about Pollock and Fontana?

The sheer brazenness of it! That really fascinated me and impressed me. I might almost say that those paintings were the real reason why I left the GDR. I realized that there was something wrong with my whole way of thinking.

Can you enlarge on the word 'brazenness'? It has connotations of morality; surely that's not what you mean.

But that is what I mean. I lived my life with a group of people who laid claim to a moral aspiration, who wanted to bridge a gap, who were looking for a middle way between capitalism and socialism, a so-called Third Path. And so the way we thought, and what we wanted for our own art, was all about compromise. In this there was nothing radical – to use a more appropriate synonym for 'brazen' – and it wasn't genuine, either, but full of false deference.

Deference to whom or to what?

To traditional artistic values, for instance. I realized, above all, that all those 'slashes' and 'blots' were not a formalistic gag but grim truth and liberation; that this was an expression of a totally different and entirely new content.

Did you always see the causes as inner and existential, rather than as formally inevitable, or as the next steps in a long evolutionary process rooted in the earliest decades of the twentieth century, or as responses to painterly problems? Was that way of thinking totally alien to you?

Yes, and it still is.

That's why I asked about your knowledge of the first generation of avant-garde artists, from 1915 to 1925 or thereabouts. You said practically non-existent; and the same goes for many artists of your generation. It had to do with universal repression of the past, the Second World War, and many other issues besides. The same went for the American artists, who had no direct experience of Fascism or the Second World War on their own home ground. They misunderstood and repressed Dada and Constructivism just as much as the Europeans did. And, if you say that Fontana and Pollock were the first who touched you so powerfully that they almost prompted you to leave the GDR, who was the next influence in this learning process? Was it Rauschenberg or Johns, or was it Yves Klein and Manzoni?

It was a slow process, of course, and for the time being I was mainly interested in transitional figures, who seemed less radical to me: Giacometti, Dubuffet and Fautrier, for instance.

Fautrier – can you reconstruct what interested you about him?

The impasto, the painterly messiness, the amorphous and material quality.

So it could be said that what interested you was the anti-artistic impulse in painting. The same applies to Fontana and Pollock, doesn't it?

Yes, everything that tried to break with the past.

And Tàpies?

I have always found him too decorative.

Too little existential weight?

None at all, to speak of; and it shows now more than ever.

There's a bit of a contradiction here. Earlier, you said that Pollock and Fontana were really important, because they conveyed a sense of crisis, because they carried an existential weight.

I tried to bring that down to the formal level, and you couldn't accept that. Which clearly means that you must have had a specific synthesis in mind from the outset, as to what meaning the practice of painting can have, and as to how it can have meaning. A synthesis well outside the conventions, as they were then defined. So you attached more importance to everything that was strongly radical in formal terms, everything that was not literary or narrative or symbolic.

Yes, because it had more to say to me.

How about the artists of the New York School, in the early 1960s? Did you see works by Barnett Newman and Willem de Kooning at the same time as Jackson Pollock?

Hardly at all. Palermo introduced me to some of the work, a bit later. Maybe at the very end of the 1960s. Then I saw, among other things, paintings by Morris Louis, which were very highly thought of.

By you?

No, I found it quite impressive that someone should just be letting paint trickle down in this way, but I didn't think highly of it.

And Kenneth Noland?

I got no more out of him. What amazed me was more the fame of these people.

Did you ever wonder how it came about that American painters interested you more than any Europeans, let alone Germans?

No, I took it for granted that Germany could be written off. With a past like that.

And what about the past before the Nazi period? Why was that not worth discussing?

I knew nothing about it.

Did you make any attempt to find out about the history of the German avant-garde?

No, or only very superficially.

Do you now see that as an issue? Does it now surprise you that Schwitters was never or hardly ever mentioned at that time? There were German artists, after all, great German artists who belonged to the avant-garde.

I came to them by way of Rauschenberg, Schwitters included.

Everything that got absorbed during the 1950s and 1960s; the way the West German artistic landscape was reconstructed after it had been reduced to provincial status by war and Fascism – all this was a highly artificial reconstruction, as we've just seen. The most important German avant-garde artists fell outside its scope altogether: Schwitters, Hannah Höch and John Heartfield were forgotten, as was the whole of German Dadaism. Reconstruction went by way of Paris painting and American painting. That is what the whole of the German Informel is based on, dismal as it is – and that's how the foundations of Modernism in Germany were relaid. That was the situation you found when you arrived.

Which is my basis.

First you see the American Rauschenberg, then you discover the German Schwitters through the American. That's an interesting paradox.

Yes, but I don't think it's that bad. And I don't regard Schwitters as the innovator and Rauschenberg as the exploiter.

That's not the point: the point is whether it means anything. Did you also see any Twombly in the early 1960s, and did that interest you?

Yes, certainly.

As much as Rauschenberg?

Almost.

And the equivalent to Rauschenberg in the European context, Nouveau Réalisme and Décollage – to leave Yves Klein right out of it for the moment – had no comparable importance for you? You didn't know the Décollage people?

Yes, I knew them all right. I thought they were interesting, but a bit old-fashioned.

Old-fashioned in what way? Old-fashioned like Schwitters?

Maybe. The technique seemed so old-fashioned to me.

How come? It seems more radical than painting, if someone sets off down the street and tears great strips off the posters on the walls and declares that to be his work.

Maybe it was jealousy, because I'd never thought of anything like that myself, and 'invention' was very much in the air then.

And how did you relate to Manzoni at that time?

Badly. I didn't like him. And least of all his 'Artist's Shit'. As far as I'm concerned, that's just about as funny as selling cans with 'Berlin Air' in them.

Or was it too radical for you, all of a sudden? Earlier on, you valued the brazenness of Pollock and Fontana. It even seemed to be a factor in your move to the West. Did Manzoni go too far?

He didn't go far enough. He got no further than the joke stage. It was only a commentary. And he wasn't painting.

Duchamp and Fluxus, Warhol and Pop Art

And what was your knowledge of Duchamp at that time?

It evolved very slowly – through Beuys, in fact. I saw the Duchamp exhibition in Krefeld in 1963,[1] which reminded me of Beuys, and that was when I really began to get interested in Duchamp.

Jürgen Harten writes that your 4 Panes of Glass of 1967 bear no relation to Duchamp, and that you therefore had no knowledge of him at that time. I find this hard to believe.

It's really hard to say. I do know that I didn't know the *Large Glass* at that time; but it may be that I had repressed the knowledge of it so thoroughly that I could make my 4 *Panes of Glass* with a clear conscience. And with hindsight I can say that my *Panes of Glass*, like the *Nude on the Stairs* [*Ema*, 1966], involve something of an anti-Duchamp attitude, because they are so plain and deliberately uncomplicated.

When did you first see any Pop Art? Did you go to the Amsterdam Pop exhibition, or did you see Pop at Ileana Sonnabend's[2] *in Paris?*

The first Pop Art I saw was shown me in reproduction by Konrad Fischer. It was a cooker, painted by Lichtenstein. And then something by Warhol, not quite so extremely anti-art as Lichtenstein, or so I thought then.

That was in 1963–64?

In '63 or '62. And then we went over to Ileana Sonnabend's, to present ourselves with our portfolio as the 'German Pop Artists'. That was when we first saw originals by Lichtenstein.

So then Lichtenstein was suddenly more important to you than Rauschenberg?

Yes, and that went on until later, when he became rather vacuous and decorative. The important artists to me then were Lichtenstein, Warhol and Oldenburg.

Can you go into more detail as to why they were important to you? Did it have something to do with the isolation of the object, as against the complicated context in Rauschenberg?

Rauschenberg was too artificial and too interesting. He hasn't got that astonishing simplification.

Instead of a complicated composition, such as you still have in Rauschenberg, which is still practically tied to the collage principle, an object in Lichtenstein or Warhol is presented as an isolated object, like a readymade.

Yes.

How about technique? Were you attracted by that perfectionist technique of Lichtenstein's?

Yes, very much so, because it was anti-painterly. It was directed against '*peinture*'.

So did you see your relationship with Duchamp in terms of a rediscovery through Lichtenstein and Warhol?

You mean the readymade quality? Certainly. But Duchamp also painted a very beautiful *Nude Descending a Staircase*.

Which you saw in Krefeld?

No, much later on, in Paris. But I knew it from reproductions. A very beautiful painting, and utterly traditional.

In terms of technique, but not in terms of the object.

In terms of the object, too. It is a nude, for all the Cubist/Futurist handling.

It's a bit of a mystery to me why you say 'Lichtenstein and Warhol, yes, but not Johns'. The distinction must lie in the manner of painting. Which means you're adopting a critical view of Warhol's and Lichtenstein's technique, too. What was it that you didn't like about Johns? Was it the complicated technique, the artistry?

Yes, because Johns was holding on to a culture of painting that had to do with Cézanne, and I rejected that. That's why I painted from photographs, just in order to have nothing to do with the art of '*peinture*', which makes any kind of contemporary statement impossible...

But when Warhol started to have his pictures done more or less anonymously, in silkscreen, that must have seemed like a slap in the face to you. This was a threat to your survival, for someone to demonstrate all of a sudden that painting is being supplanted by technology. It undermined the point of all painterly techniques, however radically simplified.

Maybe I was just admiring something that I can't do – something I'm in no position to do. The same thing happened with the Minimalists, who were also doing something I was in no position to do.

Have you ever tried leaving a photograph as a photograph, in other words adding the pictorial quality just by enlarging it, blurring it and manipulating it in that sort of way?

Rarely, and it only ever worked if it was a photograph of a painting.

The theoretical implications that were read into Warhol, his radical opening up of the definition of art, his anti-aesthetic position, of a kind that hadn't existed since Duchamp, were also present as a characteristic of Fluxus. It must have attracted you very much at that time?

Yes, it attracted me very much; it was really vital to me. Fluxus above all.

There are contradictions here that are hard to understand. On the one hand you were attracted by Fluxus and Warhol, but on the other hand you're saying 'I couldn't do that; all I wanted to do and all I could do was paint'. You align your own painting with this anti-aesthetic impulse, and at the same time you maintain a pro-painting position. To me this seems to be one of the entirely typical contradictions out of which your work has essentially evolved.

Yes, it is curious, but I don't actually find it contradictory. It's rather as if I were doing the same thing by other means, means that are less spectacular and less advanced.

So the negation of the productive act in art, as introduced by Duchamp and revived by Warhol, was never acceptable to you?

No, because the artist's productive act cannot be negated. It's just that it has nothing to do with the talent of 'making by hand', only with the capacity to see and to decide *what* is to be made visible. *How* that then gets fabricated has nothing to do with art or with artistic abilities.

From Malevich to Minimal Art

When did you first encounter the great early abstract painters? Mondrian and Malevich, for example?

In the West, at some point, late on. I don't know.

But they were just as inaccessible to you as Schwitters? It was all a thing of the past, very much more so than the New York School and Rauschenberg were?

Yes, except for Mondrian, whose work I loved at first sight, far more than Malevich and that group.

So, in 1966, when you started to paint non-figurative pictures, colour charts, did that also have something to do with a head-on confrontation with Minimal art? Was that another conflict situation, a rejection of American dominance, or was it through an evolutionary process of your own, rooted in the immediate, local context here in Düsseldorf? Was it through meeting Palermo, perhaps?

Yes, it certainly did have something to do with Palermo and his interests, and later with Minimal art as well; but when I painted my first colour charts in 1966, that had more to do with Pop Art. They were copies of paint sample cards, and what was effective about them was that they were directed against the efforts of the Neo-Constructivists, Albers and the rest.

Did you know Barnett Newman's work at that time?

No. But I came to love it later.

So your abstraction was something of an assault on the history of abstraction in Europe?

An assault on the falsity and the religiosity of the way people glorified abstraction, with such phoney reverence. Devotional art – all those squares – Church handicrafts.

And Minimal abstraction – did that interest you?

Yes, that's what turned two or three of the colour charts grey.

What about Stella? When did you see his work?

Early on, but it didn't interest me.

Did you see the Black Paintings?

I must have seen them in the 1960s.

Did you feel they were better than Vasarely and Albers?

Oh, yes.

Can you reconstruct that feeling? Why did he leave you relatively cold?

It was all too arty-crafty and too decorative, too elegant and precious.

And his symmetrical compositions didn't impress you at all?

Carpets are symmetrical, too.

And Robert Ryman – you didn't see his work until much later?

I saw a first show at Konrad Fischer's[3] in 1970 or so. I thought it was very good.

And why was that better, or different?

Because for the first time it showed *nothing*. It was closer to my situation.

Which artists were most important to you in the late 1960s?

Carl Andre, Sol LeWitt, Bob Ryman, Dan Flavin, Larry Weiner, Walter De Maria, and others.

Judd?

Not so much.

And would you say that Carl Andre had an influence on your paintings?

I thought a lot of him. But at that time I was also painting Romantic landscapes.

So the serial quality of your monochrome grey pictures has nothing to do with Minimal art? The colour charts are suddenly overtly serial paintings, either serially structured as individual works or serially arranged as a group.

The serial thing had been around since Pop Art. And as for the colour charts, especially the late ones, in those I'd tend rather to see the influence of Conceptual art: the theoretical, didactic dimension. But it all came down to the desperation of not knowing how I could ever arrange colours meaningfully – and I tried to fabricate that, as beautifully and as unequivocally as possible.

Iconography and Photography

Your photo-painting of the early 1960s does have an anti-artistic quality; it negates individual handling, creativity, originality. So up to a point you do follow Duchamp and Warhol. And your painting also negates content, by demonstrating that the motifs are picked at random.

But the motifs never were picked at random: not when you think of the endless trouble I took to find photographs that I could use.

So in every case the selection process was highly complex and explicitly motivated? So when I said in the Paris catalogue[4] that the choice of photographs was basically random, that was a highly questionable statement?

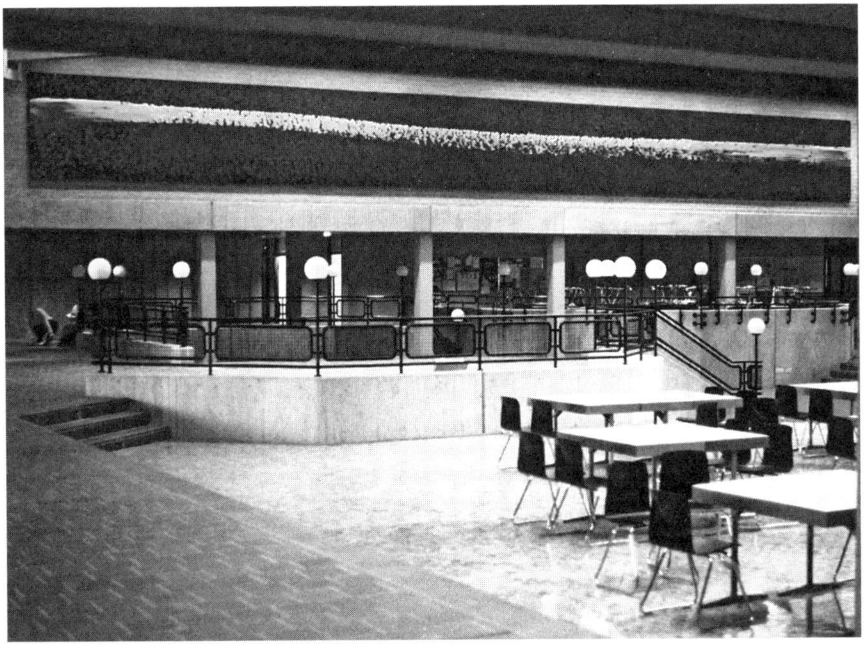

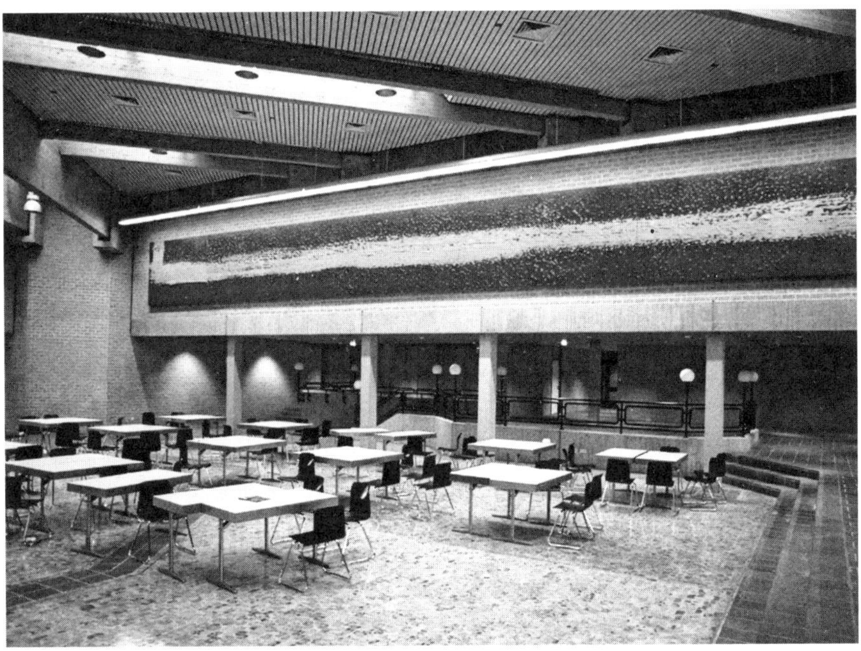

Stroke (on Red), 1979
Stroke (on Blue), Bördeschule Soest, 1980

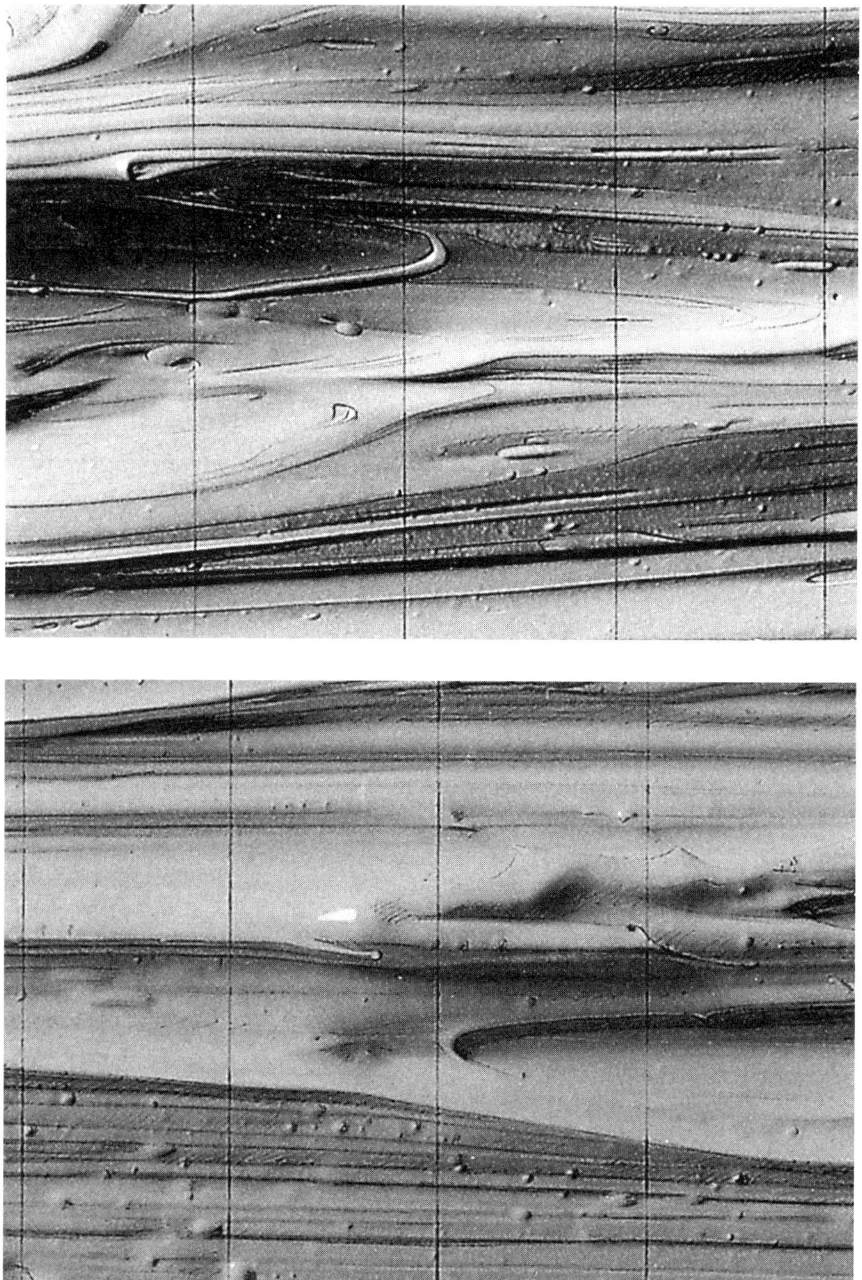

Photographs for *Blue* and *Yellow*, 1973

Maybe it was a good thing for it to look random.

So what were the criteria by which you chose photographs for your iconography?

Content, definitely – though I may have denied this at one time, by saying that it had nothing to do with content, because it was supposed to be all about copying a photograph and giving a demonstration of indifference.

And now the critics are trying to ascribe to you this iconographical concern with content. Ulrich Loock and Harten[5] talk about a Death Series: the aeroplane stands for death, the pyramid and the accident stand for death. To me it all seems rather forced, this attempt to construct a continuity for the death motif in your painting.

So you think I was looking for motifs that would be just a little bit shocking, while all the time I was totally indifferent to them?

I would agree, in that no selection can ever really be random. Every choice implies an attitude of sorts, however complex and unconscious. But, looking at your iconography in the 1960s, I find it very difficult to read into it a consistent theme of death. The Eight Student Nurses, *all right; but then there are the* 48 Portraits. *It's irrational to read a death theme into those. What have the Chile paintings got to do with the Pyramids? Or what have the Townscapes to do with the Mountain Landscapes? The iconographical elements can all be connected, but not in the sense of a traditional iconography, where you say: 'That's a death theme.' To me it seems utterly absurd to try to construct a traditional iconography for your painting.*

Maybe it is just overdoing it a little to talk about a death theme. But as to whether the pictures have anything to do with death and pain, I think they have.

But this feature of content is not the determining, the decisive element in the selection.

That I don't know, and I can't really reconstruct my motives now. All I know is that there were reasons of content why I chose a particular photograph, and why I decided to depict this or that event.

In full awareness of the fact that content can no longer be conveyed through iconic depiction? So this is another contradiction: although you knew that – for example – a death theme cannot be conveyed through straight depiction, you nevertheless tried to do just that, knowing full well that it was impossible.

For one thing, it isn't impossible at all. A picture with a dead dog in it shows a dead dog. It only gets difficult if you try to convey something above and beyond that, if the content gets too complex for straightforward depiction. But that doesn't mean that depiction can't convey anything.

Were you aware of the criteria on which you made your selection? How did you go about choosing the photographs?

I looked for photographs that showed my present life, the things that related to me. And I chose black-and-white photographs, because I realized that they showed all this more effectively than colour photographs, more directly, more inartistically and therefore more credibly. That's why I picked all those amateur family pictures, those banal objects and snapshots.

What about the Alpine Pictures and the Townscapes?

Those were done when I no longer felt like doing the figurative photo-pictures, and wanted a change from the unequivocal statement, the legible and limited narrative. So I was attracted by those dead cities and Alps, which in both cases were stony wastes, arid stuff. It was an attempt to convey content of a more universal kind.

But if you really were concerned with that kind of content, how do you explain the fact that at the same time you brought non-figurative painting into your work? The colour charts, for instance, or other abstract paintings, done concurrently with the figurative ones. You were working on two levels at once, and this confused most of your critical commentators, who started to see you as a painter who knows all the tricks and techniques, and who simultaneously discredits and deploys all the iconographical conventions. At the moment, this makes you particularly attractive to many viewers, because your work looks like a survey of the whole universe of twentieth-century painting, presented in one vast, cynical retrospective.

Now that definitely is a misunderstanding. I see no cynicism or trickery or guile in any of this. On the contrary, it all seems rather amateurish to me, the head-on way I've tackled everything, and how simple it is to read off what I had in mind and what I was trying to do. That's why I don't really know what you mean by the contradiction between figurative and abstract painting.

Let me take Table *as an example, one of your earliest paintings.* Table *already has both elements within it: a totally abstract, gestural, self-reflective quality on one hand and on the other the function of depiction. And this is surely one of the great twentieth-century dilemmas: this apparent conflict, this apparent antagonism within painting, between the functions of depiction and self-reflection. In your painting, the two run very close together. But aren't they juxtaposed in order to show up the inadequacy, the bankruptcy of both?*

Not bankruptcy, but always inadequacy.

Inadequacy in relation to what? The expressive function?

In relation to what is expected of painting.

Can that expectation be formulated?

That painting ought to have more effect.

So you would reject the accusation that is so often levelled at you, of cynical complicity with painting's lack of effect?

Yes, I would, because I do know that painting is not without an effect – I only want it to have more of one.

So the simultaneous pursuit of depiction and self-reflection has nothing to do with the two cancelling each other out; and you are just using different means to give substance to what is expected of painting?

Yes, more or less.

So, in the early 1960s you don't see yourself as the heir to a historical dichotomy, a state of fragmentation, in which no strategy is really valid any more.

And I do see myself as the heir to a vast, great, rich culture of painting – of art in general – which we have lost, but which places obligations on us. And it is no easy matter to avoid either harking back to the past or (equally bad) giving up altogether and sliding into decadence.

Which brings you, of course, to the brink of a political argument, which maybe you don't relish. But how would you explain this loss, if not in terms of politics, or social history, or just plain history? The way you put it, it almost sounds like Adorno's famous statement that 'After Auschwitz, lyric poetry is no longer possible.' Does that ring true for you?

No. There is lyric poetry after Auschwitz.

When you say that no one can paint that way any more...

By that I meant first and foremost a specific quality that we have lost.

How?

Photography is certainly one external factor involved in the fact that we've forgotten one way of painting and can no longer produce a certain artistic quality.

It can also be put in entirely functional terms, by saying that – among other things – paintings have lost their descriptive and illustrative function, because photography has assumed those functions so perfectly. The result is that the job is no longer there to be done, and the high artistic quality of old paintings, which you mention, has its material and historical roots partly in those very same descriptive and illustrative functions.

The quality can't be entirely explained away in terms of the illustrative function. All that perfection of execution, composition and so forth would still have been lost to us, even if there had never been such a thing as photography. Literature and music are in the very same mess. People praise Mozart and Glenn Gould to the skies, because the new composers can't offer the same thing any more, even though music hasn't been edged out by anything analogous to photography.

So if the loss doesn't stem from the evolution of reproductive technology, or from the experience of previously undreamt-of historical catastrophes (as Adorno suggests in the sentence I quoted), or from the destruction of bourgeois culture, or from political factors of any kind – and you've rejected all those, at least in passing, as explanations...

No, they all play their part, but I see the basic fact as the loss of the Centre.[6]

In Sedlmayr's sense? You can't be serious?

Yes, I am; what he was saying was absolutely right. He just drew the wrong conclusions, that's all. He wanted to reconstruct the Centre that had been lost.

And to reconstruct that Centre by using methods and means that were entirely incapable of achieving it. But how do you describe it, if it's so obvious to you?

I've no desire to reconstruct it.

No, but you must be able to describe it. And then it's a historical process after all...

Yes, but there are specific, new, concrete facts which have altered our consciousness and our society, which have overturned religion and therefore changed the functioning of the State. There are only a few makeshift conventions left to regulate the thing, keep it practicable. Otherwise there's nothing there any more.

Is painting one of those conventions?

No. The criteria of painting are conventions – and harmful ones, because they are ideologically defined. They block enlightenment. That's why I think so highly of psychoanalysis, because it takes away prejudices and turns us into responsible adults, autonomous beings who can act more rightly and more humanely in the absence of authorities, or God, or ideology. So it's a good thing to lose all that.

And you'd want the same for painting?

Yes.

So on one hand you see the process as irreversible, and above all impossible to reconstruct by cultural means...

That would only serve to delay it.

And political means seem to you at best problematic or questionable, or not directly available.

Politics operates more by faith than by enlightenment, so nothing is going to come of that.

But you see the role of art as a more important one than that of simply liquidating a false bourgeois cultural inheritance – though that is one of its functions, isn't it?

Liquidating? Yes, that's part of it.

But at the same time it also has another function, and that's where the contradiction comes in. What is the other function, if not a political one?

Above all, art does more than destroy. It produces something, a different image.

Of autonomy?

Yes.

And how is the painted picture supposed to constitute a model of that autonomy, here and now?

The painting is *one* important, possible way among others, one that can be used. At worst, it's on offer to those who are interested.

About your self-imposed limitation to the practice of painting – when it comes to liquidating the bourgeois inheritance while constructing the new autonomy, isn't that limitation rather a handicap? Shouldn't we suppose that there are other and more radical ways and means that will carry out the liquidation more quickly and thus also make anticipation more fruitful?

No, in this respect I'm extremely conservative. It seems to me like someone saying that language is no longer usable, because it is a bourgeois inheritance, or that we mustn't print texts in books any more but on cups or on chair legs. I am bourgeois enough to go on eating with a knife and fork, just as I paint in oil on canvas.

So, all attempts to prosecute one side of the dialectic more rapidly by artistic means seem to you to be unacceptable. Would you retrospectively criticize Duchamp, who gave up painting for this very reason?

I'm not sure that those were his reasons. But you can never take that as a sufficient reason to give up painting. To interpret Duchamp in that way, and go in for politics and criticism instead, is pathetic.

Pathetic in what way? In terms of painting's liquidation of bourgeois culture, or in terms of its capacity for anticipation?

Because it achieves nothing. It's neither artistic nor political action. It's amateur.

To put it in specific terms: would you regard it as a premise of your present-day painting that it remains in the very dilemma you faced from the start: that is, to play off the real facts of mass culture, as you see them in photography, against the esoteric and elitist conditions of high culture, in which you as an artist have a part? And that you base your work on this dialectic, assuming yourself to be exempt from the contradiction; and that in practice there is no solution that you can accept? Is this still a premise, or did it apply only to the 1960s?

I see no such premise, then or now.

But your quoted statement on Cézanne says just that. When you say: 'I consider many photographs better than the best Cézanne', that seems to express this very contradiction.

Yes, but that doesn't mean that I could ever change anything directly through painting. And it certainly doesn't mean that I could do it without painting.

Why have you so firmly rejected any concrete political intention in your own art?

Because politics don't suit me, because art has an entirely different function, because all I can do is paint. Call it conservative.

But by limiting yourself to the medium of painting mightn't you be espousing not just a conservative position but maybe also a critical dimension? Are you, for instance, calling into question the immediacy claimed by work like that of Beuys?

Naturally, by limiting myself to painting I imply a criticism of a lot of things that I don't like, not all of them connected with painting.

So you don't deny on principle that someone might validly intend to make a critical political statement through art?

I probably do deny it. But what counts is that I have to take as my starting point, my foundation, my own possibilities and my own premises.

Which you say are unchangeable...

Largely unchangeable.

Monochrome Grey Pictures and Abstract Pictures

The grey pictures were done at a time when there were monochrome paintings everywhere. I painted them nonetheless.

When you say there were pictures like that everywhere, who are you thinking of? Klein and Kelly?

Not Kelly, but Bob Ryman, Brice Marden, Alan Charlton, Yves Klein and many others.

Paraphrase as a strategy. Was that deliberate?

Not really. I thought I had every right to do it because I was doing it for a different reason, because the paintings have something different to say and also look different. It never occurred to me for a moment that this might be eclecticism.

Although at the present moment in history you have no choice but to be an eclectic.

I don't know. I don't believe that.

Why are your monochrome paintings any different? Because you painted them?

Yes, because I intended something different, because the similarity is merely superficial.

Because you regarded it as a linguistic tradition and not as an intention of your own?

But it is an intention of my own: the intention to use it to convey a different content.

The intention still stands – and so the abstract pictures, too, are intended to convey a content?

Yes.

They're not a negation of content, not painting-as-fact, not an ironic parody of present-day expressionism?

No.

Not a perversion of gestural abstraction? Not irony?

Certainly not! What kind of questions are these? How can my pictures be devoid of content, and what is this content that the Abstract Expressionists are supposed to have had as distinct from me?

They painted with a different intention in mind. Rothko, for example: he uses thinning and grading of colour to create an illusion of space, which is not simultaneously negated – as it is with you – but really represents depth, mist, shimmering, transcendence. And then, in Rothko's work, colour combination is an important element: that is, two or at most three shades or colour values are juxtaposed in a very precisely calculated, differentiated way, so that the combination generates a particular colour harmony, which is then supposed to produce a specific emotional effect.

In my work the principle's the same; it's just that different means are used to achieve a different effect.

No, because if the ability of colour to generate this emotional, spiritual quality is presented and at the same time negated at all points, surely it's always cancelling itself out. With so many combinations, so many permutational relationships, there can't be any harmonious chromatic order, or composition either, because there are no ordered relations left either in the colour system or in the spatial system.

I can't see it as a situation where composition and relationships have disappeared. When I place one colour-form next to another, then it automatically relates to that other.

Yes, but there are differently structured forms and laws governing relationships, right through to the realization that even total negation is a composition. But everything in your abstract pictures aims at abolishing traditional, relational forms of order by showing the potentially infinite variety of structurally heterogeneous elements.

Yes, but even so I still have to get all that into the right context; a context that always gets harder and harder, the more advanced a picture gets. It all starts out easy and unspecific, but gradually a context starts to take shape, and this has a coherence that is the utter opposite of randomness.

Yes, of course, but then that's a different kind of perception, and so a different form is generated – in some cases an antithetical one.

It may well be. What always is antithetical is my method, or the anticipation that, as it were, impels me to paint.

And what do you anticipate?

That something is going to come, which I do not know, which I have been unable to plan, which is better and wiser than I am, and which is also more universal. More directly, I tried to do that in the one thousand or four thousand colours, in the anticipation that a picture would emerge.

What sort of picture?

One that presents our situation more accurately; one that has more truth in it, one that has something of the future in it, so can also be interpreted as a project, a design – and more besides. Not didactic, not logical, but rather free and – however complicated – also effortless in appearance.

That's what your paintings have at their best: they seem not to try too hard, but to be produced with verve, indifference and virtuosity. But – to revert to the issue of content for a moment – how can you say that the palette-knifed surface on this painting here doesn't stand for process or materiality as such, when the painting itself has been made with such obvious emphasis on the process of its making? If you weren't interested in these qualities, you surely wouldn't use the palette knife in this way, depriving the colour, composition and structure of the painting of any possibility of generating a meaning beyond the bare materiality of the picture. It seems to me that you introduce process-related painting as just one of painting's many possibilities, while not insisting, as Ryman did, that this is its only aspect. It's one aspect among others.

Then why should I go to such lengths to make it so varied?

Because you're setting out to call off all the aspects there are, like a catalogue; because you're really trying to pursue both a rhetoric of painting and the simultaneous analysis of that rhetoric.

If all this were just a display of matter – the way the yellow, tatter-edged area rises up against the blue-green background – how could it tell a story or set up moods?

A mood? You mean it really sets up an emotional experience?

Yes, and aesthetic pleasure, too.

That's something different. Aesthetic pleasure I can see, but absolutely not a mood.

So what is a mood?

A mood has an explicitly emotional, spiritual, psychological quality.

That's exactly what is there.

Fortunately only in the weakest parts.

Surely you don't think that a stupid demonstration of brushwork, or of the rhetoric of painting and its elements, could ever achieve anything, say anything, express any longing.

Longing for what?

For lost qualities, for a better world – for the opposite of misery and hopelessness.

The longing to be able to present culture as a contemplative spectacle without losing credibility?

I might also call it redemption. Or hope – the hope that I can after all effect something through painting.

Again, this is all so generalized: effect in what sense? Epistemological, emotional, psychological, political?

All at once. I don't know.

So if you maintain that art can have this function – something that other artists would deny absolutely – then it's all the more of a paradox that you simultaneously insist on being able to do it only with the means of painting. Or, to put the question another way: do you believe that this dichotomy is concretely visible in your paintings?

Yes, possibly.

Do you believe that these are ultimately conservative paintings, conservative in the sense that Broodthaers's art seemed conservative?

In terms of the means – oil on canvas – even more conservative. I knew Broodthaers, and I had a lot of time for him, but I never really understood his pictures. Conservative – I certainly don't intend to be, and I also know that painting per se does not have to be conservative. So I can carry on in the same way, just better if possible.

The question is, how far can this schizophrenia be stretched, how far can it really be kept alive, or when does it become an empty pose – to assert this contradiction over and over again, and to act within the contradiction again and again, but without trying to get over the contradiction?

I don't know what contradiction you're talking about.

It's the contradiction of knowing full well that the means you are using won't achieve what you aim for, and at the same time not being prepared to change those means.

That's not a contradiction, it's a perfectly normal state of affairs. The normal mess, if you like. And that couldn't be changed by choosing different means and methods.

Because all means are of equal value?

No, but all similarly inadequate. The question is, what are my means, and what can I achieve with them?

But under certain historical conditions painting had different functions, and had a possibility of having an effect on its contemporary context.

If I'm thinking of political painting in our time, I'd rather have Barnett Newman. He painted some magnificent pictures.

So it is said. But magnificent in what way?

I can't describe it now, what gets to me in them – I believe they're among the most important paintings of all.

Perhaps that's a mythology that needs re-examination. Precisely because it's so difficult to describe; and because, in the encounter with paintings, acts of faith are not enough.

Acts of faith are unavoidable. They're part of us.

Do your paintings invite acts of faith, or analyses? Which matters more to you?

Either would be fine with me. In your case they invite you to analyze; others find them an invitation to perform acts of faith.

So you would be quite happy if – as Rothko demanded for his own work – someone were to fall on their knees in front of one of your paintings and burst into tears?

Unfortunately painting can't produce such an effect. Music is better off in this respect.

Chance and Open Form

What part does chance play in your painting?

An essential one, as it always has. There have been times when this has worried me a great deal, and I've seen this reliance on chance as a shortcoming on my part.

Is this chance different from chance in Pollock? Or from Surrealist automatism?

Yes, it certainly is different. Above all, it's never blind chance: it's a chance that is always planned, but also always surprising. And I need it in order to carry on, in order to eradicate my mistakes, to destroy what I've worked out wrong, to introduce something different and disruptive. I'm often astonished to find how much better chance is than I am.

So this is the level on which openness is still thinkable and credible in real terms? Chance?

It introduces objectivity, so perhaps it's no longer chance at all. But in the way it destroys and is simultaneously constructive, it creates something that of course I would have been glad to do and work out for myself.

But you don't take that personally any more? You don't regard it as a failure on your part? You see it as a generalized factor?

No, I now see it as a generalized factor, something entirely positive. Jacques Monod's Chance and Necessity,[7] and all sorts of other facts and reflections that have evolved on the subject, all confirm me in that.

Would the same principle apply to the structure of the work itself, its apparent repeatability, the apparent arbitrariness and openness of every individual painting? Is there a structural analogy to the structure of chance, in the fact that the work itself – like the separate work clusters – has no closed quality left but appears totally open?

Possibly; and, if we disregard the closed quality that every picture has to have – if it is not to be a random detail of something else, or just plain unfinished – then non-closure may perhaps be a positive quality, because it relates more closely to our reality.

Then it might be said that the compositional structure, in its openness, is the other dimension of a still-credible, substantive, Utopian factor?

That may be so. Especially because so many paintings nowadays look so stupid precisely because they lay claim to being closed works. That's the deception.

Yes, and I find this open dimension in very few artists. It's the radicalism that leads the artist to run the risk of ending up with a work that looks unfinished, infinitely reproducible and internally repetitive.

The only paradoxical thing is that I always set out with the intention of getting a closed picture, with a proper, composed motif – and then go to great lengths to destroy that intention, bit by bit, almost against my will. Until the picture is finished and has nothing left but openness.

The fiction of an openness, a total openness, just as the use of chance is not real but a fiction of chance.

I can only hope that I haven't lost my naïvety, and that I shall go on making all the same effort – which is actually quite superfluous.

What about colour – I mean, can the involvement of chance be extended to colour relationships, the colour scheme? Up to now, we have only talked about the compositional order, but I'd say that the same principle defines the relations between colours.

Not to the same extent. It sometimes happens that I mix the paint for a particular painting and then put it onto another – and this has hardly ever turned out to be a mistake. But this is really an unconscious strategy that I can use to outwit myself.

In the permutational colour paintings, you worked on a logical, consistent, random basis. There it was the form that was laid down in advance, and here in the abstracts it's largely the colour. And in contrast to the systematic manner of the colour charts, the permutations in the abstract pictures emerge naturally.

Yes, chance is natural too, and it's an element that modifies.

This freedom of colour, or this apparent arbitrariness of colour, as found in your abstract pictures, never appears in Neo-Expressionism, where the colour is always still regulated by aesthetic preconceptions, representational functions and harmonic compositions.

Yes, that's right.

The Rhetoric of Painting

What about the objectivization of the process of painting itself? You paint your big pictures not with an artist's brush but with a decorator's brush. Isn't this all part of the anonymization and objectivization of the painting process, along with permutation and chance; colour relations and compositional organization?

Certainly not.

The change in the instruments of production doesn't imply that the production of painting is once more critically called in question?

It changes the pictures only in one respect: they get louder; they are not so easily overlooked.

I was talking about the instruments – that is, the instruments also influence the perception of the picture. The fact that a monochrome was painted with a roller decisively influences the perception of the work. And in these big paintings here, where the brushstrokes suddenly turn into a decorator's brushmarks, they take on a new dimension that I would describe as a quasi-mechanical or anonymous quality.

No, not in this case. A brush is a brush, whether it's five millimetres wide or fifty centimetres.

So, in the two yellow Strokes, *their giant size doesn't add a new dimension?*

That's something different again – they only look like two strokes of a giant brush. In reality they were painted with a lot of little strokes. Here, on the other hand, it's all genuine, so to speak.

But here in the two big paintings a new dimension comes in, not only through the sheer size but also through the fact that the techniques and the act of painting have been carried to the limits of the possible.

The physical limits?

Yes, but also the limits of the perceptibility of the act, as an act of painting. And there another dimension opens up in practical terms. A dimension that is not regarded as subjective.

These are just as subjective as the small ones; they're just spectacular, that's all.

Spectacular they certainly are, even in a small format. In my catalogue text, I tried to describe how in your abstract painting the system is always 'on show', as it were – that they always have a certain declamatory, rhetorical quality. One always gets the feeling that you're showing the various possibilities just as possibilities, so that they simply stand alongside or against each other, without performing any other function.

Like making a speech that doesn't mean anything?

Yes...

A speech full of eloquence and uplift, which everyone falls for because it sounds good, which fulfils all the formal requirements of a speech and actually communicates nothing?

It doesn't sound good if you describe it that way, but you could put it differently, by saying that someone is delivering a powerfully emotive speech in order to give an analytical presentation of the resources of language, emotive persuasion and rhetoric. That is, you are making the spectacle of painting visible in its rhetoric, without practising it.

And what would be the point of that? That's the last thing I'd want to do.

You don't see the abstract pictures – in the way I have tried to outline – as a kind of reflection on the history of painting, although that's precisely what distinguishes them from all other abstract and gestural painting known to us. They not only have the rhetorical quality but also a quality of reflection on what used to be possible, reflection at the very moment when it can no longer be made use of. And I can imagine some viewers supposing that you're still earnestly practising what once was possible.

That would apply rather to the landscapes and some of the photo-paintings, which I've described on occasion as cuckoos' eggs, because people take them for something they aren't. And that was a part of their popularity – a popularity which I thoroughly approve of, on principle, and which has now totally changed. Now it's genuine, so to speak.

That would make them parodistic paintings. But the astonishing thing is that there's no parody in them.

They have a perfectly normal kind of seriousness. I can't put a name to this, so I always see them as musical. And in the structure there's a lot that reminds me of music. It's self-evident to me, but impossible to explain.

That's one of the oldest clichés that people resort to, when they are trying to find a firm footing amid the desolation of abstract painting.

That may well be. But I mentioned music in order to argue against something.

Against a catalogue of the rhetorical possibilities of painting?

I see no point in enumerating the old, lost possibilities of painting. To me, what counts is to say something; what counts is the new possibilities.

But reflection on rhetoric as a specific system of language is a highly important method, especially in present-day literary criticism. That means that people have suddenly realized the importance of looking at the linguistic conventions and the rhetorical laws behind utterances that have hitherto been examined only for their content.

Then it's just a private aberration on my part, if I always want to do something different from what I did before?

Perhaps it's not an aberration but a private dilemma, a gap between possibility and aspiration, and even so an important aspect of your work. If you were just a rhetorician, in the sense of an analytical exploration of the rhetoric of painting, there would be nothing particularly interesting about it. That's work that other people can do.

But if you refuse to see this as a rhetoric of painting, how would you define the details of the pictorial elements themselves? When one takes a look at the way elements of surface, line and colour are juxtaposed in an artificial enumeration, and with this declamatory quality, or how specific techniques of the application of colour are set out for all the world like a catalogue – some with a palette knife, some with a decorator's brush, some with an artist's brush, some smeared, some as direct traces, some as clouds of mist – there is something systematic about it all. As you were saying, it's all very well pondered and prepared, including enumeration, juxtaposition and combination.

As a whole and in every detail, its effect is emotional. It sets up moods.

That was the hard thing to figure out – whether it did, and, if so, what moods – when I said that the paintings curiously enough evoke no associations.

They do set up associations. They remind you of natural experiences, even rain if you like. The paintings can't help functioning that way. That's where they get their effect from, the fact that they incessantly remind you of nature, and so they're almost naturalistic anyhow.

But of course that then has to be defined. Not naturalistic in relation to nature?

Only in relation to nature, that's all we have.

The fact that nature appears to you as the only analogy or model that is ordered without a hierarchical structure – that you can't visualize a Utopian construct of a society that would match this ideal of nature – that is the Romantic element in your thinking.

That's not the Romantic element. It has to do with the division of labour. Some people design model societies, some design paintings, each to the best of his ability.

That's not a direct answer to my question – why nature to you is the only Utopian dimension of non-hierarchical experience; why it is unthinkable for you to argue or discuss your idea of a non-hierarchical existence in social terms; why you can only fall back on the metaphor of nature, like a Romantic.

No, like a painter. And I don't argue in social terms, because I want to make a picture and not an ideology. And what is good about a picture is never ideological but always factual.

That's just what I see in the way colour is treated like a material process; in the way colour becomes an object that is presented and modified by means of these instruments, remaining constant within these various structures and showing how it was made and what instruments were used in its making; and in the way there is practically no external reference to motivate the generation or the structure of the colour. These are all self-referential phenomena. Does this reading seem too narrow to you?

Yes, because all this effort is not there for its own sake; it is justified only if it takes all these wonderful methods and strategies and then actually produces something.

What?

A picture, and therefore a model. And if I now think of your interpretation of Mondrian, in which pictures can partly be interpreted as models of society, I can also see my abstracts as metaphors in their own right, pictures that are about a possibility of social coexistence. Looked at in this way, all that I am trying to do in each picture is to bring together the most disparate and mutually contradictory elements, alive and viable, in the greatest possible freedom. No Paradises.

Text for catalogue *Beuys zu Ehren*, 1986

In 1962 I saw a young man in the Düsseldorf Academy wearing jeans, a waistcoat and a hat; I thought he was a student, and discovered that this was the new professor, that his name was Beuys, and that he did very interesting and somehow different things.

Soon after that, in a cowshed somewhere out beyond Kleve,[1] I saw my first Beuys exhibition. I was amazed, dumbfounded, impressed – although my own affinities were with a different and far more 'official' art (Fontana, Pollock, Newman, Fautrier and the rest), which seemed to me to operate as if within a protective order, an unspoken consensus. With Beuys it was always different: he unsettled me, because he didn't play by the rules. He followed different criteria and employed different strategies; he was working for an 'expanded definition of art', which was not so much a protection as a challenge; a challenge to me, too.

Seventy artists invited to contribute one work each to an act of homage to Beuys: in the absence of any further theoretical or aesthetic conception, this is going to present a disparate picture. It is therefore going to look like a bad exhibition.

Beuys was highly critical. The customary, specialized divisions of art were always too narrow for him, and the usual collective exhibitions were more of an instrument than an opportunity to fit in... It seems that Beuys welcomed the idea of this exhibition. To me, it is one more patient and impatient attempt to overcome the helplessness of art, and I am taking part mainly because I hold Joseph Beuys in high esteem, and with him all those things that his name stands for: humanity, art, intelligence, courage and love.

Interview with Christiane Vielhaber, 1986

Early in your career you were labelled a Pop artist in the vein of the American Pop Art movement. You yourself originated the term 'Capitalist Realist'. That was in 1963 during an exhibition in a Düsseldorf furniture store.[1] *How did that description come about?*

I originally came from Dresden, where Socialist Realism prevailed. Konrad Lueg and I came up with it, for the most part ironically, since I now live in capitalism. It was certainly 'realism', but in another form – the capitalist form, as it were. It wasn't meant that seriously. It was more a slogan for that particular Happening at the furniture store.

Yet realism is something you've always portrayed in your painting.

Yes, but realism is a broad concept. One can even claim that abstract painting has its own reality.

What would that be?

Reality itself!

The reality of the image?

Yes, the reality of images! They are, of course, also imbued with a particular spirit. They spawn something. You enjoy looking at them or you don't. That's the kind of reality we use to approach these paintings.

In your case, Mr Richter, it is particularly important to find a clear terminology for your art. You have no motifs, formats or figures that reappear regularly and become recognizable. What exactly is the theme of your art?

Well, that's not quite the way it is. There are times when my work is quite easily recognizable, for example in the 1960s through the mid-'70s with the photo-paintings, which were mostly grey and looked like blurred snapshots.

How did you come up with the idea to paint these blurred photos?

I was a student, and as such you generally rely on prior models of how to make art, but these were not satisfying. Then I discovered in photos what had been missing in paintings; namely, that they make a terrific variety of statements and have great substance. That is what I wanted to convey to painting and apply to it.

Photos certainly have a great deal to do with reality. You use the term 'abmalen' [*to copy by painting*]. *Are you really just copying this reality a second time in your painting?*

No – a first time! Doing it a second time would mean it had already been painted. But it's only been photographed, this reality.

And the photo is quite a normal, conventional, modern tool these days to save us from having to draw. It's much more efficient to use a photo, because we don't even learn any more at the academy how to draw as the Old Masters did; we don't have the capability to do all that. That would mean an inconceivable period of training to be able to draw figures from sight, using models and doing studies over and over again.

But do you trust the photographs? Are they really a depiction of reality to you?

Yes, they are! I have for the most part used photos that have not been manipulated at all, or only very slightly. I've never wanted to use so-called art photography, let alone manipulated photos. Rather normal snapshots, which have the power to convey something.

And you've taken these and hung them right next to your easel?

Yes, and then copied them, as true to nature and as cleanly as possible, so that no personal signature enters the work. They should appear as anonymous as the photos, because that way they're more truthful. When I see that someone has painted something, then this act of making art is too much in the foreground. I'm not interested in what the painter thinks of the substance, but rather: what is the substance?

What function, then, does the substance or the representation of objects or of abstract painting have in your art?

In the case of representational paintings, it's empathy.

The same with objects?

It's hard to empathize with objects. With people, sure.

So a chair, for example, only expresses something about day-to-day life and about reality?

It's our chair that we use. It's actually a bit pathetic and quite banal, but it has its own spirit. I find it difficult to explain.

Are you after anything at all with your art?

Of course I am! But I'm not certain what to call it. At first there's the inclination and the wish to be able to do it. That's one thing. With that come the ardour and the fun of it. And then, secondly, independent of our aims is the pure human ability we have to do it. There's a kind of division of labour. Some people do this and others do that, and all these abilities belong to the richness of our humanity. It's a hopeful thing, to possess this ability, and a good, humanistic thing. It stands in opposition to all the unpleasant things, such as aggression and malice, war and crime.

Everything we do appears in front of this awful background. I read and hear every day that this and this many people have been killed and tortured.

In defining the function of art, then, would art be for you an ingredient of hope?

It's absolutely an ingredient of hope! To me it means this other side, which engenders hope, because we have this side in us: beauty, love, truth!! Unfortunately it's too cheap simply to say: 'That's a beautiful painting.'

You just prompted me to think of something. It's a quote from a fictional conversation with Sigmar Polke on the occasion of an exhibition in Hanover.[2] It goes as follows: 'I'm glad you're conventional, with no qualms about painting beautiful pictures. You have as much in common with Raphael as with the Surrealists and the millions of poor devils who photograph their families.'

Yes, a lot of nonsense can be created with the word 'beauty'. There's a tawdry beauty, for instance. When it's exalted, it can be quite unpleasant. The Nazis are the worst example of this. A beautiful body, a beautiful mind, and all that crap. That was a particularly one-sided, pestilent form of beauty that is simply wrong. But this doesn't mean that beauty no longer exists! Nonetheless it remains a dangerous word.

What's an example of your understanding of the term 'beauty'?

It can be a work by Mondrian, a piece of music by Schönberg or Mozart, a painting by Leonardo, Barnett Newman or also Jackson Pollock. That's beautiful to me. But so is nature. A person can be beautiful as well. And beauty is also defined as 'untouched'. Indeed, that's an ideal: that we humans are untouched and therefore beautiful.

And how does this concept of 'untouched' apply to your art?

That's an ideal case. The grey paintings, for example, a painted grey surface, completely monochromatic – they come from a motivation, or result from a state, that was very negative. It has a lot to do with hopelessness, depression and such things. But it has to be turned on its head in the end, and has to come to a form where these paintings possess beauty. And in this case, it's not a carefree beauty, but rather a serious one.

A sensuous one.

A sensuous, sensitive presence – but, no less important, also a certain beauty. Beuys has that, too! Even if he's criticized – earlier at least he was, less so today – for making disgusting smears of animal fat and felt, if you get closer to the work and surround yourself with it, you notice: it is beauty!

The beauty of the materials?

And the beauty of the truth.

The term 'truth' comes up a lot with regard to your work, and to you yourself. What is then for you the reality and the truth in your paintings?

The truth… When they have a similar structure to and are organized in as truthful a way as nature. When I look out of the window, then truth for me is the way nature shows itself in its various tones, colours and proportions. That's a truth and has its own correctness. This little slice of nature, and in fact any given piece of nature, represents to me an ongoing challenge, and is a model for my paintings.

Interview with Anna Tilroe, 1987

On what basis do you choose your format?

I choose depending on the way I feel; randomly, in other words. When I haven't done anything for a long time, I always start small, on paper.

Do you rate your work on paper as highly as the paintings?

Well, to be honest I must say it took a long time. It's only since 1976 that I have allowed myself to do that sort of small work. Before then I insisted that I should be able to theoretically justify everything I did. That theory wasn't entirely correct, but I did often believe in it. Drawing or painting on paper is more impulsive than painting on canvas. It doesn't take so much effort, and you can simply throw away anything you don't like, whereas large canvases take much more effort and time. I found that the directness of the works on paper led to randomness and virtuosity. I didn't want any of that.

It must have been a great deliverance when you were able to let go of that view?

Yes, you can be sure about that. I now get a lot of pleasure from making things. It's less possible to control and that makes the work more intimate, and closer to your feelings. Another thing that fascinates me is that the whiteness of paper creates a space that is different from canvas. I've tried to get the same effect on canvas by simply leaving the white undercoat as it is, but it didn't work. The canvas has a different quality, it has a presence, whereas paper represents a nothingness…

I am a German, and I have to live in a country divided in two. For a long time I thought that the character of my paintings was international. Until the first time I saw them hanging in an American gallery.[1] Then I suddenly saw how European they were. And how German, too: Grünewald, the Expressionists, to give a couple of names. Other people said the same. At the time I was delighted. Baselitz once

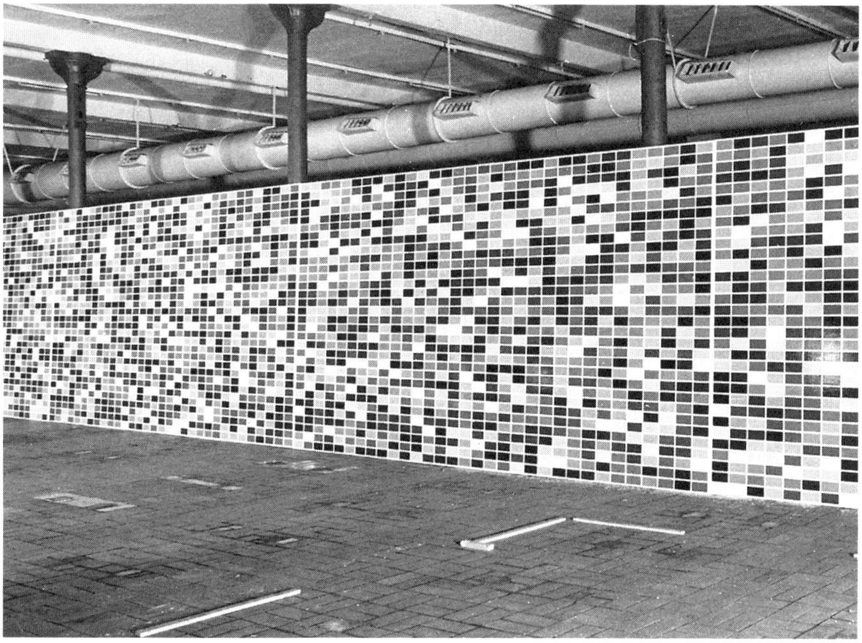

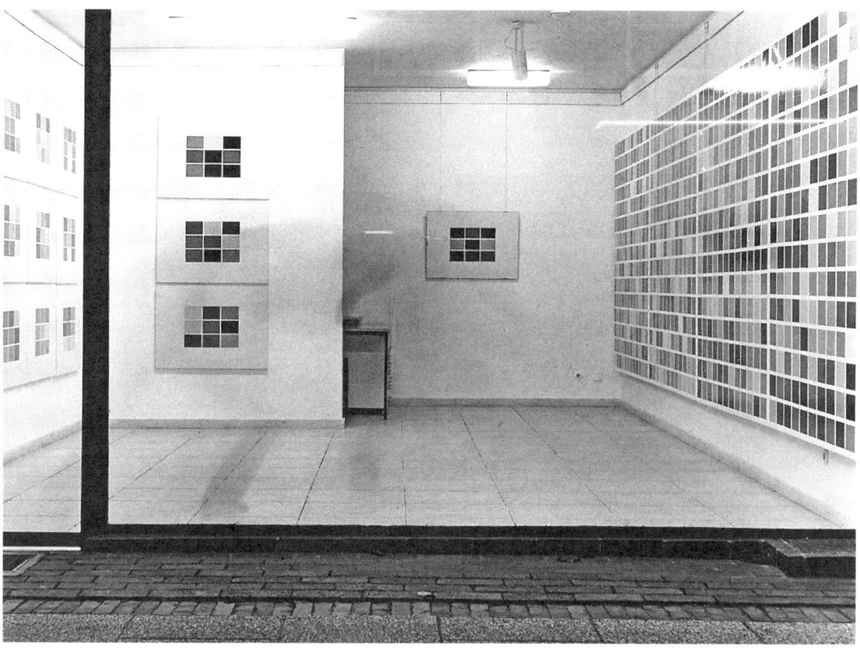

Studio shot, 1973
Kabinett für Aktuelle Kunst, Bremerhaven, 1971

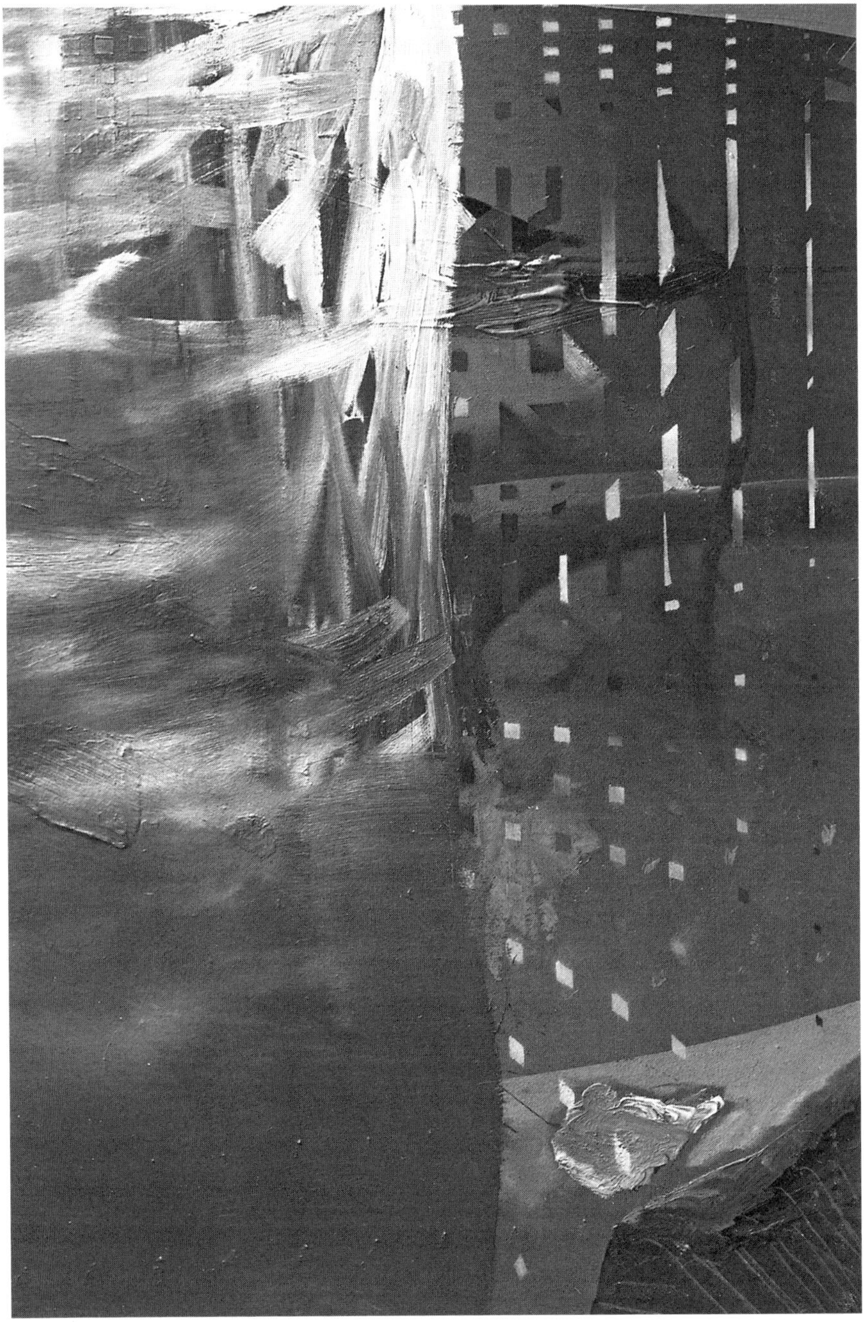

Abstract Painting, 1976 (detail)

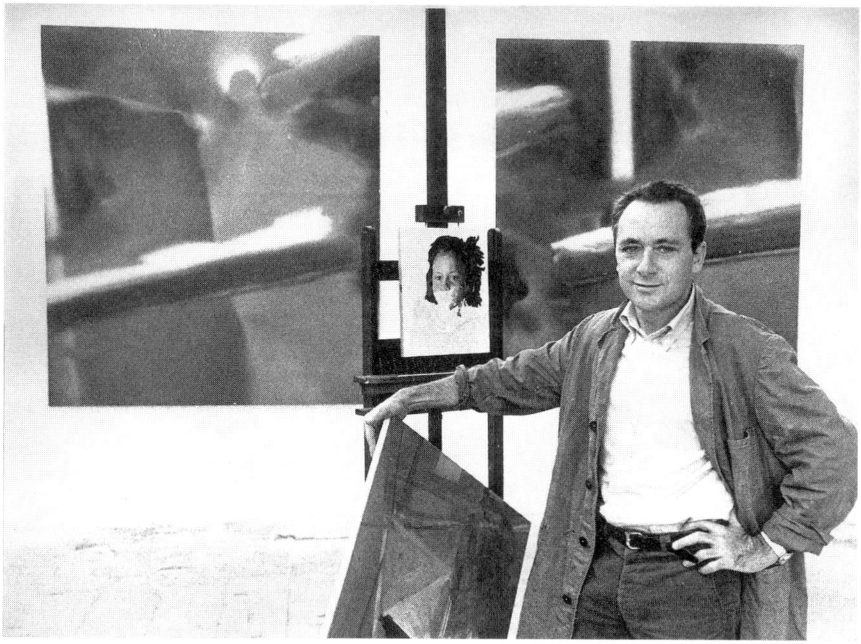

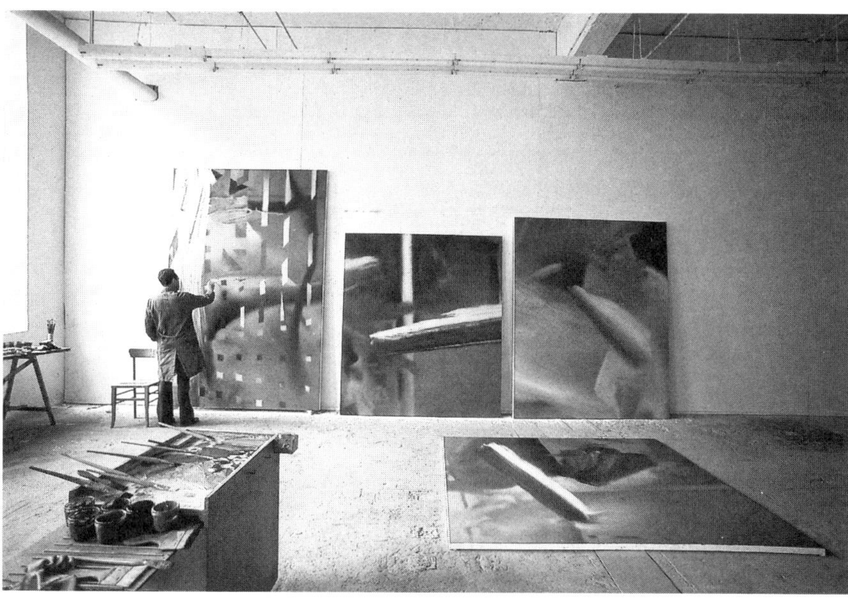

Studio shots, 1977

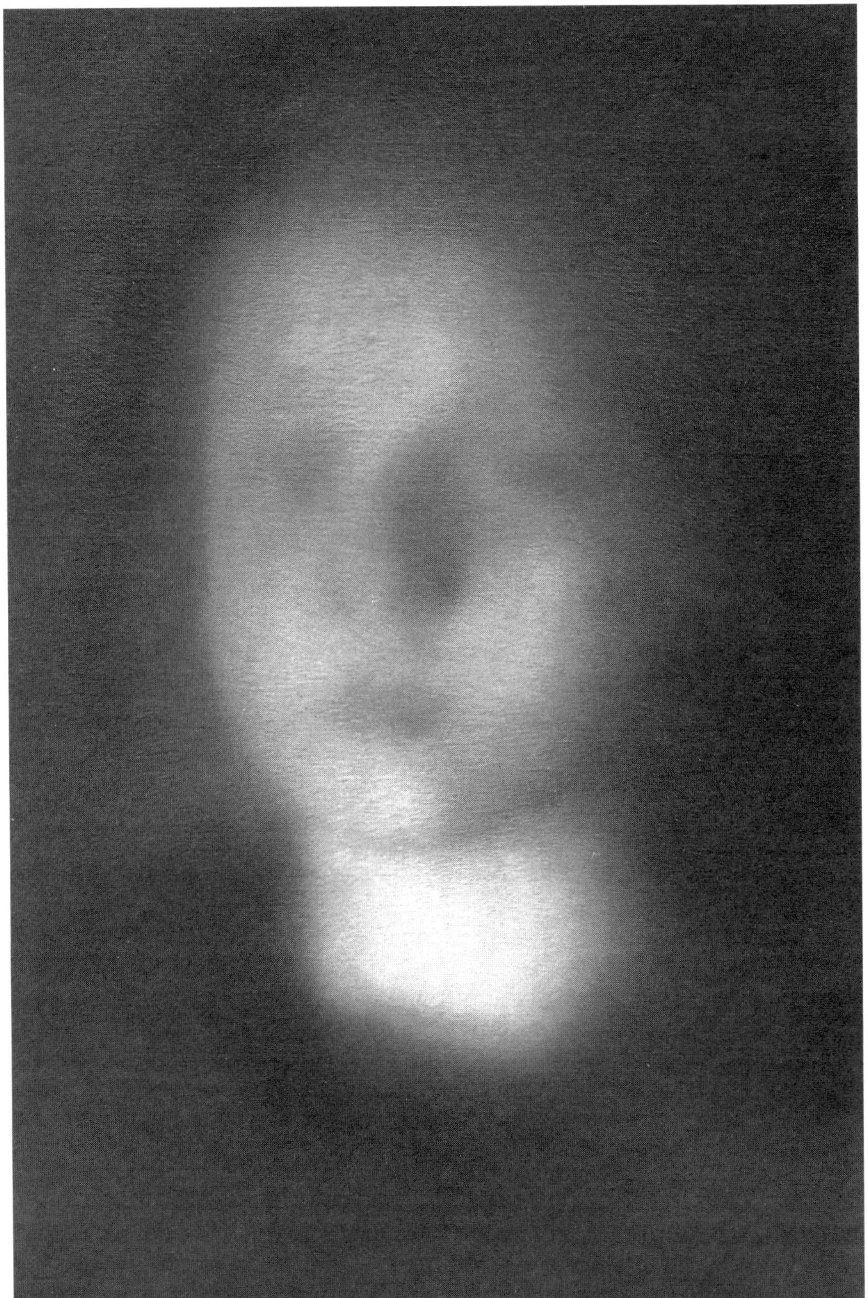

Betty, 1977

accused me of betraying my fatherland. That was in the '60s. At that time I was painting from photos and he considered that to be American. I think he meant it looked too much like Pop Art.

What does it mean to you, being a German?

It's not that I'm always ashamed, but history does concern me. What exactly happened, did we do that, what did the Russians do? This discussion is being carried on here all the time. I applaud that. There are still too many older people who say that none of it is true.

Do you have any clear memories of the war?

No, I was too young for that. But I did want to be a soldier. I was a real little Nazi. When the soldiers came through the village, I went up to them and wanted to join them. It's a question of upbringing, of course.

Did you blame yourself for that?

No. People can be brought up in any way, possibly even by apes or wolves. But I have become allergic to ideologies. And to dictatorial gallery owners.

Did you foster any Utopian ideas, or have any ideals, in your Fluxus period?[2]

I was affected by everything that was being done, and I admired it too, even the political movements, but I was very sceptical.

Nevertheless, the word 'hope' appears strikingly often in your diary.

I think that hope is one of our most important qualities. It is also a very simple quality; just a side-effect of consciousness. We are the only living beings that have a consciousness. Consciousness means knowing that I am here now and that I was here yesterday; on that basis I hope and believe that I shall be here tomorrow. It is a simple mechanism. But it is often misused and perverted.

It seems to me that in abstraction that problem is even more acute. Abstraction can easily tip over into decoration.

But take the paintings of Barnett Newman, for example. They are highly aesthetic and still good. I like his work above all, because it is the absolute opposite of mine. Those gigantic surfaces have an almost religious purity.

Didn't it upset you that your smooth grey paintings from 1974 were classified with the then-prevailing trend of fundamental painting?[3]

Yes and no. I wondered whether it were really possible for me, painting monochrome canvases, as it came so close to Minimal art. But on the other hand I thought that I should be able to do it, because at that moment it was the only way I could paint, and no other. It came straight from my heart.

At your retrospective in Düsseldorf[4] *last year it struck me that over the years your work has often fitted precisely into the spirit of the age.*

Is that so? It's quite possible, as I live now. Painting is one of the possible ways of reacting to time.

When 'wild' painting started, for example, you were doing abstract works which in the first instance also looked wild.

That's true. But I started on that in 1976. There were not yet any wild painters at that time. I had developed a tremendous dislike for the ideals of Minimal art, and was absolutely unable to paint any more grey canvases. I was completely stuck, and my only choice was, so to speak, to hang myself or to paint the absolute opposite. The same reaction later produced the 'young and wild' painters, but that's the only thing we have in common.

I seem to understand that you are not keen on present-day art. What do you dislike about it?

That it appears cynical but is not. Rather a resignation, a sort of hopelessness: no future. History is rejected and exchanged for the illusion that one can start from zero again.

Sometimes your abstract paintings give the impression of a landscape. Are you looking for realism again in abstraction?

I believe I am looking for rightness. My work has so much to do with reality that I wanted to have a corresponding rightness. That excludes painting in imitation. In nature everything is always right: the structure is right, the proportions are good, the colours fit the forms. If you imitate that in painting, it becomes false.

Do you suppress chance?

No, almost everything you see here is by chance. The moment of chance is very important, but it is guided and used. I compose my paintings. But I never look for uniformity. For a long time I wanted to bring together the things that could not be combined – and sought a form for it, a clear form. Until I saw that ultimately I destroyed it again anyway. Now I accept that the new work is slightly more diffuse. I find it has a greater richness and is more complex. I always have to cancel out the image, because at this moment I do not know what a painting should look like. For example, it has become impossible to paint a portrait. It will only be possible when there are new ideas about how a person can be portrayed at the present time. And there are no such ideas yet.

You do abstract and realistic paintings at the same time. Isn't that a great contradiction?

The means you use to organize it are the same: the same structure, the same contrasts, that sort of thing. But there is a difference in what I call the climate. For example, the landscapes are peaceful and sentimental. The abstract works are more emotional, more aggressive. I look for these differences of climate.

Letter to Manfred Schlösser, Secretary General, Berlin Academy of Arts, 16 April 1987

Re: *Sculpture Boulevard*

Dear Mr Schlösser,

Please accept my thanks for your letter of 14 April 1987, with the statement of the Academy of Arts on the dispute related to the above.

I must say I believe this 'statement' gives in too easily and uncritically to the fashionable trend of negligently staged cultural events.

It is also far too simplistic that the apologists for the Sculpture Boulevard contrive a concept of the avant-garde that justifies itself and finds its value in the mere rejection of so-called bigoted – or even labelled as fascistic – antagonism toward art. If a new arrogance of cultural leaders and artists is being fed on the old fallacy 'as long as philistines reject it, it must be good', then the demand for 'tolerance of all forms of art' is at risk of fully losing its relevance.

In this vein I think it is worth considering whether the Kurfürstendamm may be the worst possible location for this show – whether for example Metzel's piece 13.4.1981 has become merely brazen, impertinent decoration, which seems to exploit shrewdly the desperate seriousness of demonstrators; and whether the reference to Vostell's international fame will manage not to come across as calculated, arrogant intimidation.

It is not my aim to criticize works of art, but rather to remark that the grave mistakes and neglect of the organizers cannot simply be ironed out by means of retroactive, moralizing appeals. And the cynical and sloppy handling of this matter from the beginning illustrates quite clearly the mayor's role: his efforts to distance himself publicly from the sculpture project are no less despicable than his earlier support for it. In both instances he displayed neglect, incompetence and opportunism.

Berlin has brought many wonderful events to fruition that are worth the trip. But the pig-headed, militant manner in which things are being steamrollered now is simply spiritless – and hopefully not the true spirit of the times. For that reason, perhaps it is rash for the Academy to threaten the city with 'eternal disgrace'.

With kind regards,

Gerhard Richter

Notes, 1988

3 January 1988. Art is the pure realization of religious feeling, capacity for faith, longing for God.

All other realizations of these, the outstanding human qualities, abuse those qualities by exploiting them: that is, by serving an ideology. Even art becomes 'applied art' just as soon as it gives up its freedom from function and sets out to convey a message. Art is human only in the absolute refusal to make a statement.

The ability to believe is our outstanding quality, and only art adequately translates it into reality. But when we assuage our need for faith with an ideology, we court disaster.

7 January 1988. My profound distaste for all claims to possess the truth, and for all ideologies – a distaste which I have often expressed, with varying degrees of skill (and which has shown itself so clearly in my pictures, in my way of working, in my whole attitude, that I myself have repeatedly ascribed it to an innate lack of structural capacity, or of courage, or of strength, or of the formal impulse, or of potency, or of creativity) – this now receives confirmation from such people as the physicist Dürr, the evolutionary scientist Riedland, and Konrad Lorenz, who say that our sole hope of survival lies in the 'gropings of human self-doubt': in our awareness of our own limitations. And so I hope that my 'incapacity' – the scepticism that stands in for capacity – may after all turn out to be an important 'modern' strategy for humankind. Even more than before, therefore, I can assume (and, where possible, proclaim) that the absurdity (and inhumanity) of all ideology is a given fact.

13 January 1988. Art is wretched, cynical, stupid, helpless, confusing – a mirror-image of our own spiritual impoverishment, our state of forsakenness and loss. We have lost the great ideas, the Utopias; we have lost all faith, everything that creates meaning.

Incapable of faith, hopeless to the utmost degree, we roam across a toxic waste dump, in extreme peril; every one of these incomprehensible shards, these odds and ends of junk and detritus, menaces us, constantly hurts and maims us and sooner or later, inevitably, kills us. Worse than insanity.

Consolations are sold: all shades of superstition, puffed-up little ideologies, the stupidest lies.

2 March 1988. Of course, I have always declined to interpret the abject plight of art as the result of social conditions, and thus as an all-pervading environmental factor that stamps the character of art and defines its tasks and its content. I have always blamed myself for the impossibility of creating anything classically constructed and right. I was the one who was too inept to paint the 'right' pictures. But the truth is that the plight of art and of society does include everyone, and imposes on all of us the same misery and therefore the same task.

It doesn't help if I use this realization to let myself off the hook, as it were; perhaps it is necessary (and not only simple-minded and megalomaniac) for me to take it personally and to assume that the failure is my own. Because how could I ever achieve anything whatever, if I didn't assume that it was my personal business to right all wrongs?

12 March 1988. Most artists are afflicted with more than common stupidity, and this makes them even more desperate than they need be, and so they make themselves even more stupid than they really are, and so they make themselves artistically impotent – because, by panicking (consciously or unconsciously) at their own nonsense, they lose all self-respect and can produce either nothing whatever or nothing but unspeakable stupidity.

20 November 1988. To compare the Nazis' crimes with other crimes is only in a superficial sense to play them down. The real way to play them down would be to ascribe them to the Nazis alone, and thus take the easy way of acquitting oneself from guilt.

Notes for a press conference, November–December 1988 (held at Museum Haus Esters, Krefeld, February 1989)

In the early 1960s, having just come over from the GDR, I naturally declined to summon up any sympathy for the aims and methods of the Red Army Faction [RAF].

I was impressed by the terrorists' energy, their uncompromising determination and their absolute bravery; but I could not find it in my heart to condemn the State for its harsh response. That is what States are like; and I had known other, more ruthless ones.

The deaths of the terrorists, and the related events both before and after, stand for a horror that distressed me and has haunted me as unfinished business ever since, despite all my efforts to suppress it.

It is of no consequence what circumstances and chance events prompted me, early this year, to take up the theme again, to read about it, to get hold of new picture material and to start painting these pictures.

It is impossible for me to interpret the pictures. That is: in the first place they are too emotional; they are, if possible, an expression of a speechless emotion. They are the almost forlorn attempt to give shape to feelings of compassion, grief and horror (as if the pictorial repetition of the events were a way of understanding those events, being able to live with them).

The pictures raise a number of technical and professional issues, though these are of no fundamental interest to me. For instance, the objective quality of painting, imperilled or made redundant since the invention of photography; and my own reversion to a painting technique that I was using in the 1960s – an unmodern attempt at a painting based on content, a history painting.

These pictures possibly give rise to questions of political content or historical truth. Neither interests me in this instance. And although even my motivation for painting them is probably of no significance, I am trying to put a name to it here, as an articulation, parallel to the pictures, as it were, of my disquiet and of my opinion.

Reality may be regarded as wholly unacceptable. (At present, and as far back as we can see into the past, it takes the form of an unbroken string of cruelties. It pains, maltreats and kills us. It is unjust, pitiless, pointless and hopeless. We are at its mercy, and we are it.)

The experience and knowledge of horror generate the will to change, enabling us to create altered conceptions of a better reality, and to work for their realization. Our capacity to know – that is, to conceive – is also, simultaneously, our capacity to believe. Faith itself is primarily knowing and conceiving, but it simultaneously becomes the polar opposite of knowing (in that it mentally transforms the known into something different) and thus becomes the means of surviving the knowledge of horror: this strategy we call Hope. Faith is consequently an extension and intensification of the instinct to live, or to be alive. (Looked at cynically, the capacity for faith is only the capacity to generate befuddlement, dreams, self-deception, as a way of partly forgetting reality; it's a pep-pill to get work started on realizing the conception. Looked at cynically, everything is pointless.)

Deadly reality, inhuman reality. Our rebellion. Impotence. Failure. Death. — That is why I paint these pictures.

(As I said at the start: my motivation counts for nothing, as far as the pictures are concerned: they are independent of it, because they are themselves a piece of reality.)

7 December 1988. What have I painted. Three times Baader, shot. Three times Ensslin, hanged. Three times the head of the dead Meinhof after they cut her down. Once the dead Meins.[1]

Three times Ensslin, neutral (almost like pop stars).

Then a big, unspecific burial – a cell dominated by a bookcase – a silent, grey record player – a youthful portrait of Meinhof, sentimental in a bourgeois way – twice the arrest of Meins, forced to surrender to the clenched power of the State. All the pictures are dull, grey, mostly very blurred, diffuse. Their presence is the horror and the hard-to-bear refusal to answer, to explain, to give an opinion.

I'm not so sure whether the pictures 'ask' anything; they provoke contradiction through their hopelessness and desolation, their lack of partisanship.

(Ever since I have been able to think, I have known that every rule and every opinion – insofar as either is ideologically motivated – is false, a hindrance, a menace or a crime.)

Conversation with William Furlong, Jill Lloyd, Michael Archer and Peter Townsend, 1988

WF: Gerhard, could we talk about the London Paintings[1] *you're exhibiting here in the Anthony d'Offay Gallery? The first thing that surprises me are the very plain titles of the paintings, for example:* Salt Tower, Brick Tower *and* St James. *One could describe these paintings as being completely non-representational, and I don't know whether you'd be happy with the term 'abstract' being applied to them, but I wanted to ask you to begin by telling us something about how these works came into being, and about the relationship between the paintings and their titles.*

GR: Those are just names, and a name doesn't mean that much. If I give a name to my child, I can view that child as an abstract painting, whether I call him Andrew or something else.

JL: But the religious titles are very provocative. When you choose a religious title for a painting, it leads people to believe that it's about a religious experience.

GR: Their meaning has to do with the churches, not the individuals. No, they don't know that when they see and read the title.

JL: Where do they come from?

GR: From the churches, Westminster Abbey; no, they don't know that.

JL: But I assume you would see that in a religious context.

GR: That could well be.

JL: Because the paintings do have religious connotations of sorts, don't they?

GR: I don't object to [them having] that meaning.

WF: If one used the terms 'abstract' and 'figurative' to describe the two main elements in your work, would that be reasonably acceptable to you?

GR: 'Abstract' and 'figurative' are very simple terms, and they could be wrong. 'Abstract' has another meaning, but I wouldn't object to us using the terms 'representational' and 'non-representational'.

WF: I must say, my feeling is that these paintings are not really abstract – in the sense of not relating to anything – and it would appear that they have something very special in terms of their surface, how the paint is applied, and how their artistic message was crafted.

JL: Perhaps you can tell us something about the relationship between the two different forms of expression inherent in the paintings. Do you see them as opposites or as related to each other?

GR: Both are somehow realistic. Art makes artificial reality perceptible, and the other as well.

JL: So you would consider the paintings of nature to be natural?

GR: Regarding nature, I'd see them as more natural, yes, yes.

WF: But there seems to be something very special, something unnatural, when you want to transpose yourself into them. When you look at them, it's as though you were looking at nature through a filter – and, to me, they convey a strong sense of alienation and, at the same time, they appear very distant. They seem to be artificial.

GR: Yes, that's true.

JL: These paintings seem to be totally different from the abstract paintings you've made during the past few years.

GR: The new abstract paintings are quite different. Yes, yes, yes. The paintings before that had more of a structure, more composition. I can't seem to use composition as a basis any more.

JL: They are far more fragmented.

GR: Yes, yes, and destroyed.

JL: And your style has changed dramatically over the past ten years, taking a direction perhaps no other contemporary artist could have taken.

GR: Yes.

JL: Do you sense that something like that could happen again soon, and are these paintings the beginning of something new, or do they represent the end of a partially abstract phase?

GR: Yes, I have the feeling that I should be starting to do something new, but I don't know what. Perhaps I'll just continue. I really don't know. At the moment I'm in a phase where I don't have any [new] ideas.

JL: But it would appear that you enjoy painting when it's like this – you like painting without a plan. When we talked about this before, it seemed that you didn't want to apply any preconceived ideas to your work.

GR: Yes, but then I had the idea of not having any ideas. That's something different, and now I really don't have any new ideas – no vision of a new painting.

JL: But when you say that you had the idea not to have any images in your mind, you're talking about a very conscious decision. You have to try to avoid coming up with new ideas.

GR: Yes.

JL: I expect, at that moment, when you don't manage to avoid it, you just don't know what's coming.

GR: Yes, yes.

WF: Does it worry you that you're currently lacking a vision?

GR: Yes, yes, it's not very pleasant, but I've had these kinds of interruptions in the past as well – sometimes for longer, sometimes for shorter periods of time.

WF: I'd like to focus on one aspect of the paintings, if you don't mind. It is, in fact, very interesting how you created them, because, in a special way, a certain signature trait seems to be missing. Or, to put it another way, they negate the artist because they don't have a continuous, recognizable style bearing the artist's thumbprint. Surprisingly, I can't detect this thumbprint in your large photographic sculptures or your abstract paintings. I ask myself whether you did this intentionally to avoid creating a [recognizable] mark of identity?

GR: Do you think they're anonymous?

WF: They're not anonymous, but they don't display the artist's [typical] personal style.

GR: I can't judge that. My feeling is that their hands are on their hips.

JL: If that's true, then you would doubtless recognize your own paintings?

GR: My style is discernible, even if you don't recognize a single stroke of the brush on the canvas.

JL: I assume you regard a brushstroke as something subjective, a bit like the Expressionists do, and it seems as if you want to avoid that subjectivity – anything that can be seen as an expression of yourself or as feelings.

GR: I never liked the Expressionists, not the classic German ones, nor the modern variety.

JL: But when you were studying in Dresden in the 1950s, that must have been about the time that the Expressionists were very popular.

GR: Yes, but that had nothing to do with the Dresden School. That was different; more realistic, non-expressive.

JL: Dix worked there in the 1920s.

GR: But Dix wasn't typical of the Dresden School. Those people were unknown artists. If you look at the paintings of the Dresden School, you'll see they had little to do with Expressivity, and nothing to do with Dix.

JL: And what was it like for you when you came to West Germany in 1961? What did you think of abstract, expressionist painters like Götz, with whom you studied?

GR: We used a different term to describe these painters: Tachists, non-representational Tachists. That was interesting, too, but it's in the past – it's over.

JL: Did you, in contrast to the expressive, abstract artists, purposefully seek out alternatives – that is, in a conscious manner?

GR: Yes, we did try.

JL: How did that relate to the Capitalist Realism exhibition in the furniture store?[2] *There was something remarkable about that, and people still talk about it.*

GR: I'm surprised that this term became such a catchphrase. We just used it out of fun, to describe a Happening, to become better known.

JL: Did you think, 'Okay, in the East they have Socialist Realism, so we'll try out Capitalist Realism'?

GR: Yes, that's what was intended.

JL: But presumably the reference to capitalism was meant ironically?

GR: Yes, it's the wrong label. We don't have capitalist realism here.

JL: At the time, didn't you try to adopt a critical stance towards West German society?

GR: Not at all.

MA: You said there is no structure, or very little structure, in the abstract paintings. But looking back at the paintings you made up until ten years ago, you definitely started with a small, intensely painted picture from which you photographically enlarged a detail that served as the basis for a painting. Is there any similarity between those paintings and the ones here now?

GR: No, these are completely different from the ones back then. You mean the enlargement of details, the blow-ups. Yes, they don't have anything in common. When I said earlier that these paintings have less structure, I was comparing them to paintings from three or five years ago. Those had a composition and varying structure.

WF: Is there a special, dominant feeling – the idea that you're painting something from a specific vantage point – a building, say, that can be associated with the churches, the towers, and so forth? Is this something that has taken your work into a new direction, or...

GR: I don't think so, no.

WF: Is it important to you that the title contain at least a reference to a specific place?

GR: In this instance, with the London paintings, yes. Using titles is the exception. Only a few paintings have titles; it's very useful, and I can recognize them.

JL: Do the titles in these series relate to the type of change? More specifically, are the titles related to the way the paintings look and the changes you incorporated into them while you were painting them? These paintings look quite different compared to the ones last year, and they also have different titles.

GR: Yes.

JL: And is there a relationship between these things? Or perhaps you weren't aware of this when you gave them titles?

GR: It's related to other things I was interested in when I painted them – Kafka, whom I was reading at the time, or the fact that I would be coming to London to make these series. I had this on my mind, and the titles are related to that; and the titles are in colour.

JL: Did you do that to give the painting an additional dimension, so that we wouldn't just see it as an apparent abstraction?

GR: Yes, I hoped, or wished, to give them an additional dimension. I had a similar experience when I was painting from a photograph. I successively destroyed the surface until only the title remained, so that, with the tourist photos, you can hardly make out the tourists, and you don't recognize the terrible drama, which is a man being eaten by a lion – but you have the title, and that's interesting.

JL: Sometimes, in your earlier works, you used fragments of words, and the complete title wasn't visible.

GR: But that's not the case with the tourist paintings. They don't contain a single word. They only bear a title. I used fragments of words a long time ago.

PT: There's a section in your catalogue, a translation of one of your letters, in which you describe nature as being devoid of intelligence, without compassion, inhuman even. Did you mean inhuman, or anti-human, since inhuman is actually a very human term.

GR: In German we don't distinguish between this kind [and other forms] of 'human'. I think I meant 'against humans'.

PT: As in immoral?

GR: Yes.

MA: I read that and thought it was pretty interesting. Does that mean you don't really see us as connected to nature, that you view us as mere physical beings?

GR: We are connected to nature. This is a very polemical sentence.

PT: Indeed it is. It means that we, as human beings, are the only ones that can confer meaning onto nature, and, in that sense, your abstracts seem to hurl the landscapes back at the observer, making them listen inside themselves for an echo of the landscape painting, but one that has nothing to do with the landscape as such. Isn't that right?

GR: Yes, yes.

MA: How important is it in this exhibition that both forms of presentation – the abstract and the representational – are found side by side?

GR: I think people understand the abstracts and the landscapes better that way. The works are more real when shown together, but it's also possible to show only one group of paintings.

JL: Would you exhibit the photo landscapes on their own now?

GR: Not at the moment, no – more likely the abstract ones. I'm more interested in the abstract paintings. I've never tried it – just once in the past, when I only had landscape paintings.[3]

JL: So they're really just there to make the abstract paintings appear in a new light and not so that the titles confer a special meaning?

GR: The titles of the abstract paintings?

JL: Yes.

GR: Yes, yes. It's related to the hope I mentioned that they could be more significant, more important for us. I'm constantly aware of the absence of meaning. I'm only a painter.

JL: Are you saying that we have to find a way to create this meaning?

GR: Yes, I could do more. The influence of paintings is limited.

JL: In the way they can influence the public or in their inherent power to express something?

GR: Yes, with our problems. We have a lot of problems in this world, and paintings can set a lot of things straight.

WF: Let's focus on a couple of things regarding the photographic paintings. Last year I saw the very comprehensive portrait exhibition in the Museum Ludwig, which I thought was excellent, and I asked myself what the intent behind the photographic representation was as opposed to the pure paintings, which consciously emulate the photographic process – or come very close to it. Wherein lies the main difference, in your view? What are the significant differences between your painted portraits and your photographic images?

GR: You mean the photographic portraits?

WF: Yes.

GR: I have two variations: painted portraits based on photographs, and photographs of the paintings. Sometimes I give preference to the photographic variation – that's more modern, more in tune with the times.

WF: But what is it you're thinking about when you're painting these very detailed, very precise paintings that are very similar to a photograph?

GR: For me it's the only plausible modus operandi – the best representation, aside from colour. They're not in colour, and a lot of photographs I had back then weren't in colour.

JL: Do you try to make them as real, as near to reality, as possible?

GR: As real as can be, and sometimes I've succeeded in making them better than the photographs – clearer. Some of them were very small. I improved on that a bit.

JL: But sometimes there's this fine veil covering everything. It's as though this were intentional – as if you didn't want the picture to look like a perfect deception.

GR: The effect makes them appear more realistic.

MA: When you say you want them to be as realistic as possible, do you mean they should be as close to a photograph as possible, or as close to reality as possible?

GR: I don't know any painting that is better than a good photograph.

WF: But you have consciously chosen to reproduce a photographic copy. As an alternative you could have, for example, painted a portrait on the basis of the actual [living] person.

GR: This is a skill we haven't acquired. We're not capable of painting properly. Only very few artists, like Lucian Freud, are able to do so, but all others lack the ability. They haven't learnt how to. We don't have a school that teaches it.

WF: But does that also apply to landscape painting?

GR: Yes, yes.

WF: You wouldn't even consider wandering outside into the world and painting it?

GR: That's far too strenuous, having to lug all that stuff around [*laughs*].

PT: Let's talk about these paintings of yours that are based on photographs – when I contemplate them, my reaction is emotional, not because of the landscape as such, but because of the way I perceive such a landscape painting.

GR: Yes, I think I understand. That comes from the camera, right?

PT: It's as if you communicated a certain mood to me when I study your work. You force me to react to the landscape painting in a way that you expect someone to react who carries a [pre-determined notion of a] landscape within himself.

GR: That's good.

JL: I consider the landscape paintings to be pretty deceptive. They appear to be very romantic and beautiful, but they also seem quite devoid of emotion in a special sort of way. I mean, there's this undefined aimlessness in your landscapes. They're either too far away, or too close, or something else is not quite right.

GR: Aimless.

JL: Do you want us to perceive the landscapes as romantic, or do you want us to feel a little disoriented?

GR: Both. I believe that we experience these two states when we see a landscape painting. We feel nostalgic, and nostalgia encompasses these simultaneous feelings.

JL: I recall that you exhibited a painting at documenta[4] *that looked very much like a photograph, and it showed a corner of Cologne Cathedral. Why did you choose this particular cathedral?*

GR: It was a very old photo, though not ancient, from 1984, and I was in this very special mood for taking the picture.

JL: Do you study lots of photographs before choosing one to paint?

GR: I take lots of photographs. It's difficult to find something you can take a photograph of, and then you have lots of photographs and it's difficult to decide which one is right to paint.

WF: What criteria is your decision based on? How do you choose which one to paint?

GR: I really don't know.

JL: If, for example, Duchamp were to contemplate his readymades he would say, 'Well, I merely chose them.' He [really did] used to say that: because I tried to avoid picking something aesthetically pleasing, I try to avoid certain things. I'm not sure what I [actually] want, but I know what I'm trying to avoid.

GR: I try to avoid lots of things [*laughs*]; I try to avoid all things that are stupid.

MA: To return to Bill's remarks about the portrait series: they're all [based on] famous people. Is it a very personal selection? Are these all people you like?

GR: No. Some of them I hardly know, and a few of the ones I like most I haven't painted. They're not in this series.

MA: There's this painting by Kiefer – Hermannsschlacht [The Battle of Teutoburg Forest] *– and that seems to be very similar. It looks as if he studied your series. Again we find this monochrome quality, grey, black and white, and it contains entire portrait series of his personal heroes.*

GR: You said his personal heroes, and that's something completely different from me. He has shown a direction and an ideology, but I haven't, because I create the opposite of a direction – I want to destroy.

WF: Mike mentioned Kiefer, and I'd be interested to know whether you see any connection, any intrinsic relationships between your work and the work of other contemporary German artists. I'd also like to know what you think about Beuys in retrospect, seeing as you lived in Düsseldorf at the same time as he did. Do you feel that there's any link between you and these other artists?

GR: I'll say something about Beuys. I liked him a lot and, sometimes, I even loved him, but I also tried to stay away from him and not get involved.

JL: When Beuys died, you wrote in your diary notes that you believed that you, or German painters, now had a new task – that someone, in their own way, would need to continue what he had started.

GR: That's what we're doing now. We're in the process of weighing up what it means, but right now I don't have any new ideas.

PT: I'd like to ask you about your opinion of Friedrich and Corot, who are mentioned in your catalogue: there are obvious similarities in terms of atmosphere or melancholy. How close do you feel to them?

GR: I love Caspar David Friedrich, of course, and he is very different from me. He's a great painter, and strong.

JL: When I talked to you about your paintings, you spoke a lot about your interest in music. Are you inspired by music, and after listening to music are you ever inspired to paint? How does that work?

GR: I like music, I'm interested in music, but not while I'm painting, because that could distract me. But I like music.

WF: Is there some special way you might be able to integrate it into your work?

GR: No, that would be too dangerous.

Notes, 1989

14 March 1989. The word 'bourgeois', formerly a compliment, now negative in its connotations, much used, always vaguely polemical, jejune and irrelevant. 'Bourgeois' equals tidy, educated, law-abiding, in contrast to flipped-out, cheerfully dressed, ostentatiously nonconformist (e.g., Thomas Mann as against Bertolt Brecht, President Weizsäcker as against Joschka Fischer).

Just as conformism is not at all the same thing as security – the word denotes a deference to prevailing fashions, and to the prevailing climate or system, which springs from stupidity, cowardice, indolence and baseness – nonconformism is not necessarily its diametrical opposite, but often springs from a courage born of stupidity and blindness. Nonconformist laxity often originates in the confined, retarded structure of mindless insolence.

21 July 1989. Nature/Structure. There is no more to say. In my pictures I reduce to that. But 'reduce' is the wrong word, because these are not simplifications. I can't verbalize what I am working on: to me, it is many-layered by definition; it is what is more important, what is more true.

Everything you can think of – the feeblemindedness, the stupid ideas, the gimcrack constructions and speculations, the amazing inventions and the glaring juxtapositions – the things you can't help seeing a million times over, day in and day out; the impoverishment and the cocksure ineptitude – I paint all that away, out of myself, out of my head, when I first start on a picture. That is my foundation, my ground. I get rid of that in the first few layers, which I destroy, layer by layer, until all the facile feeblemindedness has gone. I end up with a work of destruction. It goes without saying that I can't take any short cuts: I can't start off right away with the work in its final state.

23 July 1989. However ineptly – desperately ineptly – I set about it, my will, my endeavour, my effort – what drives me – is the quest for enlightenment (apprehension of 'truth', and of the interconnections; coming closer to a meaning; so all my pessimistic, nihilistic actions and assertions have the sole aim of creating or discovering hope).

25 July 1989. My denunciation of ideology: I lack the means to investigate this. Without a doubt, ideologies are harmful, and we must therefore take them very seriously: as behaviour, and not for their content (in content, they are all equally false).

Ideology as the rationalization of faith; as the 'material' that credulity puts into words and makes communicable. Faith, and here I repeat myself, is the awareness of things to come; it therefore equals hope, it equals illusion, and is quintessentially human (I cannot imagine how animals get along without such an awareness); because, without this mental image of 'tomorrow', we are incapable of life.

1 October 1989. The political topicality of my *October* paintings means almost nothing to me, but in many reviews it is the first or only thing that arouses interest, and the response to the pictures varies according to current political circumstances. I find this rather a distraction.

I did make a number of imperfect attempts to formulate my motivation, which was initially 'purely human' (dismay, pity, grief), and parallel to this the theoretical components (consideration of real circumstances and of possibilities of change, which are inseparably bound up with faith and ideology; hence my critique of ideology).

I wanted to say something different: the pictures are also a leavetaking, in several respects. Factually: these specific persons are dead; as a general statement, death is leavetaking. And then ideologically: a leavetaking from a specific doctrine of salvation and, beyond that, from the illusion that unacceptable circumstances of life can be changed by this conventional expedient of violent struggle (this kind of revolutionary thought and action is futile and passé).

And then the work bears a strong sense of leave-taking for me personally. It ends the work I began in the 1960s (paintings from black-and-white photographs), with a compressed summation that precludes any possible continuation. And so it is a leave-taking from thoughts and feelings of my own, on a very basic level. Not that this is a deliberate act, of course: it is a quasi-automatic sequence of disintegration and reformation which I can perceive, as always, only in retrospect.

Of course, personal circumstances play a part in all this. On one hand, they cannot be seen in isolation from the generalized 'leave-taking' mentioned above; on the other, they have to be disregarded, because it is all too easy and too misleading to use them to explain things away in psychological terms. The upheaval that I mean has more objective causes, in the events and ideas of the world; and I am causally involved with it only in that I am receptive to the objective facts of the case and, where possible, join in formulating them.

3 November 1989. Chance as theme and as method. A method of allowing something objective to come into being; a theme for creating a simile (picture) of our survival strategy:

(1) The living method, which not only processes conditions, qualities and events as they chance to happen, but exists solely as that non-static 'process', and in no other way.

(2) Ideological: denial of the planning, the opinion and the world-view whereby social projects, and subsequently 'big pictures', are created. So what I have often seen as a deficiency on my part – the fact that I've never been in a position to 'form a picture' of something – is not incapacity at all but an instinctive effort to get at a more modern truth: one that we are already living out in our lives (life is not what is said but the saying of it, not the picture but the picturing).

4 November 1989. Andy Warhol is not so much an artist as a symptom of a cultural situation, created by that situation and used as a substitute for an artist. It is to his credit that he made no 'art'; that he touched none of the methods and themes that traditionally constrain other artists (thus sparing us the great mass of 'artistic' nonsense that we see in other people's pictures). Insofar as his avoidance of nonsense was an active one, he was an artist; but insofar as it was passive and naïve, he was no more an artist than is any mental patient whose 'works' are collected and used. The situation is complicated. It is probably true

that – though some of his works are among the most impressive things done over the last thirty years, and though his œuvre as a whole holds a decisive and outstanding importance for our age – he was still only a mediocre artist.

To take a somewhat premature example: we do not know who the Pilotys and Makarts and Lenbachs of our own time are; nor do we know whether our day even possesses a Salon art, analogous to that which existed then – an art that posterity will judge so differently.

10 November 1989. The events in the GDR, the so-called historic, democratic revolution. Moved though I am by it, in spite of the briefly flaring hopes of a happy future, a reunited Germany, I am overwhelmed by scepticism and pessimism, almost grief, sometimes rage. Rage at the shamelessly opportunistic politicians, and at the intellectuals who spouted for decades in their fanatical Marxist blindness and now sulk, unable to let go of their conceit of knowing better. Grief at the role assigned to the people, who have been systematically used – casually cooped up like convicts for 40 years, by those who would be quite happy to keep them there for another 140 – and now used in a different way and persuaded that they have created this democratic revolution themselves, by their own efforts. When it's perfectly plain that they are being sent out through the Wall, allowed into the West.

The same types who for decades cruelly oppressed and blackmailed 'the People' are inviting praise for making a few concessions. And they give ground, or twist themselves round completely, for one reason and for one reason alone – to hang on to power. Gangsters.

20 November 1989. Illusion – or rather appearance, semblance – is the theme of my life (could be theme of speech welcoming freshmen to the Academy). All that is, seems, and is visible to us because we perceive it by the reflected light of semblance. Nothing else is visible.

Painting concerns itself, as no other art does, exclusively with semblance (I include photography, of course).

The painter sees the semblance of things and repeats it. That is, without fabricating the things himself, he fabricates their semblance; and, if that no longer recalls any object, this artificially produced semblance functions only because it is scrutinized for likeness to a familiar – that is, object-related – semblance.

Even when experience or consensus more or less forbid this comparative scrutiny, we compare a white painting by Robert Ryman not with a whitewashed wall but with the intellectual experience of the history of monochromy, and with other problems in art theory; and even then it fundamentally functions in the same way. We still compare it with snow, flour, toothpaste and who knows what else.

15 December 1989. From 1933 to 1989, that makes 56 years of uninterrupted dictatorship for the East Germans. Included within that, as the necessary concomitants of dictatorship, were the catastrophes, the crimes and the constant deprivations, offset by a vast effort of lies, slander, distortion and self-deception, an effort that could have been made only under the strictest control, under extreme duress – in a dictatorship, in fact. There is a very simple and familiar logic to all this: from time to time, our capacity for hope and faith (which are the same thing in this case) has generated a delusion, or ideology, which initially energizes people to achieve some real successes, and which from the very outset makes them selectively blind: blind to all that fails to fit, blind to anomalies and crimes. Psychological repression takes place; and, when the privations and sufferings and catastrophes come along, the delusion becomes a dogma, which prevails, prohibits, controls and punishes for so long that people are transformed into patients. The GDR.

16 December 1989. Language can express only what language enables it to express.

Language is the only language of consciousness. 'What one cannot say, one does not know.'

That is why all theory is absolutely circumscribed, almost unusable, but always dangerous.

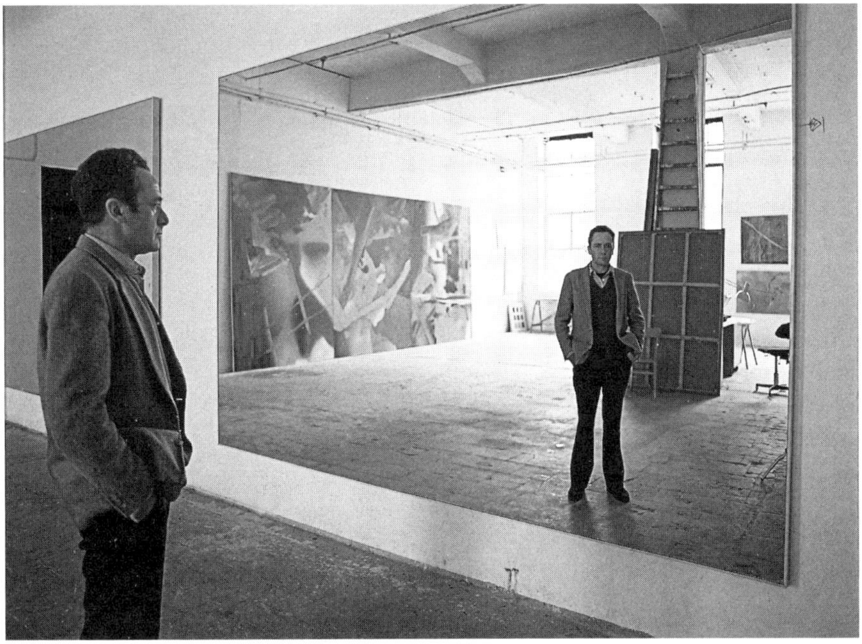

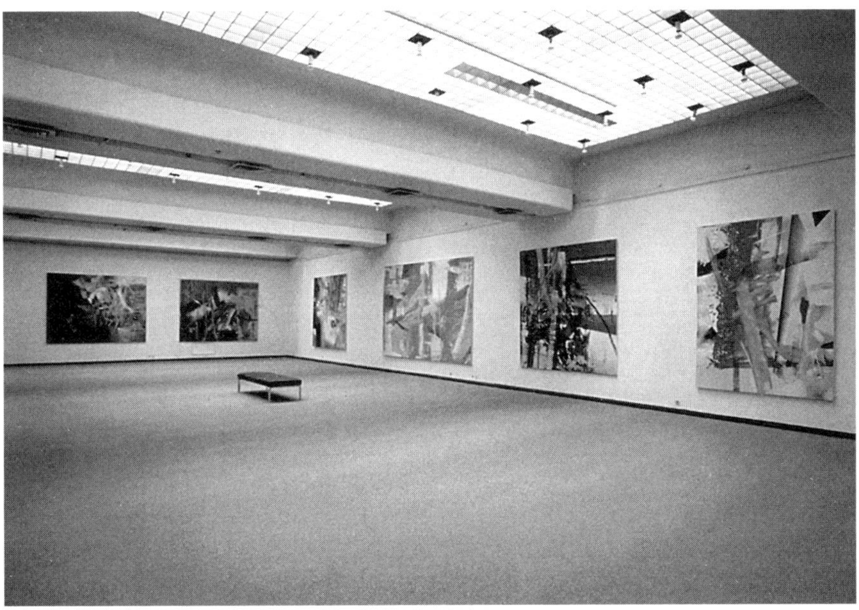

Studio shot, 1981
Städtische Kunsthalle, Düsseldorf, 1986

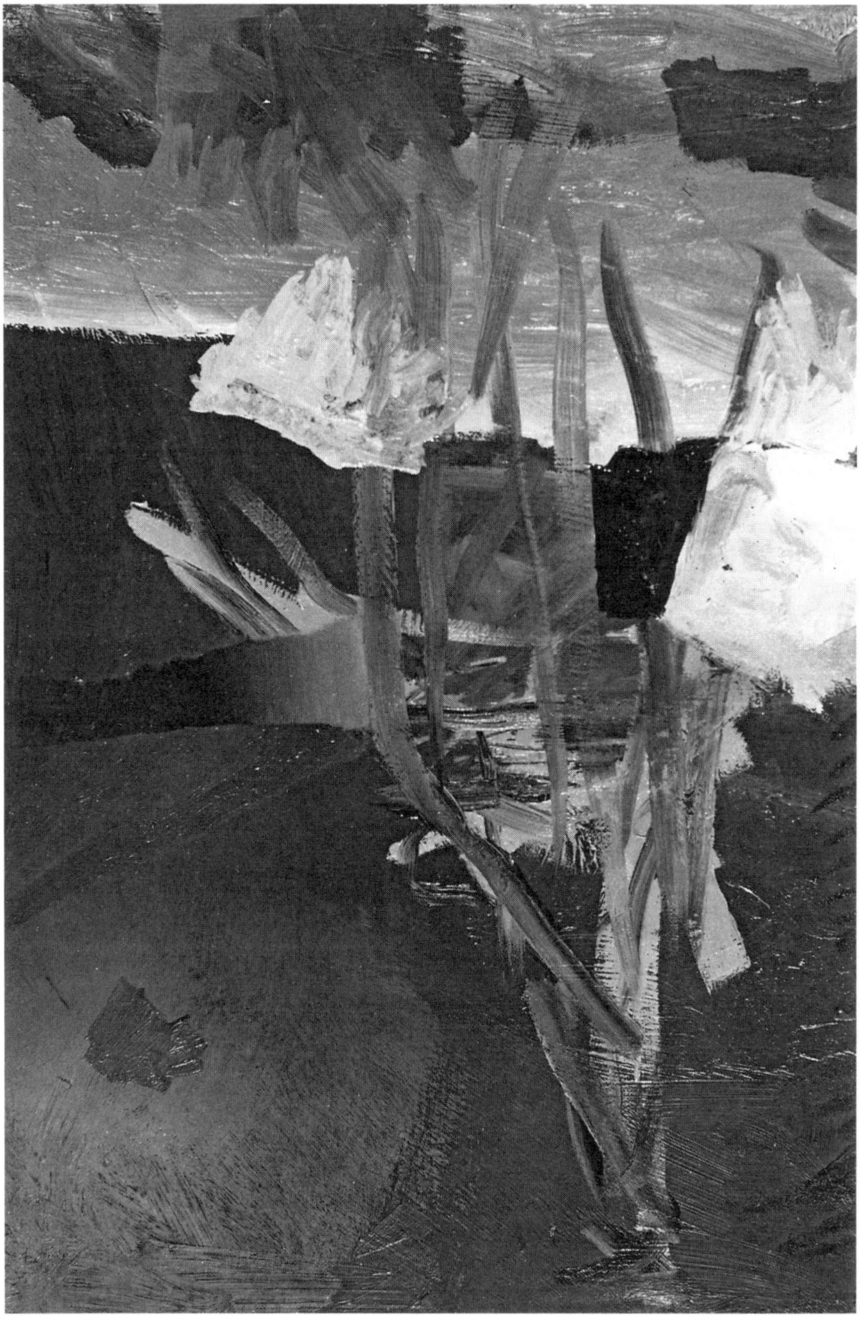

Abstract Painting, 1977

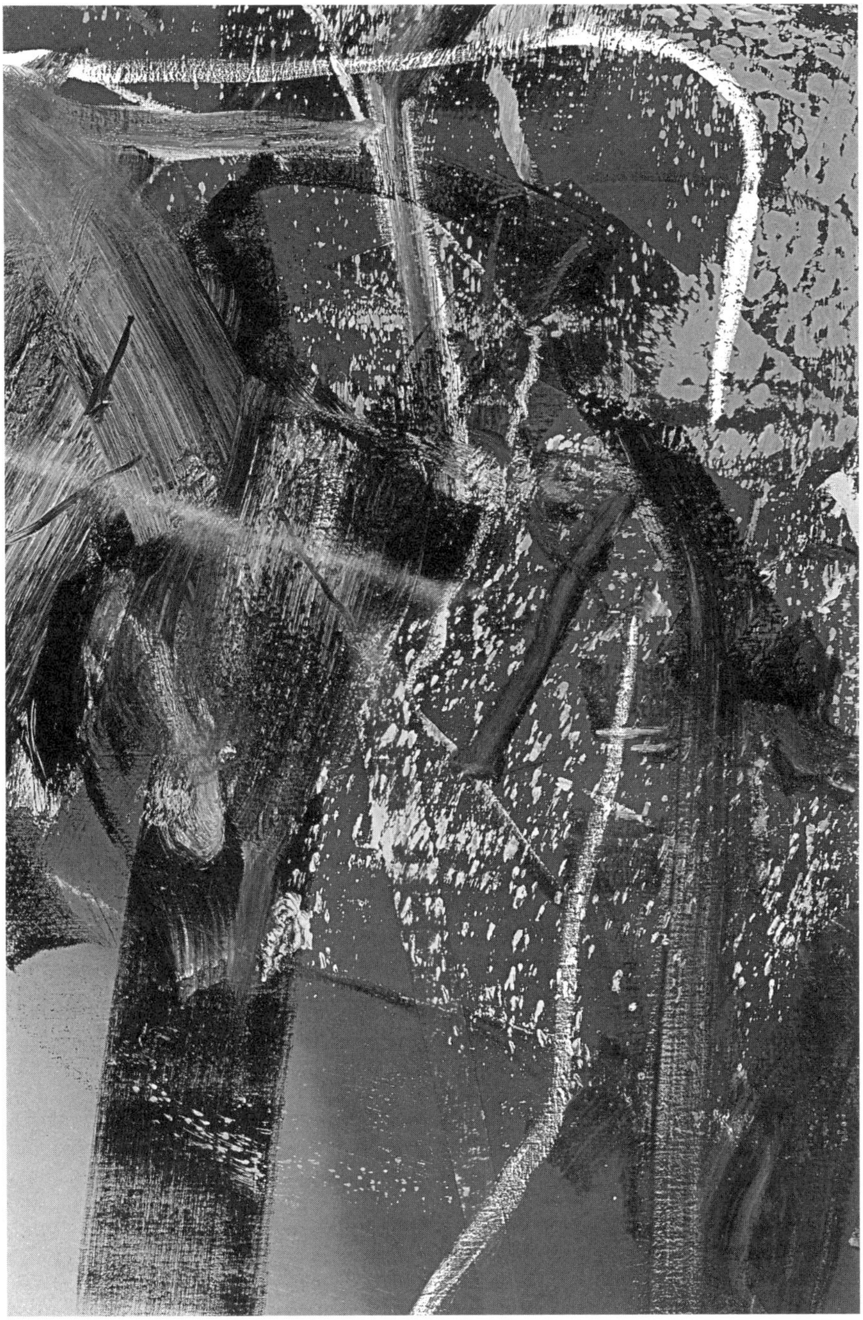

Clouds, 1982 (detail)

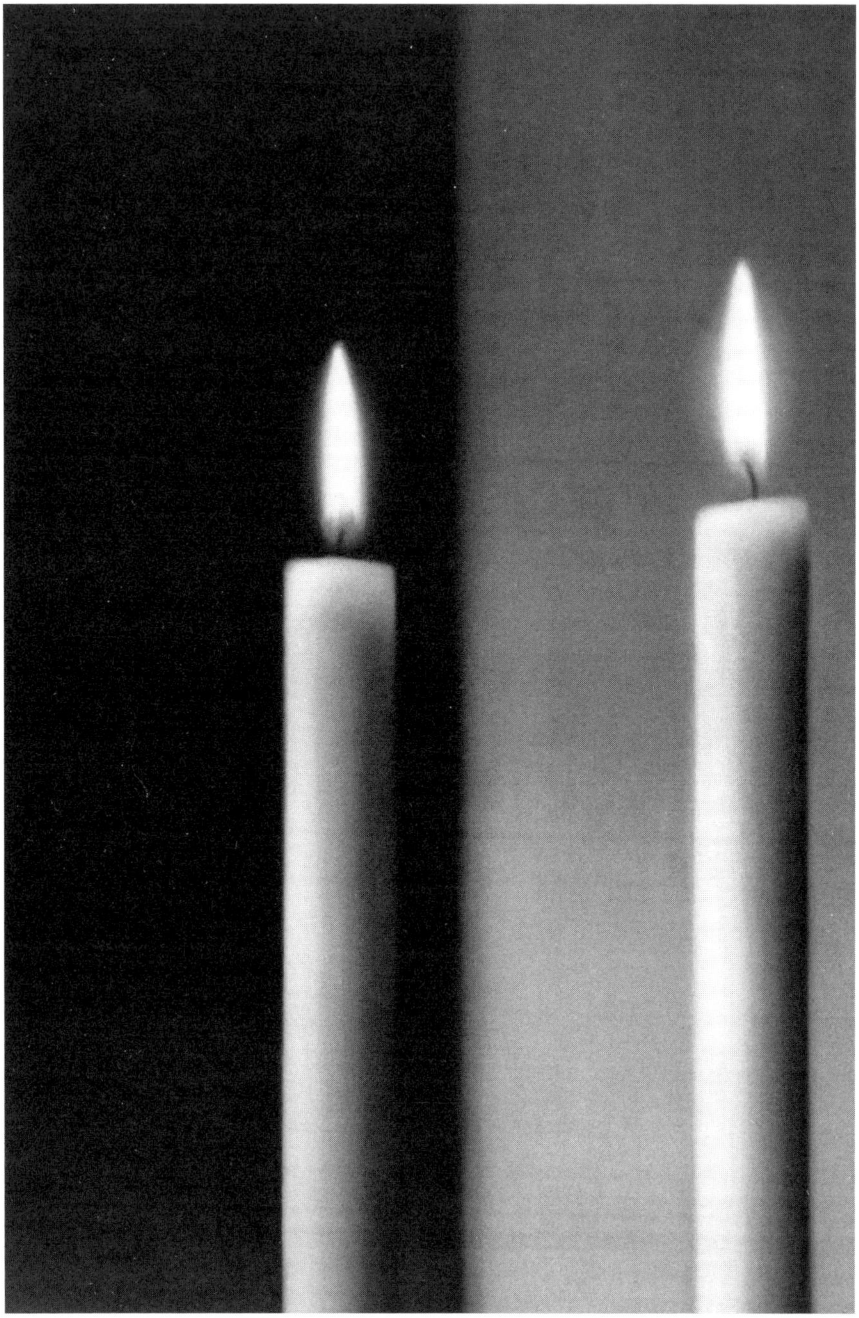

2 *Candles*, 1982 (detail)

Interview with Gregorio Magnani, 1989

Why did you decide to paint the Baader-Meinhof?

There was no special event that made me decide. I had collected some photos and the idea was in the back of my mind for a long time. It was growing and growing, so finally I said, 'I must paint this.' I come from East Germany and am not a Marxist, so of course at the time I had no sympathy for the ideas, or for the ideology that these people represented. I couldn't understand, but I was still impressed. Like everyone, I was touched. It was an exceptional moment for Germany.

The title of the series 18 October 1977 *points, among other things, to what is perhaps the most incongruous aspect of the whole Baader-Meinhof story, the three simultaneous suicides in the separate cells of a high-security jail. This is perhaps the closest you allow yourself to comment on the narrative you present. You insist on the importance of not considering it a closed case. Why?*

I tried to open it up again – to make a funeral again – but without a solution. The whole case, the entire complex of events, was not dispatched. Sometimes I have the feeling that we forgot, or that we are forgetting – throwing the entire thing away from us like garbage. Of course I can't provide an ending. I can't say, 'This is how it happened', which is not my intention. Maybe it was just for myself I tried to dispatch that complex. Working is very good for that: you come up with a sort of solution, you move things around again and again until at last they have a new order, and then you can hide them again.

Was your interest specific to the Baader-Meinhof phenomenon, as a fact in German history, or mainly in its symbolic, exemplary value?

Both. Also the symbolic event, to try to change history and fail. Baader-Meinhof was a very strong example of failure.

It was one of the last direct revolutionary attempts.

For me, ideology, extreme ideological faith, is an interesting problem. I think that we shouldn't have ideas, or Utopias, or ideologies. We don't need belief. Religion, Khomeini, Catholicism, Marxism: every belief is dangerous and wrong. It must be wrong. We can't believe we are thinking the right thing, we must be pragmatic. We no longer need belief. Perhaps it was necessary in the past, but today we have other possibilities, or at least we should create other possibilities.

To go back again is a real disaster. When you see the current wars, these people, I mean the people who actually die, are fighting for nothing: for ideas, for nothing.

Or often the ideas are excuses...

For a natural aggressivity. Yes, this is part of us, we like to kill.

You have said many times that 'Utopia is meaningless, if not criminal', yet you have chosen to paint an extreme Utopia.

This is the dilemma. I know it is part of us to build a world of ideas. I grew up with Nazi ideology and then, overnight, we had Marxism. For years Marxism told us that the capitalist system was about to collapse, and this never happened. It may happen someday, but we have to admit that we just don't know, that economy is too complex to be explained by theory. Still, when I had to read Marxist political and economic theory, I could really see its power. It wasn't simple, but it made everything so clear, you could actually see the future as a logical development of the present.

In your paintings there is pity for the Baader-Meinhof.

There is sorrow, but I hope one can see that it is sorrow for the people who died so young and so crazy, for nothing. I have respect for them, but also for their wishes, or for the power of their wishes. Because they tried to change the stupid things in the world.

Do you think Baader-Meinhof actually changed something in Germany? At least they may have undermined the respect for political and economic authority.

I don't know. On the other hand, authority is even more respected now. When the Baader-Meinhof appeared in the '70s, authority was weak in Germany, like everywhere. Now we are more pragmatic, we may not like the government, but we see its necessity. We are at the opposite end of terrorism, we want this order so that we can be a bit anarchist in our own homes. I think that this trauma changed our minds a bit, but I don't think you can explain the effects as something specific.

You've never dealt with such strong content before...

I was always afraid of this kind of subject. It's too spectacular; there is too much spectacle invested.

It's unsettling that you don't offer a stylistic change to parallel your change in content. You seem to suggest that everything can be painted in the same way.

I stepped back to twenty years ago, to the black-and-white portraits. I had hoped that I could paint these subjects in a different way, but it didn't work. I tried, but it wasn't possible; so I had to return to the former style. But it's not true that everything can be painted: I have hundreds of photos of the Baader-Meinhof, but I can't make another painting of this. I have used everything I could from those images. Yet still, for me this technique was the only way to paint. If I want to paint something, I can only paint like this. So the decision had to be made to not do something, or to do it in the old way. And in this case, I thought it was important to do these paintings.

In the '60s you did some paintings, which were derived from images of concentration camps, which you then destroyed. That was your only other attempt to deal with a tragedy which was both human and political. You said that this was a subject that couldn't be painted. What made you think the Baader-Meinhof could be painted?

I still think it wouldn't be possible for me to make paintings of concentration camp scenes. I tried to do it when I was young and even then I gave up immediately.[1] I just put the photos in the *Atlas*, where I collect all the subjects that have interested me. The concentration camps were simply terrible, without any hope, and that is something I can't paint. Baader-Meinhof is different: I tried to have some of their hope come out in the paintings.

You also suggest a sort of morbid fascination with death, a form of sadistic voyeurism.

There was no way to avoid that, even though I understood those deaths as exemplary. I hope it's not the same as seeing an accident on the motorway and driving slowly because one is fascinated by it. I hope there's a difference and that people get a sense that there is a purpose in looking at those deaths, because there is something about them that should be understood.

There is a difference in your paintings, but you seem to suggest that there is no difference in the way people look at things, whatever the reason for looking.

There are also reasons for fascination. Looking reminds us that we are the survivors, and at the same time, we see our own end, in front of us, and somehow we like seeing it.

But fascination and complicity seem to create a problem for you, insofar as you want to make 'moral' painting.

Yes, this is a problem; it's also a very old-fashioned one. The history of painting is full of images of suffering, but always as an example, our own fate.

You may also be perceived as removing Baader-Meinhof from history and consigning it to the museum. Making terrorism into an acceptable artistic subject, you also consign it to a supreme voyeurism.

I know this argument, but for me it is absolutely necessary that Baader-Meinhof is a subject for art. Art has to do with life. There must be no scene which is taboo to art, whatever risks this may entail.

The difficulty would be that you don't claim an ideological or a political purpose in your work the same way that, say, Jacques-Louis David could.

That would be almost the opposite of what I wanted to do... David painted a hero, I painted a victim. Not a victim of a particular ideology or power, just a human victim. And David also made art out of his subject – beautiful paintings with extraordinary compositions. Perhaps my work is more in-between, between documentation and art. I can't imagine how any painter today could simply make art out of this subject.

When my students at the Academy heard I was doing these works, most of them said I wasn't allowed to paint this, that I was too bourgeois, too much a part of the establishment. This seemed very stupid to me. But many young artists are going to say this is bullshit, polit-kitsch, and maybe it is possible to see the works in that way.

Except that the Baader-Meinhof was itself bourgeois, it came out of a bourgeois consciousness.

True, but do you know of any revolutionary who wasn't bourgeois? Maybe Spartacus was the last.

Do you see this series as isolated, a unique parenthesis, or are you actually revising your relation to 'content'?

Yes, this does seem a bit outside of my work. But now when I see the grey monochrome paintings I realize that, perhaps, and surely not entirely consciously, that was the only way for me to paint concentration camps. It is impossible to paint the misery of life, except maybe in grey, to cover it.

That seems much more like your approach, while this series really diverges from the way you normally deal with things.

But at the same time I always wanted to show directly what I thought, or what I felt. It would be hard to go further now. The landscape paintings now seem to be without 'obligations'. Maybe they would like to have the same seriousness as the new works, but most people don't see that, they just find them decorative.

This series renders your other works much more dramatic, especially those which have a relation to death, like the skulls, the apples...

There is actual death now; the skulls[2] were just quotations.

You are claiming a different status for these paintings from that of normal artistic production, including your own. There was no museum opening for their presentation in Krefeld, the spotlights were off, the work isn't for sale,[3] and you are allowing only certain paintings to be reproduced. You insist that this series must not be treated as consumer items. This strikes me as a Utopic gesture.

I was very afraid of the subject and that newspapers would make a big spectacle of the work. The relatives and friends of these people are still alive. I neither wanted to hurt them, nor did I want an opening with people standing around chatting and drinking wine. People visited my studio when I was working and wanted to buy a painting which they thought was saleable, like the record player, so I thought I had to do something. A gallery would just not have been the appropriate place for these images, but I realize this doesn't really change much.

What destination do you envision for this cycle?

A museum, even if they end up in storage most of the time.

A German museum?

Yes, I think it is better.

Statement on the exhibition *Bilderstreit*, 1 June 1989

After my initial misgivings regarding my participation in the *Bilderstreit* exhibition, it was made clear to me by my lawyer that a curator is within his rights to hang whatever he wishes and whatever he can get his hands on, and I not only dropped my objections, I actually sent four paintings to the exhibition. As has become apparent, it was a mistake. I did not expect that Messrs Gohr and Gachnang would be worthy of the ambitious theme, nor did I expect anything more than a Cologne-style – that is, a Werner-oriented[1] – perspective. But the fact that these two pulled off such an unsightly, boring and, in every sense, dilettante show has exceeded all my worst fears.

Conversation with Jan Thorn-Prikker concerning the *18 October 1977* cycle, 1989

I'd like to ask you about the genesis of these paintings. All of them are painted from photographic originals. Did you find the photographs first, or did you first decide on the theme and then look for the photographs?

It all comes together, the theme and the pictures that make it visible. I had kept a number of photographs for years, under the heading of unfinished business. It's hard to say how it came about that late in 1987 my interest revived, and so I got hold of some more photographs and had the idea of painting the subject.

So you researched far and wide, photographs of attacks, 'wanted' photographs, everything to do with this particular context?

Yes, everything, including photographs from the private lives of the members of the Red Army Faction [RAF], their operations, police material, everything I could dig up.

A very considerable part of your work came before you started painting at all: the research and planning stage of the pictures.

That part is highly important. But then it's nothing new. Painters in the past did the same thing. They went out into landscapes over and over again, and from their millions of impressions they chose the quite specific, definitive impression. I had a large quantity of photographs. It narrowed down all the time, and it became clearer and clearer what was really there to be painted.

What criteria guided you in your choice?

It's more or less an unconscious process. That sounds terribly old-fashioned; it's definitely no longer 'in'. These days, pictures are not painted but thought out. Anyway, the material – all the photographs just lie there for a very long time, and you look at them again and again, and then you make a start somewhere, and the choice gets smaller and smaller, the choice of photographs that might be paintable.

Were you confident from the very start that the terrorism theme was paintable?

The wish was there that it might be – had to be – paintable. But there have been some themes that weren't. In my mid-twenties I saw some concentration camp photographs that disturbed me very much. In my mid-thirties I collected and took photographs and tried to paint them. I had to give up. That was when I put the photographs together in that weird and seemingly cynical way in the *Atlas*.[1]

When I looked at the 1986 Düsseldorf catalogue and saw what you had done, it gave me a strange feeling. You were putting concentration camp photographs side by side with pornography. That seemed to me to be beyond the pale. It shocked me – but in a terrible way I found I understood it. When I was young, those pictures of concentration camp victims were the first photographs of naked people that I had ever seen. You can't imagine what a terrible crossover that was. I still have the book, but I can't look at it any more. I don't want to be reminded of that possibility ever again. Ever since, I've been aware that there are some pictures that simply must not be taken. To me, it was an unfathomable coincidence, to find you trying out such monstrous combinations. Did you never have the feeling that such picture material might be taboo?

No, never. If only because I have always regarded photographs as *pictures*. But the risk I was running was perfectly clear. There are plenty of bad examples of people hitching themselves to some big, attractive theme and ending up with mere inanity.

Death, an attractive theme?

Yes, people can't wait to see corpses. They crave sensations.

When I saw your exhibition in Krefeld,[2] *my first impression was a mixed one: 'That goes too far. That mustn't be painted.' My second impression was one of even greater horror: 'It's a wish-fulfilment fantasy: a painted, collective dream of hate.' There were a lot of people at the time who just longed to see those prisoners dead. A longing that was never expressed about the Nazi criminals. I am convinced that in 1977 many people wanted to see precisely the pictures that you have now painted. Can you understand my impression that you have painted a hate fantasy?*

I do know that the fantasy exists. But it's more complicated than that. If people wanted to see these people hanged as criminals, that's only a part of it: there's something else that puts an additional fear into people, namely that they themselves are terrorists. And that *is* forbidden. So this terrorism inside all of us, that's what generates the rage and fear, and that's what I don't want, any more than I want the policeman inside myself – there's never just one side to us. We're always both: the State *and* the terrorist.

What pictures remained unpainted?

The ones that weren't paintable were the ones I did paint. The dead. To start with, I wanted more to paint the whole business, the world as it then was, the living reality – I was thinking in terms of something big and comprehensive. But then it all evolved quite differently, in the direction of death. And that's really not all that unpaintable. Far from it, in fact. Death and suffering have always been an artistic theme. Basically, it's *the* theme. We've eventually managed to wean ourselves away from it, with our nice, tidy lifestyle.

To the same degree that it has vanished from art, it has found its way into the mass media. Television and magazines largely live on murder and crime.

Yes, but only quite superficially. In fact, all the media convey an artful, highly effective image of happiness and comfort, which then seems to be imposed on us. It's education, of a sort – educating people for something entirely false and unreal. This compulsory happiness is dangerous.

When I look at how earlier periods presented themselves, this phoney happiness is not there. The pictures dwell on the pain and suffering, the perils that threaten us as human beings. That was more realistic; such prototypes didn't give currency to the illusion that life in this world is all that wonderful. The worst thing about these illusions is that they make people even unhappier: they feel worthless and abnormal because they don't look as happy as the people who smoke HB[3] or whatever.

Happiness in former times was not a thing of this world.

No, and perhaps that was less of a lie than the lie that promises happiness here and now – the right to happiness: that's pure nonsense.

Might you as a painter have had any chance of inventing images on this theme – or is there an aesthetic necessity of some kind that means that such images must be painted from photographs?

I consider it quite simply unthinkable to invent such pictures. That's just not possible nowadays. Painters used to train for years on end, to the point where they could to some extent invent nudes. That ability no longer exists. It's gone.

I meant something different, not the loss of technical skill, not the painter's virtuosity. I'm asking whether photography sets aesthetic norms that absolutely prevent one from painting such a theme out of one's head?

I do know one such picture, by a Norwegian painter, rather Old Masterish, as phoney as Werner Tübke... Now, photography is so unsurpassed by definition, it's changed painting so greatly, there's just nothing to be said.

What do you mean by unsurpassed? As far as I am concerned, these photographs are unsurpassed in their inhumanity. Anyone would look away at once. Photographs capture a thing that it would be impossible to look at. They simply register. Finish, comma, out. They are totally impersonal. To be able to see such pictures, you need a glass wall in front of your eyes; you need the filter that a camera lens provides. In reality you wouldn't be able to look.

Photographs are almost nature. And they drop onto our doormats, almost as uncontrived as reality, but smaller. We want to see these terrible pictures, and maybe they even spare us public executions, even capital punishment. We do need that. Just think of motorway accidents, how that fascinates people. Can you explain that to yourself?

Because we're still alive. Because we got away scot-free. Because we play a privileged role as spectators. Because that single instant makes us more powerfully aware that we're alive.

That's a great advantage. But in the process we also see our *own* end, and that also strikes me as very important. And photographs can do the same thing, which is why I have never seen them as inhuman. As pictures, I don't consider them any worse, just different. They have a different effect. More direct, close to home, more immediate.

I find that astonishing. The photographs petrify me. The paintings seem to me to transcend them, to make mourning possible. It seems to me that the photographs don't permit that. They duplicate blindly.

Can I fetch you a photograph? What I can read in this – the compassion that is so directly released here – the way this young woman lies there, all the details that tell so many stories: a painting hasn't got that with the same immediacy. It's all much stronger here.

I can't understand Benjamin Buchloh, when he writes [in the Krefeld exhibition catalogue] that you intended a criticism of the 'cruel gaze' of the police photographs.

No, that's not what I meant at all.

You share that gaze, in every detail. In your painting, you participate in its horror. And yet the painting is something very different from the police photograph.

It's meant to be. Perhaps I can describe the difference like this: in this particular case, I'd say the photograph provokes horror, and the painting – with the same motif – something more like grief. That comes very close to what I intended.

Does death in this context possibly have a grandeur that it now no longer automatically has in everyday life? I am always finding news items which I collect under the heading of 'Death Without Dignity'. There's a story of someone who's been run over by a mechanical sweeper or shut in a freezer. Or people being buried standing up, because of the lack of space in Berlin cemeteries, and so on. I often wonder whether the editors realize that they're redefining our relationship with death through these stories. Stories like this are our time, it seems to me. Do you set out to involve yourself in the truth of this cruelty?

Far from it. I want to show death in all seriousness.

So why the blurring?

I first paint the pictures very precisely from the photograph, sometimes more realistically than the originals. That comes with experience. And the result is, of course, an unendurable picture from every point of view.

It reminds me of the working of psychoanalysis. As if you wanted first to cancel the repression, in order to reinstate it later. When you paint the photograph in a much bigger format, does that make it more terrible?

Partly, yes, because it's like a reconstruction of the event, just by virtue of being life-size, with all the details.

The photographer needs only a fraction of a second – but you have to spend hours creating all those details.

But it's work, after all. I feel that I'm not reduced to being a mute spectator. I have something to do. That makes it more bearable.

How do you decide on the right size for a picture?

Entirely primitive. Life-size.

The pictures of Gudrun Ensslin alive are more than life-size, something like one-third bigger than reality.

I don't know why I painted her larger than life. The portrait of the young Ulrike Meinhof is larger than life, too. Perhaps it was a vain wish...

...for life to be bigger than death? What about the format of the burial scene?

I couldn't make that life-size. The picture would have been eighty metres long. It's still the biggest picture in the exhibition, but in comparison to the event itself it's small.

The cycle consists of comparatively small pictures.

Which I'm quite glad of now, a certain plainness that I find appropriate. Two years ago, when I started to work on this theme, I thought: 'This is a gigantic theme, and these are going to be gigantic pictures.' It did come out as a cycle, but the pictures are not outsize ones – rather modest, in fact.

The RAF, as seen by you, is primarily a women's movement.

That's right. I do think that women played the more important role in it. They impressed me much more than the men.

Did you tackle the theme purely as a painter, or did you also need to know about the personalities, the politics, the events and the context? Did you read books about terrorism?

Yes, I read everything, sooner or later. Stefan Aust's book[4] was very important to me. So knowledge of the people, knowing the people, was basic to the pictures.

I was particularly struck by the portrait of Ulrike Meinhof as a young girl. It's the only picture that shows an RAF member outside the magic circle of RAF politics. It could be anybody. It's touchingly innocuous, even sentimental. Is it a special picture?

It does have a specific function in the cycle, because you see it in relation to the others. But all the fifteen pictures relate to each other.

There is always an anti-painterly element in your work. If your painting here reminds me of the blurred pictures on ill-adjusted television sets, does that bother you?

The reproductions are like that, but not the pictures themselves.

How long does one picture like this take you?

It's relatively quick. That is, applying the paint is a lengthy process, a week or so. The burial picture took longer, there were so many details to be painted, but a head would only take two days. Most of the work lies elsewhere – and that can go on for almost a year.

Can you paint anything else concurrently? Do you need a counterweight, to hold in check the depressive mood that hangs over pictures like these?

There were breaks.

But you didn't, for instance, work on colour abstractions at the same time?

No, that's not on. A break of one week, that's all right. I did paint my daughter once during that period.

Did she have anything to do with the cycle?

No, nothing. But I did find it interesting that the portrait of Ulrike Meinhof came out so much better than that picture.

Was it clear to you from the outset that this was going to be a grey cycle?

Yes, it was.

Did you ever consider painting the terrorists' victims as well? Hanns Martin Schleyer, for instance?

Never.

The scene in Victor-Statz-Strasse, with the pram as an obstacle to stop the car. The occupants' corpses on the street with blankets over them, the Mercedes?

No, never. After that you'd have to go on painting the same sort of thing. That was the ordinary crime, the ordinary disaster that happens every day. What I chose was an exceptional disaster.

What was exceptional about it?

Firstly the public posture of these people: nothing private, but the overriding, ideological motivation. And then the tremendous strength, the terrifying power that an *idea* has, which goes as far as death. That is the most impressive thing, to me, and the most inexplicable thing; that we produce ideas, which are almost always not only utterly wrong and nonsensical but above all dangerous. Wars of religion and the rest: it's fundamentally all about nothing, about pure blather – and we take it utterly seriously, fanatically, even unto death. I'm not talking about the facts. The crimes of Vietnam do have to be taken utterly seriously, but that's a different matter.

Is it the tragedy of these people that they tried to be active doers? That they refused to reconcile themselves to their own impotence – isn't that the hidden, positive core?

Yes, that's the other side – which I see, of course, despite my scepticism. That's the element of hope that the pictures were meant to contain.

Has the ideology of the RAF never interested you?

No. I have always rejected it as an ideology, as Marxism or the like. What interests me is something different, as I've just tried to say: the why and wherefore of an ideology that has such an effect on people; why we have ideologies at all; whether this is an inevitable, a necessary part of our make-up – or a pointless one, a mere hindrance, a menace to life, a delusion...

So you consider the RAF dead as the victims of their own ideology?

Yes, certainly. Not the victims of any specific ideology of the left or of the right, but of the ideological posture as such. This has to do with the everlasting human dilemma in general: to work for a revolution and fail...

Significantly, 'avant-garde' is a political as well as an artistic term. Is there a relation between art and the revolutionary impulse? What causes an established, bourgeois artist like yourself to be interested in the RAF? Surely not its actions?

Yes, the actions. Because someone is trying, with total radicalism, to change something: one can understand this, and also see it as the other side of the coin. Art is sometimes described as radical, but it isn't really – only artificially, which is something quite different.

Is painting an attack on reality, in the attempt to create something entirely new?

It's all sorts of things – an alternative world, or a plan or a model for something different, or a reportage – because, even when it only repeats or recalls something, it can still create meaning.

Recalling – that is the concept that underlies these pictures. What can one profitably remember about the RAF?

It can give us new insights. And it can also be the attempt to console – that is, to give a meaning. It's also about the fact that we can't simply discard and forget a story like that; we must try to find a different way of dealing with it – appropriately.

I sometimes feel that works of art can momentarily disable the real world. That they keep at least the idea of change alive.

Yes, certainly. It's just that I sometimes feel scared at the many demands that are made of art. Art is a perfectly natural human quality, and from that point of view it can't be called in question. You can't say that art is no good because Mozart didn't prevent the concentration camps, any more than you can say that no more poems are possible after Auschwitz. All I know is that without Mozart and the rest we wouldn't survive.

I have compared a few of the paintings with the photographic originals. Some quite fundamental changes have been made. It's clearest in the cell picture, for instance. This picture speaks impulsively, directly to the viewer. At the time, people were always arguing that a cell with a record player and books, not three books but three hundred, was as comfortable as living in a hotel. In your picture I found the reality of a cell captured with total conviction. The hell of an enclosed space with no way out.

I was very unsure about that picture, to start with. It seemed over-simplified. Everything that goes through your head, everything that I took a lot of trouble painting, had been painted out. But it holds up.

The pictures are both rigidly conceived and apparently left to chance. The motif is carefully selected from hundreds of others, but the transposition into paint seems to go its own way...

... as if against my will, or at least against all that one tends to think.

Do you subject yourself to a photograph?

It's my point of departure.

Did you mean to paint the idea of a cell? I can't imagine that.

Certainly both. I mean, that particular cell and of course also what 'cell' means. But a thing like that has to be automatic, somehow.

You have a sense of something, you see it, it's right or it isn't right? But you can't formulate it.

I notice this in abstract painting, If I read an especially good text that makes it clear to me what I have done, and I try to do the same thing again, the result is nothing but nonsense. If I work methodically, it just doesn't work. A picture has a logic that can't be verbalized until afterwards; it can't be designed. We talk about thinking a thing over, meaning over again, afterwards. I am more and more aware of the importance of the unconscious process that has to take place while one is painting – as if something were working away in secret. You can almost just stand by and wait until something comes. It has been called 'inspiration' or 'an idea from heaven' – but it's far more down-to-earth and far more complicated than that.

Are these pictures something new in your work? You have never before chosen source images with such a social charge, but only neutral ones.

That's true: I have always shied away from so-called political themes, and from anything spectacular.

But this whole cycle is built on the spectacular nature of the events concerned.

And really that is the most natural thing in the world, picking up on exceptional events. It would be absurd to have a taboo against the very thing that concerns us most. Then we'd be left producing nothing but banalities.

You're pointing with a deprecating gesture to your own abstract works. Is it part of the newness of your other pictures that they involve themselves with contemporary history? This is a very risky business. I can't imagine any painter now even trying to paint a theme such as unemployment, and yet it remains one of the central issues of twentieth-century society. Artists in the 1920s still knew how to do it. Now there's no one left who knows how it might be painted.

It is very difficult. What could one paint about unemployment, when other media cover the theme so much better?

In the Overholland catalogue in 1987, you published some journal entries that had an uncompromising tone that I very much like. There was a harshness in them that came as a welcome contrast to the banality of so many arts pages. I'll quote something: '25 November 1982. The whole art world is one vast scene of pettiness, lies, deceit, depravity, wretchedness, stupidity, nonsense, impudence. It is not worth wasting one word on it.' Aren't statements like that rather risky? You are part of this business, after all.

That's why I didn't publish them here but in Holland, where nobody was going to read them.

But publication is always...

... my wish to be unconditionally known. Only I'm a bit of a coward.

A bit of a coward and a bit courageous.

That's the only way that suits me.

Are your pictures intended to provoke?

Well, they certainly weren't meant to be boring!

These pictures always seem to take us as viewers out of ourselves, and at the same time they bring us up short – speculations and all – at the edge of the image. They answer none of the questions that they pose. I've never come across anything like this before: a picture that almost systematically jams its own signal, shoves the viewer away, and forces him to come back for more, only to start the whole thing all over again. Sometimes I have had the feeling that these are brazen oversimplifications. But in the end I feel that the success lies in the simplification.

That's the real point of the work: not to make things simple, but to reach a result, a summing-up. Initially just for oneself.

Do you see a private dimension?

Certainly. You don't take up a theme like this unless it matters to you – that's a premise. What counts is that the pictures then become universal. They are there to show themselves and not me: that would be dreadful. That's why form is so important – and that is difficult nowadays.

But you try.

Yes, because without form communication stops; because without form you have everybody burbling on to themselves, whenever and however, things that no one can understand and – rightly – no one is interested in. The form that we have in the art world today – the universally comprehensible form, that is – is entirely superficial. Openings, dealership, social game-playing: these have become the form of art. They have long since wholly or at least largely taken its place.

I have the feeling that these pictures attach themselves to an explosive historical theme, that they're an expression of your desire to endow pictures with historical weight. But at the same time they seem to me to strike a blow against contemporary art, including – perhaps especially – your own art. An attempt to say: 'Not this way.'

Yes, with all due scepticism, because I'm a part of the art world myself.

I've jotted down a quotation from Francis Bacon: 'I believe that art is recording; I think it's reporting. And I think that in abstract art, as there's no report, there's nothing other than the aesthetic of the painter and his few sensations.'

That sentence suits me very well: 'I think it's reporting.'

What about the rest of the quote?

I don't believe that quite so completely. I think that even those vacuous little abstracts on that wall over there – even those are a form of reporting.

Aren't they just authentic documents of your own inner state?

Being authentic gets you nowhere. Every picture is authentic. The worst pictures are the ones that tell you what's up with the painter and with painting in general. That's what makes them so uninteresting.

When I was preparing for this conversation and looked up your catalogue raisonné, I wondered whether there wasn't a sense of desperation in the sheer quantity of pictures. I get the feeling that there are so many pictures because you needed to search for one picture, the picture, through the many.

I don't believe in the absolute picture. There can only be approximations, experiments and beginnings, over and over again. That's what I wanted to show in the catalogue:[5] not the best pictures but everything, the whole work of approximation, mistakes and all. In my *Atlas* it's even more extreme: a deluge of images that I can control only by organizing them, and no individual images left at all.

Wasn't, for example, Jacques-Louis David's Death of Marat *(1793) more than an approximation?*

Yes, of course, there are some lucky strikes like that. There are a few almost absolute pictures. And that's the hope that keeps you going most of the time...

Have you quoted David? In the three Dead Woman *pictures, I was forcibly reminded of David, and of the space above the person in particular. The expression of dignity that these pictures contain comes through the emptiness above the closed eyes. Your picture, like David's, is elevated by the dark area above the person.*

One has half of art history in one's head, and of course that sort of thing does find its way in, involuntarily – but as to taking something out of a specific picture, that doesn't happen.

Within the cycle, these three pictures seem to me to be extraordinarily successful. How do you see it? Are they all equally successful?

I'm not sure. Perhaps this first version of the *Shot Man* isn't that good. There was an earlier one that went wrong and I had to destroy it. It's hard to say. I'm still too close to it.

The first is more like the police photograph.

That may be why I like the second version. It's calmer.

When I asked about a successful picture, you named one that you're doubtful about. Is there one that makes you say 'That's it, that's how I wanted it'?

The *Dead Woman*, those three pictures, there I agree with you; I wouldn't have any reservations about them. I like the record player. But it seems to me to be a bit unfair, talking about them like this – it's not right.

Yesterday I was watching the visitors to your exhibition. They were constantly trying to find the right viewing point, walking up and down, trying it from every angle, sometimes close up, sometimes standing well back. The viewpoint must be a particularly difficult problem here, in both senses of the word.

That's good. That's what it's about, in every sense...

What is your viewpoint? Making a record?

Partly. And also grief – compassion and grief. Certainly also fear.

Grief at what?

That it is the way it is.

Does the person you're depicting count for anything? Is it clear to you whom you're painting?

You can't really avoid that. As I said, it's only the work, the craft element, that makes it bearable. It was worse when the pictures were hanging here, in these rooms. Having these pictures around one all the time, that was unendurable. Now they're gone.

Is it important to you that the pictures be seen?

Absolutely. That's what they're there for.

What were you trying to do in these pictures?

To make pictures. To picture my own thoughts and feelings. By which I mean that my own motivation and my views about them are entirely unimportant, and ultimately beside the point: there are other professionals whose job it is to come along and talk about these things.

And yet here we are talking, and you are saying something.

Yes, of course, and I certainly don't regard myself as a blinkered specialist. But...

The RAF ought probably to be seen as an attempt to break with the idea of passive complicity, which was so important to our fathers' generation. Fascism only works if there are people who go along with it. I get the feeling that the RAF was trying to say: 'We will never again permit ourselves to be made into the accomplices of historic crimes.' That seems to me to be the starting point. Being informed, as we are, we are all now accomplices. None of us is going to say in the future, 'We didn't know.' That standard excuse of the 1950s is no longer available. We have no excuse any more. We are contemporary observers of all the crimes that are being committed today. We are all callous accomplices. Blackmailed into impotence, we are spectators of political and economic crimes that are made possible only because we connive in our own impotence.

This interests me in a general sense. The callousness, for example. The fact that we have only so much compassion in us; we tend to refuse our compassion whenever we get the chance. This makes sense, in a way; it has to do with survival strategies. But when you realize just how much we do refuse our compassion, how calmly we look on while hundreds of thousands starve or are tortured or killed – we never choke on a single forkful. This is more than avoiding compassion in order to survive: it's almost worse than killing.

And the killing goes on anyway, day after day. We can always push the responsibility off onto other people – but it's really all of us. No other species does this.

Only humanity?

Man kills as no animal kills: he kills himself, as if under a compulsion. You can't hold aloof and say it's other people, they're the criminals. That's no use, it's just self-serving glibness. This kind of thinking is dangerous. Another thing that's absurd is those people who try to make exceptions of themselves and describe themselves as peace-loving. That's just as bad as joining in personally. I'm not talking about the RAF, I'm talking about us.

The RAF began as a resistance movement against the war in Vietnam. It all ended in crimes committed by the RAF, but it all started as a struggle against the crime of war. Now there has been a historic shift. The last ten years have not been so much overshadowed by wars; it's been a decade of historic catastrophes in the production process. Bhopal, Chernobyl, Sandoz. Death tolls like Bhopal used to exist only on battlefields. The situation has got worse and worse.

Ordinary industrial production is becoming a crime against humanity and against nature. However fast the opposition movements grow, impotence grows faster still.

Our state of impotence hasn't changed much – or, to put it another way, it's not only the perils that have grown; the possibilities of doing something about them have grown, too.

With the RAF, did it interest you that here were some people who were saying, 'Thus far and no further'?

Yes, of course. But that's our daily bread, so to speak. What is really wretched is when those who want to change something fail, not just because they are prevented from succeeding, but because the means they use – and yes, that does mean their ideas – are false.

Was your experiment with history a necessary experiment?

It was necessary. I'd continue it straight away, if I could find something that works. Something that has both – that alters the painting and has an importance beyond that. Perhaps the experiment will bear fruit in future.

Is this cycle an experiment in lending weight to your painting?

Certainly. Everyone is always trying to do that. Why we never succeed, I don't know.

With a cycle like this, are you also trying to make life difficult for the art business as a consumer trade?

Impossible. The demand is so great that practically everything is swallowed up.

You can imagine a museum director buying this cycle?

They haven't got any money.

So you wouldn't sell these pictures?

No, for the moment it's out of the question. But if the interest keeps up, I'd be glad to give them to a museum on permanent loan.

Will you insist that the cycle can't be broken up?

Absolutely, even if the pictures go into store. I don't suppose any museum can afford to have fifteen pictures by one painter permanently on show. We shall have to see how the pictures hold up. That's why they are being exhibited, after Krefeld, in Frankfurt, then in Rotterdam and somewhere else after that.

Would you like to influence the public presentation of the pictures?

I would absolutely forbid any spectacle.

Can you imagine the pictures in private galleries?

No, that wouldn't be the right place for them. They can only be shown in museums.

You don't have didactic aims in view?

The pictures are not partisan; they're quite clear about that. They are hard to enlist, to make use of. Grief is not tied to any 'cause'. Nor is compassion.

What is the object of your compassion?

The death that the terrorists had to suffer. They probably did kill themselves, which for me makes it all almost more terrible. Compassion also for the failure; the fact that an illusion of being able to change the world has failed.

There is a laconic evenness in your attitude, which doesn't seem to match the emotive power. Do you wish for an illusion? Is there a wish in you for an illusion?

That wish is surely born with us.

The wish not to have to surrender to the bald fact of 'that's the way it is'? Might illusions be just as necessary as repressions?

Possibly. I don't know: maybe my hatred of ideology is mistaken, maybe I'm confusing one thing with another. Because when I say I believe it'll be fine weather tomorrow, that too has something to do with belief and illusion.

All the same, I consider belief of every kind, from astrology to every elevated religion and all great ideologies, to be superfluous and mortally dangerous. We no longer need such things. We ought to work out different strategies against misery and injustice, war and catastrophes.

Is there hope in your art? The abstract paintings formulated something like a faith in the making of beauty. In the photo-paintings it's the hope of being able to pass judgment on one's own period, or to compress one's period into a picture.

Or at least, by reporting, to help to enlighten people. To see how it is.

One entry in your journal reads like this: 'Art has always been basically about agony, desperation and helplessness... We often neglect this side of things by concentrating aesthetically on the formal side in isolation.' I'd go along with that. Except that it's a totally anachronistic position: if I look around in contemporary art, this statement is just not true. Art is more social game-playing than ever. A kind of entertainment with a phoney status element, which is often primarily about an elitist distancing of oneself from trivial amusements.

All of that is true.

A whole tribe of artists are living and working for the total opposite of your assertion. They act according to the motto: 'Profundity is out, we're glad to be superficial, and we even get paid for it.'

Walter Grasskamp once wrote that your painting was 'visual sadism': a deliberately provocative formulation, but I could immediately see why it was apt. I myself have never been able just to relax in front of your colour abstractions, as one might with pictures by Matisse, say. There is a tormenting streak in the beauty.

That may well be, but it has nothing to do with sadism.

It's not an insult to you if I say that I have never been able to find those abstract pictures just beautiful?

Far from it.

Have you ever felt the need to justify yourself for having painted the present cycle?

Not while I was painting the pictures. That came later. Here and now, for instance.

Could you have painted these pictures ten years ago?

No.

Does an artist have to be successful in order to get away with painting this subject?

I don't believe so.

Just a great painter?

A great painter – once I used to think I ought to paint like the 'great masters', and of course I couldn't. I felt it to be a terrible lack in me: I thought I basically wasn't a painter at all but a fraud, just pretending to be one. It was a long time before I realized that what I do – the desperate experimentation, all the difficulties – is exactly what they all do. That's the normal nature of the job. That's painting.

It strikes me as grotesque, of course, to hear one of the most successful German painters saying he isn't a painter at all.

OK, by now I don't mind calling myself a painter. There's no risk in that.

Was this cycle a risk, as far as you were concerned?

Certainly. But not because of possible objections from the Left or from the Right. By definition, there's always a risk – the risk of ending up with bad pictures.

Perhaps this is cynical, but after a certain degree of success there is no longer such a thing as failure. As if that were the price of success.

In market terms, that's true. By now the market would take any rubbish I might turn out. But what counts for me is something else, and so – self-criticism apart – there are still a few people whose judgment still means something. And so, if they say, 'Oh, that looks bad – he's run out of steam – you can forget him...'

Does this cycle represent a progression within your work?

Well, I don't have the feeling that I've run out of steam. I realize that these pictures set a new standard, set a challenge to me. I may be deceiving myself. It's all still too fresh. But one thing I have realized; it's hard for me to go on painting.

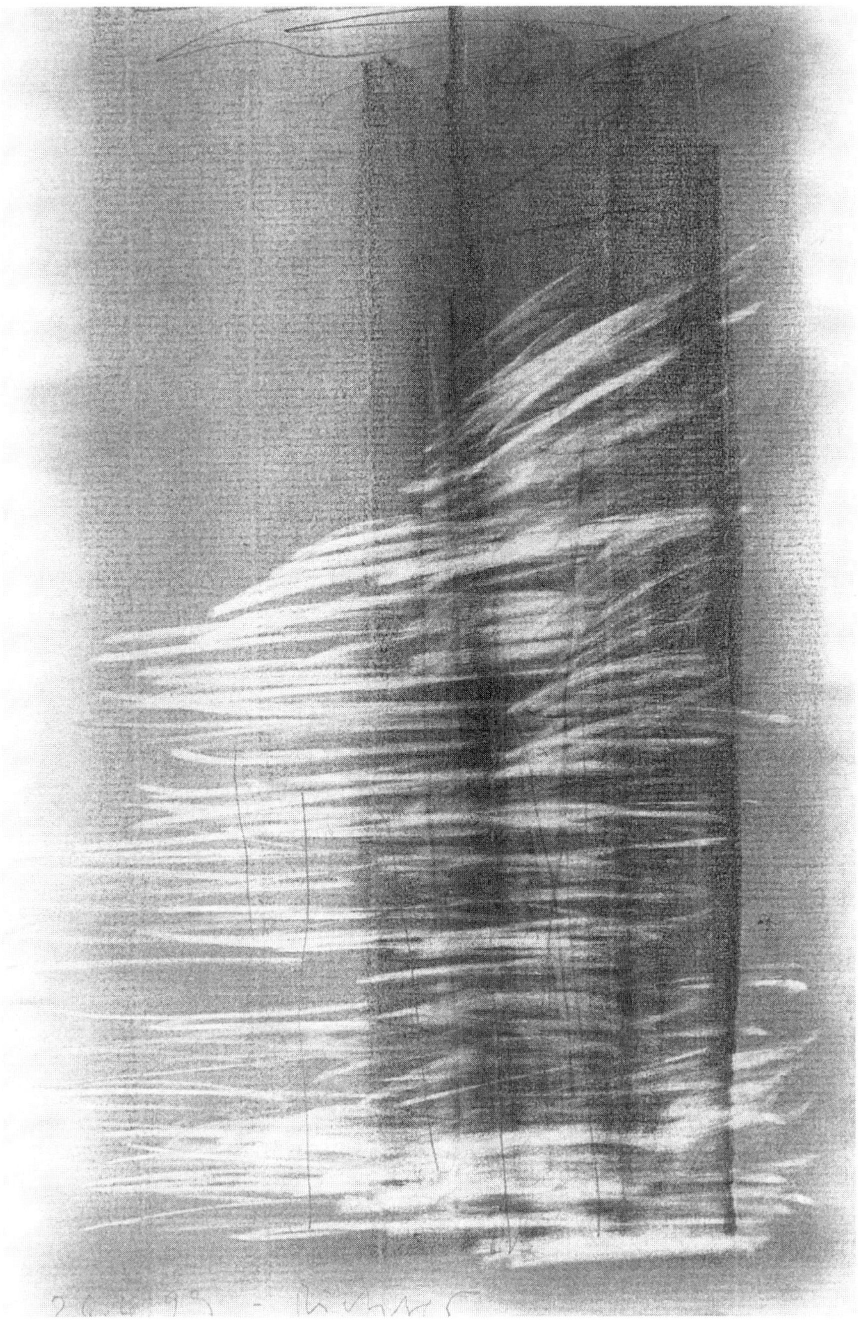

Drawing, 1999

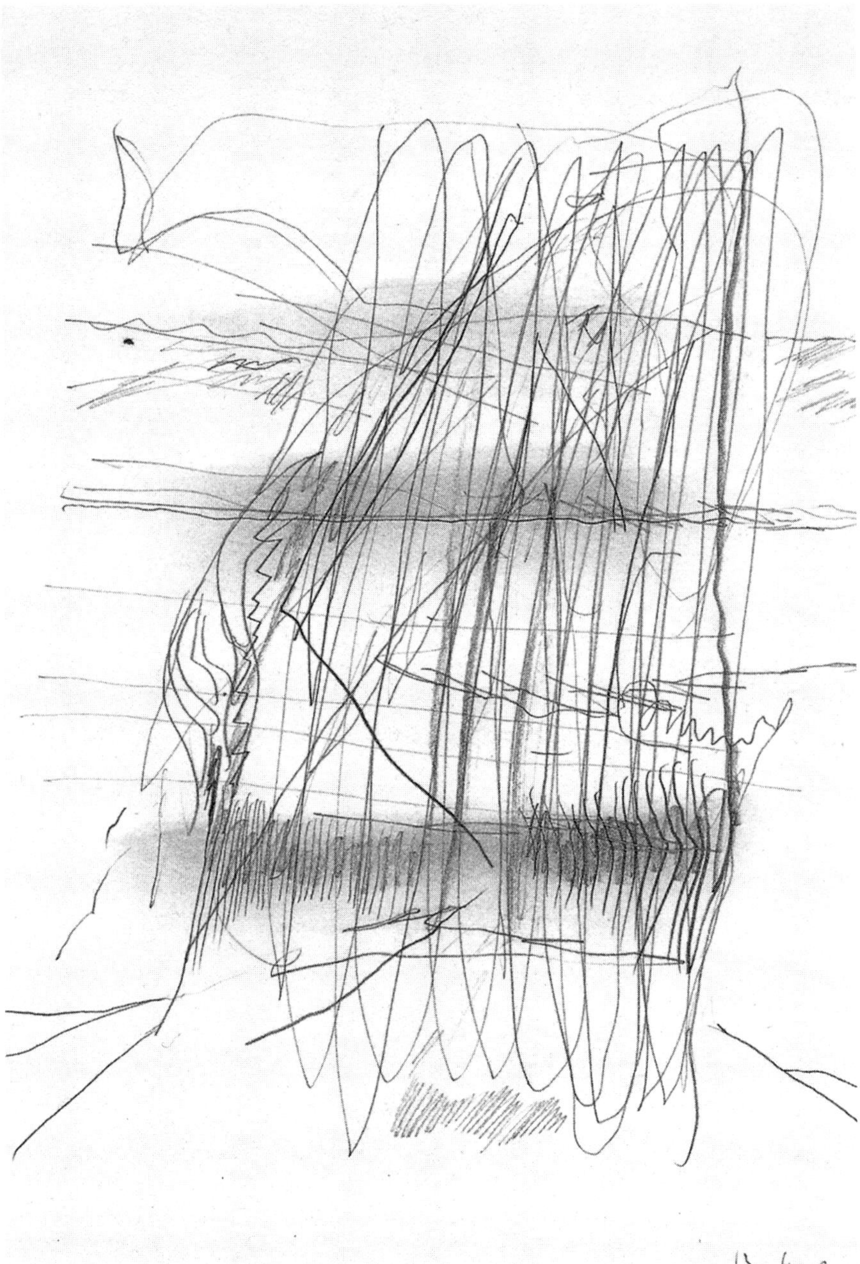

Drawing, 1998

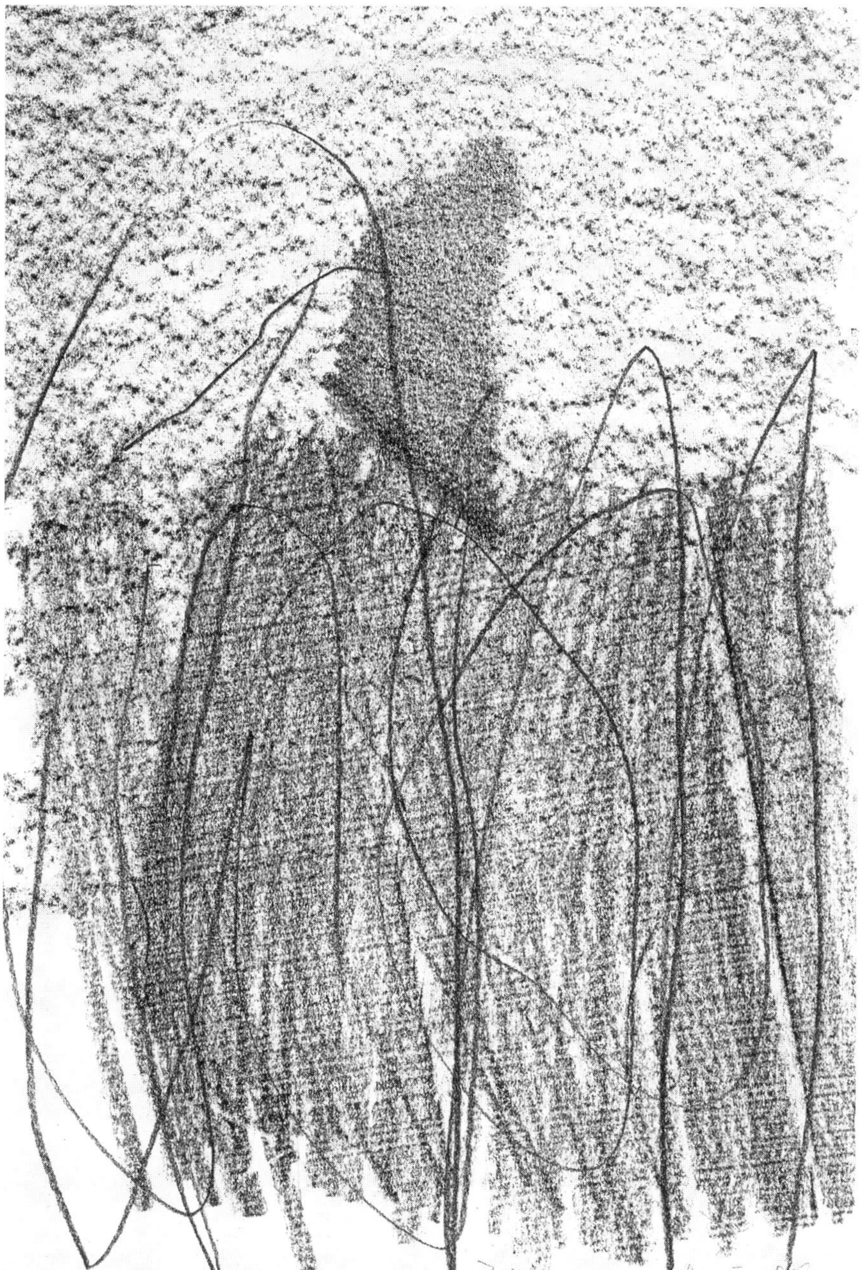

Drawing, 1988

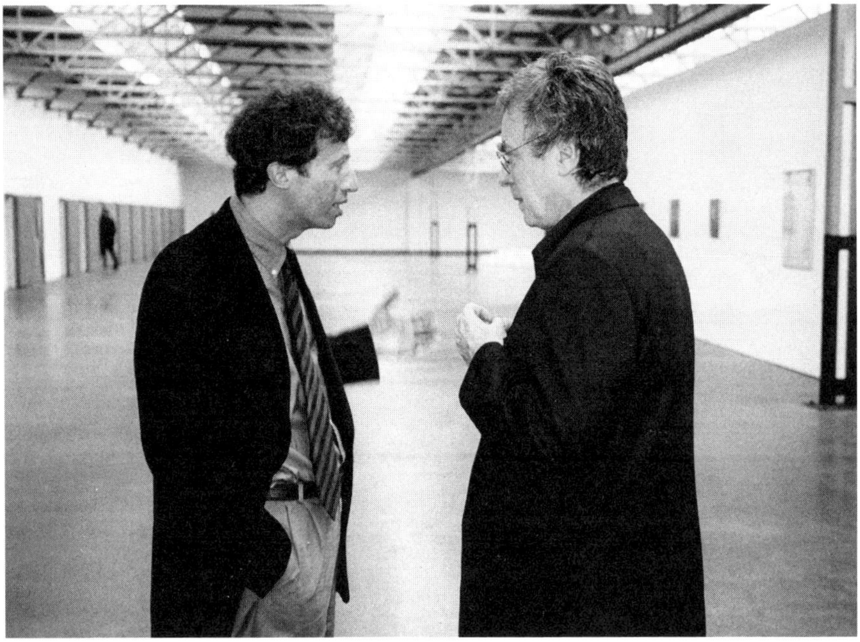

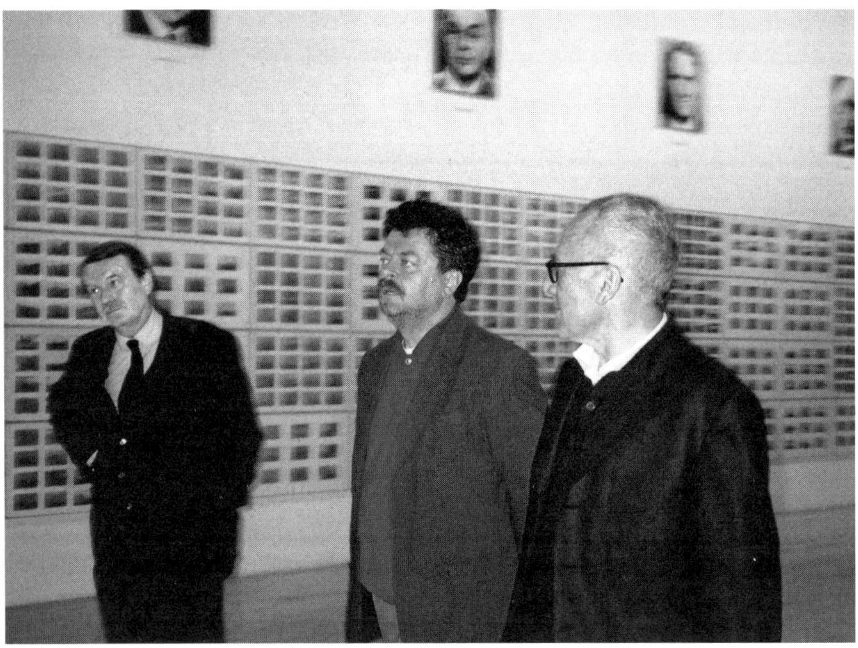

Dieter Schwarz and Benjamin Buchloh, De Pont, Tilburg, 1999
Fred Jahn, Helmut Friedel and Gerhard Richter, Kunstbau, Lenbachhaus, Munich, 1998

Letter to Walter Grasskamp on the subject of *18 October 1977*, 17 October 1989

Re: 'Gerhard Richter: *18 October 1977*'
Jahresring 36

Dear Mr Grasskamp,

Your article, referred to above, prompts me to make several comments:

I find even the very first paragraph crudely tendentious, since I cannot imagine that you are so foolish and blind as to be able to identify 'a catalogue of the most varied styles of painting, [...] which defies any possible structural sense' – nor to use in seriousness an argument against me such as that 'the paintings are comprised of over a thousand disparate pieces', or that 'the arbitrariness of the motifs' eliminates the possibility of their being 'memorable'. What is this nonsense?

And then there's your tangent on Arnulf Rainer:[1] instead of arguing empirically on why you dislike his *Hiroshima Series*, you denounce the painter and insinuate that his motivations were disingenuous. This is just as unfair as the subsequent 'parallel' you construct with my 'clever attempt, in the face of the amnesty debate, [...] to ward off the looming predictability of [my] artistic strategies'. You should be aware that in early 1988 there was no amnesty debate, and, even if there had been, certainly no such allegations can be derived from it. What you pull out of your sleeve there is just as tenuous as your own presumed prophetic talent to anticipate future strategies.

I could just dismiss all of this as helpless rubbish, but the painful thing about it is that you entangle your thinking in strategic categories, that you accuse me of your own purely tactical political sense, and in doing so you undermine any attempt I could make to clarify to you my actual motivations. Following this train of thought it's only natural that you come to the determination that the death of the RAF [Red Army Faction] members I was interested in can only be seen as the 'expression of a political – and therefore quite abstract – failure'. It seems apparent, though, there is something 'quite abstract' about you, particularly when I see now your discomfort with 'covert radicalism'. I must tell you that I've never strived for radicalism (something I've stated publicly on numerous occasions), because as a matter of fact I have other concerns. In the same way, the question of whether I am making history paintings or not could hardly be less important to me.

However, I consider not quite so unimportant your false statement that the paintings allow the viewer 'to read into them anything he wants' – because even if you saw the paintings as nothing more than a catalogue of reproductions, surely you would have imagined a huge list of everything that was not visible in them.

And then at the same time you do find a way to claim something is lacking; for example, in the case of Hanns Martin Schleyer: 'the photos of his disintegration as a hostage', and 'the ghostly shots of the crime scene with the corpse of his driver and of the bodyguards'. Sure, that sounds really striking, but it is a patently malicious misrepresentation of the theme of my work, which you go on to accuse of making it 'seem as if the government had driven' the terrorists 'to their death'. Don't even you yourself think that's a bit mean?

And at the end of all this you are 'taken aback'. Suspicion arises in you because certain photos of individuals were not allowed to be reproduced (for the protection of family members), and because I did not wish to have the paintings sold on the art market.

I can only view these suspicions as abject and cynical; and, in comparison, all your other misrepresentations become irrelevant – even the hair-raising nonsense that I paint solely 'pictures of pictures', and never of reality. This is nothing more than appalling high-school-level art theory.

Perhaps you'll notice that in taking issue here, if ever so briefly, I've actually grappled with your article; while for your part, instead of criticizing the paintings, you merely speculated about motivations and imputed strategies, thus denouncing the work.

With kind regards,

Gerhard Richter

Notes, 1990

12 September 1990. Accept that I can plan nothing.

Any thoughts on my part about the 'construction' of a picture are false, and if the execution works, this is only because I partly destroy it, or because it works in spite of everything – by not detracting and by not looking the way I planned.

I often find this intolerable and even impossible to accept, because, as a thinking, planning human being, it humiliates me to find out that I am so powerless. It casts doubt on my competence and constructive ability. My only consolation is to tell myself that I did actually make the pictures – even though they are a law unto themselves, even though they treat me any way they like and somehow just take shape. Because it's still up to me to determine the point at which they are finished (picture-making consists of a multitude of Yes/No decisions, with a Yes to end it all). If I look at it that way, the whole thing starts to seem quite natural again – or rather nature-like, alive – and the same thing applies to the comparison on the social level.

30 May 1990. It seems to me that the invention of the readymade was the invention of reality. It was the crucial discovery that what counts is reality, not any world-view whatever. Since then, painting has never represented reality; it has *been* reality (creating itself). And sooner or later the value of this reality will have to be denied, in order (as usual) to set up pictures of a better world.

5 May 1990. What sort of an occupation is this, in which you can afford to be tired, or not in the mood – in which you can be off form for days or weeks on end and not do a thing?

2 October 1990. Baselitz exhibition.[1] He presents painting as unswerving persistence, as a path without compromises, without controversy, without a Utopia, without a dream: simply being (breathing without meaning – a metaphor for the incomprehensibility of Being, which always 'only' is, brutal though it may be – which breathes, and nothing more).

The pictures are sometimes good (and in any case beyond comparison with anything else contemporary) – and occasionally inane: which is when he compromises this pure act of painting by making sentimental allusions (the *Brücke* picture[2]).

16 August 1990. Since the Rotterdam exhibition [October 1989], painting has become more laborious. At the end of December, I cancelled the exhibitions planned for this year at d'Offay and Durand-Dessert, so as to have a whole year to 'evolve' something without commitments. Since then there have been small and medium-sized pictures – very few big ones – nothing special, on the whole. Alongside this, the work for the Hypo-Bank design,[3] not very exciting either. A kind of aimless drifting. About twelve unfinished pictures in the studio at the moment: almost perversely wrong or nonsensical in the way they're laid out, without a governing idea, in the manner of a disoriented gambler who stakes a vast amount on a random card. The worst thing is that these pictures with their wantonly stupid design do have a certain quality or reality that calls for a continuation to match, but this is not really feasible. Start off by destroying them.

4 September 1990. The 'Dictatorship of the Proletariat' has long since become reality – especially here in the Western democracies, where it appears in its most bearable form. Mass society is a better name for it, because the masses have no class enemy left, and dictatorship has transformed itself into pressure of circumstances. By their presence and by their nature, the masses shape both circumstances and events in a quasi-natural way, relatively unplanned, often chaotic and potentially catastrophic. Hierarchic systems, Socialism included, are being replaced by a constantly self-reorganizing 'Aliveness' – without a plan, without an ideology, without any of those models and images (which never work anyway) of the world as it is or should be.

24 October 1990. It doesn't seem functional that we dwindle away and end our lives, just when we have learned so much. And then the next generation has to spend decades slaving to regain the same standard of experience that has been reached long before. I know that's rubbish.

The much-maligned 'art scene' of the present day is perfectly harmless and even pleasant, if you don't judge it in terms of false expectations. It has nothing to do with those traditional values that we hold high (or that hold us high). It has virtually nothing whatever to do with art. That's why the 'art scene' is neither base, cynical nor mindless: it is a scene of brief blossoming and busy growth, just one variation on the never-ending round of social game-playing that satisfies our need for communication, alongside such others as sport, fashion, stamp-collecting and cat-breeding. Art takes shape in spite of it all, rarely and always unexpectedly; art is never feasible.

Letter to Werner Schmidt, 1990

Cologne, 18 July 1990

Dear Dr Schmidt,

Many thanks for your letter asking for a few words from me – a request that is not very easy to comply with.

As to the circumstances of my departure, I can offer nothing but commonplaces – for example, that art requires freedom in order to develop, and that in dictatorships there is no art, not even bad art. Not only is this proved by the vast quantities of vapid art that is permitted to be made in the West: it has to do with an intrinsic quality in art, which makes it dependent – certainly more so than literature or music – on a specific climate. And when it comes to so-called modern art, with its declared autonomy (no longer serving a purpose and depicting something, but creating itself as a reality in its own right), then all tutelage is lethal.

Of course, reflections of this kind were not the reason why I left: my reasons were the same simple-minded ones as with all the other 'absconders from the Republic': to get away from the institutionalized lie, the suffocating tutelage. It's all a long time ago, for me, and my GDR citizenship has long been non-existent (if it was ever real to me at all).

'Citizenship Revoked': I don't really know what to say.

It may well not be a good exhibition; it may well bring together works which have little to do with each other, which make an odd mixture, which will lead to a lot of misunderstanding. But perhaps these very shortcomings, allied to a certain modesty, will be an asset in themselves.

Its other definite asset is that it is being done at all, and that a start is being made with the lengthy and wearisome process of 'coming together'. I therefore welcome this exhibition, no matter (almost no matter) what is shown in it.

I wish you the very best of luck with it, and remain

Yours sincerely, Gerhard Richter

Letter to the editor, F.A.Z. [*Frankfurter Allgemeine Zeitung*], 24 July 1990

'Locked Out'

The fact that Peter Ludwig's 'gifts' have become a nuisance, more or less, does not make his mood reflective; instead it inspires his obstinacy (see AP report, F.A.Z. of 10 July). It seems that his understanding of art is dissipating at the same pace as his power-hungry self-absorption grows. Ludwig's sentimental comments about art from East Germany are so idiotic that the colonialist attitude they contain is virtually nullified. Perhaps we should 'lock out' for a while this mixture of arrogance and bourgeois conformism.

Gerhard Richter, painter
Cologne

Interview with Sabine Schütz, 1990

A year or so ago, you caused a stir with your cycle 18 October 1977. *This group of fifteen pictures, painted in your earlier technique of blurred copies of black-and-white photographs, deals with the deaths of the RAF [Red Army Faction] terrorists in Stammheim prison. It sparked a heated and emotional debate, which went far beyond the purely artistic issues. In these works, was your concern a directly political one?*

Not directly political, and least of all in the sense of political painting, which everyone has always assumed to be left-wing – an art that serves exclusively to criticize so-called bourgeois-capitalist society. That was not my concern.

But the theme was not only highly explosive but also an explicitly left-wing one...

... which can now be regarded as buried and done with...

Exactly, and it's already history. One might ask why you came out with these pictures in 1989 and not ten years earlier.

The delay was probably necessary. But I can't precisely explain my motives for doing a thing at one time rather than another. Such things never go according to plan; it's an unconscious process. It does seem important now that, with the collapse of the Socialist system, these pictures are taking on a different and more general component, which they didn't have quite so obviously before. On the other hand, I'm wary of talking about the concerns or the messages of the paintings. I don't want to circumscribe them by imposing an interpretation.

But do you now see the terrorists purely as the victims of a false idea, which was therefore doomed to fail?

Certainly, as far as that goes. But I also feel a certain sympathy for those people, and for their desperate desire for change. I can very well understand someone finding this world, as it is, unacceptable. And they were part of a corrective – one that we shall miss in the future. We shall find another, as well as different critical approaches: less sentimental or superstitious, more realistic – and therefore more effective, I hope.

The cycle has been described as a revival of a genre largely ignored by modern and contemporary art, namely history painting. Would you agree with that?

It doesn't interest me that much. Even when I was working on the paintings, when it occurred to me that they might be regarded as history painting, and thus as something reactionary, it didn't bother me. That's more a problem for the theorists.

In a note in your journal, you say that no one can really paint the way you do, without a theme. How about this cycle? Did it have a theme?

Yes, it did. But that gloomy note of mine had more to do with the abstract pictures, and beyond that with a generalized impotence and helplessness, which can of course be turned into a theme in its own right. All the same, sometimes you have enough motivation to make all this irrelevant – and then you just paint.

When you start a painting, do you always know what you want to paint? Can it be said that you are a conceptual artist?

No, I'm not. I never know either what to paint or what the picture is supposed to look like. With the *October* cycle, as always, I had no idea what sort of pictures were going to come out of it. I had a vast assortment of photographs, and what I actually had in mind was something quite different. It was meant to be far more comprehensive, far more concerned with the subjects' lives. But then I ended up with this tiny selection: nine motifs, and a strong concentration on death – almost in spite of my intentions.

One wouldn't have expected a theme so heavy with content, from an artist who once – 25 years ago – painted a roll of toilet paper. The record player is a banal object in itself. But your relation to the object does seem to have changed markedly in the intervening time.

No, not markedly. A toilet roll is not exactly a cheerful subject either. Nor is it true that I'm now old enough to restrict myself to sad subjects. But the record-player picture is a highly charged image, of course, because the viewer knows that it's Andreas Baader's record player, that the weapon that killed him was concealed inside it, and so on. That doesn't make it a better picture, but it does get more attention, because more of a narrative can be tied to it.

Behind the fact that it used to be, say, a toilet roll or a clothes-dryer, and now it's a record player with a highly specific political significance, there clearly lies a decisive change of consciousness.

Naturally. I was younger then, and part of a very different zeitgeist, and from that point of view there might be a lot more difference between the pictures than there is. What strikes me now is the similarity – the fact that not all that much has changed. It's the same apparent indifference and absence of message. The toilet roll or the clothes-dryer, just like the record player, is a kind of 'poor person's art' – like many of the other prosaic, banal motifs.

The motif takes on a very different value in different pictures. The motif in the 18 October 1977 *series, for instance, is very different in kind from the motif in most of your earlier works. Could it be said that each group of works maintains its own specific relationship to the object and to reality?*

That must be so, but all the different pictures at different times do have one consistent foundation – and that's me, my attitude and my intention, which may express itself in different ways but never essentially changes. The variety is superficial. My own statements about my lack of style and lack of opinion were largely polemical gestures against contemporary trends that I disliked – or else they were self-protective statements, designed to create a climate in which I could paint what I wanted.

But you have also said that it doesn't necessarily matter what one paints. And by painting the clothes-dryer or the stag or the housewife you show that it really doesn't.

But then you can also see all of that as a coherent theme – and then it does matter. All these themes – the clothes-dryer, the family on the sofa, the stag – are also highly selective.

Wasn't there a touch of irony as well?

I never think that way. If I ever did admit to any irony, I did so for the sake of a quiet life. Because at some point, of course, I did care about the motifs. I didn't find the clothes-dryer ironic; there was something tragic about it, because it represented life in low-cost housing with nowhere to hang the washing. It was my own clothes-dryer, which I rediscovered in a newspaper – objectivized, as it were. Or the families – they were often people I knew. And if I didn't know them, at least they had something in common with the families and lives that I did know.

Didn't it have something to do with middle-class stuffiness?

No doubt. But what does that mean? It's not a concept that means much to me; it strikes me as arrogant.

What was it about the motif of the stag, for instance, that interested you? No one can really paint a stag these days without thinking of the word 'belling' – kitsch, in other words.

It's not the stag's fault if he's been badly painted – 'Belling Stag' over the sofa. For us Germans, in particular, relating to forests as strongly as we do, the stag does of course have a symbolic quality. I wanted to be a forester when I was young, and I was really excited when I found a real stag in the forest and took a photograph. Later I painted him, and the painting was a bit less romantic than my youthful photograph.

Again, the wedding-cake castle of Neuschwanstein also irresistibly summons up kitsch associations.

The real-life castle is a hideous monstrosity. But it does also have this other, seductive side to it, that of the beautiful fairytale, the dream of sublimity, bliss, happiness – and that's the dangerous part; that's why it's a very special case of kitsch.

I see the bomber pictures as an anti-war statement...

... which they aren't – at all. Pictures like that don't do anything to combat war. They only show one tiny aspect of the subject of war – maybe only my own childish feelings of fear and fascination with war and with weapons of that kind.

Is it possible to be fascinated by the aesthetic effect of a weapon? Isn't it always a feeling of terror, dread?

It's a mixed feeling, and it's no good suppressing the fascination.

Many years ago you described painting as 'a moral action'. What did you mean by that?

That was an inept attempt on my part to convey that it's really not all about painting beautiful pictures. It was a statement of the significance of art, and of the enormous importance that I attached to it; and the untold quantities of art that are being made and consumed at the moment do at least reveal a wholly irrational demand for art, an almost religious longing. And if art were ever in a position to satisfy this longing utterly, then that would be a great gain. Art would be something like 'faith pure and simple', which would protect us from flying off after false faiths, religions and ideologies.

You constantly stress your anti-ideological position. What do you mean by ideology?

One contemporary example is the ideology of Socialism in the GDR. People believe in such a thing against all reason – and make themselves and other people unhappy. It's a kind of psychological illness, and apparently an incurable one. It would be a lot better if we could know ourselves, see what we're really like, what we're capable of, why we kill, why we are good – and above all what is feasible. Instead of that, we 'believe'. That is a luxury we can no longer afford, on this endangered globe.

But those who are in the know, and who still proclaim these messages of salvation – aren't they perfectly well aware that they're lying?

No, certainly not. Ideology possesses people's brains so totally that there's no way left of seeing facts objectively. And the more the facts belie the ideology, the more implacably it asserts control. It's only on the behavioural level – unconsciously and instinctively – that people can sometimes escape from it. So, when Honecker wears cashmere, he's being completely natural. Then he forgets his faith, or at least bends it a little bit.

So you'd like to abolish faith?

Can't be done. We need it to survive. It motivates us; nothing would get done without it. Faith is an indispensable human quality. When I say, 'I believe that tomorrow will be Tuesday', that is an act of faith, because this Tuesday exists only in our minds. And if I then say that it will be fine weather tomorrow, that shows faith from the dangerous side, because then it gets mistaken for certainty and acted on. Which makes it seem all the worse if it then turns out cold and wet.

Intellectuals are far more endangered than 'ordinary' people or artists. They're intelligent, very good at handling words and therefore brilliant at constructing theories, and they share in the overwhelming power of words. Almost everything is prompted, forbidden or authorized by words; explained, transfigured or falsified by words. So we ought to be sceptical and not forget that there's another, highly important kind of experience. Whatever we experience non-verbally – by sight, touch, hearing or whatever – gives us a certainty or a knowledge that can lead to better actions and decisions than any theory.

A theory can also evolve empirically.

Yes, of course, it evolves out of experience and is corrected, confirmed or falsified by experience. The problem is, however, that a theory can be so logical in its own terms, so complicated and intricate – almost as complex as life – that you're compelled to go along with it because it is so convincing or so beautiful.

There is a film about your work,[1] *with the title 'My Pictures Are Cleverer than I Am'. Why is that?*

They have to be cleverer than I am. I have to be unable to follow quite all the way; they have to be something that I no longer completely understand. So long as I can grasp them theoretically, it's boring.

Quite early on, you were described as 'inconsistent', because you were always swapping levels, both in your subject matter and, even more, in your style. You have described yourself as 'uncertain'. Or is some of it about proving to yourself and to others that you can do anything?

No, it isn't that. Painting a copy of a photograph is something that can be learned. And there are so many conceivable kinds of artistic statement that I haven't made – I'm relatively limited – a bit one-sided, in fact. Never anything but oil painting.

Inconsistency is simply a consequence of uncertainty, which I certainly do tend to suffer from – but then I also regard it as inevitable and necessary.

So perhaps uncertainty is the overriding theme?

Maybe. At all events, uncertainty is part of me; it's a basic premise of my work. After all, we have no objective justification for feeling certain about anything. Certainty is for fools, or liars.

And the pictures tell no lies?

No, they make no statement at all, so they can't fool us. They tell no more lies than a tree does – though they're often less interesting.

Stylistic changes, stylistic upheavals and (perhaps) irony: all these are phenomena that have been called – ever since the word was coined – 'postmodern'. Do you give any thought to this? Do you regard yourself as a pioneer postmodernist?

I don't think so. It's never interested me much. But in a sense you could call me that – because I was never aware of belonging to the avant-garde, and that was never part of my intention. Avant-garde: that was usually too dogmatic and too aggressive for me.

In 1976 you began to paint abstract pictures, because you wanted something that you couldn't visualize in advance. In doing so, you invented a method that was absolutely new to you. Was that an experiment of some kind?

Yes. It began in 1976, with small abstract paintings that allowed me to do what I had never let myself do: put something down at random. And then, of course, I realized that it never can be random. It was all a way of opening a door for me. If I don't know what's coming – that is, if I have no hard-and-fast image, as I have with a photographic original – then arbitrary choice and chance play an important part.

How do you manage to direct chance in such a way that a highly specific picture with a specific statement comes out of it – because that is your stated intention, isn't it?

No, I don't have a specific picture in my mind's eye. I want to end up with a picture that I haven't planned. This method of arbitrary choice, chance, inspiration and destruction may produce a specific type of picture, but it never produces a predetermined picture. Each picture has to evolve out of a painterly or visual logic: it has to emerge as if inevitably. And by not planning the outcome, I hope to achieve the same coherence and objectivity that a random slice of nature (or a readymade) always possesses. Of course, this is also a method of bringing in unconscious processes, as far as possible. I just want to get something more interesting out of it than those things that I can think out for myself.

Jürgen Harten has written that your pictures are 'the painting of painting': something like a painted commentary on painting.

No, that's not right. When I listen to Bach, I can equally well say that that's music about music, because it's based on a tradition, because it's internally coherent: every note relates to another. But in the end that would mean that it means nothing and says nothing. A game of chess. What good would that be to anyone?

For many artists, the act of painting, the process, is the primary element in their work...

What counts is always the seeing. The physical act can't be avoided, and certainly it is sometimes necessary to paint with the whole body – but all in the cause. And these 'Actionists' – you only have to look at what comes out of that.

In a catalogue published twenty years ago by the Kunstverein in Aachen, Klaus Honnef wrote that you were dedicated to 'bonne peinture'. *What is the importance of 'painting', in that sense, in your pictures?*

Early on, at the Academy, I would have loved to paint like the artists I admired at that time: Manet, Cézanne or Velázquez. But I couldn't. And later on I realized that it's a good thing I can't, because that's beside the point. I'm sure that's what he meant by '*bonne peinture*'. I can't even remember what it is – presumably something like pure painting.

A painting that is exclusively concerned with itself and its own premises – and that's not what you're after?

In the first place, the basis is an intention – that of picturing the world. And painting is always only a means to this end (which is why you can't ever say that a bad picture is well painted). Nevertheless, painting and the means of painting are of important elementary facts. You can see this in a number of well-intentioned paintings, with lofty aspirations as to content, which remain absolutely inedible. This edible quality has nothing to do with self-indulgence; it's utterly basic, existential.

Has edibility got anything to do with materials and brushwork – technique, in fact?

It has more to do with seeing, I think. The rest is manual; it's no problem. Anything can be painted. It's more difficult to see whether what one is doing is any good or not. But that's the only thing that counts. As Duchamp showed, it has nothing to do with craftsmanship. What counts isn't being able to do a thing; it's seeing what it is. Seeing is the decisive act, and ultimately it places the maker and the viewer on the same level.

Many of your pictures have a different medium, photography, as an intermediary ...

... which isn't a different medium at all. It's fundamentally the same. Of course, a long time ago, I thought a picture was a picture only if it was painted. Later on I found to my great surprise that I could see a photograph as a picture – and in my enthusiasm I often saw it as the better picture of the two. It functions in the same way: it shows the appearance of something that is not itself – and it does it much faster and more accurately. That certainly influenced my way of seeing, and also my attitude to fabrication: for instance, the fact that it doesn't matter at all *who* took the photograph.

In the black-and-white photo-paintings, in particular, there is a strong emphasis on the fact that these are photographic; that they're unequivocally paintings from photographs.

I meant the pictures to have this likeness to photography – if only for the sake of the credibility that photographs have, especially black-and-white ones. There's something documentary about them. More than any other kind of depiction, you believe in them.

Isn't that a false faith?

It can be, of course. The only true reality is always the reality that we see and experience directly.

Comments on some works, 1991

Table (1), 1962

The photo for *Table* came, I think, from an Italian design magazine called *Domus*. I painted it, but was dissatisfied with the result and pasted parts of it over with newspaper. One can still see by the imprint where the newspaper was stuck to the freshly painted canvas. I was dissatisfied because there was too much paint on the canvas and became less happy with it, so I overpainted it. Then suddenly it acquired a quality which appealed to me and I felt it should be left that way, without knowing why. I destroyed or overpainted many pictures during this time. This became the first painting in my worklist; I wanted to make a new start after my work in East Germany, but also after the many pictures I had painted in the West, among which were a number of photo-paintings. I wanted to draw a line, indicating that these paintings were in the past, and so set *Table* at the top of my worklist. My earlier photo-paintings were not taken from magazines like *Domus*. There is an illustration of an early one, *Firing Squad*,[1] in one of my catalogues, which contains a partially obscured SS man. It is the sort of image that I used later on when I contrasted pornographic photographs with images from the concentration camps. I had known these pictures for a long time – I had probably come across them when I was twenty. Below the shooting scene are rows of identically painted faces along the underside of the canvas. It was very fashionable at the time to make this sort of image with its links to Pop Art. Without too much reflection, I can say that these two things, love and death – sex and crime – are two of the things that touch us most.

XL 513 (20-1), 1964

I find this image very brutal, rather like a poster. The angle of the aeroplane flying swiftly past was an image I found very interesting and something not to be found in art history, with the exception, perhaps, of Lichtenstein. There is a contrast between this picture and my other paintings of military aeroplanes. The *Stukas* *(18-1)* picture is much more decorative, while the statement in this work is that this is purely a machine of destruction. The decorative margins, or edges, in the *Stuka* picture, transform the gruesome quality of the image into something rather cute.

Terese Andeszka (23), 1964

A student researching into my work[2] has actually traced the newspapers and magazines where I found these images and has found out that many of them illustrate a collection of gruesome stories, murders and suicides which contrast with the images used. There is a contrast between the message carried by the text and that suppressed by the illustration.

Woman with Umbrella (29), 1964

It was not a sudden break from my earlier work, when I began introducing colour or painting from colour photographs. Adding colour to this work was one attempt to get more out of the picture and to add more to the painting. I tried this with several other paintings at the time – adding colour glazes to works such as the *Red Bathers*, the green *Diana* painting and *XL 513*. With this painting, I gave it a large margin: Warhol's paintings treated the image in a way that you could imagine the image continuing indefinitely either side of the canvas. With my picture the large printed margin separates the image within the painting from surrounding reality. I gave it a deliberately anonymous, neutral title, because I did not want people simply to look at it and instantly recognize Jackie Kennedy. I was very apprehensive about that sort of reaction. With a title like *Woman with Umbrella*, it doesn't reveal anything or tell any particular story. Only later, did I not mind it so much if the people were recognized. With my portrait of Elizabeth II,[3] it does not matter that she is recognized, as the title already acknowledges this. It focuses on the image of her in the tabloid press. With *Woman with Umbrella*, I was very moved by her fate expressed through gesture. It was not in any way an ironic response to what happened, or meant to be funny in the way that *Elizabeth II* was. There was another painting where I wanted particularly to conceal the identity of the depicted. It was a picture of Brigitte Bardot and her mother and I had to find a way of calling the painting *Mother and Daughter*. I wanted on no account that the identity of the pair be recognized – although now I do not care less. It was not the personality of the people that I was looking for, more a case of opening the newspaper and magazines and seeing a photograph that appealed to me as a photograph. Those were the only photos to which one gained access. Only seldom could one find private images from magazines like *Quick* and *Stern*. In those days people looked down their noses at those magazines. I used them because they published such very beautiful photographs. I did not use photos in the East, but later I was not getting anywhere and then came their use in Fluxus and Pop Art. It was the Nouveaux Réalistes who were the first to introduce reality in that form. After that I started working in a very small way, affixing shells – or a pistol – then using photos.

Administrative Building (39), 1964

This is a very banal object. Looking back on it now, it does remind you in a certain way of the type of buildings in the German Democratic Republic put up by the Party.

Great Sphinx of Giza (46), 1964

This is the sort of image well known from art history, but at the time I was not conscious of the fact that it was a grave. I was made aware of the intimate connection with death rather later on. I think it is justified to interpret this connection with death in a psychoanalytical way when looking back to this image, because it shows that I was really interested in these things at the time.

Flemish Crown (77), 1965

It looks like something from a picture by Frans Hals. In fact, it was a very cheap chandelier, the sort you could buy in department stores. I actually photographed it at my father-in-law's home and made the painting from my photograph. Most of the photo-paintings were based on found photographs, but I always took photographs myself and used them for pictures.

Kitchen Chair (97), 1965

This was a chair I owned and photographed. It was part of my search for banal objects – the chair itself, the table, the toilet roll. Although the great majority of the photo-paintings are based on photos which came from outside sources, this was one I took myself. I had always taken photographs and used several for pictures during the 1960s, although I began using my own much more in the late '60s. I mainly photographed objects, rarely taking portrait shots. The portraits I painted at this time were based on passport photographs, which I received and then turned into paintings. I began painting pictures of people with the painting *Ema (Nude Descending a Staircase)*. The photographs I used mainly came from illustrated magazines and that was the simple reason why most of the pictures were black and white.

Townscape M2 (170-2), 1968

This originally was part of a larger picture, which I cut up and made into several smaller pictures. It was an attempt to arrive at a new painting, when I considered the larger work to be unsuccessful. One part of this larger painting was then overpainted grey,[4] rather like one of the Tourist paintings,[5] painted from a photograph, then later overpainted with grey.

Townscape Paris (175), 1968

When I look back on the townscapes now, they do seem to me to recall certain images of the destruction of Dresden[6] during the war.

Grid Streaks (194-5), 1968

This is one of the pictures belonging to a group that were, in the main, despairing attempts at making paintings. I did not destroy them because they had something about them, some truth about them, which was taken up in later works. Making different attempts, trying different methods, is something I have always done.

Townscape TR (217/1-3), 1969

This came from an architectural magazine – the same sort of magazine I got the aerial views of townscapes – except these views did not appear destroyed at all, like the *Townscape Paris*. They were also minimalist in a certain way. In this painting the model does not fit together – there is a sense of discontinuity about the image. I think very few of the paintings after architectural models are successful, with the exception of this one. I was able in this painting to achieve a sense of presence. I put the paint on very thickly in black and white, creating with the two a grey. It was quite musical, almost like a fugue.

Star Picture (224/13-15), 1969

We were talking about the overpainted grey pictures in the Tourist and Townscape series. It has always fascinated me to look at scientific journals and see an almost blank illustration with perhaps four or five dots on it. They then have a caption saying that this is such and such a galaxy 80,000 light years away, approximately such and such a size, while the illustration appears to show nothing. The pictures were begun with this sort of idea in mind – the dichotomy between the image and the descriptive title which seems to have nothing to do with the image and yet be crucial to it. I was playing with this idea and might otherwise have destroyed these paintings. I was also interested in the idea that sometimes a painter can paint a picture and give it an interesting title which is so deliberate, like this one, although the painting itself is not interesting.

Sea Piece (Wave) (234), 1969

I did not have the same sort of problem that I was having with the series of detail paintings, which I was painting at the same time and which appeared endlessly repeatable and without end. I could not judge in the end which were good and which bad. Just about all the seascapes (many of which were included in the *Atlas*) depict collaged motifs. The sea and cloud sections came from different photographs then collaged together in a single image. The successful paintings were dependent on finding exactly the right mood between the combined images. There were also a couple of paintings, for example, where I used two halves of the same image of the sea. Although I had a rather bad feeling about them, I was visited by George Maciunas, who thought they were absolutely wonderful and for that reason I allowed them to survive, despite feeling they were very decorative.

Park Piece (311), 1971

This is based on a photograph of a park in Düsseldorf, where I was living at the time. At that time, I remember, it was quite fashionable to paint very large pictures. Purely on account of its size, a picture of these dimensions has an enormous presence when on display. It preceded the inpaintings and was an excuse to introduce gesture into paintings. With this painting, I just mixed up about twelve colours in large quantities and used those because it was a lot faster to paint that way. It was a commissioned work and, after I had finished it, I still had quite a lot of paint left and made other paintings using whatever colours I had left. I made a three-part, green inpainting shortly after this, which I found interesting to make, using colour from somewhere else and applying it in this automatous fashion.

Inpainting (Grey) (326/1-3), 1972

I applied the paint in evenly spaced patches, or blobs, on the canvas. Not following any system at all, there were black and white blobs of paint, which I joined up with a brush until there was no bare canvas left uncovered and all the colour patches were joined up and merged into grey. I just stopped when this was done.

Grey (334-3), 1973

The paint for the grey paintings was mixed beforehand and then applied with different implements – sometimes a roller, sometimes a brush. It was only after painting them that I sometimes felt that the grey was not yet satisfactory and that another layer of paint was needed.

Annunciation after Titian (344-1), 1973

This is one of the few occasions where I painted a series of paintings all relating to a single theme. My initial intention was to paint a copy of this beautiful Titian, which I saw in Venice, for myself, but I did not succeed. It developed into a series

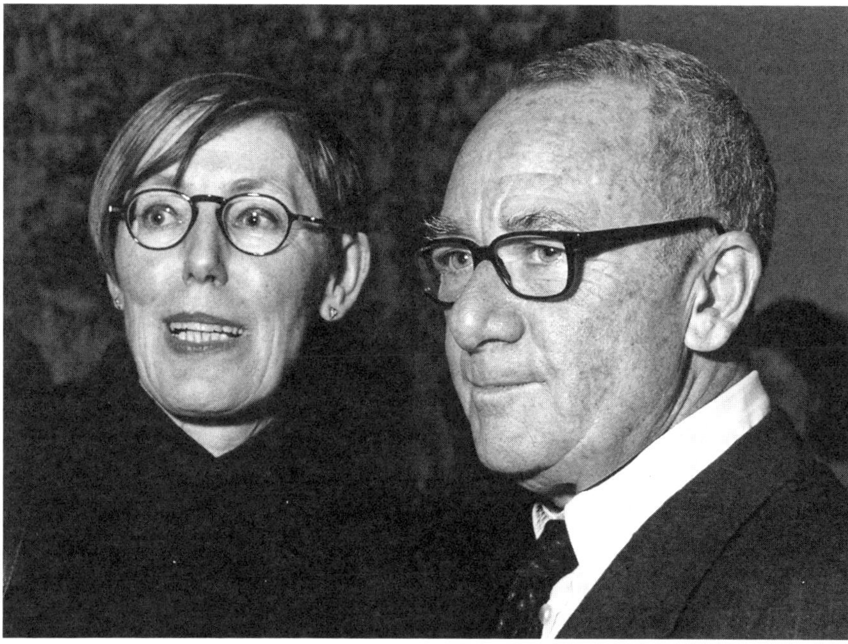

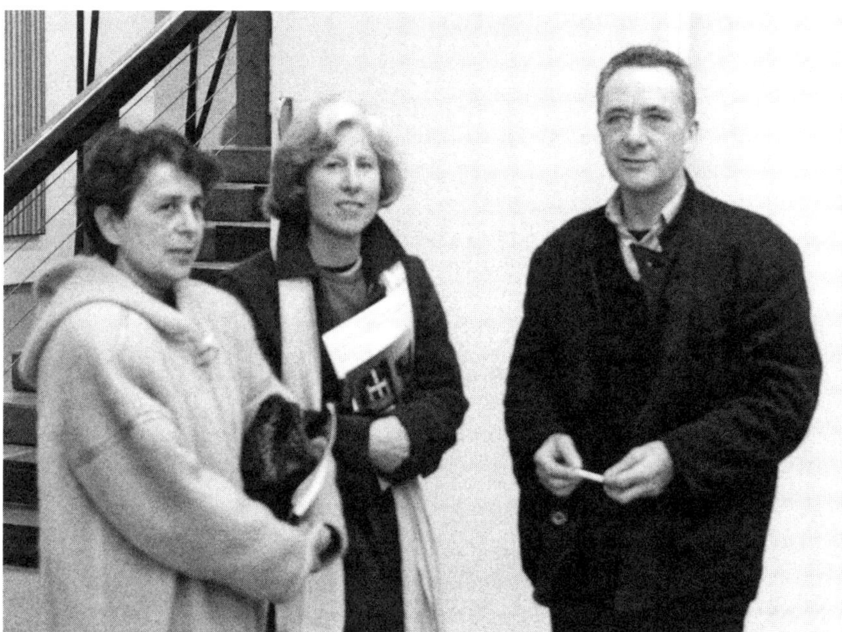

Birgit Pelzer with Gerhard Richter, 1999
Marian Goodman and Angela Westwater with Gerhard Richter, 1986

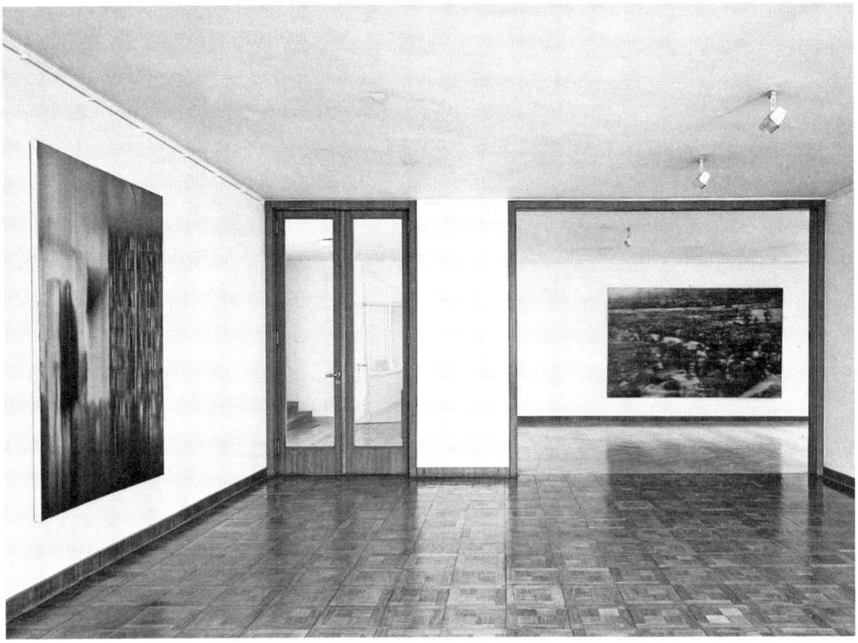

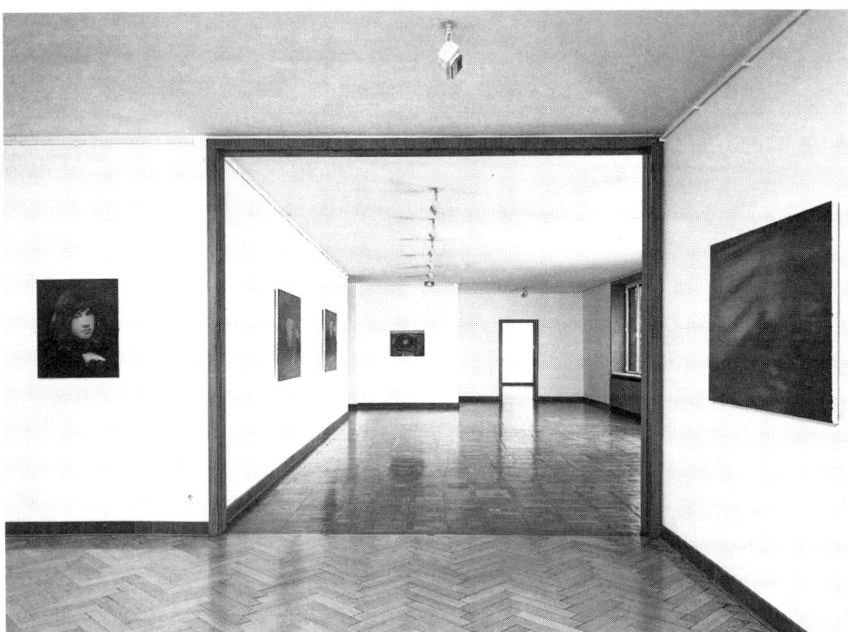

Museum Haus Lange, Krefeld, 1989

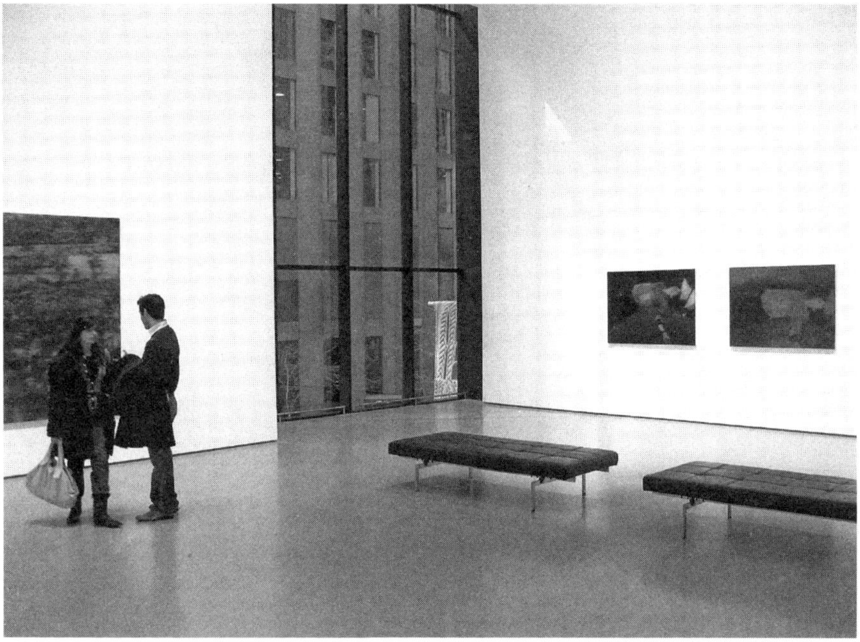

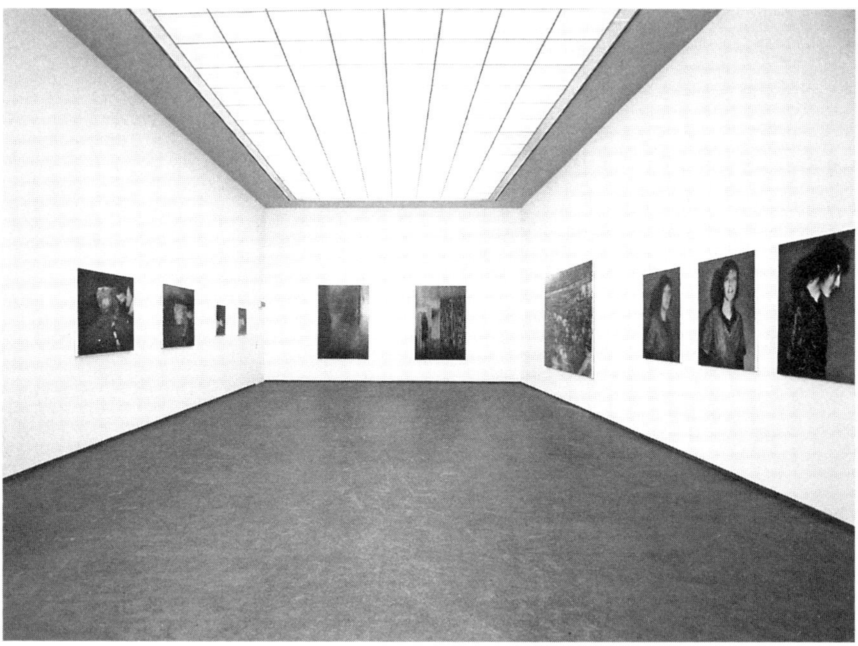

The Museum of Modern Art, New York, 2007
Portikus, Frankfurt, 1989

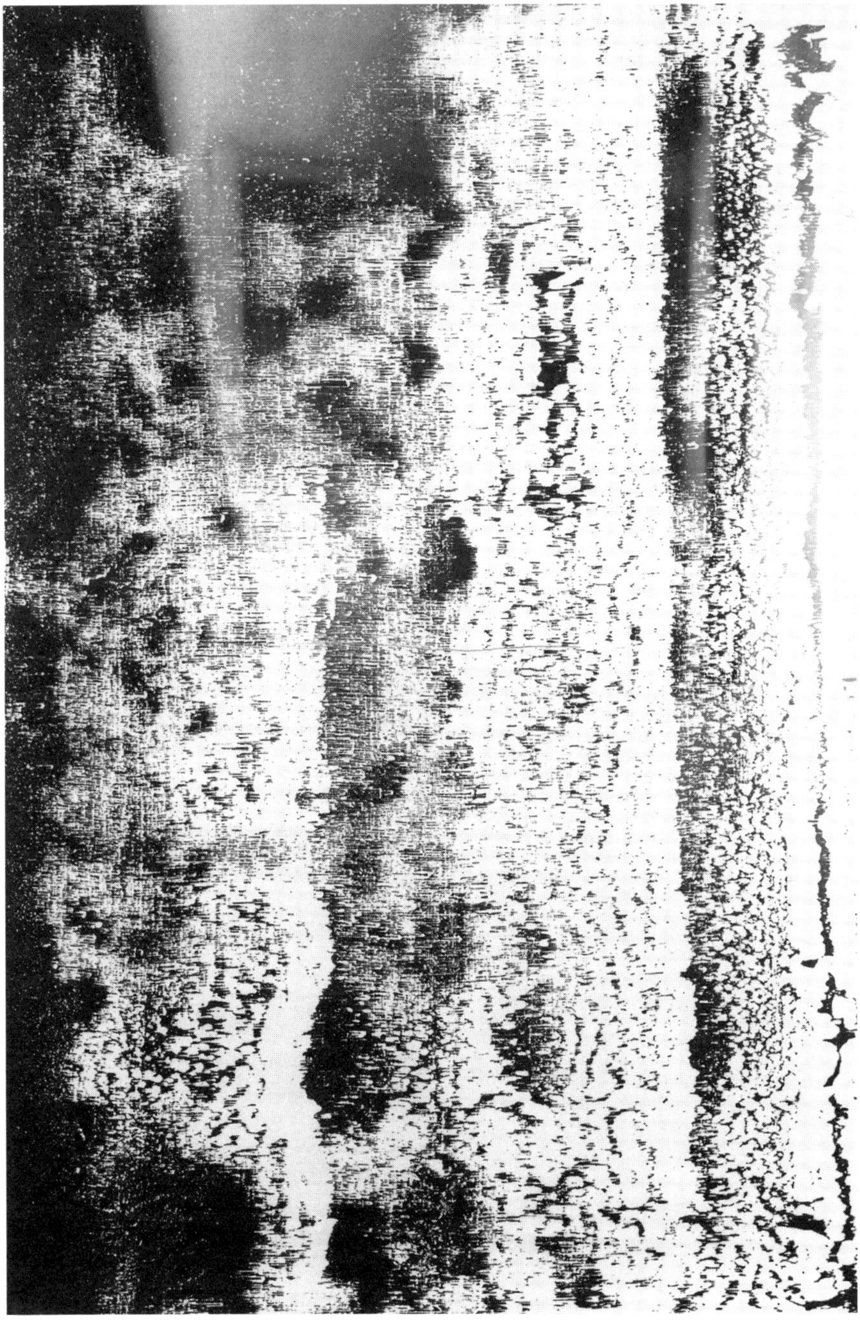

Blanket, 1988

of works, because I was unable to copy the painting after several attempts, which were then destroyed through overpainting. The whole process probably lasted about two weeks. I was drawn to the theme of the Annunciation by the feeling that if anything could be intimated to me, it would be absolutely fantastic.

1,024 Colours (350-4), 1973

I painted these series of colour charts in the hope that they might be exhibited, which did not happen at the time. The size of the canvases, the design of the grids, as well as the size of the individual boxes were subjective decisions. I was helped while painting them by students who did much of the actual work applying the paint to the canvas. I had made smaller colour charts during the 1960s, which I did not feel were as successful as the later series, which are so strong and suggestive that it makes it difficult for them to be shown alongside other paintings. I made one painting with over four thousand colour boxes, directly abutting one another in quite an impressionistic way, but with each colour repeated four times. I hoped with my colour charts to retain a picture which stood up on its own.

Abstract Painting (July) (526), 1983

The title was not given because it was painted during July. Rather, it was because it was first exhibited that month.[7] It seemed to me that certain aspects connected with the colour and the forms within the painting reminded me of feelings connected with July, so I gave it that title. There are also other paintings which I called after the months, one called *June* and the more recent diptychs *November*, *December* and *January*. In the main, the reasons for giving them these titles are personal.

Abstract Painting (576-3), 1985

In these paintings I did not apply paint across the canvas in one movement. At this time I also made a couple of enormous canvases for a private collection in Düsseldorf,[8] where I applied paint to parts of the canvas, rather than everywhere at once. Here I was trying to combine constructive elements in paintings with areas which contained destructive elements – a balance between composition and anti-composition, if you like. In paintings such as *July*, for example, there is something deconstructivist and oddly imbalanced along with something else which is carefully composed.

Forest (731), 1990

I called this series of four paintings *Forest* after completion. There was no ironic meaning intended, because of their first exhibition in a show called *Metropolis*.[9] There seemed to me a romantic mood in these four paintings that reminded me of a forest. In the blue, there is the sensation of a diffuse light, which is why I came upon this title. I applied the paint across the canvas in two separate movements; across the middle one can see a caesura.

Interview with Jonas Storsve, 1991

In 1981 the Danish painter Per Kirkeby wrote of Georg Baselitz: 'That was the end of the 1960s, and who still remembers the artistic zeitgeist that made painting almost impossible? In sheer desperation, those of us who could not keep away from the proscribed activity of painting salved our consciences by resorting to all sorts of let-outs: painting only on Sundays, painting only left-handed, turning paintings upside-down.' Did you have the same problem in the 1960s, and if so how did you solve it?

I just went on painting. But I clearly remember that this anti-painting mood did exist. At the end of the 1960s the art scene underwent its great politicization. Painting was taboo, because it had no 'social relevance' and was therefore a bourgeois thing.

Has being a painter got any simpler since then?

It hasn't got any simpler, because it does the artist no good if society accepts any and every kind of painting, if painting is consumed *en masse*, as uncritically as it has been over the last ten years. You end up feeling as forsaken as ever. It hasn't got any simpler: there's more money around, that's all.

In 1981 you exhibited at the Kunsthalle in Düsseldorf jointly with another great German painter, Georg Baselitz.[1] *How did that exhibition come about, and how do you see your own work in the context of this relationship?*

I think my painting is more fragile, more endangered and more complicated than that of Baselitz, which always seems to me to be far more confident or self-assured: it is done like a natural piece of work, with no room for doubts. This matter-of-factness and strength in his paintings is something I now value very highly. At one time I didn't like him much, and he didn't like me. We were in two different 'camps'; he was with Werner and I was on the other side, and things got quite hostile. Perhaps the exhibition was seen as an experiment, a way of bringing the two of us, or the two camps, closer together. It didn't achieve much. Done now, it might be more interesting – but I don't really believe that: what would be the point of bringing together Seurat and Manet, or Titian and Velázquez?

Whose idea was it?

Jürgen Harten, Rudi Fuchs, Konrad Fischer, Michael Werner and many others wanted it. It was a piece of showmanship. We were both sort of famous by that time, and it was as if we had to be put in the ring together. But there was no contest. We stood side by side and did nothing to each other. Even though the exhibition didn't make much public sense, and the forced comparison (which is better?) may not have achieved much, it did make me look at the pictures, his and mine, rather more closely than I would have done otherwise.

Were you influenced by Duchamp when you painted the pictures Woman Walking Downstairs *(1965) and* Ema *(1966), and when you made the* 4 Panes of Glass *(1967)?*

I knew Duchamp's work, and there certainly was an influence. It may partly have been an unconscious antagonism – because his painting *Nude Descending a Staircase* rather irritated me. I thought very highly of it, but I could never accept that it had put paid, once and for all, to a certain kind of painting. So I did the opposite and painted a 'conventional nude'. But, as I said, it was an unconscious process, not a strategy. The same happened with the 4 *Panes of Glass*. I think something in Duchamp didn't suit me – all that mystery-mongering – and that's why I painted those simple glass panes and showed the whole windowpane problem in a completely different light.

You're now working with glass again. A mirror picture is on the wall here in the studio, and in your last exhibition in London[2] *there were a number of new mirror works. Does all this still relate to the same set of issues, or has that altered with the passage of time?*

It's about glass again. This time glass that doesn't show the picture behind it but repeats – mirrors – what is in front of it. And in the case of the coloured mirrors, the result was a kind of cross between a monochrome painting and a mirror, a 'Neither/Nor' – which is what I like about it.

Do you get a similar feeling from your early representational pictures?

Yes, maybe I do. Those have the same blurred look, whereby something has to be shown and simultaneously not shown, in order perhaps to say something else again, a third thing.

In 1979 you painted a cycle of works after Titian's Annunciation[3] *(in the Scuola Grande di San Rocco). Why did you choose that picture in particular?*

Simply because I liked it so much. I saw it in Venice and thought: I'd like to have that for myself. To start with, I only meant to make a copy, so that I could have a beautiful painting at home and with it a piece of that period, all that potential beauty and sublimity. I don't really know what the period was like: maybe it was ghastly. But the theme is very beautiful. This woman to whom something is being announced: a beautiful truth, and no doubt well painted. But then my copy went wrong, and the pictures that finally emerged went to show that it just can't be done any more, not even by way of a copy. All I could do was break the whole thing down and show that it's no longer possible.

You had a long period of painting mainly abstracts, and then in 1988 you painted the cycle 18 October 1977. *In your last exhibition in London there was one additional representational painting, the portrait of your daughter* [Betty], *which was painted during the same phase. And in 1987 you went back to painting landscapes. Have you an idea for a new representational cycle?*

No, more's the pity. I'd very much like to paint figurative pictures, but I don't know how.

But you do still paint landscapes?

Not any more. I don't like any of my photographs. I'm still taking them, though not so many of them. Perhaps it's because I can imagine how it would all turn out, and I don't like it.

Might that be a similar situation to what happened in 1976, when you painted only grey pictures?

Yes, now might be the end [*laughs*].

In the cycle 18 October 1977, *you took not only your theme but also your format from history painting (the biggest picture is more than 2 metres by 3). The* Dead Man *seems even to bear a resemblance to a celebrated nineteenth-century history painting, the* Dead Toreador *by Manet.*

I don't think so. Most history paintings were much larger. I'm not really very interested in history painting, and I don't know much about it. The starting points for my *October* paintings were photographs.

Photography has always played an important part within your work, partly as a motif, but also as an autonomous medium – as in your earlier photographic multiples,[4] *or more recently in the 1990 self-portraits. What is the importance of photography within your work? Does it have equality of status with painting?*

There is never any such thing as equality of status. But I've never thought about what significance photography has for me. Painting is the form of the picture, you might say. The picture is the depiction, and painting is the technique for shattering it. Now there's painting on one side and photography – that is, the picture as such – on the other. Photography has almost no reality; it is almost a hundred per cent picture. And painting always has reality: you can touch the paint; it has presence; but it always yields a picture – no matter whether good or bad. That's all theory. It's no good. I once took some small photographs and then smeared them with paint. That partly resolved the problem, and it's really good – better than anything I could ever say on the subject.

Photography plays a very big part in present-day art. One almost gets the feeling that photography has taken over the role previously performed by painting. Does photography suit our age better than painting?

There's almost nothing left to say about photography, because it's so obvious that photography has taken away one important part of painting: the function of portraying, depicting. This has made a great difference to painting. But the invention of photography wasn't the only reason for the change. Music is passing through comparable difficulties, undergoing comparably vast changes, and those can't be traced back to any one technological innovation. There are other causes. But this is a complicated subject, best left to the specialists.

Is there a way forward for painting?

Yes. We're carrying on, and true painting has yet to come – maybe in the next millennium [*laughs*].

You also teach.[5] *Is it really possible nowadays to teach a thing like painting?*

Virtually impossible. Nevertheless there are reasons, and I don't mean reasons of artistic technique, that justify a course of study at an academy; because the conventional structures – a class, a studio, students, teachers, administration and all that goes along with it – constitute a social order in which it is possible to change both content and working practices. The academy today basically operates in the right way, even though the teachers haven't much to say and the students are pretty idle by past standards. The work being done is of a completely different kind – I hope!

Many critics speak of a constant process of stylistic change within your work, and you seem to have no single identifying characteristic. Is this a conscious tactic on your part, a way of evading all efforts to fit you into a category, or is it an unconscious need to have more than one way of expressing yourself?

More of an unconscious need – one that corresponds to my personal structure, and one that makes it unendurable for me to have to do the same thing all the time. I'm too restless for that; too uncertain, too. And in this day and age I can never imagine myself taking up an obstinate, immovable stance. On the other hand, I do perceive an unchangeable basic attitude, a constant concern that runs through all my works like a style. That's why it's quite easy to identify my pictures, however different they are externally; they're often easier to recognize and identify as 'Richters' than pictures by any other painter. And that's why it's really wrong to talk about frequent changes of style in my work. You wear different suits on different occasions; that has nothing to do with style.

How did you come to do the abstract pictures? I mean the pictures painted without photographic originals.

It's hard to put that in a nutshell. It's a long evolution – from childhood onwards [*laughs*]. Perhaps because non-representational painting is so simple to do: it's just getting colours down on paper. Totally free, or so it seems. It's still fun today. When I was eighteen, I handed in my first portfolio as an applicant for admission to the Dresden Academy[6] – it was all wild daubs, and of course they didn't take me. Much later, I took it more seriously. And I've been doing the abstract pictures, properly so called, only since 1976, when I quite deliberately accepted the random, wilful element and painted those fairly colourful, heterogeneous pictures. Perhaps I was harking back to my youthful beginnings. At all events, this kind of painting still fascinates me today; it feels like a force of nature.

Are these paintings still random and wilful?

Not directly any more. I'm more concerned now to have them evolve of their own accord. I don't work at random but in a more planned way, in the sense that I let a thing happen by chance, then correct it, and so on. The actual work consists in taking what appears, looking at it and then deciding whether it's acceptable or not. Perhaps this way of working has something in common with the readymade: the artist lets someone else – it doesn't matter who – do the work of making the objects, and the real work lies in observing the thing and deciding whether it's any good. I think the same thing is typical of our present-day art. It doesn't matter how the things are actually produced: painted, built, installed or however.

You said earlier that you took an interest in abstraction during your time in Dresden.

It was a forbidden tendency at that time, and I had no idea what it was really like. What I was doing was pretty childish.

When you crossed over to Düsseldorf in 1961, the West German art scene was dominated by Art Informel and Zero.

Yes, but at the same time there was Nouveau Réalisme, and then came Fluxus and Pop – and all that mattered much more to us.

What was your reaction? Did you feel at home in any of these movements?

For a short time I did feel that I was a Pop artist, but the main thing is that Pop and Fluxus had a decisive influence on me – like Tachisme previously. Nouveau Réalisme was never that important to me, and Zero not at all.

Your work is now shown in many different contexts. This year, you're represented in the Pop Art show in London,[7] as well as in Metropolis in Berlin.[8]

I've always really liked that – being shown in a variety of exhibitions and settings.

You don't mind critics and art historians interpreting your work in different ways?

No, I don't know exactly what it is, myself. It's only natural that there should be a number of different interpretations.

Many see your work as conceptual painting.

I don't really know what that means. It's obvious that you occasionally reflect and think about what you're doing and what you might do. In that sense, all painting is conceptual, except the painting of idiots. But I am primarily a painter, and so I'm neither a Conceptual Artist nor an intellectual.

How do you yourself see your work? Is it divided into separate groups, or do you see it as different aspects of the same thing?

I think it comes down to different aspects of the same thing – and if you like you can always subdivide and arrange that. You can put it into a lot of pigeonholes: small pictures, big pictures, medium-sized, representational pictures, colourful pictures, black-and-white pictures. But what counts is always just one thing: how I am to cope in this world, with myself and with painting.

Notes, 1992

1 June 1992. So-called circumstances cannot be changed by reason and insight; they change themselves in unpredictable ways, more or less spontaneously.

For instance, the realization of climatic damage and the prospect of a climatic catastrophe creates fear, but no effective action towards changing it.

On the contrary, fear is only a sign of our certainty that we can change nothing, and to palliate our fear we go in for displacement activities that make not the slightest possible difference; just like our ancestors, who faced up to nature armed with nothing but prayers and sacrificial offerings.

Nature goes on, as naturally merciless as ever. It creates the continual changes that we have always feared. We are helplessly and painfully at its mercy, and can do nothing but palliate and comfort ourselves.

Palliation is always childish: a few green corners in the car parks. Comfort is always a lie: false promises of a beautiful future. That seems to sum us up.

3 June 1992. Consciousness is the capacity to know that we and others are and were and will be. It is therefore the capacity to visualize, and therefore the belief that keeps us alive. Without visualizing the future, and our own goals and tasks, we should vegetate and – since we lack the instinct that the animals have – we

should perish. Belief (view, opinion, conviction, hope, plan, etc.) is thus our most important quality and capacity. And in the form of faith it can dominate us with such power and conviction that we transform it into destructive superstition. That is why we must always confront belief with scepticism and analysis.

26 June 1992. It might be for us to look on killing as part of our own nature – of the very nature that we seek to regard as our antithesis, as the inhuman, 'blind' nature of natural disasters, carnivorous animals and exploding stars.

Our behaviour conforms to this nature in two ways: on the one hand as active killing, both in wars and as civilian murder; on the other in the still more horrifying passive mode of assent (we watch the news while eating dinner; we enjoy seeing murders in films). This is because of the way we take death for granted: just as we know that we are alive, we know that we die; death comes as naturally to us as life. The instinct to stay alive limits our compassion and our willingness to help; we give our help and our pity only under duress, and when it seems to be to our own advantage.

The suppression and repression of these facts gives rise to dangerous delusions, the politics of hypocrisy, false and lying actions.

And yet to accept them would be so unimaginable and so unworkable that we knowingly and impotently prefer to allow for – that is, include in our plans – all future catastrophes.

2 September 1992. It would be easy to say that the growing and baffling complexity of the world causes and accelerates the relapse into barbarism and the destruction of civilization through sheer helplessness and apathy. But all the tradition I can pick up goes to confirm my opinion that things have never been any different, that the world has always been complex and baffling, and that civilization and art have very seldom become a reality. Murder and mayhem are the norm: unmitigated chaos.

5 September 1992. Almost every day we get the fat catalogues of exhibitions and so-called collections; we read of newly built museums, of gigantic cultural foundations of all kinds; and indeed the sums laid out from State, municipal and private funds for art and culture are dizzying. It would be interesting to find out the total sum expended for these purposes over the past ten years. Whatever it might turn out to be, it would strikingly confirm our natural lack of compassion for the poor.

19 September 1992. No religion has ever promised Paradise on Earth: only the Communists have ever been stupid enough to do that. It makes them not only frauds but murderers. Because, by transferring all the blame to others, they make themselves absolutely good, and thus rob themselves of the capacity to attempt anything good whatever.

(And anyone who believes that he can change the whole world is bound to regard any small improvement of the status quo as sabotage.)

Blasé scum.

Our own malevolence (which ranges from lack of compassion to the homicidal impulse) is something we have to accept, as we do our intrinsic fallibility and inadequacy. That is the only way we can ever enable our better sides to develop and to act.

The repression of evil creates hypocrisy, and hypocrisy is not only a 'homage to virtue' but the subtlest way of translating our own evil into reality (thus wiping out a few individuals or hundreds or thousands or millions).

Hypocrisy, being the murder weapon that suits us best, also makes it easier for us to indulge in arrogant condemnations of the killing methods of the past – which actually did incomparably less harm.

22 September 1992. Scraping off. For about a year now, I have been unable to do anything in my painting but scrape off, pile on and then remove again. In this process I don't actually reveal what was beneath. If I wanted to do that, I would have to think what to reveal (figurative pictures or signs or patterns); that is, pictures that might as well be produced direct. It would also be something of a symbolic trick: bringing to light the lost, buried pictures, or something to that effect.

The process of applying, destroying and layering serves only to achieve a more varied technical repertoire in picture-making.

23 September 1992. Because Marxist intellectuals refuse to own up to their own disillusionment, it transforms itself into a craving for revenge. And so they turn their own ideological bankruptcy into the utter bankruptcy of the whole world – mainly the capitalist world, of course, which they vilify and poison in their hatred and despair. 'Political correctness' is one of their methods, whereby they even accept the destruction of their own values in order to do more effective damage.

25 September 1992. To the depressive, all pictures become vacuous, meaninglessly painted rectangles, no matter what they represent. He sees them with the eyes of a cow – and, worse, they cause him disgust and pain.

The art world seems increasingly to suffer from this disease, and we can expect decades of misery (the price to pay for previous mania).

17 October 1992. Hypocrisy is the display of a respectability that can never be achieved. Worse still, and a public menace, is the edifice of respectability presented by ideologies: they are recognizable as tissues of lies, but indispensable as means to terror. This becomes a double hypocrisy: that of believing what is not true, and that of proclaiming what is not even believed. It also does double damage: it is like criminal assault and self-mutilation in one. This practice must make sense in some way as yet undiscovered.

17 October 1992. All this exaggerated humaneness and helpfulness – this compassion for every murderer in a death cell, every fish that perishes in an oil slick, and every dying tree – all this stands in contrast to the unprecedented vastness of the misery currently caused by war, starvation and disease; it stands in contrast to the predictably catastrophic future of an overpopulated earth whose inhabitants are going to slaughter each other and starve to death in unprecedentedly chaotic circumstances – it contrasts with the inevitable emergence of a conscious contempt for humanity and an extreme incapacity for love or mercy. It springs from the fear of all this.

19 October 1992. It might seem that we are less cruel and merciless than we were a hundred years ago, when mutual mayhem was publicly practised and accepted. And we have indeed become more sentimental: we cry when animals are maltreated, we take pity on refugees, and we do our best to protect embryos, to love gypsies and make things all right for the disabled; we can no longer stand idly by when someone dies; but we look on as thousands perish, starve and are murdered; we see and hear and read the daily growing figures that represent the misery and death of millions; we store the figures and add them up. Panic. (But most of the time we manage to salve our consciences by planting a tree.)

18 November 1992. We have no possibility of coping with the daily growing numbers of people who are unemployed, homeless, starving, dying of epidemics, persecuted and abused. What we achieve, often with desperate commitment, is

no more than a minimal, palliative gesture. We would have to turn the whole world into one vast camp, which would operate not much more humanely than Auschwitz. So we let nature take its course. We have never yet been able to do anything else.

3 December 1992. For some time now, the Marxists have been gloating again: since the collapse of Socialism, misery has grown. They still believe in a 'system' – which causes the misery if it is a right-wing system, and which would put everything right if it were a left-wing system.

8 December 1992. Artist: more of a title than a job description. It's a word that still earns you considerable respect. People associate it with splendour and misery, with the attainment of freedom and with unexampled independence. Artists' lives seem exceptional and exotic: they are ahead of their time; their works are among the loftiest works of the human race; their undaunted courage defies the incomprehension of the philistines and the persecution of the dictatorships. Artists are the truly creative ones, the geniuses; their fame and the fame of their works derives from their God-given talents and from their passionate devotion to their work, which they perform with intuition and intelligence on behalf of the community. They are always progressively minded and critical of society, always on the side of the oppressed; and, rich or poor, they are always privileged.

Understandably, everyone would rather be an artist than endure the shame of some ordinary occupation. But the artist's image is going to be adjusted, sooner or later, when society realizes how easy it is to be an artist, and to set down (on or off the canvas) something that no one can understand and consequently no one can attack; how easy it is to inflate one's own importance and put on an act that will fool everyone else and even oneself. By then, if not before, the title of artist will induce nausea.

11 December 1992. Seen rationally, what we live through, and therefore call Life, is senseless, useless, vain, unnecessary – an absurdity. Our reason chases after it, constantly supplying us with interpretations and justifications that are of course nothing but flimsy attempts to bend and block the truth.

14 December 1992. Fears of death. Our fear of death comes from the certainty of dying and the uncertainty of the way of dying. In very much the same way, we are

frightened by the predictable, catastrophic future of the world; because our minds respond to the present in terms learned from the past, we cannot see the galloping growth of population as anything but a disaster. Nor can we comfort ourselves by reasoning that circumstances themselves affect our judgment, so that we cannot anticipate the salvation that lies in the future, or think the thoughts that future events and needs will suggest.

Where catastrophes have been foreseen in the past, there has mostly been no chance of averting them: the full weight of suffering has had to be borne. ('Things are never as bad as they look' mostly has to be replaced by 'It's always worse than you think'.)

Nor is it any real comfort to know that ideas of death, suffering and dying frighten the healthy more than those who actually are suffering or dying – who often accept suffering as an all-absorbing duty, far more so than the professional duties of their healthy lives.

It is also no real comfort to know that the will to live is ineradicable until the organism is destroyed (even though a kind of endogenous opiate makes dying more bearable, and though the organism, or its will to live, generates hope in defiance of reason until the very last moment).

Hope blinds reason. It is produced by a physically and psychically intact organism as a kind of hallucinatory drug, in order to distort the realistic perception that would weaken our will to live. Animals have no consciousness, and therefore they need no hope. But they are essentially no different from us: they are possessed by the same craving for life, which forces them – as it does us – to stay alive until the last breath is drawn. Aliveness, or the craving for life, uses the organism until the latter is destroyed. It is therefore wrong to assume that the will to live is a property of the organism, nor do the genes created by the organism govern its will to live, but the reverse: it is 'Life' that creates the physical organisms for itself and uses them until death, in order to remain active as Life.

A terrifying – because utterly inexplicable – vision. Aliveness, Life, as an invisible, non-material Something; a monstrous Unknowable, by which we are abused. And the catastrophic, blind superabundance of our own reproduction, like the remorseless squandering of organisms to the point of the destruction of whole species, only goes to confirm this.

Life is therefore inexplicable, in the same way as the Big Bang and all those physical and extra-physical processes in the universe – and certainly made of the same stuff. Energy and mass: the most unsatisfactory name for it.

(If, as has sometimes been said, we are only the envelopes, the will-less tools of the genes, this only raises a chain of further questions: whose tools are the genes, and so on, down to the ultimate cause. It seems to me that no one has ever enquired as to the nature of the 'energy' which drives a virus to be alive and to reproduce itself, and which produces the virus for itself as its bearer. I did not use the relatively apt word 'energy' earlier, perhaps because it is so much taken for granted that no one asks what it is.)

30 December 1992. What counts is the world of the mind, and of art, in which we grow up. Over the decades, this remains our home and our world. We know the names of those artists and musicians and poets, philosophers and scientists; we know their work and their lives. To us, they – and not the politicians and rulers – are the history of humankind; the others are barely names to us, and the associations that they arouse, if any, are horrific ones: for rulers can make their mark only through atrocities.

No greater contrast is conceivable than that between Kafka and Kaiser Wilhelm II.

Interview with Doris von Drathen, 1992

I am not nearly so talented as you think.

As a painter?

As a talker. I've never studied it; it was never my inclination, never my skill.

Writing, on the other hand?

That happens quite rarely, too. When I'm alone and in the right mood – then it sometimes works. But talking is hard.

We were only going to talk about quite simple things, such as the question whether the analytical, aesthetic debate about your painting might obscure the pictures themselves and their power. They strike me as being painted by someone who believes in pictures.

Belief is something with many sides to it. Believing in pictures like believing in God – or believing in pictures in a practical sense, at a time when painting is rather out of favour – or believing that pictures still make sense. And that I am sure about. We're always creating pictures: take fashion, for example. We put something on because we believe in it, and we thereby offer a picture of ourselves that tells other people who we are and what we're like. The same happens in other ways: we're always creating pictures for other people to understand if they can.

So paintings, too...

Here there's a lot more to do than there used to be – because in abstract paintings, like these, there's not much to see. Here faith plays a bigger part. And often you turn out to have believed in something that isn't true.

Do you believe in your own paintings?

There are a few that I like, but I wouldn't go so far as to stand up and say I believe in them.

But surely you ought to – otherwise why go to all that trouble?

Of course, I have to believe that I can produce something useful. And the pleasure of making counts for a lot in painting – as when someone's making music. There's no room for doubt.

Doubt as to what?

That it might make no sense, or be unnecessary or passé.

Doubt as to the possibility of still making a picture you can believe in?

There are so many believable pictures in the world, and we love them; we travel long distances to see them. We need them. And there are some people who need to make pictures themselves.

How does this idea of need relate to your earlier statement that you were looking for the maximum possible indifference?

That was an attempt at self-protection – saying that I was indifferent, that I didn't care, and so on. I was afraid my pictures might seem too sentimental. But I don't mind admitting now that it was no coincidence that I painted things that mattered to me personally – the tragic types, the murderers and suicides, the failures, and so on.

If we look at the photo-paintings, the Atlas *and the abstract pictures as a coherent whole, there may be a factor in common – the idea that someone is looking for a way to grasp an appearance.*

That may be so. But what do you mean by appearance – the way reality looks, or what appears in the pictures?

I'm thinking rather of Giacometti's sense of grasping an appearance: the way your pictures duck away from the viewer reminds me of the way he tried to catch a fragment of reality by surprise; or the way Sartre describes that awkward borderline between the registers of 'there is' and 'there exists'.

That's too difficult for me. This cup: it exists, and it appears. The photograph there shows only the appearance of the cup.

And the painted picture?

The same.

Is the painted picture closer to the reality or to the appearance?

In one sense it's closer to the appearance, but then it has more reality than a photograph, because a painting is more of an object in itself, because it's visibly hand-painted, because it has been tangibly and materially produced. That gives it a reality of its own, which then as it were substitutes for the reality of the cup.

So can a painted appearance tell us more about reality?

Perhaps it can, because it's more unsettling. It's always more or less different from reality, and that's unsettling. You ask more questions.

You get close?

Yes, closer to our relationship with reality. The cup on its own is boring.

Exactly. Now let's take the Gulf War.

That's too difficult.

But this is just the set of problems we're talking about. What do you think of the theories of philosophers like Baudrillard or Virilio, who are the virtuoso commentators on the loss of our relation to reality, on the vanishing of reality? What do you think of essays like Baudrillard's, which must have appeared in German by now: 'The Gulf War Never Happened'?[1]

I think absolutely nothing of it. Things haven't really changed that much. People in the past knew about wars by hearsay, too; they were just told in a different way, that's all. It's exactly the same thing as television and newspapers nowadays. But maybe faraway wars of that kind don't always get to us any more, and we'd like to be in a real one of our own. A touch of bloodlust.

I was really thinking that maybe the theories on the aesthetic issue of 'reality loss' fail to take account of our responsibility to picture reality for ourselves. Wouldn't it be far more to the point to ask how, in a media-saturated world, we could manage to keep our consciousness wide enough awake to figure reality out, and react to it?

A small war, right here?

No, be serious. Don't you think there might be such a thing as an obligation to grasp reality, and to act on it?

But the fact that we know of the war by hearsay, or from television, is a reality. And then we have other, less passive realities as well, such as the reality I have here and now. And to me the distant, mediated reality is like an example or illustration of my own attitude or inner state. If people out there are slaughtering each other, that's not really so alien to me as all that.

Because what happens here in your studio is a kind of slaughter?

Yes, more or less.

Now I hardly like to ask what significance painting can still have, in relation to that responsibility of grasping reality.

It's hard to say whether – as people do sometimes assume – painting in the past had more effect and more reality, on the grounds that it was better understood, or more popular, or was always on view in the churches to everyone. But painting still has a reality and an effect now. It is shown and bought and discussed, and quite a lot of effort goes into all of this. And so long as the art justifies the effort, by being interesting enough, then in a sense that will do for now.

It might be possible for pictures to launch something like a leap in perception or in consciousness. Someone might suddenly look at things differently, react to them with more doubts, or with more involvement. Indifference might be overturned by pictures.

I believe it might. But I've got nothing to say on that subject.

You have no desires in that direction yourself?

Of course I have – it just doesn't do any good to take on that kind of elevated responsibility. We all know, don't we, what well-intentioned paintings look like.

Kasper König once showed your figurative paintings – the cycle 18 October 1977 *– and abstract paintings in direct succession,*[2] *in order to show that the theme is the same.*

He was right to do that. Even so, it's difficult, because figurative paintings are always more attractive than abstract ones. As soon as there are persons or objects to be seen, you get more interest.

In 1968, in the period of the grey pictures and the 4 Panes of Glass, *there is a double panel called* Way Through. *It gave me a sense of a sacrifice, in the joyous, pagan sense of the word: giving something up and getting something in return. Did it feel like leaving something behind you, shaking something off, slipping away from it, in order to get to something different?*

Certainly. And for that you always have to give something up, or destroy it, or scratch it out – as in this little abstract here.

Let's stay with scraping off for a moment. Is this removal of paint an aggressive thing?

Yes, certainly.

It has something to do with injury.

Yes, with injury, and with taking something that has been made and destroying it, subtracting it, scratching it out. And then the pleasant feeling that you can get something else in return.

Perhaps that's the basic idea of giving things up.

Getting something better.

In the very recent pictures the scraping is far more radical – and it goes deep, right down to the ground of the canvas, which is laid bare.

Yes.

Has that got anything to do with pleasure? It may be that only activity satisfies.

In a sense, yes, it does, but then you start to see what has come out of it, and then you aren't satisfied any more. So you start all over again, and again, until it's right, and then it looks quite simple – successful, somehow – as if it were perfectly easy to make and easy to repeat. But unfortunately you have to take the long way round every time. You have to put in the whole effort to paint a picture, fail, go on painting and so on.

What about the light in your pictures? In the early abstracts, or so it seems, the light is placed centrally, like the Gesù Bambino in the Early Renaissance; but in the Forest series and the Red series the light is diffuse, like light underwater. How do you place your light? Intuitively, as with everything else?

Certainly. I've never really thought about it. Somehow I tend to start off with very bright colours, and they get more and more veiled, or else brought forward again, or added on. But light is the right word, because these bright areas always have an illusionistic aspect to them.

You once painted two eagles for Marcel Broodthaers. What sort of contact was that? Did you have anything to do with his ideas?

He was an incredibly likable and fascinating man; we always greeted each other warmly, and from time to time we ate together – but to this day I still don't understand what he was doing. I like it, and I'm always glad to see it.

And the Eagles for the 'Département des Aigles'?

He asked whether we could make an exchange of works. So that's how it happened.

But you never had any affinity for his ideas.

I never got involved with them.

The Eagles do have something noncommittal or encyclopedic about them, like the 48 Portraits.

They all come from an encyclopedia. At one time I used to find encyclopedias somehow comforting.

Comforting in the sense of circumscribed and verifiable?

Yes, neutralized and therefore painless.

And why do you say 'at one time'? Don't you need that kind of comfort any more?

I'm afraid it wears off.

Looking through your Atlas I always get the feeling that I am just about to understand the system on which you based your selection, but then an image crops up that demolishes all the criteria.

I don't really understand that. I always thought there was a consistent, dominant way of seeing, a basic intention that's just there, whether I like it or not.

So can you agree with a blanket interpretation of all your work – the sort of interpretation that is attempted in this monograph here – seeing the pictures in terms of walking along an existential knife-edge?

I couldn't put a name to it.

So is such a view entirely beside the point?

No, it's not. But how can I start talking like that? I can't come along and say here I am walking along a knife-edge, right on the brink, another day and I'll kill myself.

What reason is there for continuing to paint?

Money.

You must surely have enough of that by now. You don't seriously believe that.

No, but what else am I supposed to do? Question the point of painting?

That's just it. Why is painting needed? Because it's clear that it is needed.

You can't count on that. It's like a fashion or whatever. People have a kind of blind faith in painting for a while, and then they wake up, as if from a big dream, and realize that they've been buying nothing but nonsense.

But let's get back to this idea of need. Can pictures save us? Does painting make us into better people?

In principle, yes. Yes.

Is painting better placed than other media to satisfy Sedlmayr's yearning to find a way back to the Centre?

That Centre is long since lost, and there's absolutely no point in trying to reinstate it.

But painting is possible, and necessary? In the midst of all the image overload generated by the mass media, perhaps painting is necessary so that we can still have some pictures which – without harking back to the nineteenth century – can create detachment precisely by incorporating the new experience of virtual worlds; pictures to create what Aby Warburg calls 'space for mature thought'; pictures to give the human individual some sense of his or her own autonomy?

I have difficulties of my own with concepts like detachment and autonomy, and I'm reluctant to attach a name to what it is that painting gives us. All I know is that painting is useful and important, like music and art in general – that painting is an indispensable necessity of life.

Interview with Hans Ulrich Obrist, 1993

You were uncertain about these 1962 Notes.

Yes, it all sounds rather sententious and stilted.

It begins like this: 'The first impulse towards painting ... stems from the need to communicate.'

That's certainly not wrong, but it's a bit of a truism.

In the same text you dissociate yourself firmly from the idea of Art for Art's Sake. Against that you emphasize the idea of content – not imposed content, but also not content infiltrated through the back door, of the kind you hear of nowadays.

That was an idea that was current in the East in the 1950s, a kind of ritual abuse of decadent, bourgeois art. Somehow or other I had managed to internalize the idea that art can't be Art for Art's Sake but has to be about communication; I later said the same thing in a different way.

The repetitions between one text and another bring out certain basic structures in your thinking, such as your aversion to ideologies.

That's probably innate. By the age of sixteen or seventeen I was absolutely clear that there is no God – an alarming discovery to me, after my Christian upbringing. By that time, my fundamental aversion to all beliefs and ideologies was fully developed.

This runs like a scarlet thread, as it were, through all the texts.

And on the other hand the knowledge that we need belief – which I sometimes refer to as a mania, an illusion that we need in order to survive or to do anything, a prime mover. And at the same time this vulgar materialist view that we do not essentially differ from the animals, that there is no such thing as freedom or free will – this doesn't directly come out in the texts, but those convictions were established very early on.

That sounds fatalistic.

So it may, but the important thing for me is that this kind of fatalism or negativism and pessimism is a useful strategy in life; there is a highly positive side to it, because one has fewer illusions.

Hopeless, or inescapable?

Either will do, to make us feel better, to make us create hope.

So hope is another scarlet thread?

Hope is something I always have. And the less we deceive ourselves, the more pessimistically and fatalistically we see a thing, without kidding ourselves that

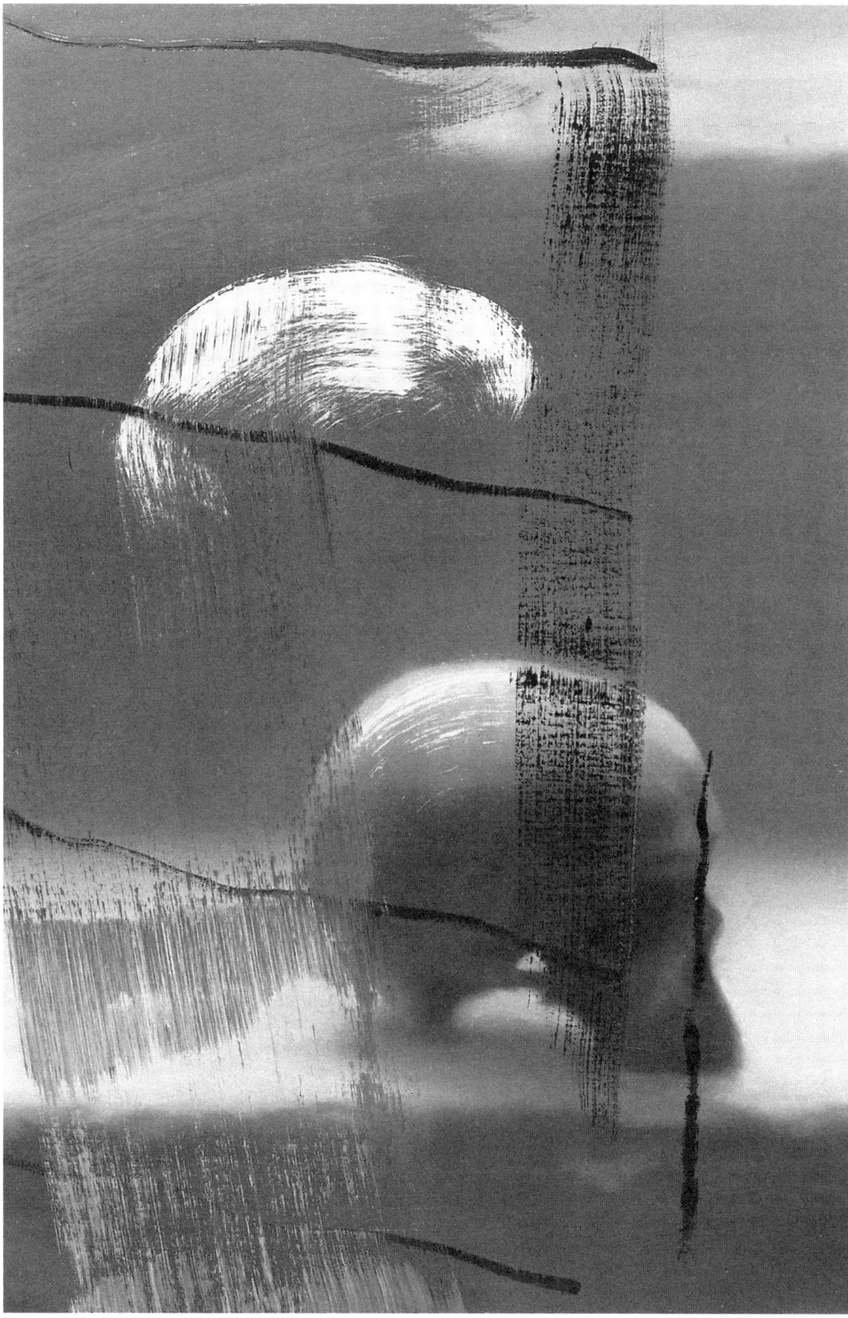

Skull, 1983

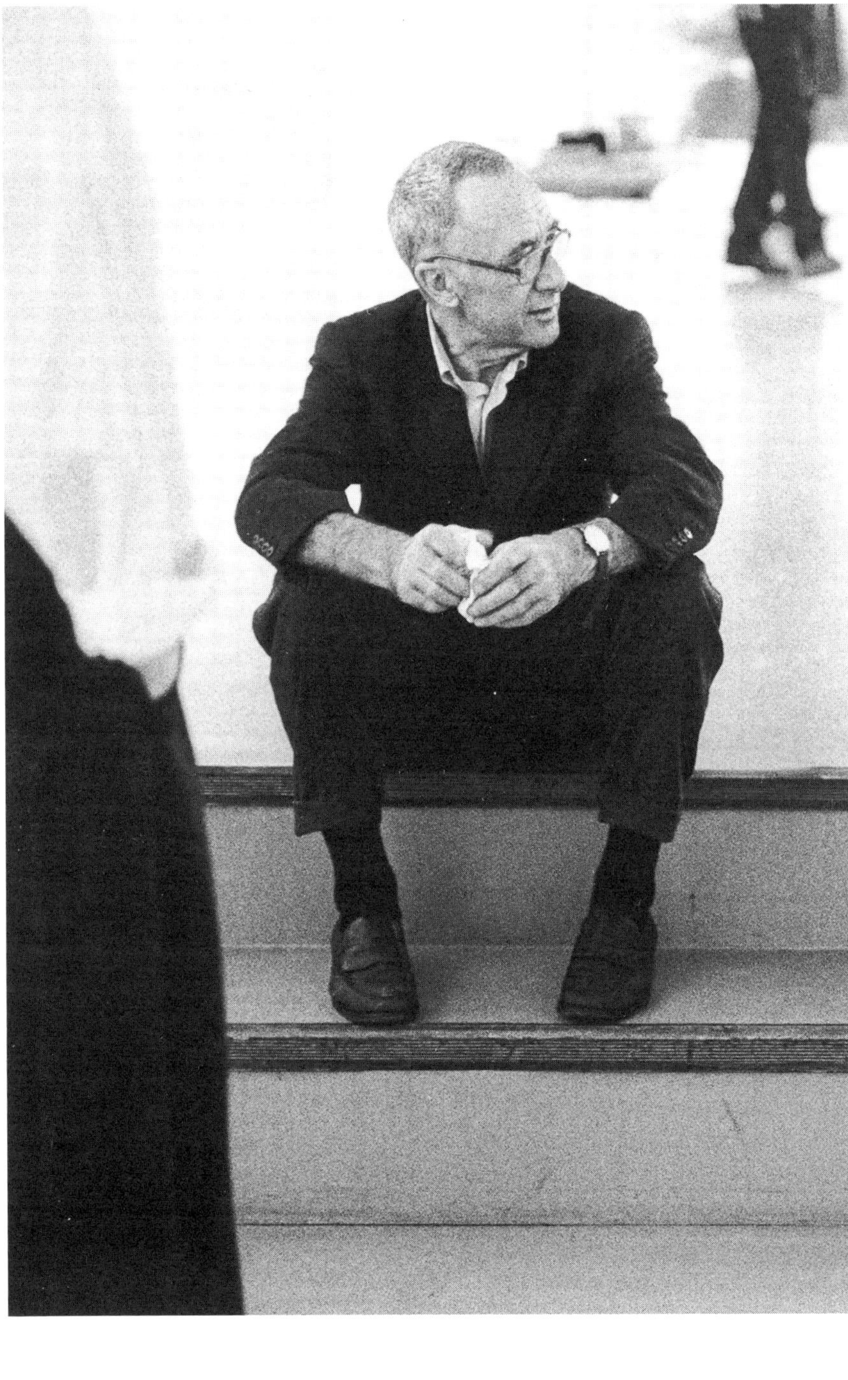

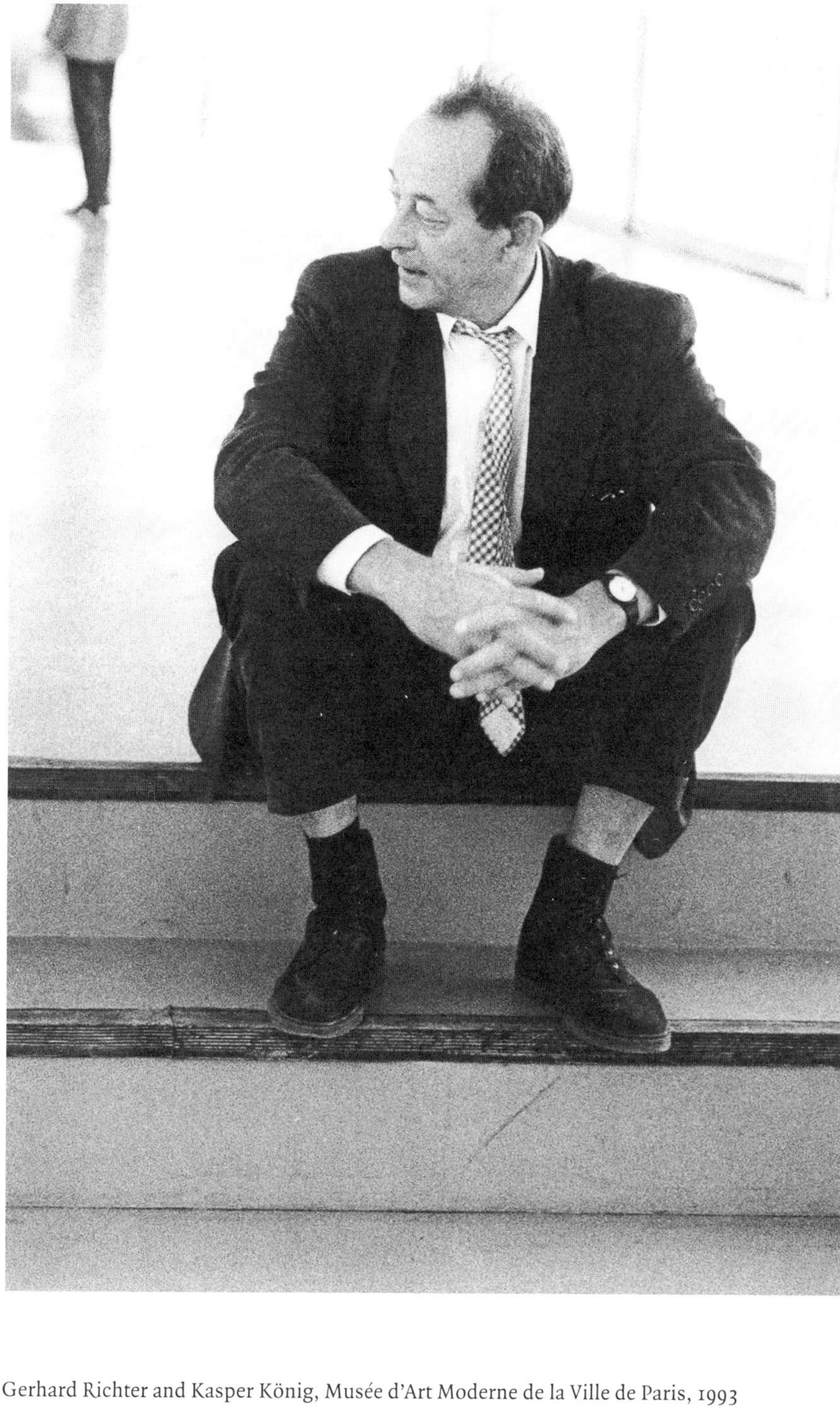

Gerhard Richter and Kasper König, Musée d'Art Moderne de la Ville de Paris, 1993

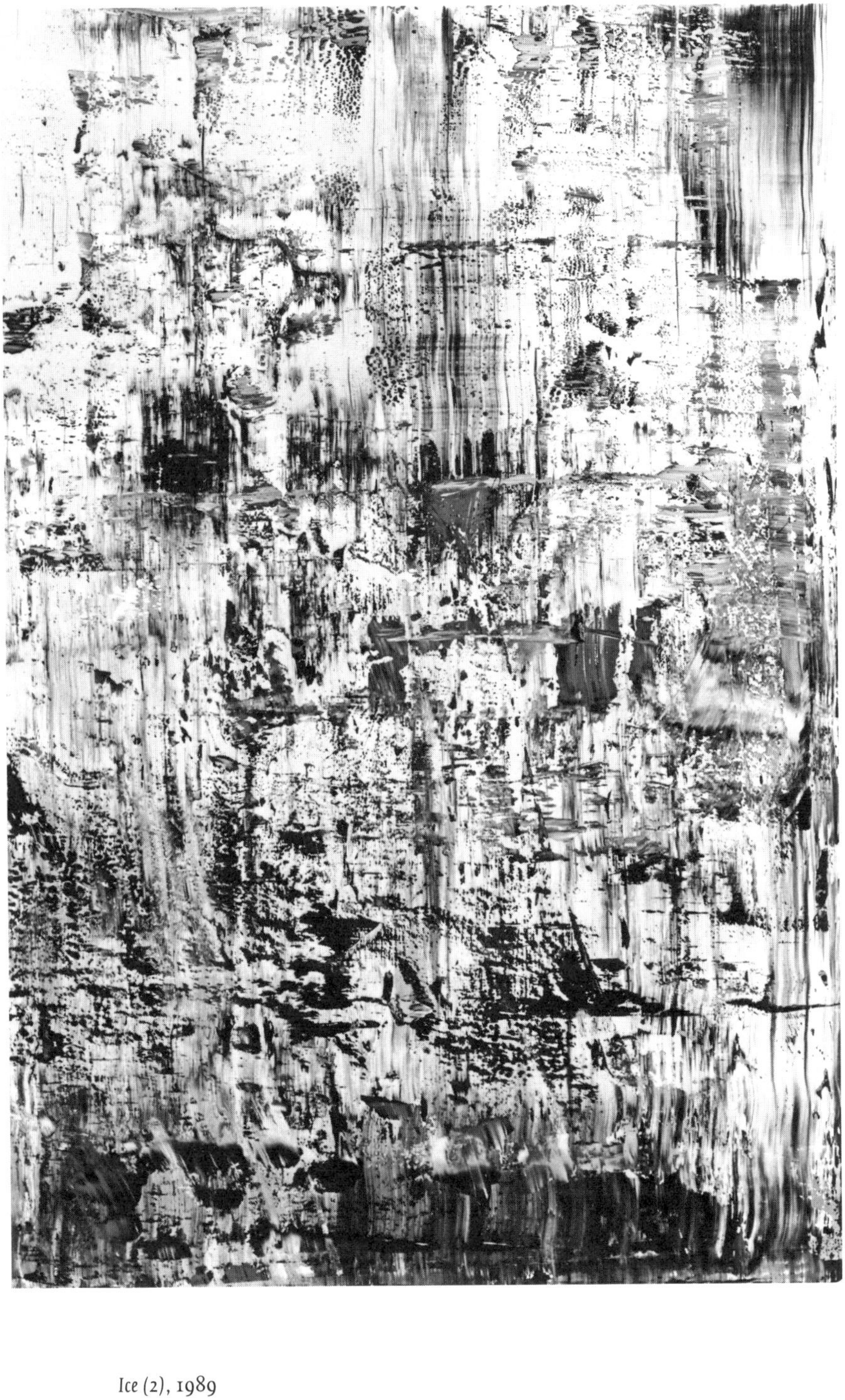

Ice (2), 1989

we have free will, or that it is possible to move a pencil from left to right by our own autonomous decision, the more we shall succeed in not succumbing to false faiths.

The press invitation to the Demonstration for Capitalist Realism[1] *makes it clear that this was a unique event, a Happening.*

And not the inauguration of an art movement.

More of a parody of all Isms.

Perhaps.

Why wasn't Polke there?

Purely by chance – maybe we'd temporarily fallen out at that time; but then, this demonstration was never meant to be all that important. We just wanted to do a little exhibition.

In the course of your conversations and texts, the word 'readymade' turns up again and again, especially from Buchloh, but also in more recent notes and interviews in which you speak of your abstract paintings as readymades – which is taking things as far as Duchamp's statement that the readymade concept expands to include the entire Universe.

I do believe in the readymade in this overriding sense, because if you confine it to art alone it tends to turn glib and illustrative: the *Plinth for the World*[2] was one example of that.

Besides the Demonstration for Capitalist Realism, *were there other, similar projects of the same kind that never came off?*

Any amount of them. In Paris, on the roof of the Galeries Lafayette, we wanted to put up a photograph of the Alps, with a cut-out for the skyline, so that Paris could have its own Alps. And there are some lovely views in the Neanderthal area; we wanted to take people out there in buses and announce: 'Here is our art.' Others later did just that.

On the one hand there was this ubiquitous reference to Pop Art: existing and available images were taken out of context, appropriated and recombined. But on the other hand the Demonstration *also reveals a connection with Happenings and Actionism.*

That's what fascinated me most, at that time. For instance, we were obsessed with the idea of holding an exhibition of Lichtenstein paintings, all of which we would paint ourselves. But that turned out to be too much work.

This scepticism about the ideas of authorship and genius has led to a number of attempts to deconstruct the Modernist claim to originality and authorship, by simply appropriating someone else's work without permission.

A terrible cop-out. Especially when a person builds his whole life on it. To do it once, as a demonstration, that I can understand.

In your response to Pop Art at that time, were you already distancing yourself from it, or were you involved in adopting or appropriating it as a movement?

My distancing was mostly about Good and Bad, and the idea or the programme didn't interest me for long anyway. And nothing has changed, really. I always thought that some were bad and some not very good, and the best were Warhol, Lichtenstein and Oldenburg. And that's the way it still is.

The Demonstration for Capitalist Realism *was an exercise in brinkmanship: it came close to a point where art dissolves into its social or political context, so that convergence must either take the form of disappearance or of a clash. And as to contextual convergence: the Happening took place in a furniture store, and it left the existing display unchanged. Art converged with a pre-existent context, but it was never about art dissolving into the context of life.*

Yes, we were rather playing with fire – to find out just how far we could go with the destruction of art. But in principle I never had the remotest desire to allow painting or art to dissolve into anything else. That kind of radicalism made no sense to me at all, though radicalism was generally regarded as the be-all and end-all at that time.

As a criterion of quality?

No, Art was the most important quality. That's why I then made fun of it all in the Polke/Richter text for Hanover,[3] and said that I was conventional and loved Raphael and beautiful paintings.

Were you then conscious of these distinct positions?

Yes, of course I was, and sometimes I had a guilty conscience about not being quite radical enough.

Not even in the Demonstration for Capitalist Realism*?*

When you're doing a thing like that, you tend to get high on it and just do it. But then when you're making something of your own again, or thinking over how terrifically radical other people are – Pollock's drip paintings, or Carl Andre's metal plates, or Arman with his containers: now that was regarded as radical. And I've never seen myself that way; I've always painted.

In spite of your constant dialogue and exchange of information with Polke and Fischer, the mechanisms of group bonding were never formalized, as they were for instance in 'Art and Language'.

That was quite deliberate. There were rare and exceptional moments when we were doing a thing together and forming a kind of impromptu community; the rest of the time we were competing with each other.

There's this text lifted from a newspaper, on a poster for Galerie Friedrich & Dahlem.[4]

Now that was a readymade, wasn't it?

Your only textual readymade known to me, except for the Perry Rhodan composite in the Galerie h catalogue,[5] and your non-statement in the book by Herzogenrath.[6]

To me it was just the same as a found photograph. But I don't think anyone twigged, because it was on the poster and just disappeared. Later I often tried out texts or text montages of the same kind.

How did the Perry Rhodan text collage come about?

We'd read the stuff, and it fitted into the Utopian naïvety of the 1960s, with all those ideas about other planets. This unartistic, popular quality, it all went together with photographs, magazines, glossies; that was the Pop side of it. All completely unimaginable today.

Another absurdist text is Polke's imaginary Richter/Thwaites interview.[7] The term 'Pop painter' turns up in that. Was it meant ironically, or did you all then define yourselves as the German representatives of Pop Art?

It was meant ironically; at that point we were trying to keep our distance from Pop. It was only at the very beginning that we were naïve enough to go off with Konrad Fischer and do the rounds of the galleries, Sonnabend and Iris Clert, and announce: 'We are the German Pop Artists.'

But the use of existing images and texts did come from the influence of Pop, which freed available, popular images from their contexts and saw them in a new way as pictures in new combinations.

Yes, of course, but maybe that can also be seen as the time-honoured practice of taking something over, setting it in a new context, and so forth. Nothing new, really.

In your texts and interviews the word 'Informel' turns up repeatedly. You don't categorically reject it, but you draw a clear line of demarcation between Informel and realism. At the same time, your work is a kind of reaction against the then-dominant stylistic and manneristic games of the Informel and Tachist school, which arose from automatism – and the term 'Informel' stands for the exploitation of that potential. What does the word 'Informel' mean to you today?

As I see it, all of them – Tachists, Action Painters, Informel artists, and the rest – are only part of an Informel movement that covers a lot of other things as well. I think there's an Informel element in Beuys, as well; but it all began with Duchamp and chance, or with Mondrian, or with the Impressionists. The Informel is the opposite of the constructional quality of classicism – the age of kings, of clearly formed hierarchies.

So in that context you still see yourself as an Informel artist?

Yes, in principle. The age of the Informel has hardly begun yet.

And this landscape here?

This is Informel, in spite of all the structure, which has rather a nostalgic look to it.

Although there's no leading idea, no leitmotiv, there's no uncontrolled use of chance either. In your pictures, chance never takes the decisions; at most, chance asks the questions.

It's the found object, which you then accept, alter or even destroy – but always control. The process of generating the chance event can be as planned and deliberate as you like.

In the same Notes you talk about the photographs everyone takes, and their function as cult objects. The banal source images reveal an unexpected, lasting, universal pictorial quality. When you said that, were you exploring the possible legitimization of illegitimate pictures – an 'illegitimate art', as Bourdieu calls it?

The legitimate pictures are the photographs – the devotional pictures that people hang or set up in their homes. We then sometimes use them for art, and that may well be illegitimate.

In the same Notes you also say that a photograph can be seen as a picture, outside the categories of High and Low, ritual photography and art. This is an important difference between you and Polke, isn't it, your refusal to go in for darkroom manipulations?

That's more of a technical, formal point; it's not that significant. I just don't like being in darkrooms. But to go back to legitimization: perhaps it's also illegitimate to bring the snapshot form too close to the readymade. Photographs are only readymades because they're so easy to produce, by comparison with painstakingly hand-painted pictures; as with a readymade, you only have to select them. The whole distinction is rather a shaky one, because it may well turn out that there are no such things as readymades at all. There are only pictures, which have value to many people or to very few, which remain interesting for a very long time or only for a few seconds, and for which very little or a very great deal is paid.

So the people who take the snaps are artists…

Yes, and when I then paint another picture of Uncle Rudi, the little officer, I'm actually watering down the true work of art achieved by those two or three private individuals who put Rudi behind glass and stood him on the sideboard or hung him on the wall. The only sense in which I'm not watering it down is that by painting the thing I am giving it rather more universality.

The displacement makes it exemplary.

Yes, and blurring was the only way of getting this done quickly. The photo-realists later painted photographs in a finicky, detailed way. I haven't the patience for that; and then there are the distracting perceptual factors that find their way in. One is the outsize format, and the other is admiration of the labour involved: the fact that it takes a whole year, the response of marvelling at the way it looks 'just like a photo'. I wanted to avoid all that by cheapening the production values. You can see that a photograph is meant, but it hasn't been laboriously copied and duplicated. This worked, and the pictures had the basic resemblance to photography without looking like copies of photographs.

You talk elsewhere about photography as drawing – or as the camera obscura, which Vermeer used – in the sense of a preliminary stage in the production of a picture. This reverses the primacy of photography, which is supposed to have given rise to Modernism by breaking down barriers. You simply use the photograph in making the picture, as a matter of course.

In the traditional practice of painting, that's the first step. In the past, painters went out into the open air and sketched. We take snaps. It's also meant to counter the tendency to take photography too seriously, all that 'Second-Hand World' stuff, which is wholly unimportant to me. Many critics thought that my art was a critique of contemporary life: criticizing it for being cut off from direct experience. But that was never what I meant.

The camera crops an image. It doesn't give the one, absolute image. The selected, partial image pushes forward and simultaneously recedes.

It's often been said that my pictures look like details. That may be so, but I can't understand it, probably because I take it too much for granted already. But maybe it was meant to refer to a certain inconclusive, open-ended quality: pictures that are cropped on four sides but can never show anything but sections, details.

And each time just one of many possibilities.

There are exceptions, of course, where it isn't one of many possibilities at all – as in the *Betty* portrait or the *Ema* nude.

And the Burnt-Out House.

Maybe the house, too. Those works tend towards the masterpiece, and if they aren't masterpieces it's just because I know that that just won't do: it's only ever like a quotation of a masterpiece, perhaps. But in principle everything is a detail.

In Betty *and* Ema *the masterpiece status just seems to creep in; I was also thinking of* Cathedral Corner.

But it can also happen with a grey picture. On a museum wall there's something masterpiece-like about it; the way it's hung.

And the other abstract paintings?

I might include pictures like *Janus* and *Juno*, for instance. But maybe only because they have such beautiful titles. There are some.

SDI, OZU. The masterpiece is the utter antithesis of the anecdote. And of the detail, and of the sequence. On the one hand you talk about the impossibility of absolute painting; on the other you bring back the concept of the masterpiece.

Perhaps that's what one is always striving for, the masterpiece; it's just that it never is one. The masterpiece seems so far outside time that one can't even strive to attain it.

In the German dictionary of the Brothers Grimm, 'masterpiece' is defined as 'an excellent, artistically perfect picture'. In his book Überwindung der Kunst [Transcending Art], *Alexander Dorner tells of a survey conducted in department stores to find the criteria of choice that defined the most popular pictures. The result is amazing. People buy colour reproductions and posters on the following criteria: (1) pictorial depth – a concept derived from centralized perspective; (2) narrative content.*

There's not much of either quality in Van Gogh's sunflowers. In that case, it's 'The Vincent Van Gogh Story' that seems to be most important. And the whole masterpiece debate is relativized by the fact that the pictures we now regard as masterpieces may well have been the perfectly ordinary consumer art of their own day.

The Mona Lisa *had its aura, even in Leonardo's lifetime. That kind of premonition of the enduring quality of a work is a well-known phenomenon.*

But at that time the word 'master' itself had a different meaning, which had far more to do with craftsmanship.

In London the Betty *portrait*[8] *suddenly had an enduring, universal, almost absolute quality; and curiously enough the same thing applied to the wider response that it got as a poster on the Underground. The masterpiece always implies this movement; you say it and then you take it back. It is one, and at the same time it isn't.*

It's slightly refracted by the historicist or nostalgic effect.

The discussion of works and artists' positions, which are important to you, comes to a head in the Buchloh interview, with a kind of reconstruction of your view of the history of art. In a much earlier interview you mentioned principally Barnett Newman, as representative of a historical position, and Gilbert & George as contemporaries.

Barnett Newman was always important. He came to me straight after Mondrian and Pollock. Newman was an ideal, because he created these big, clear, sublime fields that I could never have managed. He was my complete opposite.

Did your kinship with Gilbert & George lie in a shared interest and wish for normality at that time; the idea of disappearing into a completely banal life?

I liked them as outsiders, above all. At that time, Minimal, Land and Conceptual art were dominant. I valued all that, though I had very little to do with it. With Gilbert & George, too, I liked the very nostalgic side. They were the first people who liked my landscapes. I think what impressed me the most was the way they took their own independence as a matter of course.

Not forcing pictures into the dogmatic Modernist straitjacket?

The ideological straitjacket. Perhaps I have a kind of immunity to ideologies and fashions, because movements have always passed me by: the piety of my parents' house, the Nazi period, Socialism, Rock – and all the other fashions that made up the zeitgeist in thought, attitudes, dress, haircuts, and all the rest. To me it all seemed intimidating rather than attractive.

It's a surprise that you never mention Magritte.

He's too popular, too pretty for me. Wonderful calendar art; village schoolmaster's art. 'This is not a pipe': to me, that's just not a very important piece of information.

What seems important to me is his recurrent doubt as to the names of things.

Perhaps it got excluded because I could already see that I was in danger of painting something a bit too popular. I notice that at exhibitions: I get a very good reaction. The doormen and cleaning ladies think it's all great, even the abstract paintings. It's actually the ideal state of affairs, if you do something that everyone likes.

The Modernist rejection of any 'Art for All' sprang from a feeling of resentment, because painting had lost all its representational functions to photography. The ease with which you use photography puts the boot on the other foot – though without reviving the old unity between observer and object, or reverting to direct experience of the object. The construction of the picture now appears in a shattered mirror.

The image of the artist as a misunderstood figure is abhorrent to me. I much prefer the high times, as in the Renaissance or in Egypt, where art was part of the social order and was needed in the present. The suffering, unappreciated Van Gogh is not my ideal.

And his pictures?

I like Courbet's better.

How important was Beuys to you?

Mainly as a phenomenon and as a person. When I first saw the work, I wasn't all that interested; it was too eccentric for me. I'm increasingly in favour of the official, the classic, the universal.

Along with Manet and Ingres, Beuys is the only other artist who hangs in your studio.

Because he still fascinates me as a person more than anyone else; that special aura of his is something I've never come across either before or since. The rest are all far more ordinary. Lichtenstein and Warhol I can take in at a glance; they never had the dangerous quality that Beuys had.

In connection with the abstract paintings of the 1980s, you bring the idea of chance into play once again. Cage made chance operations out of methods based on uncertainty. But I never see chance in your work in terms of his interpretation of chance operations; you have less of the serial juggling with known elements, governed by the throw of a dice, that was usual in Conceptual art.

Except for the colour charts. Those were serial; I mixed the given colours and then placed them according to chance. I found it interesting to tie chance to a wholly rigid order.

That means giving it a form.

An architect once asked me what was so good about the colour charts; what was supposed to be the art in them. I tried to explain to him that it had cost me a great deal of work to develop the right proportions and give it the right look.

To give it a form, in other words.

Yes, because there would have been other possible ways of realizing the idea. I could paint these biscuits here in different colours and throw them across the room, and then I would have 1,024 colours in a chance form. Or in the grey pictures: if I had painted those because I couldn't think of anything else and because it was all meaningless anyway, then I might just as well have tipped out the paint on the street, or done nothing at all.

The later abstract paintings also evoke the idea of the picture as a 'model'. Is that meant in a Mondrian-like sense?

This was something that came up in an interview with Buchloh: the idea that Mondrian's paintings might be understood as social models of a non-hierarchical, egalitarian world. Perhaps that was what prompted me to see my own abstract paintings as models, not of an egalitarian world but of a varied and constantly changing one. But fortunately Mondrian's paintings are not read as models of society. Their most important quality is a very different one. It would be terrible if the *Broadway Boogie-Woogie* painting were a model of society: there would be the Yellows, the Reds and the Blues, all moving ahead in straight lines.

Roland Barthes says, 'To be modern is to know what is no longer possible.'

What is no longer possible is everything that has already been said, and all the attendant stupidities of substance and form, pseudo-intelligent messages and dishonest intentions. If you try to avoid all that, it's hard at first, but eventually it works.

This avoidance is something you once described as 'escape'; and in your earlier pictures this referred mainly to the choice of motifs.

Like Beuys's hare. He was always on the run, too. How shall I put it, escaping from falschood is always a good starting-point.

It seems to me that this idea of escape is always cropping up in the present-day world. It's an escape that faces the facts – neither a nostalgic escape into the past, nor a Utopian escape into the future.

I hope so. Although it does create more uncertainty because the Utopian or nostalgic escapees are always the ones who have the advantage of knowing where they're going.

Uncertainty as the diametrical opposite of the controlled working plan?

Basically, yes: though the whole thing may seem fairly professional, it isn't, because it's not planned and controlled: it just happens.

Whistler's 'Art happens.'[9]

Or Buren's 'It paints.'

In your Atlas *there are sketches and designs for rooms that reveal an effort to find a place to fit the pictures, to create a kind of place-specific quality.*

That sort of thing only works in sketches, because the execution would be unendurable, overblown and bombastic. But it was good to design sanctuaries of that kind, for pictures with an incredible total effect.

Utopian spaces?

And megalomaniac ones.

The Two Sculptures for a Room by Palermo,[10] *now in the Lenbachhaus in Munich, create a state of permanence without reference to the actual location.*

It's a very modest thing.

What works of yours exist in public space? The Underground station in Duisburg; the Hypo-Bank in Düsseldorf?

And *Victoria*, two large-format works in an insurance company. The two yellow *Strokes* are in a school. That's all, almost. And at BMW, rather badly hung, there are three large canvases, red, yellow, blue, each one three metres high by six metres wide – as an enlargement.

Commissioned works...

Yes, sometimes I've enjoyed doing commissioned work, in order to discover something that I wouldn't have found of my own accord. And so, when Siemens commissioned my first townscape,[11] that led to all the townscapes that followed. It's also very nice when pictures have a known place to go to.

You've always made it a point of principle not to control where your pictures go, not to decide where and how they are hung. No reliance on your own hall of fame or private museum. You've just let the pictures go.

Let them go unconditionally. They need no precautions. If they're any good, they'll always find the right place; if they're not, they'll end up in the basement, and quite right too.

Haacke, for instance, tries to get this total control. He has been trying to strengthen the artist's position.

Just imagine Giacometti making stipulations of that kind! I'm glad he didn't, so that his sculptures can be shown differently each time, now in Denmark, now in Stuttgart. Every time they look different, and yet they always stay the same. There are some frightful instances of artists who have created these imperishable monuments for themselves. A certain Herr Tiefenbach, for instance, on Capri. Embarrassing.

There are some positive examples: the Segantini Museum, the Rothko Chapel, the Earth Room.

And Walter De Maria's *Lightning Field*. And all those beautiful churches, of course – there it has worked wonderfully well.

The pictures have lasted through time, thanks to their symbiotic relationship with the space.

We're a long way away from that at the moment. Kounellis, in that curious conversation he had with Beuys, Kiefer and Cucchi,[12] talked about building a cathedral. Simulated presence. It's sometimes done for reasons of art politics, when galleries and curators want to force something through and set up artificial monuments of that kind, full of pseudo-masterpieces.

The 'New Museology' of the 1980s arose from the Beaubourg Effect, which also had its political side. Individual works from a wide-ranging collection serve to illustrate the chronological charts; the display is designed for the masses, and only stops short of the final logical step, which would be to replace the originals with copies...

Pity.

In view of this combination of haste and cultural illiteracy, it seems to me more important than ever that there are some places where one can go and pay a visit to works – the way I visit your Baader-Meinhof work in Frankfurt from time to time.

Not that that's an ideal museum, exactly. But I know what you mean.

When I saw your room in Kassel,[13] I wondered at first whether the wood was chosen by you, whether it was taking up something that is implicit in the pavilion architecture. The wood might be part of a prefabricated kit, and it ironically forces the whole thing almost down to the level of a neat domestic interior. At the same time, it strongly emphasizes the break with the 'White Cube' formula.

It was Paul Robbrecht who suggested the wood panelling. The obligatory white walls date back only sixty or eighty years.

The only other place where I've seen that kind of floor-to-ceiling hanging in relation to your work is in your own studio.

It only works in small spaces, on the private side. Whenever I've tried it on a temporary partition in a big exhibition, it's never worked.

What surprised me in Kassel was the flower piece. Was that painted after your visit to Japan?[14]

Yes, perhaps that trip did have some influence: it affected those vertical scraped stripe paintings, too.

The flower piece has remained unique in your work. But at the time it put me in mind of a cycle. It could be a starting point.

I have tried painting photographs of flowers since then, but there's nothing suitable. And when I tried to paint the flowers themselves, that didn't work either. Unfortunately. I should have remembered that it hardly ever works for me to take a photograph in order to use it for a painting. You take a photograph for its own sake, and then later, if you're lucky, you discover it as the source of a picture. It seems to be more a matter of chance, taking a shot with the specific quality that's worth painting. The same happened with the *Cathedral* picture. I took the photograph in 1984. I was not in the best of moods at that time. And when I painted it, three years later, I went on to photograph some other 'cathedral corners' of the same kind – but I didn't get one usable shot. The state of mind counts for a lot...

... a state that is specific to a time...

... and makes you receptive to something. If I went to that cathedral now, I wouldn't know what to photograph. There's no reason why, and I can't force it. I even went all the way to Greenland, because C. D. Friedrich painted that beautiful picture of *The Wreck of the 'Hope'*.[15] I took hundreds of photographs[16] up there and barely one picture came out of it. It just didn't work.

So the 'quest for the motif' has very seldom led you to a picture?

The quest for the motif is strictly for the professionals. On the other hand, when I sit down somewhere out there, more or less aimlessly and not looking for the motif, then all of a sudden the thing I've not been looking for may open up. That's good.

The flower pieces in particular raise the issue of the experiential reality of nature, which is no longer a direct experience of nature.

Because the flowers are cut and stuck into a vase...

... or because it happens via the photograph.

I think that's less important, because directly painted flowers would be no less artificial. Everything is artificial. The bunch of flowers, the photograph – it's all artificial. There's nothing new about that.

Or, to turn it round again: the Demiurge and Nietzsche's eternal recurrence of nature. The painter goes into nature and sees it as a picture created by him.

A nice idea, and one that's absolutely right, not only for painters but for everyone. We make our own nature, because we always see it in the way that suits us culturally. When we look on mountains as beautiful, although they're nothing but stupid and obstructive rock piles; or see that silly weed out there as a beautiful shrub, gently waving in the breeze: these are just our own projections, which go far beyond any practical, utilitarian values.

When did you first use mirrors?

In 1981, I think, for the Kunsthalle in Düsseldorf.[17] Before that I designed a mirror room for Kasper König's *Westkunst* show, but it was never built. All that exists is the design – four mirrors for one room.

The Steel Balls *were also declared to be mirrors.*

It's strange about those *Steel Balls*, because I once said that a ball was the most ridiculous sculpture that I could imagine.

If one makes it oneself.

Perhaps even as an object, because a sphere has this idiotic perfection. I don't know why I now like it.

At the time when you made 4 Panes of Glass *in 1967, glass was being used a lot, both in art and in architecture.*

In art, too?

Glass was used in Minimal and Conceptual art: Morris had mirror cubes, in which the exhibition space and the viewer became part of the work; and of course Dan Graham, in his Corporate Arcadia *text, shows the strong presence of glass in the architecture of that period. In mid-1960s buildings you watch the people on the lower floors working: it's transparent architecture.*

That was a social preoccupation on Graham's part. What attracted me about my mirrors was the idea of having nothing manipulated in them. A piece of bought mirror. Just hung there, without any addition, to operate immediately and directly. Even at the risk of being boring. Mere demonstration. The mirrors, and even more the *Panes of Glass*, were also certainly directed against Duchamp, against his *Large Glass*.

Duchamp comes back all the time, like a boomerang. You take up a position opposed to the complexity of the Large Glass, *and straightaway in comes the readymade idea as well.*

Maybe. But what interested me was going against all that pseudo-complexity. The mystery-mongering, with dust and little lines and all sorts of other stuff on top. I don't like manufactured mystery.

In the 4 Panes of Glass, *the artistic act was reduced to the most minimal level.*

Once again I had to take the trouble of finding the right proportion, getting the right framework. This is not a readymade, any more than Duchamp's *Large Glass* is.

Because so much work went into it.

That's right. At one point I nearly bought a readymade. It was a motor-driven clown doll, about 1.5 metres tall, which stood up and then collapsed into itself. It cost over 600 DM at that time, and I couldn't afford it. Sometimes I regret not having bought that clown.

You would have exhibited it just like that, as an uncorrected readymade?

Just like that. There are just a few rare cases when one regrets not having done a thing, and that's one of them. Otherwise I would have forgotten it long ago.

In your studio there's a little mirror, hung in such a way that one is always seeing bits of recently finished paintings reflected in it.

In this case it's a good thing that it isn't head-high, but a little higher, so that you see the mirror and not the usual mirror image, which is yourself.

Over the last two years you've made the grey and coloured Mirrors, *which you showed in the* Mirrors *exhibition at Anthony d'Offay.*[18]

Those are panes of glass with a layer of paint on the back. This means that they are somewhere in-between, neither a real mirror nor a monochrome painting. That's what I like about them.

I see the mirror as a metaphor for your work as a whole. The word 'reflect' has two planes of meaning, which bring the viewer into the picture, and thus the viewer is in two states at once. A reflective trick.

The pleasant thing is that it makes the pictorial space even more variable and more subject to chance than it is in photography.

Even more open?

Yes, this is the only picture that always looks different. And perhaps there's an allusion somewhere to the fact that every picture is a mirror.

Making fun of the Modernistic attribute of flatness.

Or rather of the view that every picture has space and significance and is an appearance and an illusion, however radical it may be, right down to the Modernist goal of the flat surface, as in the grey pictures: these surfaces, too, have once more become illusionistic.

The steel ball, by reflecting the pictorial space, is simultaneously both the receiver and the transmitter of appearance. Once the attribute of the Emperor's worldly power, it seems to have rolled out of the picture – partly as a rejection of naïve forms of New Age holism. Lately, you've often added paint to paintings or scraped it off.

Just like playing boules. Shoot; create new situations.

Conversation with Henri-François Debailleux, 1993

How did this alternation between figurative and abstract work come about?

There's no precise reason. I started doing 'figures', then, one day, all of a sudden, I started doing abstraction. And then I started doing both. But it was never really a conscious decision. It was simply a question of desire. In fact, I really prefer making figurative work, but the figure is difficult. So to work around the difficulty I take a break and paint abstractly. Which I really like, by the way, because it allows me to make beautiful paintings [*laughs*]. But also, with abstraction, I reassure myself with the fact that music is also abstract when it's not explained or sung.

Is this movement from one genre to another a game?

It's never a game. It's more of a necessity. There's always some reason that, at a given moment, motivates me to choose one path or another, a reason that simply corresponds to my state of mind – happiness or, conversely, pessimism, which was the case for the work I showed last year in Kassel.[1] There's also my desire to attempt everything.

How do you explain the difficulty you have with figurative work?

I can do abstract painting in an almost professional way. With the figure, on the other hand, it's impossible. Chance is precluded from it. You also need a particular condition and a particular angle – and you also have to be able to find them – because from the moment photography came into existence, it has precluded almost everything. Plus, when I'm painting a figure, I try to bring it to the canvas in the best way possible: it's not easy, but it is necessary, because what surrounds us is generally true, good and sometimes even beautiful. When those things are painted, we find ourselves *de facto* in the false. So they have to be 'pushed' to the point where they gain a beautiful appearance, to the point where we want to look at them. For that, they have to be as pitch-perfect as a song.

You have done every possible subject: still-lifes, landscapes, portraits, etc. Why?

Because they happen to surround us. We all need them. My method is related to an attempt to do something that might be understood by today's world, or that could at least provide understanding. In other words, doing something I understand and that everyone understands. This natural desire for communication is also found in other domains, like reading and discourse, etc. I also hate repeating myself; it gives me no pleasure whatsoever. Once I've understood something, I need to start off on new ground.

Does the exhibition have an analytical intention?

An exhibition like this one, representing thirty years of work, necessarily compresses my work, a little like the way coffee gets extracted from beans. It therefore represents a false image, but that's also just as well. It's false in the sense that one might think that the subjects were taken on solely as an exercise or a mere study of painting. At least, that's something I've often read. In reality, it represents a real commitment. That's why I have trouble understanding it when people speak of my work according to those criteria.

Do you therefore object to the idea of the second degree that is often used to describe your method?

I don't know what the 'second degree' means. When I paint a candle and a skull, it's above all painting. Yes, it's even nothing but painting. People have also said that my painting is intellectual. I don't think I'm a complete idiot, and I don't like idiotic painting, but I don't consider myself to be an intellectual. People have also spoken of conceptual painting. But everyone needs a concept!

Why is there a 'distance effect' in your painting?

I don't think it's about distance, or at least I personally don't see any distance. I am more interested in the experience of giving something form. I understand that people may say that I am distant, and yet I am the complete opposite of artists like Robert Ryman or Carl André, who are themselves really distant and closed in on themselves. For me, these images, where my feelings can be read with a great deal of precision, are, quite to the contrary, very ... exhibitionistic!

Your canvases always display perfect technique...

Unlike the period when one had to learn technique and train from the youngest age, today no one masters technique any more at all. Painting has become so easy – anyone can do it! – that it's often very bad. In this context, as soon as someone knows technique, it jumps out at the viewer. That said, for me technique is something obvious: it's never a problem. I've just remained extremely attached to a culture of painting. What's much more important to me is the attempt, the desire to show what I want, in the best way possible. That's why technique is useful for me. For me, perfection is as important as the image itself.

Conversation with Stefan Weirich, 1993

When you painted the series back then, you spent eight months focusing on details of the terrorists, studying photographs of their prison cells. What was that like for you?

It was tough. But it was, after all, related to my work. I didn't have to stare helplessly at dead bodies, but was able to do something. While I'm painting, I'm well occupied. It's a bit like being a gravedigger, if you will.

Why did you prohibit the publication and reproduction of certain paintings from the series back then?

Those were pretty hysterical times, and I had good reason to be afraid that the press would have had a field day. It would have been extremely painful for the relatives and friends of the deceased.

Photography can be very cruel. Just think of that picture from Bad Kleinen.

Reality is even more dreadful!

Would you say that photography is, in fact, a representation of reality with the sting taken out of it?

Yes, sure. Just like with any reproduction. But since reality moves on and can only be captured in a reproduction, these representations aren't quite so harmless after all.

I've noticed that your paintings really evoke curiosity – a bit like photographs. When we look at photos, we're satisfying an urge.

Yes, you're right. People always want to be informed, so we need a daily diet of pictures that show us our reality in all its facets. When you say that my paintings evoke curiosity, do you mean that a photograph piques your curiosity less than a painted photograph?

That depends on the photograph. I have an inner revulsion towards a front-page photo depicting bloodshed.

But you look at it!

Yes, that's true. But when I'm home, I turn it around and don't look any more.

Yes, it bothers you. But with painted photographs, so many details are left out or blurred that it all becomes a little more bearable, and one perhaps becomes a little more curious.

You'll be giving an exhibition of your works in the Kunst- und Ausstellungshalle in Bonn[1] – a show that's already running in Paris. Why the collaboration with Bonn? That's not coincidence, is it?

No, it's a long story. The Parisians were the first to indicate that they wanted the exhibition: it was a long time ago, and I didn't feel like doing it. Then Madrid came along, and I was even less inclined, because I know just how much work is involved in organizing an exhibition oneself. At some point, the people from Bonn came and said they would like to do an exhibition with me. That's when I realized that they have an organizational structure that's very useful, where everything is taken care of by competent people. They have enough money to engage a curator. That was very pleasant.

What's your actual role in planning the exhibition?

Three of us developed the design: Benjamin Buchloh, Kasper König and me. Then there were many discussions, resulting in a plan that was to be different from the earlier retrospectives in Düsseldorf, where the focus was more on showing the contrasts between the various themes of the paintings. The American retrospective had done this in a very methodical fashion, dividing the works into three categories: the constructivist, the figurative and the abstract paintings. It's always fun to create a new perspective, to discover new contexts of meaning.

Have you found the right kind of rooms in Bonn?

We shall see. I don't know yet. Unlike in Paris, these are lofty, grandiose rooms with lots of space for the paintings. Pomp. I hope it'll be good.

In your works you always challenge the validity of what appears to be real. In doing so you create a new reality. But that would seem to be a contradiction.

Because a painting constitutes a reality that pays tribute to the reality outside – a reality one feels unsure of.

Do you occasionally have to struggle with yourself when it comes to deciding on a topic?

No, I think my approach is that I only search for things I feel will be viable as a painting. Other things don't interest me when it comes to painting. I couldn't just paint something that deals with our world's problems. Overpopulation, hunger, wars. No, I can't do that – not directly, at any rate.

Would Hoyerswerda, Mölln or Solingen be topics for you?

No, that would simply be too current. That's more the domain of other media that record these events in an accurate manner and report on them.

How do you react to criticism? How do you respond if someone says, 'The stuff Richter does is absolutely dreadful'?

Then I say he's stupid! But nobody simply says, 'Richter is terrible' – they go about it differently. Well, there are criticisms that are annoying, and there a few that are pleasant – that touch on a nerve. And sometimes they touch on something you weren't even aware of, and that's good because you can still learn something.

What do you regard as highly important in your immediate surroundings?

The heated studio, friends, a nice home. Basically all the things others appreciate, too.

Stern *magazine wrote about you: 'Richter is one of the most important, most productive and most expensive artists in the world.' What do you think of that?*

It's not true! It's sweet and inept, like *Stern* often is.

But at the moment collectors would pay unbelievable sums just for the cloth you use to clean your brushes.

No collector has ever bought a cloth from me.

Do you measure your success by visitor numbers?

No, every time it comes from an atmosphere. Of course, visitors contribute to this, but only a few people are really moved. It's like being at a concert, where one feels the mood – although at a concert, it's more of a mass phenomenon. To my mind, it's always a few people who get the message, and that spark then touches all the others.

A musician is directly confronted by the audience's reactions.

It's like that with an exhibition, too. You just get a feel for whether it's a success or not. There's less yawning, and people don't chat as much...

So we'll be seeing quite a bit of you in the Kunst- und Ausstellungshalle?

Yes, until the exhibition opens.

What are you working on at the moment?

I hope that I'm subconsciously working on something related to my next paintings. But at the moment, I only have these compensatory tasks – exhibitions, catalogues, and bits and pieces. No time to paint.

That must be awful for you.

That's quite true.

Are you searching specifically for new goals?

No, these goals arise automatically. But quite non-specifically. I want to paint again, as soon as possible.

Conversation with Amine Haase, 1993

Mr Richter, is it true that you're a conceptualist who uses painting as a means of proving his theories – as Pontus Hulten and Kasper König have just maintained?

No. I'm like a cabinetmaker who thinks about what kind of furniture is being made at present. The cabinetmaker isn't a conceptualist either.

But what about your paintings?

I simply like to paint.

But right at the beginning of the Bonn exhibition, we see mirrors – not paintings.

That's right, but mirrors are also picture-like objects, or whatever the term is.

But they are definitely not painted works of art. Do you enjoy the confusion surrounding terms that aren't clear-cut: painting, picture, object, concept?

Conceptual art was modern, and seems to be so once again...

In Paris, some critics hailed you as the father of post-modernism. How do you feel about this, considering you were already a Pop artist, a Minimalist and the godfather of the Junge Wilde *movement?*

That's fine by me. I have my own problems to be getting on with.

Such as?

Painting.

In Bonn, much more so than in Paris, you do in fact stage far more of what you call painting. Why?

There was less room in Paris, so I couldn't 'stage' anything. The rooms in Bonn are much larger. The arrangements are the result of a 'gut feeling'. After all, there isn't a set order for the paintings that needs to be observed in each location.

But doesn't your own perception of your works – which, after all, span a period of thirty years – require an order of sorts to make them accessible?

That's basically true, but the architecture in the Bonn location is very decisive – as is most architecture, in essence, whether it's barrack-like or grandiose, as it is here.

What do you prefer – a fairly sober building, like the Musée d'Art Moderne de la Ville de Paris, or something like here in Bonn?

Initially, you have the impression that it's harder to see the paintings in Bonn: your attention is focused on the setting. But each picture stands out on its own – under quite different conditions than in Paris.

Talking of setting: why do you hang a Candle *(1983) next to the three very large and dark paintings* November, December *and* January *(1989)?*

It fits so well.

Advent in Bonn?

Yes, advent in Bonn. But I also show candles at the height of summer.

So now we're back to paintings?

Definitely.

Interview with Stefan Weirich about the 18 *October* 1977 series, 1993

When you were putting the series together, you spent eight months focusing on the topic of death. You delved into the details of the terrorists' lives, studied photographs of their cells. What was that like for you?

It was tough. But it was, after all, related to my work. I didn't have to stare helplessly at dead bodies, but was also able to do something while I was at it. While I'm painting the dead, I'm well occupied. Like a gravedigger, if you will – because he has something to do, it almost becomes a normal job. It's actually more difficult to spend the whole day in the rooms where these paintings are hanging – living with them, as it were. But as long as you're painting, it's not such a burden.

You also studied the different cultural objects left behind by the terrorists – using photographs that had been published in the press.

I only had books, and piles of photos. Lots of photos. But of course I didn't have any objects that actually belonged to them. Even the record player I only had a photo of, which I'd collected. Naturally I had far more material than I actually used.

Those were press photos.

Yes, they were from the magazines *Stern* and *Spiegel*, and from books. You know, I had actually planned to make the whole thing broader, and then I surprised myself by reducing it to the dead, to the last moment. I was going to approach the topic far more comprehensively. I was going to paint things from their lives, from their active period, but it didn't work, so I gave up on the idea of painting that.

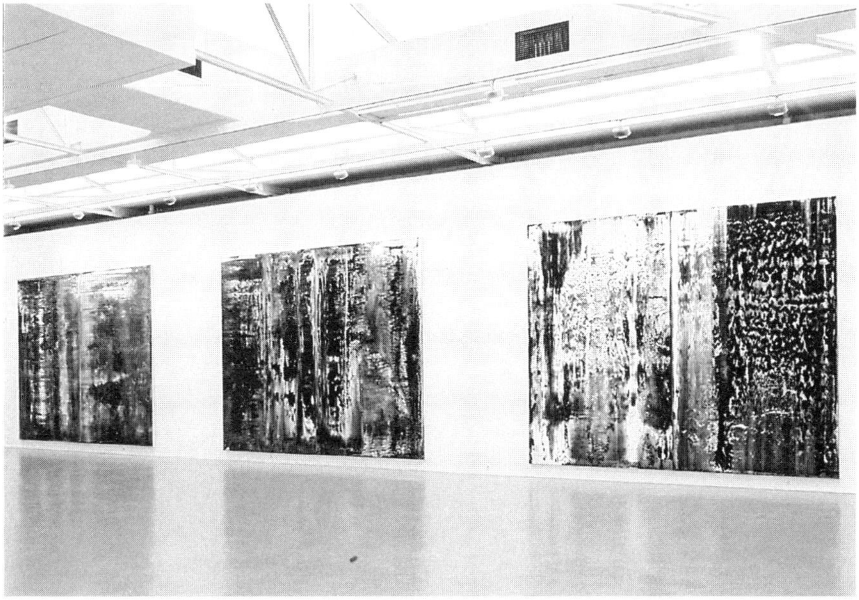

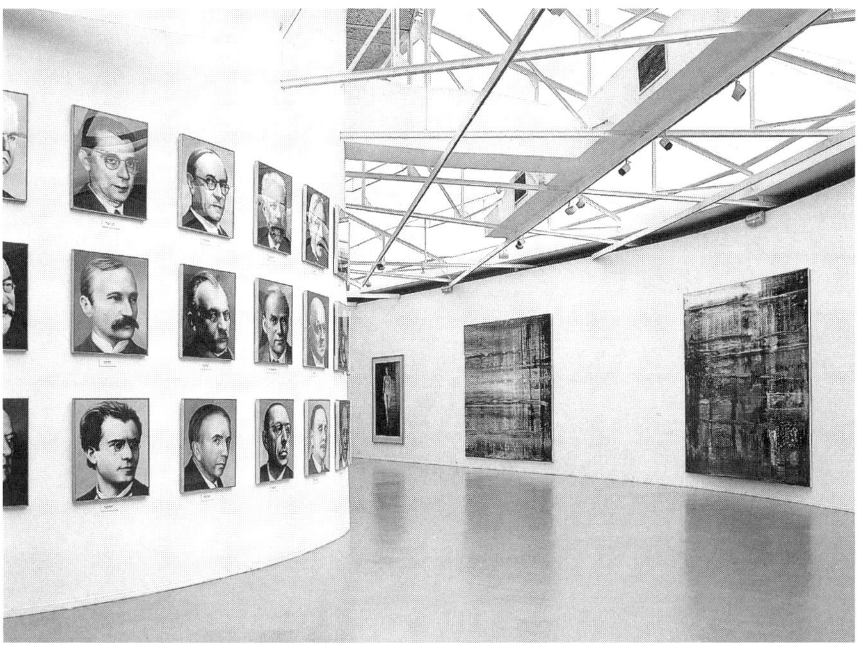

Musée d'Art Moderne de la Ville de Paris, 1993

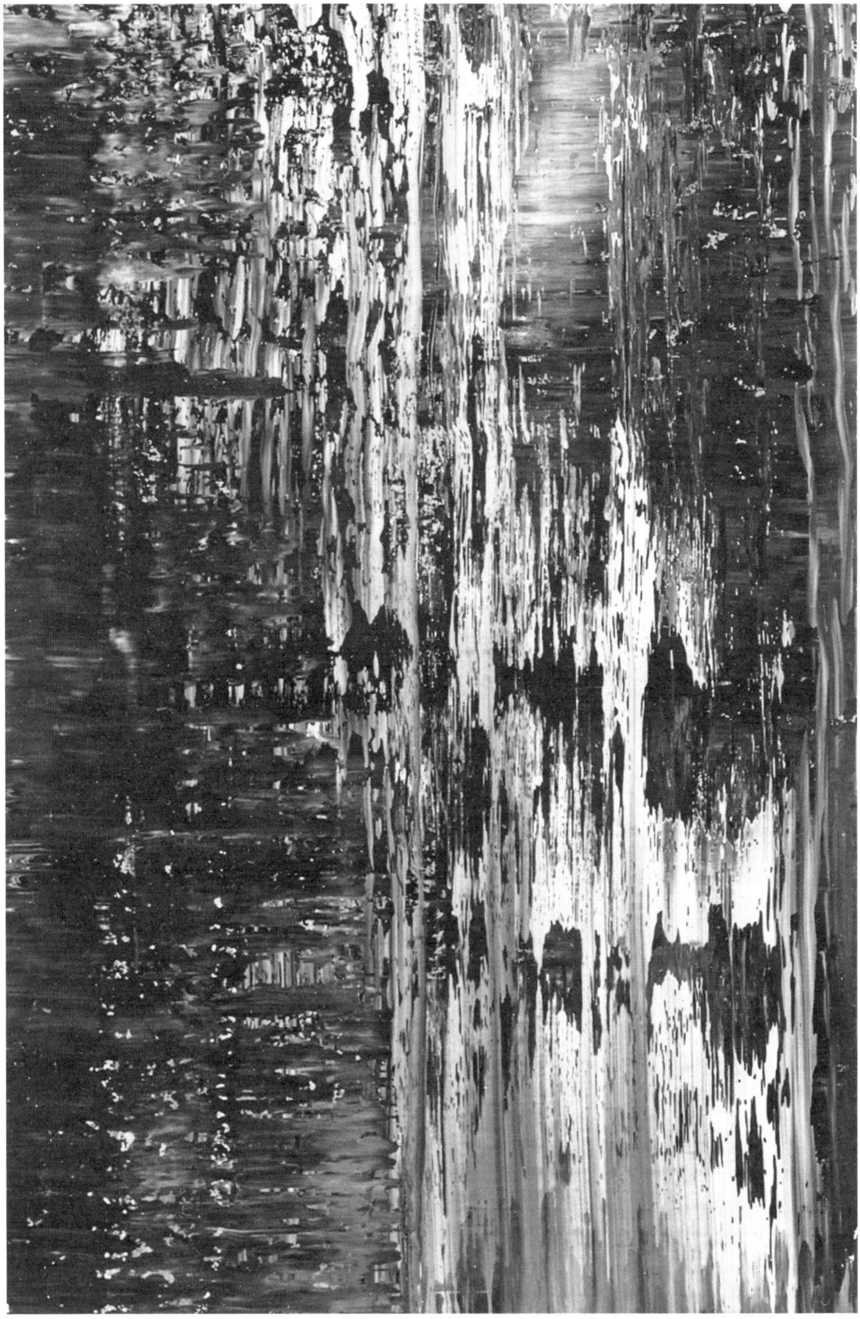

December, 1989 (detail)

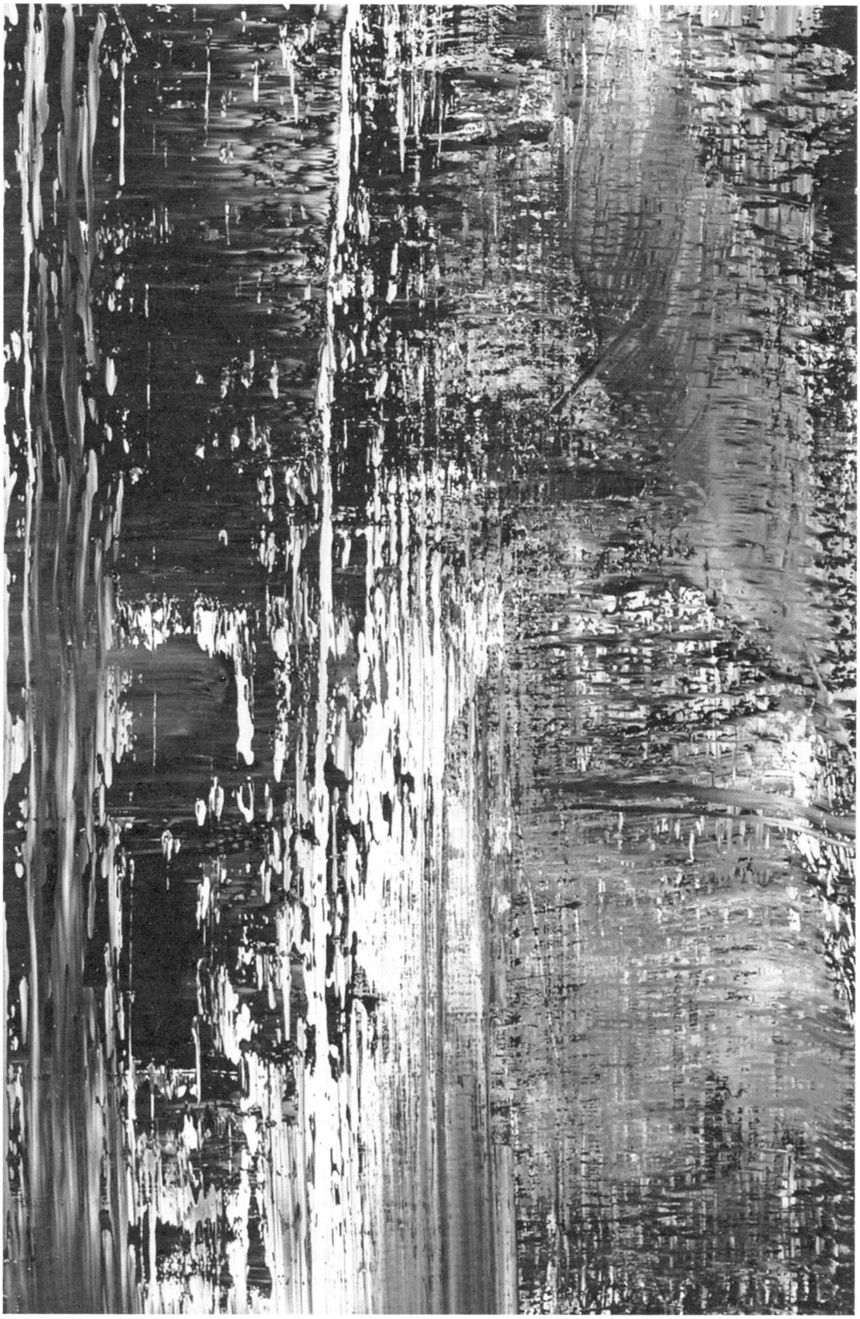

December, 1989 (detail)

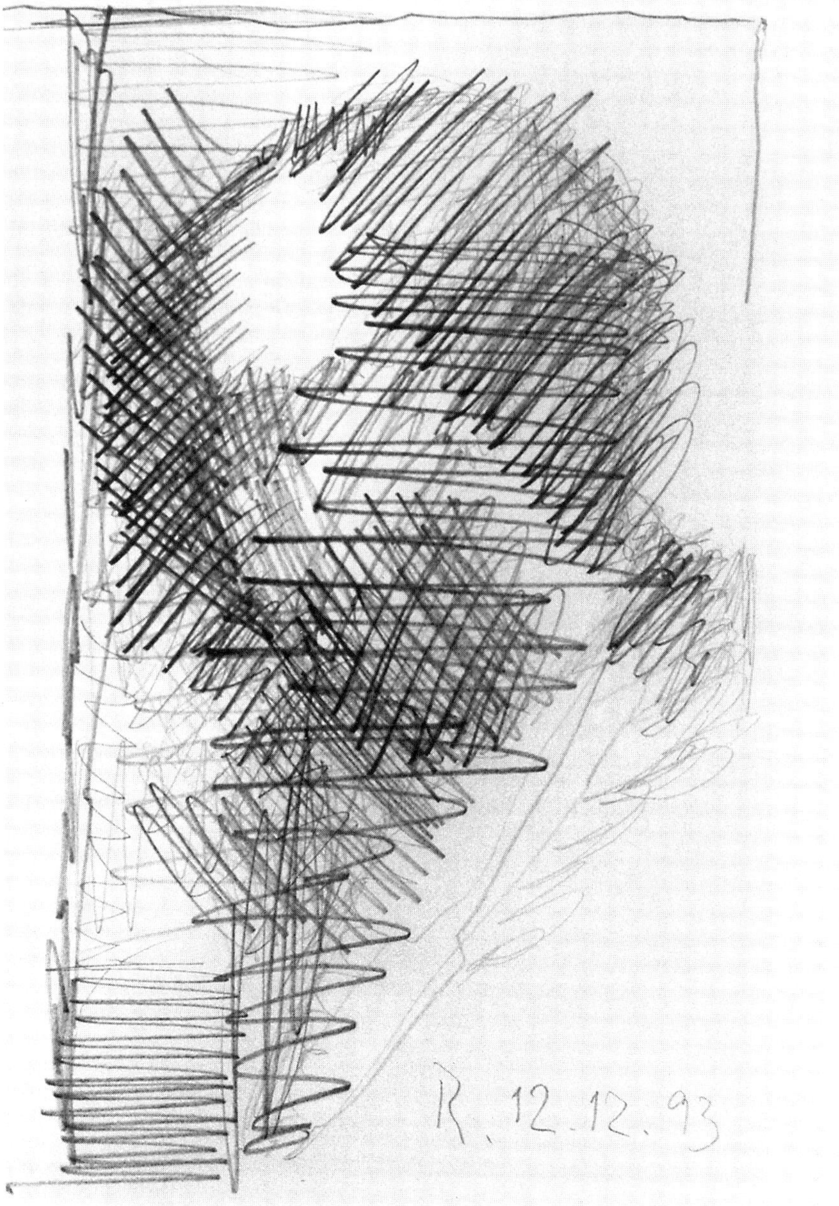

Drawing, 1993

Why did you prohibit the publication and reproduction of certain paintings from the series back then?

Those were pretty hysterical times, and I had good reason to be afraid that the press would have had a field day, because it's oh-so-sensational when someone paints something like that. It would have been extremely painful for the relatives and friends of the deceased if the whole thing had gone through the press again. I really wanted to avoid that.

Photography can be very cruel. Just think of that picture from Bad Kleinen.

Reality is even more dreadful. The smallness of the photograph almost makes it malicious – usable or acceptable. It plays it down. I mean, there are some really awful photographs, but reality just happens to be worse.

Would you say that photography is, in fact, a representation of reality with the sting taken out of it?

Yes, sure. Just like with any reproduction. But since reality moves on and can only be captured in a reproduction, these representations aren't quite so harmless after all.

I've noticed that your paintings really evoke curiosity – a bit like photographs. When we look at photos, we're satisfying an urge.

Yes, you're right. People always want to be informed, so we need a daily diet of pictures that show us our reality in all its facets. When you say that my paintings evoke curiosity, do you mean that a photograph piques your curiosity less than a painted photograph?

Interview with Susanne Ehrenfried, 1995

Were the 48 Portraits *directly influenced by the architecture of the Biennale pavilions, and do spatial conditions play an important role in your paintings? Or could these paintings have been created in a different environment (without any particular context)?*

The idea of painting the 48 *Portraits* is very old. I had had the idea for a long time, but I never actually dared to paint them. When I was invited to exhibit in Venice, I immediately realized that the architectural situation was perfect for the project. If it hadn't been for this, I probably would never have painted them. Because this work is so large in scope, it requires the right architectural setting. I was going to make about fifty paintings, but then I decided on forty-eight, because that can be divided into series of fours. The colour charts are also based on the number four.

Which of the later exhibition presentations came closest to your ideal, and why?

The presentation in the German pavilion was the most perfect. But I was also happy with the presentation in Lucerne, for example. Hanging the paintings in a row comes closest to my ideal. The Museum Ludwig did a terrible job of hanging the paintings, making them appear like a bar of chocolate.

Would you paint the 48 Portraits *exactly the same way today? What would you do differently? Would you include women in the series? And do you think Benjamin Buchloh's criticism is justified?*[1]

Buchloh's accusation is entirely congruent with current thinking and could not have been made at the time when I painted the 48 *Portraits*. It wouldn't have occurred to anyone back then. Today I wouldn't paint the 48 *Portraits* at all – not in that way, nor in any other. I used to prefer the pseudo-neutrality of encyclopedias, anonymity, and making things equal. Only including men in the series was consistent with this idea of homogeneity. If I had included women, the formal principles would no longer have been right. And it's probably also related to identity and my quest for a father figure. After all, I'm not searching for a mother figure [*laughs*].

Did the formal meaning of the term 'portrait' play an important role in the creation of your portraits? Did you analyze the traditional concept of portraits, or are such considerations of secondary importance when it comes to your motifs?

I'm afraid I'm unfamiliar with terms like these. That's not something I can answer. But, of course, portraits play a major role. I always aspire to paint good portraits, but I can't do that any more. I'm much more concerned with painting beautiful pictures.

Why was there such a long interval between the time when Betty[2] *was painted and the photograph was taken?*

Actually I always do it that way. A photograph is taken, I let it lie around and eventually I paint it.

On the whole, what do you make of people's analyses of your work in the realm of cultural studies? Do you have the impression that you are being properly understood?

None of that interests me. I don't even know what people are writing. I only know that many of my statements weren't meant the way they came across, or were wrong. Quotations are often a hindrance, and that's a disadvantage.

Why do you no longer paint works in black and white?

That would be old-fashioned. Painting is colour. My use of black and white earlier was part of my general act of refusal. It was also more authentic. Newspapers and magazines were full of black-and-white pictures.

Why don't you paint strangers any more?

In the past, I much preferred chance, but today personal relationships are more important to me.

But on a formal level there's little difference between them.

That's true. My portraits are supposed to be artificial. The artistic form is the important factor.

Did the portraits of women[3] come about in conjunction with the Romanticism exhibition?

No, I had painted them much earlier. They were only selected for this event. Butin had seen the portraits and suggested they be included. The *48 Portraits* are really the only works that were devised in that way.

Have you ever painted commissioned portraits?

Yes, in the 1960s. The portraits of Wachenfeld, Dwinger, Wasmuth, Schniewind and Schmela, for example, were commissioned works. Somehow, this way of doing things was typical in the 1960s. And that suited me very well, because it enabled me to bracket out my personal artistic preferences and allow these paintings to become products of chance. Eventually, however, I lost interest in working that way. Nowadays, no one approaches me with requests like these, because they all know: Richter doesn't do portraits on commission any more.

Interview with Hans Ulrich Obrist, 1995

In the beginning...

We begin simply [*laughs*].

The blow-up and the game with the ruler are a thread running through your work. I'm thinking, for instance, of the sketches in the Atlas *where pictures were intended to become large Utopian spaces, or the micro-studies on paper in the 1970s, which paved the way for the first large-format abstract pictures a little later.*

That's right, that happened more often.

How did the blow-up of your candle picture in Dresden come about?[1]

I don't even know any more who in Dresden had the idea of asking for a picture from me to cover the large façade. I think it was Dr Schmidt from the museum,[2] and he was also the one who suggested a candle as a motif. I then made collages of various pictures of candles on a photo of the façade and that's how what seemed the most suitable motif of the two candles came about. At first it was only intended to look pretty, but later a politically useful statement was also found in the picture.

How did the picture become politically charged?

That came about through the 13 February anniversary of the destruction of Dresden fifty years earlier which was coming up. And candles had always been an important symbol for the GDR, as a silent protest against the regime, which already made a great impression. Naturally, it was a strange feeling to see that a small picture of candles was turning into something completely different, something that I had never intended. Because as I was painting it, it neither had this unequivocal meaning nor was it intended to be anything like a street picture. It sort of ran away from me and became something over which I no longer had control. A similar thing happened with the Vienna picture.

Talking about pictures running away...

Like with children who later do things that you don't understand any more.

There's this 'Two-leg theory'. The works are present in highly specialized discursive contexts, while simultaneously having a popular dimension.

I wasn't previously aware of that, that a picture appears in a whole range of forms which I am absolutely not, or only seldom, responsible for. That's done by other people, and because they do it for another purpose it also becomes another picture. The postcard of a candle is there to send greetings and the large-format picture to drive past. I neither made nor intended either of them. A nice side-effect. To make them popular.

The form in which the same picture appears is changed by the selection of details, by the enlargement as well as the copying by CALSI (Computer Aided Large Scale Imagery). The translation is permanently there in your pictures; the translation from photo to picture which is once again reproduced. The format of the large-format picture (50 × 10 metres) brings to mind the propaganda pictures of the Russian Revolution, for instance by Altman, or Dufy's Fée Electricité.[3] *Or your monumental* Strichbild.[4]

Except that with Raoul Dufy it's not a reproduction; he himself painted it directly on the wall. And my two large lines weren't an enlargement of pictures but the enlargement of designs which I had made only for this purpose. On the other hand the picture for the Vienna Kunsthalle is a reproduction, and on top of that it's a reproduction of the detail from a picture. So it became a completely new picture, and also because its authorship is a completely different one. It wasn't even me who had the idea, that came from others, and the choice of motif was then made collectively, so it wasn't from me alone. That's a completely different way of working, rather like in an advertising agency, where I have just been working on a long-term project. That's very exciting and very contemporary. Maybe exhibitions would even be organized much better and with much more effect on the public with reproductions instead of originals.

The writer Bruce Sterling has been putting his books on the internet for several years and making them available to everyone. What is astounding is that the sales figures for his hardcovers and paperbacks have in no way sunk but have risen dramatically. In the virtual and digital world there's a great demand for the book as an object which can be handled. The same applies to exhibitions: the originals don't become any less valuable, but the distribution is much greater.

That's good – that's the only thing you should really want; to be as broadly present as possible. To expand oneself. Otherwise the others will do it [*laughs*].

Are there limits? Television?

Only because it doesn't know what to do with pictures. They only want actors, the artist in the talkshow who then makes himself totally ridiculous.

And a still picture on television?

That would be wonderful – occasionally a still picture on the box, without commentary, without music; maybe it would be a release for the viewers.

Robert Bresson[5] said that different rules are valid in each medium. In this connection maybe it would be interesting to talk about your film experiment in Japan.[6]

Where I went about it in the wrong way, rather carelessly experimented in another medium. That went completely wrong. Film is not for me.

That brings us back to your original reservations about the large-format picture.

At the beginning I thought that I had to come up with something very special – not what I can do but something completely different, something spectacular, screaming or funny. Then I have a lot of silly ideas which in the end only depress me. That's why your idea of using the river picture was very healthy. And that only a detail was enlarged I find very beautiful: it also fits in with the plan for the small book,[7] which will only show details.

The Halifax book[8] was multi-perspective and gathered various views of a picture. In contrast, the book now being put together will include frontally reproduced details of a picture. Going back to the large-format picture, at first you thought of a blow-up of a sequence of photos.

Yes, but as I said, of very special photos, which I can't even create. Now I can also imagine my photos in such a large format. Next time.

Interview with Hubertus Butin, 1995

Mr Richter, since 1991 the 18 October 1977 series has been on permanent loan to the Frankfurt Museum of Modern Art. Not only is it one of the highlights of the collection, it is also of fundamental importance to Jean-Christophe Ammann's conceptual design for the building. In that sense, the loss for the museum is doubly painful. Ammann made a great effort to try to keep the paintings there permanently. Why didn't you sell the series to him?

No concrete offer was made in Frankfurt, and, as far as I know, it couldn't have been made because the Frankfurt Museum of Modern Art has no money. I realized, of course, that Jean-Christophe Ammann wanted the museum to keep the paintings; he was very clear with me and others about this, right from the beginning, but at the same time I could never make him a promise. Because, with all respect, I always knew that the Frankfurt Museum wasn't necessarily the final destination for the paintings, and so, to my mind, it became the perfect place to loan them for a period of ten years.

So you've been using the museum as a 'waiting room'?

Not initially, since I felt so undecided about the series then. For this reason, I was very happy about Ammann's offer.

For how long will the paintings remain in Frankfurt, and how did the New York Museum of Modern Art come to be the buyer?

The series will remain in Frankfurt until 31 December 2000, after which it will go to America. Robert Storr and Kirk Varnedoe from the New York MoMA saw the paintings while the exhibition was on tour in the United States, and, apparently, they were so taken by them that they contacted my New York gallery, and eventually they got in touch with me.

The Museum of Modern Art is not an institution funded by the city or the American taxpayers, but rather a private foundation governed by a board of trustees. The board runs this temple of the muses like a big company, and the overheads and money required for purchases are largely generated through fundraising activities and through collecting donations. It's normal practice within MoMA to sell works of art from its own collection if the funds raised for a desired acquisition are insufficient – a policy which, thankfully, would be unimaginable in Germany. So what would you say if, in a few years' time, you happened upon your series at a New York auction?

You might just as well ask me what I would feel like if MoMA were flattened by an earthquake. But I'm sure the purpose of your question is to know whether the acquisition is tied to certain demands, which it isn't. I have never set conditions for a sale: in other words, every buyer has the right to re-sell the painting, stick it in his basement, or heaven knows what. Therefore, MoMA is also entitled to do as it pleases, and I think this is quite natural, since nothing remains as it is. The way art is perceived changes over time, and every painting eventually attains the status it deserves, except in a very few unfortunate instances.

Within the last five years the series has been exhibited in places like Boston, St Louis, Los Angeles, New York and San Francisco. The American public responded very favourably, generally lavishing praise on the work and acknowledging your impeccable moral integrity. Leaving all the general accolades aside, did MoMA give you a detailed explanation as to its specific interest in the 18 October 1977 series?

Robert Storr wrote to me to outline why he wanted the series for the museum, why he thinks the paintings are so good, etc. So I'd need to look at his letter again.

Kirk Varnedoe, MoMA's chief curator of painting and sculpture, announced: 'The paintings most probably remind the majority of contemporary observers of an era of violent social struggle and serve as a catalyst for current debates about some of the most inflammatory and controversial political ideas to be put forward in the second half of the twentieth century.' Varnedoe was probably thinking, amongst other things, of the wide-ranging political debates that were unleashed after the initial presentation of the paintings in Germany, which led the media to take a fresh look at this repressed historical topic. How do you see this particular American interest in the German RAF [Red Army Faction] and related topics, and, more generally, how do you rate the efficacy of political art in conservative America?

Because the Americans are far removed from the topic of the RAF, they probably relate to it in more general terms – in terms that are relevant to every modern or even unmodern country: the overall danger of ideological beliefs, fanaticism and mayhem. That's relevant in any country, including the US, which you rather sweepingly refer to as conservative. But I can also see another, more direct, link between America and the RAF – and I don't just mean the Vietnam war, which Baader and Ensslin protested against in 1968 by placing several incendiary devices in two department stores in Frankfurt. I also see a link in the fact that the attitudes and lifestyles of the so-called 1968 movement were strongly influenced by American ideals. Even the movement's inherent anti-Americanism wasn't simply a reaction against US hegemony, but was largely imported from America.

In the New York Observer, *Hilton Kramer launched a massive attack against MoMA. He's the editor-in-chief of* New Criterion, *the cultural bastion of the American neo-conservatives. As far back as thirty years ago, he agitated against Andy Warhol, claiming that 'the radical movements of the 1960s' were destroying 'the cultural ideals of an advanced civilization'. He also heaped his polemical scorn on such important artists as Robert Ryman, Cy Twombly, Jackson Pollock and Marcel Duchamp. Now he's accusing MoMA of 'mindlessly burning money and ruining its reputation' by buying the* October *paintings. He says that, with the series, you 'bestow upon the Baader-Meinhof gang the status of political saints and martyrs', and he implies that you are a sympathizer. The* Newsweek *author David Gordon has even demanded that the paintings be shown alongside portraits of the terrorists' victims. When we look more closely at the work, we can see that it is not in any way an attempt to transcend or glorify terrorism, and you have repeatedly said in public that, aside from a sense of sadness about the perpetrators, you do not sympathize with them. Nevertheless, this kind of attack by conservatives was to be expected. Did Dresdner Bank also succumb to this unfortunate misinterpretation when, in 1989, it complained that you had excluded the victims from your paintings?*

It's understandable that Dresdner Bank initially found the paintings objectionable and retracted financial support for the Frankfurt Museum of Modern Art, considering that its chairman, Jürgen Ponto, was murdered. And regarding the few press statements that criticize MoMA for buying the paintings, they can more or less be ignored, since it's obvious that they don't have much weight. And it would be quite unnatural, terrible even, if everyone praised the decision. It's perfectly fine the way it is.

Shortly after Kramer and Gordon wrote their articles, the artist Richard Serra, writing in the New York Times, *emphatically defended your work. He emphasized its uniqueness within contemporary art, and compared its influence to that of Goya's paintings and to those of the late Rembrandt. Irrespective of whether such a comparison is justified or not, it's symptomatic of the esteem that important American artists have for you. As of September, the series will be shown in a retrospective in Jerusalem.*[1] *Back in 1989, the most widely read Israeli newspaper in Tel Aviv published a major article about the* October *paintings. Do you think that the Jerusalem exhibition of the series will generate as much attention, and do you expect there to be a specifically Jewish perspective?*

I don't know enough about the situation in Israel. But the curators of the museum in Jerusalem really wanted the *October* series to be included, and they emphasized how important it was to exhibit it in their country. And the reason for this, surely, isn't just that the paintings deal with an important topic in German history, but mainly because terror and death aren't exactly unknown to the people of Israel, as is obvious when we look at the current conflicts with the Palestinians.

In 1993 the Berlin newspaper taz wrote that the series 'deals with the intensity of an ideology that, within its own illogical rationality, leads to death', because the RAF's credo was based on the blind and radical principle that altruistic action and spilling the blood of others would further revolutionary ideals. In an interview in 1989, you yourself stated that the series was intended as a general criticism of ideological thought and its ramifications. In the same vein, Jean-Christophe Ammann, the director of the Frankfurt Museum of Modern Art said, 'It is a work of art that represents the ultimate warning against ideologies in Germany in this century [...] Therefore it is a work that deals with Germany itself.' That's probably why Ammann was so shocked about the sale: 'Had he asked me beforehand, I would have said, "Whatever you do, make sure the paintings remain in Germany."' The F.A.Z. [Frankfurter Allgemeine Zeitung] *accuses you of 'neutralizing one of the lingering traumas of the post-war period by means of export'. Even considering the fact that most of the American public have responded very sensitively to the series and, unlike the German critics, immediately understood your intention, wouldn't you say that the presence of the paintings is far more important for our cultural identity and for understanding our history than they are for the Americans?*

'Neutralized by means of export' really is a rather ridiculous statement. These paintings aren't more important for Germany than for America, if only for the reason that they are not suitable for the oft-quoted task of coming to terms with history. There are other places conceived for this, such as the House of History in Bonn; there you can look at the manifestos and the equipment used by the RAF, and these exhibits would be wholly inappropriate in the United States. So things are getting mixed up here: on the one hand, there's, say, the historic material, on the other you have these paintings, which as I said deal with the topic in a general way. And one of the reasons why these depictions are so generally blurred and abstract in nature is that I most definitely didn't want to portray Gudrun or Ulrike – they are not educational material for German history.

In the selling of the October *paintings, the attention of the German public was drawn to them, and this elevated the work's domestic relevance, since it is being withdrawn from the public domain. Does your decision reflect a disappointment about the lack of interest among German museum directors – with the exception of Jean-Christophe Ammann?*

The reason these paintings are destined for New York is not because I am disappointed about a lack of German interest, but because MoMA asked me, and because I consider it to be the best museum in the world.

Strictly speaking, the transfer of the paintings to New York doesn't represent a defeat for German museums, because that could only be the case if there had been a prior conflict. Despite the great public interest, the only museum that had the courage at least to try to secure the series was the Frankfurt MMK [Museum of Modern Art]. *So the museums weren't defeated, but their lack of action is tantamount to an international, cultural and political embarrassment of the highest order. This flagrant lack of interest can't be excused, a posteriori, by claiming that there is no money because, when you take a closer look, you find that the Staatsgalerie Stuttgart recently raised 6.9 million DM for a Beckmann painting, and the Brücke Museum in Berlin purchased a Kirchner for 5 million, while the Neue Nationalgalerie intends to acquire a painting by Dix for 7.7 million. Don't you think that a work of such great social and political relevance as* 18 October 1977 *belongs somewhere like the Nationalgalerie in Berlin?*

I can't really confirm that, and I certainly won't say that these paintings 'belong' in a specific museum, be it in Berlin or in New York. I think the Nationalgalerie in Berlin is wonderful, but perhaps the *October* paintings wouldn't go very well with the existing collection. In that particular setting, the paintings might again be seen in a one-dimensional, historical light, thus attracting the wrong kind of attention. Incidentally, along with the Frankfurt Museum, the Diözesan Museum in Cologne also wanted the series. Initially, I was very fond of the idea, because I had this vision of an alternative to the populist Museum Ludwig but, then again, the specific nature of the Diözesan collection seemed too rigid a framework for my paintings. New York is the right choice.

In recent years you have frequently developed new photographic or graphic works from the motifs of previous oil paintings. I'm thinking of examples such as Kerze I und II [Candle I and II], Besetztes Haus [Squatted House], Betty *or* Ema (Nude on a Staircase). *Could you imagine creating a large-scale photographic version of the series, so that, at least, this incarnation would be domestically accessible to the German public?*

I do not think that 'the German public' wants such photographic works. But a photographic version of the paintings is not an impossibility. After all, there are two versions of the 48 *Portraits* from 1971–72.[2] So then MoMA would have a painted and a photographic version of the *October* paintings. That's not a must, though.

Interview with Stefan Koldehoff, 1995

Quite a fuss erupted here and in New York over the sale of the fifteen large Stammheim paintings. Is this because they're seen as dealing with a very German topic?

That's precisely what puzzles me – the fact that the subject of these paintings is regarded as being so specifically German. The people who are angry about their 'export' [to the US] have got something mixed up. They're investing these works with a documentary quality that simply isn't inherent in them. They were intentionally painted in an abstract manner: you don't see 'Ulrike Meinhof' or 'Andreas Baader', and there are no details pertaining to the history of the RAF [Red Army Faction]. The messages conveyed by these paintings only make sense within the context of art. In other words, they're not like the documents or artefacts you might find in places like the House of History in Bonn. Interestingly, the universal quality of these paintings always emerged quite clearly when they were exhibited abroad. Whether in London, America, or – as is the case now – in Israel, they're seen for what they are and convey a message that's pertinent to the country in which they're being viewed. And regarding Frankfurt, Jean-Christophe Ammann had always made it clear to me that he wanted the paintings for his museum, but I never promised them to him, because Frankfurt seemed less and less like the final destination for this series.

One might think that the pictures would be viewed with even more suspicion in America.

The reviews there were refreshingly different from those in Germany. People here were so disturbed by the subject that they had a hard time seeing the paintings as anything but political – or even regarded them as a kind of 'family affair'. That also explains why they made such ridiculous accusations – asserting, for instance, that a mainstream artist has no right to paint this kind of subject, or that the images were so abstract because I didn't have my own opinion. Outside of Germany, things were different: people's appreciation of the paintings wasn't hampered by expectations and prejudice.

And that's why you sold the paintings to the US?

The recipient was the main factor. We don't have a great museum like MoMA in Europe. Not even the Tate Gallery in London can match it.

Were the paintings out of place in Frankfurt?

The Frankfurt Museum wasn't necessarily the best place for them – precisely because there were obvious links between Frankfurt and the RAF. In Frankfurt they acquire this illustrative, local, documentary quality, which is detrimental to them.

Apparently there was a private collector in Frankfurt who was interested in acquiring the paintings and could have ensured that they remained in the country.

I don't know this collector. Nobody inquired about them, and no offer was made. But I'm happy no one asked me, because I would have had to have cleared it with my conscience: 'Maybe it would be better if...'

It was public knowledge that the loan to Frankfurt would end in late 1999. That's why MoMA approached you with an offer. But the paintings would also have fitted nicely into the Nationalgalerie in Berlin.

That's true. But I also think it's possible that too much political importance would have been attached to them in that collection. A museum like the Nationalgalerie has a particular structure, and its collection has a particular focus. I think my paintings would have been associated with a meaning that could have been somewhat disruptive in this context.

So no other museums expressed interest?

The only other one that approached me was the Diözesan Museum in Cologne. They want to build a new museum and their collection extends from the Middle Ages to the present. This was very tempting at first, if only as a counterbalance and alternative to the Museum Ludwig, which is a bit too populist in its approach. But, in the end, I found the religious context went a bit too far in a certain direction.

There's a heated debate in the New York papers about how the paintings should be displayed. In this age of political correctness, someone even suggested hanging portraits of the RAF's victims next to your works.

This odd suggestion was made in *Newsweek*. But opinions like these represent a small minority, as opposed to the majority, who take a thoroughly positive view of the series. I think it's completely normal that silly views are expressed as well. That's part and parcel of the debate.

Would you object to an accompanying documentary?

In Los Angeles there was a small area with information boards on the topic and with explanatory texts and photos. It was well designed. The only disadvantage with this kind of approach is that people spend more time reading than studying the paintings.

For an exhibition in London, you recently immersed yourself in the subject again by painting over 23 pages of Pieter H. Bakker Schut's book Der Prozess gegen die Rote Armee Fraktion [The Trial Against the Red Army Faction].[1] *How did that come about?*

I don't know, really. The book was lying around, and the situation was similar to the one back then: it hadn't been dealt with. I didn't know what to do with the book. So I started to paint over the pages, just as I sometimes paint over photographs. Perhaps I finally wanted to bring this topic to a personal conclusion. One or two years later, I showed the pages to a friend. He thought they were very good and advised me to keep all 23 of them together, as one work of art.

Interview with Mark Rosenthal, 1998

When did you first see Rothko's work?

It was sometime in the early or mid-1960s. The paintings were a shock. They were so serious, not wild like Warhol. Rothko's attitude with regard to painting and the job of the painter were particularly impressive to me.

What did you perceive his attitude to be?

I think it was the Art Institute of Chicago in the mid-1950s that has made a classic view of Rothko's images popular, as it says that one tends to enter *into* his canvases – not merely to look at them.

When was your next confrontation with the work?

That occurred sometime in the late 1960s, when I visited the Tate Gallery, London, to see the large series there. I came with great expectation, but the experience was a bit strange, like visiting a church. It was more an experience about mystery than about painting, I thought. Although I wasn't disappointed, I didn't identify with Rothko's work either.

Were there many of Rothko's paintings to see in Europe?

No, and I have never seen a retrospective, unfortunately.

During the 1970s, as you yourself came to work more consistently in an abstract fashion, how did you feel about Rothko?

At that time I really felt quite mixed about his work. It was both too holy and too decorative. Although the paintings apparently had a transcendental aspiration, they were used for decorative purposes, and looked overly beautiful in collectors' apartments.

Did you feel you understood Rothko's intentions?

The work had a presence that suggested a transcendental approach. While I certainly prefer that to cynicism, at the time I felt it was almost too easy to look serious and holy, just by painting dark works. There was a kind of science fiction coming from Rothko's darkness that was Wagnerian or had a narrative side, which bothered me.

This dichotomy between the holy and the decorative seems to haunt abstract painting and painters. How did you solve this dilemma, theoretically and practically, and how did your approach to that issue differ from Rothko's?

Rothko's enormous, calm paintings with their floating rectangles, where any trace of chance is removed, have something extraordinarily meditative that seems magical and mysterious. This deepness has got something religious. I myself distrust this message. This means I try to avoid every similarity with Rothko's art.

So I take it you have never related your work to Rothko's, that his attitude toward art was somehow traditional or old-fashioned?

I only identified with this seriousness, which was absolutely to be admired. At that time, in the 1970s, Barnett Newman, with his non-hierarchical structures, his non-relational colour-field painting, seemed more interesting because his work was less pretty.

Was beauty to be abandoned, then?

No, no, not at all. We need beauty in all its variations.

Did you ever share Rothko's metaphysical point of view?

Certainly. I too want that quality in general for my work, and to touch the world. But my interest only parallels Rothko; I am not influenced. His metaphysical aspirations are found in all great art. Besides, the mystery and incomprehensibility of Rothko's paintings are based on the specificity of the structures, the transcendental effects and the viewer's contemplation. The aesthetic experience in my abstract paintings is not metaphysical in the sense of being religious. Only the structure of my works is so complicated and difficult so that they are incomprehensible also. If you want, you may call it metaphysical.

Do you think metaphysical aspirations change in their details from one generation to the next?

Yes, but research or explaining such a development is very difficult.

Do you concur with the conventional view of Rothko as a Romantic?

Oh, no. For me Romanticism is the likes of Philipp Otto Runge, that is, an artist who presents a tortured view of himself. Maybe in the widest sense of the word Rothko might be a Romantic, as Robert Rosenblum suggested in his book *Modern Painting and the Northern Romantic Tradition: From Friedrich to Rothko.*[1]

Rothko was often comparing his work to music. It seems you have done the same.

I know that he had a tremendous sensitivity to music. As far as I know, he was a great fan of Mozart. I prefer Bach. Sometimes I listen to music while I paint. Since the nineteenth century, however, music has been a great influence on pictorial creativity, no matter how. Rothko's or my relation to music is not exceptional regarding abstract painting.

Have your feelings about Rothko changed in recent years?

Well, I am less antagonistic to 'the holy', to the spiritual experience, these days. It is part of us, and we need that quality.

Is there anything about you that has caused your recent evaluation of Rothko?

I suppose that I am less aggressive and militant now.

Perhaps the 1970s was a time for that?

Yes, and I am older, too.

How do you view Rothko's legacy?

He was a man who created a special art for us, and no one else will do such paintings again. I believe Rothko will be important for centuries to come.

Interview with Dieter Schwarz, 1999

The watercolours are a particular chapter in your work because they appear so sporadically, much like the drawings.

Perhaps everything is sporadic – the drawings, the paintings...

As the self-portrait[1] shows, the first watercolours were created during the time in Dresden.

That was before the Academy, when I was 17. At the time I worked a lot in watercolours, but then, at the Academy, drawing and oil-painting were taught, not watercolouring. I also can't remember that anyone at all did watercolours.

Was the watercolour regarded as inferior?

It didn't belong to the classic course of study. One drew with charcoal and pencil; afterwards one painted in oil – smaller oil sketches, larger oil studies, finally the oil paintings themselves.

And were there no antecedents for watercolours?

I can't, in any case, remember any watercolours – except for those by Emil Nolde; he couldn't be overlooked, but he was no model. In the museums, too, there were only oil paintings or at best drawings to be seen, but no watercolours.

The two sheets from 1964, Portrait of Heiner Friedrich *and* Interior,[2] *are therefore the first and for a long time the only watercolours you produced after emigrating to the West.*

So it appears, but I couldn't take these two sheets at all seriously. Two exercises from nature and sooner to be seen ironically, so that I wanted to give them to Heiner Friedrich as a joke. But then I preferred to keep them for myself.

These watercolours were not painted from photographs?

Presumably they were, since I didn't make a watercolour in Heiner Friedrich's office. The other was at home in the living room, also from a photo.

Were the two sheets individual pieces, or were there others of this sort?

No, they were individual pieces. To do more in watercolour would have been too much like a hobby, a waste of time.

The two watercolours were then incorporated into the Atlas, *and in the 1970s they were removed from it again. What sort of position did they have in the* Atlas *– that of curiosities?*

In the beginning I tried to accommodate everything there that was somewhere between art and garbage and that somehow seemed important to me and a pity to throw away. After a while, some sheets in the *Atlas* acquired another value, after all – that is, it seemed to me that they could stand on their own terms, not only under the protection of the *Atlas*.

That was the time after the exhibition of the Atlas *in Utrecht*[3] *in 1972, when the* Atlas *was altered by some of the panels being removed. It was only in 1977 that there were again watercolours – indeed, several at the same time. The one sheet is particularly striking since it was apparently painted from the abstract picture* Parachute (431-10).

Perhaps it was again an attempt to bring my abstract painting to a more serious level, no longer just painting around so carelessly and unsystematically but more consciously, being master of the situation.

Why would this watercolour be more serious?

Perhaps it was the attempt to construct abstract painting instead of burrowing half-blind through the undergrowth. And, by copying a picture here, I hoped to discover a certain regularity, to get behind the abstract pictures.

In this single watercolour, everything seems to happen at the same time and to be situated at the same level, as if planned, bound into the plane, homogeneous, which in the abstract painting appears as a sequence of events. Did this procedure prove useful?

No, or perhaps only in being able to regard it as disposed of. I realized that something like this didn't suit me and that there is no point in demanding such a reasonableness of painting.

This experiment is related to the drawings from abstract pictures, of which there are only a few. On the other hand, there exist watercolours from the years 1977 to 1978 which were used as models for abstract pictures – for example, the watercolour from December 1977,[4] *which also contains elements of drawing, or the two sheets from May 1978.*[5] *Was that a more promising procedure?*

For a while, it seemed to be so. There is a whole series of pictures painted from 'abstract' pictures, from watercolours, from oil paintings and from sections of the palette.

Some of the abstract pictures were painted with the real remains of paint on the palette as a model?

Yes, mainly from a greatly enlarged detail from the remains of paint which form there more or less by chance.

The list of sources – segments of the palette,[6] *oil paintings, watercolours – gives the impression that the watercolour moves between composition and material accumulation, and as though it were only the way of looking at it, the choice of an aspect, which makes it usable as a motif for a real picture.*

Yes, I think that sums it up.

The watercolour stands out in that it shows a sort of space; it is even underlaid with a pseudo-perspective. That clearly sets it apart from the other watercolours.

Yes, but otherwise I've avoided such stage-like elements and grid-like suggestions of space. I was more interested in a very indefinite space.

At the end of 1977 and the beginning of 1978, the first series of watercolours came about. Was there an external reason why you now devoted yourself more intensely to this technique?

It was the most suitable, and the excuse for two weeks of vacation in Davos. Small watercolours are easy to do in a hotel room.

The first watercolours are placed on the paper in such a way that a white border remains around the picture.

That's probably obligatory for drawings and watercolours, which are always placed against white.

Sometimes there are even two small watercolours on one sheet, as if they were miniatures. Were those imaginary paintings, models or studies for future pictures?

Yes, more or less – that is, attempts to somehow develop pictures, to produce them without literally making a painting of something. For that, I didn't have to fill the sheet all the way to the edge.

The formats are mostly small, one half of a sheet of writing paper. Often a grounding has been applied to it in a few broad brushstrokes, and on top of that comes a second level – a crossing out of the ground, like a negation of the primary painterly gesture, without immediately establishing a new gesture.

That seems to me typical of all abstract works, and it usually results in a sort of landscape, with all the objects that activate it.

Do landscape associations always arise for you?

I certainly didn't intend that, but it occurs to me, and I think one can't see it in any other way. Pictures simply function like the real pictures outside. Naturally, I could also orientate myself to still-lifes or portraits, but something to do with landscape is more my kind of thing.

That would mean you regard reality in the categories of painterly genres. Do these suffice to interpret or clarify what you have seen?

The other way round, I'd say: painting in the categories of reality. And whether that is sufficient or not? To me, the most important interpretation – or, better, observation – seems to be that seeing functions like this.

Were there at this point no classical watercolours that you regarded as models?

No, I can't say that there were.

In fact, watercolour had achieved no significant place in post-war art; far more, it had sooner degenerated into the domain of the hobby artist, a little derided. After the significant accomplishments in this field from the decades before the Second World War – those of Macke, Nolde, Kandinsky, Klee – there follow scarcely any other works of this sort, neither in the German Informel nor in American Abstract Expressionism. There are exceptions, of course – like Wols in Europe and Sam Francis in the United States. Did their works mean anything to you?

Wols was indeed important, but not because of his watercolours, and Sam Francis never interested me. But I'm pleased to hear that my disinterest in the watercolour was so up-to-date.

Did the watercolours of the classical modern which develop a closed form in terms of composition, colour or narrative, like those of Kandinsky and Klee, represent models that you might have considered?

I don't think I knew one of them. Also, Kandinsky never impressed me, and Klee only at a certain time.

Your first watercolours violate the demands of the technique in being executed on cheap writing paper, sometimes even on lined or graph paper where the paint does not stand as perfectly as one is accustomed to with Italian watercolour papers.

At the time, cheap paper was a possibility to avoid a certain watercolour aesthetic, the arts-and-crafts preciousness. Today one can't see things so rigidly. And one now knows, too, that whether something is good or bad isn't a question of cheap paper. I didn't want to make beautiful watercolours but to attempt something or other.

You also withheld the watercolours for a while, since they were only exhibited for the first time in 1984 in the Borgmann Gallery in Cologne.

As a matter of fact, it was only through the dealer Fred Jahn that I succeeded in overcoming my reservations about the works on paper and exhibiting them. Added to this, of course, was the fact that after ten years I could see the watercolours in a different light, and in conjunction with pictures painted afterwards, they had at least become more comprehensible to me.

This first group broke off in January 1978, and it took six years before there were new watercolours again, which means the first series was fairly unique and without direct consequences. Or did you paint watercolours that you afterwards destroyed and of which we know nothing?

I don't think so. I save such things for a while – no, there wasn't anything. There was no longer an occasion, an incentive, to paint watercolours.

In 1985 Marianne Stockebrand showed watercolours by Joseph Beuys, Nicola de Maria, Richard Tuttle and you at the Westfalian Kunstverein in Münster;[7] *then, in a somewhat altered grouping, with Palermo and Sigmar Polke at the Goethe-Institut in London.*[8] *In a broader context one might also think of the works of Georg Baselitz and Gotthard Graubner or, among the younger artists, of Thomas Schütte. These exhibitions called attention to the watercolour as a phenomenon which apparently again became a means of expression for various artists. Nonetheless, it seems to me that the ways in which these artists approached the medium were extremely different, so that one can't speak of an aesthetic paradigm that was common to all.*

Beuys always seemed to me somewhat suspicious. His works had an extremely seductive aesthetic quality, something very delicate that I always mistrusted. Palermo and Polke were preferable.

In Polke's case, the use of watercolour usually has an illustrative character as part of the drawings; it is narrative and stands in a figurative context – very different than in your case, where nothing literary can be found. In the case of Palermo, on the other hand, it's different again.

I valued him very highly and, in fact, hung watercolours by him in my room. I twice traded watercolours with him.

Nonetheless, in the case of Palermo the watercolour had another function. One could even say that the fragile appearance of this medium is of fundamental significance for his entire work; it goes together well with the drawing, but also with objects, and Palermo's pictures and objects on the other hand take on the transparent, fragmentary appearance of the watercolours. This also applies to his constructive works, which don't show the regularity and formal consequence as they were formulated by the classic avant-garde and which lent even the American abstract painting of the post-war period a self-assurance and inner strength. Palermo approaches constructive procedures and at the same time seeks his distance from them: the constructive is circumvented in an enigmatic pictorial language.

His constructive pictures have remained in my memory because they particularly appeal to me, because I can't produce such a thing. I always found it very good how he made it and that he made it – this astonished me. There was an aesthetic quality which I loved and which I couldn't produce, but I was happy that such a thing existed in the world. In comparison, my own things seemed to me somewhat destructive, without this beautiful clarity.

At the same time, your first watercolours seem more naturally pictorial and closed than those of Palermo, where the processual occupies the foreground.

Yes? I would regard them as much more confused and naturally more illusionistic than those of Palermo.

What motivated you to start again with watercolours in 1984 and to paint a series of more than 75 sheets?

That was perhaps a rediscovery or first discovery of the watercolour and its possibilities for me; perhaps it can also be explained on private grounds, and the special zeitgeist that makes such a thing possible plays a large role.

I thought your work did not react so very much to the zeitgeist.

Unfortunately, no other word for it occurs to me, but with 'zeitgeist' I mean something entirely inclusive and elementary which one cannot evade. And the effects are qualitatively very different – from grunge look to Cubism, from the dumbest conformity to the most acute opposition. Thereby one could be in such safe keeping as the Christians in the lap of God.

Then your pictures necessarily respond to that.

Yes, and I could also make watercolours that had a similar freedom. Actually, they must differ fundamentally from those of 1978: that was indeed a turning point.

That becomes clear in the appearance of the works, since everything that comes after 1984 is worked out in a different way, even produced in several attempts. In the case of the watercolours of the 1970s, one has the impression that they were painted at one go. The later watercolours differ in that they are more compact and painted all the way to the edge: they are sooner finished small pictures.

After 1984 I always used watercolour pads, in the conventional way. At any one time there would be eight to twelve pads laying side by side, and these could be handled in series, like the paintings; over the course of a few days they made various degrees of progress and then all of them, more or less, were finished.

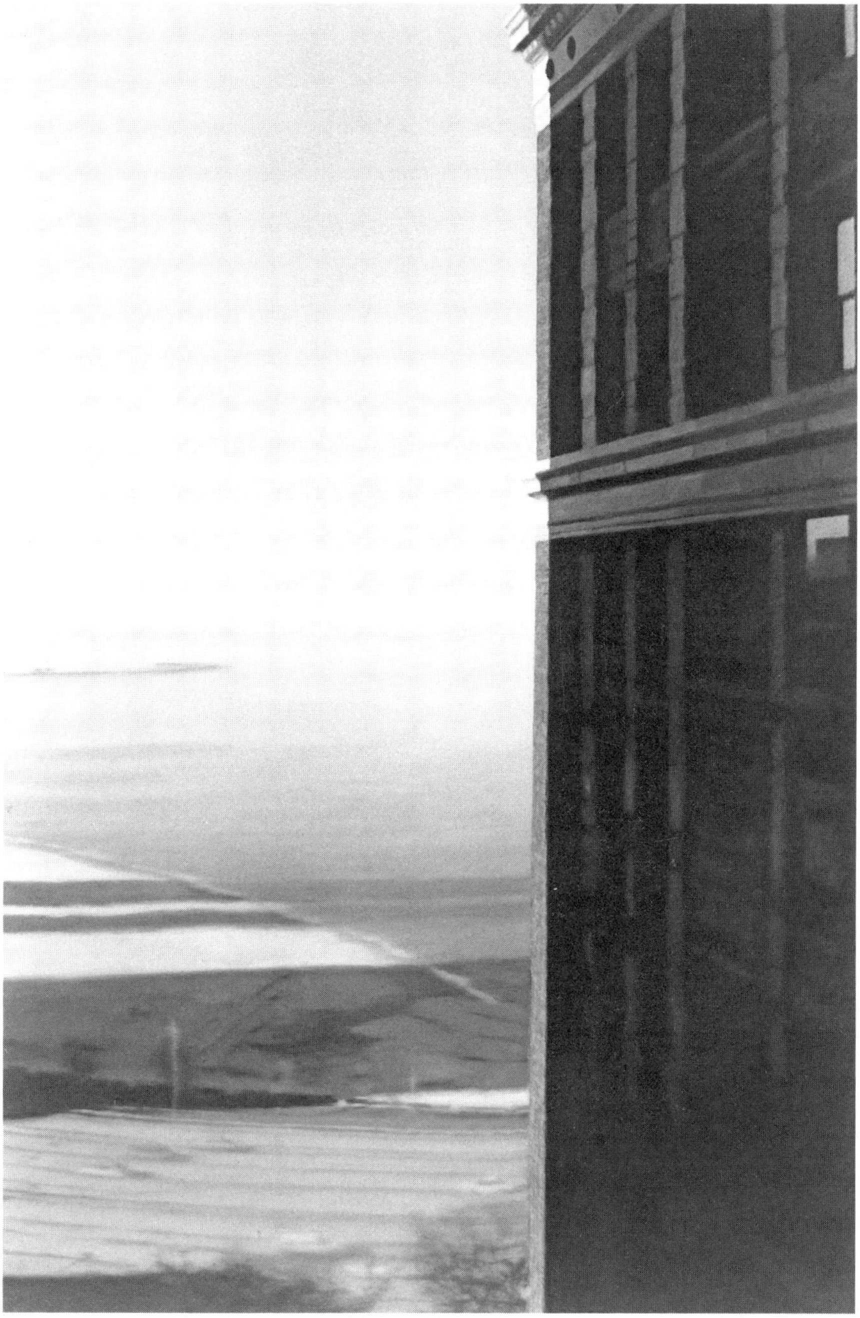

Chicago, 1992

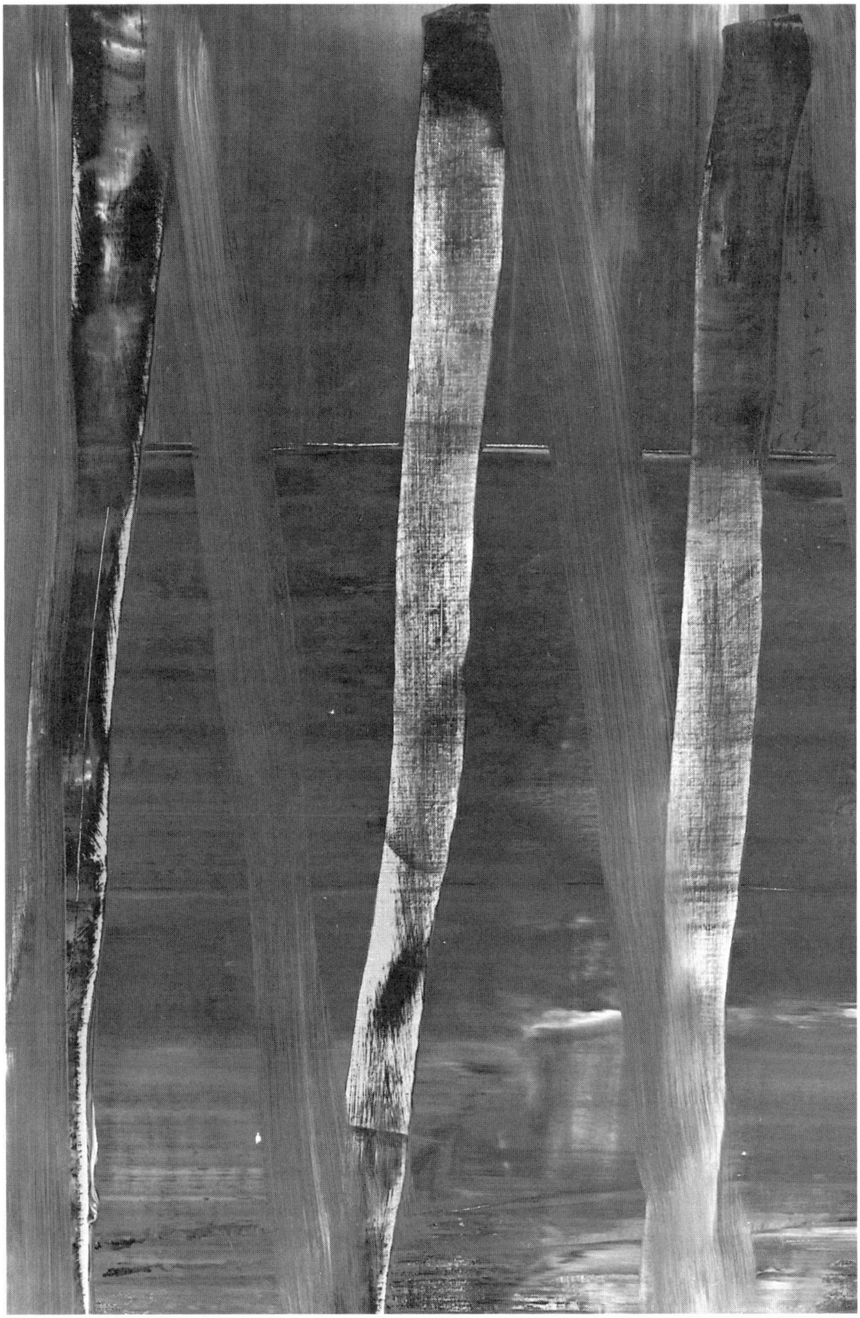

Abstract Painting, 1992 (detail)

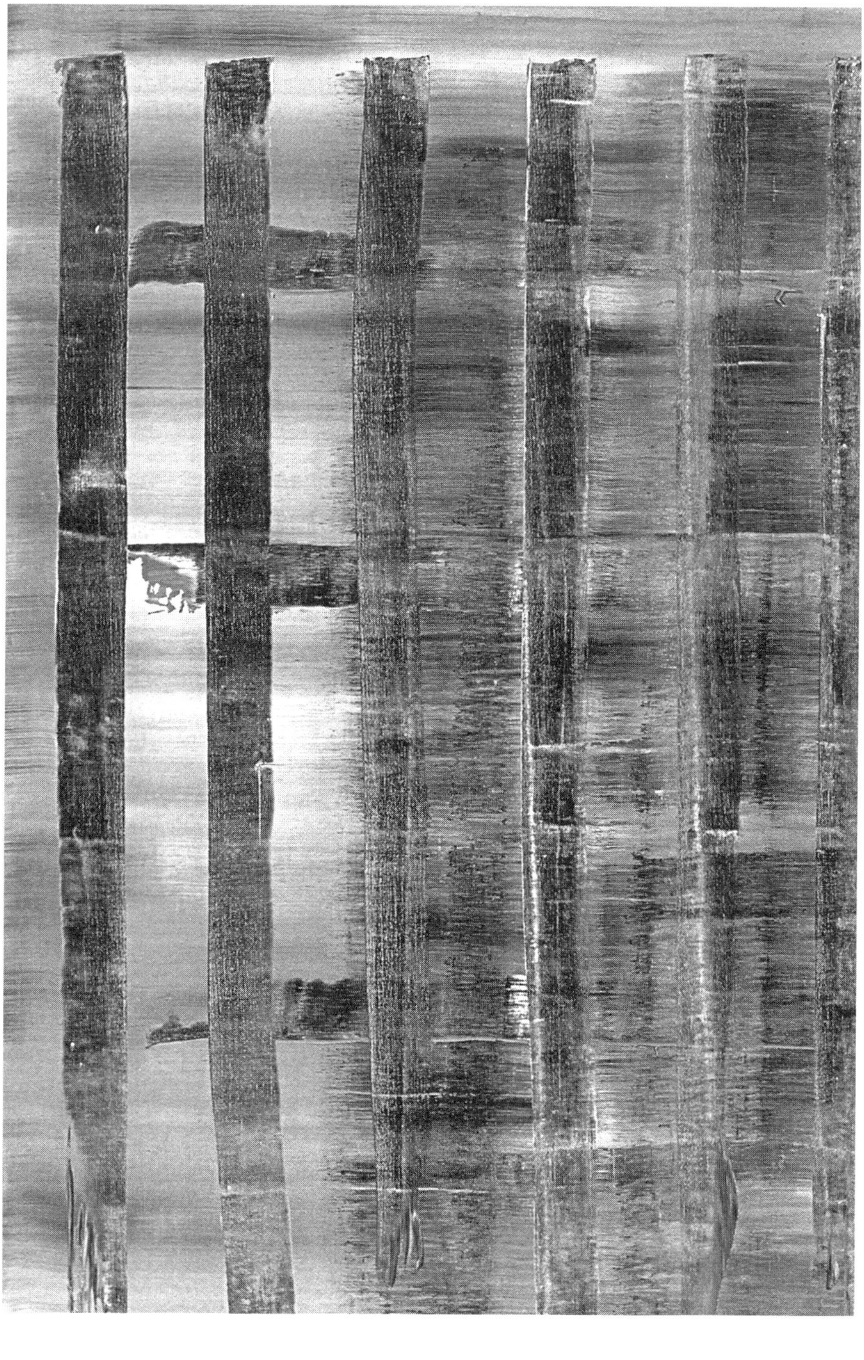

Abstract Painting, 1992

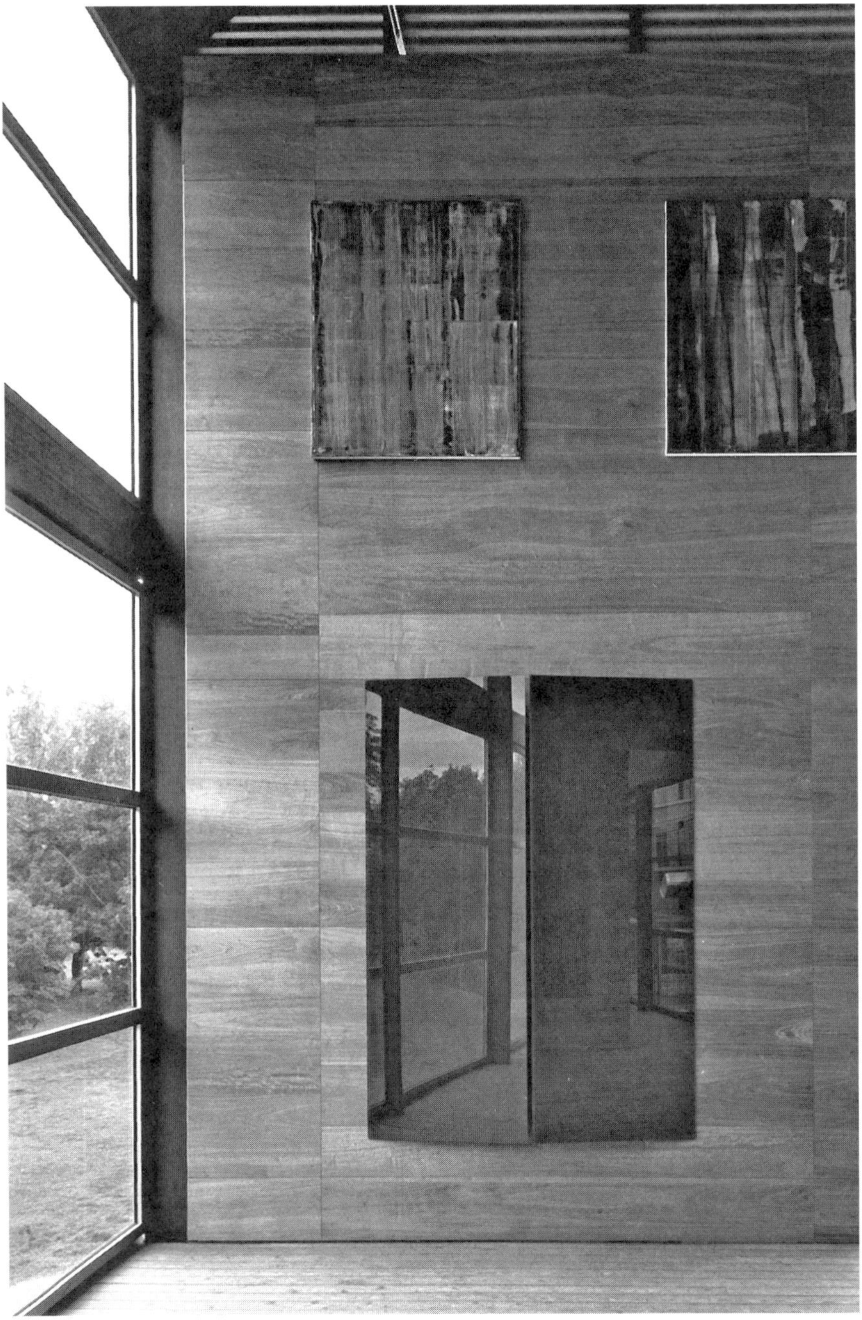

Documenta IX, Kassel, 1992

The first layer of the watercolour is applied in broad areas, usually red, blue or green, and on top of that come the traces of oil crayon...

... or the crayon is there first, so that the paint clearly beads up against the oily background. That's the reason the watercolours were so fragile: the paint didn't hold well and partly crumbled away.

It also contradicts the rules of watercolour painting that the paint is not applied to the white ground of the paper in fine glazes but almost opaquely, in drops and pools of colour.

I had to accept that when the pools of colour dried out, they could later break away. If one stands a sheet firmly on edge, it can trickle down; sometimes the loose bits of paint have to be scratched away.

Did you believe, then, that you could accomplish the same thing with the watercolours as with the pictures painted parallel to them?

Yes, it was the same sort of problem, but with different means.

What part does the format play in the attempt to show something which wasn't already present, to create something not already subjected to a certain conception or method of composition? Are watercolours and oil paintings comparable in that respect?

Yes, very similar... And yet they are so different: like a poem and a novel by the same author.

Is there another quality, another order?

Because the watercolour is more casual.

Things can emerge from this casualness that are denied to oil painting?

Yes. Working in such a way isn't technically possible, because everything would have to be ten times larger – the brush two metres long, the painter 17 metres tall, etc. That was one reason for painting the watercolours, precisely since one can't create such a thing directly on canvas.

The working process – the pouring, dribbling, spreading of paint – thus possesses a validity of its own, because the result doesn't correspond to the notion one had in the beginning.

Yes, but that's the case with the pictures, too, only in a slower, more elaborated and therefore less spontaneous way.

The respective groups of watercolours were only created during briefer periods – 1984, then only a few in 1985 and 1987, larger series in 1988, 1990, 1991 and 1992, thereafter nothing more until the last group from 1997 – and not in the continuous way you paint pictures.

Painting pictures is simply the official, the daily work, the profession, and in the case of the watercolours I can sooner afford to follow my mood, my spirits.

Most of the watercolours carry a date which replaces the title but which does not necessarily correspond to the date of production.

The year is always correct, also the month; only the day can be another. But that occurs to me only in the moment of writing it down.

In the works from 1984, the dating looks convincing because several sheets carry the same date, whereas later the dates run continuously over two to three months, and no day is left out. Surely that isn't a real chronology?

No, that's almost impossible. Also, I listed everything quite consequentially – consecutive dates for the different works on paper, so that none appears twice and everything looks credible.

In 1985 the exhibition 75 Aquarelle *was held at the Stuttgart Staatsgalerie,*[9] *and two years later came the exhibition at the Overholland Museum in Amsterdam,*[10] *devoted entirely to works on paper; afterwards there were no more exhibitions of this sort. In Amsterdam there were not only drawings and watercolours to be seen but also works in oil on paper. Indeed, such works took up much more space. The oil paintings on paper resembled the pictures even more than the watercolours did; they are actually paintings on paper. What led you to choose this technique?*

Recklessness, a failure of self-criticism. Oil on paper: it was something I hated earlier, even the name is awful. It always had something sloppy and arts-and-craftsy about it. The frivolousness bothered me.

These first works in oil on paper, however, were not fundamentally different in their conception than the painting on canvas.

For me that is an almost essential difference, and if I think of such works on paper behind glass, with mats and expensive frames, one doesn't create this sort of pleasing quality so quickly with paintings.

And yet there is meanwhile a substantial œuvre of your works on paper, particularly such works in oil on paper.

Perhaps I had hoped to do it better. But I certainly never put heart and soul into producing these paper pictures – or into exhibiting them.

Among the watercolours there are scarcely any representational ones painted from photographs or other models.

Because it is more exciting with the abstract ones, and it goes faster. It has an effect similar to my earlier enthusiasm for developing photos in the darkroom. Something is created there all by itself, which one only has to observe in order to intervene at the right moment – in that case, to stop it. Here, then, it's more a question of being able to decide than of actually making something.

Where does the choice begin, the decision?

In the beginning, one is completely free; it's almost irrelevant what is put there, and then a sort of picture comes about that usually looks quite stupid and has to be corrected until it looks better. Comparing is a help, which means it is easier for me to paint ten watercolours than one, for then I can see more clearly what is better or worse in one picture than in another.

Where is the point where you call a halt, since adding another layer could potentially go on and on?

Even for technical reasons it can't continue, since the paper doesn't stand it. But we also can't stand to continue when a thing is finally right, when every addition would only disturb.

I always thought you therefore regarded painting as a counterpole to drawings and watercolours, since you can work more systematically there.

Certainly. And painting with all its effort is a truly established profession, fundamentally solid on the one hand. The other side, of course, is crazy, unpredictable and not professional at all. For example, I'm incapable of producing a picture similar to picture X, which I painted a year before. That is also disturbing.

This means that for your work there is no abstract principle, no theory, nothing which rests behind the pictures, but that they can only be created at the moment they are being painted, out of a concentration directed toward something one doesn't know.

Yes, that is also the exciting part of it all.

Historically, the watercolour plays an important role as the less costly version of the expensive painting, the role of a more easily saleable picture. In English watercolour painting of the eighteenth and nineteenth centuries, the sheets are pushed to the most extreme representational perfection, in the manner of paintings, and due to their attractiveness even became competition for oil painting. One thinks of the watercolours of German Romanticism, which are often executed like paintings. Your watercolours of apples[11] *at least suggest this possibility.*

I enjoy painting landscapes, but for that purpose oil is such an unsurpassable technique that I could never do so in watercolours: this thin stuff would be awful, or in this way it would become a virtuoso watercolour technique. Furthermore, one can't paint in an unfocussed way.

Because in a small-format watercolour every brushstroke remains immediately visible, it tends to have the effect of virtuosity, even if not conceived to this end. One would not necessarily like to make this accusation of superficial virtuosity against painting.

That may be, yet I have nothing against virtuosity itself; it's not only fun but the prerequisite for many beautiful things.

Through the subsequent blurring, the detailed painting from a photographic source is obliterated and can only be inferred. Through the preoccupation with the representation of a motif, the self-absorbed virtuosity is also retracted. That isn't possible in this way in watercolour painting, since the technique comes more to the fore. Although you also apply means to work against it – for example, through drawing on the surface with pencil, the pulling of lines that disturb the illusion of the coloured areas.

Yet this nonetheless has a great deal of similarity to the pictures. Also the intention to permit something simple to come about instead of placing it there. Baselitz places his objects, Polke places them, and that is another procedure.

There are constants, however – like the primary colours that tend to dominate, but also particular ways in which the colours appear, how they are applied to the sheet, and individual lines that suggest a sort of handwriting. There one can recognize what was intended or desired.

With the limitation to primary colours I first of all avoid having to mix a particular tone, and it would then be less neutral, perhaps extravagant or elegant or whatever. Also, it is better to start with red, blue and yellow; the mixtures come about on their own, in any case.

At the beginning of the year 1987 there is an entire group of representational watercolours: Apples, Isa and Betty, *the* Table *in the kitchen.*[12]

I had liked the photograph of the table, and I felt tempted to paint it. But then that seemed to me too obvious – an oil painting with such a dazzling circle in the middle. On the other hand, it worked in the watercolour. I did watercolours of Betty and Isa from vacation photos. I was surprised when I saw these works again and thought how skilfully this face is rendered with a couple of brushstrokes. Yet I find this whole ploy suspect – simply the way artists do such a thing, rapidly and casually simplifying.

The assertion that something is too artistic is one you have often made. It isn't so easy to understand, since even painting has to do with an artistic manner of expression; after all, it is an artistic work and not a purely literal or mechanical reproduction.

... which I sometimes wish for myself.

What would then be the opposite term to 'artistic'?

Something severe, embittered like Caspar David Friedrich. He did not permit himself any airs and was only disagreeable.

Would it be one of the goals of painting and even of watercolour to achieve something like that?

This earnestness would be better than the unspeakable bluff with which people betray themselves.

And the watercolours possess this earnestness?

No, unfortunately not often, and there are also examples for this. I often wanted to throw away the *Apple* because I didn't find it good. Too much boredom-painting, with exciting droplets of water. And for me the other is no better, with its clumsy slopes and slipped glaze. In the oil pictures with apples, everything is more precise and combined with a bottle, but that is getting close to graphic design.

And yet your work always seeks a distance from the so-called artistic.

Maybe that's only a sort of kink of mine that's completely useless. Or a sort of megalomania.

The difference from the self-complacently 'artistic' becomes more clearly visible in the colour charts and the grey pictures, but also in the systematization of the painterly work – in that your pictures are consecutively numbered, for example. This means an emphasizing of the sequence of the pictures, posing the question of the equality or differentiation of the pictures instead of celebrating the virtuosity of the individual work. This is more difficult to recognize in the watercolours, except for the point at which they stand outside the category of this genre, as Ulrich Loock has written,[13] *and do something impossible, show something incomprehensible: out of this there results something that one would prefer not to describe with a term like 'beauty', in order not to place it into the spectrum of the possible, the comprehended.*

That pleases me!

Between the watercolours of the 1980s and those of the 1990s, on the other hand, we observe a change: the sheets from 1984 seem much more obviously composed out of disparate details than the later ones, in which the running and blending of the colours dominates.

Yet there is also nothing to see there which I would not have made myself. Even just letting things develop is something intended and is supervised, and when something occurs that is different from what was planned, that is also intentional. Sometimes it simply goes wrong, then landscapes come about like those of the greatest kitsch-specialist.

The last watercolours from 1997 were cut out of larger sheets in order to preserve the good parts. They give the impression of an epilogue or perhaps even of a conclusion. Is the genre exhausted for you?

Perhaps the entire profession. Who knows?

While the watercolours from 1984 to 1985 resemble the pictures painted at the same time, in that different layers of painting – planar and linear elements – are laid directly on top of each other, this is no longer the case in the watercolours of the 1990s. The method of painting the pictures is more severe, sometimes even approaching the monochrome, the surfaces are completely overpainted, while in some cases the paint has been scraped away in stripes down to the ground. The watercolours, on the other hand, have become more landscape-like, more playful: paintings and watercolours go their own way.

Surely the decline and fall. But what I find very beautiful is that these watercolours have so many stories to tell – almost as in a fairytale, one can recognize figures, battling serpents, red giants, boulders and clouds...

Does the association with such figures emerge only afterwards, or is it important even during the work itself?

It arises afterwards, and I am almost never irritated by it. In the course of painting, on the other hand, I try to destroy every similarity to the representational that emerges. But the similarity that seems to come about all on its own and reveals itself only later is quite in order, from my point of view.

Couldn't the watercolours get sidetracked into late Surrealism – in the succession of Max Ernst, for example?

I hope not. But there the intention was also a very different one, since the frottages were used precisely to produce these fantastic plants.

It only works, then, when it happens unintentionally, apparently arbitrarily?

Yes, because that which occurs arbitrarily and yet which has passed all the conscious controls without calling attention to itself could indeed have a higher quality.

Conversation with Paolo Vagheggi, 1999

But why turn photography into painting?

Painting is traditional but for me that doesn't mean the academy. I felt a need to paint; I love painting. It was something natural – as is listening to music or playing an instrument for some people. For this reason I searched for themes of my era and my generation. Photography offered this, so I chose it as a medium for painting.

And yet you say you don't know how to paint…

I say it half-jokingly. My generation, compared with artists in the past, has never learned to paint. Nobody has achieved that technical mastery. In the past they really studied and practised continuously. Today there's nobody you could compare, not just with Michelangelo, but even with Goethe who was self-taught but really pretty good. The art students of today refuse to study drawing, so they have no command of it. They prefer technology.

Is this going to bring about at first an end to and then a return to painting?

It won't be necessary to return to painting. I think it will always be there; I don't know how, but it won't disappear. There's a fundamental difference between creating a picture with your own hands, being able to touch it, and sitting in front of a computer screen.

You've mentioned the young. What do you think of the new generation – artists under 35?

I'm not an expert. Certainly I do go to exhibitions, get catalogues, read magazines. I've seen some interesting, exciting things, but I also see too much that's just entertainment and show, and I don't know what will still be there of it in fifty years' time. I find it's like looking at Disneyland or at a fairground. Personally I'm interested in quality; I'm much more interested in an exhibition like the one devoted to Chardin. His pictures have that special quality that is the enduring quality in art. It's the quality to be found in Mozart or Bach. It's this that the young need to understand.

How important is realism for you, or is the abstract more important?

I love figurative painting and find it very interesting. I've not done a lot of figurative work because I lack subjects. Abstract is something everyday for me, as natural as walking or breathing.

But isn't realism dead?

Realism isn't dead. It's very important for people, for they can identify with it and they can easily recognize its particular problems.

Your work has been seen as close to Caspar David Friedrich. Are there artists or periods to which you feel connected or inspired by?

I've already mentioned Chardin. I could add Raphael, Leonardo, Friedrich, Manet. It's much easier to find inspiration from the past, from the Old Masters, than it is from the moderns. I can appreciate Pollock or Fontana, both very interesting artists, but I don't find inspiration in them. I find the Romantic period extraordinarily interesting. My landscapes have connections with Romanticism: at times I feel a real desire for, an attraction to, this period, and some of my pictures are a homage to Caspar David Friedrich.

One of your pictures was sold at an auction for six billion Lire [approx. 3,100,000 Euros]. Does the market have an influence on an artist's work?

It's not me that demands these sums; it's the auctions that create them. When I'm working, I try not to think about it; I don't want to be influenced by money. But it would be difficult to live without it – especially since there are periods when I don't produce anything. I've had a year without painting. I've only recently begun to work again.

What are you painting?

For a month I've been working on a landscape[1] and on some abstracts...

Interview with Stefan Koldehoff, 1999

Leading international art experts consider you to be the most important artist alive today. However, you yourself have said that you're still striving to produce a good painting. Are you overrated by the experts?

Of course they can be wrong. On the other hand, they do have a broader perspective. I'm too close to my work to be able to see myself in such a positive light. However, I don't rate my colleagues as being better than me either. The things we do aren't *that* brilliant.

Do you experience a sense of satisfaction when you leaf through your catalogue of works or when you walk through one of your exhibitions?

Yes, there are of course moments when I'm overcome by something akin to respect or amazement – for instance, when I see an entire exhibition of my work, like now in Prato.[1] But here we're talking about works that have long since been painted and sent out into the world. With paintings still in the making, you quickly abandon any notion of being satisfied with yourself. You always hope that the next thing is going to be really fantastic, but then it turns out to be just another painting.

Are you at all interested in how your paintings are received once they leave your studio?

Yes, very much so. Naturally, I need reassurance that the ideas I put into the world with my paintings are being understood. And I'm curious to know how they're being interpreted – whether they're accepted or not.

Whose opinions matter to you? Who do you think is even competent to judge your works?

That's difficult to say nowadays. It used to be a few people I knew well – people whose opinions carried weight with me. When I was friends with Blinky Palermo, it mattered a lot to me whether he thought something was good. It was the same with Sigmar Polke and Konrad Fischer. It was all based on these short remarks: 'That one has something' – that was the best reaction of all. 'That one has something; it's not bad.' Or they'd say: 'That's no good; you can forget that.' But pithy critiques like these could only hit the mark because they were based on a strong foundation of shared values. That's also why it was possible to ignore all that high-flown, empty talk about art. Nowadays things are a bit different. Today there's the option of ignoring all the established criteria and simply saying: 'I'm doing it like this, period.' It makes things quite a bit less complicated.

When do you think an artist is important?

There are so many reasons to think that someone is important: we're currently experiencing it with [Günter] Grass. I can't read his books, except for *The Tin Drum* – and I read that a long time ago. But when Grass appears somewhere, he's such an important personality that the quality of his writing becomes secondary. [Joseph] Beuys is another one with a distinctive charisma. And then there's the other kind of importance, based on very specific achievements – like those of Thomas Bernhard, who I love because his works move me.

Did you know him personally?

I never got to know him, and I never had the desire to meet him. What would we have talked about? I'm sure he was a peculiar guy; I'm peculiar, too. Sometimes it really is better if you love the works rather than their creator.

Have you seen any art that has interested you lately?

The last thing I saw was the Chardin exhibition in Karlsruhe. There's sometimes this quality in painting – I mentioned it earlier – that can make you happy. A few small apples, and they 'have something'.

Do you look at contemporary art?

There's no way to escape it – you see it automatically while travelling, or in magazines and the many different catalogues.

You've always tried to avoid being pinned down to certain statements about your paintings. What do you think of people who nevertheless insist on interpreting your works?

Without interpretation, we wouldn't even exist; we're dependent on one another. It's only annoying when the reviews are stupid or incompetent – or when they try to be especially funny, which seems to be in vogue at the moment. Making fun of something, slating it just to make life a little easier, is a big mistake.

A few years ago you started exhibiting all the material you've used as a basis for your paintings, the so-called Atlas. *In doing so, you're laying all of the ideas you ever had, or might have had, out on the table for everyone to see. That's an exhibitionist act.*

It could be, yes. But my motivation was more a matter of wanting to create order – to keep track of things. All those boxes full of photographs and sketches weigh you down, because they have something unfinished, incomplete, about them. So it's better to present the usable material in an orderly fashion and throw the other stuff away. That's how the *Atlas* came to be, and I exhibited it a few times.

It's on show quite frequently now.

But now other people are putting it on display. The *Atlas* belongs to the Lenbachhaus in Munich – it's long since ceased to belong to me. Occasionally I run across it somewhere, and I think it's interesting because it looks different each time.

You've often insisted that your paintings don't reflect reality. But with the Atlas, *you're provoking comparisons between reality and your paintings.*

But it's precisely this act of comparison that the paintings are supposed to encourage; they're more or less inexact, false or semi-accurate reproductions of reality.

Do you sometimes need to put your paintings aside for a time?

Definitely. First they have to be moved from the studio to a second room, where they hang just as they would in an exhibition. It's a bit like a second quality-control measure. By putting them there, I can see which ones hold up under somewhat altered conditions – and which ones need to return to the studio.

Do you make this decision on your own?

Unfortunately, yes. But occasionally I'm lucky and someone happens along who's able to say more than just: 'Very nice.'

Are you under pressure to succeed?

Yes, at times. It's a horrible situation and is not at all conducive to creativity. And by this I don't mean that the work itself is causing pressure. It's rather this diffuse expectation that you have to create something new and great. It kills creativity – and when it happens, it's best to drop everything immediately.

The Vice President of the German Bundestag, Antje Vollmer, has accused you of charlatanism because she didn't think your painting for the Reichstag was appropriate.[2] *Did this bother you?*

I was surprised, because she cast her judgment so quickly: the painting wasn't even there yet. All Ms Vollmer had seen was a design sketch in A4 format. She would need superhuman powers to be able to envisage the finished product based just on this. Charlatanism definitely wasn't my problem, but rather the possibility that the project wouldn't work the way I had envisioned it, that it could have ended up being a mistake – and a very labour-intensive one at that. Doubts like these always come up during the creative process, and they often linger for a while after a work has been completed.

After it was installed, did you go and have a look to see whether the painting had the desired effect in those particular surroundings?

I did, yes. It looks good. What can I say? I wanted to present the three colours in the best possible way – or, rather, manufacture them for this space, for this purpose. It had to have a strong visible presence and be more or less tangible, like a thin pane floating in front of the wall – big and simultaneously fragile, and with a smooth, reflective surface, of course. But it would be nice if it were cleaned occasionally.

The debate about this painting does show, however, that art hasn't become quite as unimportant as you made it out to be at the beginning of this interview.

This one small debate won't prevent art from diminishing in importance. And it's not all that terrible when something that's outlived itself becomes less important. It's a natural process. The problem is when the space it leaves behind is filled with entertainment and trash. That can be pretty frightening.

Apart from one landscape, the new works hanging in your studio are mainly abstracts. How do you decide what to paint? Do you wake up in the morning and say to yourself: 'Today, I think I'd enjoy painting something abstract'?

Sometimes, yes. Painting in the abstract has a kind of normality to it, like breathing or walking. Theoretically, I could do it every day. The other paintings – the ones that are representational – are the exceptions. I have to be lucky enough to like a photograph so much that I think: 'I could turn this into a painting.' But this is happening less and less frequently, I'm afraid.

Why is that?

I don't know. Maybe I take fewer photographs; perhaps fewer of them are any good.

There's a painting over there that's based on a photograph.[3] *Why was that a good photo?*

I guess it expresses a lot. In this case, it tells of a summer afternoon, extremely hot, quiet, pleasant smells, happy feelings, children. And because of the light-dark contrasts it was a very rich picture. The darkness entering from the left has an ominous quality that threatens the beauty. It's an unusual mixture – and one that only becomes apparent at second or third glance. When you first look at it, it's just a normal photo of a summer's day. It was lying around here for a year, but it continued to pique my interest, because it 'had something'. Then I painted it. And perhaps the story I just told you is better than the actual picture. That can also happen.

But it's a story no one will know about just by looking at the painting.

But I hope they will! Just as there are people who are musically gifted, there are those who take an interest in painting. They see the story behind it. That's why they can get so obsessed with paintings.

Do you think it's okay when people interpret things into your abstract paintings?

The paintings only work because of people's desire to see something in them. Every aspect of them resembles something that's real, but the similarity only goes so far. It's the same with music: it creates moods because the sounds are similar to real tonal expressions of sadness, joy, loudness and softness. The fact that paintings come to life through this strange mechanism isn't appreciated nearly enough. Paintings present us with similarities that we attempt to categorize. They always remind us of something – otherwise they wouldn't be paintings.

To what extent can you determine the outcome when you're working the canvas with spatulas and scrapers?

It's a good technique for switching off thought. I can't consciously calculate what will emerge. Subconsciously, though, I do have an inkling of it. It's a pleasant state of limbo.

Your other projects seem to be completed – the inpaintings, the grey paintings, the colour charts. Is this true, or can we expect to see similar creations at some point in the future?

The inpaintings won't yield anything new. As to the colour charts, it's conceivable that I'll see some sense in painting-in squares once again. But sometimes I even feel that the abstract pictures have reached their limit. Even so, it's a pleasant surprise when a few do emerge that are different from the ones that came before them.

For the first time, a comprehensive collection of your sketches is being shown, in Winterthur, accompanied by a catalogue of these works.[4] *Before this, I rarely came across any Richter sketches.*

Me neither. Unlike the photographs and prints, I never catalogued, kept track of or exhibited the sketches. I sold some occasionally, but never saw myself as a graphic artist. They became more important to me thanks to the exhibition, however, and I realized that these drawings were quite interesting after all.

Are you planning more exhibitions in the future?

In two years there will be a big retrospective at the Museum of Modern Art. They're already looking around to gather together all the important works.

And when will the new paintings be on display?

Perhaps in a year. There's no hurry.

Does the turn of the millennium have any significance for you?

I always thought it was silly to attach such importance to the event. But now I realize that it does have this significance – that it automatically creates this state of contemplation and hope.

And what do you wish for yourself?

Well, after this century of grand proclamations and terrible illusions, I hope for an era in which real and tangible accomplishments, and not grand proclamations, are the only things that count.

Conversation with Birgit Grimm, 2000

Are you happy with the way your paintings were presented in the Residenzschloss in Dresden?

Yes, very much so.

Do you exert any influence on how your paintings are hung in an exhibition?

I have done in the past, and still do when I show new paintings. However, in this specific case, I didn't get involved in the organization. These works here don't belong to me any more, but to various collectors. I'm happy to see my paintings again. But the person who painted them was someone else; it's as though my brother were exhibiting them.

Your abstract watercolours have several layers of paint. Rumour has it that you don't paint your watercolours one at a time, but rather several en bloc.

Yes, several lie next to each other in a room and I work on them intermittently over the course of weeks.

Can the result still be said to be a classical watercolour?

Well, you know, people used to work pretty economically in the past, too. It's different with representational paintings where I know what I want from the start. When I'm working on something abstract, one thing leads to another – it's kind of directionless.

When someone is as famous as you are, does he still look for orientation to what others are doing?

It gets lonely, because you don't have anyone left to ask any more. Because if I ask people, they all just say: 'Oh, it's beautiful!' But that's no help to me.

But many of your paintings really are beautiful.

I always wanted to make beautiful paintings. There was a time when that was frowned upon. Today beauty is like health; everyone wants to be healthy.

Is there a message inherent in the beauty of your paintings?

Not a message, but the hope that life can be beautiful.

When a large-format representation of your Two Candles *was displayed in the exhibition hall on Brühl's Terrace in February 1995 in commemoration of the fiftieth anniversary of the bombing of Dresden, it was a moving occasion that many saw as an unambiguous condemnation of war and violence.*

That kind of thing is a fortunate coincidence. When I painted the candles, I wasn't thinking of February 13th, but I did experience feelings to do with contemplation, remembering, silence and death.

There's a pretty wild rock band called Sonic Youth that had the Two Candles *on the cover of one of their CDs. Do you listen to their music?*

Yes, I did back then, when the musicians asked if they could use the painting, but not any more.

Did the directors of the Hygiene Museum ask your permission when, in the course of renovating the building, they uncovered part of the wall painting you had made in 1956?

Yes, and I replied, 'For God's sake, it's a waste of money. You'd be better off spending the money on something of artistic value. It's only something I painted during my studies.'[1]

Your exhibition in Dresden Palace encompasses watercolours and sketches from 1964 to 1999. Why won't you acknowledge earlier works?

Because I felt like I was a student until then – someone who didn't yet know what he wanted, artistically speaking.

Do you have other memories of Dresden?

Yes, of course, those were important years for me. Seeing Dresden as an expanse of rubble, living amongst those ruins, changed my life. I don't know if the pampered youth of today could understand something like that.

As a young man, you did a photography apprenticeship in Zittau,[2] and you worked as a set painter in a theatre.[3] Have you ever been back there?

No, never. I'd like to visit Zittau sometime. Is it in Poland?

Why did you go to the West in 1961?

Because Socialism imposed its will on people and tried to tell artists what to do.

What conditions does art require in order to evolve?

It can't be the job of the State to interfere with artists. It should worry about social issues and not about how art is created.

So all that's left is private initiative?

Yes, that of the artist in his studio. Some sponsors are so omnipresent that I don't even like to appear at the opening of my own exhibitions. Another problem is that culture and art have become so commonplace – there's a danger of them becoming arbitrary products that aren't really important any more. The few things that are really good get caught in the swill [of mediocrity]. But maybe art really has lost its significance in the face of the new media.

Many still prefer to look at originals in a museum rather than at tiny images on the internet.

The question is whether people notice the difference. They don't experience anything else any more, and they can't understand why the original should be more attractive.

For years now there have been sinister proclamations about art having reached its limits – that everything has been done before.

So long as people enjoy it and it's not just children who like to paint, art can't die. It is elemental. Repetition is only boring when a painter's works are boring to begin with. Good art can't be made often enough.

Interview with Bruno Corà, 2000

You have been working for almost forty years now. What has changed from the time you started as an artist to the present day?

When I started, society was not like now. It was totally different because the revolutionary attitudes then made some sense. It was normal for young people to be against their fathers, history of art, and all these things. I have a feeling that through the years these revolutionary attitudes became bigger and bigger and they lost their sense. So today we only have this attitude to destroy our history. But this attitude to destroy doesn't really work because everything is already dead now.

Do you feel that it is difficult now to consider the sensitiveness of life? We are in a time where everything is [coarse]; there is no time for sensitivity.

Yes, that's right. People try to have no responsibilities, no values and no principles.

We try to avoid any decision about good and bad, but every [attempt needs knowledge of] the difference between good and bad. This is out of fashion.

For many years, all the art historians, art critics, journalists and many other people have identified your work with the problem of photography in our century. 'Gerhard Richter used photos as models for his paintings.' But today technology has given the artist the possibility to use the computer. Do you think this is a fashion or a necessity?

I think it's a necessity. Photography changed our way of thinking. It was a great thing, but now it isn't that interesting any more.

I'm asking you because the use of photographs was considered avant-garde: there were painters like you who chose to use photographs and it was thought scandalous. Now some artists use the computer.

Yes, but it isn't a scandal any more. It's a very normal thing.

This is conformism.

Absolutely.

To tell the truth, you used photographs like some painters had used nature. But what is the real motive of your painting, the persistence of value for the unconscious, simplicity of life, curiosity for banality. What is your deepest motive?

It's the secret of life. With respect to that, I don't understand life. I haven't made any great changes at all. I have the same interest as any painter before me. I'm interested in what I see, not in photographs. Photographs are a medium; they help me because we don't learn to paint today and it was the same for me, I didn't learn, it was out, you couldn't teach anything. I'm interested in just what I see, the portraits of the world, a human person, a landscape, whatever.

When you decide to paint a picture or you have an idea, do you know if it's going to be figurative or abstract; if you're going to paint nature, to use photographs or if the picture will be gestural or not; will your idea be objective or subjective?

There is always subjectivity.

I'll give you an example: Krieg *is abstract and* Ema *is not. Do you decide in front of the subject or in front of a deep emotion?*

What I decide to do grows in my mind and through my body.

Does it take a long time, or is it just an instant? Is it an idea that you have to develop?

It's the same experience as with writing; you have an idea but then it takes time to develop.

For example, you get up in the morning and you open your newspaper...

It has nothing to do with art. It is very seldom that I get an idea from the newspaper.

Aren't you ever stimulated by things that may happen from day to day?

I'm still waiting for something that attracts me. It may come from a newspaper or from my own photographs. I'm always waiting.

So you pass your time waiting?

Yes. I had a long period waiting for an idea lately. I waited a whole year and I didn't paint at all. One year: it was hard.

I remember when you painted Grau *[the grey paintings] and I had difficulty in penetrating into the idea behind them and I asked you why and you said you had [no] idea.*

Yes, I had no idea.

Exactly like now.

Yes, I have no idea what to paint.

But can we take these words literally that you don't have ideas; perhaps you have ideas but you don't think they are special? Is the idea on crisis still an idea?

Yes, it is.

Are you waiting for something else?

No, I wish I had ideas but they are very few now. I have done everything. What else can I do?

I remember that when you painted Grau *you painted the* Farbtafeln *[colour charts] at the same time.*

It's the same problem; no idea.

No idea; this is interesting. Because both have colour and are completely different from one another.

Yes, that's right.

They are like 'tabulae rasae'.

Yes. I like this quotation from John Cage: 'I have nothing to say and I am saying it.'

Many people write that you prefer not to have opinions and to be indifferent. I personally don't believe it, so what's your answer?

I said this thirty years ago: I have no opinions, I'm indifferent. I said it to protect myself.

Was it a way to remain free?

Yes, I was afraid to say something wrong. As you know, so many things were said by the people, by intellectuals: that was the reason.

Yes, I understand. Sometimes people think that you are cold in front of reality because whatever you paint has always the same distance. Still-life, portraits, a plane flying, a cow, photos of eight girls that have been assassinated and so on. Is it true?

I'm very surprised. How can people think I'm cold? I'm so sentimental! A painter like Mangold isn't considered cold, but I am: it's really crazy now. I am ashamed of how freely I show my work.

Because of the [equidistance] in your work people get the impression that you are indifferent to the choice of subject, but you do actually make choices. The Kerze [Candle] *was a choice.*

And at the same time it wasn't.

So if people look very carefully, they can see that there are choices in your work, there are cycles, and therefore you are not so indifferent. While you were working on your series of paintings 18 October 1977 *we had had problems in Italy similar to Baader-Meinhof which were the Brigate Rosse, or for example the murder of Aldo Moro. And nobody in Italy painted these problems with the same intensity and persistence, neither during nor after the period. For this reason some art historians associate you [with] historical painting. In your opinion what is the difference between* The Death of Marat *by David and* The Death of Andreas Baader *by Richter?*

There is a very big difference. The painting of Marat is wonderful; it is a great painting and I like it. But it is totally invented and it is very artificial... He was able to paint, not like me. I didn't learn how to paint; it was not my culture.

But many people think that you are able to paint.

They are wrong!

No, they are not wrong! We consider you the Vermeer of our time. Your art is so effective that you have nothing to learn from David. The differences between you and David are based on opinion, culture and sentiment. To be precise, David was involved in the revolution because he was among the men of the Convention. But you have never been politically involved. According to my opinion the disaster of Baader-Meinhof provoked in you a religious feeling for human death, similar to the feelings that David had for the death of Marat. Then, having this image in mind, David portrayed human death. Although you chose the image of death, I think that you prepared this painting with another idea in mind. What was this idea?

I was touched. It is hard to explain. I cannot give you a sentence or a word. That is the problem.

Well, it is enough to be touched.

I don't know why I was touched.

Letter to René Block, 17 August 2000

Dear René,

My 'report' might not turn out the way one would normally expect. But no matter how – this is the way it was:

I may have seen Arnold Bode before, but only from afar, I'm sure; I had no idea how important he was, and, quite naturally, he wasn't interested in me.

The idea for the painting came from Heiner Friedrich, who by sheer persistence hoped that this would gain some attention for himself and his artists. He somehow got hold of the photograph and explained to me how important it would be to do the painting. I was only half convinced, which is why the painting is not only half done, but also only half good.

In any case, I never liked the painting, and Mr Bode, who was to receive it as a present, apparently never liked it either. He seems to have been right in this, because he was not only able to see the need for a *documenta*; he also had a sense of quality.

That's how it was, and I send you sincere greetings,

Your Gerhard R.

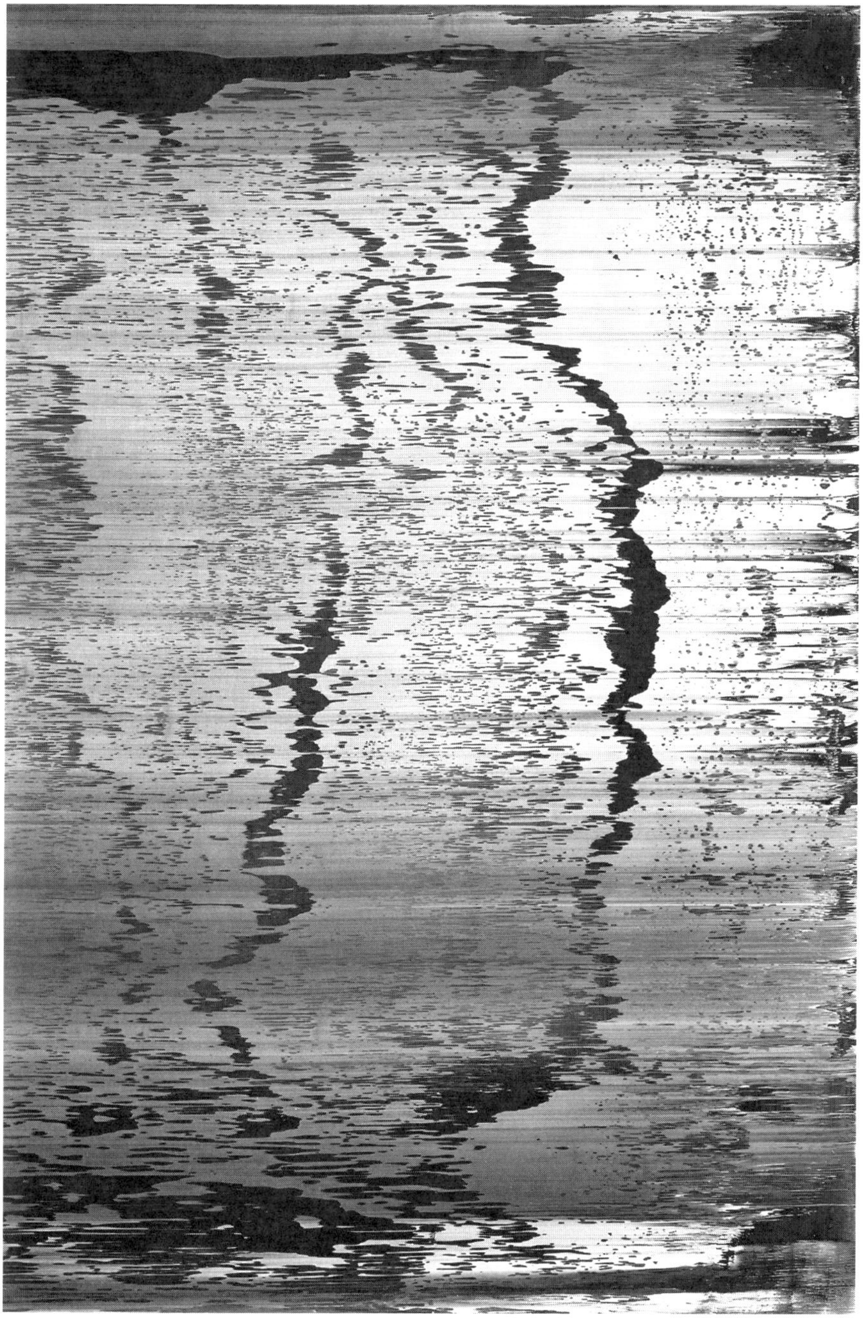

Kine, 1995

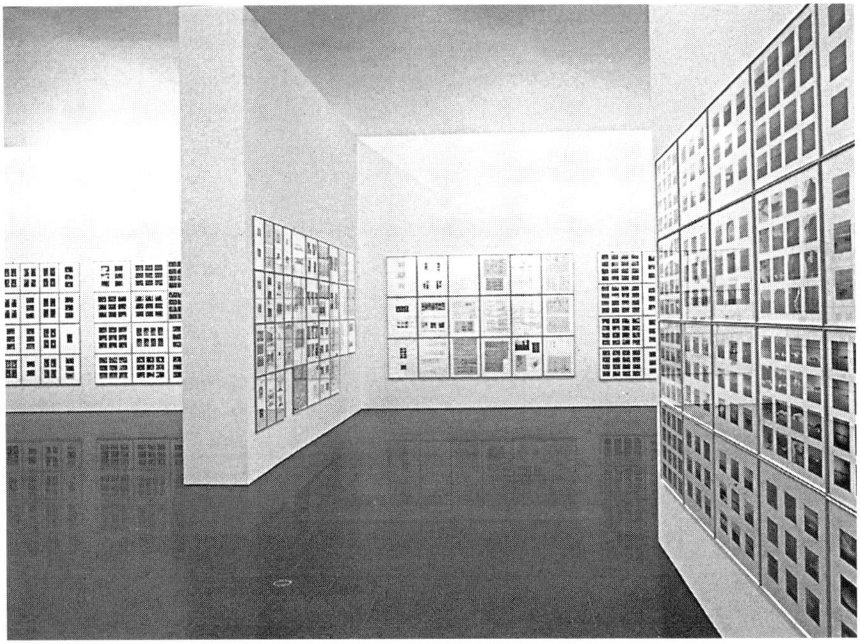

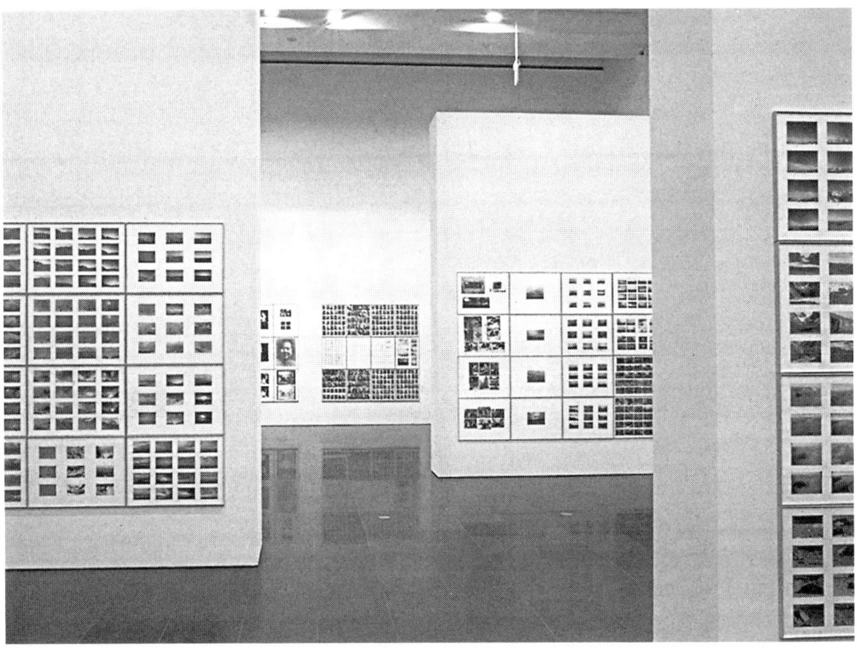

Museu d'Art Contemporani, Barcelona, 1999

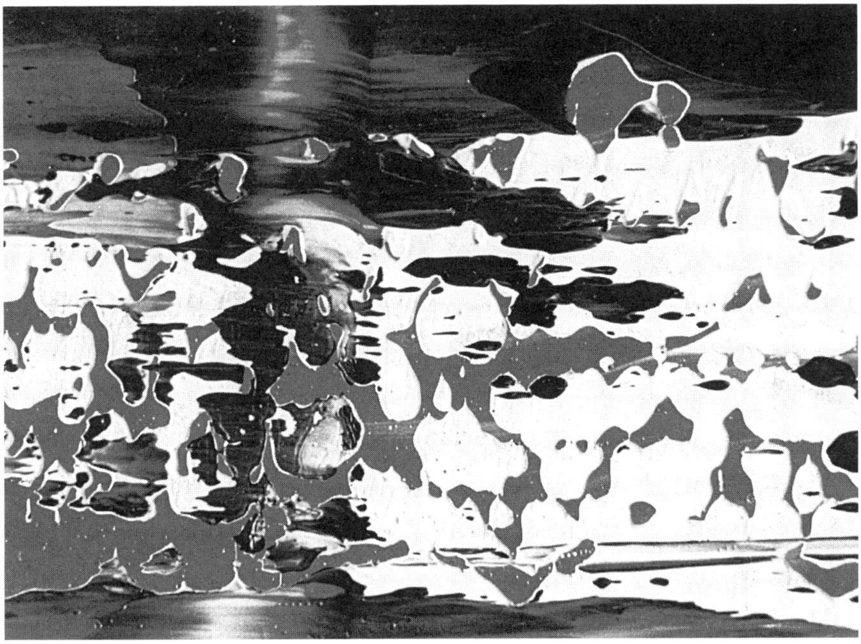

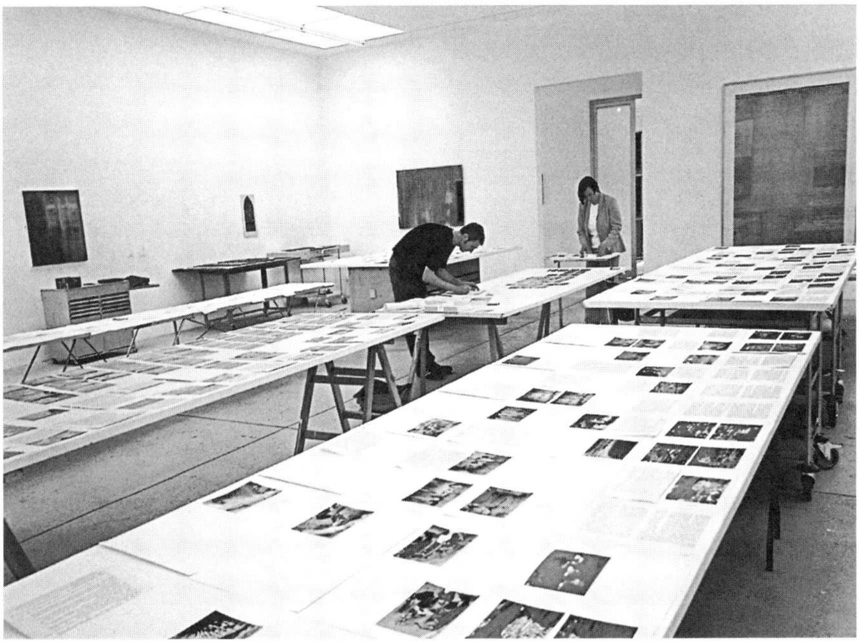

Photograph from *WAR CUT*, 2004
Montage of *WAR CUT*, 2004

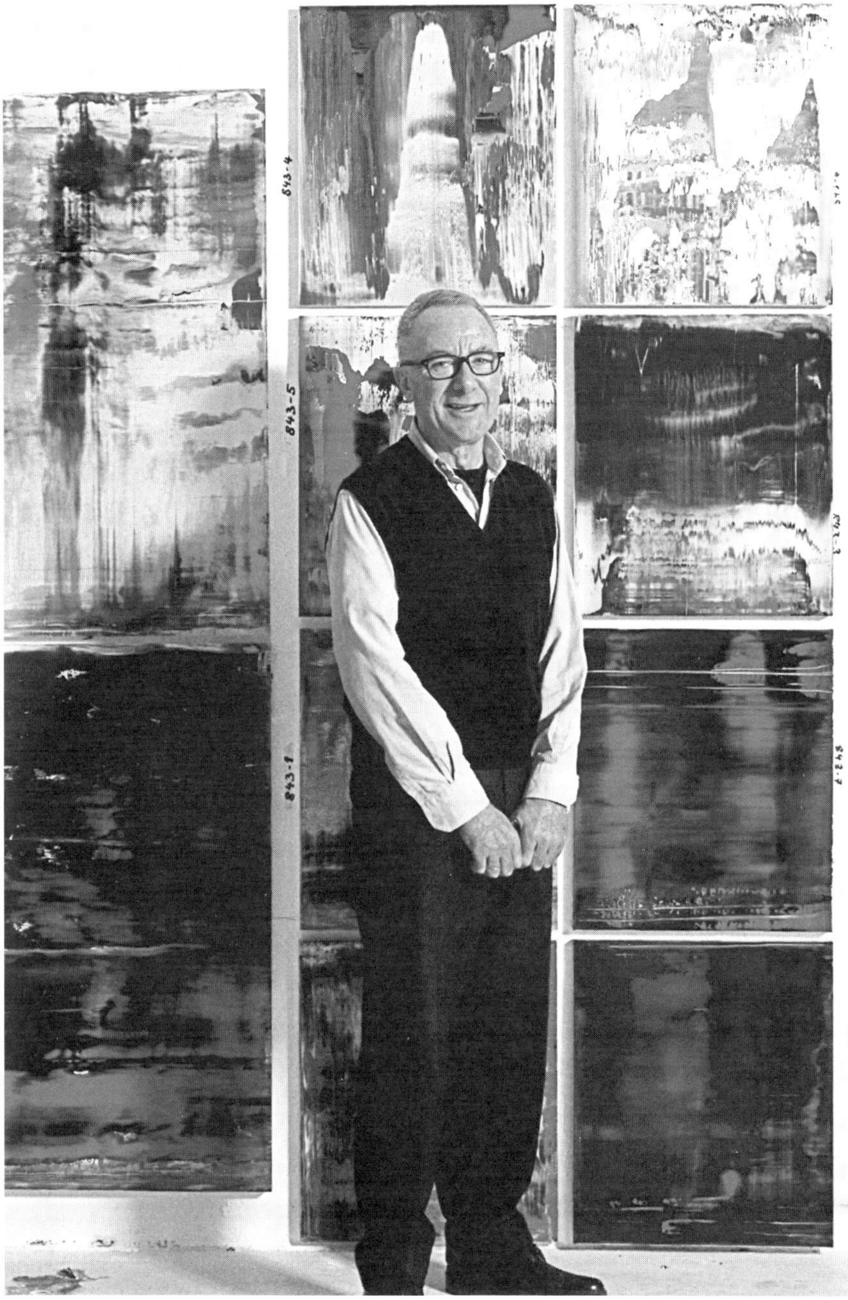

Gerhard Richter in his studio, in front of *Venetian Paintings*, 1998

Interview with Astrid Kasper, 2000

In your series S. mit Kind [S. with child] *a broad array of surface manipulations*[1] *is apparent. What prompted you to experiment with different surface structures in this particular group of works? The 'mother with child' topic evokes strong emotional identification and draws the viewer in, but this intimacy is destroyed by your artistic manipulations. Is* S. mit Kind *a good example of a work that feeds on the tension between attraction and rejection?*

If you're asking me why I chose to take many different approaches in the series *S. mit Kind*, we start with the problem that I don't even think about it, because painting is like a substitute for thinking – a different way of thinking. If, while I'm painting, I distort or destroy a motif, it's not a planned or conscious act, but rather it has a different justification: I see that the motif, the way I painted it, is somehow ugly or unbearable. Then I try to follow my feelings and make it attractive. And that means a process of painting, changing or destroying – for however long it takes – until I think it has improved. And I don't demand an explanation from myself as to why this is so. That is what your job is about... [*laughs*].

But if you contemplate the series S. mit Kind *in retrospect, can you imagine that it was the emotional subject of mother and child that, in part, made you react aggressively towards the motif?*

Well, if I acted aggressively, it certainly wasn't because of the subject – if, in fact, aggression is the right word, since a lovingly, orderly reproduction can look so stupid that it really seems aggressive. It was the same thing with the painting of these flowers over here, these yellow lilies,[2] which I copied with great care and attention to detail, and that looked so unbearable that I smudged all the nuances until the painting looked acceptable. By doing this, the lilies have become better, more ambiguous – more beautiful, that is.

When you complete a painting and then, in the end, destroy the motif, I would imagine that's not such an easy thing to do. It probably requires quite an effort...

Yes, that's true; one has invested a great deal of work. You say to yourself that you could have had it easier if you had been more result-oriented to begin with.

To return to the topic of S. mit Kind, *do you think that it might have been the intimacy of the motif that made you react so strongly in the treatment of the surfaces?*

That may be, but certainly not out of a sense of shame, or a feeling that I can't allow myself to be too private. I've never really had a problem with that.

But perhaps because it seemed too idyllic, too harmonious...

That's really the case with all realistic representations, apart from a few exceptions that are less blurred. But maybe that also has something to do with the times. Perhaps it wouldn't even be possible for me to paint in such a direct fashion today. That's why I was particularly surprised when the feminist Nabakowski[3] attacked S. mit Kind so vehemently. She worked herself up into a real temper.

I certainly asked myself why you didn't apply the kind of aggression against the beautiful landscapes that you did against the idyllic mother with child motif.

There is a painting from the S. mit Kind series[4] that I smudged and scratched more sparingly, but that has a different intention. It's more of an attempt to create a kitschy salon type of motif by really piling on the corn and the sentiment.

Yes, you vary between different gradations of surface structure in the series...

Exactly, and that is supported by the other paintings, so there is a balance within the series. It's the same as with a piece of music: there are eight little sequences – soft ones, brash ones, whatever happens to emerge.

One might draw the inference that the surface structures have become continuously more pronounced since you started, and that they play a more important role now in your photo-paintings. I'm thinking in particular of your still-life paintings of flowers from the 1990s, in which you make strong use of surface manipulation to change the motif.

Yes, that could be. But I can't explain what the exact process is, and why it's that way. I've never thought about it. All I know is what I can't do: I can't just copy something and leave it at that.

The complex surface design in your paintings disrupts my usual way of perceiving things and casts doubt on my usual criteria for observation: in your representational works, the motif becomes blurred through the smudge technique, making it difficult to recognize the motif clearly. Then again, the rich and complex surfaces of your non-representational works surpass the limits and capacities of my perceptive faculties. In short, your works take me to the limits of my cognitive abilities. Do you aim, with your paintings, to prompt the observer to think about his experiences and his way of looking at reality?

Basically your question describes exactly, almost precisely, what I want. I say 'almost', because I can't give a detailed and specific account of what it is I want to achieve. But you have immediately given me something that I most definitely want, and that is attention. That's what I want. But I don't mean a specific kind of attention. I have broader and more diverse means of achieving it. In this instance, you, as Astrid Kasper, are providing the attention through the sharpening of perception and cognition. Others want something completely different, or have completely different reasons for becoming attentive. Therefore I have not intended the precise thing that you've now discovered.

So you use different means to draw lots of attention through your paintings?

Exactly, regardless of whether it is by means of a beautiful landscape or a disruptive effect.

But if I focus my attention on the topic of perception, the question arises as to whether you are using your art to try to expand or break open the human barriers of perception and experience.

That would be great. I have a lot of wishes when it comes to painting, but my motivation has more humble foundations: to enjoy my work and to gain recognition, including the money.

In many statements that appeared in the publication Text, *you talk of painting as a model reflecting the incomprehensibility of reality. But what role does painting have in that reality? Are you trying to emphasize that reality is always tinged with insecurity, incomprehension, contradiction and complexity?*

No, those are only side-effects. I'm only trying to paint a picture that people will like, at least a bit [*laughs*].

During my intensive study of your work, I kept getting the feeling that your different artistic approaches and experiments were intended to aid you in a search for something that is universal, timeless, objective, real. Could one describe your continuous creative striving as a painter's stubborn quest for the 'absolute' picture?

Absolute – that's a word I have little use for. The word 'absolute' is simply too absolute for me. I don't know anything that's absolute. I wouldn't mind an approximation, that is, trying to get close to that state, to create something that is better, that goes beyond my rational comprehension – something that transcends.

As you emphasized in many statements during the 1980s, coincidence plays a role in the production of your non-representational works. And the smudging in the representational works can also only be controlled to a certain extent. In doing so, you introduce uncontrollable moments into your painting in an attempt to outsmart yourself.

That's always good, outsmarting oneself – in other words, to do something that's better than what the rational mind could devise.

It's particularly noticeable in paintings like the Lesende [Reading Woman] *or* Betty, *that you are striving to create a status of universal validity. I see these as great masterpieces, like those of Vermeer.*

My relation to such works of art (for instance to the paintings of Vermeer), this love, is natural and part of my flesh and my blood – it's beyond the conscious and the unconscious. It's simply a part of me, and that's why everyone makes references to such paintings. And I wish I could paint as beautifully as Vermeer. But I can't [laughs].

Your striving for universal validity, for something objective, devoid of specific details and timeless, and also the technique of smudging – all these things take you closer to the absolute picture.

The smudging makes the paintings a bit more complete. When they're not blurred, so many details seem wrong, and the whole thing is wrong too. Then smudging can help make the painting invincible, surreal, more enigmatic – that's how easy it is [laughs].

That means that you don't have an image of an absolute painting when you start on a new one...

No, not at all.

... but you do strive to create something universal.

Exactly. To create, to the best of my abilities, something that is harmonious, something comparable to a plant, a random piece of nature.

In numerous statements you made in the 1960s and early 1970s you said that you used photographs as a basis for representational paintings mainly because that gave you artistic 'leeway', freeing you from the constraints of your training and from artistic conventions. How would you explain the use of photographs as a basis for representational paintings today? Did photographs have a different function for you back then than they do now?

I think that nowadays my interest in photography is based more on tradition, on my fascination with the Old Masters and with all great painting throughout the history of art, up to the present. That's my conservative side – which I've always had, but which has become more important over the years. That's why you won't hear these trendy statements from me any more, like 'any old photograph is better than the best Cézanne'.

How does the process of choosing a motif from photographic images vary if you compare then and now? How do you choose a photograph these days?

I don't know. That has probably changed along with my interests. Today there are more children in the images; in the past there were more criminal cases. I've no idea... [laughs].

Flicking through the Atlas one can see that you really have painted less from photographs during the last few years. Have your selection criteria become more rigid?

Maybe that, too, but it's generally related to the fact that I've been taking far more photographs during these years, so I wouldn't even be able to consider painting them all. So the *Atlas* was also a means of collecting the pictures, like in a diary – a way to sort them, put them away.

So you never actually look for a photograph for a painting?

Well, in a way that's precisely what I do almost all the time. No matter what I see, the moment I look through the eyepiece of the camera, I'm thinking: painting.

With the still-life paintings of flowers and the Lesende, *the images look as though they were staged...*

The flowers are basically always staged, starting with me putting them in a vase, on a table, and then the lighting and whatever else. And with people, like the *Lesende*, it's much the same.

Paintings of yours like Ema, *the* Lesende, *the* Kl. Badende [Small Bather] *and your landscapes remind one of well known paintings by Duchamp, Vermeer, Ingres and Friedrich. How do you account for the repeated associations with these artists? You don't have an image of Vermeer's* Girl Reading a Letter at an Open Window *in your head and try to copy the image?*

No, never. But, of course, Vermeer's *Girl Reading a Letter* is in my mind or, rather, in my gut, and that influences the way I perceive things.

That means you don't consciously take other artists as role models when making representational paintings?

No, never.

But we are people in a world of modern media, and we carry a huge library of images around in our heads; images we can't simply ignore...

Exactly, but that doesn't mean we're always aware of them. On the contrary, the subconscious knowledge can be much more influential. I still recall how disappointed I was when people said that my *Nude on a Staircase* had something to do with Duchamp. I thought those remarks irrational, and needed quite some time before I could accept them.

Do you think the world of images around us has a powerful influence?

Yes, certainly. That's why we should have something like a virtual museum in our heads to help us find our bearings, to form judgments, prejudices even, to assign values and avoid running wild.

Do you believe therefore that the study or exploration of artistic traditions is a fundamental prerequisite for painters?

It enriches our lives. Just as we learn to read and write and get to know books and music, we also gain an understanding of paintings. And if we won't let ourselves be guided by what is best, we can't be good ourselves.

So you're constantly aware of artistic traditions when you work?

Certainly, because forgetting or ignoring these may be useful and fun from time to time, but we're not able to do this on a permanent basis.

All the same, don't you focus on certain paintings by Vermeer or other artists for the benefit of your own work?

There are artists who do this quite deliberately: like an advertising agency engaged in a brainstorming exercise, they conduct a strategic examination of Vermeer, or Manet (this bar by Jeff Wall[5]). I'm sure it's very interesting, but it's not my cup of tea.

But why do you so specifically pick up on Vermeer and Friedrich in your works? Have you studied them more intensely than other painters?

I always liked them [*laughs*]. And many others as well, of course. I don't think I could express in words what this specific quality is that fascinates me in many works – a quality that is also quite independent of time and that I see and love in artists as diverse as Blinky Palermo, Vermeer and Chardin. It's the same quality I detect in other areas, and it has something stabilizing to it, like a guiding light.

That means it's a particular mood and aesthetic that appeals to you particularly in the work of certain artists...

Yes, and that doesn't change much. Sometimes something new is added. During the last exhibition in Amsterdam, for instance, I discovered Saenredam[6] – a painting I hadn't seen before. I have a postcard of it hanging here now – really superb [*laughs*]. I always have postcards hanging in my place of paintings that fascinate me. They keep changing. Now it's Saenredam – over there, next to Sol Le Witt and Paul Robbrecht.

One of your prints, Übersicht [Overview], *was hanging in the Ifa-Gallery in Stuttgart.[7] It shows that you are conscious of Western cultural history, and that you don't only use and acknowledge this tradition of art, but explicitly identify with it.*

When I list my contemporaries who I like, Serra and Ryman and all the others, then I can't pretend that I think they're more important by not listing myself – I'm no worse than they are [*laughs*].

So the traditions of painting are important to you and inspire you?

Yes, definitely. We are bearers of this tradition. That's our task.

What motivates you to paint? You've worked intensively and tirelessly for forty years...

Well, I've also been eating for forty years [*laughs*].

What spurs you on?

It happens to be the activity that is most certain to make me happy. Others like to go out into their garden or whatever it is they like to do. Being able to do something for so long is really an immense privilege.

One can always discover new and exciting things in your work. But there are many artists who eventually run out of steam. Can you divulge the secret of your success?

In a way, I feel like I'm running out of steam every day – that I have no more ideas. And yet, somehow, I continue. Recently I saw Merce Cunningham on television, the dancer. He's nearly eighty, still dances, and he has students. That was very impressive.

That probably has a lot to do with passion and enthusiasm...

Or with despair; what can I say?

Your work, you as a person, and your statements are characterized by contradictions. Do you consciously nurture this in order to give your work and yourself a more enigmatic, mysterious and interesting kind of aura?

No, that's not my intention. I always dream of a very simple life where I'm satisfied, quiet and happy. That's the truth [*laughs*].

So you don't want others to be able to see what you've got up your sleeve?

No, I don't like others to see what I have up my sleeve. But I myself don't know what it is, why it's the way it is. I don't know.

That's partly what makes your work so fascinating – the fact that you're hard to pin down.

Yes, that's possible.

To conclude: do you have [an image of] an ideal viewer of your work?

No: an interested viewer.

Thank you for this interesting and stimulating conversation.

Interview with DER SPIEGEL, 2001

Mr Richter, your rhombus-shaped, red paintings were conceived for a church building. Why did nothing come of this?

In 1997 the architect Renzo Piano asked me if I could paint something for the pilgrimage centre designed by him and built near the Adriatic coast of Italy in honour of the Blessed Padre Pio. I thought the architectural design was interesting, and the very idea of building a new church appealed to me. You know, I sympathize with Catholicism, without being a Catholic myself.

What was expected of you?

The paintings were supposed to be figurative and related to the life of Padre Pio, the Franciscan Order and the stigmatization of the depicted saint. I immediately said I didn't think I would succeed in this and couldn't accept the commission. All I could do was to give something a try and then offer them the results.

Who made the decision?

A committee made up of Renzo Piano, Franciscan monks and representatives from the Vatican. They expressed their regret and declined. I can understand that.

What made the paintings suitable for a pilgrimage centre?

To me, they have a religious feel to them. But I didn't want to burden them with a title. As with all my abstract works, I started out with a vague notion and kept painting over the surfaces.

Is it possible to interpret the red rhombuses as scars, as stigmata?

Perhaps that emerges on a subconscious level, but I wouldn't feel comfortable saying it was intentional. I can't paint bleeding wounds.

These paintings were then purchased by the Museum of Fine Arts in Houston, Texas, which will loan them to the Biennale. What's left of the religious aura?

At the moment, probably only the silly newspaper catchphrase 'Rejected by the Vatican'.

Conversation with Tim Griffin, 2001

Are there any aspects of your work that American audiences fail to grasp?

No. American audiences are more accepting of my work than any other audience.

Is there anything about your works that they seem particularly receptive to?

For me, it's very impressive that audiences here prefer immediate and direct things, and, in the same way, they prefer to say things directly and without the least fear. That's good.

How have developments in new media influenced your work?

These developments make art less important. So I'm more isolated and I make fewer paintings.

Do you feel that developments in media have changed the way people see your paintings literally or analytically?

Of course, all modern media have changed the way that people see paintings. Their main effect is to make clearer differences between art and entertainment.

Are there any links, narrative or otherwise, among the abstract and figurative paintings in your current show?

The main link and common ground of both the figurative and abstract paintings is that they have the same intent: to give a picture, a visible description, to represent an image, to produce appearance, like a photo. A figurative painting shows subjects that you can recognize as a tree, house or clouds. And in an abstract painting, you can recognize only similarities, a special likeness to a tree, house or clouds – you are not able to identify what you see.

How do you see yourself in relation to the history of abstraction?

I'm not very familiar with the history of abstraction.

Is there an ethical basis for your desire to keep your political or ideological leanings out of interpretations of your work? Or are you a formalist in pursuit of depicting pure perception?

It is not that I'm keeping or withholding my political leanings – but I have only what one can see in the paintings. And of this I'm absolutely sure: I have nothing to do with formalism.

Your work has appeared on album covers – most notably, Sonic Youth's Daydream Nation. *How did this use of your imagery come about? Does this reflect your taste in music?*

I liked it a lot that Sonic Youth used my picture for a cover, but it was a rather private matter and twenty years ago. Today, I'm listening to Bach, Cage and some younger composers.

You've said: 'What counts is the world of the mind, and of art. Over the decades, this remains our home and our world.' What world of the mind and of art do you see yourself offering?

To participate in the world of the mind and art and spirit – isn't it the chance to survive?

Do you live with any art by other artists?

I have almost no paintings by other artists at home. But I see [contemporary] art every day, in catalogues and magazines, and I like to see exhibitions. It's work: sometimes a pleasure, sometimes a bore.

Interview with Robert Storr, 2002

How is it that you first began to make paintings?

When I was a child, at 15 or 16, I made watercolours, landscapes and self-portraits. I remember doing a watercolour of a group of people dancing. It was quite a nice one.

Why does it stand out in your memory?

Because I was so negative when I was young. We had moved to a new village, and automatically I was an outsider. I couldn't speak the dialect and so on. I was at a club, watching the others dance, and I was jealous and bitter and annoyed. So in the watercolour all this anger is included, at 16. It was the same with the poems I was writing – very romantic, but bitter and nihilistic, like Nietzsche and Hermann Hesse.

Did your family support your making art, or was it all on the side – private?

On the side. Maybe my mother approved. She was a bit crazy, so she thought this boy might be a genius.

So she encouraged you?

She did nothing against my efforts.

That's a lot.

That's a lot. That's true.

And when did you decide to pursue this activity professionally?

When I was 17. I had to find a job at some point; that's when I did poster painting, lettering on banners – '*Der Sozialismus lebt.*' That's a strange sentence: 'Socialism lives.'

In your case, it was also a matter of 'Socialism is a living'.

Good! And then I worked in theatre, painting scenery, for half a year. It was a city theatre, in Zittau, a small town about 100 kilometres from Dresden, where I lived in a dormitory for apprentices.

And so it was coming out of those experiences – your poems and watercolours and your work in theatre – that you decided to go to the Academy?

Yes. From the age of maybe 16 I had the feeling it would be right for me.

And what kind of a future did you imagine as an artist, at that point?

I had no idea. I just wanted to paint, to make pictures.

Did you think you were going to be a painter for public occasions or for private collectors of paintings?

A painter like all the others, like Lovis Corinth and Raphael and so on.

A famous painter [laughs].

But didn't you do a mural commission just after graduation from the Academy?

When I left the Academy, at the end, yes, I painted a large mural[1] on the theme of health and happiness in a Socialist paradise.

But you didn't see yourself continuing to make paintings of that sort – big public paintings?

Maybe for some short moment I thought this could be a future for me, making big paintings, public paintings.

I know from Ilya Kabakov, Eric Bulatov and other artists from the former Soviet Union that in the Eastern Bloc one could have a job as an official artist, a book designer, for example, and then be an unofficial artist in private. I wonder if you envisioned this kind of a double life, or if you expected just to paint pictures?

I never really thought that I would have a job in this field, painting murals or as a public artist; I did not think it was anything serious. I was most afraid of being placed in a company. That was the usual treatment.

What kind of role models were there then for being an independent artist? Who could one look to as an example of somebody who had shown that it was possible?

No one.

So it was a question of something that had to be invented.

Yes. There certainly was an underground, but I did not like it. Then there were freelance, self-employed artists. But there were no good painters among them. The independent artists, some of them, were overproud of their independence; they made a cult out of their status. I always had a bad feeling about that, their pride, their self-importance.

What kind of art could one see at that time in East Germany?

We looked very seriously at group exhibitions. At least twice a year there was a big show of work from artists' societies. In the museums it was classical art. I think the Gemäldegalerie in Dresden[2] was still closed, because only much later did the Russians come with this 'present' – they gave everything back that had been taken during the war. But there were other smaller museums, such as Pillnitz, a bit outside of Dresden, in a castle on the river. At that time there was a museum there,[3] with Caspar David Friedrich and other good painters of the eighteenth and nineteenth centuries, Rococo paintings and pastels.

You mentioned that things stopped more or less with Adolph Menzel and Impressionism?

Yes. The Russian painters like Ilya Repin and Alexander Gerasimov we could not see in the original, or very seldom; we knew them only in reproduction. Of course every year we went twice to Berlin and visited the Dahlem museum.[4] It was a big thing, to go to Berlin, to see a movie, go to the theatres and the museum.

It was forbidden at that time to go to West Berlin, but it was easy. There was no Wall.

So what kind of modern art could you see?

In West Berlin, I accidentally stumbled into a gallery once, and I can't remember anything of what I saw [*laughs*].

Was it because you were not prepared to look at contemporary art, or was it just not very good?

It was too strange. It was completely alien. In one gallery, Galerie Gerd Rosen, there was contemporary painting, and it was very decorative.

Would this be work of the '20s and '30s, or from the post-war time?

Post-war. Recent abstraction, recent work. I don't know the names, except for Bernhard Heiliger. Ernst Wilhelm Nay I learned of later. We were oriented to the French artists, to Impressionism, Matisse, Picasso and Léger.

Did you like Léger?

Yes. But I saw a painting of his last week, and I asked myself why I had liked Léger so much. It was the first time I had the feeling that this was a very stupid painting [*laughs*].

And so what other sources of information did you have then? Were there Picassos in Dresden? Did any come to Dresden in exhibitions?

No, never. But I got books and catalogues, newspapers. I had an aunt who sent me every month a West German photo magazine, *Magnum*. That was very good.

Did you use images from the magazine in your own work?

No, but it was good to look at, it was so modern.

Did you have other sources of information? Could you get Life, Look, Paris Match*?*

Unless you had a connection to an aunt, you couldn't buy them.

And what kind of work were you making then?

In school, the exercises were as realistic as possible, in the spirit of nineteenth-century artists like Menzel and Wilhelm Leibl, but not so detailed as Ferdinand Waldmüller. And then at home, it was very good, we tried to be very fresh, relaxed.

But it was still figurative?

Yes, always.

Did you work from drawings or models, or go out in the landscape?

I always painted in front of reality, never from reproductions.

So you never 'cheated' by using photographs a little bit?

No, except for one drawing, the year before I left, of bathers.

And nobody noticed?

I did not show it.

When you, Konrad Lueg and Sigmar Polke first identified yourselves as German artists, what kind of situation were you in? What were you up against? What was it like to be a young artist in Germany in 1962 or 1963?

We swam in a pool of hope. We thought, 'We'll just do it.' It was not a problem that the others, first the French and then American artists, were selling so well and at such high prices. It was not a topic. We were young, and the older German artists like Nay and Georg Meistermann were not very famous and not much liked. Their works were less expensive, and we felt that was only right because they were stupid.

Particularly in the late '60s and early '70s, the pressure not to paint was even greater in Germany than in the US. How did you manage at that time, when so many people were saying that painting was dead?

I didn't believe this. But in a sense it was familiar to me, because I knew that culture was at an end, that painting couldn't do very much any more. And as a German, I was familiar with the idea of not being worth anything. So painting wasn't worth anything, I wasn't worth anything, and then there were several other things that weren't worth anything. But nevertheless I didn't believe that. I believed in painting.

In the Academy you were surrounded by people who were primarily doing performance, installation or conceptual work of one kind or the other, weren't you?

Not so many. Blinky Palermo, Polke and Lueg were there. And we painted, although Lueg not so much. Most people who were doing performance were very stupid. There were only a few exceptions – like Joseph Beuys. But all the others were just fashion. So that wasn't such a problem.

What was your relation with Beuys in terms of his ideas about art as a social mechanism?

I always distrusted him.

In terms of his ideas about art or in general?

The social ideas were absolutely stupid. And the art was half fake, a fraud almost. But he was very interesting to us at the time. He was very engaging, the only one who was a rival to be taken seriously. He was really something to be dealt with.

And so how did you deal with him?

We observed him, the way we observed each other later.

You've said you were always attracted to madness. Was Beuys's approach a kind of madness?

Yes, I always saw a danger in him. Too much danger, the dangerous ability to fascinate other people, that was really amazing. Then to make all these claims, to fake something, to do something shabbily, to defraud ... that's why I fled from him. So that when I saw him at a party, for instance, if he was on one side of the room, I'd be on the other.

Did it also connect to his desire to create an ideology of art? Was that part of it?

Yes, I think so.

And how did you, Palermo and Polke deal with the situation when Beuys was such an overwhelming personality?

Polke had a good strategy. He made his jokes. And he is still doing this. For Palermo, though, it was not so easy, because he was a bit weak; he couldn't defend himself. Beuys sometimes had an easy game with him. He would say, 'Palermo, come here!' And this made me very furious. But then Palermo had his beautiful belief in painting. It was a paradise for him, the only ideal world.

Did you have that in common with him? Did you see painting as an ideal world?

Yes, but I see it more practically, not in such contrast with the rest of life. He had such a wild life, with drugs and so on, and so the paintings were a big contrast. It's not so with me; it's more seamless. I am proper and the paintings are proper [*laughs*]. The floor is clean and the painting is clean, you know. Back then, we wanted to make art a kind of quiet protest. Because only modern art had the power. Gilbert & George had done something classical, or neo-classical, and Palermo and I wanted to introduce a kind of seriousness. That's also when the friendship with Polke broke up.

Because of a particular incident?

No, in general. Funny, I saw him last month in Baden-Baden. It was many, many years since the last time we saw each other. He said hello, and we talked about painting.

What happened between you and Polke?

We were very close and had the same ideas; we worked together and showed together and so on. And then we drifted apart.

Why did you drift apart? Was it just that you each had your own direction, or was there a real disagreement?

Oh, no, it was not a disagreement. Just life. He took drugs, and I did not. That's all. And if you take drugs, then you have these strange friends around you. He continued to be wild and cynical and ... happy [*laughs*].

And you wanted to make something that was the opposite of that? Something more...

Serious. Classical.

Do you see yourself as a modernist?

No.

Did you ever see yourself as a modernist?

No, never. I mean, I am here, today, yes. But I never had the feeling that I was a modern artist.

Do you see yourself in opposition to modern art in some ways – or modernism, I should say, not modern art. Do you feel yourself in some ways challenged?

That's difficult, because the good modern artists, like Carl Andre, Bob Ryman, I like very much. But modern art has always only shown itself to me in trends and blowhards, so I couldn't be a modern artist [*laughs*]. There were always powerful movements or groups that today we don't even know any more.

One fascinating aspect of your work is the difference between the delicacy of some of the pictures – the blurred figures, still-lifes and landscapes – and the abstract paintings, which are incredibly tactile, and everything happens on the surface. What accounts for that change, technically? How do you read the painting?

That's a very difficult question, but they are really different, the figurative and the abstract.

How is your attitude toward the activity of painting different in each case?

I never tried to answer this question, because it is hard for me.

You mentioned that a certain abstract painting actually started out as a picture of Cologne Cathedral, and now there is only a little bit of this image visible underneath. If you did not know to look for it, you wouldn't see it. What happened between the initial image and the ultimate abstraction?

There the method of making an abstract painting is misused to cover up a bad painting. It's not as terrible as it sounds, because, as in life, one makes a virtue out of a shortcoming. But they are really two completely separate methods.

In The Daily Practice of Painting, *the book of your writings and interviews, you talk about – I presume this is more about the abstract paintings than the figurative paintings – how each step of the painting is to cancel out a cliché, an obvious thing.*

Right, that's how I described it.

How much do you know about an abstract painting when you begin it? Initially what kind of choices do you make about a colour or about the scale of a painting?

I have to have a mental picture, an image, to start. I never reach this image, but it's good to begin with it.

And do you actually get to that image and destroy it, or, once you've started, do you abandon it and just go in whatever direction the painting takes you?

I can't always reach the image in my mind – almost never, in fact – so that the abstract image I create is not quite there, but it gets to the point where I can leave it.

Is there any difference in this respect between your abstract and your figurative work, insofar as you have the technical control to push toward a very deliberate result in the figurative work if you chose to?

In order to complete a picture and say, 'This is finished, this is good', it's the same, it's always the same criterion, in both the abstract and figurative paintings.

And what are those criteria? Can you describe them?

It has to do with the surface of both, which at the end becomes erased, or more erased. Before that, they were richer, full of things. Uglier, but more precise maybe.

Well, that certainly seems true of the more recent paintings, which have gone from having very, very rich, detailed surfaces to…

Correct.

It is almost as if, when the picture gets to a certain point, you cancel it.

Yes.

Are you suspicious of virtuosity?

Yes, very. People always say that I am very virtuoso and that my pictures are, but I don't think I am. I am not!

In what way do you mean you are not?

I am not able to make a sketch of you here, just so, and that's fine. I don't have the facility to do it.

But you can make paint do a great many things.

Yes, it's easy with a photograph.

But you say you are suspicious of virtuosity. How important is it to make things hard for yourself to make a picture? Is it essential to make the process difficult in some way?

No. Ability is a given: that's not what I'm suspicious of. I hate it when people cannot do what they want to do. It goes without saying that you have to have mastery over your medium. I don't mean God-given talent but the skill that's acquired through hard work.

Are you saying that people who set out to be painters should develop the necessary skills, and that you don't have an interest in work which tries to make clumsiness a virtue?

Clumsiness is not a sign of quality for me.

Are you then suspicious of artists who stylize clumsiness, who consider awkwardness proof of their sincerity? Would you rather artists be both skilled at what they do and make their skill work for them in very disciplined ways, even make it harder for themselves?

Why should you make it even harder?

Well, you do, don't you, in certain ways?

I have no choice. It just becomes difficult. I would prefer it to be easy. Wouldn't we all?

What is the hardest thing about making a picture?

The tough part is always at the end. The beginning is always easy. So maybe you are right about making it even harder.

But where does the difficulty lie? Does the difficulty lie primarily in what the hand does or in the conception?

In the conception. To see what's wrong, this is so difficult. To make it right is easy, but to see what to make and what not to make is harder.

What not to make is important. But when you say that, is it because you have a very clear idea where a painting should end up, or because you have a very clear idea of where a painting should not end up?

I don't have a clear idea of either. I have a vague idea.

In making, for example, a figurative painting, how much do you know when you begin about how the painting is going to appear? You do have a photographic image as a reference, and you have a technique that's very much under your control. How much do you know about how the painting is actually going to look?

With figurative paintings, I know a lot. I have quite a clear concept of how it should look, but very seldom does it actually work, or come to this image. For example, I always wish to make a very detailed painting, and I am almost never able to do it.

Where the details would read clear and sure?

Clear and sharp, and as good as Vermeer of Delft. The blurring is always a kind of emergency butchering [*laughs*]. It's an emergency move at the end. To make the picture in some way attractive to look at, I blur it.

I see. Something isn't going right in the painting, and the blurring then takes care of it.

Yes, but prior to that, the situation is terrible.

The first paintings that had that quality were from the early 1960s. There is a series of portraits of a family from 1965 – Boy Baker, Girl Baker, Mr Baker and Mrs Baker – with what look like white strokes on top. Is that the first time you cancelled a painting?

With the strokes? No, I cancelled the painting by blurring. I cut the four heads off. I was trying to restore the painting because it had small cracks in it, and then I got angry and made all these marks.

Was the Table *of 1962 the first cancelled painting?*

Yes.

And what provoked you in that case to smear the image?

I painted it very realistically, and it looked so stupid. You can't paint like that, that's the problem. You can't quite stand it any more. Or very seldom. *The Reader* from 1994 is almost the way I wanted it, but that's a rare example; it is not too imprecise.

No, it is quite clear. And this is actually what you imagined?

Even better, but that's okay [*laughs*].

It's very okay! So in a way the first cases of blurring the image started out, as you say, as emergencies, either a technical emergency – cracking – or a conceptual emergency – 'I can't stand to look at something like this'. At what point did you realize that this was actually a way of painting?

That came very slowly. In the abstract paintings, there's sometimes this trick. I have to be careful not to do it, but I sometimes cover the painting with white and then everything is beautiful and new and fresh, like snow. All the misery is over, the terror.

The terrifying part of the image itself, or...

No, the way I did it, my inability to make the stupid stuff, which gets worse and worse.

And what makes something stupid in your eyes? The paint itself is innocent, you know.

I need an example of what you mean.

How do you decide whether something is good or bad? I know it's not logical, it's not something you can state easily, but...

The most important thing, in life and for humanity, is to decide what is good and what is bad. And it's the most difficult. I remember a time when it was out of fashion to judge a painting good. But all my real constructive experiences with people were about good or not good, with Polke, Palermo, Fischer or the sculptor Isa Genzken, who is very strict. 'That's ugly, terrible,' she'd say. It's very important.

And what's the difference between good and beautiful, bad and ugly?

It always means good and bad. I don't know if it is the same in English, but in German if you say it's a good painting, you already mean it's beautiful; if you say it's a bad painting, you imply also that it's ugly. It almost has moral connotations of good and evil. If we say something is beautiful, then we mean it's good.

And do you believe this?

Yes.

What if a painting is disturbing? 'Ugly' maybe is not the right word, but what if it's upsetting or makes you uneasy?

That can be a good quality, a quality you can use.

I would think that many people looking at The Reader *could easily identify the subject and can also respond to the way it is painted. On the other hand, there are paintings where the colours are mixed on the surface and mottled or unclear. Those pictures could be very disturbing to look at.*

Even then, it has to be good in some way. There has to be something that fits or resonates.

Put another way, there seems to be in the figurative paintings, especially the recent ones, a degree of gentleness, an invitation to come into the picture. In some of the more recent abstractions, though, there is a level of aggression and a closing-off of the picture. Those are very different experiences.

And both have their own criteria, and they have to be good.

Do you agree with that way of reading some of the abstract paintings?

Yes, of course.

In some of them, as you say, the white closes something off. In other cases, covering or removing the paint almost cancels the image, as if you were committing an act of aggression. Is that an accurate way to describe things?

I think so, yes.

How so?

I find that difficult to talk about at the moment.

I understand that Robert Ryman visited your studio at some point. He said to me with some perplexity that it was amazing that you could do anything and everything. My question is how do you decide what to do if you have this ability to make things in so many different ways?

I never had the feeling that I have so many abilities. I did a little landscape, and then something abstract. The day is long, so I never felt that was so special. Except I developed a bad conscience. When I saw Ryman, so thorough, so persistent, painting every day, this made me a bit nervous. I thought maybe I am not a proper painter. I really often worried that there was something missing, that I was lacking something because I was trying so many things, in all directions. I envied other artists and thought they had a quality I was lacking, especially Ryman. That changed a little after I got to know him better: I got to know his problems, and my problems [*laughs*].

And your problems were?

My problems? They are still the same. They haven't changed, but now I can see I have the right to keep on painting.

Typically, artists were encouraged to make a consistent body of work or to make a conscious progression from one idea to the next. What's striking in your work is the apparent freedom you have given yourself to move from one idea to another without worrying about how the paintings will be received. How did you arrive at the sense that this was okay?

I always hated those artists who were so consistent and had this sort of unified development; I thought it was terrible. I never worked at painting as if it were a

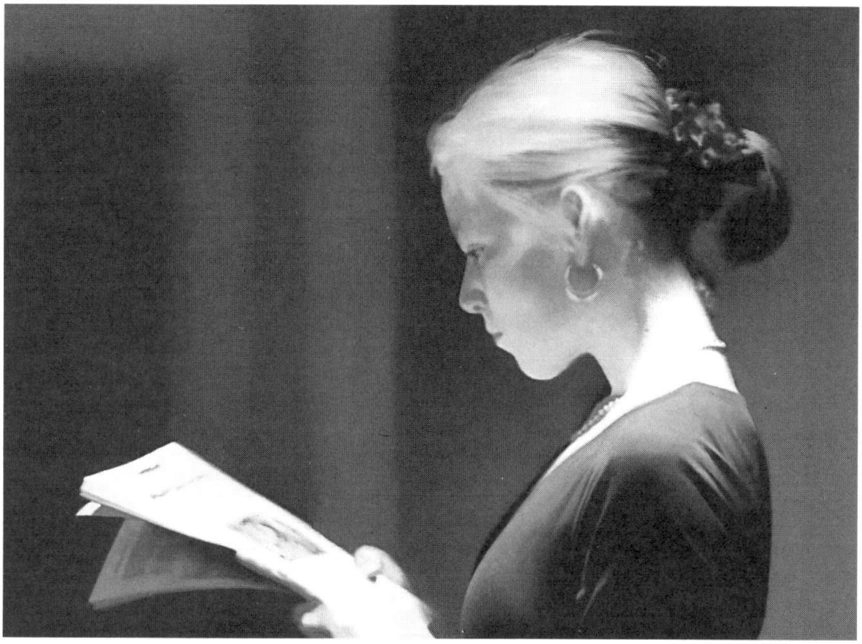

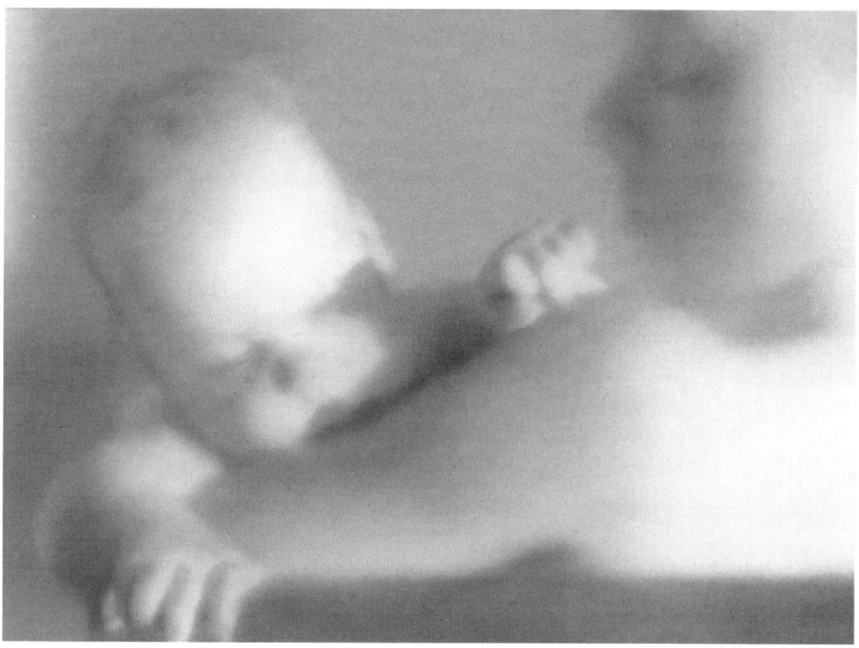

Lesende, 1994
S. mit Kind, 1995

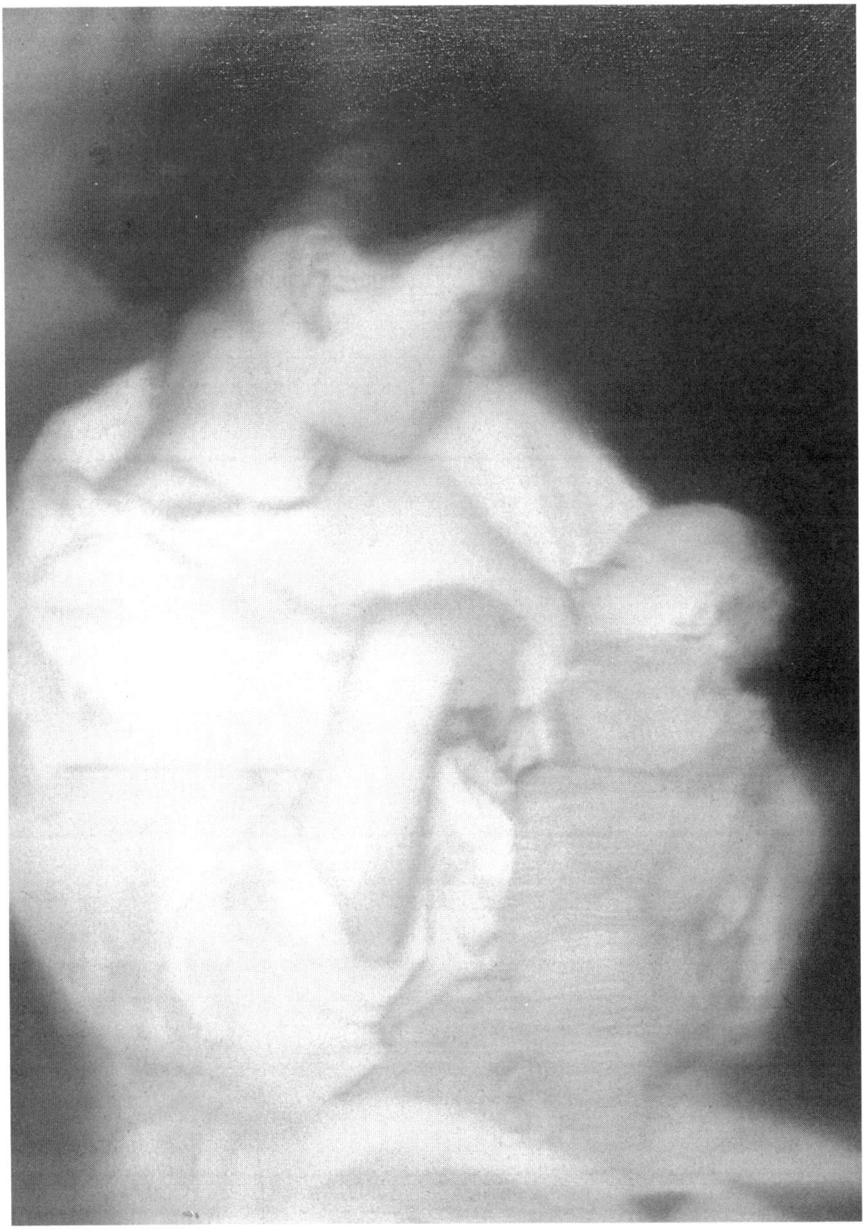

S. mit Kind, 1995

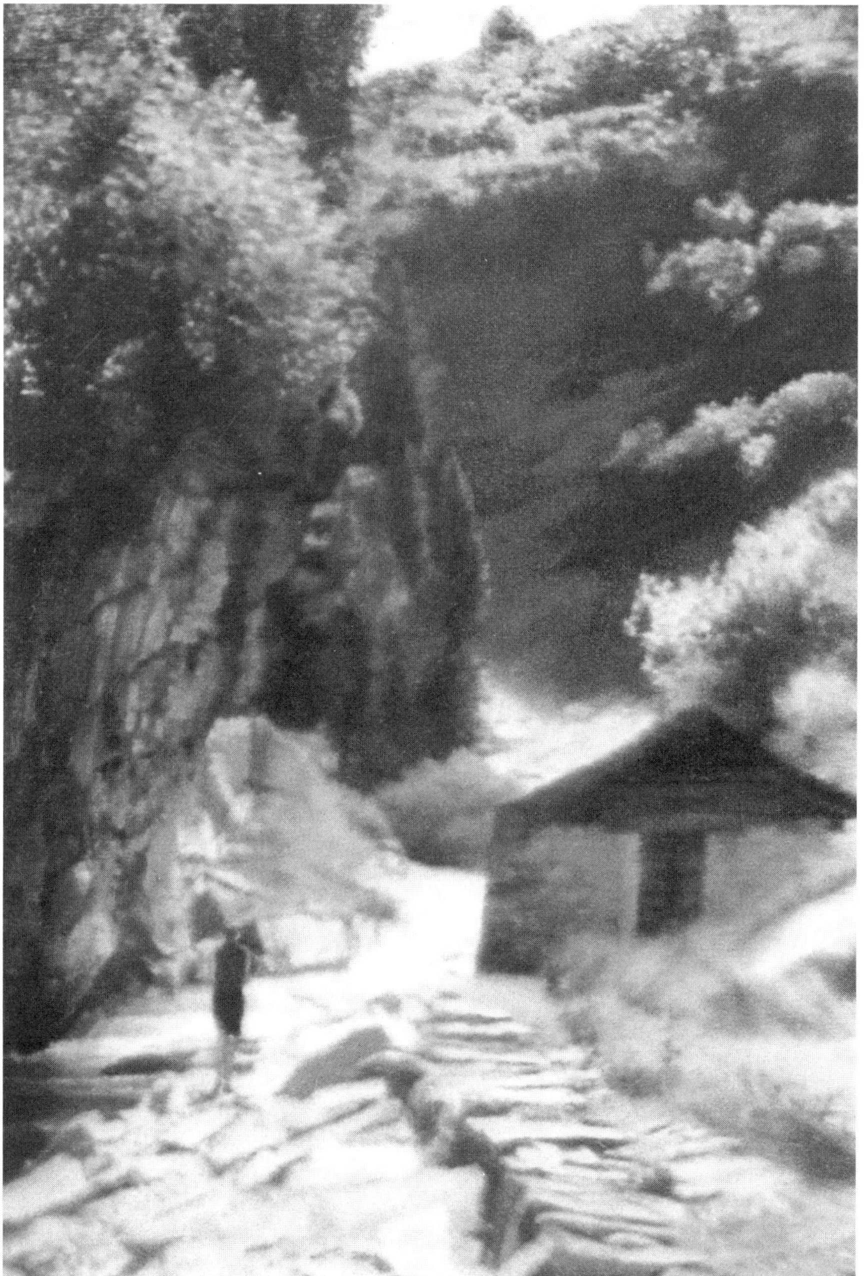

Ravine, 1996

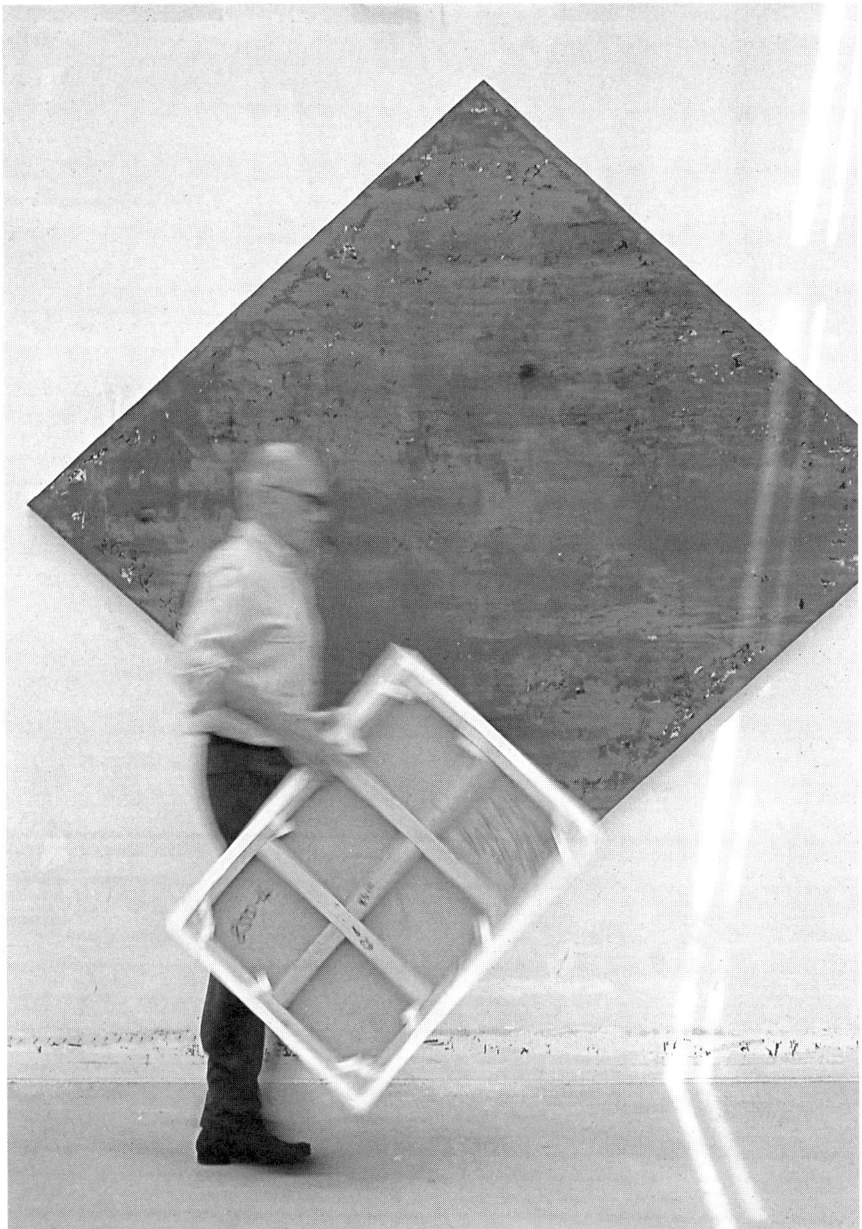

Gerhard Richter in his studio, in front of *Rhombus*, 1998

job; it was always out of interest or for fun, a desire to try something. Other artists might paint pictures for a show. They say, 'I still need large paintings.' When I was struggling financially, when I had trouble with Heiner Friedrich,[5] I couldn't be with the gallery any longer, and I had to leave. At that time, I became a teacher.[6] I would do different jobs. I didn't want to have to make paintings I would be paid for, nor did I want to have to be nice to a dealer – although I am very nice [*laughs*]. But if you force me to do something, I can't do it.

And so teaching was a way to have the freedom to...

To paint. I was never a good teacher.

In this country, even though many, many painters teach, there is always the impression that if you are teaching, it's because you are not really successful as an artist. It's striking that in Germany in particular almost all of the really interesting artists have taught, and many of them have taught for a very long time.

That has to do with the system, the civil service. You are immediately guaranteed a lifelong salary and have a certain status as a professor. Germans are still a bit crazy with the title 'professor'. All the artists are professors.

And they are not afraid that being in the Academy makes them academic?

No, you don't get better or worse. It's just a job, an extremely easy job. It's almost immoral. I have five months of vacation. And the rest, the other seven months, professors hardly need to show up. But I did; I was always very proper. It's awful!

Did you have close associations with students? Did you find that teaching actually fed your work in some way or reinforced what you were doing?

Thomas Schütte became a friend. He visits us with his family, and we always encourage each other. That is an exception.

But you didn't have the kind of relationship with students that Beuys had, for example.

No, never. Because I had no teacher, I could never imagine that students would want to hear something from me. I came into the classroom and said, 'Excuse me, I don't want to disturb you.'

You've mentioned that you did not want father figures, that you did not have a strong father yourself...

And so it was impossible for me to think that students would want me as a father. Ultimately, I learned they might.

Aside from the economic security that it gave you, did the teaching have an effect on how you thought about art? Do you in fact think that art is something that can be taught?

In the first few years, yes, I thought there was something I could maybe communicate, or somehow, with my strange manner, show some opposition and some kind of partiality. There was a need for that.

On your part?

Yes. The Academy was so bad and the teachers so corrupt, I thought I should do something.

How do you mean bad and corrupt?

In this system, you become corrupt. They were only unsuccessful artists, except Beuys, for a short time. And what they taught was truly horrible. It was so modern, the students never did what I did. I started with still-lifes, and they thought it was reactionary. But I thought this an important foundation, to learn to draw and to understand what colour is.

And that's how you taught?

Yes. It was good in the beginning. But after the times went so strange, the events of 1968 and so on, I couldn't get my position across; I couldn't offer still-life painting any more. They refused it. And of course for some students there was no need to make a still-life. Thomas Schütte, who was one of the best, or Isa Genzken, never painted a still-life. We discussed.

Do you take it as a challenge to paint subjects that other people think can't be painted, for example a still-life, even a still-life of flowers, as you've recently done?

Not consciously. But perhaps unconsciously it could be a motivation. Who knows? On the other hand, I remember that when I painted my first landscape, *Corsica*, in 1969, it was really not for the public. I thought, 'I'll do it just for fun, for me.' And I didn't expect that it would be possible to show it.

There are some very interesting parallels between the way you talk about your work and the way de Kooning talked about his. He was operating at a time when it seemed to many people – artists as well as critics – that there were certain things you could do and certain things you couldn't. And he always said, 'The minute it's obvious you cannot do something, you have to do it' [laughs]. *When it was no longer possible to paint the figure, he said, 'Fine, then I will have to paint women, because obviously it is impossible to do.' And I wonder if there isn't an element of this in your thinking as well.*

When I started the landscapes, I thought you could already sort of do what you wanted, although Minimalism and Conceptual art were still dominant. But ten years later it was more in fashion to do different things. Martin Kippenberger did everything [*laughs*].

Tacking against the wind. To go back a little earlier in our conversation, we were talking about when you took a job at the Academy and didn't want to be in a position of having to make work that was consistent for the sake of the market. I wonder if art history had special importance for you, in terms of how you approached your own work, or whether you were willing simply to step aside and do what you were compelled to do while art history took care of itself?

I am definitely inside of art history: it's my domain, my home.

And where are you inside that domain?

In the art, the painters' culture.

The culture of painters?

Yes.

But not necessarily inside an avant-garde that defines art history according to a precept?

No. That's very foreign to me.

How do artists make art history?

They never do; they never make art history. They do their job, and then after ten years it's art history [*laughs*].

There is another recent body of work which is perhaps even more surprising than the landscapes in certain ways – the paintings you made in 1995 of your wife and young child. These are very unexpected pictures.

Maybe because there are so many of them.

Both the number and the subject.

The subject? Because there are children in the painting?

Yes.

I can't quite understand why this should be so extraordinary.

It's unexpected because it seems to be very private.

Very private, yes. The only difference is that I have become more shameless. I am not as ashamed any more, and I am not afraid any more. My fears have abated somewhat. I don't feel that I have to behave properly. Somehow I finally understood that I am allowed to do what I want.

Since 1988, when you painted the cycle of paintings about the Baader-Meinhof group, 18 October 1977, *there seems to have been a decided shift in your work. The colour has changed, and the subject matter appears to be more personal. I'm thinking, for example, about the painting of your daughter,* Betty, *which was made at the same time as the Baader-Meinhof series. It's as if two sides of your mind are always working in tension with each other. How has that happened?*

I don't know what I should say to this! It has to do with age, perhaps. Or with time. Time necessitates it.

You once said that the October *paintings were a leave-taking.*

But seen like that, every painting is a leave-taking. *Betty*, of course, was a leave-taking, as were the mother-child paintings.[7]

How so?

They declare that it's over – this time, this short time.

Can paintings hold time? Is this the point of making paintings?

This is not the reason I make paintings, but yes, they can hold time a bit. That's why they are so attractive for us.

In discussing the difference between the paintings you made from snapshots and the snapshots themselves, you referred to snapshots as devotional pictures and said the paintings were different. Where does that difference lie when you begin to paint your own life in this way?

That's a real intellectual problem. Snapshots are like little devotional pieces that people have in their environment and look at. The paintings are like that a little, too, but they are less private. That may be our deepest desire, not to be private. To be public, open to the world.

When you speak about being open to the world in this way, I am struck by the fact that the paintings you made about the Baader-Meinhof group concern public events which prompted a deep response in you, whereas the paintings of Sabine with your child are personal in a different, intensely intimate way.

Like 18 *October 1977*, the mother-and-child paintings also provoked a lot of reactions and were very severely criticized.

Really? Why?

There was a crazy feminist writer in one of our best newspapers who wrote a very tough article about them.[8] And then a paper in Basel published an answer[9] that was very interesting about the paintings and beauty. One writer claimed that if I had painted sex and violence it would have been okay, but one isn't allowed to paint anything beautiful, whole or ideal. That's part of why people were outraged by the subject matter.

They see it as sentimental or kitschy?

Yes.

It is, in fact: that's why I said they are unusual paintings, because I don't know the last time that I saw an artist paint what amounts to a nativity.

They are not even that beautiful. They are a little damaged, in the way I was describing before. Again I couldn't quite hold it: they are not as beautiful as Vermeer.

So you went after them? Attacked them?

Yes. I had no choice. I had to. I didn't want to. But I really want to make beautiful paintings.

In The Daily Practice of Painting, *many of the notes seem incredibly negative, about the futility of painting, the corruption of the art world. Is the painting actually connected to those ideas, or do you think about those ideas after the painting is done? Does the painting have its own logic, its own status?*

Painting is the only positive thing I have. Even if I see everything else negatively, at least in the pictures I can communicate some kind of hope. I can at least carry on.

Interview with Jürgen Hohmeyer, 2002

Mr Richter, you said quite early on, 'People who paint are on the wrong track.' Why do you still paint?

I can't do anything else. I enjoy it, and when I don't get to paint I suffer withdrawal symptoms. But the comment about being on the wrong track is still valid.

It can't be all that wrong when the Museum of Modern Art honours you with a retrospective consisting of paintings that have become icons within the art world. Doesn't this make you proud?

Well, yes, it's a huge event. But three or four years ago, when the idea began to take shape, I had a quite different exhibition in mind – one that would focus on new and unknown works. Then I realized that four decades of painting is like a creature in its own right, something that has long since developed its own rules. Perhaps I should even worry about preserving enough space for my current works.

Many of your new, abstract paintings are dominated by pale, delicately interweaving colours. Are they symptomatic of a cooling-off of emotions?

You could say that. Age, as we know, makes us quieter, milder, more resigned. But I myself am not good at explaining why my paintings are the way they are. It probably also has something to do with the present situation. The last thing we need in this day and age, it seems, is painting.

Is this art form really doing so badly? Of course, people have always declared it to be dead, but then, every time, a 'new new painting' emerges, or 'the painting after the last painting'[1] – or whichever clever title is used in an exhibition.

Sure, and we also complained when we were young that everything had already been done – but something new emerged nevertheless.

What's changed since then?

Not just painting, but art as such, has become so unchallenging, so arbitrary and nice, that it can't be taken seriously any more. In the past, one would have said that it lacks 'social relevance'. That sums it up.

At the same time, the huge amounts being paid for your works suggest that they are considered important. So you can't really complain.

Yes, I'm successful, which is why my moaning may seem strange. But the public isn't interested in the paintings – only in the high prices. It appreciates rarity, not artistic merit.

How do you know that?

Mainly because it isn't possible to talk about paintings any more. The media feels much more comfortable with films, television productions, literature, and music as well. There's no criteria any more, only waffle.

Were there criteria in the past?

Yes, even if they were hard to define precisely. At the Academy, my friends and I knew full well who was talented and who wasn't. It was all a bit totalitarian, but all the more effective for that, and that's the way it was right through to Minimal art and Conceptual art. Under the influence of the New Realists, the *Neue Wilde* and the Transavanguardia people, the term 'good painting' was frowned upon, and quality was practically a swear word. That was the beginning of a jolly era: lots of colourful things were created, lots of museums were built, and the exhibitions got larger and larger.

But if you're honest, wouldn't you say it sounds as though you begrudge the young talents their lively ideas?

It's got nothing to do with young talents; most of the old ones are willingly playing along.

And nothing pleases your Grace?

Naturally, you get to see things that are good and pleasing on occasion. But it doesn't always have to be painting.

Could you give an example?

I was impressed by Gregor Schneider's haunted *Haus ur* at the Biennale in Venice. I went there with a negative prejudice, climbed through the higgledy-piggledy construction, came out and thought: 'Well, well, I was wrong.' I hope Schneider will persist. But that was a pretty impressive act.

Let's talk about the new generation. You painted your baby son Moritz[2] *from a photograph of him at the age of eight months and then described the paintings as 'self-portraits'. What did you mean by that?*

As an image of myself and my successor. Despite all the euphoria, there is something threatening about it. It's completely different with a daughter. And, in the case of this photograph, it was the startled look that touched me and that I can relate to. After all, we have plenty of reason to look out into the world with a shocked expression.

Shock is the principal theme of your series 18 October 1977, *dedicated to the deceased Baader-Meinhof terrorists. Since 1995 it belongs to MoMA, and it is bound to be a highlight of your exhibition there. At the time, German art critics were up in arms against the export, claiming it was a sell-out of an irreplaceable cultural treasure and document of national catharsis. You said these allegations were untrue. Do you find them more understandable in retrospect?*

No, I still think they're mendacious and idiotic. The world has become so small that there's no reason to prevent even a single piece of art from leaving the country. My series has found its ideal home.

If this series of paintings hadn't existed, would you perhaps have painted the 9/11 aircraft terrorists?

Definitely not.[3] This horrific form of global terror is something I cannot fathom. Compared to this, what happened in Germany seems almost like romantic foreplay.

But the world is small, as you said. And the ideological fixation, the obsession to improve the world that turns fanatics into killers – surely those are parallel motives? As early as 1964 you painted the Kennedy assassin Lee Harvey Oswald.[4]

I didn't think of him as a terrorist back then but as this rare kind of madman, and Kennedy's death really moved me. In any case, 9/11 didn't affect me in the personal kind of way that the terror of the RAF [Red Army Faction] did. I had come from East Germany and I was horrified to witness such ideological blindness in the West. I had plenty of friends who sympathized with it.

But you do sympathize with the concept of protest as a gesture, and you believe the RAF were entitled to that. What do you protest against?

Quite generally speaking, I'm against the fact that the majority of people are forced to live in unbearable conditions. And against the terrible certainty that one must die. I don't like that, this helplessness.

Are paintings blueprints for a better world – pretty, perfect, above criticism?

I find that definition too stringent. They can be a comfort if they contain enough mystery, like life itself. Even coming close to this state of things can make you happy.

Are you talking about your own paintings?

More likely Velázquez, or Vermeer. I couldn't admit to it so easily with my own works.

MoMA interview with Robert Storr, 2002

In the United States in the 1980s there was a burst of gallery activity, and a lot of attention was given to art coming from Europe, and from Germany, in particular. Many Americans first discovered your work all at once and, for the most part, they saw your gestural abstractions from the 1970s and 1980s next to the paintings inspired by Pop Art from the 1960s without knowing much about how these different bodies of work from a single artist were related. The assumption was that you were taking painting apart, style by style, by doing different things at the same time. So I wonder just how you understood the reception that you got back then: how comfortable or uncomfortable did you feel with this view of you as a kind of destructive painter?

I didn't notice that view. Perhaps I was glad to receive any attention at all. Some people would even claim that it was pretty smart. There was a demand for paintings that I satisfied, and at the same time there was this conceptual notion against painting – and so I served both sides. That was rather smart, a legitimation to enjoy them. Yes, pleasure without remorse. Because with this intellectual, conceptual background, you would always have an excuse. They are colourful and painterly but they are also very intellectual. Be careful [*laughs*]!

You laugh now, but in America at that time, these battles were fought very seriously. There was no laughter at all. Under the name of politics there was a puritanical belief that pleasure was bad, that the aesthetic was suspect, and that only by making anti-aesthetic, unpleasurable things could there be a justification for making paintings at all.

I remember an opening party at Marian Goodman's in the 1990s when Lawrence Weiner gave a speech that said: 'Painting is not possible any more, but Gerhard shows us that it is possible... We all knew it was over, that one could not paint abstract paintings any more. But here it is!' He got a lot of applause.

But that, in a sense, is the easy answer. The harder problem is that this rhetoric was used to say that the only way for painting to be serious was for the painter to think of it as a time-bomb that the painter had planted – you had planted – to explode the reasons for painting, one by one, until at the end of this process painting would be finished. So people said: 'It's great that he's doing this, and for now it's okay to like painting like that; but when he's done, there will be no more painting.'

Nice [*laughs*]. I didn't know that.

There is a precedent in American painting – Ad Reinhardt said: 'You must understand that I am making the last paintings possible.' As a logical gambit that's very elegant. But there is a difference between taking such a position for the challenge that it provides and actually believing it to be true.

People often declare the end of painting.

Yes, but is there a difference between how an artist says something like this – uses it as a point of departure – and how a critic arrives at and argues such a conclusion?

I don't know because I always have thought, 'This is my end.' During every crisis I have thought, 'This is it for me, but everything else will go on.' I never generalized this to be the end of painting, even though I realized that painting didn't do so well at certain points. But I conceived those times as breaks.

Back in the 1980s, Douglas Crimp wrote a famous article called 'The End of Painting' in which (in addition to misrepresenting your statement 'painting is pure idiocy') he proposed that what a painter – such as you or Daniel Buren – does under the circumstances is simply to go through the motions and critically 'enact' painting in order to prove its futility.

That is presumptuous and arrogant – or useless – because then you have to take a look at all of life. When somebody goes shopping, that's an idiotic act. Even feeding the kids is an idiotic act. From that perspective, everything is meaningless. You have to believe in the idea that it does make sense. It doesn't matter whether it is painting or working in your backyard, most of these things are so meaningless you can't even watch them.

Well, that was one interpretation, but there was also the strong view that you were a very important painter because what you were up to was undoing painting in the most masterful way. Is that true?

Yes.

Another thing I have heard sometimes in conversation is: 'Richter is no good because he always avoids taking a position. He says Yes and No, and No and Yes, in a way that suggests he is an aesthetic cynic.'

I believe that it would be a misunderstanding to call what I do cynical. I'd rather call it sentimental. I wouldn't call it professional because being cynical is not professional. Rather, what I do is naïve.

Also, my work has been accused of being cold and distant. In retrospect I think, 'How could they say that about me, about somebody who exposes himself much more than others? More than Ellsworth Kelly.' Nobody ever accuses them of being distant. I open myself up, shamelessly sometimes, and then I am told that I am cynical and that nothing means anything to me. That's why, for me, the word 'cynical' is absolutely out of place.

Why do you think people have such reactions?

One reason is that people sometimes talk about my work in terms of virtuosity.

That is an absolute exaggeration. Unfortunately I am not a virtuoso at all. I have some taste. I have an eye for bad things. But in terms of making things I am not a virtuoso, and that has always been my flaw. Today, there is almost nobody (or only a few bad examples) who has the virtuosity to draw something. I depend on the photograph and mindlessly copy what I see. I am clumsy in that regard, even though I seem very skilful. But I do have the ability to judge whether something is good or bad.

The second reason could be that I made a few remarks that have circulated, things like: 'I don't believe in anything'; 'I don't care about anything'; and 'the motifs in my paintings have no meaning whatsoever; I might have just as well painted cabbage'. These remarks gave people a certain impression of me. That's how they saw me. People still claim that only painting has an important story, never the subject.

Why did you say those things? What was the context?

I made those statements in order to provoke and in order not to have to say what I might have been thinking at that point, not to pour my heart out. That would have been embarrassing. I didn't know why I painted *Uncle Rudi* or *Aunt Marianne*. I refused to admit any kind of meaning that these paintings could have had for me. Therefore, it was much easier to say what I said.

There are personal stories attached to these images, then, but there are historical issues too. If you look at the date of these paintings – 1965 – you see that it was very early for a German artist to be making pictures about World War II that were not simply rhetorical. There were political artists making anti-fascist paintings, but to make a personal image of something connected to the war was almost unheard of. And there you were making pictures that bring that past into the open and very close to home. Did you feel as if you were in a no-man's-land when you made those paintings?

Maybe that is the main reason why the audience, as well as myself, had to fall back on a strategy of laughter. That's how it worked: people thought it was mischievous and prankish and not too serious and, therefore, it was so much easier to deal with it.

It is striking, though, that almost nobody has written about your pictures of 1962 to 1965, for example, when you made eight paintings of military aircraft – Allied bombers, fighters from the 1940s and new German jets – with regard to the specific situation in post-war Germany. These paintings were an incredibly strong statement at that time. Yet, because you worked in a manner that looked neutral, it seems as if people just ignored what was in front of their eyes. But, in fact, the images were much more pointed – and in some cases more poignant – than what anybody thought then, or even now.

We artists influenced by Pop Art refused to take anything seriously. That was important for survival. We were unable to see the statement in the work, neither the audience nor me. We rejected it; it didn't exist. Part of the reason was that there existed a different kind of painting, and Georg Baselitz was the right man for that German tradition. People thought my painting was somehow modern, but they couldn't admit that it had any kind of quality. Instead, it was somehow funny but copied from the Americans. So people thought that we were traitors. Baselitz said to me: 'You have betrayed your fatherland.'

What did he mean by that?

That I was giving in to the international style, but he remained a German. That's how it was. That was also Sigmar Polke's fate because he was painting raster dots like Roy Lichtenstein. People said that it was lousy plagiarism.

But let's shift from style to subject matter. If Lichtenstein made pictures from World War II comic books with G.I. Joe fighter planes going 'Bang', that's one thing. It is very different if you are a German artist and make a picture of American planes over Germany. And it is very different to make a painting of a German soldier, such as Uncle Rudi, *which is neither a Hero picture like Baselitz's nor a cartoon of a soldier like Lichtenstein's, but, rather, the image of a real soldier who is also your uncle.*

But this painting *Bomber* – American bomb – was forbidden. You were not allowed to take it seriously. You could only take it as a joke.

You didn't paint it as a joke.

No, but I was satisfied that it was taken as such. I would have been embarrassed if it were too serious. It was not an accusation: I wasn't accusing the Americans. I never wanted to accuse anything, except life maybe and how shitty it is. But never ... after all, they were right. Everything was fine [*laughs*]. I would have been attacked as a prosecutor.

You've explained your position to avoid declarations, to avoid rhetoric, but even without commentary, painting American B-52s and Mustangs or a post-war German fighter squadron against a social background where memories of the Allied bombings were vivid and debate over German remilitarization was in progress must have stirred many emotions and raised a lot of questions.

But there is only one painting of a German plane – the *Schärzler*.

Yes, but here we have a picture of American bombers, and a picture of fighter planes, one of the Luftwaffe Stukas, and then the Schärzler. *Altogether, there are eight pictures of military aircraft.*

I am a specialist in airplanes [*laughs*].

What I am trying to say is that I understand and accept the idea that you did not make them for polemical reasons, but the choice of subject cannot have been arbitrary. The planes are specific – none, for example, is a commercial passenger plane – and the paintings have their moment in the 1960s when Germany was beginning to look at the recent past, but also when Germany was at the centre of the Cold War and starting to re-arm.

What am I supposed to say to that?

Well, you must have been aware that while you were making neither political art nor mythological art about the ravages of war, like Baselitz, you were touching a nerve. After all, you have said: 'The Mona Lisa *is not a turnip.' There are hierarchies of subject matter: a cow, which you have also painted, is not a 1940s fighter plane or a 1960s fighter plane.*

I never knew what I was doing. What am I supposed to say now? Now I could lie here, like I am on an analyst's couch, and try to figure out my actual motives with the help of others and make sense of them. Is that what we want to do now?

I don't want to put you on the couch, but there must have been some level on which these images had meaning attached to the actual situation around you or to the past that you and others had experienced. What might have been historical denial in 1960 or 1965 is connected in an odd way with the postmodernist notion that images are just signs, arbitrary fragments of language, in a no-longer functioning system of signs. In that manner, one kind of denial, which was historically motivated, connects with another kind of denial, which is ideologically or aesthetically driven; and yet there you were making pictures that were very, very strong about things that were very, very real. When people in 1988 were surprised that you painted the October *paintings and said, 'Wait, this is different, this is a Richter unlike the one we know because he has never painted paintings with so much emotion and so much historical specificity before,' I think, 'Now wait a minute, that's not true.'*

Yes, you are right. The *October* paintings came after a period when I had done very different things and people like art dealer René Block accused me of giving in to the fine arts and losing my political edge. He said that I had been political during the 1960s and then turned to the fine arts, *beaux-arts*. After he said that I was really 'established' and colourful and aesthetic, so the Baader-Meinhof paintings came as a surprise.

Actually, my position is not at all to be a psychoanalyst but, rather, to be a close reader of pictorial texts. And there is a sense now that texts are completely open, that anything can be read in any way the reader chooses. I'm supposing that perhaps this is not the right way to go about things – or at any rate not the most productive or interesting way to read images – and that there may be intentions expressed in bodies of work of which the artist is only partially conscious or aware, which nevertheless emerge very powerfully through reiteration, and that such latent intentions have to be closely examined and seriously considered. So my question is more about now than the past, how you think about them now, how you relate these images to each other. Does such a relation stand out?

All right, I understand. That makes the questions very interesting. Sometimes I am surprised that I have never asked myself something, and sometimes one can discover something.

For example, take the painting Mr Heyde. *The man in the wide-brimmed hat whose face is turned away from the viewer was, in actuality, Dr Werner Heyde,*[1] *who was responsible for killing mentally retarded, mentally ill and chronically sick hospital patients as part of a euthanasia programme that pioneered the techniques of the 'Final Solution'. In 1959, the date included in the picture, he was exposed after having lived and worked for years in Germany under an assumed name. When you painted this picture, six years after his arrest, virtually no one had dealt in this direct way with the issue of hidden war criminals. Weren't you aware of the significance of his arrest, and wasn't it also significant that your aunt Marianne, who was a schizophrenic, was a victim of the system of medical murder he set up?*

Out of my mind, of my consciousness. I was surprised myself when many years later – I believe it was on the occasion of the exhibition *Deutschlandbilder*[2] – somebody told me that he was a war criminal.

So you didn't know who Heyde was?

I am sure I knew it. But I repressed it right away, and it became a picture like every other. I tried to show that this was a guy like every other guy that gets arrested. You can see those two policemen. I did not want to be part of the faction that accuses. I do not belong to those who present themselves as anti-fascists, because I am not. I am also not a fascist. I was disinclined to be conscious of too many things; I just wanted to let myself go. And it is still the same today.

At the time I do something, I really don't know what I am doing. Afterwards I think, 'Oh, that's why you did that, now I understand.' It's the same with the paintings. But I was much more introverted back then, and I would have refused any connection between Heyde and myself. I would have said, 'Well, it's a nice picture; it doesn't mean anything.'

So was there no conscious connection between Heyde's programme during the Third Reich and your aunt's death?

Absolutely never, not even once. It did not exist. There are no conscious connections within me at all [*laughs*]. But I am certain that I knew of it because I read it somewhere.

This raises the issue of what can be painted and what can't be painted. In Atlas, *there are images of the concentration camp*[3] *– of prisoners and bodies – and at one point you thought about making an exhibition with the pictures of the camp next to the porno pictures. Finally, you decided that it was not possible to juxtapose such things, nor even to make paintings from the documentary photos of the Holocaust. Why wasn't it possible?*

I'd say that it would have been impossible for *me*. I saw no possible moral or formal solution for how to exhibit the camp and the porno pictures as Konrad Lueg and I had planned. We had this plan in a Düsseldorf gallery, and we each collected photos; then we gave it up. It didn't work. We didn't find a way. We would have gotten a lot of attention, but it would have been unproductive and inadequate – at least inadequate.

What is the difference between an image that you can look at, incorporate into your visual memory, and one that you can paint? The camp pictures appear in Atlas, *and one sees them as part of a much wider array of pictures, yet they are not paintable. What determines that something is unpaintable?*

I believe that there is no picture that can't be painted. But there are personal limits and limits of the time, situations where the reception would go so predictably wrong that it doesn't work. It is also the personal inadequacy to not be able to give something the right form. Three years ago, I tried to use the camp pictures again, and again it didn't work. But that was my fault.

In other words, there is no such thing as an image that is absolutely taboo: there are only images that an individual cannot paint at a particular time?

Yes. I still have some photographs in the studio that I am thinking about. Who knows? There are only unfinished themes. There are some that have simply become uninteresting. A painting that is unpaintable is a painting I know would go wrong – something I can't do – one that would cause people to say: 'He meant well, but maybe he's getting old' [*laughs*]. That is the only criterion. Other than that nothing is unpaintable.

What qualities make an image that already exists in a photograph fascinating or substantial for you once it becomes a painting?

That is impossible to answer. I don't know why I like things. [*Looking at a book of images*] I like this or this. This has too much to do with Courbet, but nevertheless I like it.

I am not so much asking why a photograph makes you want to paint it, but what happens in the process of painting an image that makes the result interesting or acceptable, so that you don't destroy it or paint over it?

That is also an impossible question [*laughs*].

That won't stop me from asking.

Why doesn't it work like that? Why can't I let this go? Why can't I do this better? Why don't I know that? Like this one. [*Pointing to a canvas on the studio wall*] I don't like this one. But I don't know why. One can't answer that; at least I can't.

Speaking from the outside, I would think maybe it's the point at which there is a specific quality or experience that was not in the photograph that suddenly appears in the picture.

Yes, sounds pretty good.

And is there any way of describing or saying how this happens or even what happens?

No. But it also works the other way round. Sometimes I make a print from a painting, a multiple, using photography, and that takes a lot of time. First I have a reproduction and it looks horrible. Then I begin to change it, make it out of focus or something, or put it under plexiglass, so that it somehow becomes an independent object.

I don't think anybody anticipated this doubling back to photography[4] as a medium. In the past there had been a one-way street from the photograph to the painting, where you added and subtracted qualities from the source image. When you photograph a painting such as Uncle Rudi *or* Cathedral Corner, *what kind of transformations are you looking for?*

In the photograph, I take even more focus out of the painted image, which is already a bit out of focus, and make the picture even smoother. I also subtract the materiality, the surface of the painting, and it becomes something different.

The effect of removing the materiality from the image is very interesting, but how is that important or significant?

I wouldn't know how to say that – to say how the new quality of the photographic work is different from a reproduction.

That wasn't what I was asking, but it is an interesting question because I think some people see these works as 'just' a multiple.

The painting is better [*laughs*].

Yes, but what matters is that the visual experience is different. From your point of view what are the significant differences? From my perspective, each stage of this process seems to have a different relation to light, to the form that light assumes. In a sense, a photograph is the direct record of light, whereas a painting represents light. The second-generation photograph that comes after the painting and is the third generation of an image holds or emits light in a very different way both from the painting and the original photograph. The visual phenomenon it captures is, in a way, further refined, not better or worse but perceptually different.

I am sure that's right. But I have a problem with the term 'light'. I never in my life knew what to do with that. I know that people have mentioned on some occasions that 'Richter is all about light', and that 'the paintings have a special light', and I never knew what they were talking about. I was never interested in light. Light is there and you turn it on or you turn it off, with sun or without sun. I don't know what the 'problematic of light' is. I take it as a metaphor for a different quality, which is similarly difficult to describe. Good.

This astonishes me because it not only seems so central to what you do but to what was done by the painters that you like – Velázquez, Manet and Vermeer.

That I don't understand either. Velázquez and light. Of course, we have light, here. Without light we couldn't see each other. There is something lacking in me.

I don't mean light as a kind of metaphysical thing; I mean light as a phenomenon.

Yes, we have beautiful light, cold light, warm light, southern light; people in Italy have a different light. I do see all that. I once got into trouble with Norbert Kricke when he told me that I had to understand his sculptures in spatial terms, that they dealt with space. And I replied that there's space even in the smallest house. And he was very mad at me for being so dismissive about space, the elementary medium of sculpture. That always comes to mind when I hear the word 'light' in conjunction with painting. 'Appearance', that to me is a phenomenon.

Let me give you an example.

Now I am curious.

Okay, these are the first and the last versions of Toilet Paper. *The first one has a strong shadow, which makes the image very volumetric, and that is reinforced by the direct way it is painted. In the third version the shadows and the overall touch are softened, and the form has a kind of glow to it. In the first version, the treatment is very objective, but in the third it is atmospheric.*

Right.

These paintings have the same subject, same tonality, same technique, but the difference is the difference of light. Much later the candles and the skulls are painted in more or less the same manner as the third version of Toilet Paper. *Now, that shift in emphasis must mean something. I am not saying that it means the same thing for you as it means for me, but these two examples represent different realities or different attitudes toward reality.*

Yes, I like that because you look at the light from a practical, pragmatic perspective. Yes, I can see that. That's true. I agree. Then the light in the photograph is different. Sometimes the light is harder as, for example, in *Small Bather*. In that case, the painting is much softer and more atmospheric, while the photograph has more contrast, has a harder light, is crisper. That was the only solution. I couldn't do it softer, maybe. If I made it any softer, it would have disappeared. And I needed to spice it up. It was also good for the viewers. If it is too soft you have to be so sensitive in order to appreciate it. That would not have been possible in a photograph.

It means that you are thinking about the viewer.

The audience, yes.

When you say only the most lyrically inclined people can handle this, it is as if you are saying, 'I can see trouble coming if I make things too lyrical,' as if there were a group of people who could take this lyricism, while the rest all want something more cut-and-dried.

This edition is for a hundred people who want to have something solid. Painting is looking for just that one person. But one hundred people get that which is a bit more ephemeral and a little crisper.

It is as if you are projecting onto your audience a preference for something tough. Is this true?

Yes.

You happen to be the owner of this painting, and you like something soft.

In this case.

There is an interesting discrepancy between your acceptance, if you will, of the gentler image, and your view that in the public discourse the images have to be tougher.

Yes, stable; and I have to maintain that. The multiple has not turned into a hard picture; it has merely become a little more lively.

That's the practical answer. The buyers of this work are somewhat different.

It became a completely different object with a frame, with a sheet of plastic over the image which hangs so freely; you see the fragility. It was a substitute for the fragility of the painting. It showed all these interesting qualities that the painting does not have. I had to explain all of these relations to Dieter Schwarz who once wanted to produce them just as they were. But I said that he needed to include the frame and the distance produced by the glass and so on. That's all part of it. It has become an object, not just a picture. That's why we can't reduce it to the perkiness; it became a whole other thing.

In the beginning, you talked a lot about how important it is that the pictures you worked from are givens, readymades, pictures from an album or from a magazine. What you do is to alter that given by painting it.

Why am I changing the qualities of the photograph? Because it is too small [*laughs*]. I am a painter; I love to paint. Using photographs was the only possible way to continue to paint. I couldn't just have used a model. That was impossible and an untimely endeavour that would have cut everything short. I can't do that. Not even Lucian Freud could do that. I had to use photographs. They provided new contents that were relevant to me and to others. That was my conviction.

What contents were those?

What touches us.

But the range of subjects goes from things that are totally banal, like Toilet Paper, *to images that are not so banal, like* Mr Heyde.

To make a photo from a painting that you can put up on the wall again is comparable to making a painting from a photo. But these are the old questions where one only has excuses. Take music as an example, how some simply hear when it's right. In painting, think of the Bob Ryman exhibition in Bonn,[5] where you suddenly find a painting that has something, that looks 'right' and nobody knows why.

No, but could you describe certain qualities that give you this feeling of rightness?

I don't know how to describe that. Whether or not it has been fulfilled or how wrong it went is a different question, but the demand was, and remains, to address the things that are most important, that concern us all. And so in relation to the history of art, where nobody had ever painted toilet paper, it was time to paint toilet paper, which is not really banal.

Why?

It's important; it cannot be banal. Then there's the 'banality of evil'. It's a beautiful term – what Hannah Arendt said about Adolf Eichmann. And the same for Mr *Heyde*. This is important.

Now I am confused. In a sense, Mr Heyde *and the toilet paper are both banal and, in another sense, evil is also banal.*

And both are important. I just want to get away from the label: 'He paints the banalities of life and that's all', or 'he is one of those people who are not interested in anything'. For a while that was just fine with me. At least I was being left alone.

But now you want to get rid of that characterization?

Yes. I want to at least correct it. 'Banality' means a little bit more than unimportant.

What does it mean?

Just more. I mentioned 'the banality of evil' in order to show that banality has at some point been described as something horrific. It can be a concern to describe the banal as something terrifying. The chandelier [*Flemish Crown*] is a monster. I don't need to paint a monster; it is enough to paint this thing, this shitty, small, banal chandelier. That thing is terrifying. I've already said some time ago that in order to dissociate myself from Francis Bacon, I didn't have to distort faces. It is much scarier to paint people's faces as banal as I find them in photographs. That is what makes the banal more than just banal.

How do you mean something monstrous?

It is more terrifying to me.

I'm interested by what you said in a couple of ways. First of all, in American Pop Art, the emphasis was on ordinary commercial goods, things you buy in a store, images in magazines, and so on. More recently, Jeff Koons made a whole show dedicated to banality. But it was banality in a grotesque way, an exaggerated banality. And you are also talking about the grotesque or the monstrous, in a form that is very detached, subdued, not exaggerated. It is not a rhetorical statement that you make the image in a certain way that is very ...

Well, modest. Very small and quiet. Yes, I'd say that it is small, modest, quiet. I hope that it functions like that. That something is heard, although it approaches quietly. That was my hope. That was the trick.

Are the paintings supposed to have a certain uncanny quality?

No, but you are reminded of something. In the ideal case, somebody looks at the work and asks what this is supposed to be and why anybody would paint such a banal object. And then the person comes to think that maybe there is something more to it, that maybe the object is not that banal after all, that maybe it is horrible. It stands for something ... maybe for a terrible living room.

But not as a symbol?

No, not as a symbol. But the longer you see it, the more it becomes frightening.

For example, the Flemish Crown *is a piece of a larger reality that is frightening, not a symbol of something but part of the thing itself.*

It is an image of this horror; a detail of it.

Of ugliness?

Of the misery of this world [*laughs*]. Perhaps this special culture.

Which special culture?

A petit bourgeois culture. But I refuse to discuss it in those terms because now it turns into social criticism where I attack a certain class, the petit bourgeois, those who had this thing in the middle of their living room, the Flemish Crown. That was part of our culture, and I don't want to attack that even though I myself might have suffered under it. And although it was terrible, it was never meant to be an accusation. Now those people are all gone. There was nothing but crime and misery in those living rooms. There is only crime and misery in general [*laughs*].

So you didn't want to make a critique?

No, it's a report. Remember people; don't forget, please [*laughs*].

In general, American Pop Art concentrated on public imagery and commercial culture. But previously you told me that as German Pop artists Polke, Lueg and you wanted to represent a broader experience, a wider view of reality. I wondered if you could say something more about this larger vision in relation to the focus of American Pop Art.

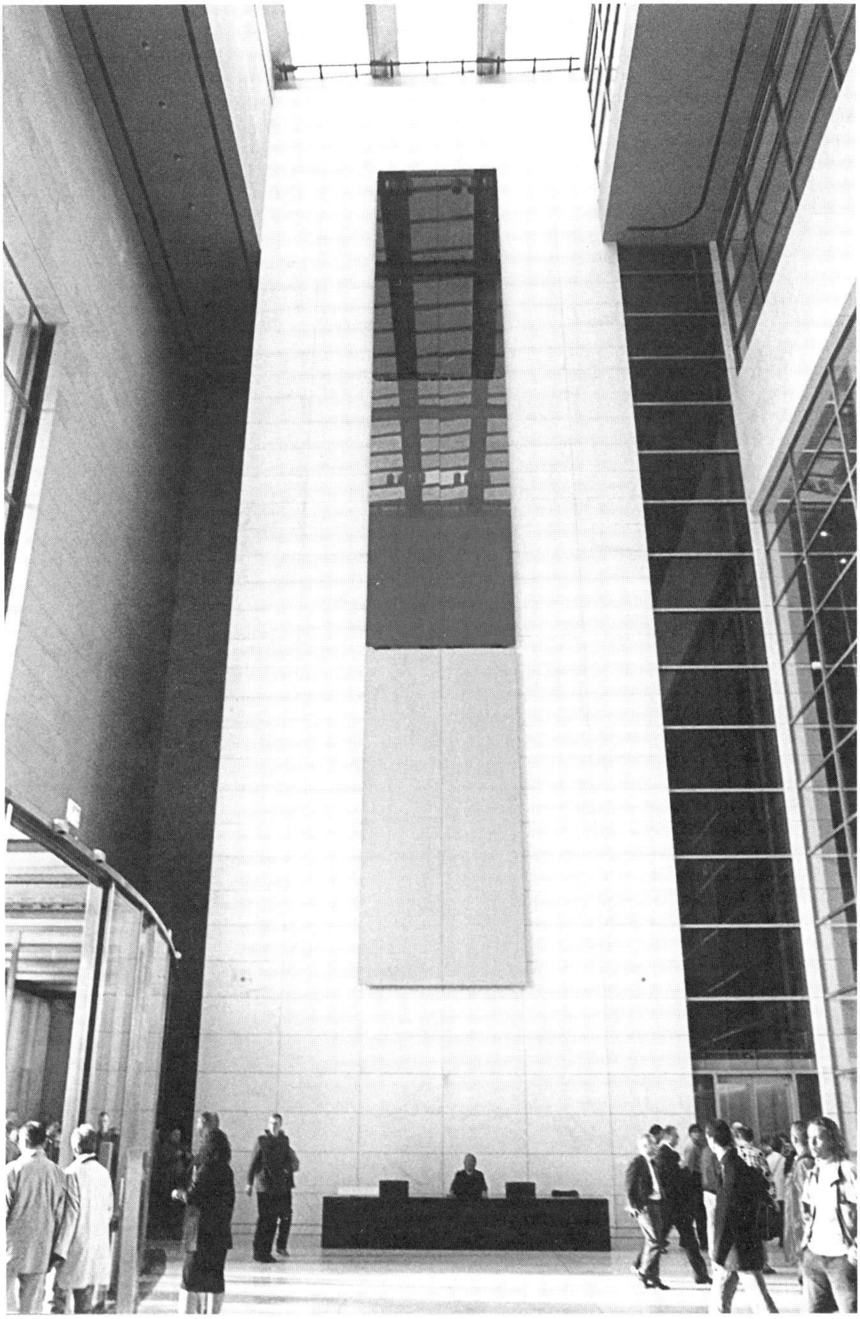

Black, Red, Gold in the Reichstag, Berlin, 1999

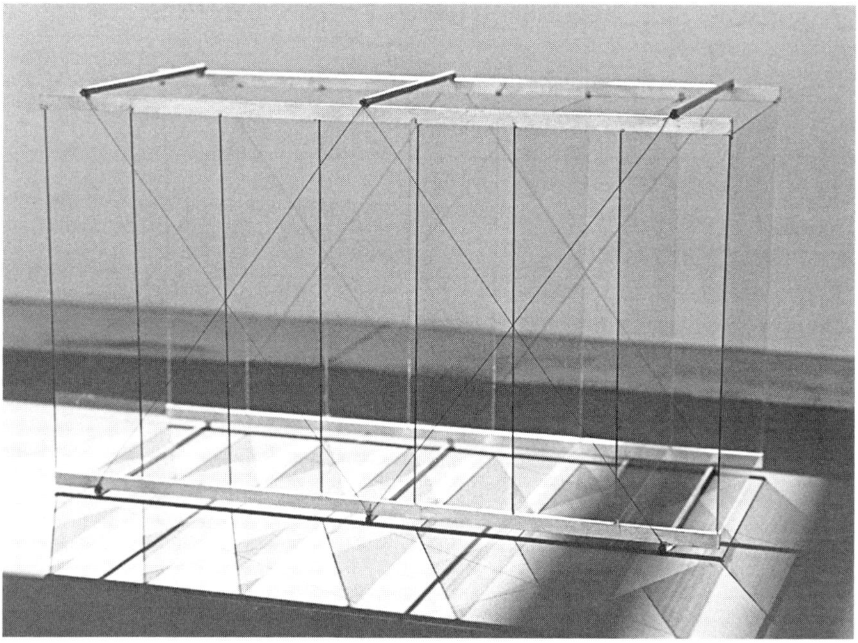

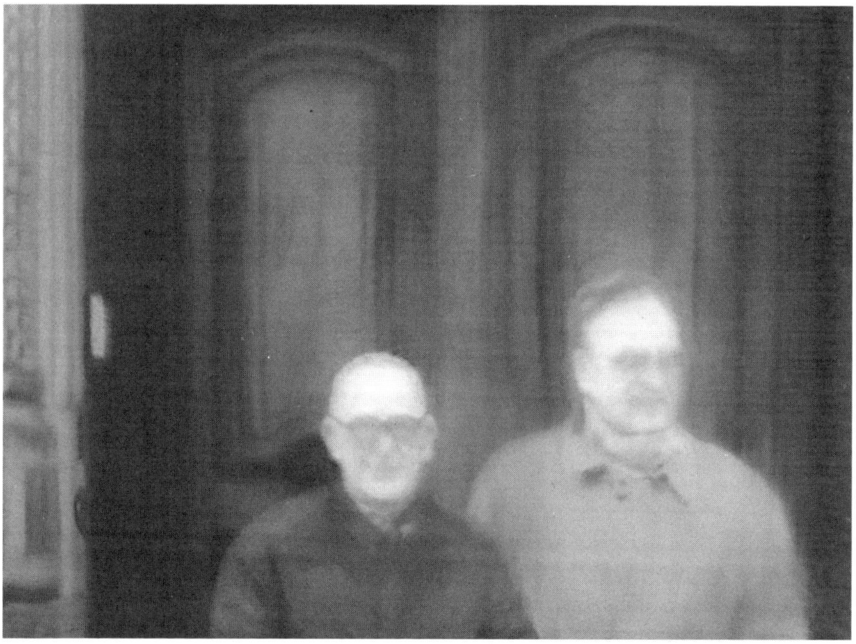

Maquette for *Standing Panes*, 2002
Court Chapel, Dresden, 2000

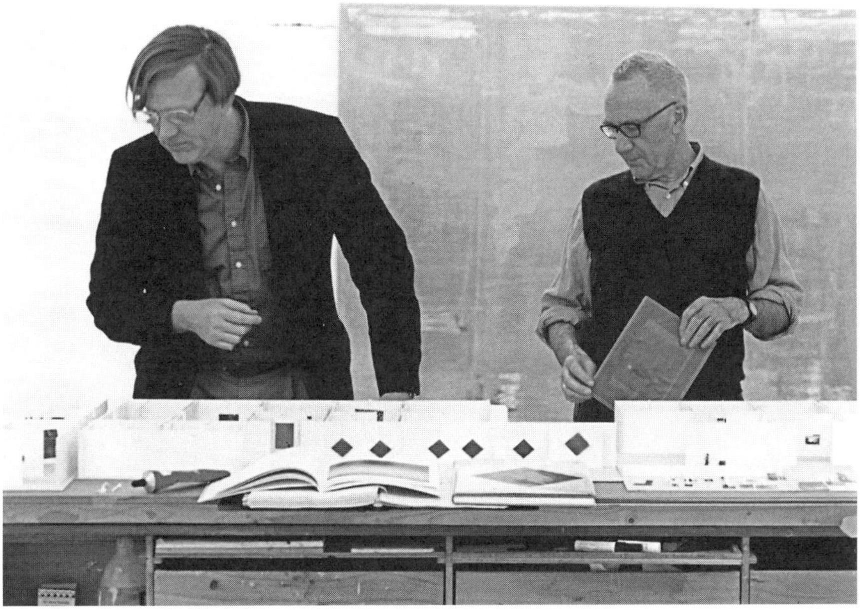

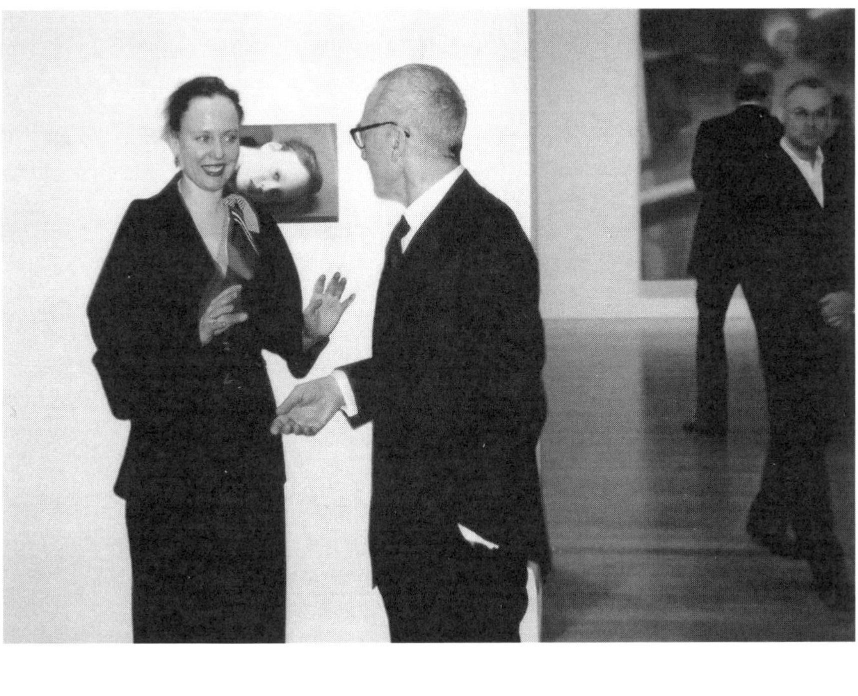

Gerhard Richter in his studio with Robert Storr, 2001
Gerhard Richter with his daughter Betty, Museum of Modern Art, New York, 2002

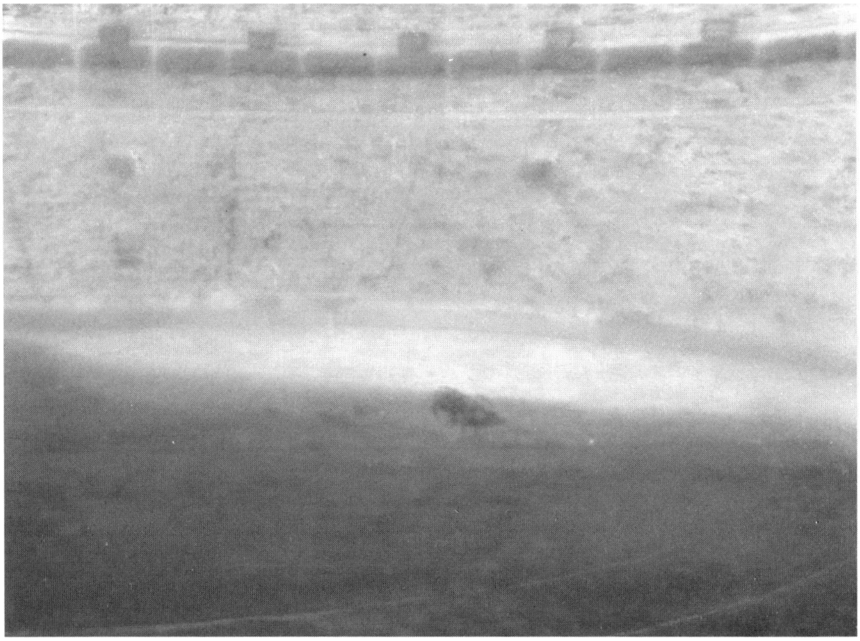

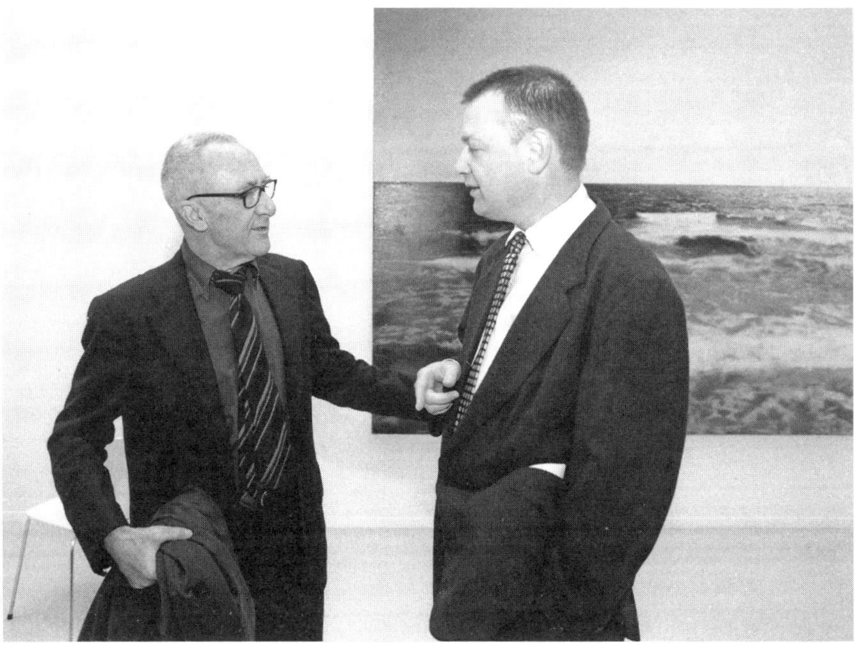

Arena, 1995
Gerhard Richter with Dietmar Elger, 1998

Maybe we didn't even have a chance. The message of American Pop Art was so powerful and so optimistic. But it was also very limited, and that led us to believe that we could somehow distance ourselves from it and communicate a different intention.

So, where does that difference lie?

It was not possible for us to produce the same optimism and the same kind of humour or irony. Actually, it was not irony. Lichtenstein is not ironic but he does have a special kind of humour. That's how I could describe it: humour and optimism. For Polke and me, everything was more fragmented. But how it was broken up is hard to describe.

Are you talking about a historical experience or a personal experience of fragmentation?

They come together, right? I don't know why. Otherwise, we would have had to play a role. Some people did that; they really participated. They imitated the Americans: optimistic, big, colourful, strong.

Lueg is more like the American Pop and you are much more…

Broken? Yes, maybe.

One American Pop artist who is definitely broken is Andy Warhol.

Yes, that's true.

Do you feel a particular affinity to Warhol?

I always liked him the most. But there is a huge difference between us, and that was the freedom that he had. People here in Germany are all very uptight. But he was not. His life story, his homosexuality – that was not possible here. Polke took some liberties, but those were very different from the freedom that Warhol had. You have to have a basis for being received like he was. That did not exist for us.

One aspect of Warhol that is very strong is his morbidity. Do you identify with that quality?

Those are paintings by Warhol I like the most, the Disaster paintings. And also some of the films. But everything else, like his huge production of commissioned portraits, was not my cup of tea.

I am less interested in Warhol than I am in you, but I think there are some telling parallels to be pointed out, and some telling contrasts. For example, when Warhol selected and transposed an image, he took things away from it; he removed information. Now you have said yourself that you have many tools at your disposal, but elimination is perhaps the most important one. Could you talk about what it means to eliminate or reduce elements of an image?

I believe that the quintessential task of every painter in any time has been to concentrate on the essential. The hyperrealists didn't do that; they painted everything, every detail. That's why they were such a surprise. But for me it was obvious that I had to wipe out the details. I was happy to have a method that was rather mechanical. In that regard I owe something to Warhol. He legitimized the mechanical. He showed me how it is done. It is a normal state of working, to eliminate things. But Warhol showed me this modern way of letting details disappear, or at least he validated its possibilities. He did it with silkscreening and photography, and I did it through mechanical wiping. It was a very liberating act.

Is the process of elimination an arbitrary one, where the results are a surprise, or did you anticipate what would be removed before actually doing it?

Well, it's in-between. You can imagine what has to be wiped out, smeared away. And then there were also accidents. In any case, it was a wonderful Utopian way to do this mechanically and not to consciously decide what has to go and what can stay. It fit the climate of the time to make everything easy and simple and happy – the Utopian climate of the 1960s. It was part of the zeitgeist to say: 'I want to be like a machine.' I don't even remember who said that. Polke said something like that, and Warhol did too. Today that's unthinkable. Now all of these paintings seem handmade, painterly, imperfect. It was different then. People only saw the similarity to the photograph, the technical perfection, which by now is outdated. Because of their age, the paintings have become so painterly and now look like old handmade paintings. Back then, they were provocative, as if produced by a machine: 'Richter paints with such perfection that the surface is like that of a photograph.'

So there's a difference in reception?

Yes.

But are you talking mostly about the critical response?

No, overall. I remember those paintings as being much more perfect. The ability to do that so perfectly was my trademark. But when you look at them today, they are far from perfect. It is rather the earlier ones that are more perfect, and maybe the later landscapes. Do you agree with this?

No.

Maybe in the 1960s one didn't see this mechanical quality; one wasn't able to see this. In terms of reception, they were said to be 'as perfect as the Americans'. And then after a while it became obvious that compared to the Americans they were not perfect but had a very European handmade quality to them.

That's true. But I also think that either there is an evolution in the work or a paradox that was always there, which is the fact that, on the one hand, technically they belong to the tradition of fine studio painting and, on the other hand, that something apparently arbitrary or mechanical has been done to pictures made in that tradition. After all, you are a master of the disruptive technique as well. The thing that makes it blur is not a machine but a bigger brush or squeegee. It was never so mechanical; it was never so arbitrary. Correct?

Yes.

And then again, you said earlier that what separated you from other artists was not simply that you have this technical command but that you have the ability to recognize when a work has achieved a certain rightness.

Yes.

So the defining quality of what you do is both a matter of the mastery of materials and a question of recognition and decision. It was never about violence done to the picture in the same way that some people have seen this kind of disruptive physicality as aggression, pure and simple.

Yes, that's true.

In some ways, what you're up to is closer to what Alberto Giacometti did than to the kind of painting that is usually described as wild or violent. It is about working away at the image and at the paint until you can see something.

Yes.

So, in that respect, your approach is similar to Giacometti's but involves a different formal language with a different set of conventions, and is being pursued at a different time.

Yes, that sounds good.

The other day, you said that when you were in East Germany you and your friends wanted to find a 'third way' between the Russian and the American models. Together, you identified your efforts with certain artists, and Giacometti was one you mentioned. Now Giacometti comes out of Paul Cézanne and a tradition you have avoided, yet, at the same time, you seem to have strived for a certain quality that was in those paintings. Is it fair to say, then, that you invented a different way of painting in order to arrive at the same place?

And this commitment to quality still clings to me like a clubfoot and makes me unfree, unproductive and impotent.

If you are impotent, the rest of us are really in trouble [laughs]. *But I didn't mean quality with a capital Q, as in a hierarchy of values but, rather, a certain feeling, a certain type of visual and emotional experience. Let's go back to basics: you paint ordinary life in a revealing but undramatic light, you use painterly languages that belie style. In a way, Giacometti attempted to do something quite similar – to capture the appearance of things that kept retreating or disappearing and then partially clicked and snapped into focus. The other day when I watched you working, the same kind of thing seemed to be happening. You have a process in which you rough in, or state, the image, then blur, or unstate, it. And after this has gone on for a while, an image becomes visible that is fundamentally different from what you started with. I don't want to force the comparison with Giacometti, but the existential aspect of his work wasn't a matter of expressive style so much as it was this pursuit of an elusive reality, a pursuit carried on without melodrama.*

Yes. I would be very embarrassed if I were staging some sentimental drama here.

It is existential and it is humanist but it is not sentimental and it is not melodramatic.

Yes. Only a bit [*laughs*].

You admit it [laughs]! That is interesting because it is as if, by way of Pop Art and mechanical reproduction that was very much of that moment, you were able to come all the way back around and answer some of the questions that confronted artists of your generation in the 1950s, except that the answers you provided don't look like anything that would have issued from the tradition in which those questions were posed.

Good.

There are three basic critical explanations for deliberate elimination or erasure in modern painting. The first one is destruction. Do you see what you do as a destructive act?

Yes, very often I have the feeling that what I do is very destructive, born out of the need and inability to construct. It is my wish to create a well-built, beautiful, constructive painting. And there are many moments when I plan to do just that, and then I realize that it looks terrible. Then I start to destroy it, piece by piece, and I arrive at something that I didn't want but that looks pretty good. Therefore I understand if somebody calls it destructive. I find that congenial but maybe it is just ... I don't know.

That makes me think, for example, of Lucio Fontana. It was said of him that in cutting and puncturing the canvas, he was attacking it, but the result is very beautiful. Does this paradox in Fontana's work relate in any way to what you do?

Maybe. I find him to be much more productive. Because even though at the beginning he and Polke and others destroyed their work out of rage and anger, later on they were able to direct those actions. I was never able to do that. I can't plan to make something look out of focus in a certain way. That doesn't work. For example, this painting [*Snow*] was created out of a different initial impulse; and this grey painting was intended to be very different from what it eventually turned into. That's why it is impossible for me to recreate them. But that's another topic. However, I already have to revise that statement I just made: there are many abstract paintings that I did plan and execute. They are mostly small and part of some sort of multiple work. For instance, I once made one hundred small paintings for Munich.[6] They simply flowed one after the other and all of them perfect. Fontana would have been amazed.

For 18 October 1977 you did several versions of some images.

Yes, those were planned like that and made according to the plan.

A second explanation for erasure or elimination is that the image is not about the act of the destruction that left it in its ultimate state, but about loss. What you see in such paintings is an absence.

I believe that Dieter Schwarz once mentioned something like that. I feel very close to this idea of seeing the pain and the loss in the work. I can't paint as well as Vermeer – we have lost this beautiful culture, all the Utopias are shattered, everything goes down the drain, the wonderful time of painting is over. It is an inclination of mine to see it that way. I don't know anybody else who is so attached to the history of art and loves the Old Masters as much or wants as much to paint like them. There are examples where I have tried to reincarnate Titian and others, but of course it didn't work out. I wanted to paint the Annunciation for myself. That is an example of how it is impossible to paint like that today. I understand why people see it that way.

So, the subject of these works is a reality that has not yet entirely disappeared but which is retreating?

It is a reality that is unreachable. It is a dream. It's over. But I am old-fashioned enough or stupid enough to hang on. I still want to paint something like Vermeer. But it is the wrong time and I cannot do it. I am too dumb. Well, I am not able to.

But I think more about visual phenomena that can be captured than the historical precedents for capturing it. What happens when the subject is not Titian but a toilet paper roll? Does that mean that reality itself, everyday reality, is something we've lost the ability to hold onto in a picture?

No, that's never the problem. I never wanted to capture and hold reality in a painting. Maybe at a weak moment I did, but I don't remember. However, that was never my intention. But I wanted to paint the appearance of reality. That is my theme or my job.

The third explanation for erasing or paring down an image is that what you are left with in the end is something irreducible and basic. Rather than performing a symbolic act of destruction or painting loss, you arrive at a distillation of the image's essential qualities.

I hope that's the case. You can say that; I can't.

But if that's the purpose of working in this way then what you finally have is neither the depicted object in itself nor a clear mirror image of the subject struggling to perceive that object, but a strange in-between entity representing the exchange of appearance between the object painted and the subject looking at it; the thing and the viewer.

That is something for intellectuals [*laughs*].

I am actually trying to describe an experience and not just a logical abstraction. The book in front of me has its own reality, and I have mine. They are separate. But when I pick it up and look at it and I try to grasp an image on the page with my eyes, those realities overlap and are confounded. Visually, I step part-way out of myself and part-way into this other world, but I can also lose my bearings and be stranded between self-awareness and awareness of the things represented in the picture.

Yes.

And that's where painting happens – at any rate, one kind of painting. If I want to make paintings about what is going on inside me then I become a surrealist or an expressionist. But I am talking about a kind of painting that is neither totally reflexive nor totally objective.

That's probably right, but you overestimate me.

You have talked about how working with photographs freed you from certain expectations. You didn't have to have style; you didn't have to have a theme in the traditional sense of the term; you could paint all kinds of disparate things. But in these early statements, you also made an issue of photography's apparent neutrality. Could you say a little bit about why seeming to be detached in this manner was so crucial for you then?

Yes, it was my wish to be neutral. I saw it as an opportunity. It was the opposite of ideology. And to be as objective as possible offered a legitimization for painting since you were being objective and doing what was necessary, enlightening, and so on.

In the 1930s, the English novelist Christopher Isherwood cast the narrator of his Berlin Stories *in a similar role by having him say, 'I am a camera,' by which he meant that he was not taking positions but merely recording what was going on around him. When you first appropriated photographs to make paintings, were you also assuming such a camera-like objectivity?*

The paintings have the advantage that I can still add a little something – because the notion of neutrality and objectivity is an illusion, of course. That is somehow impossible. Every painting automatically includes my inability, my powerlessness, my relation to reality, things that are subjective. Therefore, it was legitimate to be painted. It was not about absolute purity but about the greatest possible purity.

In many respects, Isherwood's stance was the literary equivalent of Neue Sachlichkeit *in painting during the same period, but in fact* Neue Sachlichkeit *pictures could be extremely editorial.*

That was very often the case.

And you were looking for something that was more neutral, more...

Complex.

Neue Sachlichkeit art was in part a reaction to earlier forms of modernism, in particular Expressionism, Cubism and Dada, and their fracturing and reconfiguration of traditional picture-making. A lot of Pop Art in America used modernist methods for breaking up images and recombining the pieces. For example, this happens in Warhol and Robert Rauschenberg. By contrast, your paintings are almost always whole.

Yes, that is true.

So even though you cut or crop images and reframe them inside the rectangle you paint on, you treat those edited details as complete pictorial units and, with only a couple of exceptions, you've never collaged or juxtaposed images from different sources in the same work.

I can't explain why I have such an aversion to collages. To me it always seemed cheap, and it was too sloppy, too loose. I always wanted to make a painting.

What is the appeal of making a painting, in this sense?

Well, it is somehow my duty and my task to fill the space of painting, to make a whole out of it, and everything else seems inappropriate.

Of course, Polke is a maker of collages, and your sensibility is very close to Polke's in some respects, but on this issue you are very different.

Yes, I am also the more classical one. Somebody once said that I am Goethe and Polke is Schiller, or I am Thomas Mann and he is Heinrich Mann.

Could you explain to an American audience what this distinction means?

The classical is what holds me together. It is that which gives me form. It is the order that I do not have to attack. It is something that tames my chaos or holds it together so that I can continue to exist. That was never a question for me. That is essential for life.

In terms of the situation here in the Rhineland in the 1960s, with the impact of Fluxus and Joseph Beuys, almost everybody else in your circle found themselves on the other side.

Yes, it seems as if Beuys was on the other side, and also Nam June Paik and John Cage. But Cage is really a classical man – so scrupulous in the way he holds his things together, does so little, and makes that beautiful. He never even thinks about being sloppy. Sometimes he pretends to be but he never is. He is probably even more uptight than I am and maybe more scrupulous.

You've said that in the 1960s you were very impressed by Cage's Lecture on Nothing, *in which he at one point said: 'I have nothing to say and I am saying it.' How did you understand that paradox then, and how did you relate it to your own desire to avoid making big declarative statements in your own work?*

I thought that this was born out of the same motivation that makes him use the notion of chance, which is that we can't know or say very much at all, in a very classical philosophical sense: 'I know that I don't know anything.'

Back then, when you talked about your use of photographs as the source for paintings, the range of choices you had, and the disparateness of your selection, were you thinking of the apparent arbitrariness of Cage's procedures as a model?

Cage is much more disciplined. He made chance a method and used it in constructive ways; I never did that. Everything here is a little more chaotic.

Chaotic in a sense of more arbitrary or more chaotic in a sense of more intuitive?

Maybe more intuitive. I believe that he knew more what he was doing. I might be absolutely wrong about this, but that was my impression.

You mean a more rigorous aesthetic philosophy?

Yes, the fact that he had a theory that he could name and describe. He could talk or write about what he was doing.

And you proceeded by...

From accident to accident [laughs].

But let's suppose that it was not a question of going from accident to accident but from intuition to intuition. That means that you have a hunch, you don't know the answer, and you don't know exactly why you chose certain images, and yet in some way they were connected in your mind, in some way that suggested each other or created associations as you considered them. Certainly by the time of the 48 Portraits *there was deliberateness in your choices. What kind of instinct or motivation did you have in order to move from making images of contemporary reality to making images of historical figures?*

I can only say that that's the way it was. Polke drifted away into the psychedelic direction and I into the classical. I found support in Gilbert & George where I discovered the same tendencies. And then in Blinky Palermo who was also retrieving the classical.

And Marcel Broodthaers, too?

Yes, but I couldn't understand him – ever.

But virtually all the things he refers to all belong to the nineteenth century.

But that was nineteenth-century, and I wanted something more classical.

In America, Pop addressed the present. Even though Lichtenstein painted Mickey Mouse as he had looked forty years before, still he was painting Mickey Mouse. However, in Europe, artists used a pictorial language that developed out of Pop to look at historical things. For example, Broodthaers catalogued cows in a manner that simultaneously derived from Warhol's enumeration of Coca-Cola bottles, soup cans, movie-star smiles and old-fashioned diagrams. And when Polke painted a row of books labelled Polke's Collected Works, *he made them look like they came off the shelf of an old library. When you went from making pictures of speed boats, cars, planes and Jackie Kennedy, to making the* 48 Portraits, *something of the same anachronism entered into the equation. You say that what you are striving for is a kind of classicism, but it has more dimensions than that.*

48 *Portraits* was supposed to be many things. Those were the typical neutral pictures that one finds in an encyclopedia. The issue of neutrality was my wish and main concern. And that's what they were. That made them modern and absolutely contemporary.

That's true. But who are the people in this index? They are all scientists, philosophers, writers, musicians.

Yes, clever people.

There is no painter, no artist.

That would be too close to me. People would have tried to figure out why I included that painter but not the other one. I chose figures that I had the least to do with. Of course I also had some connection to musicians and writers but there are a lot missing who I like much more than those portrayed – Sigmund Freud and Nietzsche, for example. But I didn't want to portray my favourites but the typical, the levelling; that's the reason all that was contemporary, the neutrality of the encyclopedia, which neutralizes everything and all ideology. That's why I chose many that I didn't know and took out many that I did know. It was the opposite of truth. Theodor Adorno said: 'Every artwork is the arch-enemy of another.' They can't exist next to one another. The encyclopedia makes that possible. We can do it in the world. That is the present situation.

So were you arguing against exalting cultural figures as heroes?

Not really. No, it was not my ambition to be against heroes. I love them too much. I am happy that those people exist.

Were you arguing in favour of a plural culture?

Yes, that's what it is, without endorsing it. It is a fact: we make everything the same. But it is not an attack. It is ambiguous because I hung them in a wonderfully classical way, like a shrine. This is its classical aspect, and that had to do with Gilbert & George.

In this sense, the casts that you made of Palermo and yourself [Two Sculptures for a Room by Palermo] *almost seem to belong to the row of heads in* 48 Portraits*?*

Yes, at least they have the same formal style. But we never wanted to join that line-up or saw ourselves like that. It was a formal matter. Maybe it was a polemic against the zeitgeist of egalitarianism, pluralism and this whole anti-aesthetic debate. Maybe because art was irrelevant. Maybe we made those heads and lauded the classical in order to be polemical, against the time.

I remember seeing those pieces in Munich, where I also visited an exhibition called *Italian Art Today*, with people like Giulio Paolini who made similar classical stuff. And suddenly I realized how substantial my two heads were compared to what Paolini had produced, this decorative game. I suddenly understood how dead serious mine was. That it was somehow inconsistent with the humour of Pop Art. If it was humorous, it was that way in a tragic manner.

Of course every work of art of any value has multiple levels of meaning: one can be funny and one can be serious at various levels. Paolini is funny and serious in his love affair with classical art, but the intensity of the ambivalence is lower.

Yes.

But your situation was different. Your evocation of the classical was basically a response to the whole mood of the late 1960s, early 1970s, where the general rules were: Away with the old; Everything must be relevant; and Everything must be a cultural critique.

Yes, exactly.

But that interpretation differs from what many people seem to think this work is about.

Oh, really!

Some critics seem to regard the 48 Portraits *as an empty, almost postage-stamp-like array of cultural icons. Why do you think it has had such a strong response?*

If it was only postage stamps it wouldn't be as elaborate and there wouldn't be as much trouble. It is too big and there is too much presence, and always people wonder what it is about. Women are angry because there are no women. It keeps upsetting people again and again. People are always upset when confronted with something traditional and conservative, and therefore they don't want it. You're not allowed to do that; it is not considered to be part of our time. It's over, reactionary.

Some critics explain it to themselves – make it okay to like – by arguing that it's an exercise in rhetoric, the rhetoric of a certain kind of representation of culture that questions or nullifies that culture's authority.

And as I mentioned, you also have the psychological or subjective timeliness of the father problem. This affects all of society. I am not talking about myself because that would be rather uninteresting, but the absence of the father is a typical German problem. That is the reason for such agitation; that is why this work has such a disquieting effect.

So it is about restoring a sense of history that has been broken or truncated.

It's not a restoration. It is a reference to this loss. It takes account of the fact that we have lost something. It asks the question of whether or not we need to do something. It is not about the establishment of something.

A question of whether what has been lost can be brought back or not?

Yes, but I don't believe that it comes back.

Was making the paintings a way of putting those images out to see whether they still exerted power on their own?

That was not my intention. My intention was to get attention [*laughs*]. I wanted to be seen.

Bruce Nauman once made a neon with the text 'The true artist helps the world by revealing mystic truths,' which he put in the window of his studio like a beer sign. That piece was addressed both to himself and to the public.

That's good!

And what appeared to be a declaration was really a question: 'Do you believe this? Do I believe this?' Is there any parallel between what he was doing and what you're after?

Yes, I believe that there is something like that. That's possible. But I have too much respect for Bruce Nauman to simply claim that we share the same concern, that we are thinking about the same things. It doesn't work like that.

Another way of approaching the problem might be to talk a little bit about your decision to copy Titian's Annunciation[7] *or your interest in landscape.*

It is all the same motivation.

In other interviews, you've suggested that using nostalgia or using an anachronism was a way of being subversive. But painting in traditional modes can also involve an assimilation of traditions. Were you employing these images as a tool for upsetting the fixed ideas of the avant-garde, or were you reaffirming the basic paradigms to which you resorted? Were they primarily a tool, or a goal?

That is too difficult.

Alright, but take the landscapes and the Titian copy: not only was the style in which they were painted a departure from modernism, but so were the images. The idea of someone in your position painting a Titian or painting a beautiful landscape in a somewhat romantic way was bound to get a reaction, was bound to make people say, 'What is he doing?'

On the one hand, it was a polemic against this annoying modernist development that I hated. And, of course, the assertion of my freedom: 'Why shouldn't I paint like this and who could tell me not to?' And then the affirmation was naturally there, the wish to paint paintings as beautiful as those by Caspar David Friedrich, to claim that this time is not lost but possible, that we need it, and that it is good. And it was a polemic against modern art, against tin art, against 'wild art' – and for freedom, that I could do whatever I wanted to.

Tin art?

Much modern stuff looked like aluminium. Modern, pure. Minimalism was going on at that time. I remember just a little story that took place when I was first in New York with Palermo. We had some photographs of our work – just in case.

And we showed them to someone – I think it was Bob Ryman – and I thought that he would, of course, prefer the abstract paintings, but he was only interested in my first landscape, which was *Corsica (Fire)*. And I was so surprised that he liked this painting. I thought, he is a modern artist, a real artist, not like me. But he liked it.

Well, he is a modern artist and he is a real artist, which is precisely why he would have liked it. But in that period from the late 1960s to the middle 1970s, one gets the impression that things were very hard for you.

Yes, it was at that time I lost the ground under my feet.

How so? Because the world changed on you or because you began to doubt what you were doing?

I didn't know what to do but to paint. I was 'out'.

But if I understand the situation correctly, to be out and to choose an entirely unexplored direction can also be a kind of freedom?

Well, the freedom and the comfort gained from being out were not very substantial. Being out didn't have such a positive effect. After all, I wanted to be on the inside. I don't know where I was.

But, in fact, being in that position opened up a whole different way of thinking about the work, didn't it?

I don't remember it being so different. Anyway, only much later did I realize that these crises were not something to get agitated about but that they were the normal way of working. Everybody has them. Well, maybe it is not as simple as that. There are people who work with more confidence and others who stumble from crisis to crisis. It was somewhere in-between. But I don't know if it was a special crisis; maybe it was.

I am not so much asking how you felt about it or about the immediate circumstances. I am only thinking that if you step back and look at the larger picture, here was someone associated with the avant-garde who suddenly was making pictures of traditional subject matter and making them in a classical style. That went against the grain of just about everything that was going on then, and it also went against what was expected of you in particular. And it went against what many of your supporters valued. Somehow, given these factors, you must have had some understanding of the necessity for doing all of that.

Alright. But that's what I don't know. I wouldn't know how to reply to that. Certainly the situation animated me to try different directions so that I would find something of more substance and importance. I was very sure that the big 'Detail' paintings[8] I had been making were not the direction.

Okay, let's talk about the shift toward more abstract pictures. In one statement, you have said: 'If abstract paintings show my reality, then the landscapes and still-lifes show my yearning.' In what sense do you mean that the abstract paintings show your reality?

That was later, and the reality of abstraction was what I could make directly – mentally, physically, psychologically. This was my daily challenge and those were normal difficulties; it has no relation to any kind of yearning or dream. And if it did, it would be hard to recognize it as such and I wouldn't call it a yearning. But the figurative ones were some sort of a break and recovery from everyday work. That's why I called it a yearning because there I could afford to do something romantic or nostalgic. That was a polemical remark; it has never been just like that. But in order to de-emphasize them I said they were nostalgic – a luxury.

In what sense, that the making of the abstract pictures was less about an illusion and more about a physical process?

Yes, exactly. Like a musician who has to know his stuff and has to work and to make the music, to build it.

Robert Ryman has also talked about abstract painting as being the most realist kind of painting, because everything that counts is right there in front of you – the materials, the surface. The experience doesn't depend on anything outside or beyond the painting but only on what can be directly perceived, what is 'real'. Do you mean something similar when you talk about the reality of abstract pictures?

Yes, but his reality, the one he is talking about, is different. To him it is a physically present reality, and he would probably deny any imaginary relations. At some point I said polemically that Ryman reminds us of something, tells us something. There is always some sort of narrative or reference, though I believe that he would deny that and say that to him it's all about structure or whatever.

What kind of narrative quality was in your abstract painting in the mid- to late 1970s, for example? How do you mean the narrative when you look at pictures like this?

This reminds me of a time when Buchloh asked me the same thing, and I said that I saw red rain falling here [*pointing to an abstract work of the early 1970s*] and a lake behind it, and there are broken cliffs and poles running around and one floats through spaces. He was appalled and said, 'You can't be serious! That's not true!' And I replied, 'No, it's true!' As if a child said, 'Look, mom, that's red rain, those drips right there.'

Well, first of all, I think that you can be serious about this. However, I am surprised that you see qualities so directly associated with nature. When you are making those paintings, are you actually thinking in metaphors all the time?

No, never. And I also try to avoid that something in the painting resembles a table or other things. It's terrible if it does because then all you can see is that object.

So you allow for aspects or suggestions of images in the abstract work but not actual pictures?

Not actual pictures. I just wanted to re-emphasize my claim that we are not able to see in any other way. We only find paintings interesting because we always search for something that looks familiar to us. I see something and in my head I compare it and try to find out what it relates to. And usually we do find those similarities and name them: table, blanket, and so on. When we don't find anything, we are frustrated and that keeps us excited and interested until we have to turn away because we are bored. That's how abstract painting works. That was my argument with Buchloh because I said that's how Malevich and Ryman work as well. And only like that. You can interpret the *Black Square* of Malevich as much as you like, but it remains a provocation; you are compelled to look for an object and to come up with one.

It is important whether an artist actually gives you an indication that there is such an object or teases you with the possibility that there might be one or whether the artist, in effect, lets you know that there isn't actually an image of that sort; there is something there but it is not a representation.

I just wanted to insist on the way we function. Basically we always try to identify a relation of a picture to some sort of appearance. It's not about the recognition of a particular subject matter.

Of course Leonardo da Vinci talked about looking at patterns on the ceiling and finding faces, and maybe there is a basic human tendency to do this, but whether the artist encourages or discourages this tendency is a huge issue for abstract painting.

Most artists have tried to avoid that. And still they cannot escape this mechanism. Even those paintings that are supposed to be nothing but a monochrome surface are looked at in that searching manner. The effect of these paintings depends on that mechanism. I don't even know how it could work otherwise.

In a way it does relate your abstract pictures to your figurative ones because in the figurative paintings people are reassured when they see a certain kind of image. They crave the verification of the object and long to see what they know about or bring to the object, and yet you create a distance in which that object becomes ambiguous. People want a picture that adds up to their expectations, and you do things that remove qualities from the image or cancel it out. You make paintings at the expense of pictures, or at least at the expense of the depicted object.

I don't know if you are right about that or whether I could agree. But I also don't know if I understood you correctly.

I am just saying that you use painting as a way of making it difficult for people to just read the image.

Yes, that's right.

Many of the grey abstract pictures that preceded the colour abstractions had quite painterly surfaces. By comparison, the first full-colour abstractions were anti-painterly, but the combination of hues was often very strident. In these ways the contrast between the two groups of work in touch, texture and achromatic versus chromatic effects was very dramatic. How did you first arrive at this use of colour? How was it supposed to operate in contrast to the monochrome grey paintings?

It was very sudden because I thought that it couldn't go on like that. The grey didn't work any more. That was the end. And then I started with a weird colour abstract painting that was very big and not very good and then I did the small ones. The transition was easy to make because I was working off a photo that I could enlarge.

What was the impulse behind this jump into very dramatic colour?

To do the opposite, to free myself of any constraints. I asked myself, 'Why not?' Do we want some psychoanalysis [*laughs*]?

No. If you want to offer some psychoanalysis, I'll take it, but that is not what I am asking. I was wondering about formal impulse.

Well, I never dared to show these paintings anywhere. I thought they were crazy – the early ones, that is, which, after all, I made as copies from parts of other paintings. I found that by copying those paintings I was able to construct them in an acceptable manner. You can't just show this wild stuff, those helpless smears that are absolutely random and senseless, against all rationality and taste, against everything. But then, after I had painted copies of the originals[9] I felt comfortable enough to show them – in Halifax, Nova Scotia.[10] It was a test and I realized that people took them seriously, and then I continued to make them.

That was also the time when you made your artist's book, 128 Details from a Picture,[11] *which is basically a catalogue of black-and-white photographs of the surface of an abstract painterly painting.*

Yes.

Among the last of the photo-based colour abstractions you made before you started to make direct, gestural abstraction was a picture called Faust. *Did you think at that time that assuming the role of gestural painter in some way involved a Faustian bargain?*

That was pure smugness. It was a very big and boisterous picture, and I don't remember if anything reminded me of Faust. It was a conscious decision to never declare it as being either one thing or another. Of course, in the back of my head

I thought that hopefully people would understand it as Walpurgis Night in Goethe's Faust.

I am wondering how many different levels we are dealing with here. After all, Faust makes a deal with the devil. Who is the devil in this case?

Part of it was the fear of my own courage. It was very important for me to create a painting like this. That's why I gave it such a title. But at the same time I knew it was pretentious, that it was not quite right.

But also that it was going the right direction.

But it was the last of the translations or copies. After that, all the other abstractions were painted directly.

This jump from indirect to direct painting coincides with a general turn toward painterly painting in the late 1970s and early 1980s, and to the advent of the neo-Expressionist work that came out of Europe and America.

To the zeitgeist.

Were you conscious of this general shift? Did you feel you were a part of it or independent from it? Does the term neo-Expressionist have any positive value with regard to what you were doing?

No, I was absolutely sure that I had nothing to do with that. They were mute and I was not. Silent and bad and terrible, but not me.

How do you mean silent?

Mute, dumb, dull; they had all the bad qualities. But, yes, I was certainly a child of the zeitgeist. There's absolutely no doubt about it. One is affected by what is going on at the time. But I have always been a little different from the others and somehow always stood apart from the centre.

I am using the word with a little 'e' not a big 'E', but did you intend your paintings to be read as expressive or expressionist in a particular way?

Not expressionist, no. Expressive, yes. But more in the sense of 'artificial' or something like that. That was the first time that I had the feeling that those types of paintings were cold and distant and clear – that they were not sentimental.

And the colour, the stridency of the colour, was chosen to create that effect?

I believe so. It is part of a general feeling or attitude toward life, a desire to conquer such an artificial space for oneself.

Now I am confused.

I had the hope, carried by a fresh wind, to make something free, clear, open, crystal, visible, transparent, a Utopia.

Talk a minute about the Candle paintings, which could hardly have been more different from your abstractions of the early 1980s. If I am not mistaken, they were not very well received when you first exhibited them.

Of the six I showed,[12] none sold. They later became so expensive [*laughs*].

Meanwhile, the critical response to the work was mixed, as it had been with the abstractions. At the time, it was assumed that either you were engaged in a direct satire of specific historical styles of painting or, as we discussed before, that you were engaged in a more general postmodern demolition of painting's conventions in which every style you touched on was exposed as empty.

Buchloh said 'rhetorical'. Well, there is nothing I can say to that. But I have to take back what I said about the abstractions being free from all meaning and opinion, that they are merely a crystal clear dynamic world. That is not quite right. That would be reductive because it has to do with atmospheres and contents. They are narrative and sentimental. There are certain principal intentions that are part of all the paintings. It is not that big a difference. Yet they have the character of something more clear, free, dynamic, and so on.

You seem to be saying, on the one hand, that these paintings are not to be read as traditional, serious, melodramatic gestural painting, but, on the other hand, that they still contain some ambitions for painting within the tradition to which they refer. They are neither 'retro', nor 'neo', nor part of a Duchampian game.

No.

In the final analysis, they are meant to be looked at as abstract painting.

Yes. I am reminded of when I showed my paintings in the Netherlands[13] and I talked to a critic and she said: 'It is not possible that these are real paintings; they just pretend that they are.' She liked them very much, but she said that the real quality of these paintings was that they pretended to be paintings. I believe that somehow that was her question; she did not know how to handle the paintings. That's why she said something similar to what Buchloh was talking about when he talked about 'rhetoric', that these are not really paintings.

And what did you think of that?

I am struck by the fact that these paintings are viewed according to three different standpoints: you say that the paintings are neither this nor that, Buchloh says the paintings are not paintings but rhetoric, and the woman said that they are not paintings but play at being paintings. Therefore, there has to be some truth to it.

But I am not agreeing with either of the two.

But there is something right about the woman's question, something about these paintings that sometimes look like great gestural painting but it also suggests that there is a lack of conviction that it is possible to paint like that. Unlike people like Franz Kline and others who could paint an expressionist painting with conviction – the same kind of conviction in every stroke that he paints. They had the conviction that what they were doing was good and right. And that's it. I lack that in every stroke.

In a way, though, these paintings are much more like those of Jackson Pollock than Kline or Willem de Kooning because Pollock's big all-over paintings are no longer symbolist or narrative, and the energy in them is no longer that of muscular struggle. In the great all-over works, the painting becomes, in a sense, independent. The distance that opens up between the painter and the painting is a space the viewer also can share, but the painting itself has become both intensely stimulating and formally self-sustaining, so that its persuasiveness no longer depends on the conviction or latent presence of its creator.

You are absolutely right, and now we are on a different level because I don't believe that the paintings merely pretend to be paintings. But at the time it was not possible to accept them as paintings, at least not in Europe.

But there is a big difference between a painting that is made in order to deal with convention, either satirically, critically or analytically, and a painting that accepts that conventions exist but tries to create a physical and visual reality that is as free of those conventions as possible. Does that make sense?

Yes, absolutely! The paintings have nothing to do with the articulation of theoretical conventions, of painting itself, but they have a different intention. That is absolutely right. That's why I refused to accept when anyone tried to attribute such intentions and motives to my work.

True classical art – as distinct from conservative classical or neoclassical style – may be defined as an art that accepts its own conventions, but does not simply repeat them formulaically. Rather, it uses them to transform itself and extend its range. A crucial dimension of such classical art, though, is that it is deeply impersonal. Pollock, when he painted the big all-over abstractions of the late 1940s and early 1950s, was, for perhaps the only time of his life, free of himself as a painter and thoroughly involved with the paint and the space and the process. In that sense, his was a classical art. John Cage and Merce Cunningham are classical artists in the same way. In your case, there is an irony in the fact that the painterly abstractions you started in the 1970s and continue to make have been referred to as either being expressionist or polemically anti-expressionist, but the term 'expressionist' doesn't fit either usage.

The only thing that is polemical is that I took the liberty and made the paintings the way they are, without regard to whether they were reminiscent of something explosive or expressionist.

From my perspective, though, the irony is that you have approached a style – expressionism – which for many people cannot, by definition, be classic, and you have demonstrated the contrary, that it is possible to make a visually exciting, physically expansive, even aggressive picture that is classical in that it is not about the painter in any obvious way, and not emotional in the most banal sense.

Yes, that sounds very good.

The other model we inherit from the early modernists is that of Kandinsky, the idea of abstraction as a metaphysical or transcendentalist art. Now at one point you said: 'Abstract paintings are fictive models that make visible a reality we can neither see nor describe but whose existence we can postulate.' Do you in fact view your abstract paintings – either the grey paintings, the colour paintings, or both – as being as much about the yearning for transcendent states of being as the landscapes are about a yearning for the beauty found in nature?

If I understood you correctly, I would say that the landscapes are closer to such an intention than the abstract paintings. They are further removed from a stated intention to be models of a reality. You mentioned Kandinsky – I can't stand any of his paintings or the work of most artists similar to him who have said, 'I am like a child,' as if they could invent the world from the very beginning. I don't relate to any of that stuff. I was not interested in anything of the kind. I thought they were all stupid.

But I wasn't talking specifically about Kandinsky's words or his style but of the kind of aspiration for modern abstract art with which he was associated. It's a tendency with which Mondrian, Rothko and Newman were also connected, a drive to find a pictorial means for referring to philosophical or spiritual ideas, for representing things that, in essence, cannot be represented. Does that make sense to you at all?

Yes, but you put it somehow in a naïve way. It's not that simple. But every art, whether it is philosophy, literature, music or painting, can touch something; it can't depict, never depicts. And I believe the painters you mentioned were talking about depiction, and that's impossible. There is some truth to the idea of the paintings being models of a world, but the word 'model' seems to be the wrong term. Because one might really take it for a model in the sense that 'this is what it looks like in a different world' and that is not how it is meant. I have to distance myself from the concept of the 'model'.

But apart from your own painting, do you think that this is something art can do?

Yes. A painting can help us to think something that goes beyond this senseless existence. That's something art can do.

And you think it can still do that despite everything you've said?

Yes, absolutely.

And do you think it does happen?

Yes, from time to time. And I am certain that we will find different forms and maybe then painting becomes obsolete, but we will always need something, right?

But many people seem to think that the possibility of making art that is significant in that way has simply been used up. They believe too much of history and too much experience argues against such idealism.

Our time looks as if we finally got over all of the nonsense, got rid of our need for a larger scheme, forgot history, rejected art and rejected our fathers so that everything will be free and animalistic, techno-animalistic. I don't believe in any of that. That's just a movement. It is probably unavoidable. We now have the techno-animalistic age. It begins. But what will we do when everything is needless and meaningless?

Do you think that there is actually such a dramatic change going on right now, a change more dramatic than what went on in the 1960s?

Maybe, yes. Today there are more *facts* that are changing. All the great things such as the computer world, the internet and genetic engineering are very real and very important. Compared to that, the 1960s were just a dream. The 1960s were nothing real, only dreams – strawberry fields [*laughs*].

Maybe that is the occasion to talk a little bit about the October *paintings. After all, the idealism of the Baader-Meinhof group and how it went wrong are the subjects of the work, and the act of completing the works was implicitly idealistic as well insofar as it set a high standard for what painting could do, how much it could communicate. You seem to believe that idealism in an aesthetic context is possible but that in a practical, political context it is dangerous. Is that a fair summation?*

It is impossible to exist without idealism. I always imagined that I was one of the few who could live without idealism in order to discover later that all that time I was full of illusions. Even when I was against it, I *believed* in my opposition to it. It's a difficult subject.

When did you think of yourself in these terms, of having no illusions?

Maybe during the time I made the *October* paintings when I dealt with the subject matter and took notes and cursed the ideologues. When I realized that I myself *believed*, that I was euphoric, that I was carried by belief, I realized, this is wrong – it is merely a belief itself.

To whom did you find yourself opposed in this situation?

The opposition were primarily the terrorists, but it was also the faction of the art world that was possessed by big beliefs. I remember the kind of worship around Malevich and others. I could never participate in that. I was never

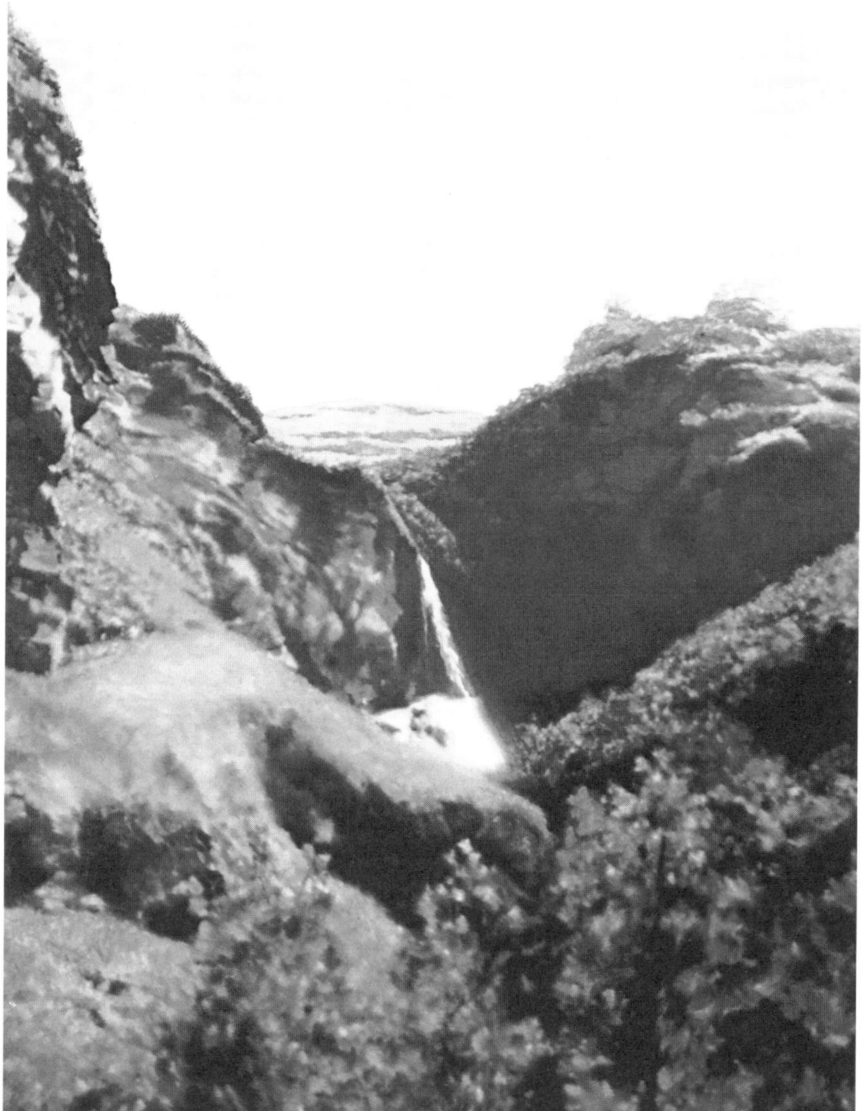

Waterfall, 1997

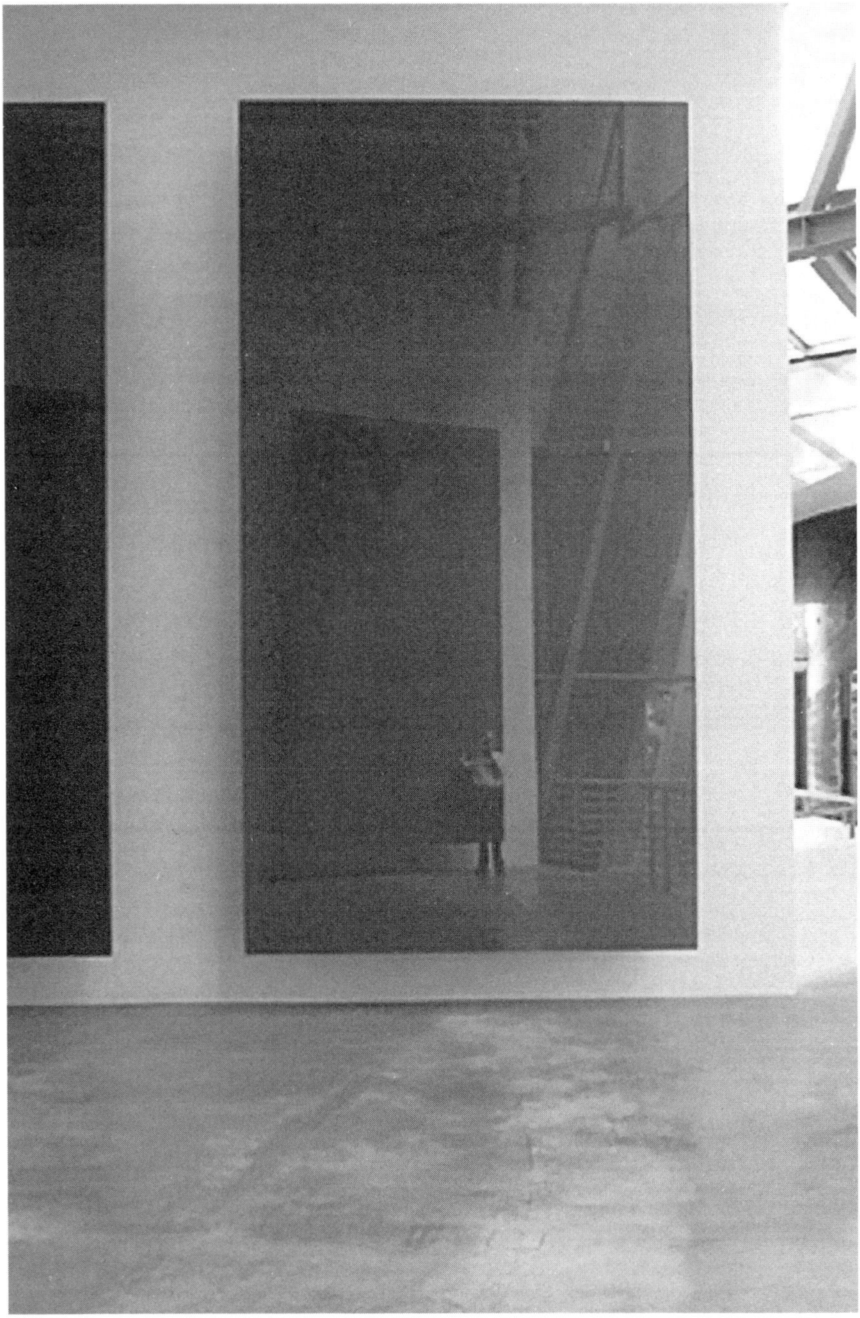

Guggenheim Bilbao, 2004

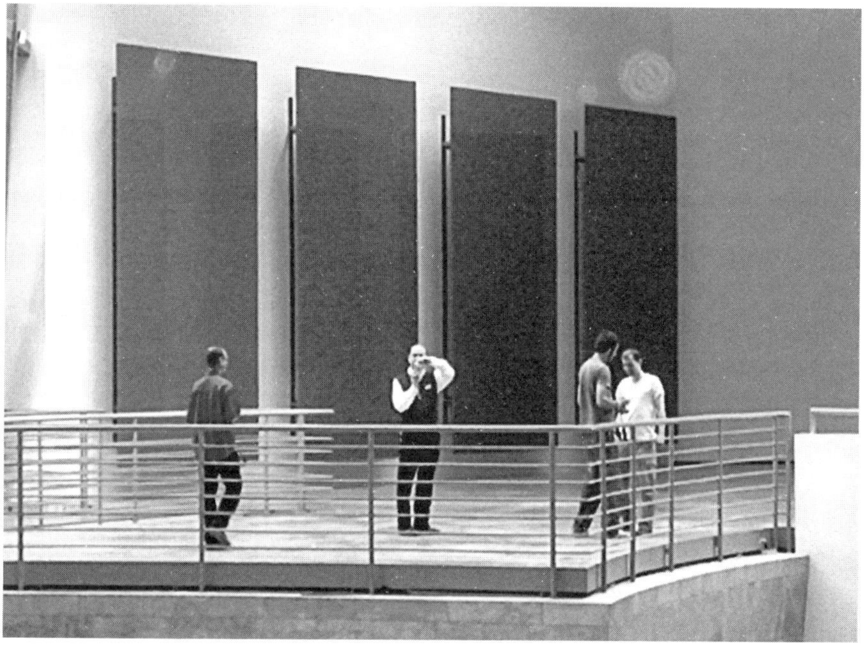

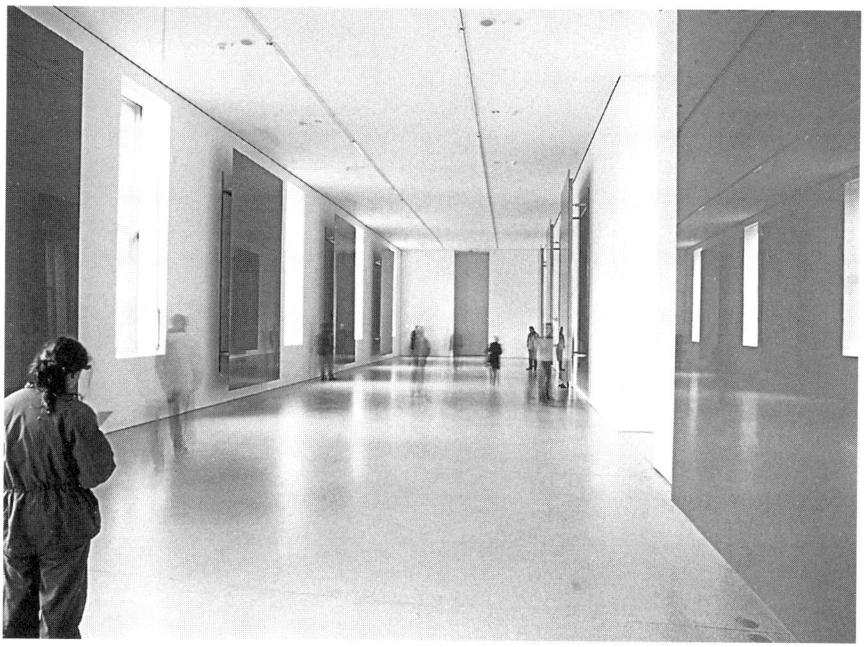

Guggenheim Bilbao, 2004
Guggenheim Berlin, 2002

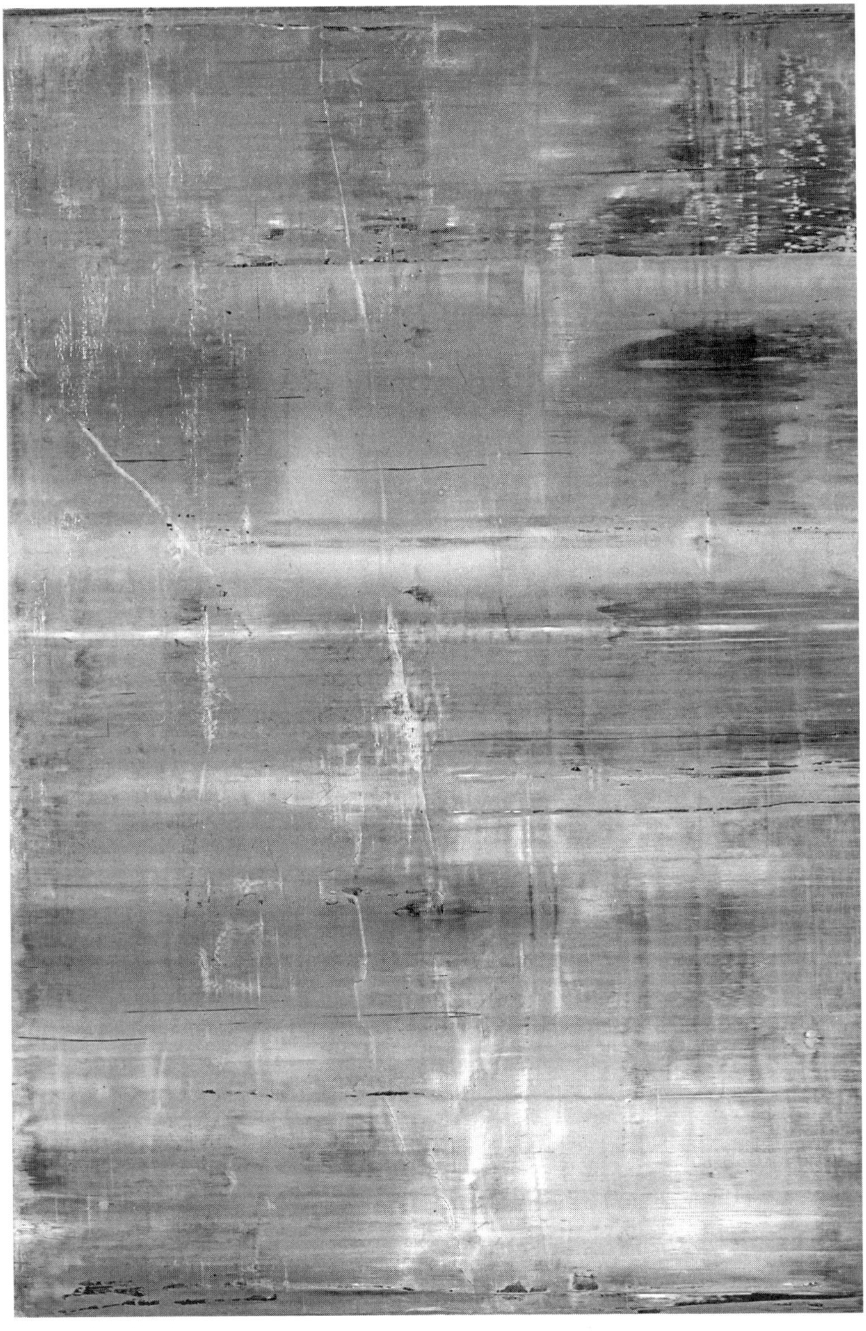

Abstract Painting, 2000

interested in that. I never shared any of those beliefs. For me the government was the smaller evil because it believed the least. They were merely gangsters, of the sort that are always around in any period. But those who were full of beliefs, they were dangerous. I was convinced that the government had no ideology whatsoever, whether it was Helmut Schmidt or Helmut Kohl. I was against believing, as such, against the fact that one could poison so many brains and have such power. I thought I was free from belief.

But in a way your resistance converted you to a kind of belief even though you didn't accept the opinions of the members of the Baader-Meinhof group whom you were painting. You were forced to acknowledge that belief of an intensity such as theirs has value.

In the end I was just as unfree. I was carried by some sort of belief.

In many ways 18 October 1977 *marks a turning point in your work. The landscape paintings, the Titian paintings, even the* 48 Portraits *are still engaged in a game of hide-and-seek with tradition, but after the* October *paintings you seem to paint your subjects with less distance. Take the flower paintings, for example. They are less shy about being beautiful paintings than the early landscapes. Likewise, the portraits that you have done of Sabine are very different from previous portraits you've painted of people close to you. There's an intimacy to these images that is different in quality from earlier works.*

What about *Ema*? The staircase?

Yes and no. It is a very beautiful picture, but...

But it is also a demonstration.

Yes, there's something between you and the picture. An idea.

Yes, it is staged. And the little nude of Sabine [*Small Bather*] is not staged.

I am not thinking of the nude so much as the pictures of her reading. Those are really in a realm with Vermeer, not in style, not historical reference, but because it allows the viewer to look into a private situation – with great reserve, but one can look. Do you think such a change has occurred?

If I could take an impartial look at myself I would say: 'That guy has matured a little, he has gained some sovereignty, he is older.' That sometimes happens in painting. If I would not be sitting here, that's what I would say. Same with Velázquez: when he became older his paintings became better. Nice. Thank you for this [*laughs*].

As you get older, you paint better, but you paint better not for technical reasons, not for formal reasons, but because you have a different understanding.

With a little more ease.

Or, to choose a different word, with greater permission. When you are young, people around you say, No, you can't do this or that, and then also a voice inside says No to the things that matter most. But it is as if, after the Baader-Meinhof paintings, you gave yourself permission to make pictures with a different quality. Is that true?

Yes, even though there were a lot of backlashes, and I produced a lot of garbage in-between. For example, the difficulties I am having now. I can see this beautiful quality that you just described in a few paintings, once in a while, and then suddenly it disappears and then it resurfaces again. It is not as if this quality has become the rule now. That would be wonderful.

I guess I am not talking about beauty alone, but also about the overall resistance to change abating in some degree.

Yes, but that's not true either. If I could count on that being a constant feature now, then all paintings would be much more relaxed – but they are not. There are always exceptions. But you are right; something has changed, but not enough.

So what is it? What is the obstacle?

The constraints persist. You said that when one is young that there are a lot of restrictions, and I still am subject to those restrictions. Only sometimes am I free of them, maybe more often than before, I don't know. I wish that I could give myself those permissions and that freedom on a more regular basis, but I can't. Otherwise there wouldn't be as many forced paintings.

These pressures are...?

I don't know where they come from. They exist. Yesterday we saw the catalogue of Goya drawings, and I realized that when Goya was very old he made much more relaxed drawings. He was allowed to make things that way. Or there is somebody like Matisse. And I was a little bit jealous because I have not yet achieved this permission. But now we have talked much too long about this, and this is not even our topic. I am sorry.

Along with granting oneself permission to do certain things, there can also be an element almost of defiance. For example, in the last five years you've made a number of images that raised the hackles of the avant-garde.

I don't know.

You made a series of pictures of Sabine with your son – almost as if she were a Madonna with Child. And you made a multiple of the cross.

Oh yes [*laughs*].

Did you anticipate the negative reactions that those works received in some quarters?

Well, I don't know much about that. People don't tell me these things. Sometimes I simply hear something through others. I only came across it once myself in a critical review of the *Small Bather*. That's where I finally read it. The review was titled 'Holy, Holy, Holy', and then it went off. I understand why they get upset, but when they tell me that this is reactionary, I don't understand it.

I don't agree with it, but I think I understand it. This is a period when there is almost no room for the kinds of words that you have used recently to discuss the October *paintings, like 'faith' or 'belief', or as far back as the early 1960s when you talked about art as being a substitute 'religion'. Using such vocabulary or making allusions to such traditional symbols or iconography is extremely provocative, given its misuse by fundamentalists or people in positions of power: you can be misunderstood in many, many ways. And perhaps the question is not how many ways you can be misunderstood but how would you like to be understood?*

I don't know how I would like to be understood. Maybe as the keeper of tradition [*laughs*]. Rather that than any other misunderstandings.

As a guardian of an aesthetic tradition or as a guardian of a philosophical and moral tradition?

Whatever you can get [*laughs*].

Interview with Babette Richter, 2002

I'd like to begin by talking, quite generally, about the interview situation itself. What's it like for you? Do you feel ambivalent about it, or is it just basically agonizing to be asked to define yourself?

No, it's ambivalent, like everything in life. To begin with it's tempting, and it only becomes agonizing when it doesn't work, when one fails. And I then feel it's an obligation and I think, 'You should be able to manage that; surely a person must be intelligent and competent enough to manage that.' And there's a degree of vanity involved, the illusion that you're saying something quite unique, important and amazing. In reality nobody is amazed, and, if you're lucky, what you say is just about presentable.

To what extent do you experience a discrepancy between the language you can convey and the ideas you have in your head? Everyone knows the difficulty: you say something, and, really, you wanted to express something completely different, or you had a different image of it in your mind.

That involves the interesting effect, the disappointment, when you realize you have ideas that can't be justified. Everyone knows the situation. For example, you think, 'If I could have things my way, I would tell people quite simply what the score is and what is wrong with this, that and the other.' One often feels totally sure of oneself, no matter what the topic. And then, when you are asked to say something, you can't utter a single word – not a single sentence – because it's too complicated; it's only simple in your imagination. It's the same with interviews. If things get awkward, you can hide behind a torrent of words; that's something I've learnt. That way, you do at least say something.

Is making yourself understood also a problem, the feeling that the other person isn't in the least getting what you're saying?

Yes. There are some very silly interviews, or very embarrassing ones. After all, I'm not so proficient that I can react elegantly, no matter what. The latest embarrassment was an interview I gave in New York, where I asked myself afterwards, 'Why didn't you say this and this? Why did you answer at all?' The questions were put in such a way that I was dumbfounded. I think the first questions were: 'What have you got against language? What don't you like about it?'

How is one supposed to reply to that? Then let's not bother to have this conversation?

Exactly! In any case, my response should have been cooler. Politicians are good at that.

Do you also see a danger, occasionally, of letting too much of yourself out?

I used to see that danger all the time, and I was intent on not revealing too much of myself. It's partly the fear that one will engender opposition – and the fear that a certain response will be painful, if one happens to be talking rubbish. And then there's the fear that it will be too intimate, that one will expose oneself and seem pathetic. Then again, the more interesting interviews are the ones that touch on the intimate. In a way, they can't be private enough, but when I feel intimately involved, I get very angry with myself.

Which interviewers have you liked best? Which were the conversations where you felt most comfortable? Which ones did you think of as highly productive?

There are really only two, Buchloh and Storr, because they know a lot about the subject matter, and because I feel that they understand me. Also because they weren't afraid to attack me – that is, to challenge what I had said.

I see a relationship between certain terms you use again and again. Those are terms like silence – and, in that context, concealment, loss, absence and hurt. When you talk about painting, those terms are: smudging, destroying, subtracting, scratching, covering over and eliminating. What meaning do these terms have for you?

Oh, now it's getting complicated. Yes, that's the way it is, so there must be some truth in what you say...

There is this ambivalence within you, between opening up and shutting out, exposing something that is simultaneously taken away; the introvert artist who is silent, but who is also popular because he and his paintings display his intimate side. What is the relationship between what you can say and do, and what you paint?

I don't know how to answer that offhand. But I'd like to get back to what you said before, that is: the view, the accusation, that I am non-committal verbally and in my work, meaning that I am politically indifferent, neither left-wing nor right-wing, but maybe both at the same time. The fact is that I can't see that as a flaw. It's more of an instinctive thing, and a wisdom that is extremely desirable because it makes you more critical, and it shows that nothing is as clear and simple as people like to believe, with all their neat and unambiguous statements and slogans; even though such simplifications are more attractive, more interesting.

Those simplifications aren't necessarily more interesting, though...

No, but a slogan provokes opposition, because if everyone just had a choice between deciding on the merits, in the sense of a yes or no answer, it would be pretty boring, don't you think?

Yes, in the sense that slogans are compact, one-dimensionally correct – in other words, black or white, and therefore catchy. Let's talk about your paintings. Nowadays you don't paint in black and white any more?

Yes, that's true.

Did your earlier black-and-white paintings have a different quality for you, a different meaning than the colour ones? For example, was black and white a way of distancing yourself more, or was it a means for you to try to illustrate objectivity?

Basically it was just more unusual, back then, to create black-and-white oil paintings, and more real, because all the newspapers, the daily diet of photographic material, including television, was black and white, and the photo albums and photography itself – all of it was black and white, which is difficult to imagine these days. That's why it imbued a sense of reality into painting that represented something completely new. Looking at them now, the likeness to photographs, the documentary quality, aren't as evident, because the paintings just seem like paintings. But black-and-white photography has managed to retain a unique quality; the F.A.Z. [*Frankfurter Allgemeine Zeitung*] still uses black-and-white photographs, even if the majority would probably prefer them to be in colour.

The last black-and-white paintings were part of the RAF [Red Army Faction] series. These paintings deal with the topic of ideology, with the failure of ideas, with ideology seen as fanatical belief, as illusion. When it comes down to it, they are death paintings. They are about the possibility of portraying death, and they represent a study of the topic. Is death a recurring theme for you?

Increasingly so; it's in the nature of getting older, so to speak.

How did you personally experience the rebellion of 1968?

I could never really relate to the ideas and slogans of the student movement, though I was somewhat drawn to its anti-authoritarianism, probably because of a father-complex of sorts...

Which brings us to the three paintings Uncle Rudi, Mann mit Hund[1] *and* 48 Portraits. *How are they linked to your father image?*

[*Laughs*] I think I'd rather tell you that in private...

But surely we can talk about problems to do with fathers: the paintings show the loss of a father figure – the photograph of the lost, small and beaming uncle as an officer; the strange snapshot of your father, who almost comes across as a clown; and the intimidating encyclopedia portraits of various male role models. They all pertain to the image of the lost father.

Yes, absolutely, and I have even less difficulty admitting to it since it's the experience of an entire generation, the post-war generation, or even two generations that lost their fathers for all sorts of reasons – some literally, who had fallen in the war; and then there were the others, the broken, the humiliated, the ones that returned physically or mentally damaged; and then those fathers that were actually guilty of crimes. Those are three types of fathers you don't want to have. Every child wants a father to be proud of.

Proud, in this context, refers to the father's function as a role model. The absent, failed or criminal father represents the absence of a figure one can identify with. What did your father represent for you, in this context? What father figures did you have later on? Were there specific role models, or father figures?

Yes, certainly, but the problem was that they were usually dead already – people like Goethe or Van Gogh – or they were far away, like Picasso and Gérard-Philippe.

Van Gogh?

Yes, as a young man I wanted to be crazy like Van Gogh.

And how does the image of your mother manifest itself?

I really don't know what to say about that. My mother ... that's something so normal: you just have one. What can I say?

But a mother-child relationship isn't all that self-explanatory: people have different ideals of how a mother should be, and different notions about the role of women, which have to do with a more or less problematic relationship with their mothers. How do you view the paintings you have made of women?

Well, I did notice again, just recently, looking at all the combined paintings of women in the New York exhibition,[2] that I was surprised at how contradictory the images were. There are the images of idealized women, starting with the *Ema* nude, where she really seems to be descending the stairs like an angel coming down from heaven. Then there's the painting of the daughter, which is also an idealization since its essence is a longing for culture, for the beauty in art which we no longer have, which is why she turns away. Then we have the *Lesende* [Reading Woman], which is also an idealized image because she is so taken by Vermeer, the artist-god, that she tries to represent a similar beauty. Who knows, maybe those are desired ideals. And then there's the other side, the victims. The black-and-white paintings of women have more to do with their everyday lives, which only attract attention when something untoward happens to them – when they become victims, like the eight student nurses, and others. The *Isa* paintings were based on photographs I took. And I never painted my mother as such; there's only a family portrait in which she appears.[3]

You just mentioned idealization in the portrayal of women. Could Ema *be seen as an indirect, hidden idealization, and could* Sabine mit Kind [Sabine with Child] *be seen as a direct religious, icon-like idealization of the mother figure?*

Despite all their similarities with images of the Madonna, they still don't have anything to do with an idealized mother figure. They are far too individualistic, in every respect – even if they are, at times, painted in such a way that the figures can't be identified. It may be that the nude on the stairs, with its religious connotations, also appears a bit like the portrait of the saviour. But I basically don't know what I was thinking, or what my intention was, so I can't offer an interpretation. Somehow, I've always strictly refused to try and make things understandable or to analyze my motifs: the paintings themselves were always the message. For instance, the fact that I photographed your mother on the stairs wasn't planned or intended as such, and neither was the painting that resulted from it. And the fact is that I hardly dared show it to anyone. That's how old-fashioned it was. Glass, metal and Pop were fashionable.

In what context were the later Betty *portraits conceived, the lying-down one and the turned-away one – though, really, there are three, including the blurred, out-of-focus one?*

The three motifs weren't painted on the same day, but round about the same time. The blurry one was also a lying-on-the-table one, an image which I then turned upright and made out of focus because the facial features weren't right any more.

At that time I was between ten and thirteen years old. When did you paint them? When was the lying-down one made?

I did the one with the head resting on the table at a time when I was only painting abstract works. There is a photograph where the painting is on the easel, in the studio on Brückenstrasse.[4] The whole room is full of abstract paintings, except for this one. That was like a luxury, or a compensation, a counterbalance.

And the other one was also painted at a time when you were focused in a different direction.

Yes, that was at the time of the Baader-Meinhof series, or maybe shortly afterwards; I don't remember exactly when I painted it, though I tried to work it out once before. But it's definitely a nice story that I painted as a counterbalance to the terrorist series.

The brittle and aggressive quality of these paintings is also apparent to me, though. The portrait of me lying down ... this deathly paleness ... this cut-offness ... this vulnerability. And the one with the averted face also has a strange, mysterious aura. The facelessness ... this eerie nothingness I'm looking at.

Yes, the averted head reminded me of Hitchcock back then. I'm sure this fact isn't relevant in terms of art history, but rather psychoanalysis. I was relieved, however, when no one else saw this connection.

The averted, turned-away face has something to do with parting and also with death. This act of not-showing plays on uncertainty and the unknown. The film uses similar devices to create a sense of foreboding.

Yes, sure, but in the film, Perkins turns the chair with the mother around so we get a frontal view of her as a decayed corpse, which is the paramount horror, but also the resolution of the mystery. I don't think that the *Betty* painting has anything to do with this theme.

The first abstract paintings, those garishly colourful works – about which my schoolmates commented 'What kind of a mess is that?' – caused a stir, precisely because they weren't messy, but came across as rather distanced, cold and artificial. You yourself thought they were insane at the time. What sort of insanity was it? Did it have something to do with breaking down barriers? How do you view these paintings today?

As more of a product of their time than I thought back then. Minimalism and Conceptual art had lost their appeal. There was a renewed desire to rebel, to provoke, to challenge values. It's like a climate change that affects the whole world, like a 'Rebel Without A Cause' or whatever the film title is. This upheaval, as it can be described in retrospect, happened everywhere at the same time, but was given different tags: depending on their stance they were called *Die Junge Wilde*, or Constructivists, or Post-modernists, or whatever people called them. In any event, it was a time of upheaval for me, too, a kind of craze if you like, which carries you and lets you be very productive. But one thing that went along with this process was scepticism – the constant awareness of certain traditions or skills I had attained, and these things accompanied me like watchmen. And that's why people reacted by assessing my works as 'cold' or 'distanced'. In fact, however, I only became an intellectual painter because I was always the opposite of fashionable, and fashion was all that silly, funny, spontaneous, ugly stuff that could be produced on the fly.

Which current movements within art influence you nowadays?

There aren't any such movements or fashions at the moment, or they are emerging mainly within the electronic media so I'm hardly aware of them. Traditional art is practically dead, by which I mean this huge, complicated entity – with all its wonderful aesthetic and moral aspirations – that used to be called art. That's been sidelined completely, and doesn't have any sort of public relevance any more; on the contrary, it's increasingly denigrated.

That sounds very old-fashioned. How do you see your role in this? As a critic of the times, or as a painter upholding traditional and classic values?

I am the exception that is tolerated; perhaps not even that. But I wasn't referring to myself just now, but rather the zeitgeist, the role of art in the public sphere.

In your last interview with Robert Storr, you relate the term 'classic' to order, orientation, stringency and precision. In the same context, you evoked the spectre of slovenliness as an antipole to these values. Do you equate bad, slovenly behaviour with loss of orientation, form and content? Or what did you mean?

All that is true, but in the interview I was referring to [John] Cage's method of coincidence. Even if he left everything to chance, which is an impossibility, and even though he talked about this in an extremely seductive way, Cage still applied so much attention to the realization of a work that even the most banal sequence ended up being a highly artificial product. I was influenced by this, of course – by the knowledge that coincidence can only become something beautiful and useful when we put our stamp on it.

So coincidence needs to be re-integrated into a tidy system, one that structures it in a strictly conservative order. Is this order – a tidiness also apparent in your studio, and all your dealings – a necessity? Does it convey a sense of security and give you orientation? Does it give you the grip you need to attain greater freedom, or can it also be an obstacle?

It gives me confidence and saves me time, so it's something quite functional, and very useful. And sometimes it is also a bit of a trick, such as when I can't be bothered to do the actual nitty-gritty work. And there's the obsessive tidiness, but that's not so much of a problem for me.

You've always been very fond of German classics, like those by Goethe or Thomas Mann. Did you study them in your youth as well? Were they role models?

Yes, always – Goethe particularly, and Nietzsche and Beethoven. It was my mother who put me onto them.

And which painters were your role models?

Oh, that always kept changing: there are so many that I couldn't even list them all. But I could name a few all-time favourites that I liked even better as I got older. Artists like Raphael, Velázquez, Vermeer or Manet. But the day-to-day role models weren't such gods, but rather quite normal painters.

In 1970 you said that priests and philosophers had died out and that we didn't need them any more, because art could do the job for them. Back then, you saw art as a very superior discipline, as 'the highest manifestation of hope'. What's your view now? What, to your mind, does art have to do with religion or philosophy today? What can it convey differently or better, and what can't it explain?

If you subtract the youthful polemic, I can say that nothing much has changed in my view of art. And occasionally Schopenhauer, Nietzsche and other clever people strengthen me in my belief that art is the only thing that keeps us going at all and that gives, if not meaning, then at least a little hope to existence.

So what did you mean when you said once that painting is idiocy?

Another one of those clever slogans, but when it comes down to it everything becomes idiotic when one isn't convinced of it – if one doesn't believe in it.

What does faith mean for you? What do you believe in?

In a lot of things. For one thing, belief is a normal part of everyday life, something we use all the time in everything we do: 'I believe that I will catch the train, that the meal will be good, that I will accomplish this and that, and etc.', and we apply belief in much the same, natural way when it comes to the big things, like ideologies, convictions, religions and so forth. There's no way around it; we can only know about this and be conscious of it, so we don't get too blind in our beliefs. Of course, all this happens quite naturally and inevitably. One can see this by looking at people in wretched conditions – in prison camps, hospitals and old people's homes, where their suffering is meaningless and they have no hope: in other words, where they don't have the freedom to decide whether to continue like that or not.

You describe faith as a natural process, as a hardwired motivation, as the only apparent means of dealing with reality and, in a way, making it more bearable. Our subjective and, more or less, voluntary beliefs enable us to grasp things about reality and existence that we can't know via our objective faculties. But belief, in this sense, is also the product of the will to live, of a subconscious survival instinct, that we cannot control ourselves. This motivating force, this faith, seems to rule us in the same way that an animal is the prisoner of its inner impulses. That's why Schopenhauer said, rather sarcastically, that death is really preferable to life, because the will to live, our principal drive, is not in essence a conscious thing, and, hence, not bound by reason. But if belief is merely seen as the product of a will to live, as an instinctual fear of death, how do you explain religious belief – which is, per se, linked to the concept of personal sacrifice, as in Christian martyrdom, on the one hand, and, on the other hand, the fanatical suicide bombers, who also see themselves as martyrs while they are blowing themselves up and bringing death to others?

Distress forces us to create the illusions we need to survive, and various beliefs and religious meanings are available to make our existence bearable and invent a make-believe world. That can be anything – everything is possible, from the cheapest, tackiest superstition to the most complex belief systems.

So what meaning does the little golden multiple cross have for you in this context?

The golden cross isn't anything very specific, and it's meant to be a bit polemical. For one thing, of course, it's a symbolic gesture expressing the highest respect for our Christian culture, which stretches back two thousand years. That's my home, those are my roots, it's a tradition I have the highest regard for and which is far more complex than its critics could ever fathom. The cross coincided with the banning of crucifixes in schools, which provoked a desire on my part to protest against the ruling. So I was happy that I had made it.

In one of your notes you described nature as being inhumane, and said that its stupidity was bottomless. That's very close to the ideas of Rosset, who talks about the idiocy of what is real. Rosset describes reality, in its inevitable idiocy and gruesome presence, as an assault on life and on reason. Our desire to make reality meaningful is therefore destined to fail. All humans can do is helplessly lament their pathetic existence and try and keep reality at arm's length.

Yes, but the fact that we have this urge, that we try to see the positive, is what makes us alive – the fact that we don't just grin and bear it, but try to make it comprehensible. That's what makes it all a little easier, even when the truth is unpleasant.

Yes, the urge to acquire knowledge is incredibly powerful, and we want to dig deeper and deeper, even if we come up against boundaries that, ultimately, are there to protect us. Maybe we don't actually want to go all the way. How do you deal with nature as a painter, with the nature you described as stupid and inhumane?

Pictures of landscapes convey only beauty, and that's basically all I want to show, and capture, if possible. We don't have much choice in the matter. For example, the only reason we think a landscape is beautiful is that collective experience tells us so and prompts us to like it or reject it. That is, if I look out of the window now and the sun is shining, I'm automatically happy. Our photo albums are proof of this, because we are constantly trying to capture the sun, because the sun represents the opposite of misery, drudgery and death.

And so, at the end of this conversation, we return to the topic of death. The inevitability of death is something we have difficulty accepting, and we cannot grasp this fact by means of reason.

Yes, but there is another comfort, for in a way the assumption that we must die is based on an error. The error lies in the idea that I, the person I am here and now, must die at some point. The reason this is wrong is that the person who will die one day will be someone completely different and not the me who is sitting here now. That's true the other way round, too: the person I was, say, two years ago, has long since died. Of course, the problem with this model is that one can't think in terms of rigid timeframes. That's the problem: how to comprehend the ever-growing past, dealing with someone who, in a way, no longer exists, but who, of course, is very similar to me. I find all that far too puzzling.

That's a nice thought, that reason is not capable of seeing you as simultaneously non-existent. With that, you're also broaching the subject of schizophrenia – the idea that the individual can see himself as another by being a completely different person in the past than he is now, and will be someone else again in the future. In that way, the thought that one will die becomes practically impossible – impossible as a thought concerning the person that I see myself as now. In other words, as long as I'm not actually dying at this moment, my death is a long way off and has nothing to do with me. On the other hand, my very consciousness, my self-appraisal – which shows me as I am, which remembers how I was – is itself split off from my being. Reason gets marred by the paradox of self-reflection, which is a product of the discrepancy between real feelings, thoughts about myself, memories and the knowledge of being finite. As a sensitive, vulnerable being, I have to respect my subjective self: that is, I have to hide my imperfection and mortality from the other being, and from myself.

But you can't wholly succeed in this, because the facts do weigh on you, the fact that you will die, and the spectre of the past, because these things do become the present. The inevitability of future death becomes current fear and remembering what is no more can also cause pain in the present.

Thanks for the conversation. Maybe we'll do another interview some time.

About Blinky Palermo, 2003

I don't remember when I first met Palermo... At the Academy! At the time, I was friends with Lueg and Polke. At the Academy, they always held this semester walk-around in February, and that's when I saw them hanging there, those little paint-on-paper works Palermo made – tiny little pictures, paint-on-paper, and everyone agreed, 'Yes, he's good!' And that's how we met. He was with Goller. Yes, I thought that was interesting, how someone could do something that was so tranquil. I don't know how we came to be friends. I think Polke got to know him first. He was in this clique with Imi Knoebel – you know that lot? Chris Kohlhöfer was one of them. I don't remember that much, it's such a long time ago – more than thirty years! In the end, he took my studio in Harkortstrasse because I moved into another one, and at the time we still visited each other, but then he kind of drifted off into the drugs scene, while I was always more rooted. That's why we lost touch. And they were all heavy drinkers. The time I spent with Kohlhöfer, right in the beginning ... it was just amazing, and when I came to his studio I liked his stuff. He had this really decrepit little studio, and in the middle of this mess was a picture made of pure fabric, clean and clear, as if it were surrounded by a halo! It was a beautiful sight! It impressed me. And we had this sense for what's good and what's bad: that was something marvellous!

There was this immediate understanding when we saw something – a painting – and said, 'That has something!' That was good, that was really good about us. Back then was also the period when art wasn't relevant enough. Painting, above all else, was completely irrelevant to society. Yes, it was horrible, and we sometimes felt as if we were reactionaries.

My wife, Ema, sewed the fabric pictures for him. That's how we got to own a Palermo. It was nice and had a kind of charm! We'd known each other for about eight years. He visited us a lot, frequently accompanied by his girlfriend, a strawberry blonde called Kristin. She brought a child along, a boy, who was living with them. I always thought it was rather strange. The boy was seven years old, maybe. Then the three of them moved to Mönchengladbach. First they lived on this road, an extension of Corneliusstrasse, in Düsseldorf. We were there sometimes. I was more the solid, bourgeois type. We all drank when I joined them occasionally, in the old part of Düsseldorf. Palermo was a heavy drinker, and it was painful to watch – yes, but there's nothing one could do. When I tried to talk to him about it, he always played it down, saying, 'Yeah, yeah, I'll give up soon.' I have a different attitude today. If I'd had the authority, I might have been able to tell him something, something psychoanalytical perhaps. In those days everyone laughed about that kind of thing – about therapy. There was no such thing as being health-conscious. Freud already existed, but not for us – that's the price one pays. It was a period full of illusions.

Beuys liked him, he loved Beuys, and Beuys had a certain hold over him. That wasn't the way it was with us. I don't like that ... when people become dependent, like he did, in a different way, with Friedrich, the gallery owner. And Dahlem – he also had a certain power over Palermo. We almost had a fight once, Friedrich and me. We stood facing each other with clenched fists, ready to fight over Palermo, shouting, 'You're coming with me!', 'No, you're staying!' – words to that effect. He gave him money and was like a father figure. Palermo was fatherless; he was an orphan. Living with Kristin's child seemed weird to me – I didn't know about such things, since I didn't have a child back then. I didn't even know that she had left... Did Kristin leave? After that he was in Sri Lanka with Babett, where he died, – suffocated – over and out.

He had taken over my old studio. There were rumours about who collected all his works after his death – cleared everything out – I haven't got a clue as to how and what. It's a touchy subject.

I was at the funeral, the burial. It was movie-like in an odd sort of way. We were there, Rückriem and me, and Marlies Grüterich, an art critic from Cologne, and I don't remember who else. A whole table full of people. For some reason, I can only remember those people, but I'm sure there were quite a few more – definitely. Then we walked in the direction where the grave was, and the Friedrich crowd joined from the side. Friedrich and Thordis went to the grave and immediately disappeared again. It was so odd that they didn't come to the funeral meal. After the burial we all toasted Blinky. It was a big table. Who paid for it all? Not his trusty gallery owner! Konerding was there, too. He's dead now. It was in Münster.

I was at the Friedrich country residence once, in Kirchberg. Holger [Heiner Friedrich's brother] was there as well. Blinky didn't come along that time, but there was that terrible Dahlem guy. My memories aren't pleasant, but I really couldn't say how my relationship with Friedrich ended. I had a contract with him once,[1] as an artist, but then I dropped him.

I advised Palermo to drop Friedrich as well. They already had a special kind of relationship. Heiner was an interesting guy, someone obsessed with power.

There was this party at Six's, with Bridget Polk – the fat lady from the Warhol factory.[2] And then the three of us got undressed and jumped about naked. We just did our little performance and got dressed again. That was for the benefit of the others, so they had something to shriek about. We didn't do anything; we were just naked. Bridget always made 'tit prints' of her breasts.

I'd like to tell more – I have such pleasant memories of how we sat there, my wife Ema doing her sewing and us drinking coffee; it was so pleasant and relaxed. And Blinky with his unwashed hands, always holding a cigarette, his yellow hands. He was so charming, so nice. I was always amazed when we were in a bar, how he'd look at the women with this devoted gaze and then manage to take one home with him. I found that pretty impressive. Maybe I was a little jealous, as well, that someone who had absolutely nothing, no money and always got drunk, could manage that sort of thing. But it was his home – this bar and the atmosphere there. That was also the period when Kristin was working behind the bar and he lavished his attentions on her.

Oh yes, I was in New York with him – that was nice. I'm not sure any more when that was. 1970, maybe. That was the first trip to New York for both of us. We'd booked a fortnight with a group – cheap flight, cheap hotel – and we went home after ten days because we were so exhausted from walking, walking, walking. We got fed up and felt like we were Europeans for the first time, and we actually felt a bit proud. It was a nice feeling to be aware of it – to realize that we were Europeans, were different, more complicated – and they're so 'straight' and always have to completely simplify matters, and we don't. He always returned to the hotel late, when I was already sleeping. He was so interested in jazz. He went to these bars where they played jazz, as you could in those days.

During one of these periods when we spent a lot of time together and he occasionally worked in my studio, that's when we made our joint paintings. I don't remember exactly, but the first time there were these two boards,[3] and

I started painting one of them grey, and I said to Palermo: 'Join in. You do one, too.' It was quite good. We both took this grey paint and started spreading it around the canvas with our fingers. The boards were two times one metre, and together they measured two metres square. Later they were exhibited, and then they broke. That's how it started! After that it just so happened that we'd occasionally do something together. One such occasion was when those two Polaroid pictures were lying on the table. I'd taken them of a light bulb, and I said: 'I'm not sure I should paint them, they're too abstract.' And he answered: 'Oh well, I'll simply add another one, then it'll be even more abstract.' That's how the Krefeld brown-beige paintings[4] came to be. Those two were also on canvas.

Then another project came about. I really liked the wall paintings he did.[5] He had simply painted a room in the classic colour ochre yellow, with a neat frame left unpainted – about a hand's width – top, bottom, left, right – colour fields. It was classical in the modern age back then [*laughs*] – it had this wonderful, slight whiff of tradition. I liked it very much, and then I said that what it needs are sculptures[6] in a room like that. Yeah – do it! We made those ourselves. I made a plaster of Paris mask of his face, he helped me with mine, and I modelled the rest to fit – the head, the hair, the ears, the back of the head.

These two heads are permanently exhibited in Munich.[7] Of course, the walls aren't there, but the Munich people painted the walls yellow, as a tribute to Palermo. It's the typical Munich ochre colour. It's been done 'like the original'. There isn't a sign saying: 'This is a work of art by Palermo.' The only things on display were my two sculptures. They were only united with the Palermo walls for one exhibition. It wasn't a condition that the sculptures had to be shown with the Palermo walls. Back then, after the exhibition, I took the sculptures back home with me. And later still I had them cast in bronze. All in all, there are three pairs. One pair made of plaster of Paris, two made of bronze. I never learned how to do that. There are many specialists who make bronze casts. I did it in plaster of Paris back then. There is some fun to be had from making models. I never took lessons in sculpting.

Statement for 100 *Artists See God*, 2004

A monochrome grey painting, oil on canvas, in any common size, is simply the only possible representation/image of God. That is obviously very simple, too simple; of course when I made this grey painting I neither intended to express a conception of God nor would I be able to make such a painting.

Conversation with Christiane Hoffmans, 2004

You haven't given up the idea of giving some of your paintings to the city of Dresden, have you?

No, on the contrary, I'm very much interested in making that happen. But they were too quick to tell the press about what we had in mind, because if I have an idea for a painting, I can't just go along and say, 'Here I am, I've painted this lovely picture.' Fortunately the fuss surrounding this has died down again.

And what's the next step?

That doesn't just depend on me. There's a collector, who wishes to remain anonymous, who wants to loan a few Richter paintings to Dresden. I'll be meeting him again to discuss which paintings he'll give them, and for how long. The thing is that it doesn't make as much sense for me to furnish the museum with paintings on my own. I know that this collector owns quite a few Richter paintings, and if he were to give them about ten, and I also gave them ten, that would be ideal. And then one might think about approaching this or that collector of my paintings, and they could also contribute something.

Your relationship to your native city of Dresden is still very strong, even after an absence of more than forty years.

I have a special feeling for Dresden because I was born there and because I rediscovered it after the Wall fell, after all those decades. I wouldn't have thought that such a feeling of belonging was possible. It's an unusual collection of buildings one finds there – the small city centre, the architectural chunks that stand out in the cityscape, strangely awkward, unsymmetrical. I would like my paintings to have a home there, a few from each creative period so that people will know: that's where one can see the Richter paintings.

Apart from personal reasons, does your decision also have a political dimension?

I hadn't considered that, but that's automatically a part of it. I'm always troubled, and suffer along with them, when things are looking rough.

And have you also devised similar plans for Cologne, your second home?

Cologne is a wonderful city – the place where I live.

An interesting differentiation.

Perhaps my feelings for Dresden will subside again. But the people of Dresden are in any case more in need than the people of Cologne. Perhaps there could be some kind of push for the Galerie Neuer Meister in Dresden. Then they could get up the courage to do something again.

And your archive?

I can say the least of all about that, because I'm not well versed in these things. I don't really know what exactly an archive is.[1] I have an office here that works, that's orderly and contains everything, and at the moment I don't see any reason to give it to them. But then I saw that there are a few things in Munich, and in Hanover, and in Nuremberg, and now I'm beginning to fathom what an archive is, but it's really something for widows.

When do you think a decision will be made?

By the end of May, I should think. The first step would be to take a few paintings to Dresden and hang them there to see how they look in those spaces. It would be really great if it works out with those paintings.[2] I would be very happy to see those paintings in Dresden.

Interview with Jan Thorn-Prikker on the work *WAR CUT*, 2004

Can you say something about the abstract painting that served as a starting point for WAR CUT?

That picture was done long ago, in the 1980s, so the Iraq War wasn't involved. I was slightly surprised when the Musée d'Art Moderne de la Ville de Paris bought the picture; there are more attractive works, not so rough and harsh. But about two years ago I took close-ups of the work in the museum without knowing what I might use them for. When the war started, I heard all these conflicting opinions. I thought newspaper reports were salutary – impotent and ineffectual as everything else in the face of catastrophe – but their plain presentation of the facts consoled me.

Do you include all the articles published about the Iraq War in the paper on the first two days, or did you leave out some?

I left out some. My layout determined what I included or didn't include. It was not something I had specifically in mind before I started. I wanted to vary the layout, to move from empty to full and back again. I had a general plan, a sense of balance. But the specific arrangement evolved as I worked on it, until at some stage there were 324 pages. I read most of the texts only after I placed them with the pictures. I read them as literature, which was very pleasing. I was not looking for straightforward narrative, which is maybe also why I chose that particular abstract painting. Some of my other abstract pictures are less ambiguous. Their atmosphere is either very agitated or tranquil or almost storylike in their narrative flow, so that they seem nearly representational or surreal. This picture had none of that. It was close to being uncommunicative, which I don't mean negatively.

The Iraq War was a television war. Why did you reject using those images?

WAR CUT only very indirectly involves reality. Even the facts in the newspaper articles somehow become unrealistic in this context. I removed the headlines and bylines from the articles. I respect the writers, but I like to think that maybe by removing the headlines I contributed toward having these texts read as literature. It would be like taking a newspaper photo and putting it in a museum as an oil painting, which is I suppose what I did with Baader-Meinhof.

Then would you say that WAR CUT *was also a kind of plea: 'Look closely at these texts; they talk about your world'?*

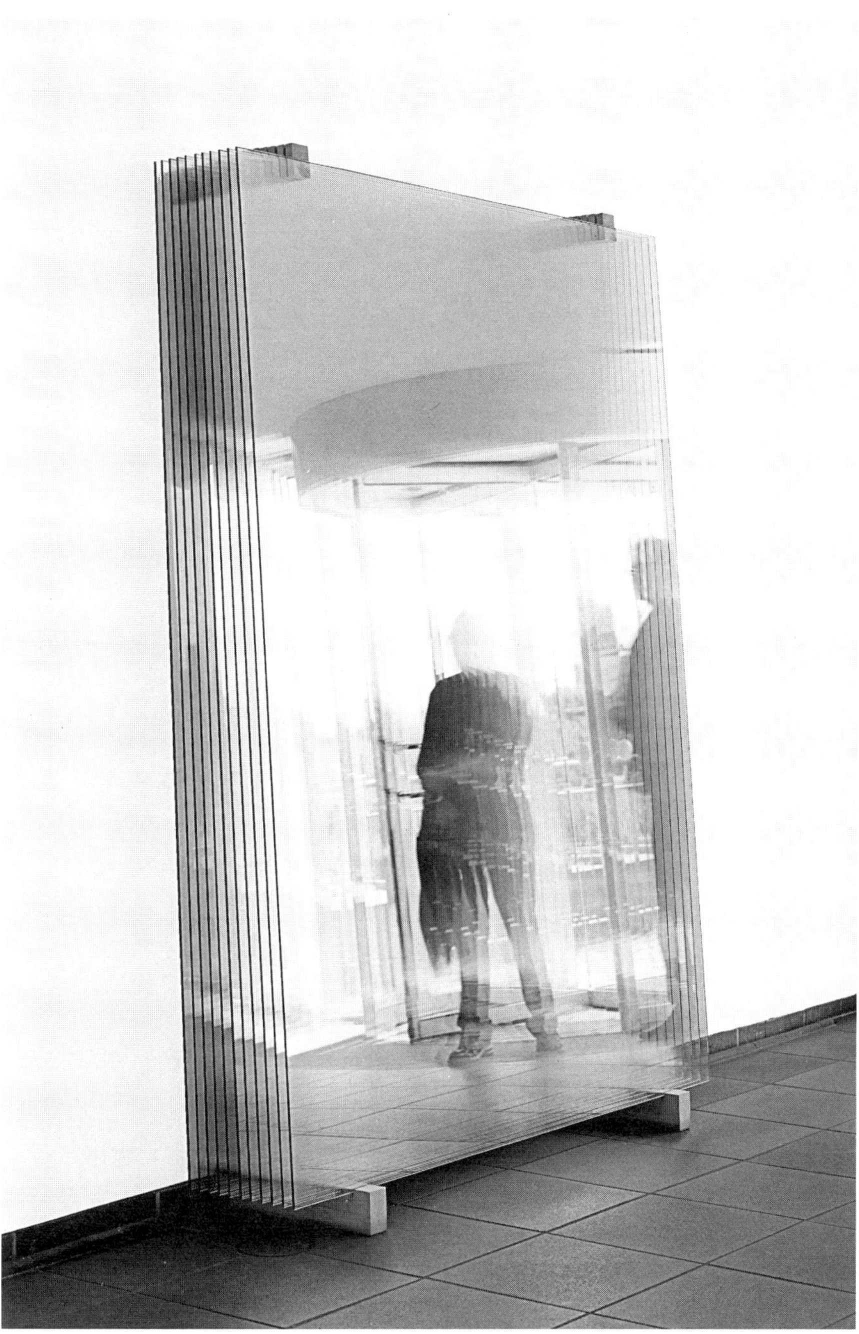

11 Panes, 2003

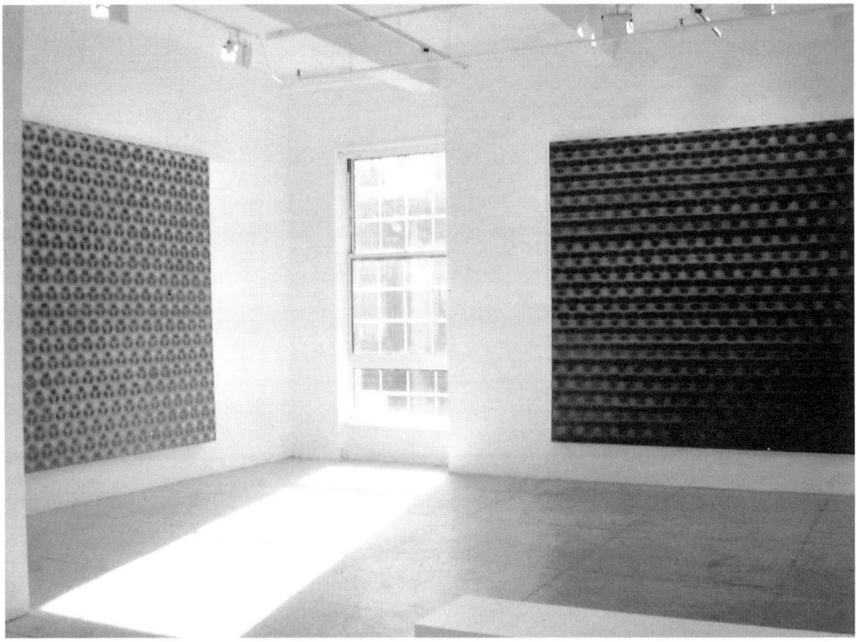

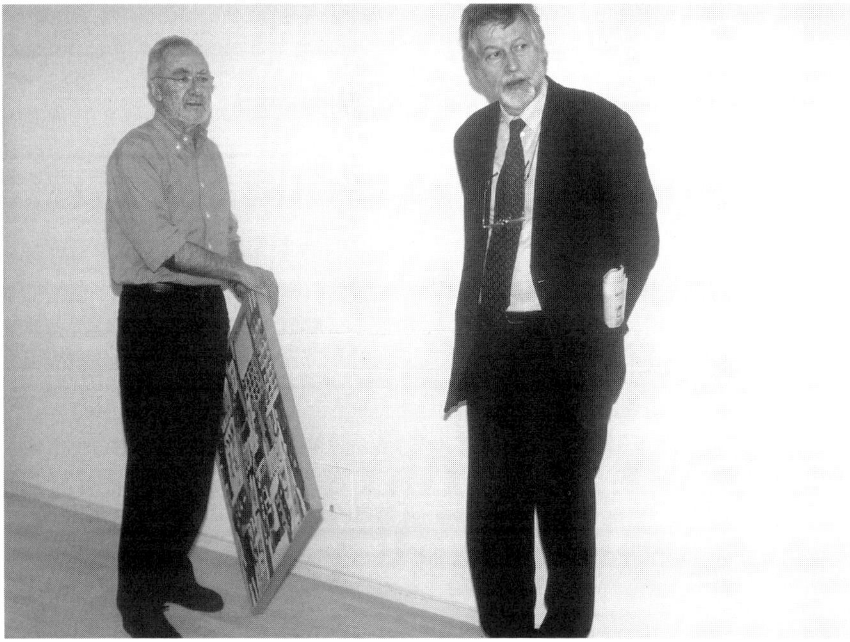

Marian Goodman Gallery, New York, 2005
Gerhard Richter with Armin Zweite, 2005

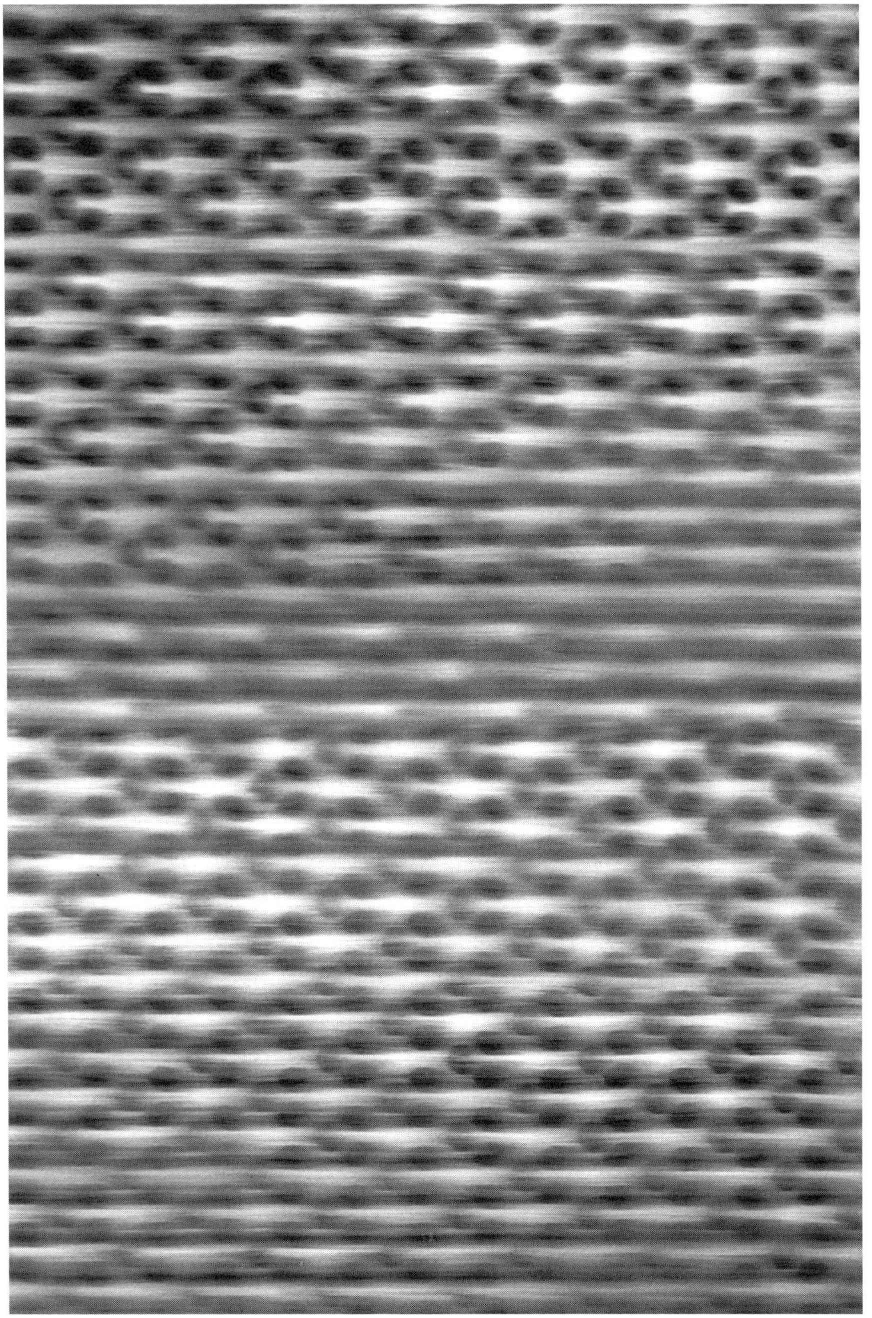

Silikat, 2003 (detail)

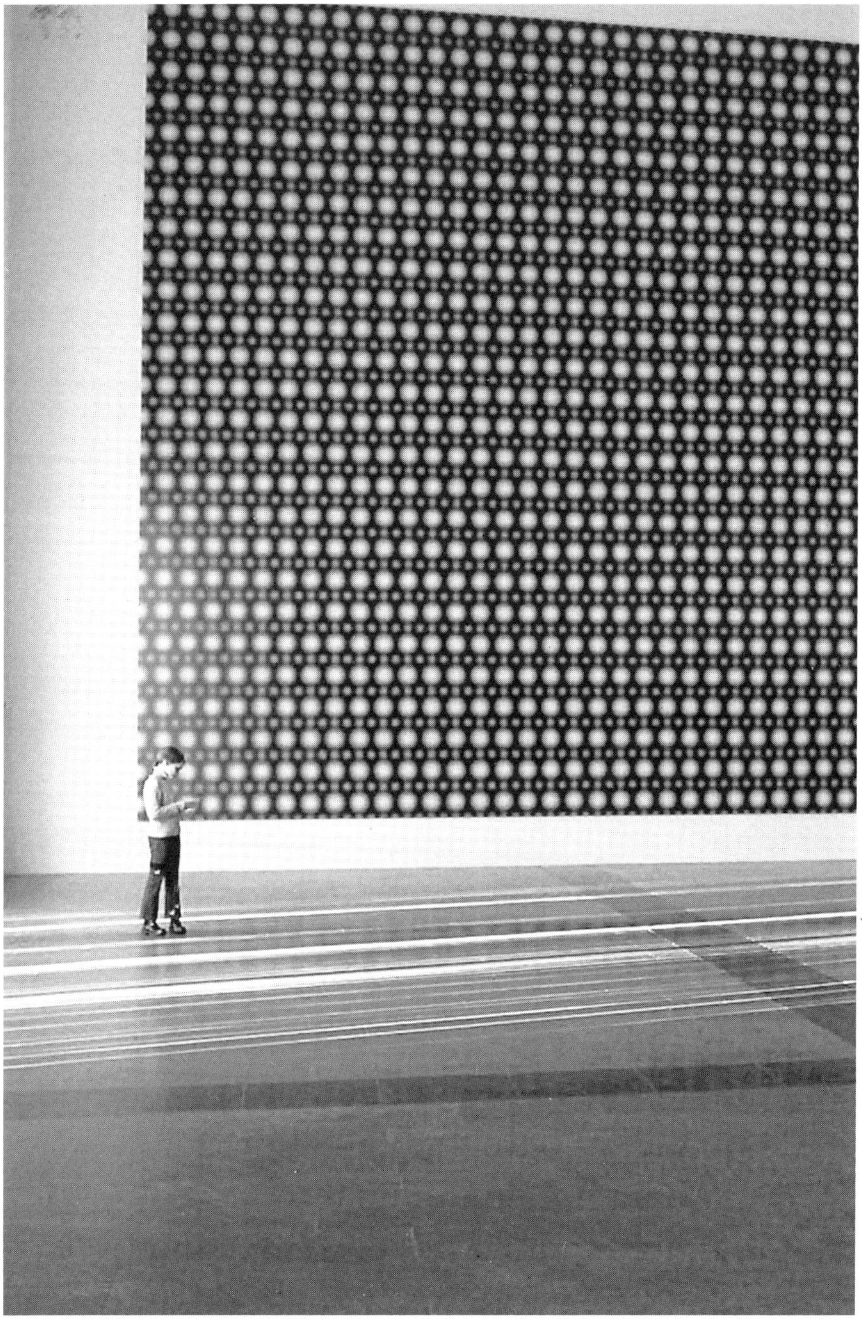

Strontium, K20 Düsseldorf, 2004

Yes, but also I mean that the texts now survive longer than the single day when they were in the newspaper.

Why did you use the Frankfurter Allgemeine Zeitung?

Because I have been reading it for forty years.

Why March 20 and 21, 2003?

The outbreak of war is the date that people remember. Just like the start of Hitler's war on September 1, 1939. On the other hand, it seems to me that March 20 and 21 didn't have an impact comparable to, say, September 11, 2001.

Did you order the texts chronologically?

No, only approximately. After all, I had this strict framework where every page had fixed arrangements and magnitudes. But that still left sufficient latitude for preferences and specific confrontations with images, and for a certain breadth of themes. The real gift for me was the fact that chance could bring about wonderful combinations.

Could you say something about the unusual form of WAR CUT?

My approach to form is very simple. Whatever is real is so unlimited and unshaped that we have to summarize it. The more dramatic events are, the more important the form. That is why people marry in a church and why we need a priest for a funeral.

With WAR CUT, *did you give these dramatic events form by putting them between book covers?*

The book covers and the way the material between them is treated. And the way texts and images influence one another, change their meanings, with the images changing incomparably more because they are much more open and ambiguous.

But the images and texts are placed alongside one another almost blindly. You have great trust in the chance occurrences involved in such form.

Form is all we have to help us cope with fundamentally chaotic facts and assaults. Formulating something is a great start. I trust form, trust my feeling or capacity to find the right form for something. Even if that is only by being well organized. That, too, is form.

As for chance, consider John Cage. His musical compositions were never a total appropriation of a chance acoustic event. He devised an ingenious system to build structures from dumb abundance. And he devoted even more skill to giving form to this succession of sounds. That is the absolute opposite of chance, nature and rubbish.

When people hear you say that form is the most important aspect, that could easily be understood as meaning that you are unconcerned about the politics or the human cost of the war.

No, no. In this case the facts are so overpowering, the contents so crucial, the form is also all the more significant. We need it simply to be able to deal with the subject matter.

How did you decide how to arrange the texts with the photographs?

My method was to attach a number of texts to a number of images without having to think about whether something would be better positioned to the left or the right, above or below; or whether a specific image fit together with a particular text or not. Most did fit together, and only a few inappropriate or banal conjunctions had to be changed. The images are always arranged in accordance with – what shall I call it: aesthetic criteria? I placed these images so that a connection develops in terms of colours, structures and other characteristics. It all starts somewhat casually. It was like putting together a story or a film, which begins somehow or other, has tranquil and wild, nasty and fantastic passages, and then once again fades away, ending in white. A dream.

Once you put a text alongside an image, both lose their independence. It immediately establishes a relationship.

Some images match the cruelty and the madness described in the texts shockingly well. And others can even serve as illustrations when the texts speak of deserts and other landscapes.

WAR CUT *seems to show aerial photographs. Oil fields on fire. Pools of oil, blood – things that in reality aren't depicted. Sometimes ghosts, death heads, hideous faces emerge from the images.*

I have nothing against that.

Your book is contradictory. As an artist's work it says, 'That's how things are. That's how the world looks.' However the same book simultaneously says, 'That's unacceptable. Things can't continue like this.' The book both raises a protest against the world as it is and confirms that state of affairs.

Yes, that is also why I wanted to try and see this war from a completely different angle. Admonitions, protests and such are not my thing.

To what extent is WAR CUT *an attempt at coming to grips with a war? I've met a few people who reacted to* WAR CUT *with something close to annoyance. They say that you take everything and simply throw it together – that this is merely a simulation of sympathetic interest. They say that you could just as easily have made a collage with anything.*

Of course that isn't the case. Anyway, it's not possible. How could one be in this world without feeling dismayed by it? Even if one paints flowers and gingerbread.

Do you think your book involves a sense of mourning?

Yes, and rage, too. Mainly rage because war is upsetting, because it demonstrates our impotence, because obviously we can't prevent it, because we cannot assess it anywhere near adequately. That becomes apparent in the many different judgments, prejudices and simplifications we hear and read. That is also why I absolutely avoided expressing an opinion, which is completely useless here and obstructs the attempt to come somewhat closer to the truth. In addition, my opinion is certainly just as wrong as that of my friends who almost all greatly simplify matters, condemning the war and grumbling about Bush in a way that is close to kitsch. That is not my way.

I certainly don't think the war is unnecessary. Otherwise it wouldn't happen. And we are certainly far from being able to do without wars. But I did not have so much cause to mourn. September 11 horrified me to a greater extent.

Does the fact that you belong to the generation that experienced World War II influence your feelings about war?

Yes. Those experiences are present, like an underlying theme.

But you keep the wound fresh. Whether you mean it that way or not, that is a way of expressing sympathy.

Yes, it is. But the greatest pleasure was to complete this book. Then it was fun to have produced something beautiful. I found my way back to painting. That was a new beginning after a long intermission. After all, I hadn't painted for two years. It was good to produce something like this. Something storylike, something fantastic. The absolute opposite of war.

Interview with Jan Thorn-Prikker, 2004

What was the starting point for your latest endeavours in Dresden?

The flood,[1] of course. It mobilized something that had lain dormant. When Helge Achenbach asked me two years ago if I would participate in the charity auction for Dresden, I didn't hesitate to suggest they take my largest painting, a painting with a certain knock-on effect that would also fetch a fair sum.

The auction was very successful, and your painting, Fels [Rock] *(1989), was sold for 2.6 million Euros.*

I was very happy about that. And then the person who bought it gave it to the city as a permanent loan, which was more than I ever could have hoped for.

So, once again, your preoccupation with Dresden was triggered by a destructive force, this time the force of nature. It's a coincidence, but perhaps it's not that irrelevant. Distress commands attention.

... and touches the heart [*laughs*]. I had been back to Dresden before, but it didn't preoccupy me. It was nice to see everything again, this strange baroque ensemble: Brühl's Terrace, the Hofkirche, the Zwinger, the palace, the opera, the Gemäldegalerie. I realized that all that had a lot to do with my development; that it represented a unique cultural experience which influenced me greatly, more than I had ever realized.

I had been to Dresden once prior to that, in 1986, to take part in the *Positionen* [Positions] exhibition,[2] which was part of the cultural exchange programme – at that time between East Germany and West Germany.

I was there two or three times after that. Once I went with my daughter, to show her everything, and ten years ago I visited with my wife. And then, in the year 2000, I went again, with Benjamin Buchloh,[3] to see the exhibition *Zeichnungen und Aquarelle* [Drawings and Watercolours].[4]

What's the connection between the charity event and the installation of a Gerhard Richter room in the Albertinum museum? Did the museum become aware of you due to the event and realize then that you were originally from Dresden?

I think so. The contacts at museum level only came about after the flood – not until February of this year, in fact, when Martin Roth said to me, 'You must come to Dresden: we want to have a Richter room in the Albertinum – and we also want a Richter archive.' So I drove there immediately, or rather I flew.

What exactly are the plans for Dresden?

They involve three rooms that were reserved up until now for contemporary art.

The collection consisted of donated works of art, acquired works and works on loan – and was thus a little haphazard. The roughly 350 other works will be taken down today [21 June 2004]. The space will then be renovated room by room before the pictures are re-hung, albeit in a different order. We've discussed this. Ulrich Bischoff, the director, and his staff will present a different order based on certain categories. Perhaps the walk-round on the second floor will then pass through six exhibitions, starting with Caspar David Friedrich and ending with Richter.

About forty of my paintings will be on display, eleven from private collections and the rest from my own. It will be an overview of the last forty years. It'll be quite nice.

What's behind their interest in having your archive?

That's also a nice idea the people from Dresden had, and I hope it will turn out to be do-able. The archive would consist of, and make accessible, everything that has been printed – all the catalogues, books, posters, the essays, the press reports, the catalogue raisonné with comprehensive information about every painting, and so on and so forth. There's a lot of stuff that needs to be stored, organized and made accessible. So it would be the primary source for anyone who's interested. And, of course, it would be far more efficient than my studio office could ever be.

For some time now, you've been focusing on the beginnings of your own biography in Dresden.

I didn't plan it that way. When I came to Dresden last April with my wife and the children, I was amazed that I could remember street names I thought I had long since forgotten, and then I visited places where I used to go as a child, as a teenager and as a student.

You were born in Dresden but spent your first years in Zittau?

Near Zittau, in Reichenau. We moved there when I was three years old because my father was offered an apprenticeship. I don't remember why that was, just as I don't remember the reasons for our second move to Waltersdorf, which is also near Zittau. That was in 1942 or thereabouts.

In the decisive and formative years of your childhood, between 1939 and 1946, your father was away at war, and when he returned from American imprisonment he was really always absent for you.

... and after that I – or we, my family – were so alienated from him that we didn't know how to deal with each other. This wasn't a unique case either.

You were ten years old when you came to Waltersdorf.

Yes, that's why my memory of it is much clearer, because that's where I had my crucial experiences. The end of the war, the change of system, the first post-war years. All those adventures and the beginnings of understanding, philosophical outlook, my professing to be an atheist, and so on.

You were living in Waltersdorf when Dresden was destroyed. Were you aware of what had happened?

That was a long way away, almost eighty kilometres as the crow flies. I remember that we were out on the street during the bombing raid because it was being reported on the radio, and people were saying, 'Can't you hear the thudding?' I think they were imagining it. But we certainly knew that something terrible was happening.

In 1945 you were thirteen years old. Can you remember what Dresden was like before the bombing?

Only very vaguely. It was only a few months ago that I suddenly remembered Grossenhainer Strasse, building number 18b, where I was born. Then there was Tieckstrasse, where my great-grandmother lived, not far from the original Circus Sarrasani building, where as a young lad I could see the elephant stalls through the cellar windows. My great-grandmother's sewing box, made of armadillo skin. A man falling from a ladder – something that, according to my parents, only I had seen. All these odd memories bubbling up to the surface...

Spending the war in a small village where there were no bombs, where no one was being driven away...

... was nerve-racking enough. The retreating German soldiers, the convoys, the low-flying Russian planes shooting at refugees, the trenches, the weapons lying around everywhere, artillery, broken-down cars. Then the invasion of the Russians, some of whom were also just poor devils like us – the ransacking, rapes, a huge camp where us kids sometimes got barley soup.

An exciting time?

Yes, I thought it was great. I envied the soldiers who were allowed to take part in the war. I was fascinated, like all kids, or all boys. I wandered through the trenches. Then the Russian planes came, the ones that had shot up the convoys. I thought it was all marvellous. I envied the soldiers sleeping in the barn. It took a soldier to bring me to my senses. You snotty little brat, you should get a right spanking. That gave me a fright. That gave me something to think about.

Did the grown-ups talk about the war with you?

Yes, they did. It was sad when my mother's brothers fell in battle. First one, then the other. I'll never forget how the women screamed. When the postman comes and brings the telegram: 'Fallen for the people and the fatherland' – I remember that very well, even the little details. First we thought it was the other brother who had died. Then we read it again and realized that it wasn't Fred at all, it was the handsome one, Rudi.[5] And the two women screamed again, and much louder.

How did you spend your time in Waltersdorf? Were you a member of an organization? Were you ever politically active?

Automatically, so to speak, with the change of system. At the age of fourteen, I immediately joined the Free German Youth and was active as a treasurer. Then I joined the Liberal Democrats, but also left them, all out of conviction. And then I was very active on the artistic side – I was a member of an amateur theatre group and took lessons in painting. Those first few years after the war, in the village, they were incredibly nice.

Suddenly there were libraries, housed in the expropriated properties. Cesare Lombroso's *Genius and Madness*, Hesse, Stefan Zweig, Feuchtwanger, all that standard middle-class literature. It was a wonderful, carefree time ... made it easy to forget the dark side of things.

Chaos as opportunity – as a chance to catch one's breath in between two eras?

Yes, certainly. It was, of course, a very haphazard period before I went to the Academy – a bit of school, a few jobs, half a year as a scene painter, half a year as a poster artist, finally a whole year as an industrial painter.

What does that mean?

I applied to the Academy when I was eighteen and was rejected, but the examiners suggested I go and find a job in a nationalized company. I found a position in a large clothing factory in Zittau, and after a year the company delegated me to study at the Dresdner Academy.

You were nineteen years old then. What state was the Dresdner Academy in directly after the war?

Some buildings, or parts of buildings, were still intact, especially in Güntzstrasse where I was first and where all the first-year students studied. What I remember vividly is that very often, practically every day, we would walk through rubble to get from one building to the next, from Güntzstrasse to Brühl's Terrace and back. The whole city was strewn with rubble.

You came from a vocational school, a place where one isn't normally trained to be an artist. Where did the impulse come from? Who was the person who triggered your interest in the arts?

My mother was very interested in art. But she had nothing to do with fine art. We had a few books on the subject. Pompeii and Dürer, Corinth and things like that. I liked to paint, sketched a lot, started to collect art prints, wrote poems – the usual development. And then you meet people who have the same interests, and then you end up at the Academy.

What were your first impressions of the Academy?

For a start, it was something really great to be admitted to the Academy at all, and even the wrecked building on Brühl's Terrace was very impressive. It was great being a part of all that, and the fact that the teachers were real artists. But, bit by bit, the magic wore off, and everyone developed their own strategies for coping with the increasingly strict regime. Having to get up at eight every morning was symptomatic of the other loathsome things, of subjects like social science, political economy and Russian. Aesthetics was also a horrible subject, because there was this guy who tried to prove to us which paintings were Socialist art and were therefore good.

Just to reiterate: we're talking about an academy during East Germany's formative years. That must have been an odd situation – a liberal climate to begin with, which then got more rigid year on year. Eventually they committed themselves dogmatically to the ideal of Socialist Realism.

That's how I experienced it. It became increasingly ideological. For example, we weren't able to borrow books that dealt with the period beyond the onset of Impressionism because that was when bourgeois decadence set in. Or formalism: that was the other term synonymous with evil. The only exceptions were artists who declared their commitment to Communism. Guttuso, Picasso, and a few others – they were allowed to produce formalistic paintings. And I tried to benefit from this exemption by learning from Picasso and Guttuso, and the paintings I made became increasingly bad and strange.

I can imagine that you were willing to adapt to their demands, but, at the same time, you were unable to paint the way they expected you to.

Yes, certainly, I was young. The result was neither fish nor fowl – a kind of decorative modernism. And when I went on to present these things in one of the annual Dresden exhibitions, my name was actually mentioned in an English radio programme.[6] That seemed to me like inappropriate fame – the wrong kind of attention – and I felt a bit embarrassed. At the same time, I didn't like the dissidents who had, or who developed, a kind of haughtiness.

You tried to live in harmony with the system?

Yes, that was really what I always aspired to, even though I thought differently. After all, we had this grand illusion of a 'third way'. That was the promising mixture of Capitalism and Socialism. I also remember that I was often thankful for negative news about the West – that is, reports that revealed how terrible the system was. That's the only way to exist in that kind of regime, otherwise one would have to be constantly ashamed that one is still living there. So this 'third way' was kind of an idealistic dream.

In 1959, two years after finishing your studies at the Academy, you visited documenta II.

In search of an acceptable form for representational art, congruent with a 'third way'. But it was the works by Pollock, Fontana and Fautrier that really made a lasting impression.

The main focus of documenta II *was on American painting. Back then, Werner Haftmann declared abstract art to be a worldwide language. So why did Jackson Pollock and Lucio Fontana impress you so much? Their works aren't exactly what you'd call representational.*

But radically different, ruthless – it was incredible that something like that should be displayed there.

Returning to Dresden [Jan-Thorn-Prikker shows Richter different photos of Dresden, before and after the bombing raids].

Here all the memories get mixed up – the real ones and the others, from pictures, from childhood photographs. It's easy to get confused occasionally.

The golden statue of Augustus on the horse in the Neustadt opposite the House of German–Soviet Friendship. On the right you get to Tieckstrasse, and over to the left is Grossenhainer Strasse, where I was born.

The Postplatz: that was important on June 17th. That was the centre of activity, and we rushed there while the painter Harald Metzkes stayed in the Academy and continued painting. There was a motorcyclist I shouted at to turn his clattering engine off, because one of the protesters was giving a speech, saying that we had nothing to lose but our chains. But the fact that Metzkes kept painting annoyed me, because I saw it as a symbol of unconcerned painting.

The Old Market Square, the Church of the Holy Cross. All intact. Probably Prager Strasse, seen from the main train station. Only vague memories, nothing concrete. When I went back, later, there was nothing left, only rubble and more rubble, just like in the picture.

That must be the street leading to Güntzstrasse. I remember the romantic Elias cemetery, wild and overgrown. The courtyard of the Academy. There, in that yard, I was first shown two books with photographs of the concentration camps and the horrors that had taken place there. I was in my early twenties. I'll never forget it. It was like a document, with reportage photos. Awful records. Perhaps it was even an American book. Because I remember wondering afterwards why East Germany hadn't made more of a fuss about it. It was almost like a secret book.

It was like irrefutable proof of something we had always half known.

Here the typical wallpapered walls with remains or traces of furnishings. The bits that were left, remnants of walls, fire walls extending over several storeys, like paintings.

For a long time East Germany was the country with the insurmountable border, a country whose citizens couldn't travel where they wanted. Were you able to travel abroad?

Yes and no. A total ban on travel wasn't imposed until the wall was built [1961]. Until then there was the big window: West Berlin. I managed to travel to West Germany practically every summer. I applied for permission, my professor signed the papers and I was allowed to go. Heinz Lohmar,[7] I liked him. I was in Paris once. I thought I'd bump into all these artist types, but I didn't see anyone.

Did you go to Italy?

No, not back then. But once I travelled via Warsaw to Moscow and Leningrad. The train arrived in Berlin and went straight on to West Berlin. I remained seated, gave my suitcase to left-luggage, went back to Dresden and said to my then-wife, 'Come on, we're getting out of here.'

So it was a spur of the moment decision?

No, it had been planned. The Moscow trip just provided the impetus to leave immediately. That was in 1961, shortly before the wall was built.

During that period, tens of thousands of people fled East Germany. So you shared the general view, prevalent at the time, that one couldn't live there?

Yes, exactly.

What bothered you most about East Germany? It's not as if you were suffering. You were a young painter, had commissions – you were at the beginning of a promising career.

Well, things weren't all that rosy, but I was doing relatively well. I already owned a motorbike, and later a car, a Trabant. The thing that was really unbearable was the hopelessness, the pressure to succumb – how shall I say? – to compromise, to fall in line. I had the feeling that society couldn't yield the things that were right for me, that I needed. There were colleagues who adapted better to the system or who lived in a state of resistance whilst doing their thing. But that wasn't for me. I prefer to be accepted [*laughs*].

Do you need the official recognition?

I'll put it like this: I never wanted to be a misunderstood artist, an outsider, a bogeyman. Never. Even fifty years ago I found the thought satisfying that, whenever culture blossomed, artists tended to be part of the establishment rather than freaks; that their status as highly qualified masters made them part of the elite. We still benefit from that today.

Did the youthful atheism you mentioned earlier have something to do with Nietzsche? Your family, after all, was staunchly Protestant.

My father, yes. But the public climate was very much anti-Christian. And, apart from Nietzsche and Schopenhauer and my mother's liberal ethics, there was also this book – I think the author's name was Selbmann, an economist, a Marxist, who wrote a kind of treatise on the world. About dialectical materialism. It impressed me a lot.

To me, dialectical materialism was an attempt to explain the world scientifically. There was always an answer to every question about why things are as they are. That satisfied my need for objectivity. As far as I was concerned, materialism was a philosophical branch of objectivity. Can you relate to that?

In my youth, I think I would have seen it exactly the same way. In confirmation classes it dawned on me that I simply couldn't believe in God. I was shocked, and afraid of course. I was fourteen at the time.

Later on you always emphasized the 'non-ideological', the desire not to be duped by an ideology, not to follow an ideology. That seems to be rooted in these early experiences. Faith is not for me, you are supposed to have said once.

That's beginning to change.

I think there's a fundamentally religious tenor in your work. There are the Vanitas motifs, for instance; the sublimity inherent in many motifs. Hanging here today, in your studio in Cologne, is a plan for a church window.[8] *And not least, there are the two crosses you made as objects. Basically they just represent the proportions of your own body, in height and width. The cross is you yourself, standing, with your arms spread out.*

I sympathize with the Catholic Church. I can't believe in God, but I think the Catholic Church is marvellous.

What do you find so impressive?

Our global Christian culture has formed us. I'm thankful for the great art, the music, the most wonderful architecture, for the literature and the philosophy, which happens to be thoroughly Catholic even when it preaches absolute atheism.

Everything you worship in art is derived from this value system. So is religion something you'll gladly grin and bear?

Well, no, it's a little more than that. When we had our two children christened here in the cathedral, my attitude towards the church had already radically changed, and I had slowly begun to realize what the church can offer, how much meaning it can convey, how much help, comfort and security.

But even that isn't, in essence, a religious justification for religion, but a practical and aesthetic one. You have high regard for the power of its rituals and the sense of security conveyed through its grand language of forms. The meaningful word, the space that shields us, the grand painting, the guiding vision, the sound of music. The faith in something that is greater than we are.

Everything we need.

Was literature important for you in Dresden?

Very much so. Above all, Thomas Mann. And when I took this passion with me to the West, I had to discover that it made me appear like a bit of a fool. He wasn't progressive or radical – he was bourgeois, and these were the important catchwords of the time.

Was it possible for you to continue with anything in the West, or did you have to start everything from scratch?

When I arrived, it was more like being at zero. It was also frightening, this sudden freedom, which was essentially nothing else but being abandoned. In my anguish, I went to study at the Academy in Düsseldorf, so I would have a home. Luckily I met a former fellow student from Dresden. He lived in Düsseldorf, explained to me that Düsseldorf was a centre of modern art, and let me stay at his place for the first few weeks. So I stayed and didn't go to Munich, which is where I had initially thought I needed to go.

So in 1961, aged twenty-nine, you became a student again – a 'late painter'?

And because I looked younger than my age and was a bit childish, people didn't notice so much. Polke was nine years younger than me. Konrad Fischer was seven years my junior. Palermo, eleven years. Everyone was younger than me. And my contemporaries, the Zero people,[9] seemed like the older ones to me.

What did you think of your teachers?

Back then all you had to do was find one professor who would allow you to take part in his drawing class and you were a bona fide student. The friendliest seemed to be Ferdinand Macketanz, and I stayed with him for about a semester, then I changed to K. O. Götz, who I found more interesting, and who also had the more interesting students – Konrad Fischer, for example.

When I was with Macketanz, I painted like I was obsessed, varying in style between Dubuffet, Giacometti, Tàpies, and many others. Kind of a crash-course in post-war painting... Later I burnt everything in the yard of the Academy. One thing I thought was great about K. O. Götz was that he would come into the studio and say, 'Don't let me disturb you.'

So your love for Picasso lasted precisely until you arrived in Düsseldorf, and then it was over. After that, you could paint as you wanted?

Well, it took at least a year until I even roughly knew what I wanted, what interested me, and what suited me best.

Did Düsseldorf give you lots of inspiration back then?

Oh yes, it was incredibly exciting, with all those exhibitions and events, all those artists. And then I was incredibly lucky to find the right friends at the Academy: Sigmar Polke, Konrad Fischer and Palermo. We experienced everything together, the first Happenings, the Fluxus events:[10] these things had an enormous effect on me.

But Fluxus was also a bit of an odd, slapdash kind of affair.

It didn't seem like that to me at the time, and if you ignore the hangers-on, there are quite a few that remained loyal to the concept – Nam June Paik, Beuys and Cage, of course.

Does John Cage belong to Fluxus? To me he was like the big star whom I regarded as a separate entity from Fluxus. He was 'the artist' and the others were 'the movement'.

I felt the same way. And, later on, I started to love his music, and it became something of an exemplary artistic symbol to me.

Regarding documenta II *in 1959, you mentioned that you were impressed by the work of Jackson Pollock and Lucio Fontana. Were there other important artistic influences later on? Someone who you could 'catch up with and overtake', to quote a phrase the Soviets used.*

The Pop artists were impressive, the whole movement, but particularly Warhol and Lichtenstein. Then came Minimal and Conceptual art, and that was similarly impressive, but a little more painful, because it was so current that it made Pop Art seem old. Luckily that's only part of the truth, and the enjoyment in painting remains the most important factor anyway.

[Thorn-Prikker and Richter look at a photograph of a mural painting in the Dresden Hygiene Museum.]

For my diploma.[11] 1956. Five by fifteen metres.

The whole history of art seems to be represented here: Botticelli's Venus*, Manet's* Breakfast on the Grass*, Matisse's* The Dance*.*

How could it be any other way? Art history was the big compulsory subject, and it more or less told you who was worth emulating.

Was that a chore or more a natural part of the curriculum?

It seemed natural, also laborious, but all in all a wonderful thing – a treasure, so to speak, because it conveyed the basic criteria and set the scene. Nowadays I guess that's a bit unpopular.

Nowadays any reference to tradition and craft is a red flag in modern art. But, turning back to the painting, which also represents an odd mixture of the 'strength through joy' aestheticism of the Nazis and the typical East German approach to painting. Two representations of aesthetic idiocy…

Yes, and that's why it has this aura of clinical conformity. The young artist was trying to give it a modernist sheen.

[Another photograph.] *This here is a mural painting for the Socialist Party headquarters. Police on horseback suppressing a workers' demonstration.*

Even more modernistic, in the style of Guttuso. But I never had a problem with the fact that I painted that sort of thing once. In a way, I quite like the naïve vigour, the pleasure in being able to produce a situation, and I also like that element of impertinence towards the ideology – it's all just theatre. I was aware of that. In any event, I'm glad this image now only exists as a reproduction.

When did you start doing what you wanted to do?

To some extent I've always done so. But to be able to do so completely, as it were, I needed to leave East Germany. Otherwise I might always have had to compromise, or create theatre.

[They look at different photographs of paintings.] *There's the* Stag *that is only properly painted in the middle. Is that an unfinished painting?*

It's a finished painting, courtesy of Konrad Fischer. He came in, saw the painting, and said, 'Why don't you leave it? It's good like that.' I did a double-take and thought, 'Yes, he's right.' That was our thing: spontaneous judgment.

Will the Stag *be on display in Dresden?*

No, in Dresden there'll be *Dead*, a nice painting. The dead man was found beneath an ice block.

Do you remember the story behind it?

No, not any more. It must have been a body that was found when the ice melted after a particularly hard winter. In my fantasy it's always the North Sea, though there probably aren't any such huge ice blocks there. A tragic accident.

I agree that the painting has something tragic, but at the same time there is something comical.

Something wretched, pathetic, attaches to this man, the way he lies there as though it were nothing special.

Back then the so-called Cold War was raging. But in the 1960s, the ice began to melt; people actually talked about a thawing of relations whenever there was a glint of liberalization somewhere within the Eastern Bloc. Sometimes one even thought that the Cold War ice itself could thaw. The painting is extremely charged. At the same time, nothing in this story contributes to a better understanding of the image. The painting is not metaphorical. How large is it?

One metre high, and one and a half metres wide. I'm certain I painted it from a magazine, though I didn't cut out the corresponding story. But there's a doctoral thesis that pinpoints the exact source.

Would this motif also have been imaginable in a three-metre version?

No, that would have destroyed it. I wanted to lift the image out of the smallness and anonymity of the paper, and present it, but without making it larger than life. That was a wonderful effect, that that was even possible: paint something, with oil paint on canvas, hang it on a wall, or in an exhibition, and that's enough to make the motif appear as something different. It becomes a painting, attains a meaning and relevance. It becomes more visible, and, above all, more important.

Let's turn now to the working process. First you reproduce the image with a preparatory sketch, and then you colour it in. Skilled workmanship, square for square. How much room does the artist have in this reproductive process?

To start with, it's drawn as accurately as possible. Then you have a picture that has been copied from a photograph, with all the details, and it looks very ugly. Then I start to smudge it. That destroys much of the photographic detail.

Was something smudged here as well?

Yes, it was. Here, in this painting, I noticed the clumsy positioning of the shoes, which I decided to leave. A minor blemish.

Could you have presented the same motif, the same size, as a photograph?

I've tried that occasionally, but it never works. It isn't just paint on canvas that does it, or the artisanship; it's the otherness of it, more or less, the difference compared to a photograph, which is itself mysterious, like the whole process. And the painting needs to reflect the mystery and, if possible, amplify it. If I had only copied it as accurately as possible, it would have been very boring.

At the time you came to Düsseldorf, action painting was in vogue. So what turned you on to photo-painting just then? That wasn't exactly abstract art.

It was Pop Art, and then Fluxus. Pop Art was the external impetus. From Fluxus I got the irreverent attitude. And the Pop artists had a very impressive answer to abstract art. We're doing something new, something that is totally taboo and where your criteria don't apply.

Spite? Being anti-bourgeois, and especially anti-authoritarian, was popular.

Sure. The anti-authoritarian aspect was always part of me, even if it was never obvious.

You have a reputation for being a highly skilled craftsman, and extremely proficien. Are those qualities prerequisites for art?

Generally speaking, it's no longer necessary for painting pictures. A bit of dexterity definitely helps, and some people are inherently more skilful, more practically minded than others. But nowadays it's not a pre-condition or criterion.

So where does art hide? Because it's equally true that not everyone can paint like you. So what is specifically artistic about your paintings . Where's the art in what you do?

First of all, it's pleasure – the pleasure of doing it. And then being able to see it – to see whether it looks good or not, whether it's presentable. To recognize whether it has a visual substance, a message, the required quality that destines it to be a work of art. Just the ability to see. That's why Duchamp is so important: his readymade is nothing but a process that emphasizes the basic skill at the heart of the matter: the ability to visualize something. This process is much more important than the end result. Anyone can produce a result, but to know what is to be executed, that's the important thing.

A clever view. An intelligent feeling. The whole thing seems to be about a zone that lies somewhere between knowledge and emotion. Is a consciousness of quality a kind of subconscious emotional intelligence? That's not a skill one can acquire.

It seems to me that not many people have the desire to delve into this. When I was a student and someone would tell me a painting didn't look good and was partially wrong or badly painted, I went to great lengths to find out what it was that looked bad, which criteria had been applied to come to such a conclusion. Of course, at first, you don't understand a thing; you don't see anything – the good bits or the bad. But as time goes by you develop the ability to see, the ability to recognize quality. And it seemed to me that the most important thing was that the criteria for quality were very broad, meaning that one could discern a recurring and comparable quality in Chardin and Palermo and Carl Andre and Vermeer, and so on and so forth. But the daftest response I got once, after voicing a criticism was, 'That's how I intended it.'

[The two of them are looking at a reproduction of *Motor Boat* (1965).] *Do you remember where you took this photograph?*

I don't remember any more. It might have been an advertising shot[12] that was done in documentary style. The illusion of happiness and leisure time. Have you ever driven in a motorboat? Terrible, isn't it?

As with the painting in the Hygiene Museum, the topic is: joie de vivre. In the Hygiene Museum we have the Eastern version; ten years later we get the joie de vivre of the West. Leisure time.

Definitely more realistic than the Eastern version.

People like you and me.

... in pursuit of happiness. Or on their way to Schreckenstein [Castle].

Behind us, on the wall, there is an abstract painting. The painting bears the title March, 1994. *Why is it called* March? *Was it painted in March, or did you want to capture the atmosphere of March?*

Both. It is a little reminiscent of thawing, of pre-springtime.

I want to remind you that you have painted seasonal scenes on several occasions.

Ah yes, there was a *July* once, and then, in 1989, *November, December, January*. These very large, somewhat dark paintings, pretty inspired.

So when one of your paintings is named after a month, with you we can be sure that it's actually related to the season. It's not just a date painting, like with On Kawara, *for instance.*

That's true. I only use the date as a title with sketches and watercolours. That gives them an air of a diary entry.

You have used the key term 'thawing' in relation to the content of this abstract painting. But that is very condensed. If you just hear the word you're a long way off from seeing your abstract painting. I always find it very difficult to put an abstract painting into words. How would you describe your own painting to someone you're talking to on the telephone? How would you convey what you have painted?

I would say it's about two and a half metres high and two metres wide. The paint that was applied has been vertically scratched off. Pretty evenly, like a wooden fence. Underneath there are mainly horizontal brushstrokes, or marks made with a palette knife. It has reddish and light blue tones, and darker, soft brushstrokes underneath that have partly been scratched away. And with the traces of white the painting gets a light feel, like a Chinese watercolour, a lightness. And, to my mind, the remnants of snow convey a certain optimism, like just before spring. That's why I like it.

Is your thesis-like method of description supposed to imply that there is no abstract art, that March *is not an abstract painting?*

The term abstraction is used very vaguely within the world of painting. Whenever something isn't recognizable as a concrete object like a table or a chair, then it's declared to be an abstract painting.

Which is an abstraction of what?

Of reality [*laughs*]. From the old convention that pictures are images of objects.

A moment ago you explained how your abstract painting took its cue from a seasonal mood. Could one say that our brain always insists on being able to categorize things as recognizable? Whatever is abstract cannot remain so; it must be translated into recognizable reality. The brain wants to recognize the world.

That's exactly what 'abstract' art feeds on. From this mechanism, that if we want something, we recognize it and give it a label. And because some elements in the *March* painting have a certain likeness to real events, we generate associations.

Your reference to the title and the seasonal mood helps me to 'read' the painting more easily, but if I'd first seen it hanging in a museum, I wouldn't have looked at the title, but would have tried to view it as spontaneously and unfiltered as possible. This painting also has a kind of magic, by which I mean something that cannot be explained and which even a title can't begin to define. It's not a message. It also has a very natural, individual presence. A colour tonality one can submit oneself to, or which one passes without being touched by. In this part of my consciousness, I perceive it as 'abstract'. Would it be possible to say that an abstraction is, in part, an abstraction of something, a suspension of reality? And, on the other hand, that it's something like one's own inner world?

Yes, I'm sure one can see it that way. That sounds good to me.

The painting with the title Grey *from 1973 will also be shown in Dresden. You've often painted grey pictures in the course of the decades. Can you say something about that?*

Difficult topic. The grey is certainly inspired by the photo-paintings, and, of course, it's related to the fact that I think grey is an important colour – the ideal colour for indifference, fence-sitting, keeping quiet, despair. In other words, for states of being and situations that affect one, and for which one would like to find a visual expression.

A grey suit, a grey tank, a grey mouse – are those associations that are intended? Grey also seen as the representation of crisis?

Sure, yes. Crises are a normal part of life, as long as they don't become pathological.

Paint it grey, even when there's nothing more to say?

That's roughly how Cage put it: 'I have nothing to say and I am saying it.' I always thought that was a wonderful quote. It's the best chance we have to be able to keep on going.

Do the grey paintings that keep cropping up in your work also tell of an ongoing crisis within art? Of art which, depending on the context of its time, always reaches points of change, points where it can go no further? Something along those lines?

Certainly, but there is the other side as well, the desire to create something whole, something holy, which cannot be improved upon. Something that is perfect in itself, natural and without blemish. A grey painting allows you to get close to this ideal.

In Berlin you presented eight grey paintings behind glass, in the spaces of the German Guggenheim. They seemed to be a totally different grey from the earlier grey paintings.

That's the result of past efforts to try and find the right kind of grey.

... which, fortunately, cannot be simply produced. In Dresden you present a work that consists of eleven glass panes arranged in a staggered fashion. The glass used is more reflective than normal glass. How did this work of art come about?

It was just a coincidence that there were eleven panes left stacked together in my place – and I was quickly fascinated by them. I played around with them for quite a while, and, thus, five different versions emerged – each made up of eleven panes, in various proportions, with this highly reflective glass or with normal glass.

And why eleven?

Of course I also tried it with ten, nine or twelve, but it always seemed to be wrong; either one was missing, or there were too many. So eleven it remained. I also like the number eleven. It's not as neat as ten, nor as significant as twelve, but it isn't without interest either, if only because it makes so many people ask: why eleven?

And it reminds me of 9/11.

... which is fine by me.

Over the years, glass has become increasingly important in your work. In 1967 you made your first glass object, the 4 Scheiben [4 Panes of Glass]. *What's the essence of your relationship to glass? You noted on a sketch: 'Glass – Symbol (see everything, understand nothing)'. The closest thing to the readymades are your mirrors. The one from 1986 will be exhibited in Dresden. What do you see in the mirror?*

Myself. But then I immediately see that it functions like a painting. Just more perfectly. And just like a painting, it shows something that isn't there – at least not there where we see it.

So the mirror would be the perfect artist?

Exactly.

'How much morality does art require?', 2004

I don't know the Flick Collection, and the people who are currently heaping so much praise on it don't know it either – that's a pretty horrible game right there. Names are dropped, values and standards are proclaimed, but in reality all that happens is that we see how quick and easy it is to establish a so-called top-notch collection these days.

Given enough money, almost anyone can do it. And if Mr Flick then goes along and lends his collection to the people of Berlin for seven years, many act as though this were a gift to the nation. The moral aspect of all this, insofar as it can even be separated from the aesthetic aspect, seems wholly disgusting to me.

Gerhard Richter

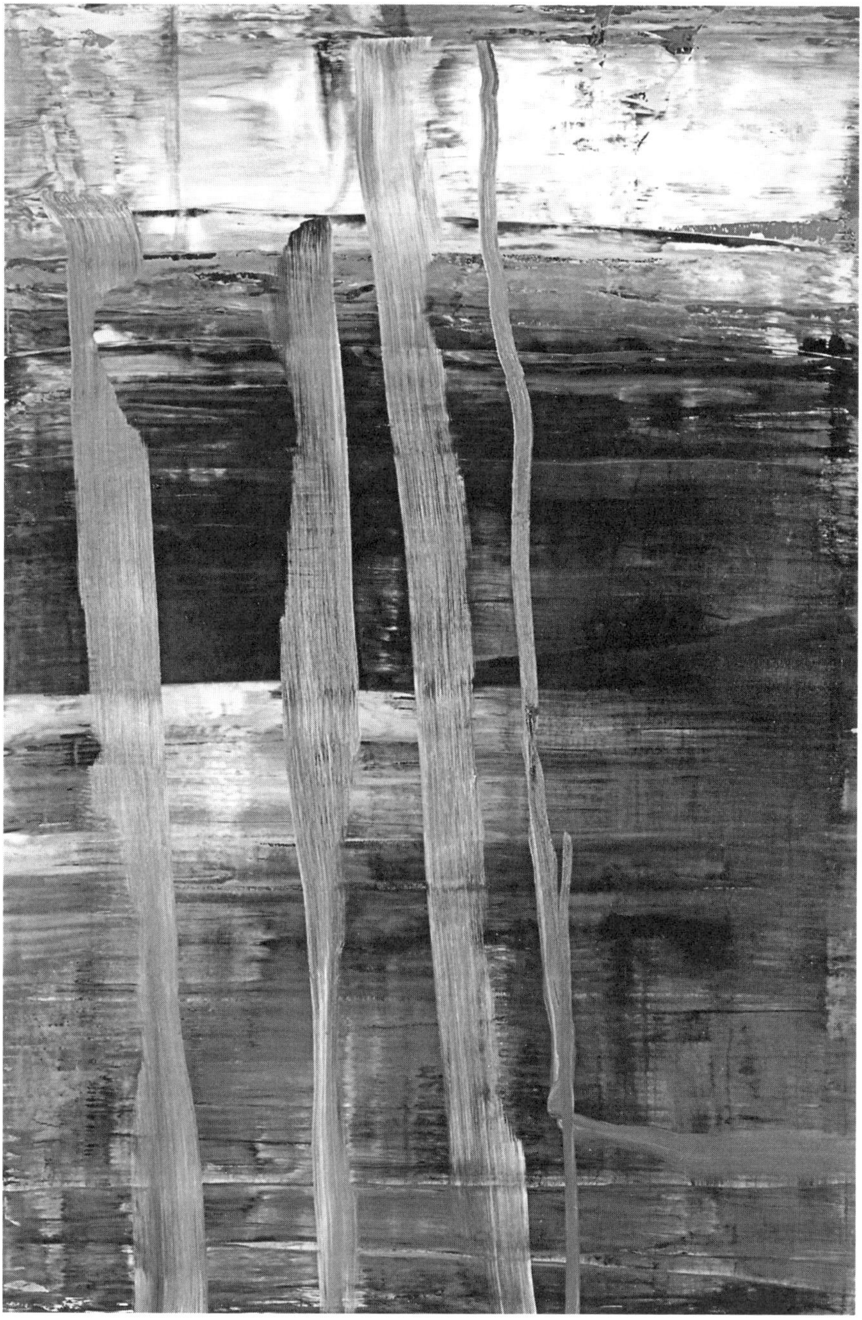

Forest (2), 2005

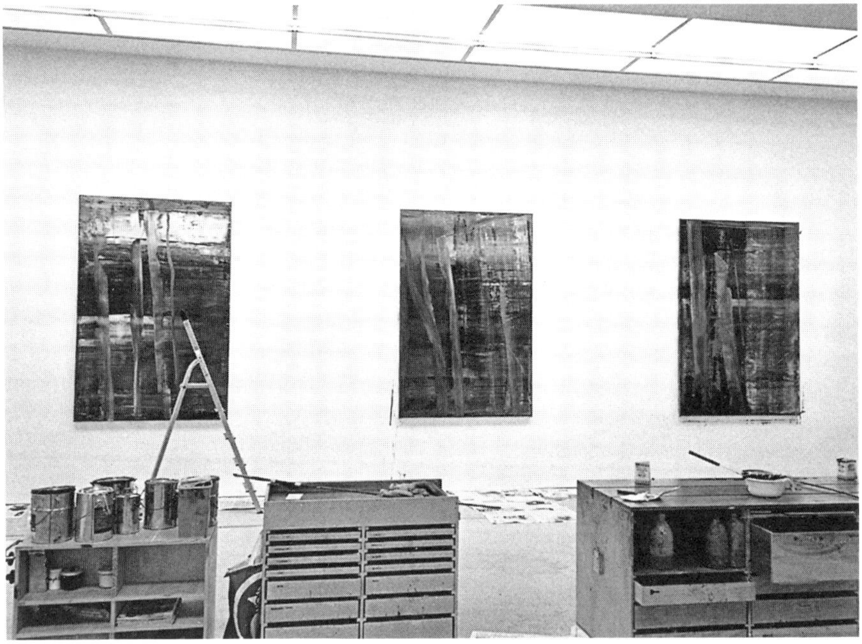

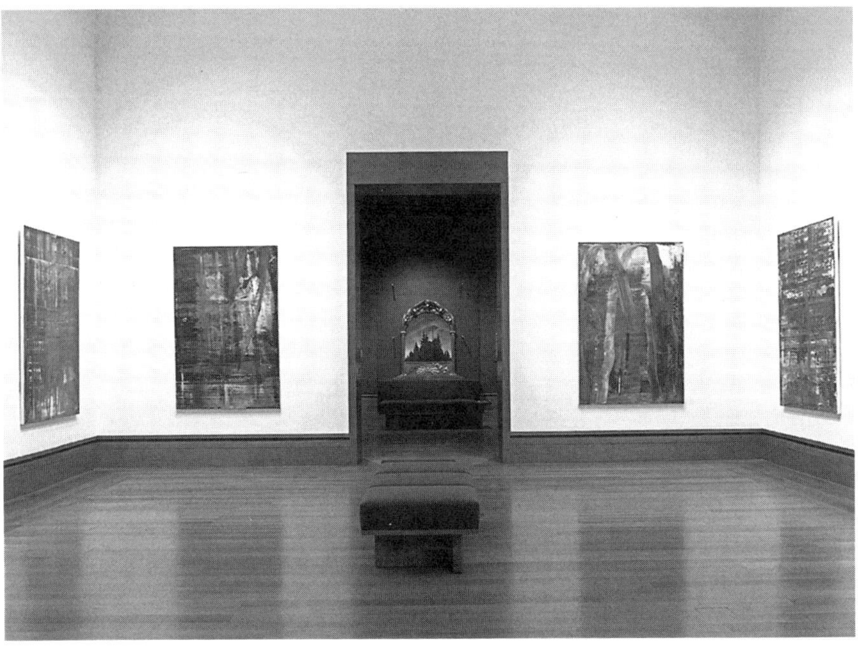

Studio, 2005
J. Paul Getty Museum, Los Angeles, 2006

Conversation with Stefan Koldehoff, 2004

Mr Richter, how did your idea for the print Kerze II[1] *in 1988 come about?*

It came about gradually. It was not any man's or woman's idea; it just came about. When the poster for the exhibition in Goslar was finished, people said, 'That's really nice, but the writing gets in the way.' Well, then we did something without writing. And when it came to signing it, I signed in huge handwriting out of irony, or perhaps it was just mischief.

Why are some of the prints signed 'Joseph Beuys' or 'Georg Baselitz'?

I was just being silly when I signed 'Beuys' and 'Baselitz' as well. It was high spirits, not a provocation. I didn't intend to upset anyone; it was a sign of my good mood.

Why then specifically Beuys and Baselitz?

To me they had always been the most famous and the best artists. I'm sure I also signed a couple with 'Polke'.

Was that a game you played with the expectations of the art market as well?

I didn't look at it that way then, that there were expectations. They were only fulfilled later – in a rather perverse way, because it got so expensive. I understand that someone paid $26,000 at auction, and that's definitely at least $25,000 too much.

Especially considering your motif was produced as a simple offset print.

That was normal. Since the beginning I've preferred offset printing for my kind of graphic work.

Why, exactly?

I didn't like the 'handcrafted' ethos – the cult surrounding delicate prints and handmade things. I always thought: that's not what it's about. It's really about motifs that should be so interesting on their own that you want to reproduce them. And it's definitely not about making some 'added virtue' with added value attached to it. Of course it has to be cleanly and handsomely copied, and we've always done our best at that. But we did not want to be part of this tradition: that was too much artifice for me.

Is that still the reason today why your graphic work is done in offset print?

Yes. It can be just as beautiful.

The aesthetic value is meaningful?

Yes, always. The quality of the paper, the print, the size of the borders – all these things play a role together, and must become a complete whole, as good as can be.

Did Candle *sell well in Goslar back then?*

I don't know. That print wasn't meant so seriously. I wouldn't have thought that it would become such an item.

In the meantime it's one of the most expensive prints you've ever done...

Yes. Those are the miracles of life.

In an exhibition that has now gone around the world from its starting point in Bonn, only your prints and editions are being shown. Is it okay with you that these works are separated from the rest of your œuvre?

You can separate anything, so it's certainly justified. It's like that in nature: I could write a book that first dealt with all the evergreens and then with all the different kinds of roses, even though they're all plants. So I can exhibit someone's landscapes alone, or also just the prints. It's all interesting.

The editions at the Bonn exhibition were sold out five minutes after opening. Do you feel that people are still interested in the motif, or do they just care about the signature? That brings us back to the question about Candle.

[*Laughs*] You mustn't rob me of the illusion that the piece worked, that it looks good, and that's the reason it's being bought.

You once said how important beauty is in your motifs. Is that also the case for your graphic reproductions?

Yes. Absolutely.

Are you still searching for motifs?

No, I always find them somehow. I don't browse through newspapers looking for pretty images, but they do come to me eventually.

Interview with Benjamin H. D. Buchloh, 2004

What motivated you to seek out microscopic photographs as the models for your new paintings?[1] *What did you think you saw in them, other than the disintegration of matter into molecules?*

I waited far too long for a motif to finally fall into my hands that fascinated me, that I absolutely wanted to paint. This is how the four large new paintings came about. I called them *Structures* because they happen to form kind of a structure. And because in some cases I don't even know what kind of substance the illustration is supposed to depict. Only the original, the microscopic photograph from the popular science magazine, has any claim to illustrating science.

Obviously these paintings go beyond any claim to a merely scientifically exact illustration, which of course wouldn't lead to much. Unlike the scientific photographs, the paintings have something rather sombre about them. Indeed, in many respects they resemble the earlier blurred paintings just as much as the early abstractions, or for example even the Tube *paintings. And despite the putative similarity of their motifs, or the possibly comparable technique, these new paintings have a completely other quality. Such rigid seriality, and the nearly mechanical repetition of an ornamental structure, have appeared quite rarely with you, if ever.*

It is true that this is a first. Actually, saying so is itself rather suspect, because ultimately all of this was played out long ago, serial abstraction, Minimalism, etc.

But it's still not Op Art, even though the paintings do indeed seem to take up a moment of pseudo-scientific, technological art in the 1950s, that moment when art believed it had to become entirely scientific. And so the new paintings also bear very peculiar relationships to our immediate present. In the confrontation with overwhelming technological developments, digital electronics for example, which in the recent past have influenced and controlled our ways of perceiving the world more than we could ever have anticipated, painting has now gained an entirely new, if precarious, status and value.

But my early Tube, Stripe and Curtain paintings do have something to do with these new paintings here.

And would you say that earlier motifs and processes are repeated here, or is this a completely new form of painting for you?

Naturally the technique is repeated, and the paintings in many respects resemble my old paintings. And I'm also not sure why they nonetheless strike me as different, that is, more topical.

Were these new paintings not projected, then?

No, they were; even in cases where I have drawn them with the aid of a stencil. Or when they are only done by some printing process – it would still be projection.

The template allows you to transfer the structure?

Yes, so that each individual form is in the right place, and always looks the same. Afterward they are painted in, as mechanically as possible, and further painted over until all the brushstrokes have been painted away, and everything becomes as blurred as the microscopic photo and similarly mysterious-looking. As pure drawings, these patterns look very much like Op Art, like Bridget Riley or Sol LeWitt, but also very beautiful from the right place.

Have you always appreciated Bridget Riley's paintings?

Yes, of course. This shimmering look has always been something that I liked. I was just missing the illusionistic fuzziness.

Your new paintings are indeed very hard to describe. At first blush, I would say, their structures are quite cell-like: they convey an experience between hermetic seriality and control, between computer cells and mass structures. They articulate a quite deep scepticism, not to say, hopelessness.

Yes, that's true. You've come quickly to the point. I have also thought, at times, that perhaps this really is a quite terrifying thematic, like getting closer to the end, in the direction of death and dissolution, down to the very elements, where all that is left are these dread atomic structures. And that would then be in keeping with the other works, with the *Panes of Glass*, which also have this side because they look like gates onto nothingness. There you have it.

These microscopic photos have, for some reason, really captured your interest. And what you just said about the glass pieces, I hadn't yet ever seen in that way, though of course it's very compelling. But the question remains – if reflection on death is indeed one of the points of departure for these paintings – how far one can push that reading into a generalization of experience. Even if these paintings stem from a private reflection, they are still public, and that would necessarily have to do with a general, societal situation.

There is, of course, also a general human situation in death...

Yes, but wouldn't it be unsatisfying to try to limit it to forms of a natural, private, biological death, or to psychosomatic or scientific models? Does that mean that you don't see the societal and historical components, which I've already precipitously introduced to my interpretation, quite as clearly?

No, that doesn't mean that at all. These others, the general dimension absolutely has to be there, otherwise it would be totally uninteresting.

The dimension of experiencing total control and forced conformism, a kind of isolation for each individual structure, each of which is entirely self-contained. The uncanny aspect of these new paintings is their cell-like massing, or their massed cell divisions, if one were to look at it as a societal model. For me, that then immediately becomes a political metaphor and a metaphor for social organization. And I know that this won't suit you at all. But unlike nearly every example from your long history of abstraction, these paintings have something almost ornamental about them. And the transition from painting into pure ornament – doesn't that bother you? Isn't that a dangerous tendency?

Yes, it certainly did bother me. Painting ornaments is of course the dumbest thing one could do. But it seems to me that my paintings show more than a few ornaments.

For the dialectic between ornament and banality gives these images a strangely sinister dimension. They prompt me to try to think of the historic moment, if ever, when so-called abstract painting became total ornament, but without becoming decoration. That seems to me to be a practically unknown, if not impossible, dialectic. You define these images in a double negative: they are neither decorative ornaments, nor pure abstraction.

Although I use both.

And it becomes even more interesting when one realizes that not only do these abstractions have a photographic basis, but so does the ornamental structure itself. That is a further contradiction, for an ornament is actually never photographic.

Here, of course, it is photographed arrangements of atoms that just happen to look like ornaments.

And your painterly abstraction was also never explicitly photographic. Although it has become clearer through the years that even your abstract colour paintings have a very strange relationship to photography, so far no one has managed to come up with an intelligent way to formulate it.

No.

Your abstract paintings are essentially just as photographically mediated as all your other paintings. They have always had a technical, physical, if not to say a downright chemical dimension, and so find themselves at the polar opposite of an abstraction dedicated to the painterly expression, gesture, or the purely chromatic, whatever that might be.

Yes, that's true. That surely has to do with the fact that any abstract daubings can be easily reconciled with a realistic photograph. These are two illusionistic modes of creating images that are brought together there.

The chemical and the optical?

The photographed reality and the real colour traces.

That is of course also what Roland Barthes says about photography, that it has a fluid, chemical dimension – specifically, the materials with which the photographic print is made –

and an optical and iconic dimension in which the light and optics of the camera create an image.

Yes, and that might also explain why I have always come back to this great interest in painting over photographs. But I am more interested in the optical dimension, that is, the creation of appearance.

So you constructed these paintings in a very strange, in-between place. And then there is also the important question, to come back to this again, of which range of readings is acceptable for you. That is to say, whether it begins simply with the chemical and physical molecular structures, as you have described it yourself, by which they take a form of experience, or of knowledge, as the point of departure for your painting. This could be entirely possible. Or whether, on the other hand, you were seeking a different form, in which the ornament was frozen as a model of that which cannot be experienced, and in its inability to be experienced dissolves into an ornament.

Yes, absolutely.

So what you're saying is, painting as the greatest form of hope, as the only form of hope, as you put it so well some time ago, is not exactly what I would take away from these pictures.

Art, the highest form of hope!

Is this the highest form of hope as your mature work, or is this painting at the dawn of the new century?

It would seem that it's my mature work, but in that case I suppose I should like it to be something else...

A different mature work, or another way of painting? How could it be different?

A bit lighter, more relaxed. Not so serious and full of tension.

But it's good to be tense, isn't it?

Exhausting, though. I'd prefer to paint like Matisse.

But of course that's not at all your predisposition.

That's why I dream of it now and again.

Has there ever been anything like it in your painting? Perhaps in the flower still-lifes?

They are too melancholic.

In the portrait Betty? *Or in the portraits of* Sabine with Child?

No, not there either; perhaps there never has been anything like it for me. At most in my watercolours, they have a certain casual quality. And that's of course also why those are your favourite paintings...

Well, your guess is quite correct. It is a bit strange that from the very beginning your work has had such a strict prohibition against the hedonistic dimension of painting. And this is actually true to this day. For, even in the large colour abstract paintings, in which some of your interpreters have thought they saw chromaticist or even symphonic joy – it isn't there either. For those are always tones or constellations of colour, which cannot be discharged as symphonic joy, nor do they point to any promising future. Correct?

Yes, that's what I was afraid of.

And so, the way one can see colour in, say, Matisse as the colour of the body or as natural colour, or as a corresponding to sensory experiences, or even to the experience of happiness – has that never been conceivable in your use of colour?

No, that's correct, a kind of tense cheeriness, something shrill or, also, evil.

That's a wonderful contradiction. What exactly is that, a tense cheeriness?

... an artificial one, one with gritted teeth, that conveys a threat as well.

A kind of technically directed cheeriness. Your painting definitely has that aspect. But why do you think, then, or what is the reason that you as a German painter have never had a basis for painting like Matisse, not that you never wanted to achieve it? Do you think it has to do with the fact that the motivations for art in your generation were radically different from the outset?

The circumstances were at any rate quite different, and so I never had a chance at that kind of painting. And when I see other artists who pretend to have this kind of casual approach, then it of course becomes immediately clear that they can't possibly ever have even one of the qualities that Matisse and Bonnard had in their time.

Do you think that the difference is primarily national and cultural, or more historically determined?

They go together: my national situation was also my historical, and vice versa.

So it is historically specific, then. And so does the prohibition against hedonism also have to do with the fact that you are a post-war German artist? That your experience as a German after the Second World War and after the Holocaust has inevitably concerned you in your work and has shaped you deeply? Do you also believe, then, that there is something quite specifically German in your work, or is it more that you are an international artist? Because there is something a bit strange, after all, that you, as a German artist, have such an enormous international reputation.

Certainly, yes, the past has been absolutely formative for me.

Your painting could only be understood, from its very beginning, as mediated by technology and photography, which of course was never the case for Matisse. For him, painting was only ever conveyed in a painterly and aesthetic way, and to all appearances was not even touched by technology or photography. But there were other French artists for whom this mediation by technology and photography was incredibly important.

Do you mean contemporaries of Matisse?

Duchamp, for example, who was of course somewhat younger, but not so much younger that one couldn't make the comparison.

But doesn't Duchamp belong to another age entirely?

Perhaps not so much any more. That's why it's so curious that you should just now bring up Matisse again, of all people. This is, by the way, the first time that I've ever heard you speak of Matisse.

Well, I've certainly complained about him a lot.

But then it is also interesting to consider how many painterly positions, despite all the historical 'prohibitions', have been reached by means of traditional modes of painting.

Thank God.

Further, what are we ultimately looking for in this kind of painting? A degree of differentiation that can no longer be reached by means of a technologically mediated mode of painting? When you say that even you still wish to achieve a hedonistic aspect in your painting, is that because this kind of painting might allow you a measure of differentiation that the current, technologically mediated forms of painting don't allow for? If you were, then, actually to lift the ban on hedonism that you internalized early on, what then would your painting even look like? What would you expect to gain from it?

None of this is even conceivable for me.

But if painting, for you, is about absolute individualization and differentiation, why can't you go as far as Matisse?

I'm too old by now. And even if I were twenty years old today, then maybe I could play around on the computer and post some kind of drawings and clips on the internet, really relaxed, entertaining things that people actually need. Luckily, though, this is not our topic.

Now this might seem a rather odd question, but how does it happen that you have only painted your son Moritz? What if you were to paint a portrait of your daughter Ella, an image that wouldn't – like the Moritz portrait – derive from a clearly Oedipally charged situation? Wouldn't that be quite in the vein of painting beyond the ban on hedonism? Wouldn't that demand an entirely different kind of painterly differentiation? Or would your painting balk at such a project, for the simple reason that time has run out for that?

I'm quite struck, because you have touched on such a relevant matter. Why haven't I painted her yet? Sometimes I'm on the spot, like when Ella asks: when are you going to paint me, anyway? Or her mother says: you painted your first daughter, and then the boy, but now you're going to have to paint Ella, too, aren't you? But nothing comes to mind, except perhaps that beautiful Velázquez portrait of a young girl...

Oh, the portrait of an Infanta?

The *Infanta*, yes. Wonderful. But honestly, I have yet to hit upon an idea for a painting of Ella. Perhaps because I have too few problems with her. Then, too, it is quite a hindrance that several of my earlier paintings have become such monuments, that is, they demand that I now produce an even more beautiful painting. That's the worst.

But it is of course very interesting to ask oneself whether this project mightn't be too deeply in conflict with your own art, epistemologically speaking. For if art is still supposed to be the highest form of hope, isn't it then a double paradox that it is so entirely unable to articulate these very different forms of experience, because you have always based your painting on negation, on refusal, and on criticism?

I don't know. My *Woman Reading* is not like that. And there are also other paintings, for example, the portrait of Betty. This painting is obviously not based on criticism and refusal. Nor would that be the case with a possible portrait of Ella, of course. Who knows, perhaps I might soon be able to make the necessary time to do it at my leisure. That would take care of a lot of things ... and my painting could go on, too.

How do you see the current situation of your work, and of artists in general? Has it changed radically in the last thirty years, or is it basically the same situation under a different guise? For example the nexus at which art, in our day, connects with power structures. This relationship has become considerably closer, at least in contrast with the period in the 1960s and '70s when the dialogical relationship between art praxis and power structures was much more controversial. And now both of these spheres have become nearly inseparable. That is, even a mode of art production that could still understand itself as criticism and opposition is immediately confronted with a praxis of reception that can assimilate anything and transform it into investment property.

Yes, though I'd actually have to call that a hopeful outlook. Because for me, it has always been the case, the only possible case, that art is inseparable from power relations, and that both mutually influence and enable each other. And exactly this was the Utopia and great fallacy of the '60s, when we thought that we could dismantle all that.

Did you ever share in this Utopia?

Yes, up to a point, back then.

So now this false belief has been corrected, and everything looks like it's in its proper place?

Now it looks more truthful, but shockingly ugly – the form of power and the art.

Oh really? Was there ever a beautiful governing power?

Almost beautiful, but only when that power was combined with art, when it was almost art in itself. And really we are now so clever and talented that we could create such a form of rule for ourselves. That is the whole point, after all. Unfortunately, though, it often misfires.

Do you really believe in what you're saying just now? And do you also believe that cultural praxis is no longer a form of dissent, or is incapable of producing a negation any more, but rather immediately becomes subsumed under existing power structures? Do you believe this is a situation one should just accept?

Ideally, yes. Ideally that would also be a situation that would unite all oppositions, all divergences and make something out of them. That's the common goal.

What is the goal?

We want to make the world a beautiful place.

Do the powers that be want that, too?

The powers that be, too, yes.

Ah well, so those in power don't want to be exploitative? They don't want to be controlling?

Governing power has to have control; that's why we chose it in the first place. And everyone wants to exploit; we need that, it's our nature.

We need to be exploited and oppressed?

Yes, except it's not exploitation and oppression, it's normal existence.

Do you mean to say, that doesn't exist any more? That has been done away with?

It never existed. Any more than the Devil ever has. These are all just simplifications that allow one to place blame elsewhere.

So you are saying that we have come a long way, in the historical development of subjecthood, or of the emancipation of the subject from power and exploitation? We've really reached an ideal community of free human beings? And, in so doing, made art superfluous?

Of course we haven't achieved all that. Far from it: right now it all seems irredeemably horrid, and we are quite far from being able to make art superfluous. Anyway the day will never come when we won't need art; for that we are far too malicious.

What role does art play with respect to evil? Art as a governess for our improvement?

That, too, naturally, and for our enlightenment, and much more.

Art as the governess for the world? Art as the world's reconciliation?

Absolutely.

Or art as the spiritual exercise of sublimation, in order to demonstrate for us how one should sublimate properly?

Yes, to be sure, that's part of it. We have to sublimate. I can't just kill you right now. I have to behave myself with you.

That is, have the registers in which negation is articulated become something other than the expressly political? Is negation formulated on the level of physical experience, the level of cognitive, perceptual, intellectual experience?

That may all very well be, but far beyond such tasks of negation and criticism, all I am only interested in any longer is the aesthetic accomplishment of art.

Yes, but aesthetic experience is still a form of collective perception that applies to everyone. And if art should barge in and say '... this is a reductive form of perception that I find unbearable; this is a model of experience that deadens me; this is a form of interaction that makes me suffer' ... then isn't that also a form of political intervention?

Well, as far as the fine arts are concerned, they do look a bit meagre in terms of their capacity for intervention.

Don't you believe that your art can do it?

My art? Oh no, I belong to a field of art that has become very unimportant and has hardly anything left to say.

The greatest living painter says that about his art?

My success has nothing to do with it: it hasn't allowed me to do what we're talking about right now, that is, this success in itself is no proof that painting today still has any generally valid social relevance.

In earlier conversations, you have always denied that painting could come to any definite end. How do you judge this situation now, after the experience of your big and tremendously successful show at the Museum of Modern Art in New York?

Maybe all those people came in order to see the end of painting, a last flare-up, before it's over.

Why do you think that there is no painting any more?

Because I never see it any more. Films, however, which in contrast to so-called painting have something to say, something to offer. It is kind of astonishing that painting is even still exhibited, and when you see on top of that how much effort the art critics put into poetizing meaning around these paintings, then the laughable role of painting today really becomes clear.

So you see painting as an already dying culture. Is that with sadness, or with satisfaction?

With sadness. There were times when this culture came to life. For example after the war, first in France, or then in America. There you had wide swathes of the Western world believing that a Barnett Newman was something wonderful and exciting. There's really not much of that left any more.

Yes, and now wide swathes of the Western world and the American world see that the painting of Gerhard Richter is something totally unique. Your exhibition in New York spawned an almost cult-like following, endless queues at New York's Museum of Modern Art, such that we were all asking ourselves how it is even possible that so many people want to see it? What do they see in it? And why do they want to see it?

I can't say I know why. Probably, as I said, these people wanted to see the last flicker of post-war painting.

And is that what you represent?

Yes, I represent that. After that, though, is the end.

So you are the last great painter?

When you put it that way, I don't know how else to answer.

And the technical moment, the virtuosity in the creation of your paintings, isn't that an additional argument, or is that even the secret of your success? That is, it's not just that you are the last great painter, but rather that you are the last painter who really knows how to do this in a technical sense?

That could be.

And isn't it objectionable to you that virtuosity should become a cult?

Well no, virtuosity has something beautiful about it. I do like it.

Like Yehudi Menuhin? A great violinist of painting?

A great violinist of painting!

Do you believe that painting is really about the preservation of masterful, individualist, artisanal production? Or don't you much rather think that it's about the conceptual, cognitive and perceptual foundations of the work of art, which can be saved in painting?

It all fits together, though. Menuhin's virtuosity is only enjoyable when he is using it to play a wonderful piece.

At the same time, in the new paintings it is nonetheless very clear that you are just using the means of painting to take up a particular situation, or are trying to document a structure...

... which is very unpainterly. Exactly as in my *Panes of Glass*. There at any rate painting ceases entirely.

Well, isn't what you want to preserve there this extreme ambiguity of your work, a contradictoriness unimaginable for anyone else, which really can only be produced by painterly means?

No, it could be produced by other means as well. For my *Panes of Glass*, the same criteria apply as I use in judging a painting by Chardin. That's what it's about, for me.

What about when, in the present moment, you paint the structure of silicate?

In the end it doesn't matter what I paint, it's always about this same quality.

Wouldn't that be conceivable with other means?

Yes, quite naturally, with what have you – with video, film, photography and so forth, no boundaries.

So it's more about a specific definition of the differentiated subjectivity, not specific techniques that need to be rescued?

I would never want to rescue a technique.

But shouldn't specific forms of subjectivity or of differentiated experience be saved, against the social project of total desublimation? You are a conservative person, and when one is conservative one wants to save everything, right?

Yes, absolutely, I want that. Preserving certain values, I consider that a quite natural desire; everyone does it. And that's why I also believe that here on this planet, despite all our most horrifying strayings, we are in principle on the right path. Sometimes.

What makes you so confident? The present...

... even the present has its moments of promise...

Conversation with Georg Imdahl, 2005

Mr Richter, is the design you've developed really specific to this location? In other words, is it only suitable for Cologne Cathedral?

Yes, of course, it was devised specifically for this place. But for half a year now I've also had an offer to do something for the cathedral in Reims, quite independently of this. I haven't started on that yet, but the preliminary talks about the project will be held in the near future. And one thing is clear: I couldn't repeat what I did here with the squares.

Could a concept like this one for Cologne also work in a secular environment?

Yes. A smaller, similar version already exists in a Bauhaus-style family house in Berlin.[1] It's in the stairwell, but the window there has lead frames, which don't really fit properly with the design.

What was the major challenge for you when you started work on the church window in Cologne Cathedral?

It was very difficult. After everything I've seen of modern church windows, I have to say: there's really no such thing. When I looked through the catalogues of the glass companies that had said they could execute my design, I couldn't find anything I liked, and a lot of it was simply dreadful. Maybe we've lost the ability to make something like that.

Will your design fill the entire arched window located in the southern transept facing Roncalliplatz? That would be a huge project.

Yes, it goes from the top to the bottom, twenty metres high.

Your work always contains a touch of transcendence. But there aren't any obvious clues to suggest religiosity or belief. Does belief play a role in your work?

What exactly is belief? Something similar to a basic characteristic in us humans. There is a longing for it. I wish I had the capacity for it.

What does it mean for you to be able to produce a work of art for Cologne Cathedral?

That's a difficult one: sometimes I don't want to admit to myself that this really is something fabulous. It's something unique. The cathedral is there for all time, and then to have a window that is such a focal point, and the southern one at that, with the bright light coming through – that really is a gift.

Conversation with Bertram Müller, 2005

When you see your old Düsseldorf paintings again, such as the portraits of the gallery owner Alfred Schmela and Karl-Heinz Hering, the former director of the Arts Association, and, on top of that, the landscape near Hubbelrath, is it a moving experience for you?

Yes, of course I'm touched. My career started in Düsseldorf. Düsseldorf was where it all began.

And what about your K20 painting from last year, which is being shown in this exhibition – would you consider that to be related?

That was more of a coincidence. I had photographed the museum to get a better idea of where I would be exhibiting, and this painting arose from that photograph. The important thing was the segment with the windows.

Unlike in other exhibitions, was it your intention with K20 to provide a view of Grabbeplatz outside, and from there to allow people to look inside?

Yes, I insisted on it. I don't like rooms you can't look into or out of.

SPIEGEL interview, conducted by Susanne Beyer and Ulrike Knöfel, 2005

Mr Richter, your paintings fetch record prices at auction. You're considered the world's most expensive artist. The more famous you become, and the more worldwide acclaim you receive, the more pronounced your reputation grows for being shy and unapproachable. Is it advantageous to be perceived as an expensive mystery?

Certainly, though I don't see myself as a mystery. I'm just fairly reserved. I was never that good with words – I don't enjoy talking – and that makes me a little shy. I'm also fundamentally sceptical towards myself, hence towards others as well. And that's why I'm never sure if what I do is right or whether it's any good.

We can't believe that, coming from the world's most sought-after artist.

But you have to. I've always admired that wonderful self-assuredness in others. For example, the inbred confidence of my colleague Georg Baselitz. He can just walk onto a stage and start talking. Or, in the past, as a student at the [Dresden] Academy, I was always amazed that my fellow students could be so enamoured with their own creations that they could sit in front of them and sing their own praise. When I paint, I tend to be disappointed that the result is just another painting.

Just another painting – that art collectors would give their right arm for. Mr Richter, your modesty comes across as coquetry.

There's not much reason to be smug. Why shouldn't I be a little deferential in the face of all the masterpieces in the history of art? You can't really philosophize about the essence of art anyway. It's impossible to explain, let alone prove, what's so good about a painting by the Dutch master Pieter Saenredam – you can only see it. But there is one consolation: uncertainty can be quite a motivating force.

Are people who lack confidence better artists?

I have no idea. After all, I don't know how Mr Rubens felt.

But we do have the impression that you're coming out of your shell. In the last few years you've rediscovered your fondness for the city of your birth, Dresden, and you've publicly proclaimed your happiness about this. You've given important works to the Albertinum in Dresden, and you plan to establish a Richter Archive there, with material pertaining to your life and work. Are you perhaps in the process of dismantling the mystery surrounding yourself?

Again, there is no mystery. But at the age of seventy-three, I don't think I have as much reason to be shy. There's no point. It's just not possible to always do and say the right things. These days I have a more relaxed attitude towards many things.

And yet you must have always been sure of yourself as an artist. In the 1960s you were attacked for painting pictures from photographs, which was unusual and confused many people. But you continued without wavering.

Well, at least for me personally there's always been a part of me, a kind of instinctive knowledge, about what is good and what is bad. I see many landscapes, take photographs of hundreds of them, and paint one or two. This is proof to me that I know what I want – a fact that seems to give me a certain sense of self-assuredness.

Aren't the prices that your works command reason enough to feel self-assured? We're talking about millions of dollars being bid at auctions. There must be more than one collector who has become rich by selling one of your early works.

When you hear about these record sums, it's flattering, of course, but at the same time it's shocking. Above all, this kind of thing is not a good source of motivation. In fact, when I'm in a bad mood, I see this kind of success as a sign that something has gone askew in the world – that the buyers know nothing about art, and that I somehow conned them. And they do indeed tend to pay far too much for art. There is a huge discrepancy between the true value and relevance of art and the insane prices people are paying for it.

What's so terrible about spending a lot of money on art?

There are buyers who bid via telephone for a work of art they've never actually seen. That's not art appreciation – it's neglect. And it's a factor that contributes to diminishing culture. People's appreciation of art, their interest in art, is waning. Perhaps all people want to do is invest their money. But they don't need art.

You bet they do. People are visiting your exhibitions, in particular, in droves – even if you don't always make things easy for them by making sure they have a hard time interpreting your universe of images. They find sensuous landscapes next to austere colour fields or sumptuously colourful abstractions. It was once said that your art is 'relentlessly neutral'. Even critics seem unable to define what you're about.

Why should they be intrinsically wiser than the average person who's interested in art? They simply have the unfortunate task of having to instantly define what these works of art mean. This leads them to make claims like my works are paintings about painting, or that they represent abstract concepts, clinical virtuosity, a refusal to commit, a cover up – and who knows what else.

Those terms have all been used to describe your work over the past thirty or forty years. And they're all wrong?

Yes, because it's all much simpler: my art is a lot more accessible than that of most of my colleagues. I hardly hide anything. On the contrary, I'm almost embarrassed about showing myself and my life so openly in my paintings.

Today we know that many of your portraits are of members of your family, and we know their history. Take the painting of your aunt Marianne, for instance, who was killed in February 1945, or your uncle Rudi, wearing a Wehrmacht uniform. Why were the biographical references in your paintings ignored for so long?

I had no desire for people to discuss these matters. I wanted them to see the paintings, not the painter and his relatives, otherwise they would have somehow given me a label, reached a premature conclusion. In truth, factual information – names or dates – have never interested me much. Those things are like an alien language that can interfere with the language of the painting, or even prevent its emergence. You can compare it to dreams: you have a very specific and individual pictorial language that you either accept or that you can translate rashly and wrongly. Of course, you can ignore dreams, but that would be a shame, because they're useful.

Nowadays, all of your works and your biography are examined meticulously. A few years ago, when you presented paintings showing your wife Sabine and your young son Moritz,[1] *they were seen as a revelation – as Richter's declaration of a new sentimentality. There were stories about it in the arts sections of every newspaper.*

This kind of reporting leads away from the paintings. It satisfies a different need: the craving for gossip. It's something I can understand. After all, when I'm at the dentist leafing through *Bunte* [magazine], I find the gossip entertaining, too. But biographical details have limited relevance when it comes to understanding a work of art, and, of course, you have to know the painting first. People like to think that Francis [Bacon]'s paintings are so much easier to fathom because they've been told that he was gay.

In early September a book by the journalist Jürgen Schreiber[2] *will appear about your aunt Marianne, who became a victim of euthanasia in the 1940s. Your first father-in-law, a medical professor in Dresden, was involved in such atrocities. All this is documented in the book, which uses a painting you made of your aunt as its starting point. Does this bother you?*

Well, these things get published, whether I like it or not. What does bother me, of course, is the way it's marketed – with sensationalist headlines like 'The Painter's Secret', or 'A Family Drama'. That really is very tacky. I haven't actually read the book, but it will be like Jürgen Schreiber's article in *Der Tagesspiegel* a year ago,[3] just with more details and based on far more extensive research. If the book holds what the article promises, I'll be very pleased.

Why?

Because it's always interesting to discover something about yourself you weren't previously aware of. These are family histories that, by being clarified in hindsight, are easier to understand – or they're stories that would not have come to light at all. In this way, the paintings of my aunt, uncle, father and so forth gain an additional dimension in retrospect.

It's clear that you've always painted, and still paint, members of your family. Is this a way to help you cope with problems?

Only about one per cent of my paintings show family members. Do they help me deal with problems? It's likely that these problems can only be depicted. But photographs, private ones and others, keep appearing that fascinate me so much that I want to paint them. And sometimes the real meaning these images have for me only becomes apparent later. A striking example of this is the small painting *Horst with Dog*. When I painted it, I just thought it was funny – pleasantly similar to the humour of an artist like Sigmar Polke. But when I saw it displayed in New York thirty years later, I was a little shocked because it seemed to me that the father was portrayed as a predominantly tragic figure.

Horst with Dog *was acclaimed as a curious portrayal of your father, Horst Richter. In it, he comes across as a tragic clown figure. Dietmar Elger, your biographer, called you a fatherless son because your father was in the war and you hardly saw him when you were a child. But the* New York Times Magazine *intimated that Horst Richter was not your real father.*

And that's true. But things like that aren't exactly unheard of.

You were born in 1932. Did you know, as a child, that this man was not your father?

I knew it pretty early on.

Was the difficult relationship with your parents part of the reason you got on the metro train in East Berlin in 1961 and fled to the West?

No, that had nothing to do with my parents. If anything, it was more to do with my parents-in-law, who already lived in the West and helped to ease the transition. But the severing of all close relationships to friends and colleagues was extremely hard for me. There was only one reason for leaving – the [East German] regime, which choked the life out of everything.

In the West you experienced fatherhood yourself for the first time in 1966. Do you think this experience brings people closer to their own parents?

That's hard to say. In the late 1960s nobody was interested in family values – and certainly not in fathers. Looking back, the progressives in the 1960s and '70s, with all of their pompous behaviour, just seem pathetic. Intoxicated with naïve illusions about prosperity and social change, they fostered a disdain for authority that was simply irresponsible. Children were left to their own devices. I wasn't much better, except that I had more qualms about it. The portrait of my daughter, Betty, which I painted much later, and which shows her turned away from the viewer, could be seen as expressing a degree of sadness about this fact.

This back view of your daughter is a world-famous icon.

Yes, it's very popular. I heard that it's the most frequently reproduced piece of modern art. It is, after all, rather attractive, painted with subtlety. It has nice colours, and the dark, monochrome background forms an interesting contrast to the shining glory of the flower pattern on the bathrobe my daughter is wearing. And – you can't see her face. I was unsure about that at first. I felt it was too much like a film, like something akin to Hitchcock's *Psycho*.

The thriller is about a murderer who keeps talking to his mother, whom we only catch an occasional glimpse of from behind...

... and in the end he turns the chair around and we see the disfigured face of his mummified mother. Pretty frightening.

Thinking of that while viewing the painting Betty *really would be a rather horrific association.*

But, fortunately, that doesn't come to mind. The averted face may be a somewhat hackneyed way to introduce a sense of mystery into the portrait, but the core emotion, surely, is one of painful regret related to loss and separation – something along those lines. But, of course, I was not aware of this when I painted it.

You had problems with your father, hence problems with being a father yourself?

An entire generation was saddled with this. Like many people my age, I never had the experience of having a father I could look up to. Most of our fathers were away in the war for a long time, and they either didn't return or they came back shattered and broken – and as perpetrators. This trauma of a generation tainted by their fathers has had repercussions right up to the present day. Perhaps that's why terrorism had a different quality here than in other places. Back in the 1970s, it was essentially a reaction against these fathers who had failed in every respect.

War and terrorism appear to be subjects that haunt you. Your legendary series 18 October 1977 *is about* RAF *[Red Army Faction] terrorists. The fifteen paintings show faces, cells in Stammheim Prison, corpses, a funeral. Together these form a disturbing kind of nightmare. At first, these paintings were frequently damned by critics, but today they're referred to as 'altars', and in 2002 the* New York Times *honoured them as being 'quite simply the only great work of art about terrorism to date'. But looking around your studio now...*

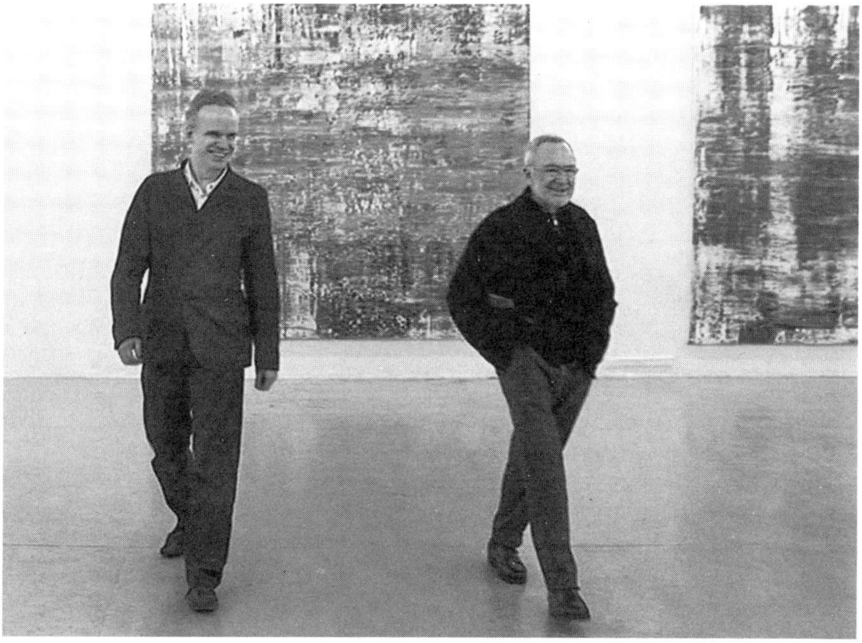

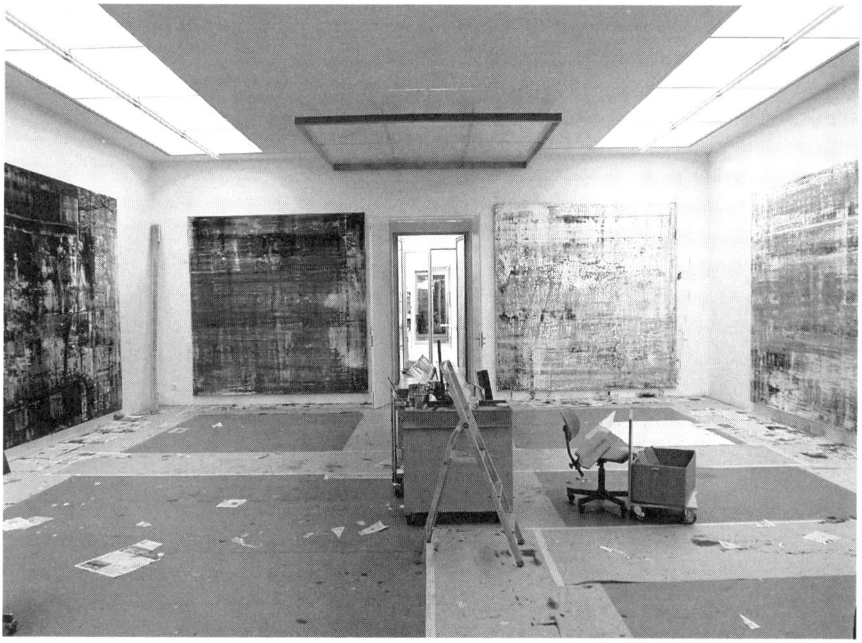

Hans Ulrich Obrist with Gerhard Richter, 2007
Cage in Richter's studio, 2006

Cage, 2006 (detail)

... all my work is non-realistic, only abstract paintings.

But one small painting here does show something less abstract: you can make out what appear to be the towers of the World Trade Center.[4] Is this a new topic for your work?

I'm afraid not. These here are only failed attempts. I couldn't get this stereotypical image of the two towers, with the smoke billowing out of them across the deep blue sky, out of my mind. Finally, I tried to paint it, but it didn't lead anywhere. Even while I was painting, I realized that this was the wrong approach.

What will happen with this painting?

I'll destroy it, or I'll paint over it at some point, since the canvas is still usable. Who knows, maybe the right visual idea will emerge for this topic, for the topic of terrorism.

A painting by Gerhard Richter about 9/11 would guarantee worldwide attention. But it would also be a risk, since there would be a great danger of being misunderstood. Hardly any of your colleagues have dared to deal with the subject.

When it comes down to it, the only thing that interests me about this topic is fanaticism. No matter how one describes it – as belief, conviction, ideology, a plan or a vision, depending on one's viewpoint – it always boils down to an image of a reality. What fascinates me, and shocks me, of course, is that this ability to imagine, which has so much power, which can unleash such passion and spur us on and motivate us to accomplish incredible things, can also lead to the most terrible crimes. But there's one area where this fanaticism can be thoroughly expressed without harming anyone – the world of art. If you look at it like this, Beuys's idea that 'all humans are artists' is a very attractive dream.

Beuys, of all people, is the complete opposite of you. Beuys stood for a provocative form of anti-aestheticism. But your paintings – whether realistic or abstract – celebrate beauty, even when your topics are controversial.

Beauty is problematic, because we no longer have a consensus as to what it actually is. Part of the problem is that the term 'beauty' is, or sounds, so hackneyed. The same applies to words like 'good' or 'truth'. But this doesn't diminish the value of these kinds of ideals, or the fact that people need beauty. For me, beauty has always been a factor in determining the quality of a work of art, regardless of its form or the era in which it was conceived.

Beauty – more so than ugliness – is considered a polemical term. Many feel that it is outdated and thus provocative.

Viewed simply, beauty is the opposite of destruction, disintegration and damage. This means it can't be separated from form, without which nothing can be created. And the most important aspect, as far as I'm concerned, is that it is only form that makes it possible to understand things and thus build a society. The opposite would be authentic babble, and that is just antisocial.

But the term 'authenticity' is often heard in current debates about art.

I can already see a tendency in the art world towards the disintegration of form, and this reflects what's happening in society as a whole. Form as a universally valid, ideal value is no longer popular. Form has become a nuisance: it's so much easier to jump on the bandwagon and blather on about authenticity, individualization, artistic freedom and self-realization. But this is basically as irresponsible and wrong as thinking of everything in terms of ratings and polls: it tempts people to lie. Everything has to be as comfortable as possible for the customer or voter, and no matter how stupidly he behaves, you have to keep telling him how great, how fantastic, he is.

Aren't you being a little unfair? The essence of contemporary art lies in the versatility of its forms and styles, in the way it affects people in different ways, entertaining or disturbing them.

It's understandable that artists want to do their own thing. But the consumer should be capable of choosing, judging and knowing what he wants. Nowadays, the criteria are lacking.

That sounds as if you're advocating a return to the academic rigidity and standardized aestheticism of past centuries.

That's not what I mean. When people complain about a botched work of architecture, for example, it's generally the architect who's accused of egotistical self-expression and of having created something truly awful. But the person who should be blamed, first and foremost, is actually the client, who didn't have the competence to decide what kind of a building he wanted or what it should look like. I realize that things are a bit different when it comes to contemporary art – it's so autonomous that it can't be commissioned any more. You have to accept whatever the artist delivers and then play a game of make-believe, like in *The Emperor's New Clothes*.

Can you give us an example?

The statue of Willy Brandt[5] in the Social Democratic Party headquarters in Berlin. It looks like a zombie. But the party members act as if they were blind and think they're honouring Willy Brandt with a piece of modern art. The people of Salzburg face a similar predicament. Having encumbered themselves with a dubious work in honour of Mozart, they also have to act as if they had no eyes.

You mean the Mozart sculpture by the not unrenowned artist Markus Lüpertz, which was recently unveiled in Salzburg and which shows the composer naked, as an arm amputee, and with surprisingly feminine attributes?

Why doesn't anyone complain? I don't know where this lack of judgment in matters of art comes from. It's as though we've forgotten how to use our eyes. One thing certainly contributed to this development – the Nazis, with their defamation of modern art as 'degenerate'. That had a disastrous effect and hugely undermined people's ability to judge for themselves. Later there arose a reverse line of reasoning with a very intimidating effect: people who dared to reject contemporary art were accused of being narrow-minded philistines with right-wing or even fascist tendencies. This kind of attitude encourages people to close their eyes and shut their mouths rather than risk being accused of being narrow-minded.

Would you like art to be more elitist, more rigorous in the way artists are trained?

Initially, it would be a matter of general education – for all segments of society. And, of course, it would be determined by the cultural aims of society as a whole. Naturally, the academies would need to play a key role in this process. In the past, I complained that we have far too many, and far too mediocre, academies. I have a more relaxed attitude now, meaning that I believe that our relentlessly changing society has a need for academies that train far larger numbers of artists in a variety of ways. In a sense, you can compare it to tourism, which has long since abandoned the principle of enabling the 'happy few' to travel around the world. But that still leaves the problem of quality, which is based on an unwavering desire to go beyond what has already been achieved. You can't get anywhere without ideals.

What's your opinion on the young generation of artists from Leipzig? Their paintings are colourful and accessible – their success can be measured by the increasingly mind-boggling sums being paid for their works.

Nicely illustrative and perfectly non-committal. It's a tradition in the east of Germany and could already be seen in the era of the DDR. Artists like Willi Sitte and Werner Tübke belong to this school of narrator. But it doesn't interest me: I find it too pragmatic and formalistic.

This generation of artists, in their mid-thirties, is not only regarded as pragmatic and commercially oriented, but also surprisingly conservative. That's something that should appeal to you, since you're considered a long-time champion of bourgeois values.

I haven't been able to discover any truly conservative side to these young artists. And, incidentally, the term conservative isn't really socially acceptable yet: it has negative connotations, just like right-wing, bourgeois or backwards. It's certainly not in vogue. And you're not a conservative just because you have a tastefully designed apartment. A conservative attitude is harder to live by. In fact, I would say that many of my left-leaning friends could be described as conservative, if only because of their work ethic and their attitude towards art and global issues. They all want to conserve or protect something, and they're basically as bourgeois as Golo Mann – I just bought one of his books while on vacation on [the island of] Usedom.

The historian Golo Mann's conservatism can be traced back to the major turning points in his life, starting with his flight from Nazi Germany in 1933. Do you see parallels to yourself? You've also experienced major turning points in your life, having lived in four different eras in German history: the Nazi period, the German Democratic Republic, and the old and new Federal Republic.

Perhaps. When you've experienced so much lunacy and have managed to remain relatively unscathed, you tend to want to preserve what's good, remain sceptical, and not trust the latest hype. I've had a great deal of luck.

Mr Richter, thank you for talking with us.

Conversation with Roberta De Righi, 2005

Mr Richter, why are you not in agreement with Jürgen Schreiber's book, Ein Maler aus Deutschland [A Painter from Germany]?

Unfortunately it did not turn out to be a good book – something I had not expected. I found Jürgen Schreiber's article in the *Tagesspiegel*[1] a little over a year ago quite impressive – the same with the talks about his research and the consuming passion with which he's been pursuing this topic. He had brought a great deal of facts together – facts I had known nothing about and that I generally found very interesting. But with each page I had more doubts, and it took a lot of effort to read the book through to the end.

How so?

Schreiber has pumped this stirring topic up into a book: he mixes facts, contrives connections between things, decorates it all with his own imagination, and drags intimate details into the light that don't serve to support the topic itself, but rather apparently only prove the pleasure he takes in snooping around.

But it must have been clear to you from the beginning that in all likelihood some painful things would come to the surface in a book project like this.

No, not at all. And it's not just about a couple of little sensitivities here. I'm upset about the quality of the book, about the attitude and the jargon, both of which actually stand in the way of the express desire to get closer to the truth.

Schreiber does continually try to emotionalize, and he tends toward inventing stories, for example when he describes your grandmother visiting your aunt in the asylum. As a reader, you keep asking yourself how he could know this.

He doesn't know it. How could he anyway? These are conjectures. The same applies to his descriptions of Heinrich Eufinger,[2] where he becomes unbearably subjective. The author writes that he 'could positively smell the brilliantine' and talks about his 'uneasy gaze from small and narrow eyes'. That kind of thing is not only untrue, it's absolutely stupid.

With this simple equation of physiognomy with personal character, the author quite disturbingly approaches Nazi racial theories.

That, too. But Eufinger came across quite differently to me back then. There was nothing of the Nazi about him: he was highly educated, competent, a really impressive guy. I knew nothing about his role in the forced sterilizations, much less about his collaboration in Nazi eugenics and euthanasia. And his status in the SS was explained to me as a kind of honorary membership.

Did you know nothing more, or did you just not want to know?

In the early 1950s we really had other problems to deal with.

And when you painted Aunt Marianne *did you know anything about their joint history?*

I only knew that she'd been killed, but very little about her life and next to nothing about her suffering. That is certainly one thing the Schreiber book accomplished: it retroactively gave me the story behind the painting.

Interview with Jeanne Anne Nugent, 2006

The Getty exhibition is an affirmation of a German tradition in painting, a very complex and, at times, troublesome history. With Caspar David Friedrich heavily represented at one end and you at the other, one might get the idea that you are the standard-bearer of painting for Germany. How might you feel about that?

Positively, although perhaps I'd prefer to say 'trooper' rather than 'standard-bearer', joining forces with those who feel an allegiance to tradition, and especially to a tradition that owes something to Friedrich. I'm very happy to be counted as part of that.

What does tradition mean to you? Was it always important for your work?

Tradition was simply a given, a valuable cultural heritage that set standards. Of course having an attitude like that put me outside the trend that thinks it fashionable to decry tradition, and to talk about the end of history and of art. You know more about it than I do.

Yes, the end of art and the death of painting have become commonplaces of art history. However, in the 1960s that stance wasn't all that alien to you, was it?

It's true that when you're young you tend to spout provocations, and if the time seems right for it, you come up with some pretty brash proposals, like sinking Venice or flattening the Alps. One shouldn't take all of that too seriously.

Your artistic career is closely connected with Dresden. You were born there, moved further east during the war, and returned in the 1950s to attend the Dresden Academy of Fine Arts. Your earliest watercolours from the 1940s seem to have been influenced by Romantic landscape painting, and perhaps also by Die Brücke *and* Der Blaue Reiter. *How did you first become aware of these artistic movements?*

From books and from the little folios with art prints that you used to get then –

I remember Diego Velázquez, Albrecht Dürer, Lovis Corinth – but that was before my time at the Dresden Academy. It was simply a matter of what was around, what we saw and bought for ourselves.

It's very important that it was in Dresden that you first became familiar with the great tradition of German painting.

Yes. My time in Dresden fundamentally and powerfully influenced me, although I wasn't really aware of it at the time. I realized it later. However, as far as the 'great tradition of German painting' goes, I received a very patchy account of that due to the ideological slant on art as it was taught to us, and the attitudes about modern art that were more or less mangled by the time they reached us from the West.

Of course it's a problematic story, but you painted quite a bit and knew a lot about tradition nonetheless.

But the point is that I never tried to paint like Rembrandt or Raphael or Friedrich; I wouldn't have been able to paint like them anyway – I just wanted to see if I could capture that mysterious, lasting quality that so many of those old paintings have.

That's the thing I find so interesting about your work. It always has had a lot to do with history, German history, German art history, and the history of art more generally. Yet your work is modern, new and, one might say, mysterious.

Maybe a specific example could shed some light on that. The five paintings I did on Titian's *Annunciation*,[1] you know the ones. When I saw Titian's painting in the Accademia I just wanted it for myself, for my apartment, so I decided to copy it as far as I could. But I couldn't even manage a semi-presentable copy. So then I painted five variations on the Annunciation that didn't have much to do with Titian's *Annunciation* but that I was quite happy with.

Yes, but I must say that many of your works from the GDR have a similar effect, for instance The Supper *with Adolph Menzel, Pablo Picasso and Mona Lisa, and other works from that time were very ...*

... typical of my attitude? Yes, but the quality was really very poor, forgivable for a student maybe...

No, they were clever; clever responses to tradition, in my view. I know The Supper *wasn't a 'great painting', but the idea that you were so young and could see that this problematic history had something comic about it was quite perspicacious. To put all those art-historical figures together at a dinner table suggested to me your sense of what I would call the absurdity of a 'cut-and-paste' tradition.*

If you like.

What do you understand by tradition, especially in the sense of knowing a tradition well enough to break with it? And when that happens, what is it that gets broken?

The urge to break with a tradition is only appropriate when you're dealing with an outdated, troublesome tradition: I never really thought about that because I take the old-fashioned approach of equating tradition with value (which may be a failing). But whatever the case, positive tradition can also provoke opposition if it's too powerful, too overwhelming, too demanding. That would basically be about the human side of wanting to hold your own.

The value of those traditions also might be about timelessness...

Yes, that is the most important effect of true quality, that it's as simple as it is mysterious, that it's just naturally there but completely incalculable. And it's not confined to a particular discipline or era: you can find it in Giotto, John Cage, Johann Sebastian Bach, or whomever else.

The experimental freedom of your adolescent work changed after you entered the Dresden Academy. On the one hand the formal training resulted in a number of accomplished figure drawings, still-life paintings and portraits. On the other hand Socialist subject matter was introduced and you began to tackle complex multi-figure compositions with increasing confidence. Although it was a long time ago, perhaps you could comment on whether you had a sense that you were giving something up when you moved from the experimental watercolours to your academic training, or whether at first the new programme seemed positive, a legitimate step forward towards a new art?

I did notice a loss of spontaneity and freedom, but I just accepted the training as necessary, unavoidable toil.

Could you say how much the nature of the training has influenced you since then?

Although it would seem totally outmoded today, this is the training I had, and even as a student I was convinced, and still am, that it was exactly right. The craft skills we learned developed a feeling for materials, and drawing and painting from life were invaluable for the development of the eye. The one-sidedness of the 'do's and don'ts' could also be taken as positive because it encouraged one's capacity to resist and oppose. If we couldn't check books out, we just studied them all the more closely in the reading room, and the things that were absolutely forbidden became all the more exciting.

So which books and catalogues did you have access to in the Dresden Academy library?

Well, you could borrow anything up to Edouard Manet, but everything after that, from the Impressionists onwards, could only be consulted in the reading room.

I see, so they were there.

Yes, but not nearly so many as the classics, and the closer you got to the present, the fewer there were. The only exceptions were contemporary artists who were card-carrying members of some Communist party – like André Fougeron, Renato Guttuso and the rest – you could borrow books about them. And the excuse we were given for their 'formalism' was that they were forced to go along with Western modernism in order to survive. Utter nonsense – which of course made it very easy for us to form our own opinions.

The daily schedule of classes at the Academy took up practically the entire day. How did you manage to experiment with any real freedom when you were faced with such ideological constraints?

With a little vigilance you soon found the gaps in the barrage of rules, and of course, most importantly, you also had like-minded friends.

Artistic friendships always have been important to you, naturally beginning in East Germany. Many of your fellow students in Dresden who remained there throughout the Cold War – people like Wieland Förster,[2] Wilfried Werz[3] and Helmut Heinze[4] – became leading exponents of artistic trends within the GDR. They are all representational artists, but they all distanced themselves from the didactic art propagated by the State. It seems to me they were taking the same 'third way' that you have talked about in connection with your own work when you were in the GDR. How did these friendships add to your education at the Academy?

They were part of it, probably the most important part of all.

And that's when the idea of the 'third way' came up?

Yes, for sure.

A third way – wasn't that a bit idealistic?

Oh yes, the dream of an intact world – in the midst of so many political fronts.

And at first you, too, were idealistic about Socialism, weren't you?

No, never in fact. The ending 'ism' was enough to make me immune to any susceptibility in that direction.

I see. I think it's astonishing that you got away with that attitude and painted such a great number of pictures in the GDR.

For a start, the GDR wasn't the same kind of dictatorship that prevailed in Nazi Germany, and it was possible to create your own space to some degree. And then, I just really relished painting – in fact, any kind of work – which can be a great help in all sorts of difficult situations.

So you found a way to cope with the system in the GDR and produced a lot of pictures that are both idealistic and technically well painted. Among the personal works there are some very accomplished family portraits, such as Die Lesende (Ema)*, among others. These are* *positive images from the GDR, if I can put it like that. Despite everything, you found the freedom to pick out the things that were worthwhile for you, so that you could develop there.*

So it would seem.

The Leipzig painter Werner Tübke is one of the only artists in the Getty exhibition who also worked in the GDR. You left, but he stayed. He is almost unknown in the US, although the next generation of artists who studied with him and his colleagues Bernhard Heisig and Wolfgang Mattheuer at the Leipzig School has made its mark here in the US. Tübke's work sought to combine history painting with Socialist themes. Your work also engages with tradition, but its resistance to any kind of instrumentalization gives your pictures a completely different motivation. You seem to want to demonstrate resistance in your work. Is that true?

I certainly did not want to demonstrate resistance because that would have meant countenancing that very instrumentalization. I just want to paint pictures.

I realize that you do not wish to be compared with Tübke...

On the contrary, why not compare? But I've already talked about the difference when we were discussing the *Annunciation* pictures: Tübke wants to paint as wonderfully as the Old Masters, and he is unusually gifted at it; he's a great illustrator. I can't do that, and I don't want to either.

Of course. He's harking back to a tradition of sheer skill, but strictly speaking he always had a very narrow view of tradition, whereas your view is much wider. Is that just an East/West issue, or something else?

Actually, it has nothing to do with that – if it does at all, then it is only in the sense that Socialist Realism demanded precisely that kind of illustrative dexterity. In the West, Tübke would have found completely different applications for his extraordinary talent.

The role of photography in your work has been much discussed over the years. When I was researching your early career in Dresden, I was surprised to discover how much you used photography when you were still in the GDR. You didn't just turn to it as a tool when you were painting, or as a means to document your own work, you also photographed works of art that were banned by the State. Could you say a few words about the need for that?

It's not that unusual – people are forever photographing things they can't take with them. So if I could only see a painting in the West, or only once in a catalogue, of course I would take a picture of it. But I also think I was probably more curious and impatient than most.

But I was really astonished when I found so many photographs of works of art that you took for your artist friends – for instance, the shots from a book about Henry Moore.

You photographed the entire book! After I saw the photographs I realized that, yes, of course, you learned something else from those modernist genres and traditions, a different approach, wouldn't you say? And at the same time you took a lot of pictures of your own works, and the works of others in exhibitions and books in the West. Photography became a part of your particular 'way of seeing', didn't it?

Could be. But whatever the case, this technology presented a wonderful chance to document something I had seen, and then to see it again as a small image. For me it's a way of constantly training my eye. And a way of appropriating things that comes more naturally to me than words.

In doing so, you took a path that ran counter to the dominant ideology, because books on Henry Moore and Picasso were not officially available. It is unusual that you worked so intensively with the camera in those days, and then later, after you left, it's as though you reinvented your work through the camera.

By painting from photographs?

Yes. But in the GDR you used photography not just to preserve things but also to internalize them and visualize them. Is that right?

Sure. But for me this practice is so natural that I can't explain anything about it to you – I don't know anything about it.

Right, okay. But my question is about the early influences. Don't you think the social and historical circumstances of your education also influenced your very way of seeing?

Yes, of course. Naturally.

In the 1960s the contrast between the art schools in East Germany and the Düsseldorf Academy of Fine Arts hardly could have been greater. Many people don't realize how much you had experimented with Informel before you started on your first series of photo-paintings in the West. This is largely because you burned those abstract works when you were at the Düsseldorf Academy. You were rather sceptical about Informel in those days.

It's more that I was sceptical about my own attempts...

Yes, but later you revisited Informel...

It's not that I had anything against Informel art, it was just that I couldn't be part of that; I had to find my own way...

And later, in revisiting Informel, you achieved a certain elegance in your work through painterly qualities, and perhaps, in spite of yourself.

I think I know what you mean – in the sciences and in mathematics there are elegant solutions, but in art elegance is a slightly derogatory word. I have no objection to either the one or the other kind of elegance.

Along with elegance and painterliness comes expression. Yet, as a young man, you frequently spoke out against expressivity. Later it was: no, I want expressivity. Why?

It's true that I'm not really drawn to the so-called Expressionists, although it has little to do with the individual painters, some of whose pictures I might like a great deal. I just don't like the propaganda-style slogan, the label 'Expressionism' that's attached to a certain crude brand of dilettantish painting.

But your work does have something to do with expressivity.

I should hope so! Pictures that don't express anything, that say nothing, would be completely uninteresting.

Let us turn now to your new paintings in the Getty exhibition: the twelve abstract paintings that make up the series entitled Wald,[5] *which might be translated as 'forest', 'woods' or 'woodland'. The title evokes a literal connection with the subject of many of Friedrich's paintings but, for me, the new abstract series comes closer to Friedrich in mood and atmosphere, more so in fact than your earlier Friedrichesque landscapes based on photographs. Is this apparent to you? How might you explain that?*

That's too difficult for me; I'm bad at interpreting art. I can only confirm that you are right about the affinity to Friedrich, but I can't explain why. Whatever the case, I agree that these twelve abstract, intricate, scratchy paintings have much more to do with the spirit of Friedrich's paintings. Because of their superficial similarity to Friedrich, my smoothly painted landscapes [the earlier photo-paintings] are somewhat embarrassing in the connection to Friedrich. It's a very different relationship that comes through the two groups of my work.

Yes, and about fifteen or sixteen years ago you already used the title Wald *for four large-format abstract paintings.*

Yes. Those abstract paintings[6] are more homogenous than the twelve new ones, and their predominant blue tone connects them more readily with Romanticism. The new work presents a different kind of 'forest', if we want to take the title that literally, or it simply might be that I've gone further with the idea.

We're nearly finished, but I do have to ask – is there a 'German spirit' in painting?

I believe so, yes. But I'd rather not know the details.

Notes for a press conference, 28 July 2006

I first came up with the idea for the colour-chart pictures back in 1966, and my preoccupation with the topic culminated in 1974 with a painting that consisted of 4,096 colour fields.[1]

Initially I was attracted by the typical Pop Art aestheticism of using standard colour-sample cards; I preferred the unartistic, tasteful and secular illustration of the different tones to the paintings of Albers, Bill, Calderara, Lohse, etc.

A little later, I became more interested in the neutral and systematic categorization of the colours we can see and, in conjunction with that, their coincidental appearance within the painting. In this way, I could avoid creating a colour scheme, or any result that might be representational, and only had to determine the format of the painting, the proportions of the grid and the quality of the material. The paintings created in this manner tend towards total perfection and convey the idea of a practically endless number of possible pictures.

While engaged in the – unsuccessful – attempt to calculate how many coincidental combinations of a painting would be possible, I began to understand that, basically, all coincidental paintings would look equally undefined, and that it would take perhaps a thousand years of continuous coincidental juggling before a representational motif might emerge.

Turning to the colour-classification methodology:[2]
The starting point are the four pure colours red, yellow, green and blue; their in-between shades and scales of brightness result in colour schemes containing 16, 64, 256 and 1,024 shades. More colours would be pointless because it wouldn't be possible to distinguish between them clearly.

In the above-mentioned painting with 4,096 colours, only 1,024 different shades were used: these were, however, deployed four times each. This large number of small coloured squares was intended to create a pointillist effect and to allow for, amongst other things, the appearance of coincidental representations. Aside from all theory and interpretation, I take pleasure in the purely visual aspects of these paintings.

In early 2002, the master builder of the cathedral suggested that I develop a glass design for the southern window. The guiding principle was the representation of six martyrs, in keeping with the period. I was, of course, very touched to have such an honour bestowed upon me, but I soon realized that I wasn't at all qualified for the task. After several unsuccessful attempts to get to grips with the subject, and prepared to finally concede failure, I happened upon a large representation of my painting with 4,096 colours. I put the template for the window design over it and saw that this was the only possibility. I wrote to the master builder, telling her that I wouldn't be able to realize the suggestions made by the cathedral chapter, but that I would send her a draft anyway – one that, to me, seemed like the only viable way to design the window.

After that there was a pause of several months, and then the work started on the model, with test patterns and a number of design concepts. The special requirements of the material – that is, coloured squares that could be made of glass – meant that the colour scale had to be reduced to 72 different shades. In reality, there will be about five or ten times as many shades, because each manually manufactured tone is produced as a large sheet of glass which encompasses clearly visible variations of the desired shade. So the scale will span about 500 different shades, and each will appear about twenty times in this window. All in all, the glass work will be made up of 11,000 squares measuring 94 × 94 millimetres each. Half of these (i.e. 5,500) will be allotted by means of a random generator, the others will be like a mirror image of the ones randomly allocated.

Gerhard Richter/28 July 2006

Interview with Hans Ulrich Obrist, November 2006

Going through the many interviews that you have given, I noticed that the topic of architecture is almost never mentioned, which is strange because architecture has played a central role in your exhibitions, and you have had many conversations with architects over the years. And then there is also the architecture of your house that you designed yourself. I was wondering why the subject of architecture almost never comes up in your interviews.

Architecture was, or is, a kind of hobby, an inclination I have to fiddling around and building things. Putting up shelves or cupboards, or making tools, or designing houses ... it always has a functional or social motivation. If social changes are in the air, I am gripped immediately by the desire to build, and I think that I accelerate or anticipate changes in my life by doing so, at least in draft. In the case of my house, that was anticipation: in other words, first build, then change one's life.

In other words, it helped to trigger a change...

Yes, first came the house, and then came the family, and the house was filled.

Could it be that the house produces reality?

[*Laughs*] Yes, with this house I anticipated my vague desire for new social conditions. And the shape of the house was directed in a rather naïve, polemical fashion against the dissolution of architecture. In other words, it was altogether conservative: symmetrical, clearly structured, robust.

Against the then-prevalent deconstructionism?

Yes, and that hasn't got any less crazy to this day.

So it was a reaction against...

... all this wild stuff. Sure, I realize the dangers of an austere position in architecture, such as is represented by Ungers. And there are other brilliant architects like Foster and Renzo Piano, for example. But when I saw [Piano's] Klee Centre in Berne, which looks like a hall for equestrian sports, I thought it was simply dreadful. It has nothing to do with Klee; it could be filled with anything at all. There is probably a patron in Berne who wants to throw his money down the drain. It's terrible, too, to leave everything to the architect. Basically it's the clients' fault – they no longer know what they want. Anyone will go over the top if he has no limits to keep to.

Yet one counter-example that immediately comes to my mind is the new building for the Walker Art Center in Minneapolis. In this case a brilliant client brought forth a remarkable architecture. The museum as an amplifier. But in the case of your house it was a very different situation, because you weren't the architect's client; you sketched the house, and became the architect yourself. You had an architect, but he only played an advisory role.

I had built a number of models. For the details and for the total implementation, I certainly needed an architect to show me what things looked like, what I was looking for. That's the difference between me and Wittgenstein,[1] who designed everything down to the last rod and screw. I have no inclination whatever to succumb to this extreme form of building mania.

So you made the drawings, the ground plan, and designed the structure?

Everything, every room and the whole archaic ground plan, the cross and the square wings, this splendid symmetry, and if I'm lucky, the result will be a piece of timelessness.

I'd be interested to know if there were architects who were important for you, who influenced or inspired you?

No particular architects. Rather, I had a general interest in buildings, irrespective of when or by whom. Of course there are names, Palladio and the Bauhaus architects and Ungers ... everything that looked good.

Mies?

Yes.

Gropius? Le Corbusier?

Gropius, yes. Corbusier is a bit too round and colourful for me.

You've been friends with Ungers for a long time.

I've always liked Ungers. In the '80s he designed the architecture for the Westkunst exhibition organized by Kasper König,[2] which I liked very much. There were numerous assaults against his display. But I've always said how much I liked it, which helped Ungers. Since then there's been a link between us ... but the fact that we get on so well has a human side, too.

Are you interested in the work of Herzog & de Meuron?

I used to be, but today I think the dissolution has gone too far. Yet, when I think how critical I was about the Gehry museum in Bilbao, I have to admit that, although I didn't think much of it when I went there, I was fascinated and it made me think.

Time and again artists have turned their hand to architecture. That also has something to do with the interest in light. History comes up with various examples of the idea of the artist's studio. Joan Miró, for example, had a studio built for him in Majorca by José Maria Sert, the exponent of Spanish Modernism. How must a room function if it's to be of any use to you as a studio?

Better than the one I have now. But somehow I'd be frightened of having a perfect studio: I'd rather have one as defective as it is.

How did you find the documenta *room that Robbrecht designed for your pictures in 1992?*

I liked it very much. It worked very well as an exhibition space. But I wouldn't like a studio like that.

The room was clad in wood.

That was good, and that's why I've done my office like that.

In your place the high doors are striking.

Yes, they're 3 metres high; I like that. No one is made to look small with a door like this. On the contrary, they look taller. It may sound paradoxical, because with my 1.7 metres I would fit almost twice over.

Another feature of your house is that it opens towards the inside while being closed off towards the outside. It is almost invisible from the road...

Maybe these days I'd be less concerned to close myself off like this, but this district here in Hahnwald [on the outskirts of Cologne] was already a bit difficult for me and I gradually had to get used to having such strange neighbours.

So it was a question of sealing yourself off?

Yes, of seclusion, of not being disturbed. The house itself is open all round. It took me a year to notice that you can't live here without an alarm system, that with twelve external doors on the ground floor, more or less unsecured, you could be butchered and no one would notice. That's something I changed root and branch.

Another aspect of your relationship to architecture is, of course, with your exhibitions. Very often for your paintings you have designed rooms completely. You have many drawings of these displays.

Sometimes they're Utopian but they are always for real rooms, in order to stage the exhibition properly and present the pictures as well as possible.

When did this actually begin? There are Utopian room configurations at a very early stage, even with the Atlas *in the 1960s.*[3]

That's when it began. It's simply one of my inclinations – to want to have beautiful rooms. In many cases I insisted on the room having a window. For example, in 1986 in the Kunsthalle Düsseldorf, the first thing I did was have a window unblocked.[4]

You were also the first to come to grips with the very problematical room situation in the German Guggenheim in Berlin, and you did it by opening a window to the street.[5]

That was part of the work, so to speak. It was time-consuming to unblock the windows, and because of the angle of the panes of glass it was also expensive. Now, in Düsseldorf, at the exhibition in the Kunstsammlung Nordrhein-Westfalen,[6] I have integrated windows into the room once more, so that you can see in from the outside and, above all, so that you can see out from the inside.

Is this the window as a 'display feature'?

I don't know what that means, but I think it's a bad thing that museums no longer want to have any windows at all, if possible. The buildings are all so air-conditioned and equipped with such sterile lighting that no windows are needed any more.

Like this underground situation in the Lenbachhaus in Munich,[7] where your Düsseldorf exhibition is currently touring.

I was very unhappy about that. In fact it made me ill to think about it. That's not architecture, that's a station platform, it's un-architecture. A proper play needs a stage, and pictures need architecture. It's quite simple.

There's also an interesting drawing that you made of a museum for the 1,000 grey pictures, a barracks with 1,000 rooms. One picture per room. This mutual relationship between the picture and the room is very important for you. And then there is the room that you did with Blinky Palermo in the early '70s. How did that come about?

I found his murals very good, and when I once went into the gallery in Munich where he just had painted the walls ochre, I said, more as a joke, 'Something's missing; maybe next time we should set up two sculptures.' And that's just what we did in Heiner Friedrich's gallery in Cologne.[8]

Another example is your joint exhibition in the Galerie Ernst in Hanover.

Oh yes, the exhibition for Salvador Dalí[9] with Palermo in Hanover; only two pictures by me and all around, beneath the ceiling, the black stripe by him – highly staged, pretty good.

Although you did that for the Surrealist Salvador Dalí, didn't you?

Yes, out of conviction. Although, or because, Dalí was, for modern painters, the one with the worst reputation, a reactionary bourgeois kitschmonger. We wanted to do something to counter this opinion.

But Dalí is not an artist you really admire.

No. Palermo didn't particularly like him either. But we also realized that he was a brilliant painter, who had painted wonderful, crazy paintings. In this sense, an undifferentiated negative judgment is entirely inappropriate, in fact blind.

In contrast to the previous project with Palermo, which became a permanent room, and now functions in the Lenbachhaus like a little chapel, this Dalí room was only temporary.

Could it be reconstructed?

I could still imagine that, albeit not really without Palermo. It wasn't even possible to reconstruct it in the Lenbachhaus in Munich. All that's left are the two sculptures, and with the typical ochre, the whole thing recalls Palermo; it is therefore more in the way of a homage to him.

By you to him?

By me and the Lenbachhaus.

In terms of exhibition displays and architecture, another interesting aspect is your work with mirrors and glass panels, which is also something that begins in the '60s with the rooms. They're a continually recurring element. And in recent years you have also done these piled-up glasses...

You mean the eleven panels of glass leaning against the wall? Well, after the framed panels, which I had properly planned and designed, the leaning panels are more of a gift. That is to say, I found them here in my studio. The glazier had leant them against the wall. And they were left there till I discovered them.

A readymade, so to speak...

So to speak. Because they were deposited in my studio for other purposes. And there weren't eleven, but five or six, and they looked better and better. It was a step-by-step process. First you get it into the right light, out of the corridor into the studio. Next the right beams (you have to try out the best number) and at some stage or other the piece is finished. At that time I was expecting Kasper König, and I wasn't sure whether he would see these eleven panels at all. But he saw them at once, and said he would like them. I was of course delighted.

Few of your works react to rooms in the sense of a response to, or a critique of, a room.

Like for example the *Eight Grey*, which was first installed in the Berlin Guggenheim, or the *6 Grey Mirrors* for Dia:Beacon. Although both series were conceived for a particular room, they would of course be possible in a different room.

So in the case of the three BMW pictures,[10] *which were commissioned exclusively for this one particular foyer, or of the 20-metre strokes for the school in Soest, they would still be conceivable elsewhere, wouldn't they? And in the case of the* Black, Red, Gold *installation for the Reichstag?*

Well, the flag's dimensions are too extreme for it to fit anywhere else. Quite apart from the content; for something like the *Black, Red, Gold*, the Reichstag really is the right place.

There are a number of smaller versions and editions of this flag. Interestingly, the commissioned work led in turn to other works.

I wasn't commissioned to depict the German flag. I was stimulated by the theme, even though Palermo existed[11] and that famous flag by Jasper Johns. I also once had a 1 × 1-metre version of the flag in my living room, but that didn't work; it was too intrusive, having to look at this black, red and gold all the time.

It's a constant oscillation. On the one hand you have a flag, and on the other you can look at it as abstract.

Yes, in Berlin the flag motif is not obtrusive, of course. And the whole depiction is so enormous there, it has so much elegance that it puts you in a good mood [*laughs*].

How did the BMW pictures come about? Were they commissioned, too?

I was taking photos of palette structures and paint residues, which I then greatly enlarged and painted. The commission came at just the right time, in other words when I could put to use what I was doing at the time. With *Strontium* it was even better: I was just experimenting with pictures on that theme when I had this enquiry from Herzog & de Meuron for the de Young Museum[12] and I was provided with precisely what the *Strontium* motif needed – perfect printing technology and this extreme dimension of more than 9 × 9 metres.

Did it only work on that wall?

No, it also looked very good on another wall, for example in the K20 in Düsseldorf, maybe even better than in the de Young Museum. I only know this from a photograph, and there it is disappointing, dead and empty like the photo of a model.

In respect of architecture, we still haven't talked about the church windows. When I was here a year ago, I went out to this little chapel on the outskirts of Cologne. That wasn't a commissioned work; what you did was hang an existing photograph. How did that come about?

A friendly printer had given me a 60-year-old photo[13] which fascinated me greatly. It was an aerial view of the southern part of Cologne taken by the US Air Force in February '45, with a ruined bridge and countless bomb craters.

That's reminiscent of your townscapes…

… because they also look as if they've been bombed to pieces. But in the photo it was, if anything, the other way round. Because the photo itself had been through the wars, so to speak, I had it processed and retouched, so that it looked like a brand new, immaculate photo. We made an edition of it, and this one large photo for the church.

Now you're working on another project for a church, a window for Cologne Cathedral.

Yes, that's an enormous thing. The starting point for the design is a picture, a colour plate dating from 1974. The principle is unchanged: a number of different colour tones are placed at random in a particular grid. And the window is filled up like that.

It consists of lots of little squares, like the 1974 colour plate.

Yes, only in a different field: it's not square, but the shape of the Gothic window. And the size of the squares is different, and the spectrum of colours is narrower.

Why is the number of colours smaller?

It's limited to 72. Of course, we could have far more different-coloured pieces of glass made but, for one thing, the colour tones must be distinguishable from a distance, and for another, the scale should be balanced. In other words, if there were 500 shades of red but only 100 different shades of green, the whole thing would have a red cast. So we had to develop a balanced colour scale.

I also see associations with the 1,000 grey pictures in the 1,000 rooms. Both are examples of 'ars combinatoria'.

Oh, really? But here with the cathedral window we're talking about something quite concrete, something real, and it's a very special location which carries a greater burden of history and importance than almost any other. It is all so overwhelming that any supplementation with modern art often comes across as inhibited, false, silly or kitsch. In order to avoid this danger, I have taken the place as it is: what does the cathedral look like, how is it used? And in so doing, I've avoided wanting anything special. So: no depictions of saints, no message and, in a certain sense, not even art. It was just to be a radiantly beautiful window, as good and beautiful and with as many meanings as I could make it here and now.

Illustrating nothing? Depicting nothing?

Nothing like that. Simply this very simple design, realized optimally. Of course, I wasn't able to have these ideas before the design, but at the start I had to try out all possible picture ideas, accompanied by dissatisfaction at all these useless ideas – until I then saw a reproduction of my old colour-field pictures and was even a little frightened, because it fitted so well.

Your large-scale pictures often oscillate between micro and macro elements. You see this particularly in the Stroke, *but you can also see it in respect of your details in the* WAR CUT *book.*[14] *I wanted to ask you something else about this to and fro of micro and macro. In your Munich exhibition, the last room with the silicate provided an almost autonomous zone. It was almost a room within a room: it was my favourite room in the exhibition.*

Good! That all hangs together. I was fascinated by the motif, because while imaging technology in microscopes has advanced to the point where you can really see an atom, you can never see it sharp. I find that important, because it sets a limit.

You can't go any further.

One can't go any further; there's really an end-point, simply because there's nothing there that can be seen. A new quality starts there. That's fascinating in itself! And as a fact, this event shows itself quite simply as lack of sharpness, as a little out-of-focus photo.

The first 'original'[15] *came from the* Frankfurter Allgemeine Zeitung *newspaper. Is the* F.A.Z. *a permanent source?*

[*Laughs*] That's how it is with newspapers, you get used to the daily delivery of news from the world. And even though they annoy me every day, I like them.

The F.A.Z. *was also the trigger for* WAR CUT. *The book started as a small project: I'd invited you to Paris and you photographed a lot of details from one of your books there. What followed had a lot to do with chance...*

To start with, I had no idea what I was supposed to do with the photos. They lay around in the studio until the Iraq War broke out and I read all the reports in the newspaper.

Then the random encounter produced a major construction.

Perhaps because the events that the newspaper articles were describing to me were just as incomprehensible as my abstract detail photos. In any case, I saw a connection.

You spent months sticking them this way and that.

A few weeks certainly, before the final layout was there – order versus chaos, in other words. It was good.

Maybe we could talk about the studio. Actually there's a whole exhibition of new pictures and drawings on show here.

The drawings[16] have only just been begun. But the twelve pictures[17] are finished. Only it's difficult to say anything about them: for me they're still too fresh to understand. You know what's meant by stable fever? No? When horses are kept in the stable too long before a race, they run better. That was doubtless the case with me in this series.

Then it went quite quickly?

Well, a few months. And now I wouldn't know what else to do with them. They seem to be finished and maybe not too bad.

The smaller picture here shows the Twin Towers?

Yes. Probably September 11 bothered me more than I expected. The big drawings also have something to do with that theme; maybe at the time so did all the pictures, even if you can't see that now.

On September 11 you were on the way to your last New York exhibition[18] *when the aeroplane was forced to land in Halifax. Now there's the next New York exhibition. These twelve pictures are among the darkest of your abstract pictures.*

Apart from the elegant *December*, *November* and *January*, which have more black. The new pictures here are more spontaneous, more abrasive, less aesthetic, somewhat painful. The little picture of the two towers was very colourful to start with, with the garish explosion beneath the wonderful blue sky and the flying rubble. That couldn't work; only when I destroyed it, so to speak, scratched it off, was it fit to be seen.

As a drawing it was already hanging here a year ago. So it was at the same time the first and the last drawing.

Yes. But I'm worried about exhibiting it. On the one hand, it's a perfectly harmless picture, small, and not at all sensational. On the other, it has such a spectacular title, *September 11*. I should keep it, and if it still looks all right, maybe I'll exhibit it one day later on.

Finally, are there any unfinished or unrealized projects which you would like to see completed?

Build some new houses. Realize something of the Utopias which we dreamt up some forty years ago, practical things like traffic systems in the Ruhr, nice social housing[19] on the Rhine meadows in Oberkassel [in Düsseldorf].

Have you designed any social housing?

Some pretty wooden models, dilettante, but with a deep conviction that the world can and must be made better.

You did realize your own house!

I could imagine how it might be improved.

What changes would you make?

I'd change the location, raise the level of the plot a bit. Make the house a bit more practical, and build the four wings a metre longer – in other words, not seven metres long, but eight. That would be better – for the stairs, too. And then of course a much better studio.

Interview with Hans Ulrich Obrist, 2007

For now let's start at the beginning. I wanted to ask you what it means for you to participate in the Biennale under Robert Storr[1] this year?

I take particular pleasure in the fact that Robert Storr is doing this international exhibition. He's a professional in the best sense. And the Biennale is indeed a wonderful and important event – in all likelihood it's the best there is, despite the moaning that goes on. So I'm really glad I can be there and can show my paintings there.

Can we talk about the new paintings? This is the first time this unbelievable new cycle has been shown.

It's a series of six large, rectangular paintings,[2] and they have a special significance for me insofar as I still don't fully understand them. They were planned completely differently: that is, I wanted to paint them from photos I had prepared two years ago; photos of various atomic structures comparable to the silicate series[3] or the strontium picture[4] from 2004. These six photos promised beautiful, serious, somewhat disturbing paintings. And then when I had begun with the first painting, in late August, I suddenly lost the desire to work on it and proceeded to destroy what I had already painted, to paint it over without being conscious of what I wanted and where I wanted to go, and I just kept on painting like this somehow. This peculiar state of hopelessness, perplexity and high spirits kept on long enough for me to finish all six paintings. Of course from time to time during the work I have fantasies about how the paintings could finally look. For example, at one point I thought the paintings would have to be completely white, with very little adumbration – like large drawings in oil on canvas.

Something like the large white paintings that were exhibited in Japan?[5]

Yes, something like that. These concepts always get me very excited, but mostly they will have disappeared the next day, or a week later. And then I would start up again, nonsensically. In this way they definitely are my freest paintings. And I never even thought it possible they would be finished: I had no concept of final results. But then they were finished after three months, which means there was nothing more I could do with them. I was almost upset about it.

Because of a sudden emptiness afterward?

Yes, that too. That's often the case when something is finished, and one feels superfluous and useless. But in this case that finished state of the paintings came

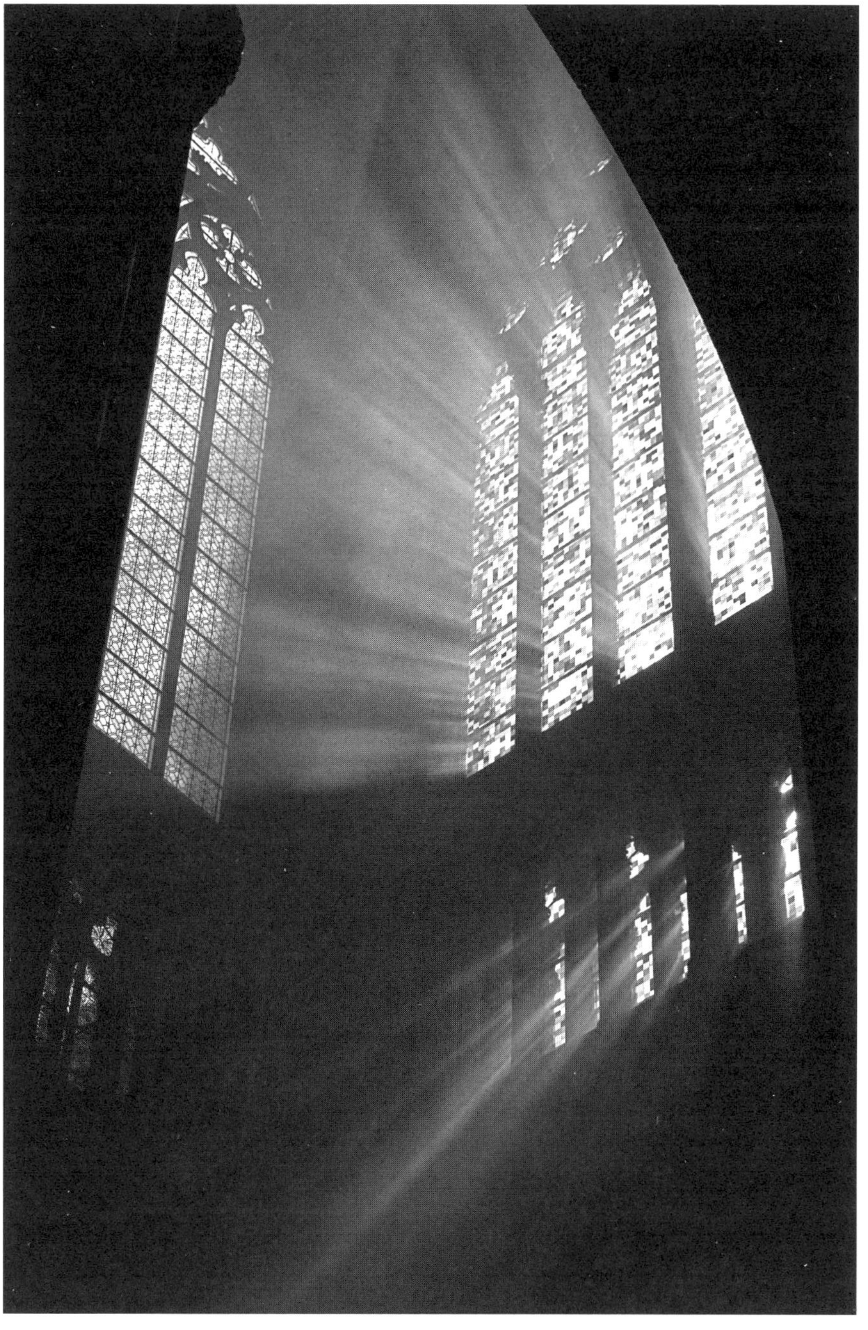

Cathedral window, Cologne, 2007

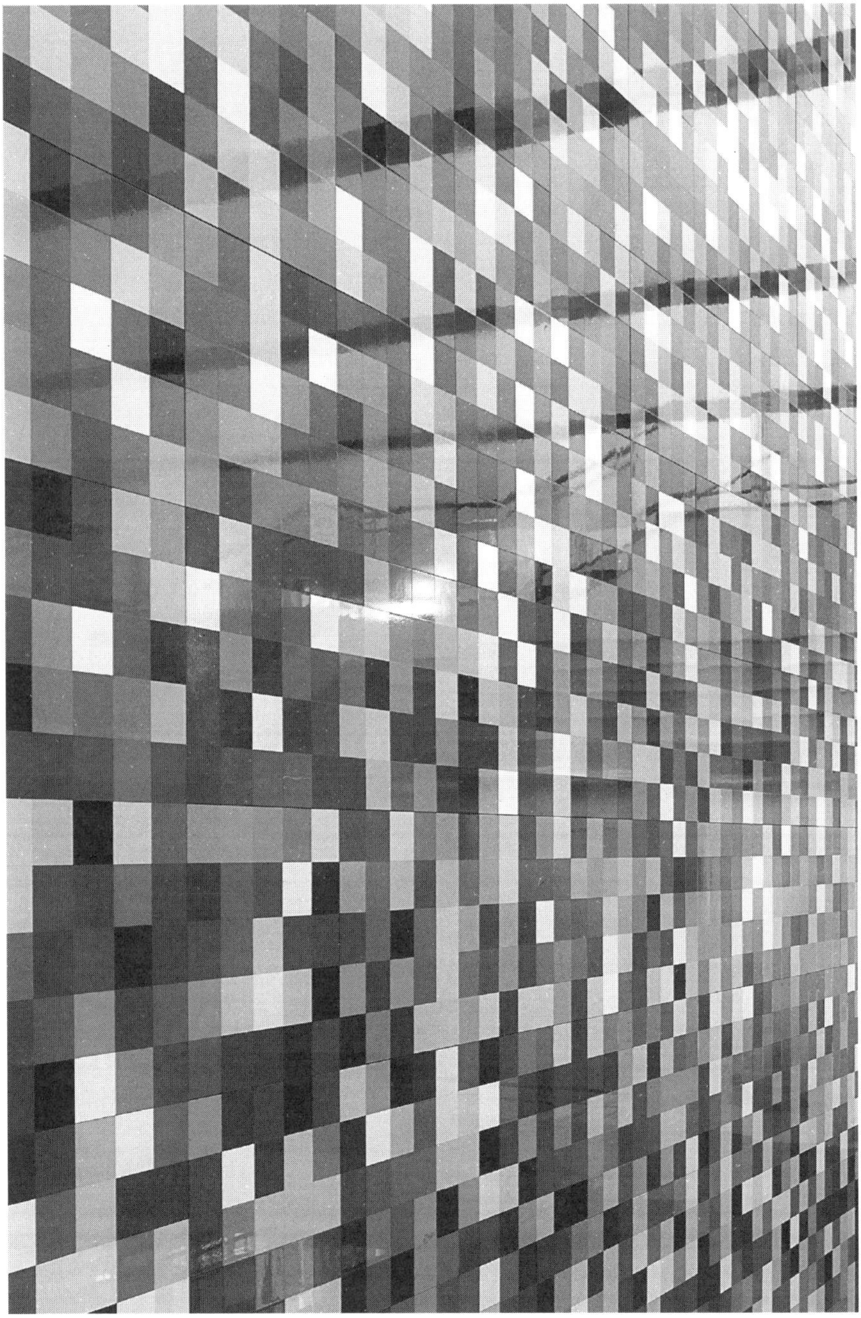

4,900 *Colours*, 2007 (detail)

quite unexpectedly, in fact almost disappointingly. I think I had felt I would be able to – or would have to – paint them forever. In any case, they were done, and the next problem was that I did not know what the paintings showed, and how I could title them. And there it was you who helped me with a question. You asked me what music I'd been listening to during that period of work, and I answered: Cage!

And with that you'd found your title.

In hindsight I have to say: rightly so. Because just then I had discovered – or rediscovered – the *Complete Piano Music* by John Cage, and had been listening to it almost exclusively for a while, and I still enjoy it today. Around twelve CDs, all of them with Steffen Schleiermacher. Wonderful. Of course such a title is only indirectly linked with the paintings – it doesn't actually describe anything; it simply guides one's perspective in a certain direction, toward certain connections and similarities. But of course it signifies more than just a name. In any case, the title is also meant to honour and express admiration for the music.

Cage has had a longlasting impression on you. You also once said that his 'Lecture on Nothing' impressed you: 'I have nothing to say and I am saying it'...

Yes, that's true. Oddly enough another connection just occurred to me, a visual similarity. Yesterday once again I saw this beautiful Guardi postcard,[6] the *Laguna grigia*, a wonderful little picture I'd once seen in Milan. I enjoy these kind of connections.

And that brings us back to Venice...

Into the grey lagoon of John Cage.

Wonderful! Perhaps we can speak a bit more about Cage and coincidence. You have spoken often about the concept of coincidence in Cage's and your own work, and it seems to be the case that coincidence plays a role again in these unplanned paintings...

Yes, a definitive role, even in the abstract paintings. Despite all my technical experience, I cannot always exactly foresee what will happen when I apply or remove large amounts of paint with the scraper. Surprises always emerge, disappointing or pleasant ones, which in any case represent changes to the painting – changes that I have to process first in my mind before I can continue. One can see, or rather hear, a great example in Cage's work of how extensively, cleverly and sensitively he treats this coincidence in order to make music out of it.

You also spoke of Cage's discipline. You were interested in the notion that coincidence is only possible with a great deal of discipline. The same applies to these paintings.

Yes, otherwise they would just be smears of paint. Even with the colour charts and now with the cathedral window these coincidences are only useful because they've been worked out – that means either eliminated or allowed or emphasized; in short, brought into a particular form. That is skilful and artistic.

When I saw your Cage paintings for the first time, in your atelier, you were not yet certain if the cycle would have five or six paintings. It was as if the five paintings belonged together, but the sixth was a part of the series yet also not... Can you say something about this? I believe all six are being shown in Venice.

Yes, the question of five or six was solved in time, because the first painting quite obviously belongs to the series, even if its appearance is somewhat different, somewhat softer than the following five. It now has the sense of being an introduction.

These new paintings are...

... more spontaneous, more free, not planned.

I would like to ask again – because something quite new is happening with the paintings that wasn't there before – can we possibly encapsulate what it is?

That's difficult for me to say. In the first place, I'm glad that I'm gradually able to recognize what the paintings show, that something is being conveyed, that they actually depict something, something quasi-real. But it will take some time yet before I can describe what that is.

You once said that in your abstract paintings there is a search for a likeness, which is always there...

Yes, it's always there. I think all abstract paintings function that way. We aren't capable of viewing paintings without searching for their inherent similarity with what we've experienced and what we know. To see what they offer us, whether they threaten us or whether they're nice to us, or whatever it might be...

A question about construction and deconstruction – because it's very interesting that this cycle began, like many of your abstract paintings, with an image which was then destroyed. And there are these several phases of image, as you've documented them photographically in this book, where one can see all the painted-over images which no longer exist. It's actually a rather destructive act, and you agreed as we looked at them that this destructive act exists, but that alongside it there is the desire to create a well-built, constructive painting.

Yes, it's quite exciting to work that way, with destroying and building up, and wrecking again and so on. That's effectively a prerequisite – otherwise nothing will result. Only in figurative paintings is it any different; there the destruction and construction are not as obvious.

Do you think these are optimistic paintings?

... I'm beginning to...

I thought the grey paintings in your New York exhibition were much darker by comparison...

... which I exhibited in 2001 with Marian?[7] They were actually a light grey, like bright dust and fog, but rather melancholic.

Somehow the Cage paintings bring a more optimistic quality ... something of the principle of hope.

That may lie in a certain aggression and unpredictability they possess, which makes them more optimistic than the grey New York paintings.

And what is coming next? The paintings are finished, and it's always interesting to look toward the future...

I have no idea! Whether something new will come is a matter of my age and of fortune. I hope it will, and I'm ready for it.

We haven't yet spoken about the light in these paintings, about cold light, warm light, southern light, northern light... How would you describe the light in these paintings?

[*Laughs*] Now that I've referred to the Guardi, with its gentle southern light from the lagoon, I think I have to describe it as northern light.

Perhaps that's the paradox of the light in Engadin [in Switzerland], where the south and the north – like Finland and Italy – collide.

Wonderful! Yes, Nietzsche described that so well. That's exactly what it is: the light of Sils Maria.[8]

Final question: there is this wonderful little text by Rainer Maria Rilke called Advice to a Young Poet, *and I'd like to ask you what is your advice here in 2007 to young painters?*

[*Laughs*] Don't be easily led astray, and don't give up believing in art. That's all.

Wonderful. Many thanks for this interview.

Appendix

Source citations, annotations and commentary

The original volume of Gerhard Richter's texts, edited by Hans Ulrich Obrist, was published in German in 1993: *Gerhard Richter: Text. Schriften und Interviews* (Frankfurt/Leipzig: Insel-Verlag). In 1995, this volume was translated into English by David Britt and published as *Gerhard Richter: The Daily Practice of Painting. Writings 1962–1993* (London: Thames & Hudson/Anthony d'Offay Gallery). The present volume includes not only newer material generated since 1993, but also numerous older texts not previously available. Texts not found in earlier editions have either been printed here in their original English translations (with orthography and punctuation standardized throughout for consistency) or have been translated especially for the present volume.

The headings and titles used in the 1995 publication have been retained. For new material, even if previously published elsewhere, we have used titles similar in format to those chosen in 1995. As a result, these new titles are not necessarily identical to those found in the original publication of each text, though wherever possible we list the appropriate bibliographical information.

Titles of artworks have been given their English names as they appear in *Gerhard Richter: Catalogue Raisonné 1962–1993* and *Gerhard Richter: Catalogue Raisonné 1993–2004*. If a work does not appear in either catalogue, a literal translation has been supplied in square brackets.

Finally, various persons, events and topics are marked in the texts with footnote references corresponding to the commentaries on the following pages. Any obvious mistakes in spelling or content have been corrected.

Dietmar Elger

Abbreviation for references to the previous edition: *Gerhard Richter. The Daily Practice of Painting: Writings 1962–1993*, London, 1995, is hereafter referred to as *The Daily Practice of Painting*, 1995.

Letter to Professor Heinz Lohmar, 6 April 1961
Previously unpublished.
Translated from the German by Ben Posener.

A letter by Richter to his former teacher at the Dresden Academy of Fine Arts, written only weeks after his escape with his wife Ema from East Germany through Berlin to West Germany. The original copy of the letter is held in the Academy's archives.

1 *Professor Lohmar*: Born in 1900 in Troisdorf, near Cologne, the painter Heinz Lohmar taught mural painting at the Dresden Academy of Fine Arts. As a mentor he was extremely supportive of Richter.
2 *journey to Moscow and Leningrad*: Just prior to his escape, Richter had taken a study trip to Moscow and Leningrad. At the time of his return, via West Berlin, he deposited some of his luggage there in anticipation of the pending escape.

Notes, 1962
First published: *The Daily Practice of Painting*, 1995, pp. 11–15.

1 *I did not come here*: Richter refers to his escape from East Germany (i.e. from Dresden via Berlin to Düsseldorf) in March 1961.

Letter to a newsreel company, 29 April 1963
First published: *The Daily Practice of Painting*, 1995, pp. 15–16.

A letter signed by Gerhard Richter to Mr Schmidt at the *Neue Deutsche Wochenschau*, Düsseldorf, dated 29 April 1963. The letter also functions as the press release for the exhibition in a former butcher's shop in Düsseldorf, at Kaiserstrasse 31a, by artists Manfred Kuttner, Konrad Lueg, Sigmar Polke and Gerhard Richter. They were able to rent the space from the city of Düsseldorf for 40 DM. The exhibition was to be the only exclusive joint presentation by the four artists, who were friends. On one further occasion their work appeared together in a larger group exhibition (*Neodada, Pop, Decollage, Kapitalistischer Realismus*, René Block Gallery, Berlin, 19 June–5 November 1964). The exhibition at Kaiserstrasse 31a opened on Saturday 11 May 1963 at 11 a.m., and ran through 26 May. Gerhard Richter's works *Party* (2-1) and *Dead* (9) were on display.

An identical typescript, signed by all four artists and addressed to Cent-Fox and *Fox-Tönende Wochenschau*, Düsseldorf, is to be found in the Manfred Kuttner archives. For a facsimile, see: 'Ganz am Anfang/ How it all began. Richter, Polke, Lueg & Kuttner', *Sediment*, 7, 2004, p. 72. In a conversation with Susanne Küper, Manfred Kuttner claimed they sent their press package to film production companies, newspaper editors, museums and galleries as far away as the United States. See also:

Susanne Küper, 'Konrad Lueg und Gerhard Richter: Leben mit Pop – eine Demonstration für den Kapitalistischen Realismus', in *Wallraf-Richartz-Jahrbuch*, Vol. LIII, 1992, p. 305, note 27.

1 *Capitalist Realism*: The term appears for the first time in this press release. Although a number of stylistic terms are listed with question marks on the invitation card ('Pop-Art? Imperialist Realism? Anti-Art?'), there is no explicit reference to 'capitalist realism'. Presumably the term is meant as an ironic reference to the East German Socialist Realism movement, which at least two of the four artists, Richter and Manfred Kuttner, had come to know in the GDR. The René Block Gallery in Berlin held a solo show entitled *Gerd Richter. Images of Capitalist Realism*, from 18 November 1964 through 5 January 1965.
2 *German Pop Art*: In the autumn of 1964, Richter and Konrad Lueg travelled to Paris and introduced themselves to, among others, the gallery owners Iris Clert and Ileana Sonnabend as 'German pop artists'.
3 *We*: Richter wrote the letter on behalf of the other artists participating in the exhibition, Manfred Kuttner, Konrad Lueg and Sigmar Polke.

Manfred Kuttner was born in 1937 in the town of Greiz, in Thuringia. From 1956 to 1959 he studied along with Richter at the Dresden Academy of Fine Arts. When Richter taught an evening course in drawing in 1957 as part of his degree requirements, Kuttner was among his students. After Kuttner's escape to the West in March 1960, he began his studies under Gerhard Hoehme the following semester at the State Art Academy in Düsseldorf. He later switched, along with Richter, to the studio of K. O. Götz. In 1962 they gave their first exhibition together in the Galerie Junge Kunst [Young Art Gallery] in Fulda (8–30 September 1962), which had been arranged by their fellow student, Franz Erhard Walther, who came from Fulda.

Konrad Lueg's original name was Konrad Fischer. He was born in 1939 in Düsseldorf. He used his mother's maiden name as his artist name. From 1958 to 1962 he studied at the State Art Academy with K. O. Götz (among others), where he became acquainted with Richter. The two organized a demonstration on 11 October 1963 in the Möbelhaus Berges [Berges Furniture Store] entitled *Leben mit Pop – eine Demonstration für den Kapitalistischen Realismus*. Konrad Fischer opened his own Düsseldorf gallery in 1967 at Neubrückstrasse 12. Richter exhibited here for the first time in 1970 (11 April–7 May). Konrad Fischer-Lueg died in 1996 in Düsseldorf. Extensive information on Konrad Lueg the artist can be found in the catalogue *Ich nenne mich als Künstler Konrad Lueg*, Kunsthalle Bielefeld, 1999. A book on his gallery, the Konrad Fischer Galerie, is also available: *Ausstellungen bei Konrad Fischer, Düsseldorf Oktober 1967–Oktober 1992*, Bielefeld, 1993.

Sigmar Polke was born in Oels, Lower Silesia, in 1941 and went to Düsseldorf in 1953. In 1962 he began studies with K. O. Götz as well. Richter and Polke exhibited together only once, in 1966 at Galerie h in Hanover. A combined catalogue and artist's book was published (see also: 'Text for exhibition catalogue, Galerie h, Hanover, 1966', written jointly with Sigmar Polke, pp. 36–44).

Programme and Report: The Exhibition *Leben mit Pop – eine Demonstration für den Kapitalistischen Realismus*, Düsseldorf, 11 October 1963

First publication (programme): Untitled, in *Brennpunkt Düsseldorf. Joseph Beuys. Die Akademie. Der allgemeine Aufbruch*, 1962–1987, exhib. cat., Kunstmuseum Düsseldorf, 1987: fig. p. 100.

First publication (report): 'Bericht über *Eine Demonstration für den Kapitalistischen Realismus* von Konrad Lueg und Richter, am Freitag, den 11. Oktober 1963, in Düsseldorf, Flingerstrasse 11 (Bergeshaus)', in Rolf-Gunter Dienst, *Pop-Art. Eine kritische Information*, Wiesbaden, 1965, pp. 138–140.

First English publication: *The Daily Practice of Painting*, 1995, pp. 18–21.

The programme and report were written jointly by Konrad Lueg and Gerhard Richter. The programmes were numbered sequentially by hand in a demarcated field on the upper right-hand corner and were distributed to the audience. The typescript of the report is held in the Konrad Fischer-Lueg archives, as is the original copy of the scripted announcements read over public address at the event. Richter exhibited the following works: *Mouth (Brigitte Bardot's Lips)* (11-1), *Pope* (destroyed: for an image, see *Gerhard Richter. Bilder, Paintings* 1962–1985, exhib. cat., Städtische Kunsthalle Düsseldorf, 1986, p. 20), *Stag* (7) and *Neuschwanstein Castle* (8). A complete description of the event can be found in Susanne Küper, 'Konrad Lueg und Gerhard Richter: Leben mit Pop – eine Demonstration für den Kapitalistischen Realismus', in Vol. LIII of *Wallraf-Richartz-Jahrbuch*, 1992, pp. 289–306. See also: 'Ganz am Anfang/How it all began. Richter, Polke, Lueg & Kuttner', *Sediment*, 7, 2004.

1 *Professor Beuys*: Joseph Beuys was born in Kleve in 1921. He studied from 1947 to 1951 at the State Art Academy in Düsseldorf under Ewald Mataré, and was himself named professor there beginning in the summer semester of 1961. Richter reports that he initially thought Beuys was one of the students when he first met him at the Academy.
2 *Messrs Schmela and Kennedy*: Richter and Lueg had constructed two papier-mâché figures, of the Düsseldorf gallery owner Alfred Schmela and of American president John F. Kennedy, and integrated them into the demonstration at the Berges Furniture Store. To raise

funds, Richter had also designed floats for the Düsseldorf carnival parades. After the exhibition, the Kennedy figure was acquired by Kasper König, and the Schmela figure was bought by the Cologne restorer Wolfgang Hahn. For images of these works, see: *Aufbrüche, Manifeste, Manifestationen*, exhib. cat., Städtische Kunsthalle Düsseldorf, 1984, fig. p. 103 (Schmela), fig. p. 106 (Kennedy).

3 *14 pairs of roebuck antlers*: For the demonstration, Richter had borrowed the antlers from his father-in-law, Professor Heinrich Eufinger (see 'Conversation with Roberta De Righi, 2005', note 2).

4 *texts from furniture catalogues*: The text fragments were taken from the store's catalogues and read over loudspeaker. For example: 'Is your room a single or double? Here this question is solved with the wide Swedish bed. The wardrobe displays alternating wood with glass doors.' Or: 'Valuable, authentically styled furniture, which we see in palaces, museums and well-maintained bourgeois homes, has always been made of birch and cherry woods.'

Notes, 1964

First published: *The Daily Practice of Painting*, 1995, pp. 22–24.

In the statements listed as 'Notes, 1964', published in the 1995 edition, Richter also refers to the groups of work *Türen* [Doors] and *Vorhänge* [Curtains], which were begun in 1965 in the case of *Vorhänge* (with the exception of No. 36a), and in 1967 in the case of *Türen*. At least some portion of this text, therefore, was written after 1964 and not before 1967.

1 *I worked as a photographic laboratory assistant*: Despite this statement, Richter never in fact worked as a photographic laboratory assistant. As a young man in Waltersdorf, he had had the opportunity to develop his own prints in a darkroom belonging to the father of a schoolfriend. His mother had given him a camera for Christmas 1945.

2 *Götz*: Karl Otto Götz, born in Aachen in 1914, taught from 1959 to 1979 as Professor of Painting at the State Art Academy in Düsseldorf. After Richter had begun his studies in the winter semester of 1961–1962 with Ferdinand Macketanz, he switched the following semester to Götz's studio. Richter remained there until he left the academy without a degree at the end of the summer semester in 1964.

3 *Gaul*: Winfred Gaul (1928–2004) had studied from 1950 to 1953 at the Stuttgart Art Academy, and lived in Düsseldorf from 1955. K. O. Götz writes in his memoirs: 'I recall the student exhibition in February 1962, where [Richter's] informal paintings were hung in the dark lower hall of the academy. Then shortly thereafter he began making signal paintings [*Signalbilder*]. When the painter Gaul visited me at the academy and looked in on my class, he was

surprised that among other things there were signal paintings on the wall. Gaul was also doing signal paintings at the time, and moaned, 'Something new has just appeared on the art scene and they're already doing it at the academy.' (K. O. Götz, *Erinnerungen und Werk*, Vol. 1b, Düsseldorf, 1983, p. 912.)

4 *Contact with like-minded painters*: The fellow students Richter, Manfred Kuttner, Konrad Lueg and Sigmar Polke discussed their work and planned strategies together for presenting it to the public.

Poster text for the exhibition *Klasen und Richter*, Galerie Friedrich & Dahlem, Munich, 1964

First publication (exhibition poster): *Gerd Richter. Fotobilder, Portraits und Familien* at the Galerie Friedrich & Dahlem, Munich, 10 June–10 July 1964.

First English publication: *The Daily Practice of Painting*, 1995, p. 26.

Richter's exhibition *Fotobilder, Portraits und Familien* took place simultaneously, though in separate spaces, with an exhibition by Peter Klasen at the Galerie Friedrich & Dahlem, Munich. This was Richter's first solo exhibition. The poster is printed on both sides. On the obverse are multiple reproductions of Richter's painting *Stukas* (18-1), 1964. On the reverse side were small images from other works, a list of the work on exhibit, and the text printed here. The text is a newspaper report found by Richter, which he uses and reproduces here as if readymade. Konrad Lueg and Richter had similarly found and employed the spoken catalogue texts at their demonstration at the Berges Furniture Store.

1 *Klasen*: The painter Peter Klasen was born in Lübeck in 1935. He studied from 1956 to 1959 at the College of the Arts in Berlin. In the same year he moved to Paris, where he still lives today.

2 *Galerie Friedrich & Dahlem*: The gallery was founded in 1963 by Heiner Friedrich, his wife Six, and their partner Franz Dahlem. Heiner Friedrich had taken notice of Richter via Kasper König, who was living at London at the time, and recommended in early 1964 that Friedrich visit the young Richter in Düsseldorf. Heiner Friedrich was Richter's most important gallerist in the 1960s.

Interview between John Anthony Thwaites and Gerhard Richter, written by Sigmar Polke, October 1964

First published: *The Daily Practice of Painting*, 1995, pp. 26–28.

This text is a fictitious interview between Richter and the art critic Anthony Thwaites, written by Sigmar Polke. Less than a year later, in July 1965, an almost identical interview appeared, in which the art critic Albert Schulze-Vellinghausen acted as interviewer, and in which the same questions were now answered in the collective 'we' by Polke and Richter together. Along these lines, the first answer read: 'We have a lot of work, and are well developed artistically, and also mentally and physically. We pull the expander front and back. And if you saw our new pictures, Mr Thwaites, you would collapse!' The typed manuscript is held at Gerhard Richter's atelier, and bears his hand-written gloss: 'the interview invented by Polke, slightly altered for a catalogue which was not published.'

Letter to Heiner Friedrich, 23 November 1964

First published: *The Daily Practice of Painting*, 1995, pp. 28–30.

1 *catalogues and posters*: Richter refers to the catalogue from his exhibition with René Block in Berlin, *Gerd Richter. Bilder des Kapitalistischen Realismus* (18 November 1964–5 January 1965), as well as to the poster from his joint exhibition at the Galerie Parnass in Wuppertal, *Neue Realisten. Konrad Lueg, Sigmar Polke, Gerd Richter* (20 November–31 December 1964).

2 *Jährling*: Rudolf Jährling had founded the Galerie Parnass in 1949. The exhibition with Richter, Lueg and Polke was one of the last shows in his gallery, which closed on 5 June 1965 with the Happening *24 Stunden* [24 Hours].

3 *Block's*: René Block opened his gallery in September 1964 with the exhibition *Neodada, Pop, Decollage, Kapitalistischer Realismus* (16 September–5 November 1964), in which Richter, Lueg, Polke and Kuttner also participated. The solo show by Richter, after a presentation by Stanley Brouwn, was just the third exhibition of the new gallery.

4 *Hague Realists*: The exhibition *Neuer Realismus und Pop Art* was held at the Academy of the Arts, Berlin (20 November 1964–3 January 1965), and had been shown at the Gemeentemuseum, The Hague, and in Vienna.

5 *catalogue text by de la Motte*: Manfred de la Motte: 'Gerd Richter oder der kapitale "Kapitalistische Realismus"', in *Gerd Richter. Bilder des Kapitalistischen Realismus*, exhib. cat., Galerie René Block, Berlin, 1964.

6 *I've noted some of it down*: Presumably Richter is referring to his 'Notes, 1964', printed here (see pp. 21–23).

7 *Rome exhibition*: The exhibition referred to here, in the Galleria la Tartaruga in Rome, was not actually realized until 1966 (20 January–20 February 1966).

Notes, 1964–1965

First published: *The Daily Practice of Painting*, 1995, pp. 30–39.

In his letter to Heiner Friedrich, dated 23 November 1964 (see pp. 25–29), Richter refers to some notes he had made – presumably a reference to a portion of the notes printed here.

1 *Dalí's*: Salvador Dalí (1904–1989). In 1970 Richter had in fact done an exhibition at the Galerie Ernst in Hanover with Blinky Palermo under the title *Für Salvadore Dalí* (10 October–6 November 1970). Shown there were Richter's large-format paintings *Detail (Red-blue)* (273) and *Detail (Grey-lilac)* (274), 1970, each 200 × 300 cm.

2 *Bacon's*: Francis Bacon (1909–1992). In 1962 Richter had painted *Papst* [Pope], in addition to other paintings, which leaned heavily on Bacon's style. For images, see: *Gerhard Richter. Bilder, Paintings 1962–1985*, exhib. cat., Städtische Kunsthalle Düsseldorf, 1986, p. 20.

3 *contemporary Fluxus events*: Events that Richter had attended as a visitor included: *NEO-DADA in der Musik* at the Düsseldorf Kammerspiele (16 June 1962), *Festum Fluxorum Fluxus* at the State Art Academy, Düsseldorf (2–3 February 1963) and the *Festival der neuen Kunst – Actions/Agit-Pop/De-Collage/Happening/Events/Antiart/L'Autrisme/Art Total/Refluxus* at the Polytechnic College in Aachen (20 June 1964).

Text for exhibition catalogue, Galerie h, Hanover, 1966, written jointly with Sigmar Polke

First published: *Polke/Richter*, exhib. cat., Galerie h, Hanover, 1966.

First English publication: *Gerhard Richter*, exhib. cat., 36th Venice Biennale, German Pavilion, Venice, 1972, pp. 27–33. *The Daily Practice of Painting*, 1995, pp. 39–56.

Sigmar Polke and Richter exhibited together from 1 to 26 March 1966 at August Haseke's Galerie h in Hanover. The following of Richter's paintings, all done in 1965, were on display: *Tiger* (78), *Uncle Rudi* (85), *Two Women with Tart* (95), *Stool in Profile* (98) and *Man with Two Children* (96). A catalogue was printed to accompany the exhibition, which Richter later described as 'demonstrative', in contrast to his commercial gallery exhibitions. The catalogue is also listed by both painters in their respective catalogues raisonnés of artist editions (*Sigmar Polke. Die Editionen 1963–2000*, Ostfildern-Ruit, 2000, cat. no. 2, pp. 12–13; *Gerhard Richter. Editionen 1965–2004*, exhib. cat., Bonn Art Museum, 2004, cat. no. 3, p. 126). Nonetheless, the catalogue only contains an image of one work by each artist, in Richter's case, of *Uncle Rudi* (85). The text, which consists of a collage of text fragments either written or collected by the artists, is accompanied by eleven candid and posed photos of both artists. For this purpose Richter and Polke quoted heavily from the Perry Rhodan science-fiction series. The figures listed in the catalogue alongside the artists – including Perry Rhodan, Atlan, Gucky and Lieutenant Afg Moro – all come from these adventure stories. Factual information about Richter's and Polke's career and work is printed, while in other places the two artists' own ironic writings and quoted text fragments are so closely mixed together that it is difficult for the reader to separate reality and fiction. The handmade clippings of texts and images are contained in August Haseke's archives (see also: 'Ganz am Anfang/How it all began. Richter, Polke, Lueg & Kuttner', *Sediment*, 7, 2004, fig. p. 97).

1 *Perry Rhodan*: Richter enjoyed reading the science-fiction periodical containing adventure stories about the title character Perry Rhodan, which first appeared in 1961.

Interview with Dieter Hülsmanns and Fridolin Reske, 1966
First published: 'Dieter Hülsmanns: Das perfekte Bild' (Interview), in *Rheinische Post*, Düsseldorf, 3 May 1966.

First English publication: *The Daily Practice of Painting*, 1995, pp. 56–58.

Notes, 1966
First published: *The Daily Practice of Painting*, 1995, p. 58.

Biographical information, 1966
Previously unpublished.
Translated from the German by Ben Posener.

The original typescript is held in the Zentralarchiv des internationalen Kunsthandels, Cologne.

1 *Waltersdorf*: Although Richter was born in Dresden on 9 February 1932, on numerous occasions he listed Waltersdorf, where he was later raised, as his birthplace. This erroneous information has persisted even through the present in many iterations of the artist's biography. Regarding the background of this situation, Richter recently commented that he was often told he should replace the common family name 'Richter' with the place name 'Waltersdorf', just as the artists Emil Hansen, who was from Nolde, or Karl Schmidt, who came from Rottluff, had done. Although he did not take this step, in the 1960s he repeatedly used Waltersdorf instead of Dresden as his birthplace.
2 *photo lab operator*: See 'Notes, 1964', note 1.
3 *Move to Düsseldorf*: Together with his wife Ema, Richter escaped in March 1961 through Berlin to West Germany.
4 *Art Academy Düsseldorf*: Richter arrived in summer of the same year in Düsseldorf and began studies during the winter semester of 1961–1962 at the State Art Academy. After the first semester he switched to the studio of Karl Otto Götz, where he remained until the end of his studies in the summer of 1964.
5 *Hemden* [Shirts]: Richter refers here to works done in 1961 and 1962 in which he affixed shirts to the canvas and painted over them. These paintings make reference to the work of Alberto Burri or Antoni Tapiès. After he had

exhibited examples of this style at the Galerie Junge Kunst [Young Art Gallery] in Fulda (8–30 September 1962, joint exhibition with Manfred Kuttner), Richter destroyed these paintings.

Statement, 1967
First published: Untitled, in *Art International*, March 1968, pp. 54–55. Translated from the German by Ben Posener.

1 *The nudes*: *Easter Nudes* (148), *Student* (149), *Spanish Nudes* (150), *Wee Girls* (151), *Nude* (152), *Sisters* (153), *Bathers* (154), *Diana* (155), *Gymnastics* (156), *Olympia* (157), all from 1967.
2 *Doors*: Two works from 1967, *5 Doors (I)* (158), *5 Doors (II)* (159).
3 *The Chirico-like emptiness*: Reference to the depiction of empty Italian town-squares in the paintings of the *pittura metafisica* of Giorgio de Chirico.

'Work Overview', 1968
First published: 'Arbeitsübersicht', in *14 × 14. Junge deutsche Künstler*, exhib. cat., Staatliche Kunsthalle Baden-Baden, 1968. Translated from the German by Ben Posener.

1 *Film about V. Bradke*: At the exhibition *Volker Bradtke* Richter screened the only art film he had made, nearly fourteen minutes long in black and white. The project was part of a running exhibition series called *Hommage à Schmela*, which ran from 9 to 15 December 1966 in the Galerie Schmela, and which featured a different artist every day. Other artists involved were Sigmar Polke, Konrad Lueg, John Latham, Heinz Mack and Joseph Beuys. Richter's exhibition took place on Tuesday 13 December 1966. In addition to the film, he also showed the large-format painting *Volker Bradke* (133), as well as numerous photo-portraits of Bradke. The name has varied spellings. While the invitation card made in Richter's handwriting uses 'Bradtke', one can also find the spelling 'Brandke' in text on the photographs which document the exhibit.

Interview with Rolf-Gunter Dienst, 1970
First published: Rolf-Gunter Dienst, 'Interview', in *Noch Kunst*, Gütersloh, 1970, pp. 192–199.

First English publication: Rolf-Gunter Dienst, 'Interview', in *Gerhard Richter*, exhib. cat., 36th Venice Biennale, German Pavilion, Venice, 1972, pp. 19–21.

The Daily Practice of Painting, 1995, pp. 60–64.

1 *advertising and stage painter*: Richter worked for six months starting 1 April 1949 as assistant to a sign painter in Zittau. On 1 February 1950 he began as an apprentice set painter at the Zittau State Theatre, but was fired on 15 July

because he refused to paint the theatre stairwell together with his fellow apprentices.

2 *photographic laboratory assistant*: See 'Notes, 1964', note 1.

3 *Happening*: The exhibition *Leben mit Pop – eine Demonstration für den Kapitalistischen Realismus*, at the Berges Furniture Store in Düsseldorf, 11 October 1963 (see 'Programme and Report: The Exhibition *Leben mit Pop – eine Demonstration für den Kapitalistischen Realismus*, Düsseldorf, 11 October 1963', pp. 17–20).

4 *Art Informel*: Among the most important German representatives of Art Informel were Ernst Wilhelm Nay, Emil Schumacher and Richter's teacher at the Düsseldorf Art Academy, K. O. Götz.

Note, 1971
First published: *The Daily Practice of Painting*, 1995, p. 64.

Comments regarding resale rights, 10 December 1971
Previously unpublished.
Translated from the German by Ben Posener.

Richter wrote this statement, which bears no addressee, on the planned change in his resale rights, in response to a letter from the gallery owner Rudolf Zwirner dated 9 December 1971. Zwirner's letter was written to Konrad Klapheck, Richter and Blinky Palermo, as a handwritten note indicates. Zwirner describes in the letter the severe consequences of a change in legislation (raising the resale tax rate from 1% to 5%), and requests to speak with the artists over the next few days. Richter's original typescript is held in the Zentralarchiv des internationalen Kunsthandels in Cologne.

Interview with Rolf Schön, 1972
First published: Rolf Schön, 'Unser Mann in Venedig', in *Deutsche Zeitung*, 14 April 1972, p. 13.

First English publication: Rolf Schön, 'Interview', in *Gerhard Richter*, exhib. cat., 36th Venice Biennale, German Pavilion, Venice, 1972, pp. 23–25.

The Daily Practice of Painting, 1995, pp. 71–75.

The interview took place before Richter's participation in the Venice Biennale (11 June–1 October 1972) and was published in the Biennale catalogue.

***Documenta* survey, 1972**
First published: Untitled, in Klaus Staeck, ed., *Befragung der Documenta oder Die Kunst soll schön bleiben*, Göttingen, 1972, p. C 1.7.
Translated from the German by Ben Posener.

Klaus Staek's publication for *documenta* 5, edited by Harald Szeemann, appeared even before the exhibition opened on 30 June 1972 (exhibition ran through 8 October). The volume contains reprints of a questionnaire answered by a number of artists participating in *documenta*, such as Giovanni Anselmo, Dan Graham, Jörg Immendorff, Sol LeWitt, John Salt and Richter.

1 *hyperrealism?*: See 'Interview with Peter Sager, 1972', note 2.

Conversation with Mathias Schreiber, 1972
First published: Mathias Schreiber, 'Ein gutes Foto von mir gibt es nicht', in *Kölner Stadt-Anzeiger*, 14 June 1972.
Translated from the German by Ben Posener.

1 *portraits of poets and thinkers*: Reference to the group of work entitled *48 Portraits* (324/1-48) from 1971 to 1972.

Interview with Peter Sager, 1972
First published: Peter Sager, 'Gespräch mit Gerhard Richter', in *Das Kunstwerk*, July 1972, pp. 16–17.

First English publication: *The Daily Practice of Painting*, 1995, pp. 66–71.

The interview appeared on the occasion of Richter's exhibition at the German Pavilion of the Venice Biennale from 11 June to 1 October 1972.

1 *Palermo*: Blinky Palermo was born Peter Schwarze in Leipzig in 1943. When he was adopted, his name became Peter Heisterkamp. Later he chose the artist name Blinky Palermo, after an Italian mafioso. Beginning in the winter semester of 1961 he studied at the State Art Academy in Düsseldorf. Richter became acquainted with him at the student exhibition in spring 1963. In 1970 they travelled together to New York. They also exhibited twice jointly: *Für Salvadore Dalí* at Galerie Ernst, Hanover (10 October–6 November 1970), and at the Galerie Heiner Friedrich, Cologne (21 April–15 May 1971), with a mural painting by Palermo and Richter's *Two Sculptures for a Room by Palermo* (297-1). Three paintings in Richter's catalogue of works were also done jointly with Palermo: *Finger-marks* (253) of 1970 and *Untitled* (303, 304) of 1971. Richter later said about their friendship: 'We didn't have a competitive relationship because we were so different. I always acknowledged that he could create a certain stillness in his work – that was foreign to me' (Dietmar Elger: *Gerhard Richter. Maler*, Cologne, 2002, p. 227). Blinky Palermo died in 1977 during a trip to Ceylon. See also Richter's characterization of his friendship with Palermo: 'About Blinky Palermo, 2003', pp. 450–453.

2 *New Realists*: This term refers to the American so-called photo- or hyperrealists, such as Chuck Close, Richard Estes, Ralph Goings, Malcolm

Morley and the Swiss artist Franz Gertsch, all of whom were presented quite prominently at *documenta* 5 in Kassel in 1972 (30 June–8 October).

3 *Carl Andre*: Born in 1935 in Quincy, MA. On 21 October 1967, Konrad Fischer (Lueg) opened his gallery with an exhibition by Carl Andre.

Letters to Wulf Herzogenrath, 1972
First published: Wulf Herzogenrath, ed., *Selbstdarstellung. Künstler über sich*, Düsseldorf, 1973, pp. 18–19.

First English publication: *The Daily Practice of Painting*, 1995, pp. 76–77.

Richter's two letters of 2 November and 22 December 1972, to the then-director of the Kölnischer Kunstverein [Cologne Art Association], Wulf Herzogenrath, were printed out of alphabetical order at the front of Herzogenrath's book. The photo included by Richter does not depict himself, as claimed, but rather Mr Schmettka, the security guard of the Düsseldorf State Art Academy where Richter had been teaching since 1971. The book contains self-portraits by Joseph Beuys, Erwin Heerich, Otto Piene, Günther Uecker, Timm Ulrichs and Stefan Wewerka.

1 *Rau*: Johannes Rau was the Minister of Sciences in the North Rhine Westphalian state government. On 11 October 1972 he fired Joseph Beuys from his professorship after he had refused to decline any applications from students wishing to study with him. Richter was among a number of other artists and intellectuals who signed a letter of protest against the 'career or teaching debarment'.

Notes, 1973
First published: *The Daily Practice of Painting*, 1995, p. 78.

1 *'The centre cannot hold'*: Richter refers to the polemic by Hans Sedlmayr (*Verlust der Mitte*, Salzburg, 1948), in which the author argues against abstract painting as the global language of art, and laments the lack of the human figure as an artistic credo.

From a letter to Jean-Christophe Ammann, February 1973
First published: *The Daily Practice of Painting*, 1995, pp. 78–81.

The letter was written in connection with Richter's exhibition at the Lucerne State Museum, of which Ammann was the director at the time. The exhibition took place from 21 January to 25 February 1973.

1 *Biennale*: Richter's exhibition in the German Pavilion at the 36th Venice Biennale (11 June–1 October 1972).
2 *Glass*: *4 Panes of Glass (160)*, 1967.

Interview with Irmeline Lebeer, 1973
First published: Irmeline Lebeer: 'Gerhard Richter ou La réalité de l'image', in *Chroniques de l'art vivant*, 2, February 1973, pp. 13–16.
Translated from the French by Will Bishop.

1 *Konrad Fischer's gallery*: Richter's first exhibition at the Konrad Fischer Galerie took place from 11 April to 7 May 1970. Richter later recalled: 'I enjoyed the show at Fischer's, with my broken little pictures hung so closely together.' (Dietmar Elger: *Gerhard Richter. Maler*, Cologne, 2002, p. 226).
2 *photo-realists*: See 'Interview with Peter Sager, 1972', note 2.
3 *180 tones*: *180 Colours (300/1-4)*, 1971, lacquer on canvas, each 200 × 200 cm.
4 *steel balls*: Indeed in 1989 and 1992 Richter produced three editions of balls made of gleaming stainless steel (see *Gerhard Richter. Editionen 1965–2004*, exhib. cat., Bonn Art Museum, 2004, catalogue nos. 70, 76 and 77).

Statement, 10 October 1973
First published: Untitled, in *Der Löwe. Theorie, Dialoge, bildende Kunst*, 5, 31 July 1975, p. 15.
Translated from the German by Ben Posener.

1 *The hyperrealists*: See 'Interview with Peter Sager, 1972', note 2.

Interview with Gislind Nabakowski, 1974
First published: Gislind Nabakowski, 'Zur Verkündigung von Tizian', in *Heute Kunst*, July–August 1974, pp. 3–5.
Translated from the German by Ben Posener.

The subjects of this interview are Richter's paintings based on Titian's *Annunciation* (*c.* 1530) at the Scuola di San Rocco, Venice. Richter had viewed Titian's work during a visit to Venice in preparation for his exhibition at the German Pavilion at the 1972 Biennale. Five paintings resulted in 1973, *Annunciation after Titian*, work nos. 343/1-2 and 344/1-3.

1 *a similar context*: Richter refers here to the so-called Heisenberg uncertainty principle (lit. 'fuzziness') discovered in 1927 by the German physicist and Nobel Prize winner Werner Heisenberg, which claims the impossibility of determining the location and speed of atomic particles with exact precision, but that either one factor or the other can be determined to the detriment of the other value.
2 *Uecker's*: Günther Uecker (born in 1930 in Wendorf, Mecklenburg; lives in Düsseldorf) formed the artist group Zero, together with Otto Piene and Heinz Mack. From 1963 to 1970 Richter had his atelier right next to Günther Uecker's, at the address am Fürstenwall 204. Uecker and Richter exhibited together at the exhibition series 14 × 14 at the Staatliche Kunsthalle in Baden-Baden (5–14 April 1968).

3 *professor at the Art Academy in Düsseldorf*: Richter taught painting from 1971 to 1994 at the State Art Academy in Düsseldorf.

Text for catalogue of group exhibition, Palais des Beaux-Arts, Brussels, 1974: 1,024 Colours in 4 Permutations
First published: '1024 Colours in 4 Permutations', in *Carl Andre, Marcel Broodthaers, Daniel Buren, Victor Burgin, Gilbert & George, On Kawara, Richard Long, Gerhard Richter*, exhib. cat., Palais des Beaux-Arts, Brussels, 1974.

First English publication: *Pier + Ocean*, exhib. cat., Hayward Gallery, London, 1980, p. 114.

The Daily Practice of Painting, 1995, pp. 81–82.

Gerhard Richter participated in the exhibition at the Palais des Beaux-Arts (9 January–3 February 1974) with the four large-format colour murals *1,024 Colours* (350/1-4) of 1973.

From a letter to Edy de Wilde, 23 February 1975
First published: Untitled, in *Fundamentele Schilderkunst/Fundamental Painting*, exhib. cat., Stedelijk Museum, Amsterdam, 1975, p. 57.

The Daily Practice of Painting, 1995, pp. 82–83.

Gerhard Richter participated in the exhibition, which took place from 25 April to 22 June 1975, with the paintings *Grey* (348, 349, 361-1, 361-3, 366). Other artists exhibited included Alan Charlton, Raimund Girke, Robert Mangold, Brice Marden, Agnes Martin, Edda Renouf, Robert Ryman and Jerry Zeniuk.

Text for catalogue of *Acht Künstler – acht Räume*, Mönchengladbach, 1975
First published: Untitled, in *Räume*, exhib. cat., Städtisches Museum, Mönchengladbach, 1976.

First English publication: *The Daily Practice of Painting*, 1995, p. 84.

Richter's artist statement appeared in the catalogue *Räume* [Spaces] as a quotation included in the text about the artist Johannes Cladders. Richter participated in the exhibition, which took place from 29 August to 8 October 1976, with the eight-piece work *Grey* (367/1-8), of 1975. The museum had acquired the piece shortly before the exhibition began. Other artists exhibited included Carl Andre, Marcel Broodthaers, Daniel Buren, Bruce Nauman and Ulrich Rückriem, as well as the architect Hans Hollein, who had designed the new museum building, which opened in 1982 on the Abteiberg.

From a letter to Benjamin H. D. Buchloh, 23 May 1977
First published: *The Daily Practice of Painting*, 1995, pp. 84–87.

This letter, fragments of which were published in 1995, is printed in full for the first time here.

1 *Benjamin H. D. Buchloh*: Richter had met Buchloh in 1972 at the Galerie Rudolf Zwirner in Cologne, where Buchloh was working as an assistant. Buchloh later helped Richter with the concept and hanging of the exhibition at the Musée national d'art moderne, Centre Georges Pompidou, Paris (1 February–21 March 1977) and wrote the text for the accompanying catalogue.
2 *new pictures*: Referred to here are Richter's 'soft' abstract paintings, as he describes them, which he painted from small abstract sketches. The sketches were photographed by him and projected onto large-format canvases and painted over in a photo-realist manner. Examples from this group of work are *Abstract Painting (417-424)* from the same year. Two of these, *Abstract Painting (421 and 422)*, were to be exhibited at *documenta* 6 in Kassel (24 June–2 October 1977), but were taken down by Richter just before the opening, after discussions with the curators about the presentation of his work. Both paintings can still be seen in the exhibition space in several press photos that were taken at the time.
3 *outsize blow-up*: The process of transferring small sketches onto large format, as described in note 2 above.

Answers to questions from Marlies Grüterich, 2 September 1977
First published: *The Daily Practice of Painting*, 1995, pp. 88–90.

This text consists of written answers by Gerhard Richter to interview questions posed by Marlies Grüterich. The interview was not published at the time. A typed script is on file at the Gerhard Richter atelier.

1 *three of these*: This actually refers to the two works *Abstract Paintings (421 and 422)*. On the reasons these were not shown at *documenta* 6, see: 'From a letter to Benjamin H. D. Buchloh, 23 May 1977', note 2.
2 *fellow artists in the GDR*: At *documenta* 6 in Kassel in 1977, official representatives of East German art participated: Bernhard Heisig, Wolfgang Mattheuer, Willi Sitte and Werner Tübke.

Interview with Amine Haase, 1977
First published: Amine Haase, 'Malerei als Schein', in *Rheinische Post*, Düsseldorf, 16 September 1977.

First English publication: *The Daily Practice of Painting*, 1995, pp. 92–95.

From a letter to Benjamin H. D. Buchloh, 29 September 1977
First published: *The Daily Practice of Painting*, 1995, p. 96.

Interview with Marlies Grüterich, 1978
First published: Marlies Grüterich, 'Gerhard Richter', in *Poetische Aufklärung in der europäischen Kunst der Gegenwart bei Joseph Beuys, Marcel Broodthaers, Daniel Buren, Jannis Kounellis, Mario Merz, Gerhard Richter – Geschichte von heute und morgen*, exhib. cat., Halle für internationale neue Kunst, Zurich, 1978, pp. 87–88.
Translated from the German by Ben Posener.

1 *catalogue for the Fundamental Painting exhibition*: See commentary to 'From a letter to Edy de Wilde, 23 February 1975'.

Interview with Bruce Ferguson and Jeffrey Spalding, 1978
First published (in English): Bruce Ferguson and Jeffrey Spalding, 'Gerhard Richter', in *Parachute* 13, Fall 1978, pp. 31–33.

1 *Zero*: Düsseldorf artist group, founded in 1957 by Heinz Mack and Otto Piene. From 1962 Günther Uecker was also a member of the group, which was officially terminated in 1964.
2 *Nulle*: The Dutch artist group 'Nul' was founded in 1960. It followed similar practices to those of the Düsseldorf Zero artists. Among its most well known members were Jan Schoonhoven and Henk Peeters.
3 *Fluxus*: Düsseldorf was the centre of the international Fluxus movement. During that time Richter visited the following related events: *NEO-DADA in der Musik* at the Düsseldorf Kammerspiele (16 June 1962) and *Festum Fluxorum Fluxus* at the Düsseldorf State Art Academy (2–3 February 1963).
4 *Picabia*: Richter refers to Francis Picabia (1879–1953) and his stylistic shift between ironical erotic nudes, reduced abstractions and complex transparency paintings, in which he layered multiple painted or drawn motifs.
5 *cloud painting in the National Gallery of Canada*: *Cloud (270/1-3)*, 1970, each 200 × 300 cm.
6 *upcoming show in Eindhoven, Netherlands*: *Gerhard Richter. Abstract Paintings*, Stedelijk van Abbemuseum, Eindhoven (8 October–5 November 1978). The exhibition was also shown at the Whitechapel Art Gallery, London (14 March–22 April 1979).
7 *Reality and Abstraction*: Reference to the exhibition *Dalla natura all'arte, dall'arte alla natura*, at the Venice Biennale in 1978. Richter's two large-format *Grey Paintings* (each 250 × 200 cm) of 1973 and 1974 were shown, as was his *Townscape F (177-3)*.
8 *The recent Chicago exhibition*: *Europe in the Seventies. Aspects of Recent Art*, Art Institute

of Chicago (8 October–27 November 1977). The exhibition was also shown at the Hirshhorn Museum and Sculpture Garden, Smithsonian Institution, Washington (16 March–7 May 1978), the Museum of Modern Art, San Francisco (23 June–6 August 1978), the Fort Worth Art Museum (24 September–29 October 1978) and the Contemporary Arts Center, Cincinnati (1 December 1978–31 January 1979). Other participants included Giovanni Anselmo, Bernd and Hilla Becher, Daniel Buren, Hanne Darboven, Jan Dibbets, Gilbert & George, Richard Long, Mario Merz, Panamarenko, Klaus Rinke and Gilberto Zorio.

9 *National Gallery*: See note 5 above.

10 *Winnipeg Art Gallery*: There is no work by Richter contained in the collection of the Winnipeg Art Gallery.

11 *first one-man show in New York*: This refers to the exhibition *Gerhard Richter. New Paintings*, which took place from 14 January to 11 February 1978 at the Sperone Westwater Fischer Gallery. Richter's actual first solo exhibition in New York, however, took place in 1973 at the Reinhard Onnasch Gallery (15 September–15 November 1973).

12 *A show in London*: See note 6 above.

Author's note, August 1979

First published (in English): 'Author's Note', in 128 *Details from a Picture (Halifax 1978)*, Halifax, 1980, p. 65.

The details referred to are from the 1978 painting *Halifax* (432-5).

Letter to Benjamin H. D. Buchloh, 30 August 1979

Previously unpublished.
Translated from the German by Ben Posener.

This letter to Benjamin H. D. Buchloh, who taught at the Nova Scotia College of Art and Design in Halifax, and who edited the publication series, discusses various possible formulations for the text to 128 *Details from a Picture (Halifax 1978)*, Halifax, 1980. The final version of the text is printed in the book (see 'Author's note, August 1979', p. 113).

1 *oil study*: The work bears the title *Halifax* (432-5), 1978, 52 × 78 cm.

2 *exhibition 17 PICTURES*: The exhibition took place from 4 to 18 July 1978 at the Anna Leonowens Gallery in Halifax.

3 *large-sized 'pictures'*: Richter refers to the so-called 'soft' *Abstract Paintings* (Work nos.: 417-424, 428-430, 434-440, 444).

Letter to Birgit Pelzer, 25 March 1980

Previously unpublished.
Translated from the German by Matthew Price.

A letter from Richter on the subject of the large-format, so-called 'soft' *Abstract Paintings* (Work nos.: 417-424, 428-430,

434-440), exhibited at the Stedelijk van Abbemuseum, Eindhoven (8 October–5 November 1978), and at the Whitechapel Art Gallery, London (14 March–22 April 1979).

1 *The Ausschnitte from 1970–71*: Reference to the following works: *Detail (Brown) (271)*, 135 × 150 cm, *Detail (272)*, 140 × 140 cm, *Detail (Red-blue) (273)*, 200 × 300 cm, *Detail (Grey-lilac) (274)*, 200 × 300 cm, *Detail (Green-grey) (275)*, 200 × 130 cm, all from the year 1970, and *Detail (Makart) (288)*, *Detail (Karmin) (289)*, *Detail (Kreutz)*, each 200 × 200 cm, as well as *Detail (291)*, three parts, 250 × 375 cm, all from the year 1971.
2 *The Striche*: Reference to *Stroke (on Blue) (451)*, 1979, four parts, 190 × 2,000 cm, *Stroke (on Red) (452)*, 1980, four parts, 190 × 2,000 cm. Both pictures were created for the 'Public/Industrial Art' [*Kunst am Bau*] project at the Kreisberufsschule [Regional Vocational School] in Soest, where they are still on display today.

Description of design for the 'König-Heinrich-Platz' Underground Station, 1980 (together with Isa Genzken)
First published: Gerhard Richter and Isa Genzken, 'Beschreibung der Konzeption für die Gestaltung des U-Bahnhofes ‚König-Heinrich-Platz', in *U-Bahn-Kunst in Duisburg* (insert), Wilhelm-Lehmbruck-Museum, Duisburg, 1992.
Translated from the German by Ben Posener.

1 *Isa Genzken*: Born in 1948 in Bad Oldesloe. After studying for several semesters in Hamburg and Berlin, she transferred to the Düsseldorf State Art Academy in 1976 and studied in Gerhard Richter's studio. In 1983 the two were married. They divorced in 1994.

Notes, 1981
First published: *The Daily Practice of Painting*, 1995, pp. 96–99.

1 *The big Strokes*: See 'Letter to Birgit Pelzer, 25 March 1980', note 2.
2 *Berges furnishing store*: This refers to Konrad Lueg's and Richter's Happening in 1963 at the Berges Furniture Store. See 'Programme and Report: The Exhibition *Leben mit Pop – eine Demonstration für den Kapitalistischen Realismus*, Düsseldorf, 11 October 1963', pp. 17–20.

Text for catalogue of *documenta* 7, Kassel, 1982
First published: Untitled, in *documenta 7*, exhib. cat., Vol. 1, Kassel, 1982, p. 443.

The Daily Practice of Painting, 1995, p. 100.

Richter participated in *documenta* 7 (18 June–29 September 1982) with five large-format *Abstract Paintings*: *Yellow-green (492)*, *Red (493)*, *Lilac (494)* and *Orangery (495)*, two parts, each 260 × 400 cm, as well as the picture *Oldenburg (489)*, 225 × 175 cm. All the works date from 1982.

Interview with Amine Haase, 1982
First published: Amine Haase, 'Kunst ist die höchste Form der Hoffnung', in *Kölner Stadt-Anzeiger*, 15 September 1982, p. 33. Translated from the German by Matthew Price.

This interview was conducted on the occasion of Richter receiving the Arnold Bode Prize on 22 September 1982.

1 *large-format works of yours*: See commentary on 'Text for catalogue of *documenta* 7, Kassel, 1982'.

Notes, 1982
First published: *The Daily Practice of Painting*, 1995, p. 101 (note from 14 June 1982); *Gerhard Richter. Werken op papier 1983–1986*, exhib. cat., Overholland Museum, Amsterdam, 1987, p. 4 (note from 25 November 1982).

The Daily Practice of Painting, 1995, p. 101.

Richter still occasionally puts down notes in writing. Some of his notes from 1982 to 1986, relating to the exhibition of works on paper at the Overholland Museum in Amsterdam (20 February–20 April 1987), were published in the accompanying catalogue. In the 1993 German edition of Richter's texts, further notes through the year 1992 were included. Christiaan Braun writes in the catalogue introduction (p. 3): 'During a visit to Gerhard Richter's atelier during the preparation for our exhibition, he spoke of his diaries. It seemed a good idea to allow the artist to speak for himself through a selection from his personal notes, since many art critics have struggled with the challenge of classifying his work. The selection includes some very personal entries, and for this reason alone I am grateful for his willingness to allow these to come to public light on this occasion. These notes were often written at night, not as statements but as instantaneous reflections of a particular mood or disposition. In this regard they are comparable to the works on paper, which also have more personal spontaneity than the paintings. For this catalogue, he selected the entries that relate to art.'

The Daily Practice of Painting, 1995, features an entry not published at the time of the exhibition.

Notes, 1983
First published: *Gerhard Richter. Werken op papier 1983–1986*, exhib. cat., Overholland Museum, Amsterdam, 1987, pp. 4–5 (notes from 27 January, 2 June and 11 June 1983); *The Daily Practice of Painting*, 1995, pp. 102–107 (notes from 18 March, 13 May, 8 June and 3 November 1983).

The Daily Practice of Painting, 1995, pp. 101–107.

See also commentary on 'Notes, 1982'.

1 *Minimal Art*: Richter means American Minimal art, which he had come to know from 1967 onwards, primarily through exhibitions by Carl Andre, Sol LeWitt and Fred Sandback at the Konrad Fischer Galerie in Düsseldorf, and Donald Judd at the Galerie Heiner Friedrich in Munich.

Notes, 1984
First published: *Gerhard Richter. Werken op papier 1983–1986*, exhib. cat., Overholland Museum, Amsterdam, 1987, pp. 5–7 (notes from 15 April, 23 April, 15 June, 6 September, 21 September, 19 October and 27 December 1984); *The Daily Practice of Painting*, 1995, p. 108 (notes from 16 April 1984, erroneously dated 16 January 1984).

The Daily Practice of Painting, 1995, pp. 107–111.

Notes from 27 December 1984 printed in *Gerhard Richter. Werken op papier 1983–1986* were not included in *The Daily Practice of Painting*, 1995.

See also commentary on 'Notes, 1982'.

1 *Goldberg Variations*: In 1984 Richter finished the edition *Goldberg-Variationen*, which consists of 120 individually painted LPs of Glenn Gould's recording. Richter contributed fifty of these to the portfolio *Hommage à Cladders* at the Mönchengladbach Museum Association (see *Gerhard Richter. Editionen 1965–2004*, exhib. cat., Bonn Art Museum, 2004, cat. no. 60).

Interview with Bruno Corà, 1984
First published: Bruno Corà, untitled, in *Terrae Motus*, exhib. cat., Fondazione Amelio, Istituto per l'Arte Contemporanea, Naples, 1984, p. 145.

First English publication: *The Daily Practice of Painting*, 1995, pp. 111–112.

The exhibition and catalogue for the project *Terrae Motus* were inspired by the gallery owner Lucio Amelio from Naples, who responded to the terrible earthquake on 23 November 1980 in southern Italy with this initiative. Other participants in the project included Joseph Beuys, Christian Boltanski, Enzo Cucchi, Gilbert & George, Keith Haring, Mario Merz, Robert Rauschenberg, Cy Twombly and Andy Warhol. Richter donated the work *Static (487)* of 1982 to the Fondazione Amelio, Istituto per l'Arte Contemporanea, which exhibited it from March 1983 through late December 1984 in the Villa Campolieto in Naples.

1 *Glenn Branca's band Static*: Reference to *Static (487)*, 1982. In the following year Richter painted *Glenn (532)*. In 1983 Richter and Isa Genzken (see 'Description of design for the "König-Heinrich-Platz" Underground Station, 1980 [together with Isa Genzken]',

note 1) designed a poster for a concert featuring Glenn Branca and his band at the Düsseldorf Art Academy on 24 May 1983. See also: *Gerhard Richter. Editionen 1965–2004*, exhib. cat., Bonn Art Museum, 2004, cat. no. 59.

Interview with Wolfgang Pehnt, 1984
First published: Wolfgang Pehnt, 'Gerhard Richter. Kunst wird kritiklos aufgenommen unter dem Motto: Nun macht mal, es ist ja alles ganz interessant', in Werner Krüger and Wolfgang Pehnt, eds, *Documenta-Documente. Künstler im Gespräch*, Cologne, 1984, pp. 118–131.

First English publication: *The Daily Practice of Painting*, 1995, pp. 112–118.

The interview was in fact conducted in 1982 in connection with *documenta* 7 in Kassel (18 June–29 September), and was broadcast on Deutschlandfunk radio on 4 July 1982 as part of the series 'Art and Artists'. For the printed edition, the discussion was edited and shortened. Other artists interviewed were Georg Baselitz, Bernhard Becher, Joseph Beuys, Bernhard Leitner, Richard Paul Lohse, Markus Lüpertz, Meret Oppenheim, A. R. Penck and Salomé.

1 *A picture like this*: Reference to the *Abstract Paintings* from 1976.
2 *from 1952 to 1957*: Richter was accepted at the Dresden Academy of Fine Arts in the winter semester of 1951–52. After his four-semester core programme, he transferred to Heinz Lohmar's studio for mural painting. He graduated in 1956, having completed a thesis project with a mural at the German Hygiene Museum in Dresden. As a result of his successful studies, Richter received a post-graduate fellowship and financial aid for three further years at the Academy, where he had his own atelier.
3 *Happening*: This refers to the demonstration *Leben mit Pop – eine Demonstration für den Kapitalistischen Realismus*, held on 11 October 1963 at the Berges Furniture Store (see pp. 17–20).

Notes, 1985
First published: *Gerhard Richter. Werken op papier 1983–1986*, exhib. cat., Overholland Museum, Amsterdam, 1987, pp. 7–10 (notes from 20 February, 22 February, 28 February, 18 May, 28 August, 13 November and 27 December 1985); *The Daily Practice of Painting*, 1995, pp. 120–121 (notes from 25 March and 30 May 1985).

The Daily Practice of Painting, 1995, pp. 118–123.

See commentary on 'Notes, 1982'.

1 *Hausmann's Nude, Back View*: Richter refers here to a photographic nude, *c.* 1930, by Raoul Hausmann, which was included as an illustration in the following newspaper exhibition review: Katharina Hegewisch, 'Hanteln statt Rüschen. Das Aktfoto: ein Panorama im Münchner

Stadtmuseum', *Frankfurter Allgemeine Zeitung*, 21 February 1985, p. 23.

2 *lacquer studies*: A number of these studies are contained in Richter's book *Atlas*, plate 413 (Helmut Friedel, ed., *Gerhard Richter. Atlas*, Cologne, 2006).

3 *The Kiefer exhibition*: At the time this entry was made (25 March 1985), there had been no recent solo exhibition by Kiefer. It therefore remains unclear to what Richter's observations refer.

Interview with Dorothea Dietrich, 1985
First published (in English): Dorothea Dietrich, 'Gerhard Richter. An Interview', in *The Print Collector's Newsletter*, 4, September/October 1985, pp. 128–132.

The interview took place on 5 March 1985 in New York on the occasion of Richter's exhibition at the Marian Goodman Gallery and Sperone Westwater Gallery (5–26 March 1985).

1 *abstract works from photos*: The phrasing is unclear. The reference is to the so-called 'soft' *Abstract Paintings* that Richter painted from photographs which themselves were made from small sketches he had done. For examples, see the *Abstract Paintings* (417-424, 428-430, 434-440, 442-444, 446, 460).

2 *With that book it came pretty much to an end*: This statement is in reference to the 1972 edition of *Atlas van de foto's en schetsen*, from an exhibition at Hedendaagse Kunst, Utrecht (1–31 December 1972). The work on *Atlas* was hardly 'pretty much' complete, though, as Richter assumes here. In 1989, 1997 and 2006 new and ever more comprehensive editions of *Atlas* were published.

3 *published a book about them*: *Gerhard Richter. Aquarelle*, Munich, 1985. The book appeared in conjunction with the exhibition of the works at the Graphic Collection of the Staatsgalerie Stuttgart, from 19 January through 17 February 1985. In addition to the watercolours, three paintings were exhibited.

4 *Glenn Branca*: See 'Interview with Bruno Corà, 1984', note 1.

5 *Tatlin*: *Tatlin*, 17.11.1982, graphite on paper, 29.7 × 21 cm. For a reproduction, see: *Gerhard Richter. Zeichnungen 1964–1999*, catalogue of works, Kunstmuseum Winterthur, 1999, cat. no. 82/24, fig. p. 237.

6 *Manifesto of Capitalist Realism*: This refers to 'Programme and Report: The Exhibition *Leben mit Pop – eine Demonstration für den Kapitalistischen Realismus*, Düsseldorf, 11 October 1963' (together with Konrad Lueg) (see pp. 17–20).

7 *is undeterminable?*: The interview ends – in the German original as well as in the printed American edition – with this open-ended question.

Notes, 1986
First published: *Gerhard Richter. Werken op papier 1983–1986*, exhib. cat., Overholland Museum, Amsterdam, 1987, pp. 11–15 (notes from 18 February, 21 February,

25 February, 17 March, 18 March, 21 March, 28 March, 21 April, 25 April and 12 October 1986); *The Daily Practice of Painting*, 1995, p. 132 (notes from 25 October 1986).

The Daily Practice of Painting, 1995, pp. 124–132.

See commentary to 'Notes, 1982'.

1 *Kucki, Kia and Klemente*: Richter refers offhandedly to the Italian painters of the so-called *arte chifra* movement: Enzo Cucchi, Sandro Chia and Francesco Clemente.

Interview with Benjamin H. D. Buchloh, 1986

First published: Benjamin H. D. Buchloh, 'Interview with Gerhard Richter', in *Gerhard Richter. Paintings*, exhib. cat., Museum of Contemporary Art, Chicago/Art Gallery of Ontario, Toronto, 1988, pp. 15–29.

The Daily Practice of Painting, 1995, pp. 132–166.

1 *Duchamp exhibition in Krefeld in 1963*: This major Marcel Duchamp retrospective was actually presented from 19 June through 1 August 1965 in the Museum Haus Lange in Krefeld, Germany. It had been previously shown at the Gemeentemuseum in The Hague, and later also in Eindhoven, Berne and Hanover. In a letter to his Munich gallerist, Heiner Friedrich, Richter wrote on 25 June 1965, 'I saw the Duchamp exhibition in Krefeld; it was very interesting to me.'

2 *Ileana Sonnabend's*: Richter's trip to Paris with Konrad Lueg was in the spring of 1963, just after the opening of the group exhibition with Kuttner, Lueg, Polke and Richter on Kaiserstrasse 31a in Düsseldorf (11 May 1963). Richter, Lueg and others introduced themselves in Paris at the Ileana Sonnabend Gallery, as well as to Iris Clert, as 'German Pop Artists', though no opportunity for an exhibition resulted. Nonetheless, in 1966 Ileana Sonnabend wrote to Richter with a request for some information from him, having nominated him for a prize. The following year she visited Richter at his atelier in Düsseldorf.

3 *first show at Konrad Fischer's*: The first Robert Ryman exhibition was held by Konrad Fischer from 21 November through 17 December 1968 in his gallery on Neubrückstrasse 12. Six multi-piece works from the *Classico* series of 1968 were shown.

4 *Paris catalogue*: *Gerhard Richter*, exhib. cat., Centre national d'art et de culture, Georges Pompidou – Musée national d'art moderne, Paris (1 February–21 March 1977).

5 *Loock and Harten*: Ulrich Loock, 'Das Ereignis des Bildes', in U. Loock and D. Zacharopoulos, *Gerhard Richter*, Munich, 1985, p. 118; Jürgen Harten: 'Der romantische Wille zur Abstraktion', in *Gerhard Richter. Bilder, Paintings 1962–1985*, exhib. cat., Städtische Kunsthalle Düsseldorf, 1986, pp. 21–22.

6 *loss of the Centre*: see 'Notes, 1973', note 1.
7 *Jacques Monod's Chance and Necessity*: Jacques Monod, *Zufall und Notwendigkeit. Philosophische Fragen der modernen Biologie*, Munich, 1971 (originally: *Le hasard et la nécessité*, Paris, 1970).

Text for catalogue *Beuys zu Ehren*, 1986
First published: Untitled, in *Beuys zu Ehren*, exhib. cat., Städtische Galerie im Lenbachhaus, Munich, 1986, p. 482.

First English publication: *The Daily Practice of Painting*, 1995, pp. 166–167.

In 1986 the Städtische Galerie im Lenbachhaus in Munich presented the exhibition *Beuys zu Ehren* [Homage to Beuys] (16 June–2 November) in honour of the 65th birthday of the recently deceased artist. Alongside works by Beuys, the work of his artist colleagues and friends was shown. Richter participated with *Abstract Painting (596)* of 1986 and *Two Sculptures for a Room by Palermo (297-2)* (1971/1984).

1 *a cowshed somewhere out beyond Kleve*: Together with Konrad Lueg, Richter visited the so-called *Stallausstellung* [Stable Exhibition] by Beuys, which took place in a former cowshed in Kleve from 26 October through 24 November 1963. The exhibition was organized by Franz Josef and Hans van der Grinten, and displayed work from their joint collection.

Interview with Christiane Vielhaber, 1986
First published: Christiane Vielhaber, 'Interview mit Gerhard Richter', in *Das Kunstwerk*, 2, April 1986, pp. 41–43.
Translated from the German by Matthew Price.

1 *Düsseldorf furniture store*: Reference to Richter's and Konrad Lueg's demonstration and exhibition at the Berges Furniture Store. See 'Programme and Report: The Exhibition *Leben mit Pop – eine Demonstration für den Kapitalistischen Realismus*, Düsseldorf, 11 October 1963' (together with Konrad Lueg), pp. 17–20.
2 *an exhibition in Hanover*: See 'Text for exhibition catalogue, Galerie h, Hanover, 1966, written jointly with Sigmar Polke', pp. 36–44).

Interview with Anna Tilroe, 1987
First published: Anna Tilroe, 'Sensaties voor het oog', in *Volkskrant*, 20 February 1987, p. 20.
Translated from the Dutch by Gregory Ball.

This interview was conducted on the occasion of the exhibition *Gerhard Richter. Werken op papier 1983–1986*, Overholland Museum, Amsterdam (20 February–20 April 1987). At several points in the original interview, the discussion is interrupted with commentaries by the interviewer, which are left out here.

1 *an American gallery*: Richter had his first solo exhibition in an American gallery in

1978 at the Sperone Westwater Fischer Gallery in New York (14 January–11 February 1978). The reference here, however, appears to be to the 1973 exhibition in the New York branch of the Reinhard Onnasch Gallery in Berlin (15 September–15 November 1973).

2 *Fluxus period*: Reference to the demonstration and exhibition *Leben mit Pop – eine Demonstration für den Kapitalistischen Realismus*, by Richter and Konrad Lueg at the Berges Furniture Store in Düsseldorf (11–25 October 1963).

3 *fundamental painting*: Richter participated in the exhibition *Fundamentele Schilderkunst/Fundamental Painting* at the Stedelijk Museum, Amsterdam, in 1975. See 'From a letter to Edy de Wilde, 23 February 1975', pp. 91–92.

4 *retrospective in Düsseldorf*: *Gerhard Richter. Bilder, Paintings* 1962–1985, Städtische Kunsthalle Düsseldorf, 18 January–23 March 1986.

Letter to Manfred Schlösser, Secretary General, Berlin Academy of Arts, 16 April 1987

First published: *Gerhard Richter: Text. Schriften und Interviews*, Frankfurt/Leipzig, 1993, p. 159.

Translated from the German by Matthew Price.

This letter represents Richter's position on the Berlin city art project *Skulpturenboulevard* [Boulevard of Sculpture], located on the Kurfürstendamm for the city's 750th anniversary celebration in summer 1987. Participating artists included: Frank Dornseif, Brigitte and Martin Matschinsky-Denninghoff, George Rickey and Wolf Vostell. Olaf Metzel's piece, a mound of red and white police barricades, caused great controversy.

Notes, 1988

First published: *The Daily Practice of Painting*, 1995, pp. 170–173.

See commentary to 'Notes, 1982'.

Notes for a press conference, November–December 1988 (held at Museum Haus Esters, Krefeld, February 1989)

First published: *The Daily Practice of Painting*, 1995, pp. 173–175.

These represent Richter's notes and thoughts before the press conference on his exhibition of the fifteen-part series *18 October 1977*, which was shown from 12 February through 18 April 1989 at the Museum Haus Esters in Krefeld. A second, more complete typescript is held at the Gerhard Richter atelier.

1 *Once the dead Meins*: Richter had made a painting of the dead terrorist Holger Meins, but did not include it in the *18 October 1977* series, and in fact later painted it over (*Abstract Painting (686-9)*, 1988).

Conversation with William Furlong, Jill Lloyd, Michael Archer and Peter Townsend, 1988
First published: *Audio Arts Magazine*, Vol. 9, No. 4, London, 1989, cassette recording, side A.

First published in written form: William Furlong, *Audio Arts. Beunruhigende Versuche zur Genauigkeit*, Leipzig, 1992, pp. 231–242.

The present version follows the written publication. Translated from the German by Ben Posener.

The conversation took place in London in connection with Richter's first solo exhibition at the Anthony d'Offay Gallery (11 March–16 April 1988).

1 *London Paintings*: These are: *Tower 1–6* (*646/1-6*), 1987, *Brick Tower* (*643-1*), 1987, *Flint Tower* (*652-1*) and *Salt Tower* (*652-2*), both 1988, as well as the group *St James, St Andrew, St Bridget and St John* (*653/1-4*), all 1988.
2 *furniture store?*: Reference to Richter's and Konrad Lueg's demonstration and exhibition in the Berges Furniture Store. See 'Programme and Report: The Exhibition *Leben mit Pop – eine Demonstration für den Kapitalistischen Realismus*, Düsseldorf, 11 October 1963', pp. 17–20.
3 *landscape paintings*: These are mentioned in connection with the following exhibitions: *Gerhard Richter. Städte*, Galerie René Block, Berlin (17 January–5 February 1969); *Gerhard Richter. Zwei Seestücke* 1975, Kabinett für aktuelle Kunst, Bremerhaven (29 November 1975–4 January 1976).
4 *documenta*: *documenta* 8, Kassel (12 June–20 September 1987). Richter's work *Cathedral Corner* (*629-1*), 1987, 122 × 78 cm, was shown.

Notes, 1989
First published: *The Daily Practice of Painting*, 1995, pp. 176–182.

See commentary on 'Notes, 1982'.

Interview with Gregorio Magnani, 1989
First published (in English): Gregorio Magnani, 'Gerhard Richter', in *Flash Art*, May/June 1989, pp. 94–97.

1 *gave up immediately*: From the joint project with Konrad Lueg, referred to here, Richter's only remaining work is the collected material in *Atlas*, plates 16–23 (Helmut Friedel, ed., *Gerhard Richter. Atlas*, Cologne, 2006).
2 *the skulls*: In 1983 Richter painted a group of small-format pictures with skulls as the motif, *Skull* (*545/1-3, 547-1, 548/1-2*). One of these pictures combines the motif with a candle, *Skull with Candle* (*547-2*).
3 *the work isn't for sale*: In 1995 Richter sold the *18 October 1977* series, which had been on loan to the Museum of Modern Art in Frankfurt, to the Museum of Modern Art, New York. The works were not shipped to New York until 2000, however – at the end of the term of loan

in Frankfurt. See also: 'Interview with Hubertus Butin, 1995', pp. 322–26, and 'Interview with Stefan Koldehoff, 1995', pp. 327–29.

Statement on the exhibition *Bilderstreit*, 1 June 1989

First published: 'Ein Kratzer ohne Folgen? Diskussionsbeiträge von Künstlern, Sammlern, Kunstvermittlern', in *Kölner Stadt-Anzeiger*, 1 June 1989, p. 9.
Translated from the German by Matthew Price.

This statement of Richter's was cited in an article to which the sculptor Heinz Günter Prager – the former director of the Abteiberg Museum in Mönchengladbach – and the Cologne collector Udo Brandhorst also contributed, amongst others.

1 *Werner-oriented*: Richter accuses the exhibition's curators of favouring artists who were represented by the Galerie Michael Werner in Cologne. Those who participated in the exhibition included Georg Baselitz, Per Kirkeby, Markus Lüpertz and A. R. Penck.

Conversation with Jan Thorn-Prikker concerning the *18 October 1977* cycle, 1989

First published: Jan Thorn-Prikker, 'Wir sehen auch unser eigenes Ende. Ein Gespräch mit dem Maler Gerhard Richter über den Zyklus *18. Oktober 1977*', in *Frankfurter Rundschau*, 29 April 1989, p. ZB3.
First English publication: Jan Thorn-Prikker, 'Gerhard Richter, 18 October 1977 = Gerhard Richter, October 18, 1988', in *Parkett*, No. 19, March 1989, pp. 124–165.

The Daily Practice of Painting, 1995, pp. 183–207.

1 *in the Atlas*: See Helmut Friedel, ed., *Gerhard Richter. Atlas*, Cologne, 2006, plates 470–479.
2 *your exhibition in Krefeld*: The first presentation of the *18 October 1977* series, at the Museum Haus Esters, Krefeld, from 12 February through 18 April 1989.
3 *people who smoke HB*: Reference to a common brand of cigarettes in Germany.
4 *Stefan Aust's book*: Stefan Aust, *Der Baader-Meinhof-Komplex*, Hamburg, 1985.
5 *in the catalogue*: *Gerhard Richter. Bilder, Paintings 1962–1985*, exhib. cat., Städtische Kunsthalle Düsseldorf, 1986.

Letter to Walter Grasskamp on the subject of *18 October 1977*, 17 October 1989

First published: 'Brief an Walter Grasskamp', in *Gerhard Richter. 18. Oktober 1977* (press reports), Cologne, 1989, pp. 111–112.
Translated from the German by Matthew Price.

Richter's letter to Walter Grasskamp is in response to the latter's article on the series *18 October 1977* ('Gerhard Richter: 18. Oktober 1977. Erborgte Radikalität', in *Jahresring 36*, Cologne, 1989, pp. 220–29).

1 *tangent on Arnulf Rainer*: Richter refers to the series *Hiroshima* by Arnulf Rainer, with painted-over photos of the victims and of the city after the atomic bomb was dropped on 6 August 1945.

Notes, 1990
First published: *The Daily Practice of Painting*, 1995, pp. 218–221.

See commentary on 'Notes, 1982'.

1 *Baselitz exhibition*: Richter refers here to the solo exhibition *Georg Baselitz* at the Städtische Kunsthalle Düsseldorf from 28 July through 9 September 1990. The exhibition had previously been shown at the Kunsthaus Zurich.
2 *the Brücke picture*: Reference to the painting *Der Brückechor* by Georg Baselitz, dated 1 August 1983. For a reproduction, see: Andreas Franzke, *Georg Baselitz*, Munich, 1988, pp. 202–203.
3 *Hypo-Bank design*: Reference to two works done in 1991, *Zwölf Spiegel für eine Bank* [Twelve Mirrors for a Bank] (740) and *Sechs Spiegel für eine Bank* [Six Mirrors for a Bank] (741). These were commissioned for the Hypo-Bank building in Düsseldorf, designed by Oswald Mathias Ungers. Sol LeWitt also participated as an artist on the project. For reproductions, see: *Oswald Mathias Ungers, Gerhard Richter, Sol LeWitt*, Hypo-Bank, Düsseldorf, 1991, design plates and colour plates.

Letter to Werner Schmidt, 1990
First published: Untitled, in *Ausgebürgert. Künstler aus der DDR und aus dem Sowjetischen Sektor Berlins* 1949–1989, exhib. cat., State Art Collections, Dresden, 1990, pp. 30–31.

First English publication: *The Daily Practice of Painting*, 1995, p. 222.

A letter from Richter dated 18 July 1990 to Werner Schmidt, the General Director of the Dresden State Art Collections and curator of the exhibition *Ausgebürgert. Künstler aus der DDR und aus dem Sowjetischen Sektor Berlins* 1949–1989. The exhibition was held at the Albertinum in Dresden (7 October–12 December 1990) and at the Kleine Deichtorhalle in Hamburg (10 January–1 March 1991).

Letter to the editor, F.A.Z. [*Frankfurter Allgemeine Zeitung*], 24 July 1990: 'Locked Out'
First published: 'Ausgesperrt', in *Frankfurter Allgemeine Zeitung*, 24 July 1990, p. 8. Translated from the German by Matthew Price.

Richter's letter to the editor in response to a news report in the 10 July 1990 edition of the *Frankfurter Allgemeine Zeitung*, p. 31, in which the paper reported on criticism made by the collector Peter Ludwig of the directors of the Museum Ludwig in Cologne, and their policy of refusing to display publicly the work of artists from the former GDR. Ludwig had lamented that works by East German artists, which he and his wife had donated to the museum that bears their name, were left undisplayed in the basement.

In June 1990 Georg Baselitz had expressed his aversion to the prominent representatives of art from East Germany, Bernhard Heisig and Wolfgang Mattheuer, to the magazine *art. Das Kunstmagazin* ('Ein Meister, der Talent verschmäht', in *art. Das Kunstmagazin*, June 1990, pp. 54–72): 'Not artists, not painters. Neither of them has ever painted a painting. They have merely worked on restoration and reconstruction, but never created anything. It's all quite boring. They are interpreters who have merely filled the requirements of the system in the GDR' (p. 70). And continuing: 'There's no jubilance in their painting; they're just assholes' (p. 70). Richter responded to this with a letter to the editor the following month: 'Baselitz is right, and I could not have expressed it better (though perhaps more politely) myself' (Gerhard Richter, Letter to the Editor, in *art. Das Kunstmagazin*, July 1990, p. 6).

Interview with Sabine Schütz, 1990
First published: Sabine Schütz, 'Gerhard Richter', in *Journal of Contemporary Art*, New York, Fall/Winter 1990, pp. 34–46.

The Daily Practice of Painting, 1995, pp. 207–218.

1 *a film about your work*: Viktoria von Flemming, 'Meine Bilder sind klüger als ich', NDR, 1987 (updated and expanded edition, 1992).

Comments on some works, 1991
First published (in English): *Gerhard Richter*, exhib. cat., Tate Gallery, London, 1991, pp. 125–130.

Richter's commentary on pictures exhibited at the Tate Gallery, London (30 October 1991–12 January 1992). The comments are taken from a conversation with the exhibition curator, Sean Rainbird, during preparation for the opening. The complete interview no longer exists.

1 *Firing Squad*: A reproduction of the work *Erschießung*, 1962, 170 × 200 cm, can be found in the catalogue *Gerhard Richter. Bilder, Paintings 1962–1985*, Städtische Kunsthalle Düsseldorf, fig. p. 19.
2 *A student researching into my work*: Ingrid Misterek-Plagge, '*Kunst mit Fotografie*' *und die frühen Fotogemälde Gerhard Richters*, Münster/Hamburg, 1992. The publication also contains the author's recollections of a conversation with Gerhard Richter (pp. 329–330).
3 *portrait of Elizabeth II*: *Queen Elizabeth (168)*, 1967, 62 × 53 cm.
4 *overpainted grey*: *Townscape M1–9 (170/1-9)*, 1968, nine parts, each 85 × 90 cm. Richter painted over the eighth panel *(170-8)* in monochrome grey.
5 *like one of the Tourist paintings*: The four-part series *Tourist (368 to 370-1)* was done in 1975. The first picture *Tourist (grey)*

(368) was painted over in grey by Richter.

6 *the destruction of Dresden*: At the age of thirteen Richter experienced the air attacks on his native Dresden on 13–14 February 1945 from Waltersdorf, about 70 km away.

7 *exhibited that month*: *Gerhard Richter, Ausstellungen bei Konrad Fischer*, Düsseldorf, July 1983. The work is reproduced in colour on the invitation card.

8 *a private collection in Düsseldorf*: Reference to *Abstract Painting (green)* *(588/1-3)* and *Abstract Painting (blue)* *(589/1-3)*, 1986, each three parts, each 160 × 150 cm.

9 *a show called Metropolis*: *Metropolis*, Martin-Gropius-Bau, Berlin (20 April–21 July 1991). Four large-format pictures from 1990 were exhibited: *Wald 1–4* *(731-734)*, each 340 × 260 cm.

Interview with Jonas Storsve, 1991

First published: Jonas Storsve, 'Gerhard Richter. La Peinture à venir', in *Art Press*, September 1991, pp. 12–20.

First English publication: *The Daily Practice of Painting*, 1995, pp. 223–231.

1 *Georg Baselitz*: *Georg Baselitz – Gerhard Richter*, Städtische Kunsthalle Düsseldorf (30 May–5 July 1981).

2 *last exhibition in London*: *Gerhard Richter. Mirrors*, Anthony d'Offay Gallery, London (22 April–17 June 1991). Richter's mirror works with the following work catalogue numbers were exhibited: 485-1, 735-1, 735-2, 736-1, 737 and 739-1.

3 *Annunciation*: Reference to Richter's five paintings from 1973, *Annunciation after Titian* *(343/1-2, 344/1-3)*.

4 *photographic multiples*: This refers to the photo-editions that were made of photographic images painted by Richter, such as the *Eight Student Nurses* *(130a)* of 1966, *Olympia* *(157a)* of 1967, and the *48 Portraits* *(324a)* of 1972, which all exist as one-off photos. Richter later produced these kinds of work in printed editions. Amongst these are the works *Betty* (1991), *Ema (Nude on a Staircase)* (1992), *Kl. Badende* [Small Bather] (1996), *Ravine* (1997), *Cathedral Corner* (1998), *Orchid* (1998), *Uncle Rudi* (2000) and *Mr Heyde* (2001). (For reproductions, see: *Gerhard Richter. Editionen 1965–2004*, exhib. cat., Bonn Art Museum, 2004.)

5 *You also teach*: Gerhard Richter held a professorship in painting from 1971 to 1994 at the Düsseldorf State Art Academy.

6 *Dresden Academy*: Richter had applied unsuccessfully for admission to the Dresden Academy of Fine Arts for the winter semester of 1950–51. He was told he should first work and prove himself at a state-owned business, and on this advice he began as a commercial painter at Dewag, a textile factory in Zittau. One year later he was admitted to the Academy.

7 *Pop Art show in London*: Reference to the *Pop Art Show*, Royal Academy of Arts, London (13 September–15 December 1991). The exhibition was later shown at the Museum Ludwig in Cologne (22 January–21 April 1992). Richter's early pictures *Folding Dryer* *(4)*, 1962, *Swimmers*

(90), 1965, and *Alfa Romeo (with Text) (68)* also from 1965, were shown.

8 *Metropolis in Berlin*: *Metropolis*, Martin-Gropius-Bau, Berlin (20 April–21 July 1991). Richter exhibited the four abstract pictures *Wald (1-4) (731-734)* of 1990.

Notes, 1992
First published: *The Daily Practice of Painting*, 1995, pp. 242–251.

See commentary on 'Notes, 1982'.

Interview with Doris von Drathen, 1992
First published: Doris von Drathen, 'Entretien avec Gerhard Richter', in *Les Cahiers du Musée national d'art moderne*, Centre Georges Pompidou, Paris, No. 40, Autumn 1992, pp. 86–89.

First English publication: *The Daily Practice of Painting*, 1995, pp. 231–240.

1 *'The Gulf War Never Happened'*: Jean Baudrillard, *La Guerre du Golfe n'a pas eu lieu*, Paris, 1991.
2 *in direct succession*: After presenting the *18 October* 1977 series at Portikus in Frankfurt from 29 April to 4 June 1989, Kasper König showed the three 1989 large-format abstract paintings *November (701)*, *December (700)* and *January (699)* from 12 to 19 December 1989.

Interview with Hans Ulrich Obrist, 1993
First published: *The Daily Practice of Painting*, 1995, pp. 251–273.

This text represents the closing interview by Hans Ulrich Obrist for the 1995 edition of Richter's texts.

1 *Demonstration for Capitalist Realism*: Reference to the Happening *Leben mit Pop – eine Demonstration für den Kapitalistischen Realismus* by Richter and Konrad Lueg at the Berges Furniture Store in Düsseldorf on 11 October 1963. (See 'Programme and Report: The Exhibition *Leben mit Pop – eine Demonstration für den Kapitalistischen Realismus*, Düsseldorf, 11 October 1963', pp. 17–20.)
2 *Plinth for the World*: Reference to the sculpture *Socle du Monde* (1961) by Piero Manzoni.
3 *Polke/Richter text for Hanover*: See 'Text for exhibition catalogue, Galerie h, Hanover, 1966, written jointly with Sigmar Polke', pp. 36–44.
4 *Galerie Friedrich & Dahlem*: See 'Poster text for the exhibition *Klasen und Richter*, Galerie Friedrich & Dahlem, Munich, 1964', p. 23.
5 *Galerie h catalogue*: See 'Text for exhibition catalogue, Galerie h, Hanover, 1966, written jointly with Sigmar Polke', pp. 36–44.
6 *book by Herzogenrath*: See 'Letters to Wulf Herzogenrath, 1972', pp. 68–69.
7 *imaginary Richter/Thwaites interview*: See 'Interview between John Anthony Thwaites and Gerhard Richter, written by Sigmar Polke, October 1964', pp. 24–25.

8 *the Betty portrait: Betty (663-5)* from 1988.

9 *Whistler's 'Art happens'*: James Abbott McNeill Whistler (1834–1903) was born in Lowell, MA, but worked principally in Great Britain. He was friends with Oscar Wilde. His painting was influenced by the Pre-Raphaelites and was considered a forerunner to Impressionism. Whistler's most famous painting, *Arrangement in Grey and Black: Portrait of the Painter's Mother*, 1871, 144.3 × 162.5 cm, is held by the Musée d'Orsay in Paris.

10 *Room by Palermo*: The original installation in 1971 at the Galerie Heiner Friedrich, Cologne, included a mural by Palermo and two busts mounted on columns by Richter, *Two Sculptures for a Room by Palermo (297-1)*. The installation was remounted by Richter in 1984 at the Städtische Galerie im Lenbachhaus in Munich. In lieu of the original plaster busts, the remounted version includes one of the two bronze originals (*Two Sculptures for a Room by Palermo (297-2)*).

11 *my first townscape: Cathedral Square – Milan (169)* from 1968. This painting, made for the Siemens branch in Milan, was auctioned at Sotheby's, London, in 1998, and is currently at the Park Hyatt Hotel in Chicago.

12 *with Beuys, Kiefer and Cucchi*: A closed conversation between Joseph Beuys, Jannis Kounellis, Anselm Kiefer and Enzo Cucchi was held in 1985 at the library of the Basel Kunsthalle. It was later published as a book. See Jacqueline Burckhardt, ed., *Ein Gespräch/Una Discussione*, Zurich, 1986.

13 *your room in Kassel*: At *documenta 9* (13 June–20 September 1992) Richter displayed his work in a modest, panelled room in one of the pavilions constructed at the Karlsaue. Twelve *Abstract Paintings*, as well as the grey double mirror *Abstract Painting (765)* and the photo-realist *Flowers (764-2)*, both from 1992, were shown.

14 *your visit to Japan*: Richter left on 16 September 1991 for a two-week trip to Japan, with the intention of finding material for a film version of *Atlas* (see Dietmar Elger, *Gerhard Richter. Maler*, Cologne, 2002, pp. 403–405). The film was never completed.

15 *the wreck of the 'Hope'*: Richter's trip to Greenland took place in 1972 over two weeks. As he later explained, 'I wanted to take photos that resembled *Gescheiterte Hoffnung* by Caspar David Friedrich. That was my project.' (See Dietmar Elger, *Gerhard Richter. Maler*, Cologne, 2002, p. 254.)

16 *hundreds of photographs*: Richter took numerous photographs during the trip, many of which were integrated into his *Atlas* (Helmut Friedel, ed., *Gerhard Richter. Atlas*, Cologne, 2006, plates 332–359), and were published as a separate art book (EIS, Galleria Pieroni, 1981; see also, *Gerhard Richter. Editionen 1965–2004*, exhib. cat., Bonn Art Museum, 2004, cat. no. 58). These photos were the basis of the four large-format works of 1975, *Seascape (375 to 378)*, as well as the paintings *Ice (476)* from 1981, and *Iceberg in Mist (496-1)* and *Iceberg (496-2)*, both from 1982.

17 *the Kunsthalle in Düsseldorf*: Reference to the exhibition *Georg Baselitz – Gerhard Richter*, which took place from 30 May through 5 July 1981 at the Städtische Kunsthalle Düsseldorf.

18 *Anthony d'Offay*: Reference to the exhibition *Gerhard Richter. Mirrors* at the Anthony d'Offay Gallery in London (22 April–17 June 1991). On exhibit were several *Abstract Paintings* and numerous mirror works (see 'Interview with Jonas Storsve, 1991', note 2).

Conversation with Henri-François Debailleux, 1993

First published: Henri-François Debailleux, 'Monter ce que je veux', in *Libération*, 5 October 1993, p. 36.
Translated from the French by Will Bishop.

This interview was conducted on the occasion of Richter's retrospective at the Museé d'Art Moderne de la Ville de Paris (23 September–21 November 1993).

1 *last year in Kassel*: At *documenta 9* (13 June–20 September 1992) Richter exhibited several *Abstract Paintings* (752/1-3, 756/2-4, 757, 760, 762/2-4), as well as the still-life *Flowers* (764-2) from 1992, and a mirror work, *Abstract Painting* (765). Richter's participation is documented in the catalogue *Gerhard Richter*, Marian Goodman Gallery, New York, 1993.

Conversation with Stefan Weirich, 1993

First published: Stefan Weirich, 'Wieder mal malen', in *Bonner Rundschau*, 26 November 1993.
Translated from the German by Ben Posener.

This conversation is largely identical to the following published interview with Stefan Weirich: 'Gerhard Richter', in *Bonner Illustrierte*, December 1993. It was held on the occasion of the artist's retrospective at the Kunst- und Ausstellungshalle der Bundesrepublik Deutschland [Art and Exhibition Hall of the Federal Republic of Germany], Bonn (10 December 1993–13 February 1994).

1 *in Bonn*: *Gerhard Richter*, Kunst- und Ausstellungshalle der Bundesrepublik Deutschland, Bonn (10 December 1993–13 February 1994). The exhibition was previously shown at the Musée d'Art Moderne de la Ville de Paris (23 September–21 November 1993), and later travelled to the Moderna Museet, Stockholm (12 March–8 May 1994) and the Museo Nacional Centro de Arte Reina Sofía, Madrid (7 June–7 August 1994).

Conversation with Amine Haase, 1993

First published: Amine Haase, '"Wie ein Schreiner", Conversation with Gerhard Richter in Bonn', in *Kölner Stadt-Anzeiger*, 11–12 December 1993, p. 37.
Translated from the German by Ben Posener.

The conversation was held at the press conference for the Gerhard Richter retrospective at the Kunst- und Ausstellungshalle der Bundesrepublik Deutschland, Bonn (10 December 1993–13 February 1994).

Interview with Stefan Weirich about the *18 October 1977* series, 1993
First published: Stefan Weirich, 'Aus dem Leben', in *Die Tageszeitung*, 28 December 1993, p. 12.
Translated from the German by Ben Posener.

Interview with Susanne Ehrenfried, 1995
First published: Susanne Ehrenfried, 'Gespräch mit Gerhard Richter am 8. August 1995', in Susanne Ehrenfried, *Gerhard Richter. Das Portrait bei Gerhard Richter*, Vienna, 1997, pp. 219–221.
Translated from the German by Ben Posener.

1 *Buchloh's criticism is justified?*: Benjamin H. D. Buchloh, 'Die Malerei am Ende des Sujets. Kapitel 4: Das Sujet als Specimen: Achtundvierzig Portraits', in *Gerhard Richter*, Kunst- und Ausstellungshalle der Bundesrepublik Deutschland, Bonn, 1993, Vol. II (texts), pp. 37–45.
2 *Betty*: *Betty* (663-5), 1988, 102 × 72 cm. The photographic model for the painting was taken in 1977.
3 *portraits of women*: The interviewer is making reference to the exhibition *The Romantic Spirit in German Art 1790–1990*, at the Royal Scottish Academy and The Fruitmarket Gallery, Edinburgh (28 July–7 September 1994), at the Hayward Gallery, South Bank Centre, London (29 September 1994–8 January 1995), and at the Haus der Kunst, Munich (2 February–1 May 1995). Together with three abstract paintings, Richter showed both versions of the *Lesende* [Reading Woman] (799-1, 804), each dating from 1994.

Interview with Hans Ulrich Obrist, 1995
First published (in English): Hans Ulrich Obrist, 'An Interview with Gerhard Richter', in *Gerhard Richter* (foldout), museum in progress, Vienna, 1995.

This interview by Hans Ulrich Obrist took place in September 1995 on the occasion of the unveiling of a 10 × 54-metre reproduction of the painting *River* (823), 1995, on the façade of the Vienna Kunsthalle (December 1995 through March 1996).

1 *your candle picture in Dresden come about?*: In spring 1995 a monumental blow-up of Richter's *Two Candles* (512-3), 1983, was hung at the Brühl Terrace in Dresden.
2 *Dr Schmidt from the museum*: Prof. Dr. Werner Schmidt was the then-General Director of the Dresden State Art Collections.
3 *Dufy's Fée Electricité*: Raoul Dufy's monumental mural *Fée Electricité* was made in 1937 for the Paris World's Fair,

and can be seen today at the Musée d'Art Moderne de la Ville de Paris.

4 *Strichbild*: See 'Letter to Birgit Pelzer, 25 March 1980', note 2.

5 *Robert Bresson*: The French film director Robert Bresson (1901–1999) first worked as a painter, switching to film in the 1930s. He made his first short film, *Les Affaires publiques*, in 1934.

6 *your film experiment in Japan*: See 'Interview with Hans Ulrich Obrist, 1993', note 14.

7 *plan for the small book*: Gerhard Richter, *Abstract Painting 825-11. 69 Details*, Zurich/Berlin/New York, 1996.

8 *The Halifax book*: Gerhard Richter, *128 details from a picture (Halifax 1978)*, Halifax, 1980.

Interview with Hubertus Butin, 1995

First published: Hubertus Butin, 'Mit der RAF ins Museum of Modern Art. Gerhard Richter im Gespräch', in *Neue Zürcher Zeitung*, 23 October 1995, p. 21. Translated from the German by Ben Posener.

This and the following interview by Stefan Koldehoff were conducted in reaction to press reports that Richter had sold the *18 October 1977* series to the Museum of Modern Art in New York for an undisclosed sum. At the time, in 1995, the paintings were on loan by the artist to the Museum of Modern Art in Frankfurt. In 2000 the series was transported from there to New York, and from 5 November 2000 to 30 January 2001 was presented as part of the exhibition *Open Ends* at the Museum of Modern Art. A separate catalogue on the series by Robert Storr was printed: *Gerhard Richter. October 18, 1977*, Museum of Modern Art, New York, 2000.

1 *retrospective in Jerusalem*: *Gerhard Richter*, The Israel Museum, Jerusalem (19 September–3 December 1995).

2 *48 Portraits from 1971–72*: By 1972 Richter had already produced a photo version of the *48 Portraits (324/1-48)*: *48 Portraits (324a)*, 48 photographs on cardboard, each 70 × 55 on 100 × 75 cm. The Museum Ludwig, Cologne, holds this work, as well as the painted version. In 1998 a further photographic version of the *48 Portraits* was produced in an edition of 4 + 2 copies (see *Gerhard Richter. Editionen 1965–2004*, exhib. cat., Bonn Art Museum, 2004, cat. no. 94).

Interview with Stefan Koldehoff, 1995

First published: Stefan Koldehoff, 'Stammheim in New York', in *Die Tageszeitung*, 28/29 October 1995, p. 15. Translated from the German by Ben Posener.

1 *The Trial Against the Red Army Faction*: Gerhard Richter, *Stammheim*, Anthony d'Offay Gallery, London, 1995.

Interview with Mark Rosenthal, 1998

First published (in English): Mark

Rosenthal, 'Gerhard Richter', in *Mark Rothko*, exhib. cat., National Gallery of Art, Washington, D.C., 1998, pp. 363–366.

The interview was conducted on 11 April 1997.

1 *From Friedrich to Rothko*: Robert Rosenblum, *Modern Painting and the Northern Romantic Tradition: From Friedrich to Rothko*, London, 1975 (German edition: *Die moderne Malerei und die Tradition der Romantik*, Munich, 1981).

Interview with Dieter Schwarz, 1999
First published (in English): Dieter Schwarz, 'About Watercolors and Related Things', in *Gerhard Richter. Aquarelle/Watercolors*, exhib. cat., Kunstmuseum Winterthur, 1999, pp. 17–27.

This interview was conducted on 26 June 1999 in the artist's Cologne atelier. It was printed in the catalogue for the retrospective of his works on paper, which was first shown at the Kunstmuseum Winterthur (4 September–21 November 1999), then at the Kupferstichkabinett [Engraving Collection], Dresden State Art Collection (15 January–19 March 2000), the Kaiser Wilhelm Museum, Krefeld (9 April–18 June 2000), and at De Pont, Tilburg (1 July–8 October 2000). Dieter Schwarz's catalogue of Richter's drawings appeared in conjunction with the exhibition.

1 *the self-portrait*: *Selbstbildnis* [Self-Portrait], 1949 (for a reproduction, see: *Gerhard Richter. Aquarelle/Watercolors 1964–1997*, exhib. cat., Kunstmuseum Winterthur, 1999, colour fig. pp. 5, 17).

2 *Portrait of Heiner Friedrich and Interior*: For reproductions, see: *Gerhard Richter. Aquarelle/Watercolors 1964–1997*, exhib. cat., Kunstmuseum Winterthur, 1999, colour fig. p. 29.

3 *Utrecht*: *Gerhard Richter. Atlas van de foto's en schetsen*, Hedendaagse Kunst, Utrecht (1–30 December 1972).

4 *watercolour from December 1977*: *Vorlage für abstraktes Bild*, 1977 (for a reproduction, see: *Gerhard Richter. Aquarelle/Watercolors 1964–1997*, exhib. cat., Kunstmuseum Winterthur, 1999, colour fig. p. 40). The watercolour is the model for *Abstract Painting (436)*, 1978, 200 × 250 cm.

5 *the two sheets from May 1978*: Each of these is titled *Vorlage für abstraktes Bild*, 1978 (for reproductions, see: *Gerhard Richter. Aquarelle/Watercolors 1964–1997*, exhib. cat., Kunstmuseum Winterthur, 1999, colour fig. p. 51). The watercolours are models for *Abstract Painting (437)*, 1978, 200 × 335 cm, and *Abstract Painting (442)*, 1978, 200 × 300 cm.

6 *segments of the palette*: For a list of these works, see 'Letter to Birgit Pelzer, 25 March 1980', note 1.

7 *the Westfalian Kunstverein in Münster*: *Wasserfarbenblätter* [Watercolour Sheets], Westfälischer Kunstverein [Westphalian Art Association], Münster (14 June–28 July 1985).

8 *Goethe-Institut in London*: *Watercolours by Joseph Beuys, Blinky Palermo, Sigmar Polke, Gerhard Richter*, Goethe-Institut, London, 1987.
9 *Stuttgart Staatsgalerie*: *Gerhard Richter. Aquarelle*, Graphic Collection of the Staatsgalerie Stuttgart (19 January–17 February 1985).
10 *Overholland Museum in Amsterdam*: *Gerhard Richter. Werken op papier 1983–1986*, Overholland Museum, Amsterdam (20 Feb ruary–20 April 1987).
11 *watercolours of apples*: For reproductions, see: *Gerhard Richter. Aquarelle/Watercolors 1964–1997*, exhib. cat., Kunstmuseum Winterthur, 1999, colour fig. pp. 90–91.
12 *Isa and Betty, the Table in the kitchen*: For reproductions, see: *Gerhard Richter. Aquarelle/Watercolors 1964–1997*, exhib. cat., Kunstmuseum Winterthur, 1999, colour fig. pp. 88–89.
13 *as Ulrich Loock has written*: The interviewer is referring to the following text: Ulrich Loock, 'Aquarelle von Gerhard Richter', in *Gerhard Richter. Aquarelle*, exhib. cat., Staatsgalerie Stuttgart, 1985, pp. 5–9.

Conversation with Paolo Vagheggi, 1999
First published: Paolo Vagheggi, 'La fotografia salva la mia pittura', in *La Repubblica*, 11 October 1999.
Translated from the Italian by Judy Gahagan.

The conversation was conducted on the occasion of Richter's exhibition at the Centro per l'Arte Contemporanea Luigi Pecci/Museo d'Arte Contemporanea, Prato (10 October 1999–9 January 2000).

1 *landscape*: *Sommertag* [Summer's Day] (859-1), 1999, 117 × 82 cm. See Richter's comments on this painting in 'Interview with Stefan Koldehoff, 1999', p. 352.

Interview with Stefan Koldehoff, 1999
First published: Stefan Koldehoff, 'Gerhard Richter. Die Macht der Malerei', in *art. Das Kunstmagazin*, December 1999, pp. 18–20.
Translated from the German by Ben Posener.

1 *Prato*: *Gerhard Richter*, Centro per l'Arte Contemporanea Luigi Pecci/Museo d'Arte Contemporanea, Prato (10 October 1999–9 January 2000).
2 *painting for the Reichstag was appropriate*: *Black, Red, Gold* (856), 1999, coloured, enamelled glass, 2,043 × 296 cm.
3 *based on a photograph*: *Sommertag* [Summer's Day] (859-1), 1999, 117 × 82 cm.
4 *catalogue of these works*: *Gerhard Richter. Zeichnungen 1964–1999*, catalogue of works, Kunstmuseum Winterthur, 1999 (exhibition: 4 September–21 November 1999).

Conversation with Birgit Grimm, 2000
First published: Birgit Grimm, 'Schönheit und Hoffnung. Gerhard Richter über Aquarellmalerei, glückliche Zufälle und seine Dresdner Jahre', in *Sächsische Zeitung*, 18 January 2000, p. 13.

Translated from the German by Ben Posener.

The conversation was part of the press conference for Richter's exhibition of works on paper held at the Kupferstichkabinett [Engraving Collection] of the Dresden State Art Collection (15 January–19 March 2000).

1 *painted during my studies*: Richter's mural for the German Hygiene Museum in Dresden was done in 1956 as his thesis project at the Dresden Academy of Fine Arts in the mural programme of Professor Heinz Lohmar.
2 *photography apprenticeship in Zittau*: Richter never actually apprenticed in photography. As a youth he had, however, had the opportunity to develop film in a darkroom belonging to the father of a schoolfriend.
3 *set painter in a theatre*: On 1 February 1950 Richter began as an apprentice set painter at the Zittau State Theatre, but was fired on 15 July because he refused to paint the theatre stairwell together with his fellow apprentices.

Interview with Bruno Corà, 2000
First published (in English): Bruno Corà, 'Gerhard Richter', in *Carte d'Arte*, June 2000, p. 9.

The interview was in conjunction with Richter's exhibition at the Centro per l'Arte Contemporanea Luigi Pecci/Museo d'Arte Contemporanea, Prato (10 October 1999–9 January 2000), which was curated by Bruno Corà.

Letter to René Block, 17 August 2000
First published: Untitled, in *das fridericianum magazin*, 5, Autumn 2000, p. 41.
Translated from the German by Ben Posener.

This is a letter from Richter dated 17 August 2000 to René Block on the background to his painting *Arnold Bode (33)* of 1964. The facsimile printed in the *fridericianum magazin* is complemented with a text by Block with his recollections of the first showing of the painting at the exhibition *Gerd Richter. Bilder des Kapitalistischen Realismus* at the Galerie René Block in Berlin (18 November 1964–5 January 1965). Block also recalls the appearance of Arnold Bode at the exhibition.

Interview with Astrid Kasper, 2000
First published: Astrid Kasper, 'Abschlussinterview vom 15.12.2000', in Astrid Kasper, *Gerhard Richter. Malerei als Thema der Malerei*, Berlin, 2003, pp. 232–239.
Translated from the German by Ben Posener.

1 *surface manipulations*: *S. mit Kind (827/1-8)*, 1995. Richter had painted over the photorealistic motifs in some of the

paintings by using a scraper to create abstract images, and by removing the paint in spots with the palette knife.

2 *these yellow lilies*: *Lilies* (870-1), 2000, 68 × 80 cm.

3 *Nabakowski*: Gislind Nabakowski, 'Heilig, heilig, heilig. Trügerischer Weichmacher-Realismus: Gerhard Richter in Nîmes', in *Frankfurter Allgemeine Zeitung*, 18 July 1996, p. 36.

4 *painting from the S. mit Kind series*: *S. mit Kind* (827-7), 1995, 36 × 51 cm.

5 *this bar by Jeff Wall*: Jeff Wall, *Picture for Women*, 1979, Cibachrome in illuminated display case, 163 × 229 cm.

6 *Saenredam*: Pieter Jansz Saenredam (1597–1665), Dutch painter and draughtsman, best known for his architectural representations.

7 *Ifa-Gallery in Stuttgart*: The exhibition *Gerhard Richter. Übersicht* was put together by Richter for the Ifa and shown from 22 September to 5 November 2000 at the gallery of the Institute for Foreign Affairs (Ifa) in Stuttgart. Since then the presentation has been on an international tour of museums and cultural institutions.

Interview with DER SPIEGEL, 2001
First published: 'Wunden kann ich nicht malen', in *DER SPIEGEL*, 14 April 2001, p. 165. Translated from the German by Ben Posener.

Interview on the six-piece group *Abstract Painting, Rhombus* (851/1-6) of 1998, which were rejected as paintings on commission for a pilgrimage centre in Italy, but were presented at the Venice Biennale (10 June–4 November 2001), and have been acquired since then by the Museum of Fine Arts in Houston.

Conversation with Tim Griffin, 2001
First published (in English): Tim Griffin, 'The Richter Scale. The ever-ambiguous Gerhard Richter continues to shake up the art world', in *Time Out*, New York, 4–11 October 2001, p. 59.

This conversation occurred on the occasion of Richter's exhibition of new work at the Marian Goodman Gallery in New York (14 September–27 October 2001).

Interview with Robert Storr, 2002
First published (in English): Robert Storr, 'Gerhard Richter. The Day is Long', in *Art in America*, January 2002, pp. 66–75, 121.

The published text is an abbreviated version of an interview that took place on 17 and 18 October 1996.

1 *a large mural*: See 'Conversation with Birgit Grimm, 2000', note 1.

2 *the Gemäldegalerie in Dresden*: The Gemäldegalerie was reopened, in its original home designed by the architect Semper, on 3 June 1956, after the Soviet Union had returned the contents of the collection.

3 *a museum there*: The Dresden State Collection's Gemäldegalerie began as early as 1951 to show parts of its collection at Schloss Pillnitz, among which was a painting by Caspar David Friedrich.

4 *the Dahlem museum*: The Gemäldegalerie in Berlin-Dahlem maintained one of the most significant collections of European painting from the thirteenth to eighteenth centuries. The holdings were transferred in 1998 to the Gemäldegalerie at the Kulturforum in Berlin.

5 *trouble with Heiner Friedrich*: In August 1972, Richter terminated his working partnership with the Galerie Heiner Friedrich in Munich.

6 *became a teacher*: In the summer semester of 1971, Richter assumed his professorship at the Düsseldorf State Art Academy.

7 *mother-child paintings*: Reference to *S. mit Kind (827/1-8)*, 1995.

8 *a crazy feminist writer*: See 'Interview with Astrid Kasper, 2000', note 3.

9 *published an answer*: Thierry Chervel, 'Wie die Schönheit möglich ist. Eine Ausstellung in Nîmes zeigt neue, ungewohnt private Bilder von Gerhard Richter', in *Basler Zeitung*, 20 August 1996, p. 38.

Interview with Jürgen Hohmeyer, 2002
First published: Jürgen Hohmeyer, 'Mein Ebenbild bedroht mich immer mehr', in *Frankfurter Allgemeine Sonntagszeitung*, 3 February 2002, pp. 21–22.
Translated from the German by Ben Posener.

This interview by Jürgen Hohmeyer took place on Richter's seventieth birthday.

1 *'the painting after the last painting'*: *Das Bild nach dem letzten Bild*, Galerie Metropol, Vienna; Museum het Kruithuis, s'Hertogenbosch, 1991. Richter participated in the exhibition with the work *Grau (334-1)* from 1973. The exhibition *New new Painting* took place in 1993 at the Städtische Galerie Göppingen, without Richter's participation.

2 *Moritz*: *Moritz (863/1-3)*, 2000.

3 *Definitely not*: In a later interview of 2005 Richter mentioned a painting that showed the burning Twin Towers of the World Trade Center. He claimed the work failed and he either destroyed it or painted over it (see 'SPIEGEL interview, conducted by Susanne Beyer and Ulrike Knöfel, 2005', pp. 498–508). In 2005, however, Richter did a group of four large-format drawings which reveal the silhouette of the Twin Towers within their abstract structures (for reproductions, see: *Gerhard Richter*, exhib. cat., Marian Goodman Gallery, New York, 2005). A photograph of Richter's atelier printed in the catalogue shows the sketch for the drawings on his easel.

4 *Lee Harvey Oswald*: *Oswald (16)*, 1964, 130 × 110 cm.

MoMA interview with Robert Storr, 2002
First published (in English): Robert Storr, 'Interview with Gerhard Richter', in *Gerhard Richter. Forty Years of Painting*, exhib. cat.,

Museum of Modern Art, New York, 2002, pp. 287–309.

The interview was conducted for the catalogue of the artist's seventieth birthday retrospective at the Museum of Modern Art, New York (14 February–21 May 2002), Art Institute of Chicago (22 June–15 September 2002), San Francisco Museum of Modern Art (11 October 2002–14 January 2003), and Hirshhorn Museum and Sculpture Garden, Washington, D.C. (20 February–18 May 2003).

1 *Dr Werner Heyde*: *Mr Heyde (100)*, 1965, 55 × 65 cm. The following book on the Heyde case is available: Klaus-Detlev Godau-Schüttke, *Die Heyde/Sawade-Affäre*, Baden-Baden, 2001.

2 *Deutschlandbilder*: *Deutschlandbilder. Kunst aus einem geteilten Land*, Martin-Gropius-Bau, Berlin (7 September 1997–11 January 1998).

3 *the concentration camp*: Helmut Friedel, ed., *Gerhard Richter. Atlas*, Cologne, 2006, Plates 16–20.

4 *doubling back to photography*: Such photographs based on paintings are in the appendix of *Gerhard Richter. Editionen 1965–2004*, exhib. cat., Bonn Art Museum, 2004, and include, for example: *Betty (663-5)* (cat. no. 75), *Ema (Nude on a Staircase) (134)* (cat. no. 80), *Toilet Paper (75-3)* (cat. no. 83), *Kl. Badende* [Small Bather] *(815-1)* (cat. no. 87), *Ravine (837-1)* (cat. no. 90), *Cathedral Corner (629-1)* (cat. no. 97) and *Uncle Rudi (85)* (cat. no. 111).

5 *Bob Ryman exhibition in Bonn*: *Robert Ryman – Retrospektive*, Bonn Art Museum (22 March–27 May 2001). The exhibition was previously on view at the Haus der Kunst in Munich (8 December 2000–18 February 2001).

6 *one hundred small paintings for Munich*: *Fuji (839/1-110)*, 1996, oil on Alucobond, each 29 × 37 cm (or 37 × 29 cm). For a reproduction, see: *Gerhard Richter. Editionen 1965–2004*, exhib. cat., Bonn Art Museum, 2004, cat. no. 89, colour fig. p. 238. These 110 pictures were made to support the purchase of the *Atlas* by the Städtische Galerie im Lenbachhaus, Munich.

7 *Titian's Annunciation*: *Annunciation after Titian (343/1-2, 344/1-3)*, 1973.

8 *'Detail' paintings*: Richter's so-called 'soft' abstract paintings, made between 1977 and 1980 based on photographic enlargements of small abstract sketches (work nos.: 417-424, 428-430, 434-440, 442-444, 446, 460).

9 *copies of the originals*: Richter is referring to the large-format 'soft' abstract paintings. See note 8 above.

10 *Halifax, Nova Scotia*: *Gerhard Richter. 17 PICTURES*, A. Leonowens Gallery, Halifax (4–18 July 1978).

11 *128 Details from a Picture*: Gerhard Richter, *128 details from a picture (Halifax 1978)*, Halifax, 1980.

12 *Of the six I showed*: *Gerhard Richter*, Galerie Hetzler, Stuttgart (6 November–4 December 1982). Four of the candle paintings were shown (work nos. 498-1, 498-2, 499-2, 510-3) at prices between

DM 16,000 and DM 24,000.

13 *my paintings in the Netherlands*: *Gerhard Richter. Abstract Paintings*, Stedelijk van Abbemuseum, Eindhoven (8 October–5 November 1978).

Interview with Babette Richter, 2002

First published: Babette Richter, 'Glauben. Gespräch mit Gerhard Richter', in Babette Richter, *Der Andere. Interviews – Versuch einer Annäherung*. Cologne, 2002, pp. 38–58. Translated from the German by Ben Posener.

An interview of Richter by his daughter, Babette (Betty) Richter, who has been painted by him several times: *Betty* (425/4-5), 1977, and *Betty* (663-5), 1988.

1 *Mann mit Hund*: *Horst with Dog* (94), 1965, 80 × 60 cm.

2 *the New York exhibition*: *Gerhard Richter: Forty Years of Painting*, Museum of Modern Art, New York (14 February–21 May 2002).

3 *family portrait in which she appears*: *Family* (30), 1964, 150 × 180 cm.

4 *studio on Brückenstrasse*: *Betty* (425-4), 1977, 30 × 40 cm.

About Blinky Palermo, 2003

First published: Untitled, in *'To the people...' Sprechen über Blinky Palermo*, Cologne, 2003, pp. 72–78.

Translated from the German by Ben Posener.

1 *contract with him once*: Richter signed his contract with the Galerie Heiner Friedrich on 1 May 1966. The contract guaranteed Richter a monthly payment for exclusive representation of his work and had an initial period of two years. It was modified after the first year. For more details, see: Dietmar Elger, *Gerhard Richter. Maler*, Cologne, 2002, pp. 151–153.

2 *the Warhol factory*: Actually named Brigid Berlin, she belonged to Andy Warhol's so-called 'Superstars' in the 1960s. She acted in Warhol's films, including *The Chelsea Girls* (1966) and *Imitation of Christ* (1967–69), and he later employed her as a telephone receptionist at the Factory.

3 *two boards*: *Finger-marks (with Palermo)* (253), 1970, two parts, 200 × 200 cm. The piece no longer exists.

4 *Krefeld brown-beige paintings*: *Untitled (with Palermo)* (303, 304), 1971, each two parts, 150 × 325 cm. For many years the paintings were on loan from a private owner to the Kaiser Wilhelm Museum in Krefeld. Today they are in a private collection in America.

5 *wall paintings he did*: Reference to Palermo's mural at the exhibition *Palermo. Wandmalerei*, Galerie Heiner Friedrich, Munich (15 February–3 March 1971).

6 *sculptures*: *Sculpture for a Room by Palermo* (297-1), 1971, each 174 cm high, plaster, painted grey. The joint exhibition of Palermo's murals and Richter's sculptures was held from 21 April to 15 May 1971 at the Galerie Heiner Friedrich in Cologne.

7 *in Munich*: The bronze of *Sculpture for a Room by Palermo (Richter)* (297-2) is exhibited along with Palermo's murals (as reconstructed by Richter) at the Städtische Galerie im Lenbachhaus, Munich.

Statement for *100 Artists See God*, 2004
First published: Untitled, in *100 Artists See God*, exhib. cat., Independent Curators International, New York, 2004, p. 56.

Richter's contribution to the catalogue accompanying *100 Artists See God*, which was shown from 7 March to 27 June 2004 at the Jewish Museum, San Francisco. The piece Richter selected to show at the exhibition was the small-format grey painting *Grey* (341-5), 1973, 46 × 46 cm.

Conversation with Christiane Hoffmans, 2004
First published: Christiane Hoffmans, 'Ein Zuhause für meine Bilder', in *Welt am Sonntag*, 2 May 2004, p. 90.
Translated from the German by Ben Posener.

1 *what an archive is*: On 1 February 2006 the Dresden State Art Collections created the Gerhard Richter Archive.
2 *if it works out with those paintings*: On 20 August 2004 the Galerie Neue Meister at the Dresden Albertinum opened a new collection centre with over forty Gerhard Richter works from the museum's collection as well as on loan from the artist and from private collections.

Interview with Jan Thorn-Prikker on the work *WAR CUT*, 2004
First published: Jan Thorn-Prikker, 'Je dramatischer die Ereignisse sind, desto wichtiger ist die Form.' Ein Gespräch mit dem Künstler Gerhard Richter über seine Arbeit *WAR CUT*', in *Neue Zürcher Zeitung*, 29–30 May 2004, p. 45.

First English publication: Jan Thorn-Prikker, 'A Picture Is Worth 216 Newspaper Articles', *The New York Times*, Section 2, pp. 26–27.

Interview by Jan Thorn-Prikker in conjunction with the appearance of the book project *WAR CUT* (Paris/Cologne, 2004). The book combines 165 facsimiles of complete articles from the *Frankfurter Allgemeine Zeitung* on the Iraq War (2003), with 216 photographic clippings prepared by Richter from *Abstract Painting* (648-2), owned by the Musée d'Art Moderne de la Ville de Paris.

Interview with Jan Thorn-Prikker, 2004
First published: Jan Thorn-Prikker, 'Gerhard Richter im Gespräch mit Jan Thorn-Prikker', in *Gerhard Richter im Albertinum*, exhib. cat., Galerie Neue Meister, Albertinum, Dresden, 2004, pp. 74–88.
Translated from the German by Ben Posener.

Published in the catalogue which accompanied the opening of the Gerhard Richter rooms at the Galerie Neue Meister, Dresden Albertinum, on 20 August 2004.

1 *The flood*: Reference to the flood of the Elbe River in August 2002.
2 *the Positionen [Positions] exhibition*: The exhibition *Positionen. Malerei aus der Bundesrepublik Deutschland*, with works by eleven painters – Horst Antes, Willi Baumeister, Raimund Girke, Gotthard Graubner, Anselm Kiefer, Konrad Klapheck, Ernst Wilhelm Nay, Sigmar Polke, Richter, Emil Schumacher and Günther Uecker – was shown in the Neue Berliner Galerie at the Altes Museum, Berlin (31 October–30 November 1986), and at the Albertinum, Dresden State Art Collection (10 December 1986–12 January 1987). A scaled-down version of the exhibition was shown later at the Sprengel Museum in Hanover (25 January–28 March 1987).
3 *Benjamin Buchloh*: During this trip, a photo was taken of Buchloh and Richter, which the latter used later as a model for the double portrait *Court Chapel, Dresden* (865-3), 2000, 80 × 93 cm. The photo was not, however, taken in front of the Hofkirche, but at the entrance to the Academy of Fine Arts at the Brühl Terrace in Dresden.
4 *Zeichnungen und Aquarelle [Drawings and Watercolours]*: The exhibition *Gerhard Richter. Zeichnungen und Aquarelle 1964–1999* was shown at the Kunstmuseum Winterthur (4 September–21 November 1999) and from 15 January to 19 March 2000 at the Kupferstichkabinett [Engraving Collection] of the Dresden State Art Collection.
5 *the handsome one, Rudi*: Richter did a portrait of his uncle in 1965, *Uncle Rudi* (85), 87 × 50 cm.
6 *an English radio programme*: Richter participated in a number of exhibitions after his studies, among which were the *Kunst-Ausstellung Dresden* 1957 and the *Ausstellung Junge Künstler* at the Albertinum in 1960. The work lauded in a BBC radio broadcast was an urban landscape Richter had shown at the Dresden Christmas exhibition in 1959.
7 *Heinz Lohmar*: See 'Letter to Professor Heinz Lohmar, 6 April 1961', note 1.
8 *church window*: This refers to Richter's design for a stained-glass window in the south transept of Cologne Cathedral, completed in 2007. See also: 'Conversation with Georg Imdahl, 2005', p. 496.
9 *Zero people*: The Düsseldorf artist group Zero, founded in 1957 by Heinz Mack and Otto Piene. From 1962 Günther Uecker was also a member of the group, which was officially dissolved in 1964.
10 *Fluxus events*: Richter visited events as a spectator, including the following: *NEO-DADA in der Musik* at the Düsseldorf Kammerspiele (16 June 1962), *Festum Fluxorum Fluxus* at the Düsseldorf State Art Academy (2–3 February 1963) and the *Festival der neuen Kunst – Actions/Agit-Pop/De-Collage/Happening/Events/Antiart/*

L'Autrisme/Art Total/Refluxus at the Aachen Polytechnic (20 June 1964). A photograph taken at the latter event by Heinrich Riebesehl shows Richter together with Blinky Palermo and Manfred Kuttner (see Dietmar Elger, *Gerhard Richter. Maler*, Cologne, 2002, fig. p. 81).

11 *For my diploma*: Richter's thesis project in 1956 was a mural at the German Hygiene Museum in Dresden. The mural was painted over after Richter's escape from East Germany in March 1961.

12 *advertising shot*: Richter used a motif from a Kodak advertisement which was published in the illustrated *Stern* (11 July 1965, p. 83).

'How much morality does art require?', 2004

First published: 'Wie viel Moral braucht die Kunst?', in *Die Zeit*, 16 September 2004, p. 49. Translated from the German by Ben Posener.

Richter's contribution in response to a *Die Zeit* newspaper survey regarding the opening of the Friedrich Christian Flick Collection at the Hamburger Bahnhof, Berlin, and the controversy surrounding the Flick company's involvement in wartime production under the Nazis. Artists such as Hans Haacke, Luc Tuymans, Thomas Schütte, Marcel Odenbach and Thomas Struth, whose works are in the collection, were asked to contribute to this debate on the question 'How much morality does art require?'

Conversation with Stefan Koldehoff, 2004

First published: Stefan Koldehoff, '26 000 Dollar sind 25 000 Dollar zuviel', in *Monopol*, October/November 2004, p. 34. Translated from the German by Matthew Price.

This conversation accompanied an article by Anne Zielke on the edition *Candle I* (1988) in the magazine *Monopol* ('Das Wunder von Goslar', in *Monopol*, October/November 2004, pp. 27–33). The article reports on the print's extraordinary increase in value over the course of the preceding years.

1 *Kerze II*: This actually refers to the edition *Kerze I*, 1988 (see *Gerhard Richter. Editionen* 1965–2004, exhib. cat., Bonn Art Museum, 2004, cat. no. 64). The model for this motif is the painting *Candle* (512-1), which Richter reverses here in reproducing it.

Interview with Benjamin H. D. Buchloh, 2004

First published (in English): Benjamin H. D. Buchloh, 'Interview', November 2004, in *Gerhard Richter*, exhib. cat., Marian Goodman Gallery, New York, 2005, pp. 59–70.

1 *new paintings*: Buchloh is referring to the paintings *Silikat* (883-7), 2003, *Silikat* (885/1-4), 2003, *Abstract Painting (Skin)* (887/2-3), 2004, and *Strontium* (888), 2004.

Conversation with Georg Imdahl, 2005
First published: Georg Imdahl, 'Das südliche Fenster und seine Erstrahlung', in *Kölner Stadt-Anzeiger*, 3 February 2005, p. 24.
Translated from the German by Ben Posener.

A conversation with Georg Imdahl on the subject of Richter's design for a stained-glass window in the south transept of Cologne Cathedral. See also: 'Notes for a press conference, 28 July 2006', pp. 517–518.

1 *family house in Berlin*: *Glasfenster, 625 Farben* [Stained-Glass Window, 625 Colours] *(703)*, 1989, 273 × 268 cm.

Conversation with Bertram Müller, 2005
First published: Bertram Müller, 'Natürlich bin ich gerührt', in *Rheinische Post*, 2 March 2005, p. A8.
Translated from the German by Ben Posener.

The conversation was held as part of the press conference for the exhibition at the K20 Art Collection of North Rhine Westphalia, Düsseldorf (12 February–16 May 2005).

SPIEGEL interview, conducted by Susanne Beyer and Ulrike Knöfel, 2005
First published: Susanne Beyer and Ulrike Knöfel, 'Mich interessiert der Wahn', in DER SPIEGEL, 15 August 2005, pp. 128–132.
Translated from the German by Ben Posener.

1 *your wife Sabine and your young son Moritz*: Reference to the eight-part series *S. mit Kind (827/1-8)* of 1995.
2 *Jürgen Schreiber*: Jürgen Schreiber, *Ein Maler aus Deutschland. Gerhard Richter. Das Drama einer Familie*, Munich/Zurich, 2005.
3 *article in Der Tagesspiegel a year ago*: Jürgen Schreiber, 'Das Geheimnis des Malers', in *Der Tagesspiegel*, 22 October 2004, pp. 1, 4–5.
4 *World Trade Center*: In 2005 Richter did a group of four large-format drawings which reveal the silhouette of the Twin Towers within their abstract structures (for reproductions, see: *Gerhard Richter*, exhib. cat., Marian Goodman Gallery, New York, 2005). A photograph of Richter's atelier printed in the catalogue shows the sketch for the drawings on his easel.
5 *the statue of Willy Brandt*: Richter is referring to the 3.4-metre-high bronze sculpture of Willy Brandt by Rainer Fetting, of 1996, which is located in the SPD's Willy Brandt Building in Berlin. Rainer Fetting answered Richter's criticism of the work in the Berlin tabloid B.Z.: 'It didn't upset me. I know what I think about his work. His technique, with its painting-for-painting's sake, can be found in any textbook. That's not very creative. Gerhard Richter's paintings are boring.' (Michael Zöllner, 'Zicken-Krieg der Super-Künstler', in B.Z., 13 October 2005, p. 23).

Conversation with Roberta De Righi, 2005
First published: Roberta De Righi, 'Mit jeder Seite neue Zweifel', in *Abendzeitung*, 7 September 2005, p. 17.
Translated from the German by Ben Posener

Richter's view on the book by Jürgen Schreiber (*Ein Maler aus Deutschland. Gerhard Richter. Das Drama einer Familie*, Munich/Zurich, 2005).

1 *article in the Tagesspiegel*: See 'SPIEGEL interview, conducted by Susanne Beyer and Ulrike Knöfel, 2005', note 3.
2 *Heinrich Eufinger*: Professor Heinrich Eufinger was the father of Richter's first wife Ema, whom he married in 1957. Eufinger was born in 1894 in Wiesbaden and died in 1988 in Wilhelmshaven. From 1935 to 1945 he managed the State Women's Clinic in Dresden-Friedrichstadt. After the war he was imprisoned for three years. From 1950 to 1956 he managed a clinic in Burgstädt. In 1956 Eufinger and his wife fled from East Germany.

Interview with Jeanne Anne Nugent, 2006
First published (in English): Jeanne Anne Nugent, 'Interview with Gerhard Richter', in *From Caspar David Friedrich to Gerhard Richter. German Paintings from Dresden at The J. Paul Getty Museum, Los Angeles*, exhib. cat., J. Paul Getty Museum, Los Angeles, 2006, pp. 113–117.

The interview is a compilation of several discussions held in May and June 2006.

1 *Titian's Annunciation*: *Annunciation after Titian (343/1-2)*, 1973, each 125 × 200 cm, *Annunciation after Titian (344/1-3)*, 1973, each 150 × 250 cm. See also: 'Interview with Gislind Nabakowski, 1974', pp. 85–90.
2 *Wieland Förster*: Born in 1930 in Dresden. Studied from 1953 to 1958 at the Dresden Academy of Fine Arts. He is a freelance sculptor living in Berlin.
3 *Wilfried Werz*: Born in 1930 in Berlin. Studied from 1951 to 1956 at the Dresden Academy of Fine Arts. He is a stage designer living in Berlin.
4 *Helmut Heinze*: Born in 1932 in Mulda, Saxony. Studied from 1950 to 1957 at the Dresden Academy of Fine Arts, where he took up a professorship in sculpture in 1979. He lives in Kreischa, near Dresden.
5 *Wald*: *Wald (1-12) (892/1-12)*, 2005, each 197 × 132 cm.
6 *Those abstract paintings*: *Wald 1-4 (731–34)*, 1990, each 340 × 260 cm.

Notes for a press conference, 28 July 2006
Previously unpublished.
Translated from the German by Ben Posener.

Richter's notes for a press conference held on 28 July 2006 at the construction site office of Cologne Cathedral, where a presentation was held for his design for a stained-glass window in the south transept. See also: 'Conversation with Georg Imdahl, 2005', p. 496.

1 *4,096 colour fields*: The first of these paintings, from 1966, was *Ten Colours (135-1)*, the last of them, from 1974, was *4,096 Colours (359)*.
2 *colour classification methodology*: See also: 'Text for catalogue of group exhibition, Palais des Beaux-Arts, Brussels, 1974: 1,024 Colours in 4 Permutations', p. 91.

Interview with Hans Ulrich Obrist, November 2006

First published (in English): Hans Ulrich Obrist, 'Gerhard Richter', in *Domus*, January 2007, pp. 117–125.

The initial interview was conducted in July 2005, but was revised extensively by Richter and finally completed on 14 November 2006.

1 *Wittgenstein*: The philosopher Ludwig Wittgenstein built a cabin in Norway in 1914 as an architect, as well as a home for his sister Margarete Stonborough on Kundmangasse in Vienna.
2 *Westkunst*: The exhibition *Westkunst. Zeitgenössische Kunst seit 1939*, curated by Kasper König, took place from 30 May to 16 August 1981 at the Cologne Exhibition Centre.
3 *Atlas in the 1960s*: For reproductions, see: Helmut Friedel, ed., *Gerhard Richter. Atlas*, Cologne, 2006, panels 221–252.
4 *a window unblocked*: Richter is referring to his retrospective, *Gerhard Richter. Bilder 1962–1985*, which took place from 18 January to 23 March 1986 simultaneously at the Städtische Kunsthalle Düsseldorf and the space in the same building belonging to the Düsseldorf Art Association for the Rhine and Westphalia.
5 *by opening a window to the street*: For the exhibition *Acht Grau* at the Deutsche Guggenheim, Berlin (11 October 2002–5 January 2003), Richter had the window dressings removed so that the outdoors would be reflected on the grey surfaces of his paintings.
6 *exhibition in the Kunstsammlung Nordrhein-Westfalen*: *Gerhard Richter*, K20 Art Collection of North Rhine Westphalia, Düsseldorf (12 February–16 May 2005).
7 *Lenbachhaus in Munich*: *Gerhard Richter*, Städtische Galerie im Lenbachhaus, Munich (4 June–21 August 2005).
8 *Heiner Friedrich's gallery in Cologne*: Reference to the exhibition *Richter/Palermo*, Galerie Heiner Friedrich, Cologne (21 April–15 May 1971).
9 *exhibition for Salvador Dalí*: *Gerhard Richter/Blinky Palermo: Für Salvadore Dalí*, Galerie Ernst, Hanover (10 October–6 November 1970).
10 *three BMW pictures*: *Red (345-1)*, *Yellow (345-2)*, *Blue (345-3)*, 1973, each 300 × 600 cm.
11 *even though Palermo existed*: Richter is referring to the group of work *To the People of New York*, from 1976, consisting of thirty-nine panels. Palermo used only the colours black, red and gold.

12 *the de Young Museum*: The architects of the de Young Museum in San Francisco, Jacques Herzog and Pierre de Meuron, commissioned Richter to supply an installation for the museum. In 2004 the work *Strontium (888)*, c-print, 130-part, 910 × 945 cm, resulted, and was included in the exhibition *Gerhard Richter* at the K20 Collection of North Rhine Westphalia, Düsseldorf (12 February–16 May 2005). Thereafter the work was permanently installed at the de Young Museum. For reproductions, see: Helmut Friedel, ed., *Gerhard Richter. Atlas*, Cologne, 2006, plate 748.

13 *60-year-old photo*: Richter was given the photo by Heinrich Miess, who later published the four editions with the image. For reproductions, see: *Gerhard Richter. Editionen 1965–2004*, exhib. cat., Bonn Art Museum, 2004, cat. nos. 113–116, pp. 263–266.

14 *in the WAR CUT book*: Suzanne Pagé and Hans Ulrich Obrist, eds, *WAR CUT*, Paris/Cologne, 2004.

15 *The first 'original'*: The model for the graphic reproduction *First View*, 2000, appeared on 26 July 2000 in the *Frankfurter Allgemeine Zeitung*. For a reproduction, see: *Gerhard Richter. Editionen 1965–2004*, exhib. cat., Bonn Art Museum, 2004, cat. no. 112, p. 262.

16 *The drawings*: (4 drawings). For reproductions, see: *Gerhard Richter*, exhib. cat., Marian Goodman Gallery, New York, 2005.

17 *the twelve pictures*: *Forest (1-12) (892/1-12)*, 2005, each 197 × 132 cm.

18 *your last New York exhibition*: *Gerhard Richter*, Marian Goodman Gallery, New York (14 September–27 October 2001).

19 *nice social housing*: For a reproduction, see: Helmut Friedel, ed., *Gerhard Richter. Atlas*, Cologne, 2006, panel 259.

Interview with Hans Ulrich Obrist, 2007

First published: Hans Ulrich Obrist, 'Gerhard Richter', in *L'UOMO Vogue*, May/June 2007, pp. 206–213.
Translated from the German by Matthew Price.

1 *Biennale under Robert Storr*: Robert Storr, curator of the 2002 Gerhard Richter retrospective at the Museum of Modern Art, New York, was curator of the 2007 Venice Biennale (10 June–21 November 2007).

2 *a series of six large, rectangular paintings*: Reference to the paintings *Cage (1-6)*, 2006, oil on canvas, 290 × 290 cm (nos. 1, 3, 4), and 300 × 300 cm (nos. 2, 5, 6).

3 *the silicate series*: *Silikat (885/1-4)*, 2003, oil on canvas, each 290 × 290 cm. The works were acquired in 2006 by the Art Collection of North Rhine Westphalia in Düsseldorf. See Kunstsammlung Nordrhein-Westfalen/Kulturstiftung der Länder, *Gerhard Richter. Silikat*, Düsseldorf, 2007 (PATRIMONIA series, vol. 322).

4 *the strontium picture*: *Strontium (888)*, 2004, c-print, 130 parts, 910 × 945 cm, was commissioned for the Fine Arts Museum of San Francisco, designed by Swiss

architects Herzog & de Meuron – De Young Legion of Honor, San Francisco.

5 *white paintings that were exhibited in Japan?*: The comment refers to the single edition *Snow White*, 100 reproductions of which were printed by the gallery Wako Works of Art in Tokyo in 2006, and published in a book of the same name.

6 *Guardi postcard*: Francesco Guardi (Venice, 1710–1793), *Gondole sulla laguna (laguna grigia)*, Museo Poldi Pezzoli, Milan.

7 *exhibited in 2001 with Marian?*: Richter is referring to the *Abstract Paintings (867/1-3)*, 2000, oil on canvas, each 175 × 250 cm. The exhibition took place at the Marian Goodman Gallery, New York, from 14 September to 27 October 2001.

8 *Sils Maria*: In 1992 Richter exhibited at the Friedrich Nietzsche House in Sils Maria (July 1992–March 1993), curated by Hans Ulrich Obrist. The majority of the works on show were painted-over photographs.

Picture Credits

p. 2: Timm Rautert
p. 28 below: Reiner Ruthenbeck, Düsseldorf, 1963, © VG Bild-Kunst, Bonn, 2008
p. 51 below: Carlo Catenazzi, Art Gallery of Ontario
p. 150: Henning Lohner, Los Angeles
p. 220: Jerry Spiegel, New York
p. 243: © Anne Gold, Aachen
p. 265 above: © GAECHTER+ CLAHSEN, Fotografen SWB, Atelier BINZ39, Zurich, 1998
p. 265 below: © Heinz Jokisch, Düsseldorf
p. 267 above: Dietmar Elger, Gerhard Richter Archive, Dresden
pp. 290, 291: © Manfred Leve, Nuremberg
p. 313 below: André Morin, MAM/ARC, 1993
p. 364: Hubert Becker, 1997
p. 388: © Hubert Becker, 1998
p. 409: © Peter Dibke, 2002
p. 411 above and below: © Sabine Moritz-Richter, 2001/2002
p. 458 below: © Wolfgang Kuehn, Meerbusch
p. 482 below: © J. Paul Getty Museum, Los Angeles
p. 503 above: © Belz / Hamann
p. 529: © epd-Bild / Guido Schiefer
Artwork photography: Friedrich Rosenstiel, Cologne

Index

Although Gerhard Richter avoids classification of his works, they have been placed here, where possible, into categories for ease of reference under 'Richter, Gerhard, artworks'.

Numbers in *italics* refer to illustrations.